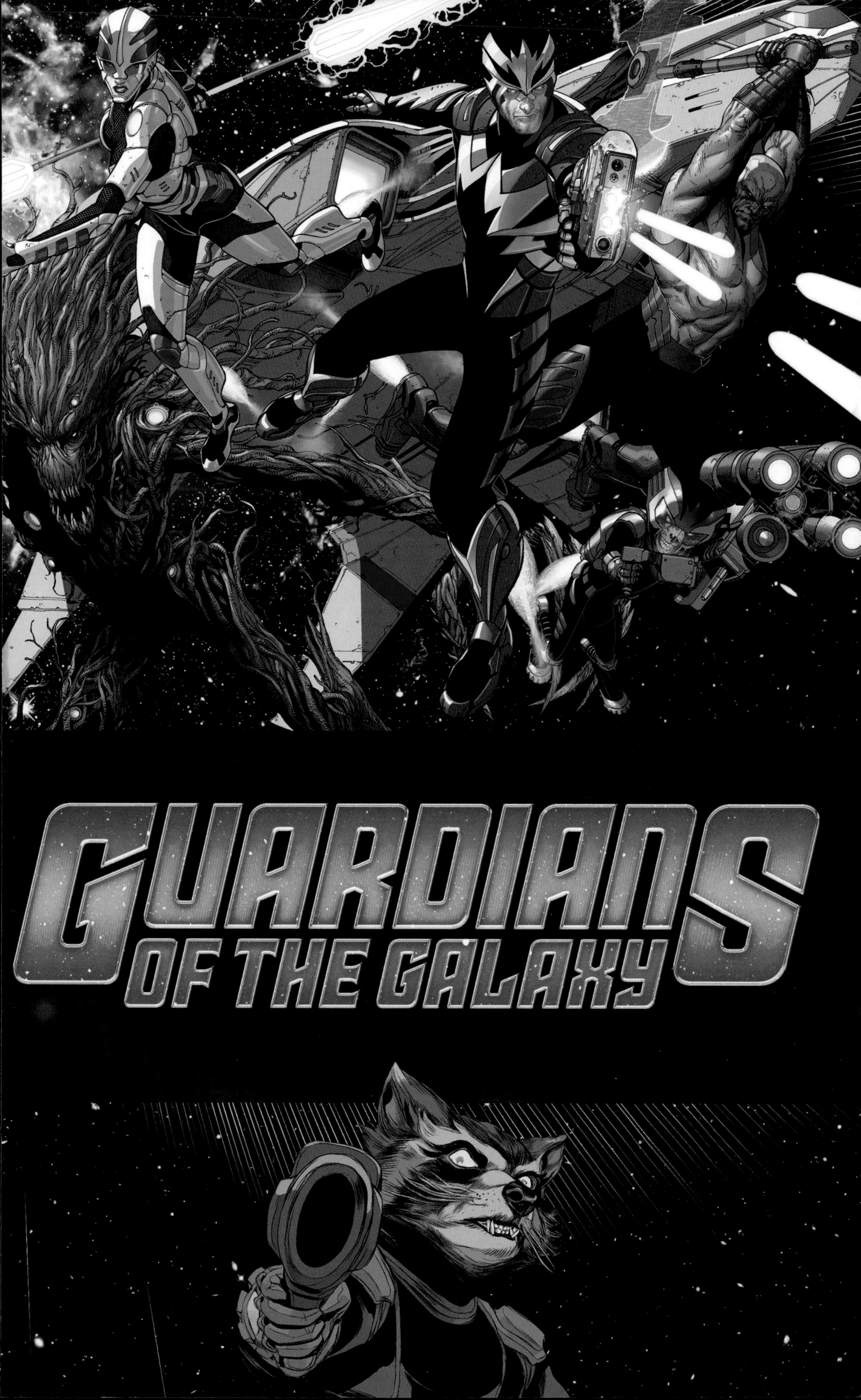
GUARDIANS
OF THE GALAXY

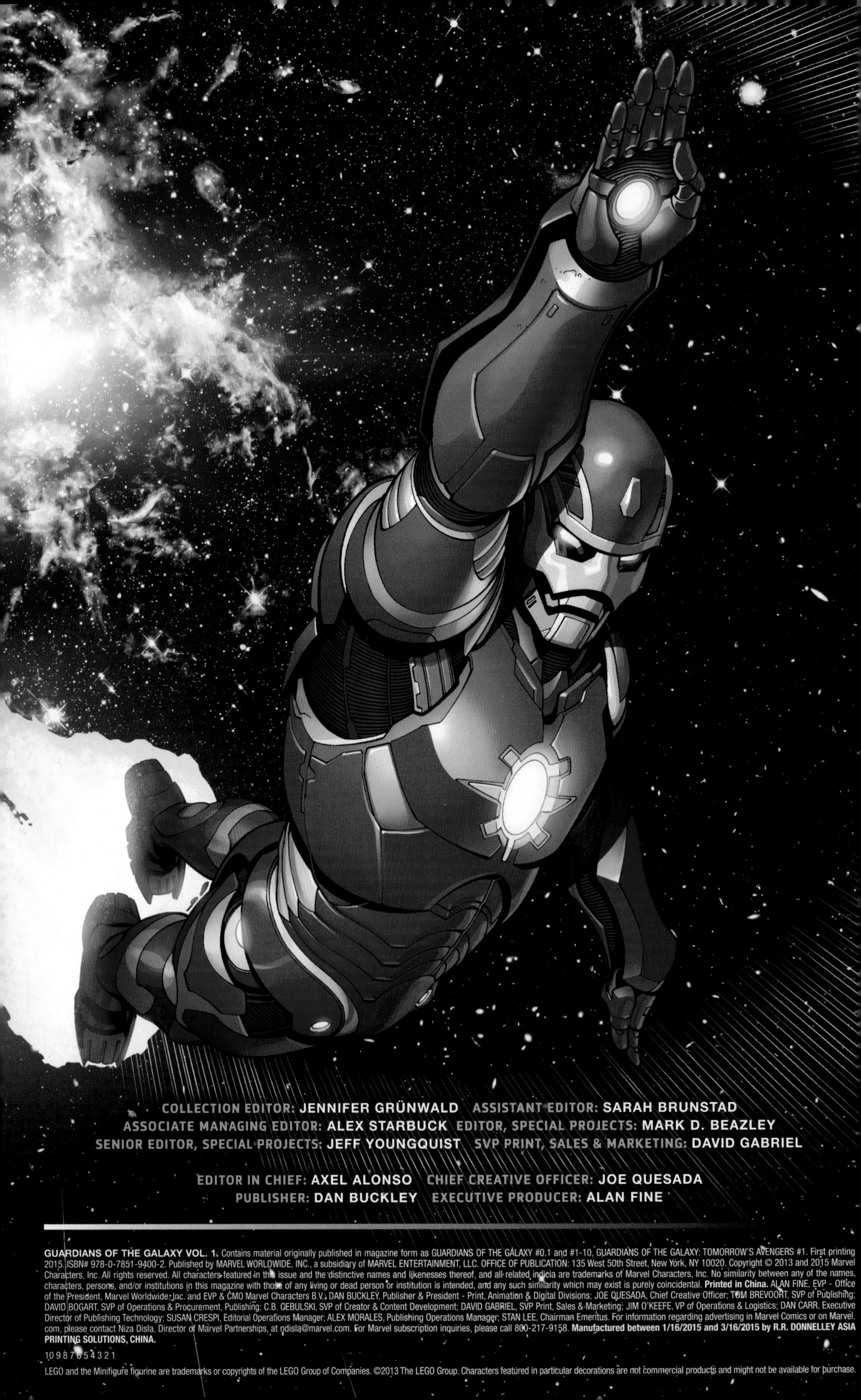

COLLECTION EDITOR: **JENNIFER GRÜNWALD** ASSISTANT EDITOR: **SARAH BRUNSTAD**
ASSOCIATE MANAGING EDITOR: **ALEX STARBUCK** EDITOR, SPECIAL PROJECTS: **MARK D. BEAZLEY**
SENIOR EDITOR, SPECIAL PROJECTS: **JEFF YOUNGQUIST** SVP PRINT, SALES & MARKETING: **DAVID GABRIEL**

EDITOR IN CHIEF: **AXEL ALONSO** CHIEF CREATIVE OFFICER: **JOE QUESADA**
PUBLISHER: **DAN BUCKLEY** EXECUTIVE PRODUCER: **ALAN FINE**

GUARDIANS OF THE GALAXY VOL. 1. Contains material originally published in magazine form as GUARDIANS OF THE GALAXY #0.1 and #1-10, GUARDIANS OF THE GALAXY: TOMORROW'S AVENGERS #1. First printing 2015. ISBN# 978-0-7851-9400-2. Published by MARVEL WORLDWIDE, INC., a subsidiary of MARVEL ENTERTAINMENT, LLC. OFFICE OF PUBLICATION: 135 West 50th Street, New York, NY 10020. **Printed in China.** ALAN FINE, EVP - Office of the President, Marvel Worldwide, Inc. and EVP & CMO Marvel Characters B.V.; DAN BUCKLEY, Publisher & President - Print, Animation & Digital Divisions; JOE QUESADA, Chief Creative Officer; TOM BREVOORT, SVP of Publishing; DAVID BOGART, SVP of Operations & Procurement, Publishing; C.B. CEBULSKI, SVP of Creator & Content Development; DAVID GABRIEL, SVP Print, Sales & Marketing; JIM O'KEEFE, VP of Operations & Logistics; DAN CARR, Executive Director of Publishing Technology; SUSAN CRESPI, Editorial Operations Manager; ALEX MORALES, Publishing Operations Manager; STAN LEE, Chairman Emeritus. For information regarding advertising in Marvel Comics or on Marvel.com, please contact Niza Disla, Director of Marvel Partnerships, at ndisla@marvel.com. For Marvel subscription inquiries, please call 800-217-9158. **Manufactured between 1/16/2015 and 3/16/2015 by R.R. DONNELLEY ASIA PRINTING SOLUTIONS, CHINA.**

10 9 8 7 6 5 4 3 2 1

STAR-LORD   GAMORA   ROCKET RACCOON   GROOT   DRAX   IRON MAN

GUARDIANS OF THE GALAXY

WRITER: **BRIAN MICHAEL BENDIS**   CONSULTANT, #5-8: NEIL GAIMAN

ISSUES #0.1, 1-3
PENCILERS: **STEVE McNIVEN** (#0.1, 1-3) & **SARA PICHELLI** (#2-3)
INKERS: **JOHN DELL** WITH **MARK MORALES** (#2), **STEVE McNIVEN** (#2-3) & **SARA PICHELLI** (#2-3)
COLORIST: **JUSTIN PONSOR**   COVER ART: **STEVE McNIVEN, JOHN DELL** & **JUSTIN PONSOR**

ISSUES #4-7
PENCILERS: **SARA PICHELLI**
WITH **OLIVIER COIPEL** & **MARK MORALES** (#6, PP. 3-8) AND **VALERIO SCHITI** (#7, PP. 8-13, 20)
COLORISTS: **JUSTIN PONSOR** WITH **IVE SVORCINA** (#6, PP. 3-8)
COVER ART: **SARA PICHELLI** & **JUSTIN PONSOR**

ISSUES #8-9
ART/COLOR/COVER: **FRANCESCO FRANCAVILLA**

ISSUE #10
ARTIST: **KEVIN MAGUIRE**
COVER ART: **KEVIN MAGUIRE** & **EDGAR DELGADO**

LETTERER: **VC'S CORY PETIT**   ASSISTANT EDITOR: **ELLIE PYLE**   EDITOR: **STEPHEN WACKER**
ANGELA CO-CREATED BY TODD McFARLANE & NEIL GAIMAN

TOMORROW'S AVENGERS

WRITER: **BRIAN MICHAEL BENDIS**
ART: **MICHAEL AVON OEMING** & **RAIN BEREDO** (DRAX), **MING DOYLE** & **JAVIER RODRIGUEZ**
(ROCKET RACCOON) AND **MICHAEL DEL MUNDO** (GAMORA & GROOT)
LAYOUTS (DRAX, ROCKET RACCOON, GAMORA): **YVES BIGEREL**
LETTERER: **VC'S JOE CARAMAGNA**   COVER ART: **MING DOYLE**
EDITOR: **SANA AMANAT**   SENIOR EDITOR: **STEPHEN WACKER**

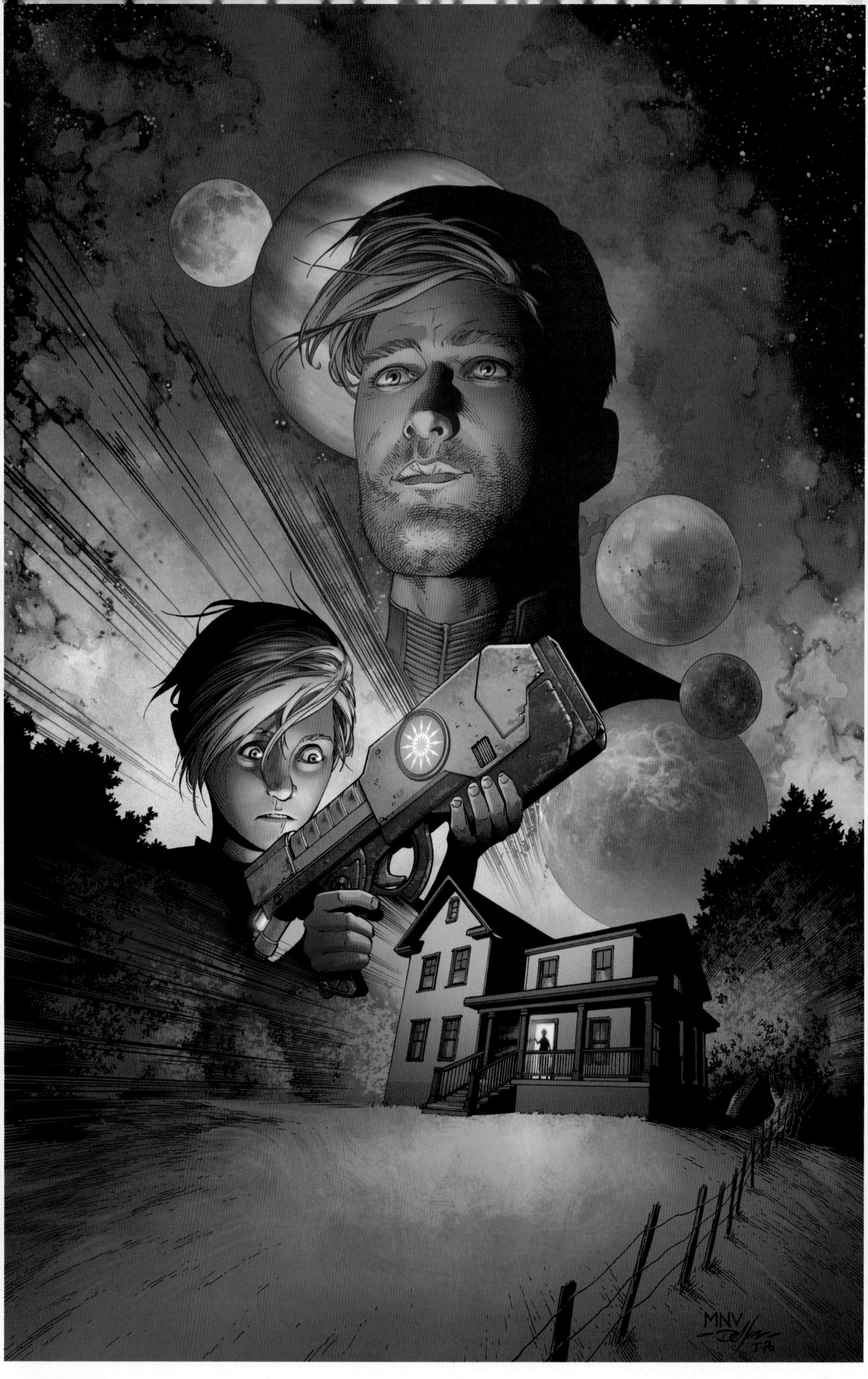
MNV

0.1

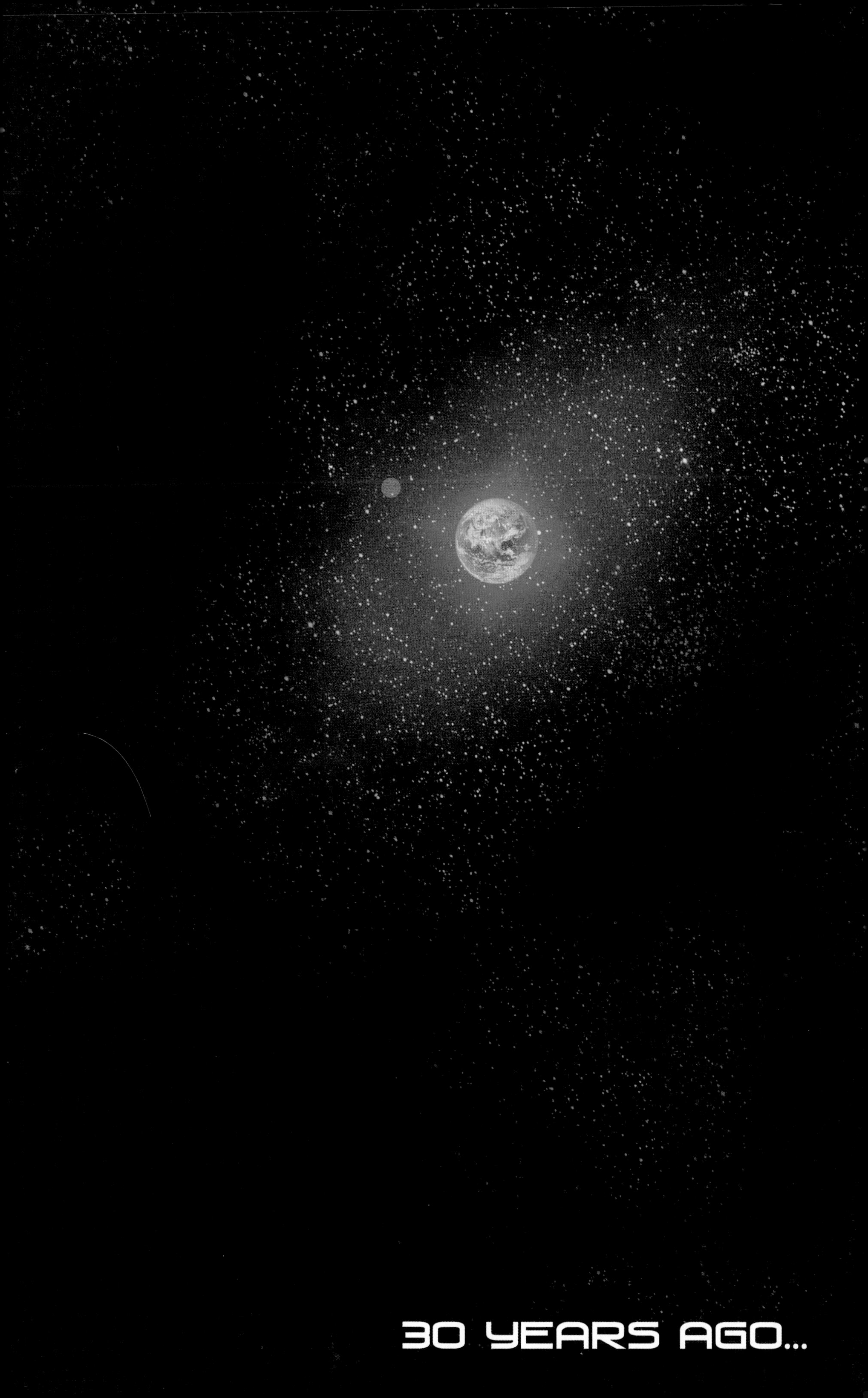
30 YEARS AGO...

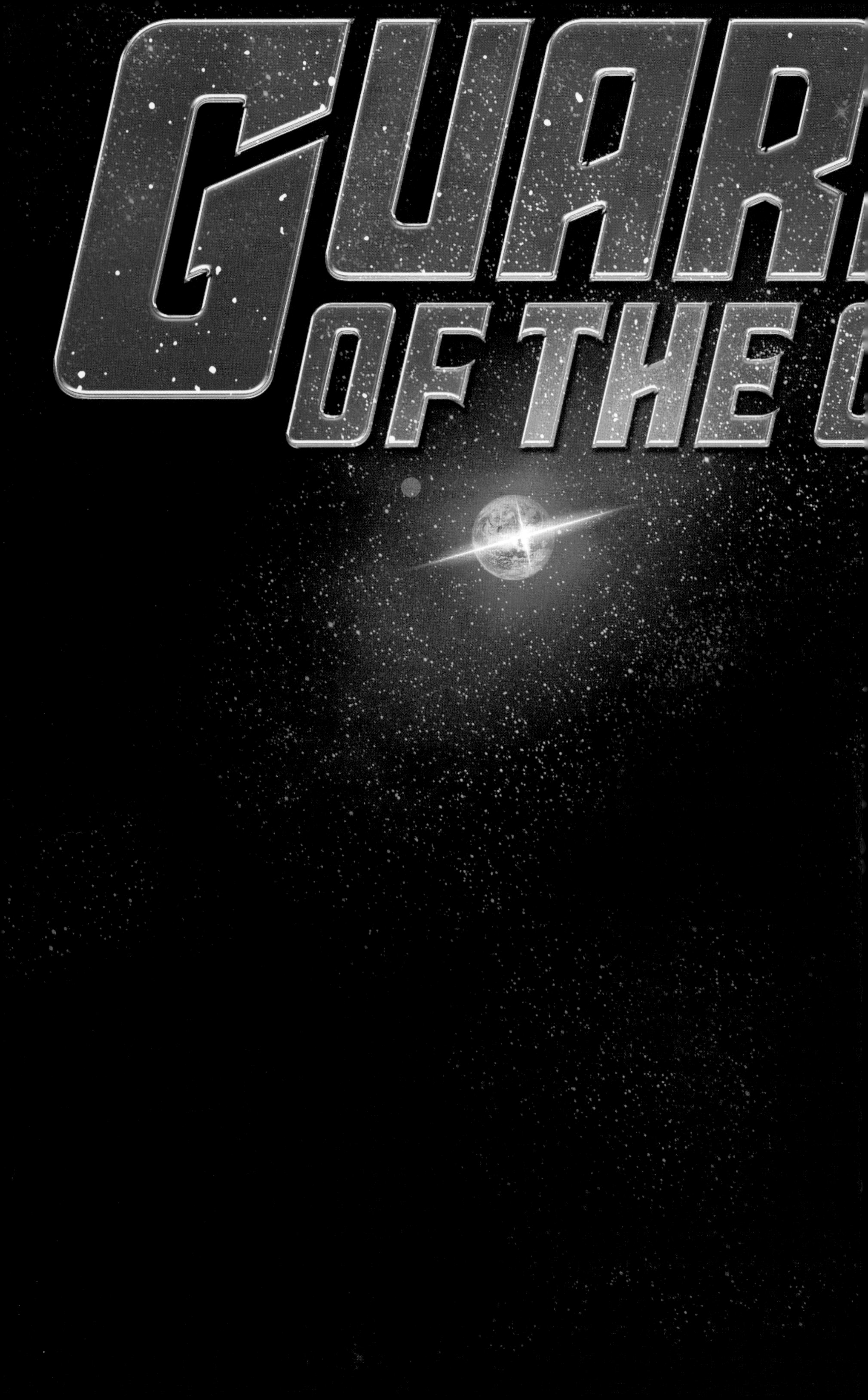
OF THE

DIANS
ALAXY

"NO.

"NO,
MOM.

"HE BROKE UP
WITH *ME!!*"

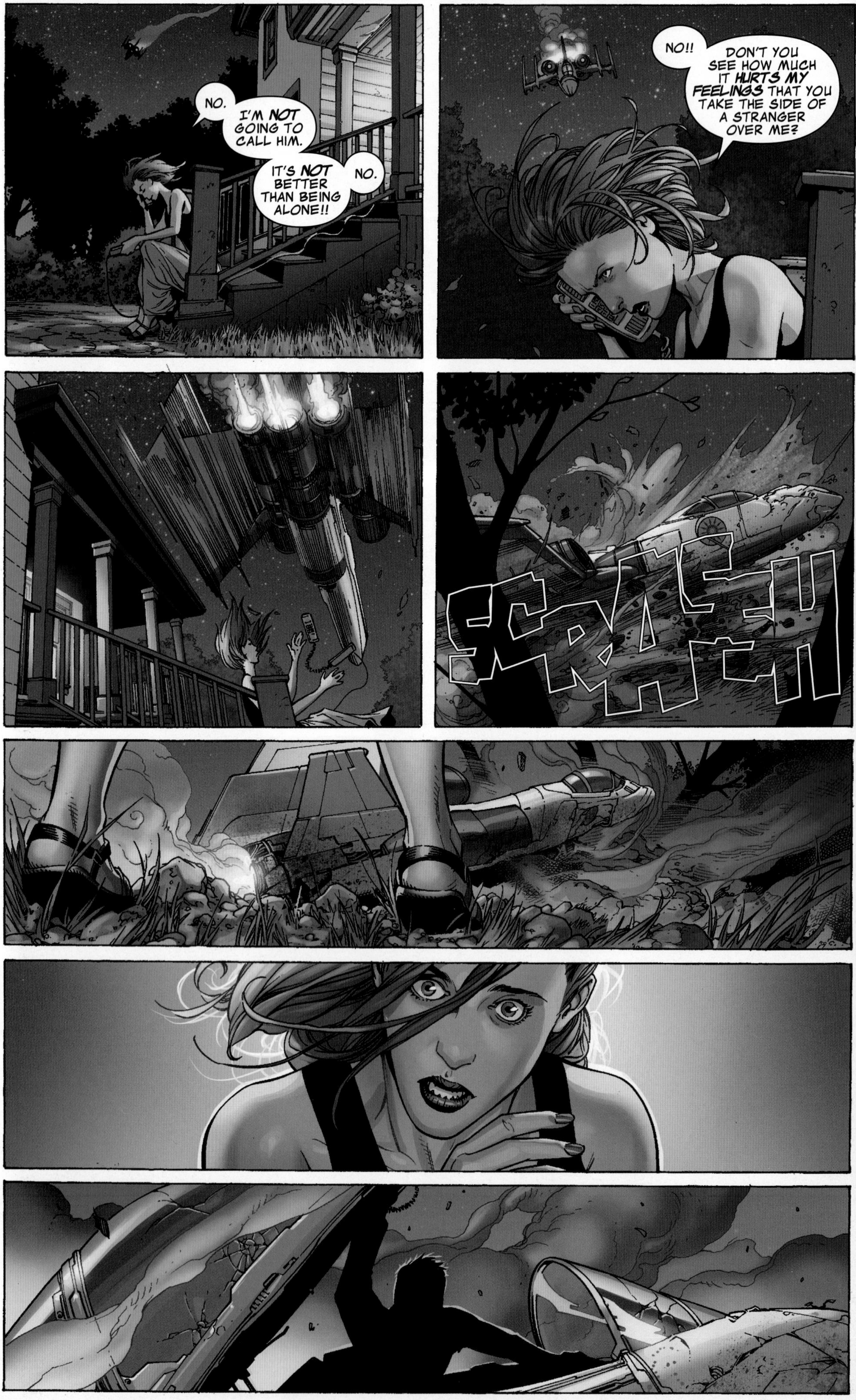
NO.
I'M NOT GOING TO CALL HIM.
IT'S NOT BETTER THAN BEING ALONE!!
NO.
NO!!
DON'T YOU SEE HOW MUCH IT HURTS MY FEELINGS THAT YOU TAKE THE SIDE OF A STRANGER OVER ME?
SCRATCH

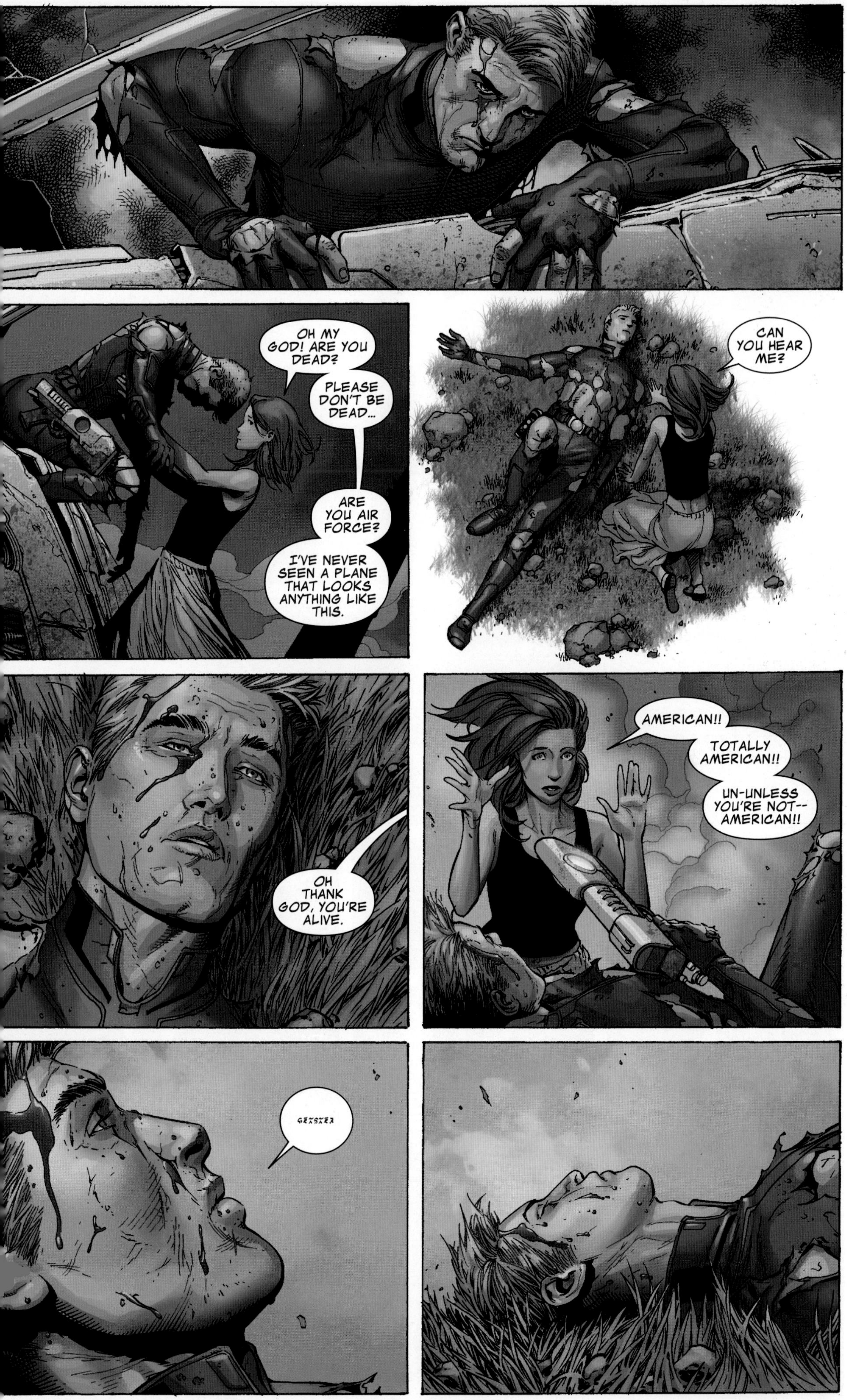
OH MY GOD! ARE YOU DEAD?
PLEASE DON'T BE DEAD...
ARE YOU AIR FORCE?
I'VE NEVER SEEN A PLANE THAT LOOKS ANYTHING LIKE THIS.
CAN YOU HEAR ME?
OH THANK GOD, YOU'RE ALIVE.
AMERICAN!!
TOTALLY AMERICAN!!
UN-UNLESS YOU'RE NOT--AMERICAN!!

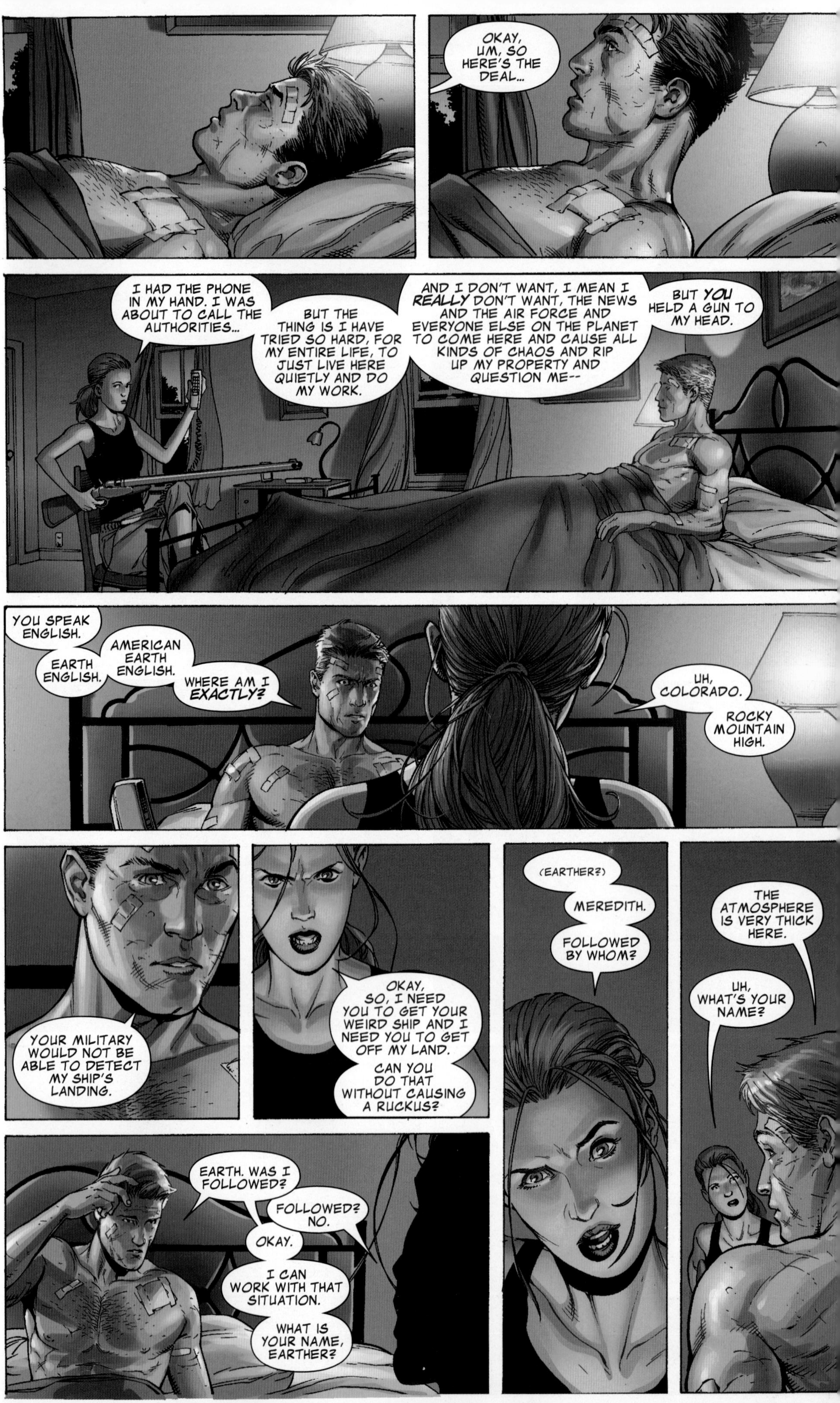
OKAY, UM, SO HERE'S THE DEAL...
I HAD THE PHONE IN MY HAND. I WAS ABOUT TO CALL THE AUTHORITIES...
BUT THE THING IS I HAVE TRIED SO HARD, FOR MY ENTIRE LIFE, TO JUST LIVE HERE QUIETLY AND DO MY WORK.
AND I DON'T WANT, I MEAN I REALLY DON'T WANT, THE NEWS AND THE AIR FORCE AND EVERYONE ELSE ON THE PLANET TO COME HERE AND CAUSE ALL KINDS OF CHAOS AND RIP UP MY PROPERTY AND QUESTION ME--
BUT YOU HELD A GUN TO MY HEAD.
YOU SPEAK ENGLISH.
EARTH ENGLISH.
AMERICAN EARTH ENGLISH.
WHERE AM I EXACTLY?
UH, COLORADO.
ROCKY MOUNTAIN HIGH.
YOUR MILITARY WOULD NOT BE ABLE TO DETECT MY SHIP'S LANDING.
OKAY, SO, I NEED YOU TO GET YOUR WEIRD SHIP AND I NEED YOU TO GET OFF MY LAND.
CAN YOU DO THAT WITHOUT CAUSING A RUCKUS?
EARTH. WAS I FOLLOWED?
FOLLOWED? NO.
OKAY.
I CAN WORK WITH THAT SITUATION.
WHAT IS YOUR NAME, EARTHER?
(EARTHER?)
MEREDITH.
FOLLOWED BY WHOM?
THE ATMOSPHERE IS VERY THICK HERE.
UH, WHAT'S YOUR NAME?

MY NAME IS J'SON OF SPARTAX.

YOUR KINDNESS IS APPRECIATED.

I HOPE I WILL BE ABLE TO RETURN IT.

ARE YOU A PILOT?

I'M FROM SPARTAX. I AM OF THE THRONE.

IS THAT-- WHAT IS THAT?

I WILL NEED TO FIX MY SHIP AND GET BACK TO MY PEOPLE. I WILL TRY TO DO SO AS QUICKLY AS I CAN.

OH MY GOD. ARE YOU KIDDING ME?

ARE YOU FROM-- ARE YOU FROM SPACE?

I'M FROM SPARTAX.

I'VE TOLD YOU THIS A FEW TIMES.

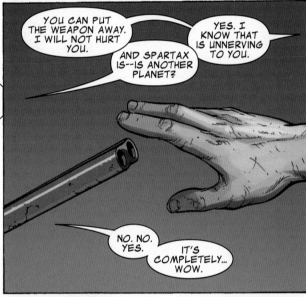

YOU CAN PUT THE WEAPON AWAY. I WILL NOT HURT YOU.

YES. I KNOW THAT IS UNNERVING TO YOU.

AND SPARTAX IS--IS ANOTHER PLANET?

NO. NO. YES.

IT'S COMPLETELY... WOW.

DO YOU-- DO YOU NEED A TOOLBOX OR--?

YOU'RE A FUNNY EARTHER.

NO. I HAVE THE TOOLS. BUT IT MAY TAKE SOME TIME.

EARTHER?

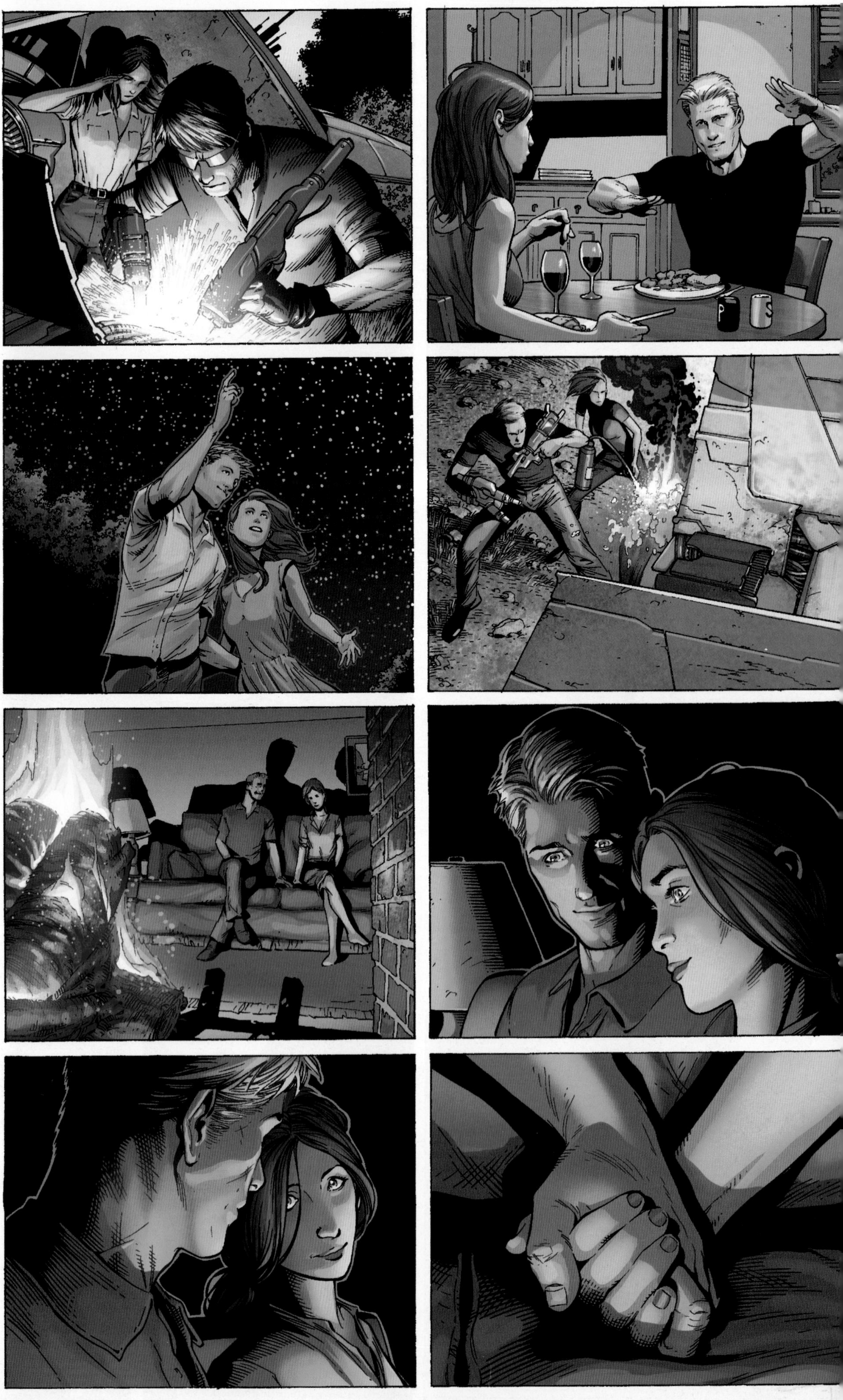
P
S

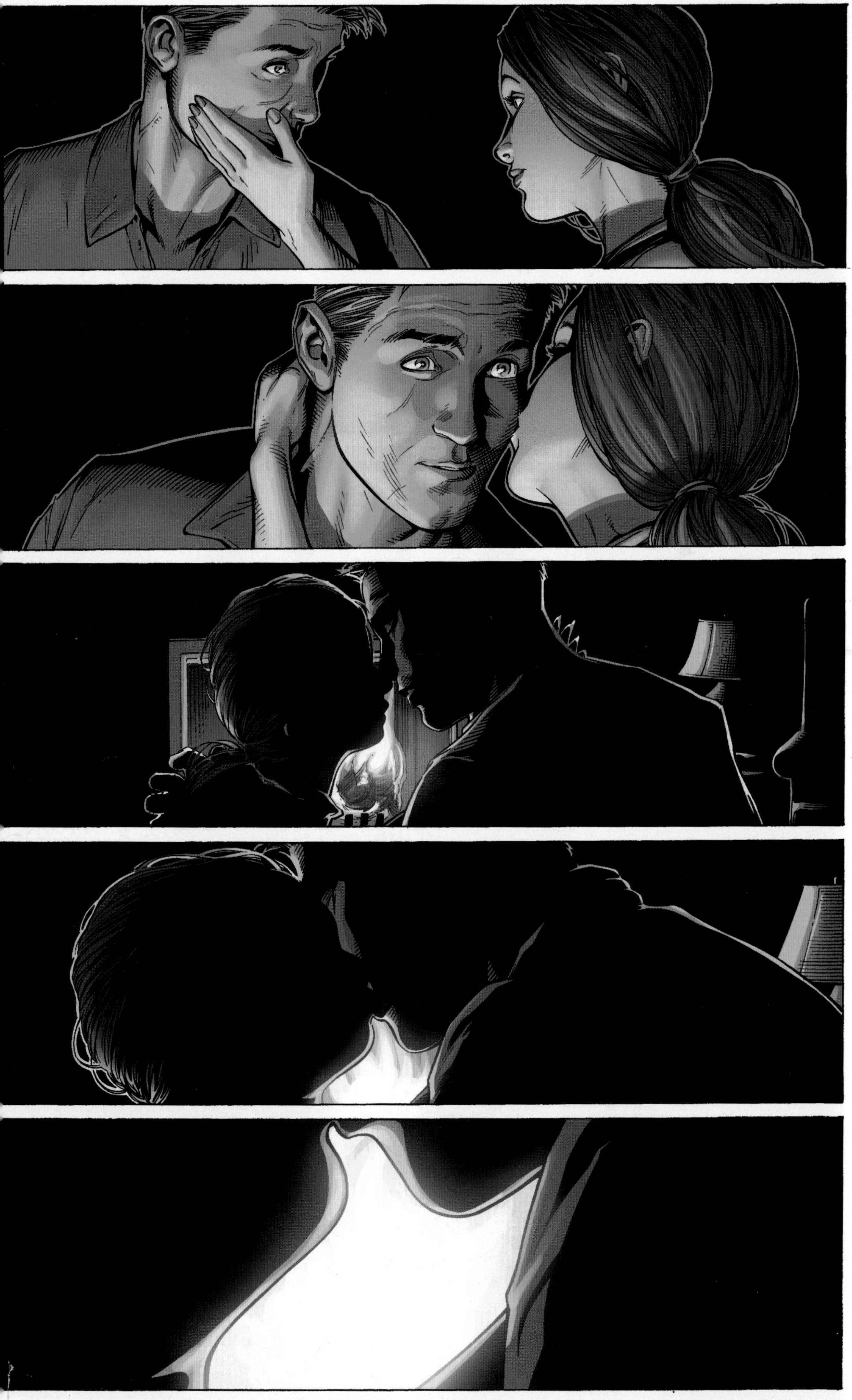

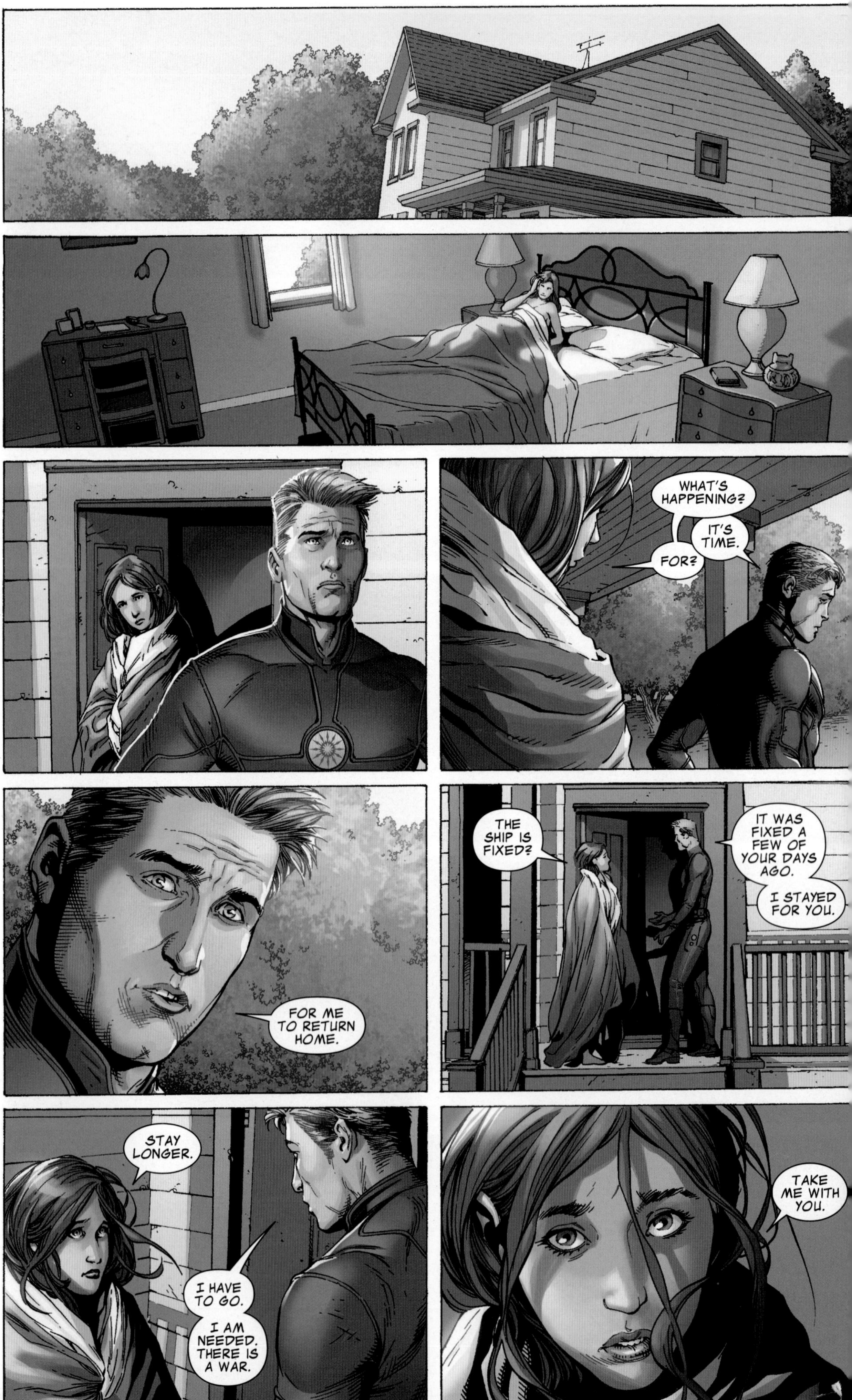
WHAT'S HAPPENING?
IT'S TIME.
FOR?
FOR ME TO RETURN HOME.
THE SHIP IS FIXED?
IT WAS FIXED A FEW OF YOUR DAYS AGO.
I STAYED FOR YOU.
STAY LONGER.
I HAVE TO GO.
I AM NEEDED. THERE IS A WAR.
TAKE ME WITH YOU.

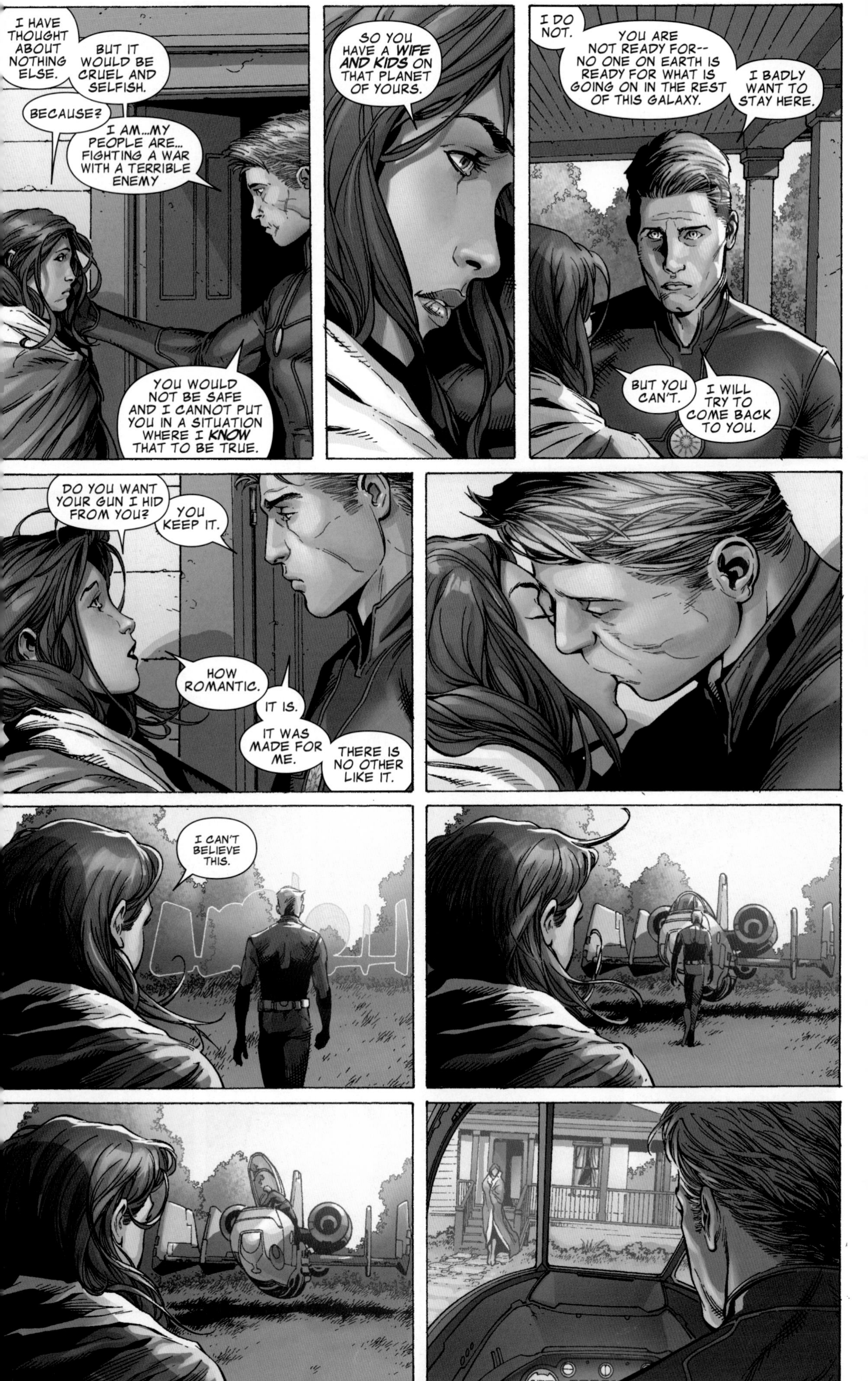
I HAVE THOUGHT ABOUT NOTHING ELSE.
BUT IT WOULD BE CRUEL AND SELFISH.
BECAUSE?
I AM...MY PEOPLE ARE... FIGHTING A WAR WITH A TERRIBLE ENEMY
YOU WOULD NOT BE SAFE AND I CANNOT PUT YOU IN A SITUATION WHERE I KNOW THAT TO BE TRUE.
SO YOU HAVE A WIFE AND KIDS ON THAT PLANET OF YOURS.
I DO NOT.
YOU ARE NOT READY FOR-- NO ONE ON EARTH IS READY FOR WHAT IS GOING ON IN THE REST OF THIS GALAXY.
I BADLY WANT TO STAY HERE.
BUT YOU CAN'T.
I WILL TRY TO COME BACK TO YOU.
DO YOU WANT YOUR GUN I HID FROM YOU?
YOU KEEP IT.
HOW ROMANTIC.
IT IS.
IT WAS MADE FOR ME.
THERE IS NO OTHER LIKE IT.
I CAN'T BELIEVE THIS.

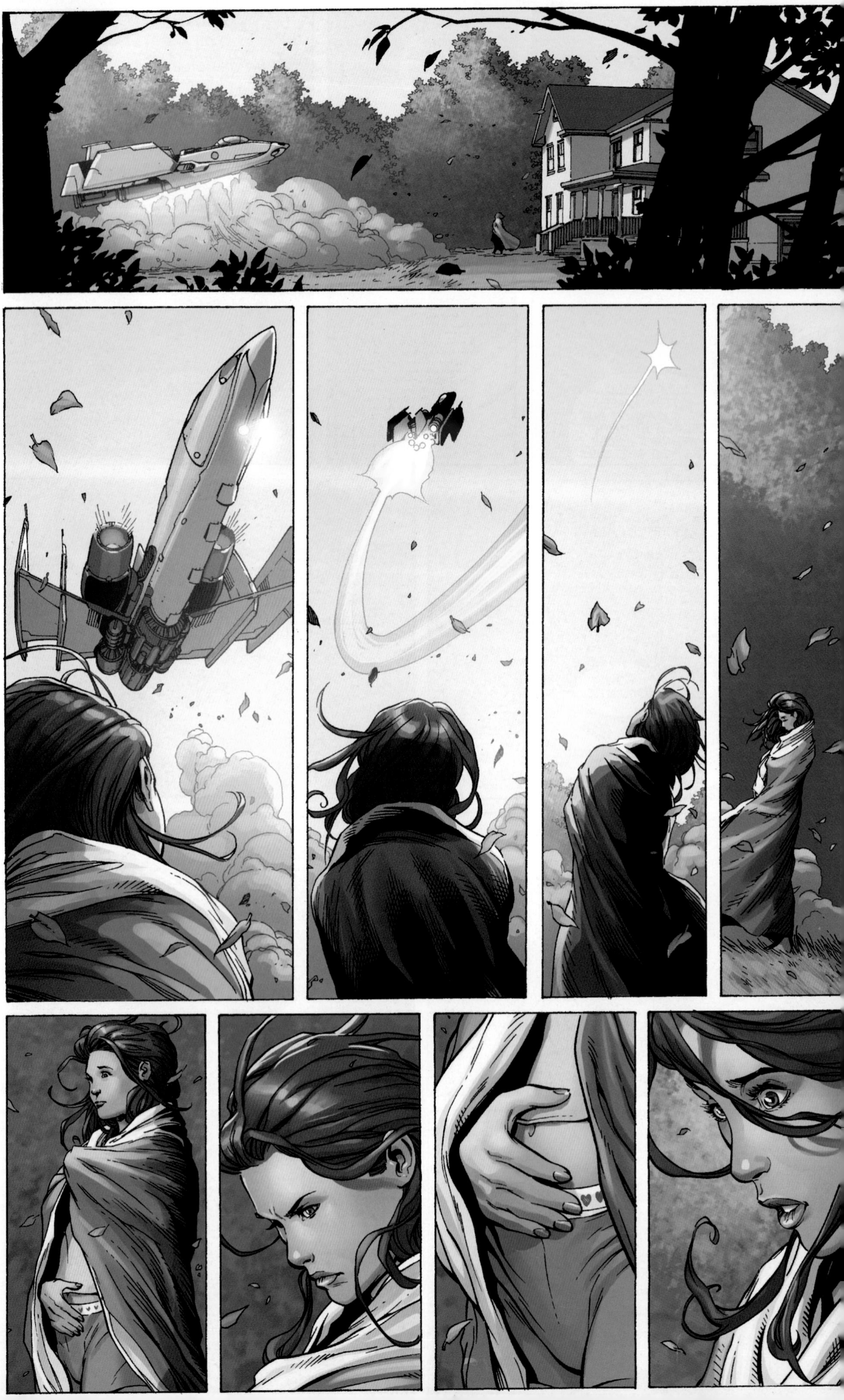

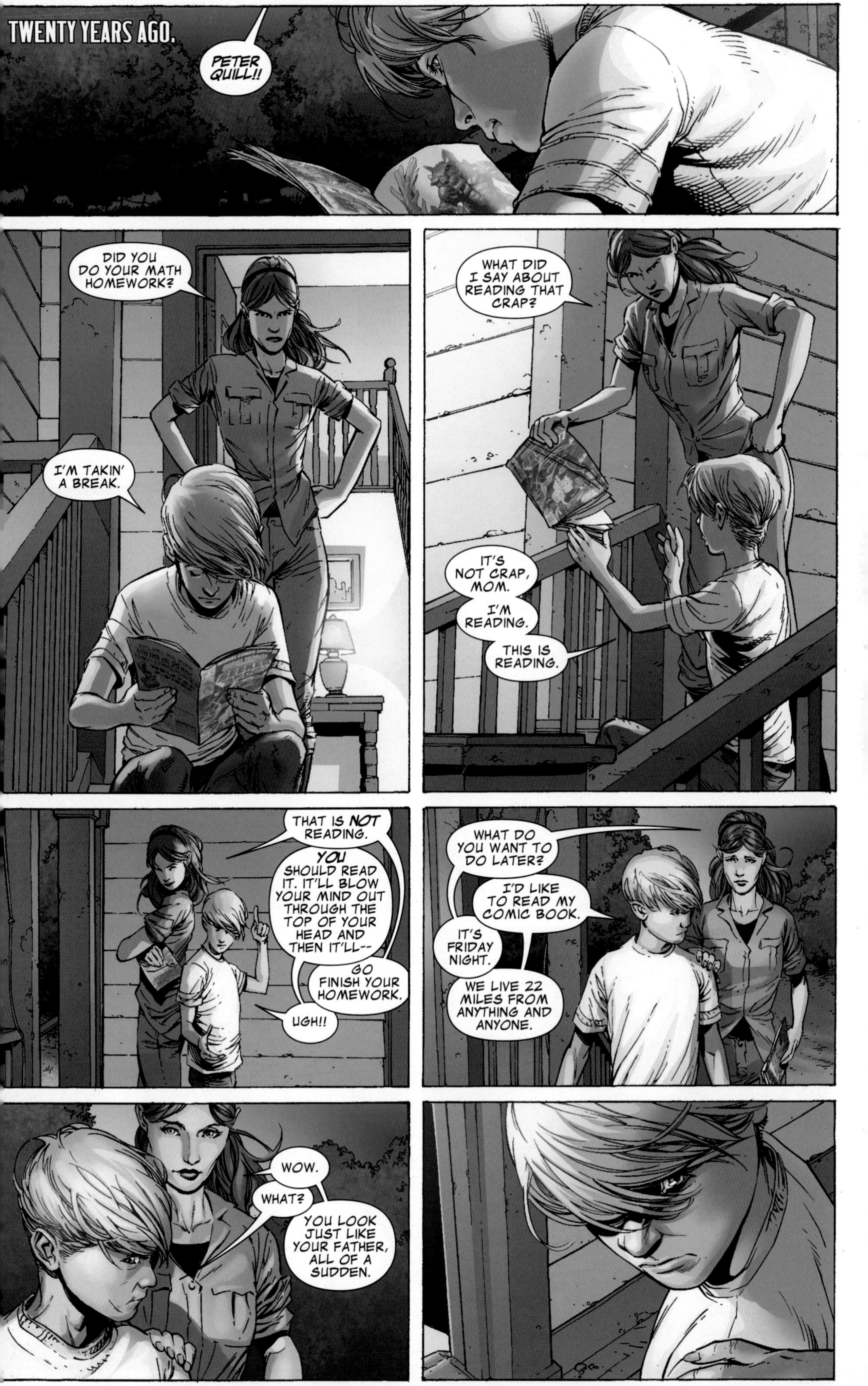
TWENTY YEARS AGO.
PETER QUILL!!
DID YOU DO YOUR MATH HOMEWORK?
I'M TAKIN' A BREAK.
WHAT DID I SAY ABOUT READING THAT CRAP?
IT'S NOT CRAP, MOM.
I'M READING.
THIS IS READING.
THAT IS NOT READING.
YOU SHOULD READ IT. IT'LL BLOW YOUR MIND OUT THROUGH THE TOP OF YOUR HEAD AND THEN IT'LL--
GO FINISH YOUR HOMEWORK.
UGH!!
WHAT DO YOU WANT TO DO LATER?
I'D LIKE TO READ MY COMIC BOOK.
IT'S FRIDAY NIGHT.
WE LIVE 22 MILES FROM ANYTHING AND ANYONE.
WOW.
WHAT?
YOU LOOK JUST LIKE YOUR FATHER, ALL OF A SUDDEN.

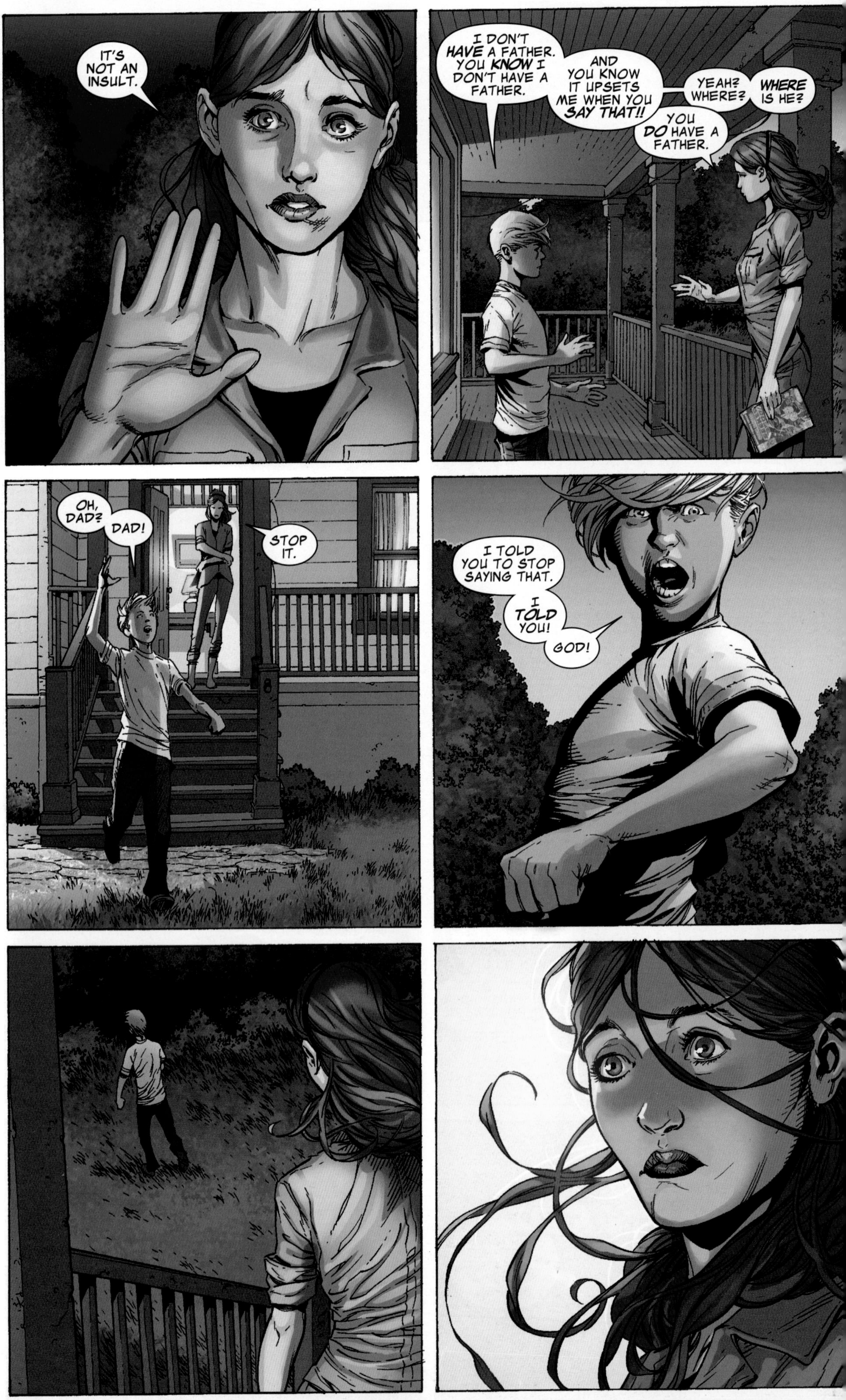
IT'S NOT AN INSULT.
I DON'T HAVE A FATHER. YOU KNOW I DON'T HAVE A FATHER.
AND YOU KNOW IT UPSETS ME WHEN YOU SAY THAT!!
YOU DO HAVE A FATHER.
YEAH? WHERE?
WHERE IS HE?
OH, DAD?
DAD!
STOP IT.
I TOLD YOU TO STOP SAYING THAT.
I TOLD YOU!
GOD!

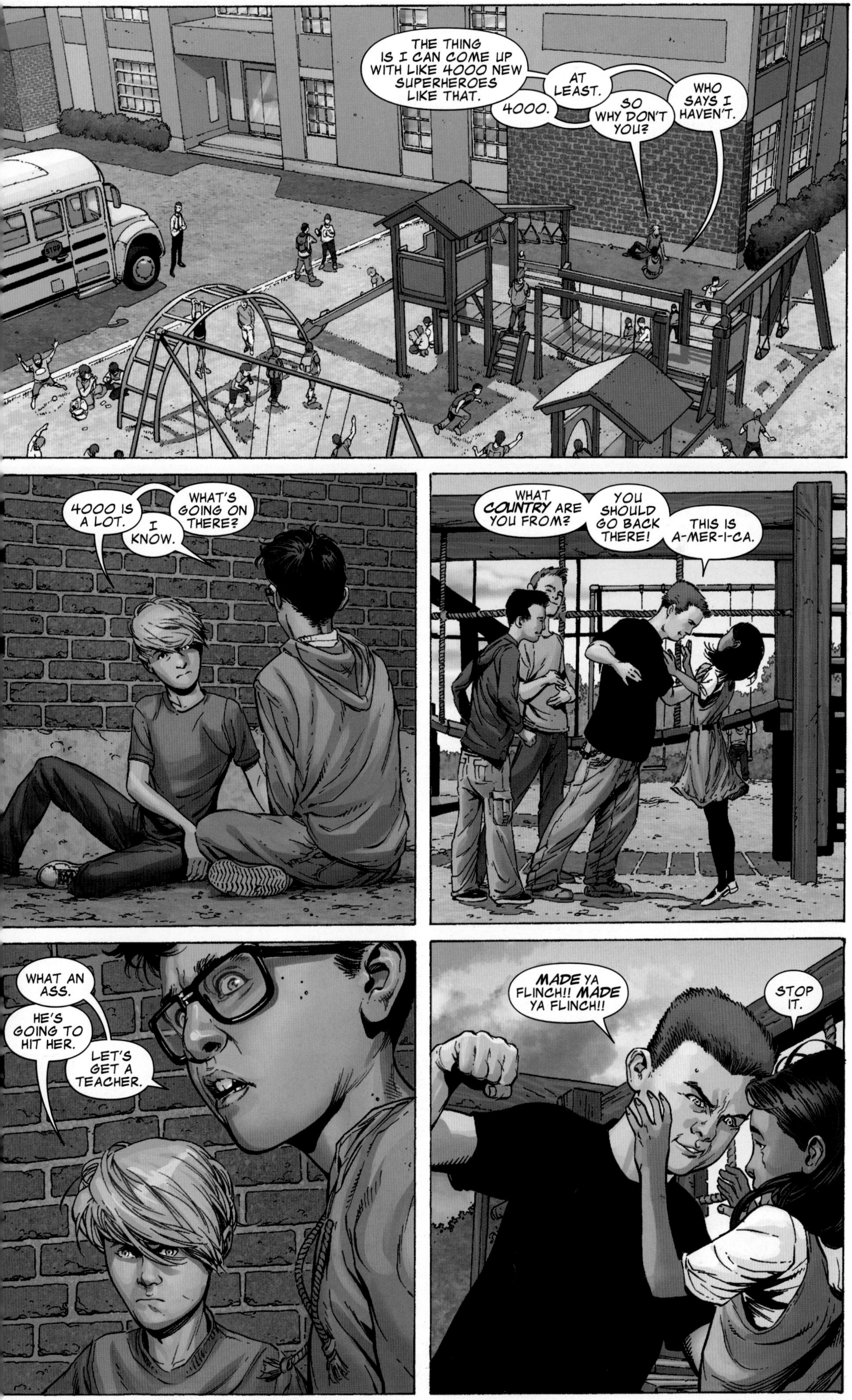
THE THING IS I CAN COME UP WITH LIKE 4000 NEW SUPERHEROES LIKE THAT.
4000.
AT LEAST.
SO WHY DON'T YOU?
WHO SAYS I HAVEN'T.
4000 IS A LOT.
I KNOW.
WHAT'S GOING ON THERE?
WHAT COUNTRY ARE YOU FROM?
YOU SHOULD GO BACK THERE!
THIS IS A-MER-I-CA.
WHAT AN ASS.
HE'S GOING TO HIT HER.
LET'S GET A TEACHER.
MADE YA FLINCH!! MADE YA FLINCH!!
STOP IT.

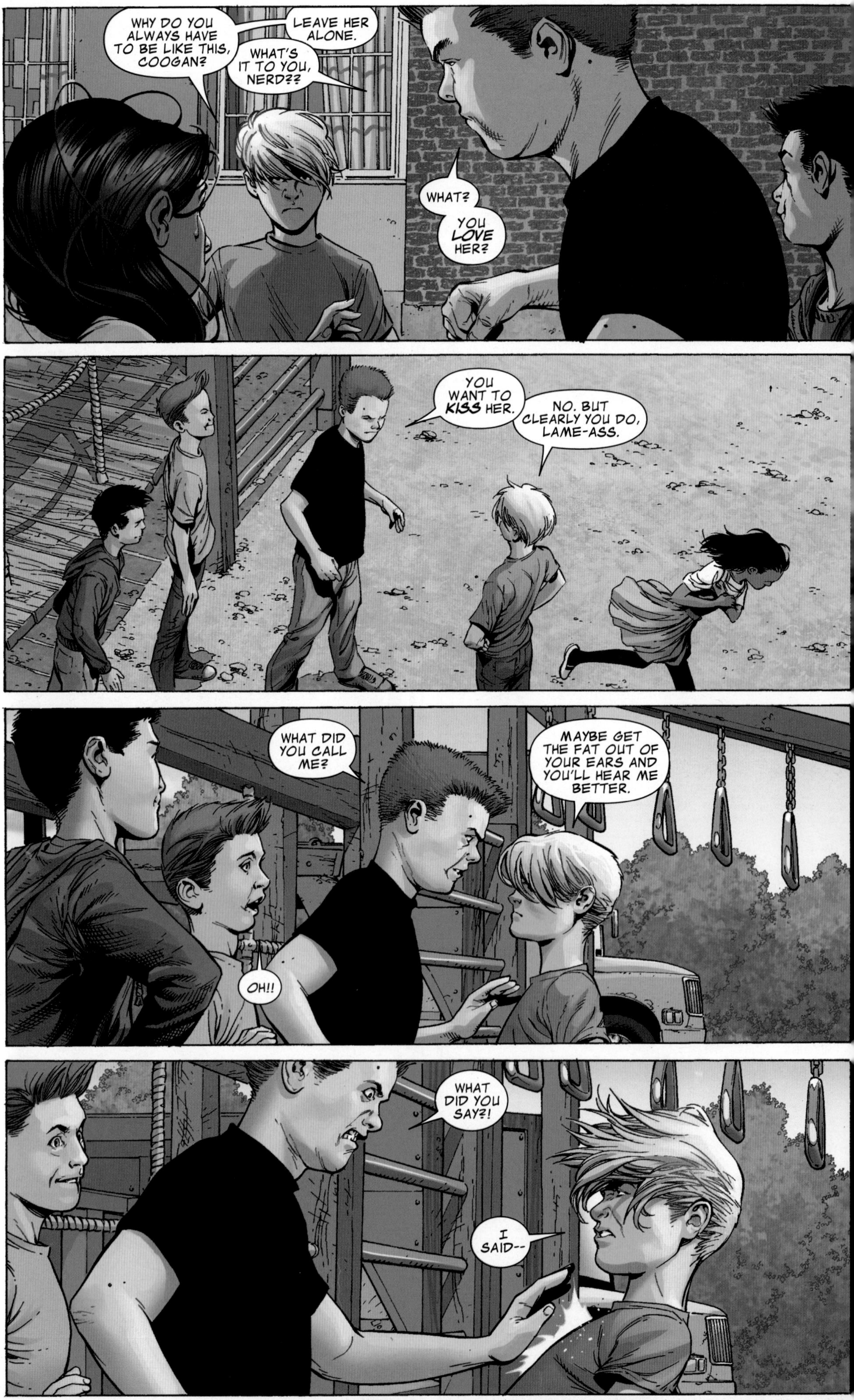
WHY DO YOU ALWAYS HAVE TO BE LIKE THIS, COOGAN?
LEAVE HER ALONE.
WHAT'S IT TO YOU, NERD??
WHAT?
YOU LOVE HER?
YOU WANT TO KISS HER.
NO. BUT CLEARLY YOU DO, LAME-ASS.
WHAT DID YOU CALL ME?
MAYBE GET THE FAT OUT OF YOUR EARS AND YOU'LL HEAR ME BETTER.
OH!!
WHAT DID YOU SAY?!
I SAID--

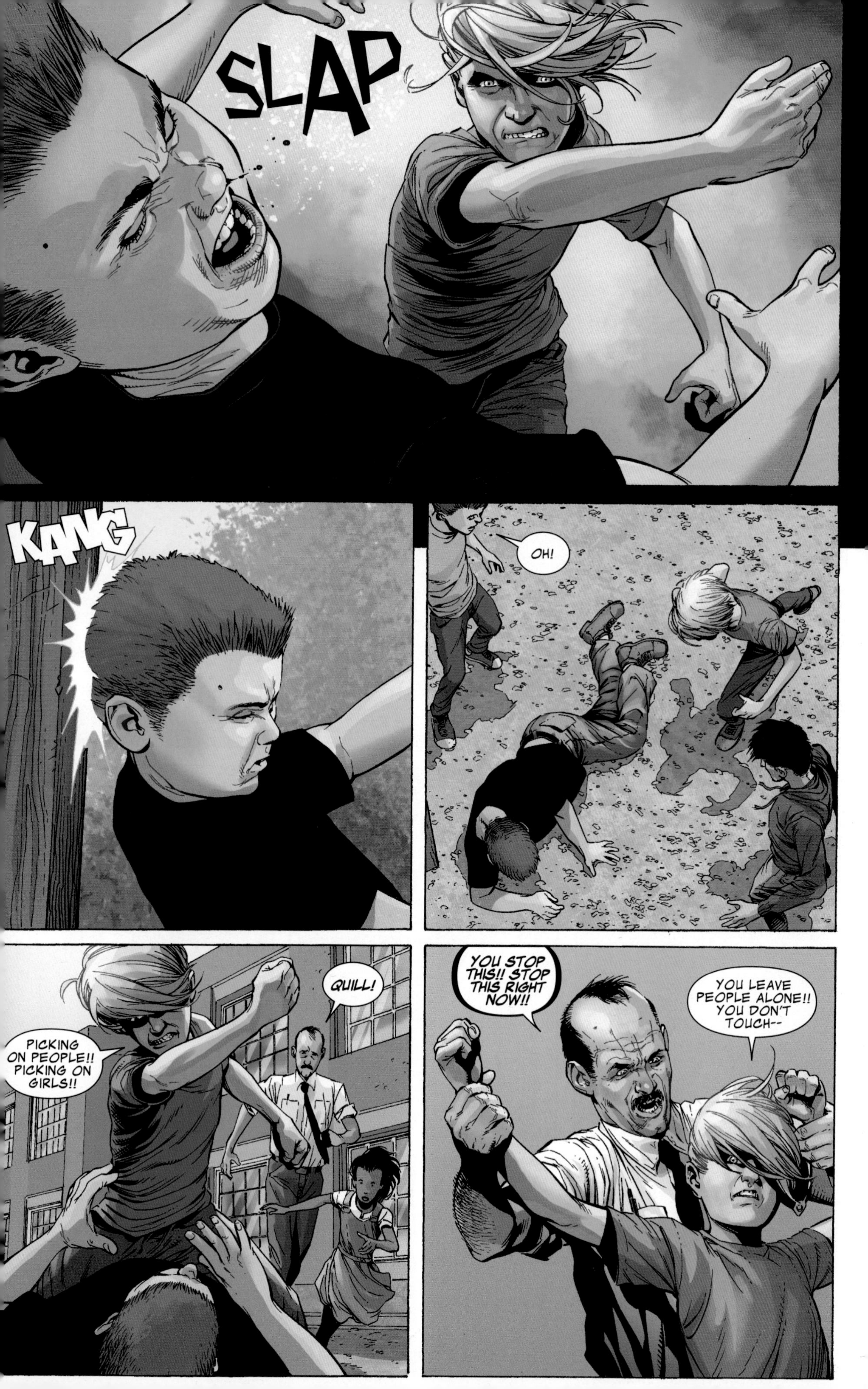
SLAP
KANG
OH!
QUILL!
PICKING ON PEOPLE!! PICKING ON GIRLS!!
YOU STOP THIS!! STOP THIS RIGHT NOW!!
YOU LEAVE PEOPLE ALONE!! YOU DON'T TOUCH--

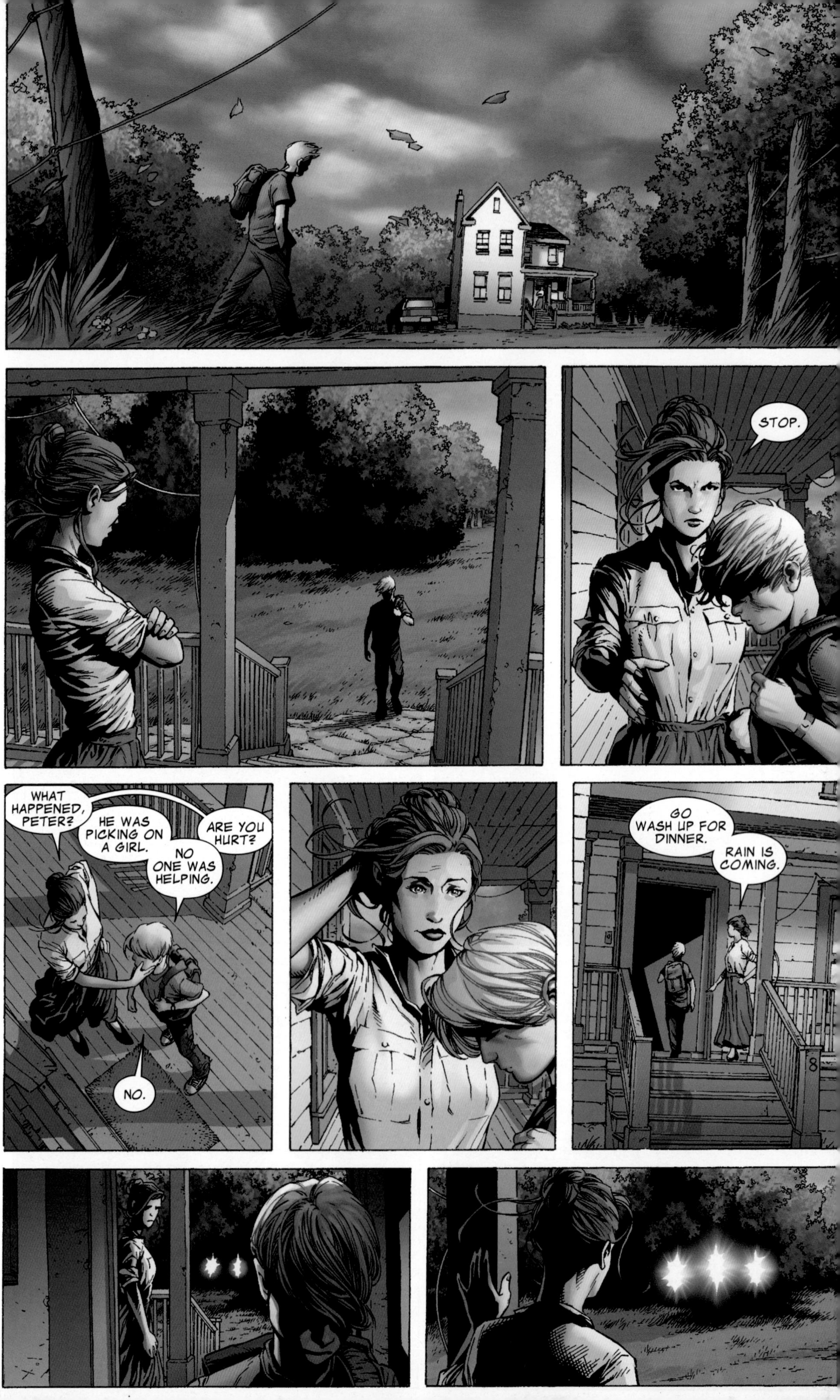
STOP.
WHAT HAPPENED, PETER?
HE WAS PICKING ON A GIRL.
NO ONE WAS HELPING.
ARE YOU HURT?
NO.
GO WASH UP FOR DINNER.
RAIN IS COMING.

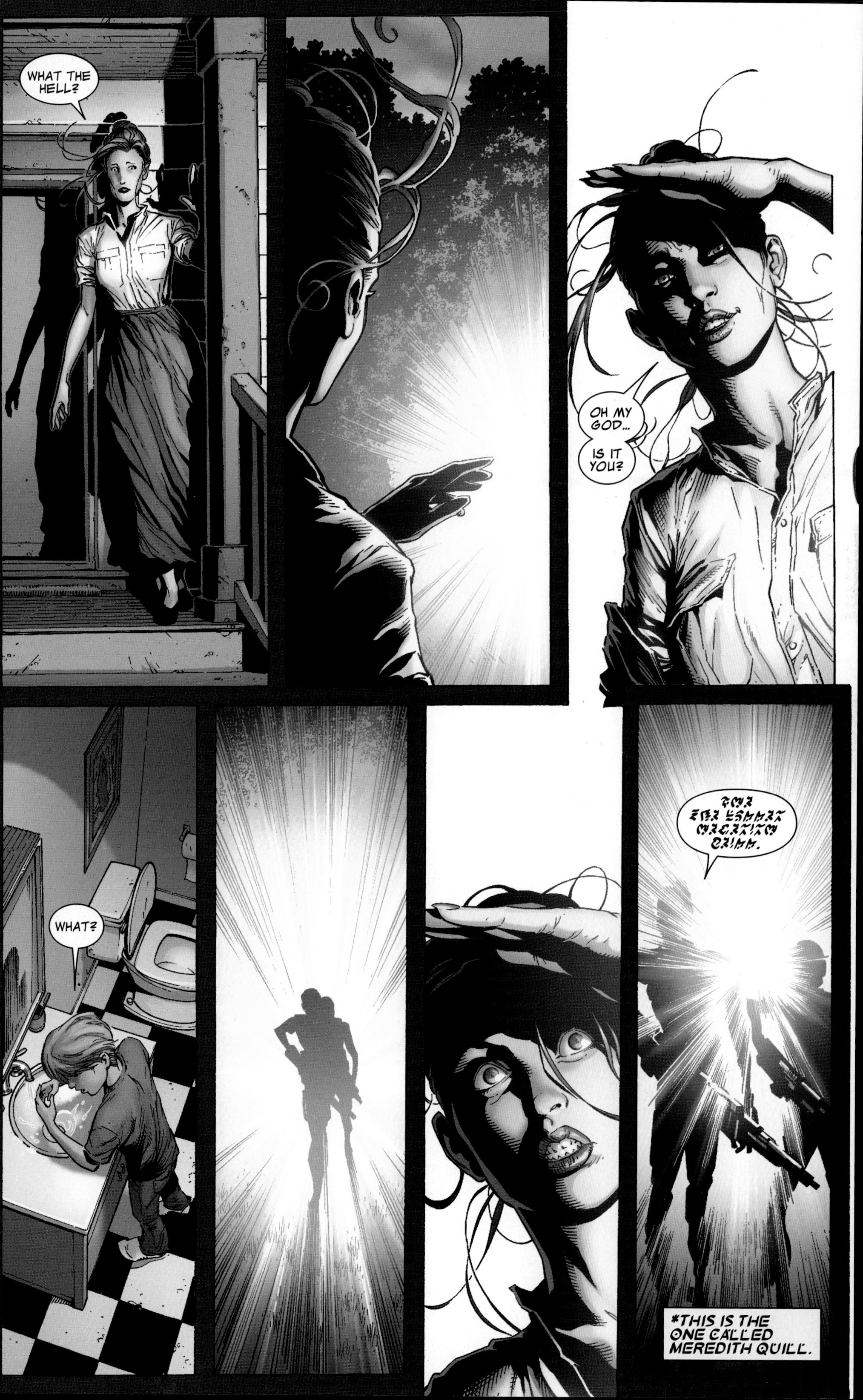
WHAT THE HELL?
OH MY GOD...
IS IT YOU?
WHAT?
*THIS IS THE ONE CALLED MEREDITH QUILL.

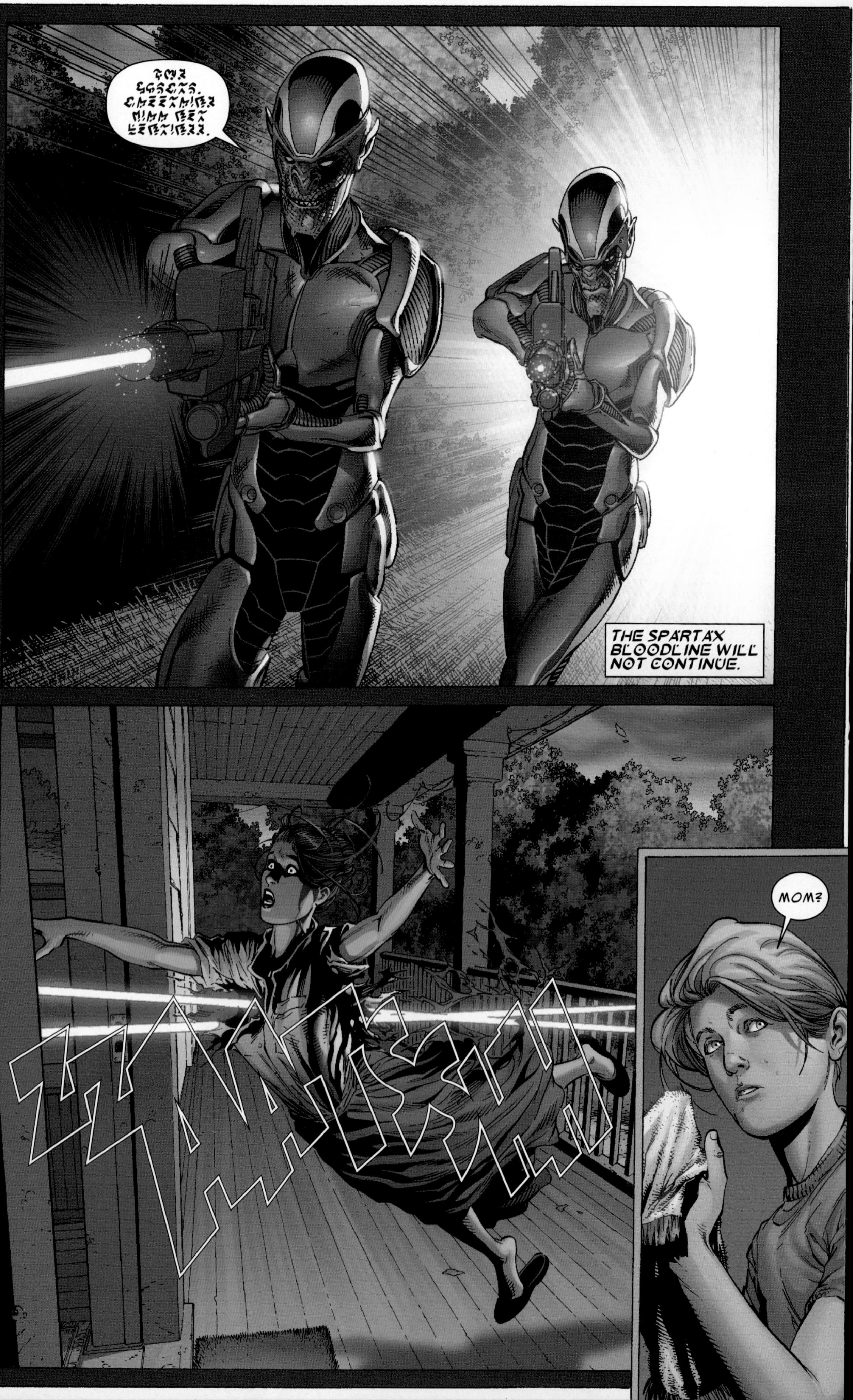
THE SPARTAX BLOODLINE WILL NOT CONTINUE.
MOM?

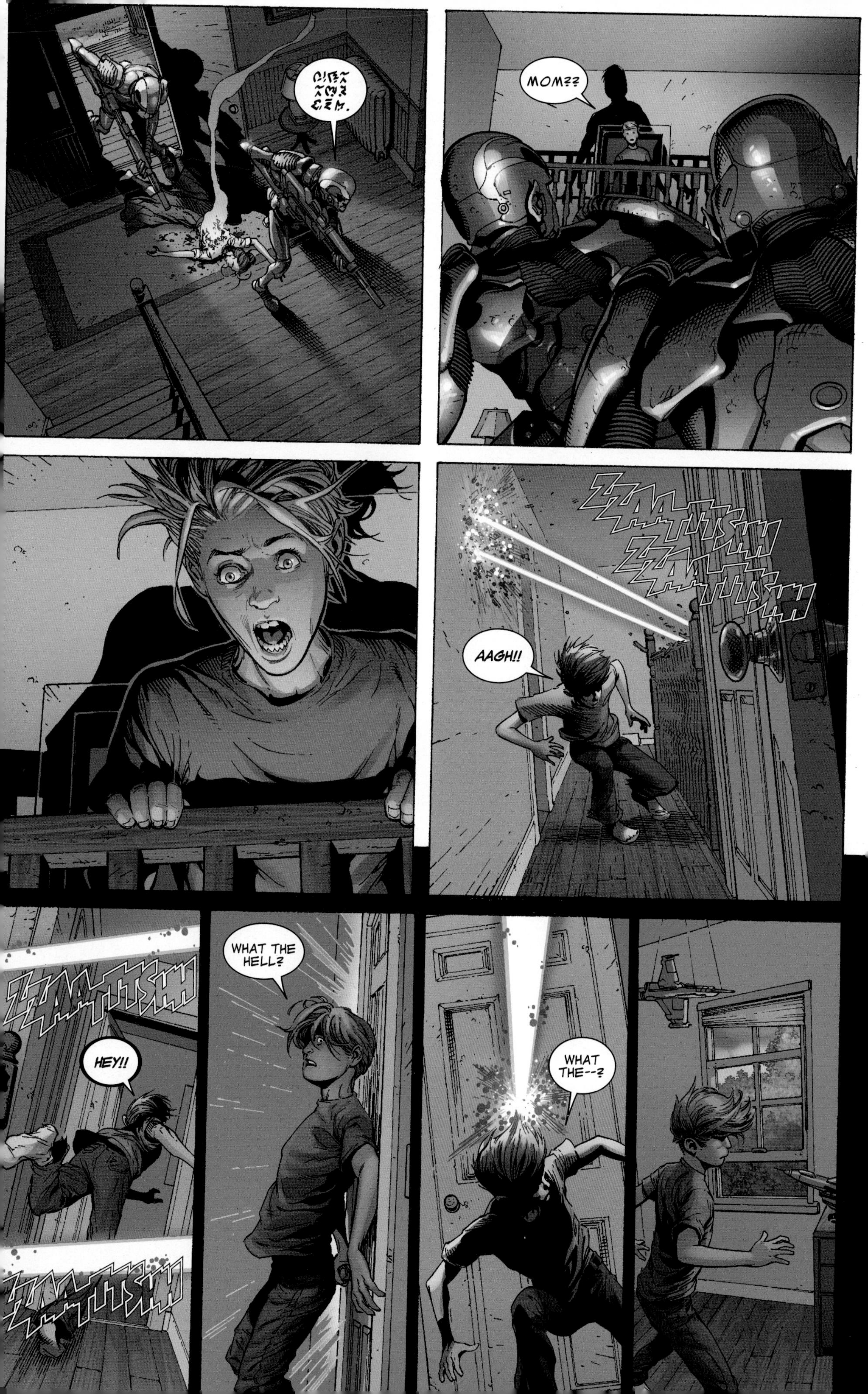

MOM??
ZZAATUTSHH
ZZAATUTSHH
AAGH!!
ZZAATUTSHH
HEY!!
ZZAATUTSHH
WHAT THE HELL?
WHAT THE--?

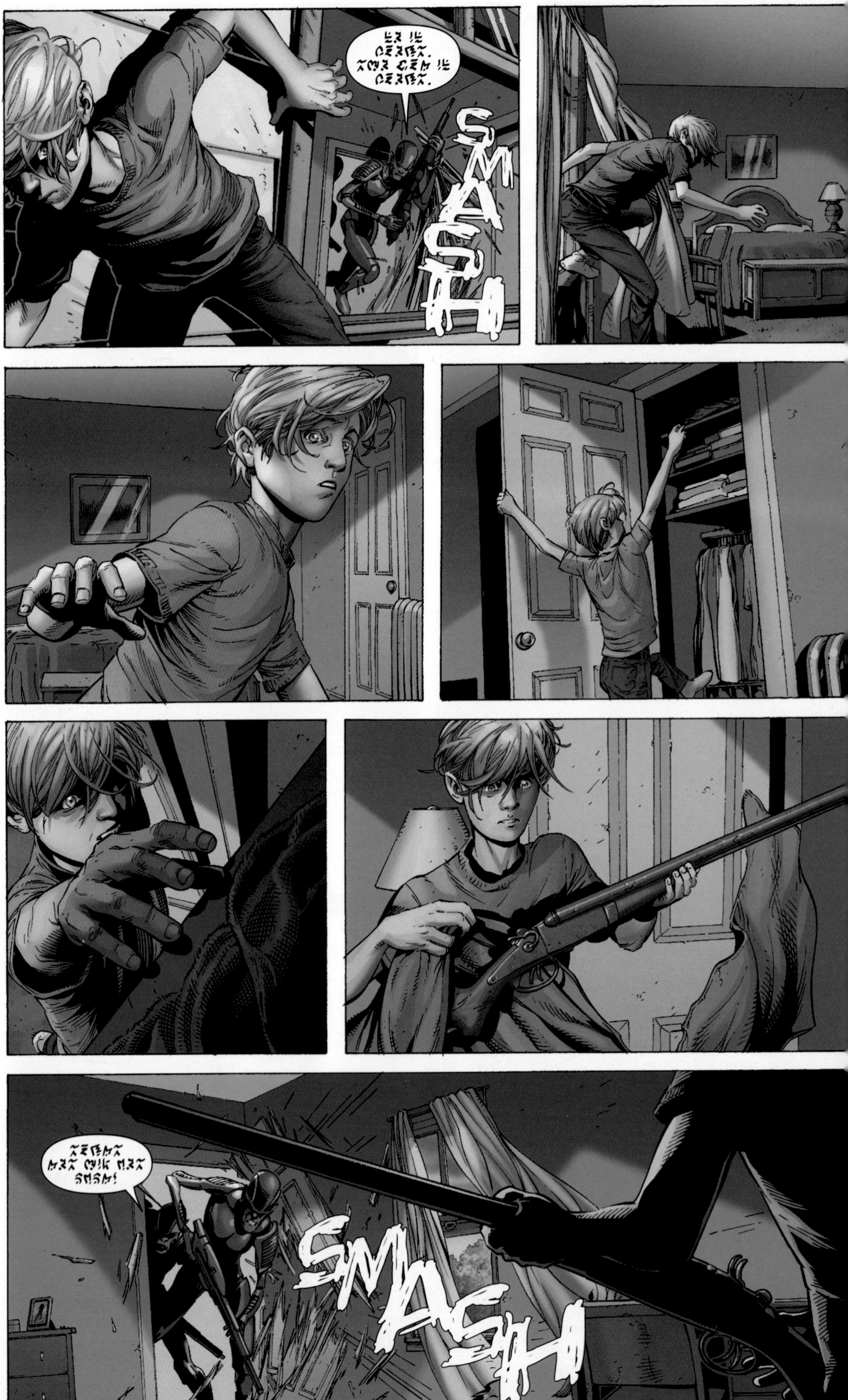
SMASH
SMASH

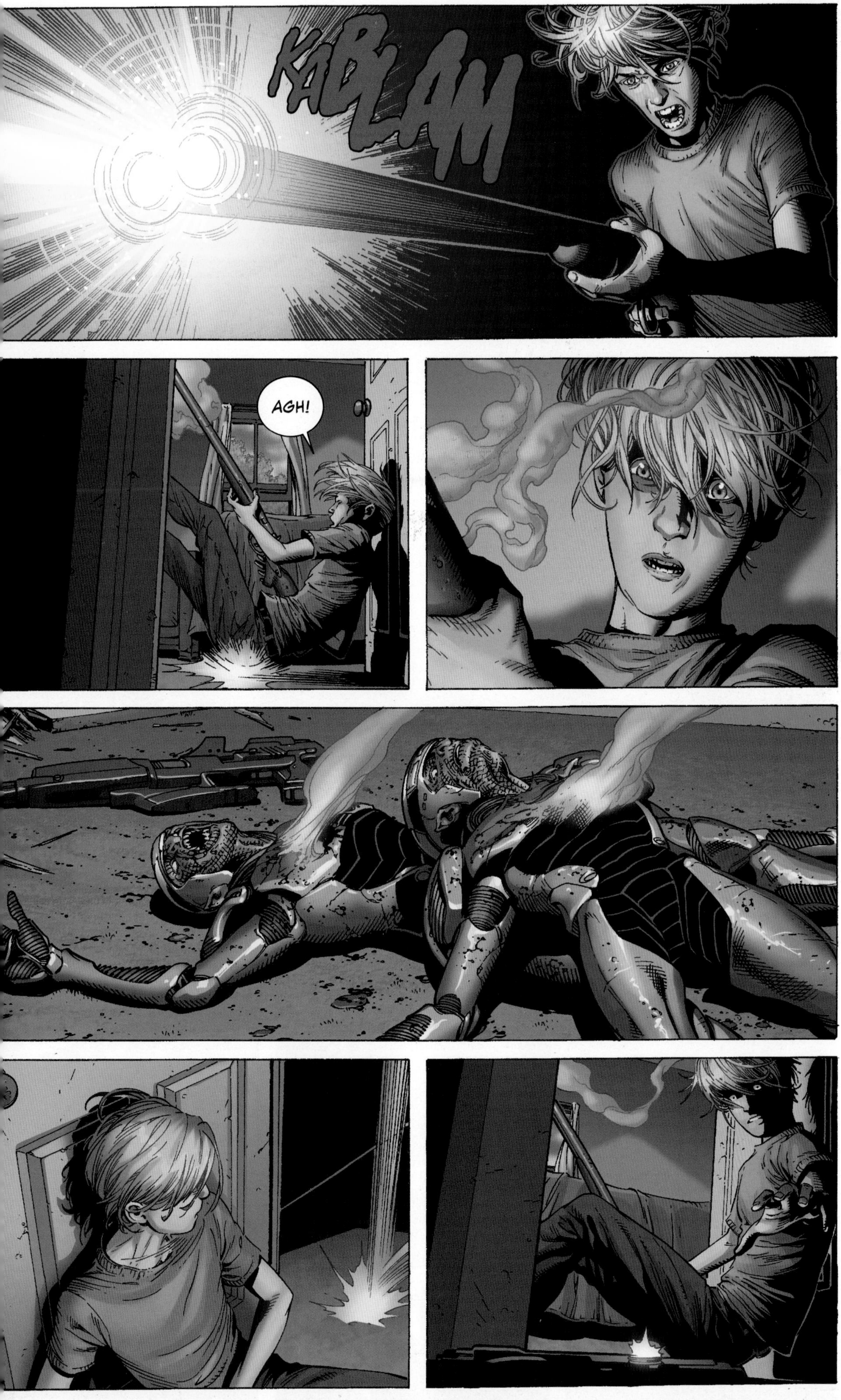
KABLAM
AGH!

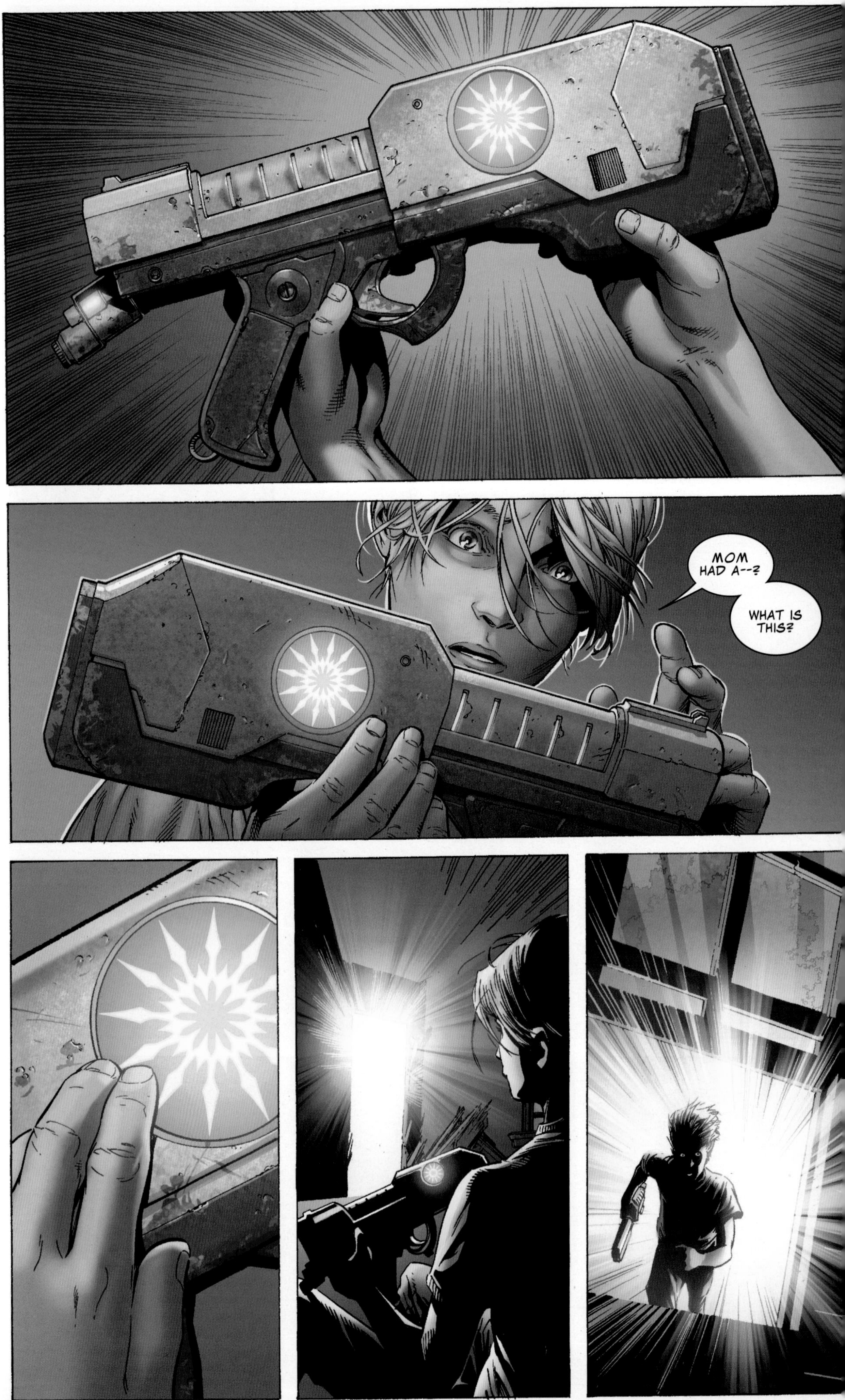
MOM HAD A--?
WHAT IS THIS?

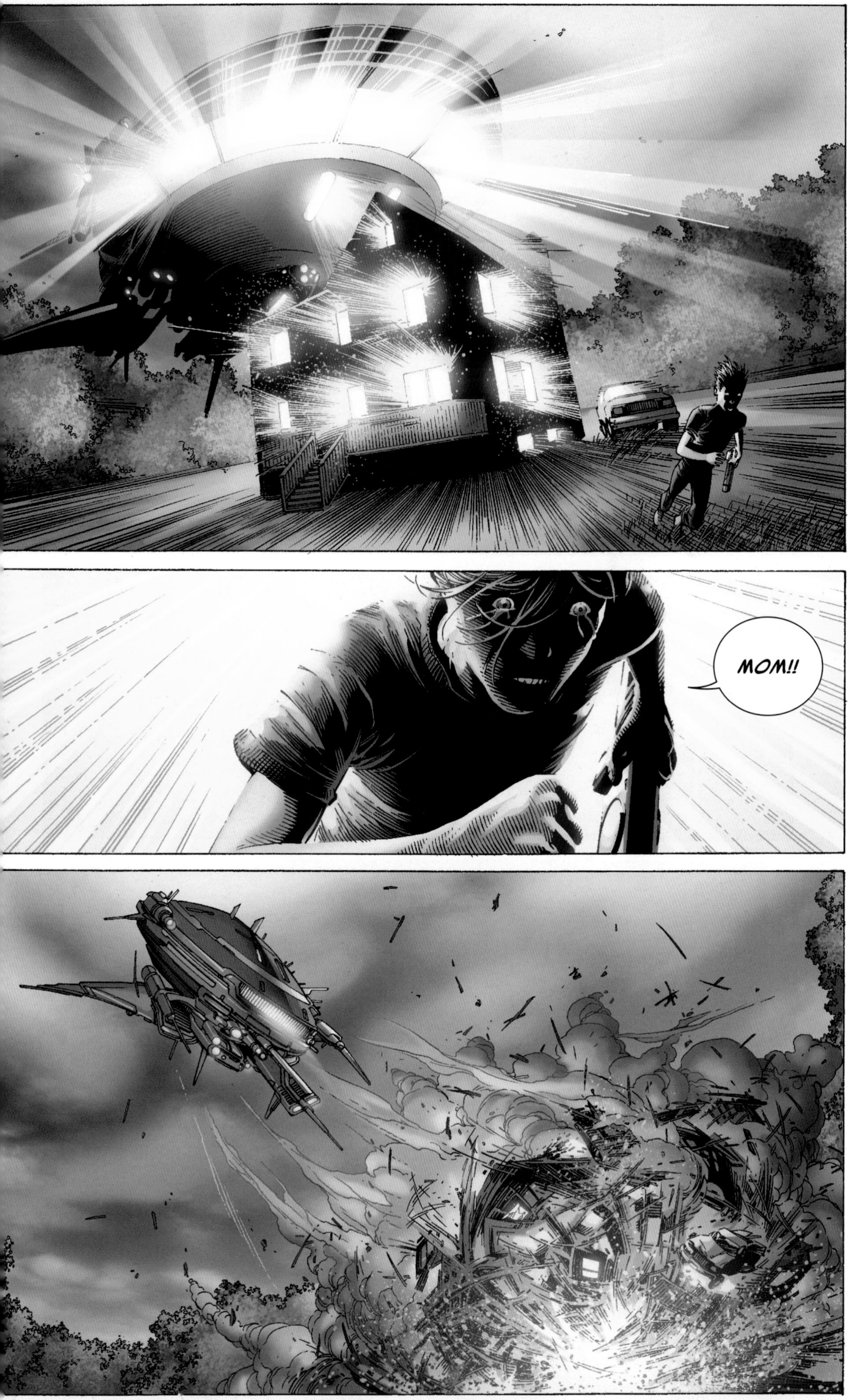
MOM!!

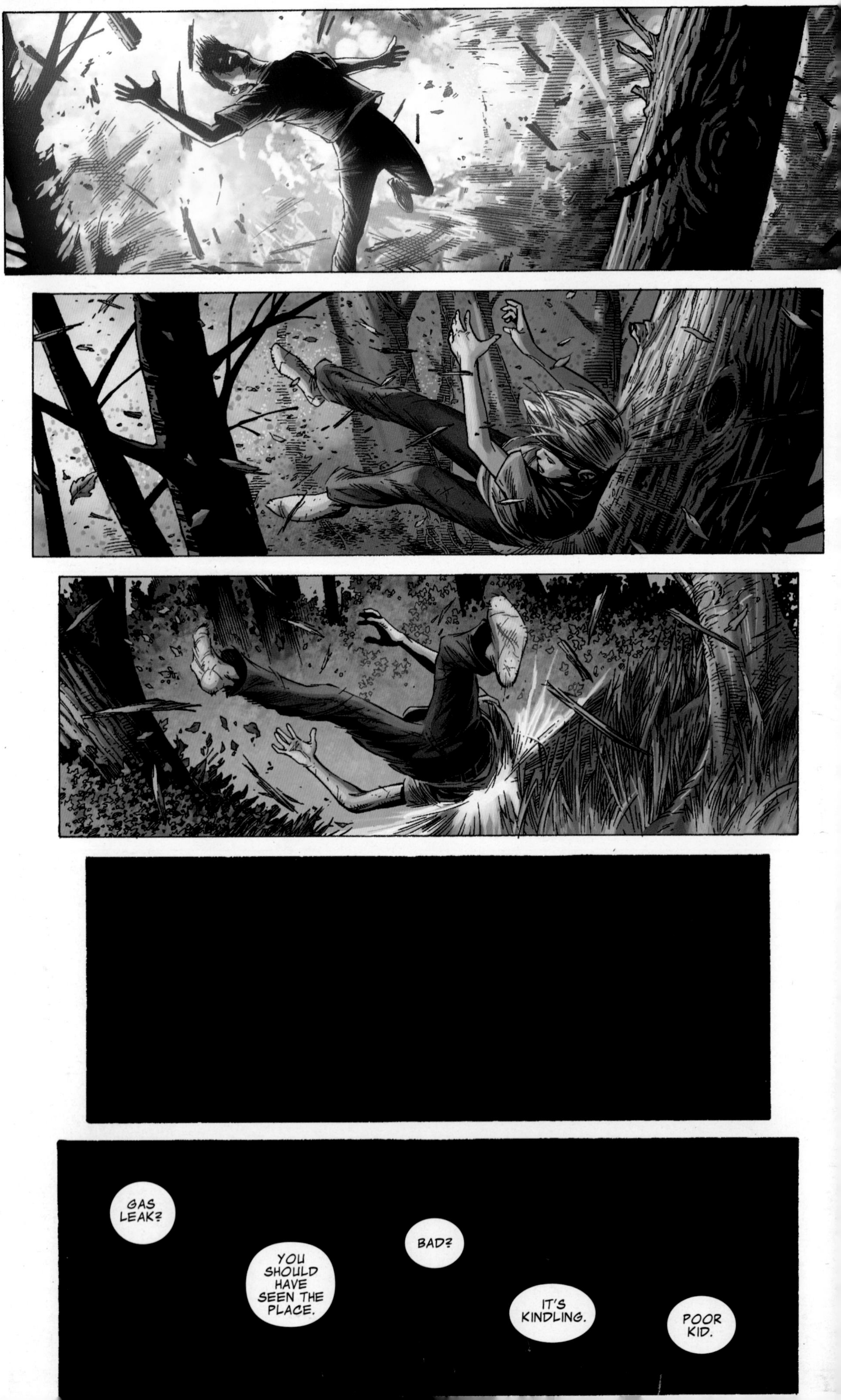
GAS LEAK?
YOU SHOULD HAVE SEEN THE PLACE.
BAD?
IT'S KINDLING.
POOR KID.

4000...
UH, I THINK HE'S AWAKE.
PETER?
PETER, DON'T TRY TO TALK.
NURSE HOLLOWAY, CAN YOU TELL THE FRONT DESK THE PATIENT IS AWAKE?
WE'LL NEED SOMEONE FROM CHILD PSYCHIATRIC DOWN HERE ASAP.
PETER, DO YOU REMEMBER MEETING ME YESTERDAY?
NO.
THAT'S OKAY.
YOU WERE PRETTY OUT OF IT.
DO YOU REMEMBER WHAT HAPPENED TO YOU?

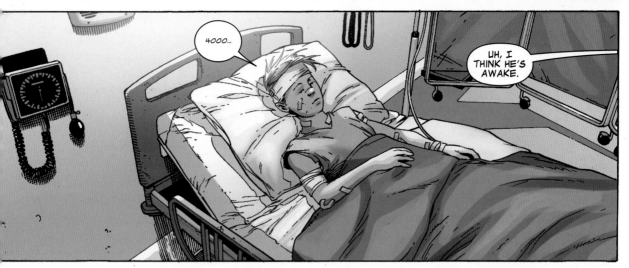

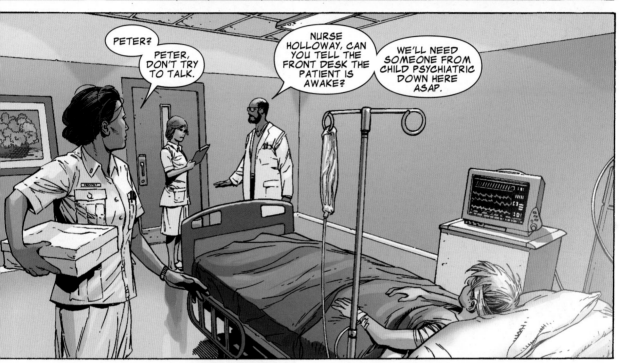

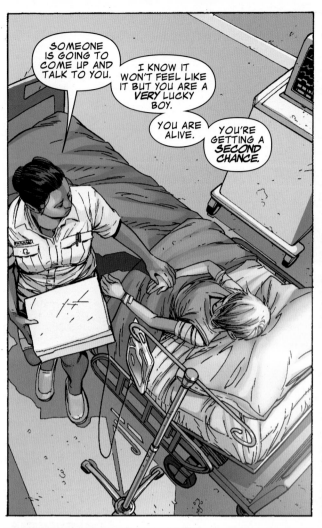

SOMEONE IS GOING TO COME UP AND TALK TO YOU.

I KNOW IT WON'T FEEL LIKE IT BUT YOU ARE A *VERY* LUCKY BOY.

YOU ARE ALIVE.

YOU'RE GETTING A *SECOND* CHANCE.

OH, AND THE PARAMEDICS FOUND YOUR SPACE TOY.

I THOUGHT YOU WOULD WANT IT.

I KNOW IT'S NOT-- IT'S SOMETHING, AT LEAST.

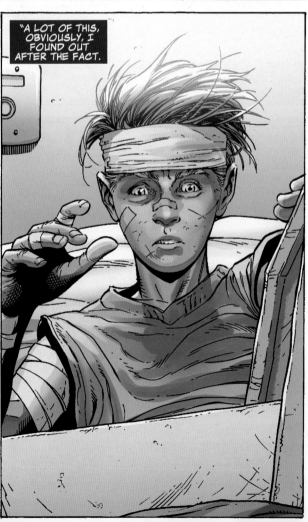

"A LOT OF THIS, OBVIOUSLY, I FOUND OUT AFTER THE FACT.

"BUT THE QUESTION WAS...WHY?

"WHY DID A BUNCH OF ALIENS FLY HALFWAY ACROSS THE GALAXY TO WHACK A 10-YEAR-OLD BOY...?"

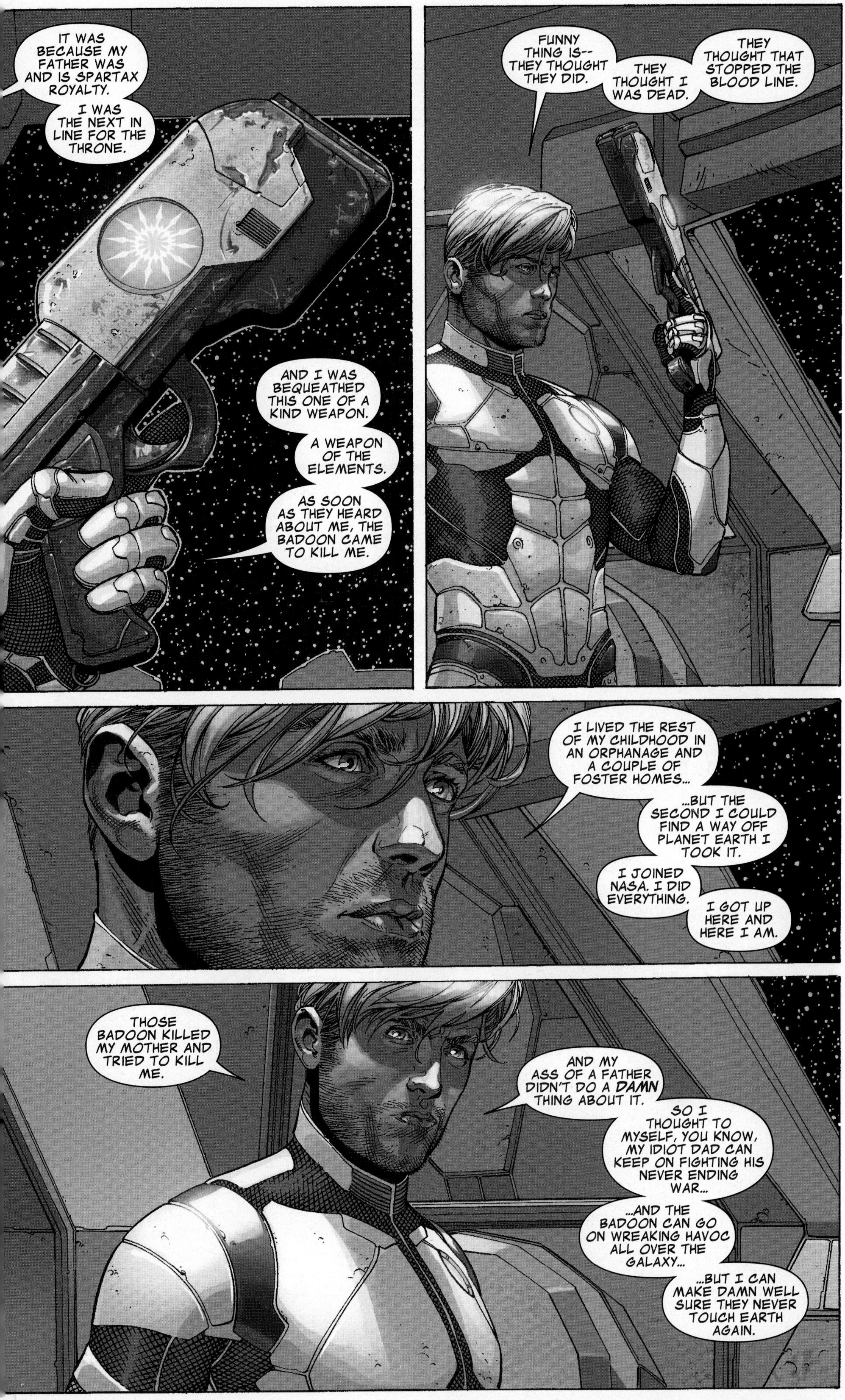
IT WAS BECAUSE MY FATHER WAS AND IS SPARTAX ROYALTY.
I WAS THE NEXT IN LINE FOR THE THRONE.
AND I WAS BEQUEATHED THIS ONE OF A KIND WEAPON.
A WEAPON OF THE ELEMENTS.
AS SOON AS THEY HEARD ABOUT ME, THE BADOON CAME TO KILL ME.
FUNNY THING IS-- THEY THOUGHT THEY DID.
THEY THOUGHT I WAS DEAD.
THEY THOUGHT THAT STOPPED THE BLOOD LINE.
I LIVED THE REST OF MY CHILDHOOD IN AN ORPHANAGE AND A COUPLE OF FOSTER HOMES...
...BUT THE SECOND I COULD FIND A WAY OFF PLANET EARTH I TOOK IT.
I JOINED NASA. I DID EVERYTHING.
I GOT UP HERE AND HERE I AM.
THOSE BADOON KILLED MY MOTHER AND TRIED TO KILL ME.
AND MY ASS OF A FATHER DIDN'T DO A DAMN THING ABOUT IT.
SO I THOUGHT TO MYSELF, YOU KNOW, MY IDIOT DAD CAN KEEP ON FIGHTING HIS NEVER ENDING WAR...
...AND THE BADOON CAN GO ON WREAKING HAVOC ALL OVER THE GALAXY...
...BUT I CAN MAKE DAMN WELL SURE THEY NEVER TOUCH EARTH AGAIN.

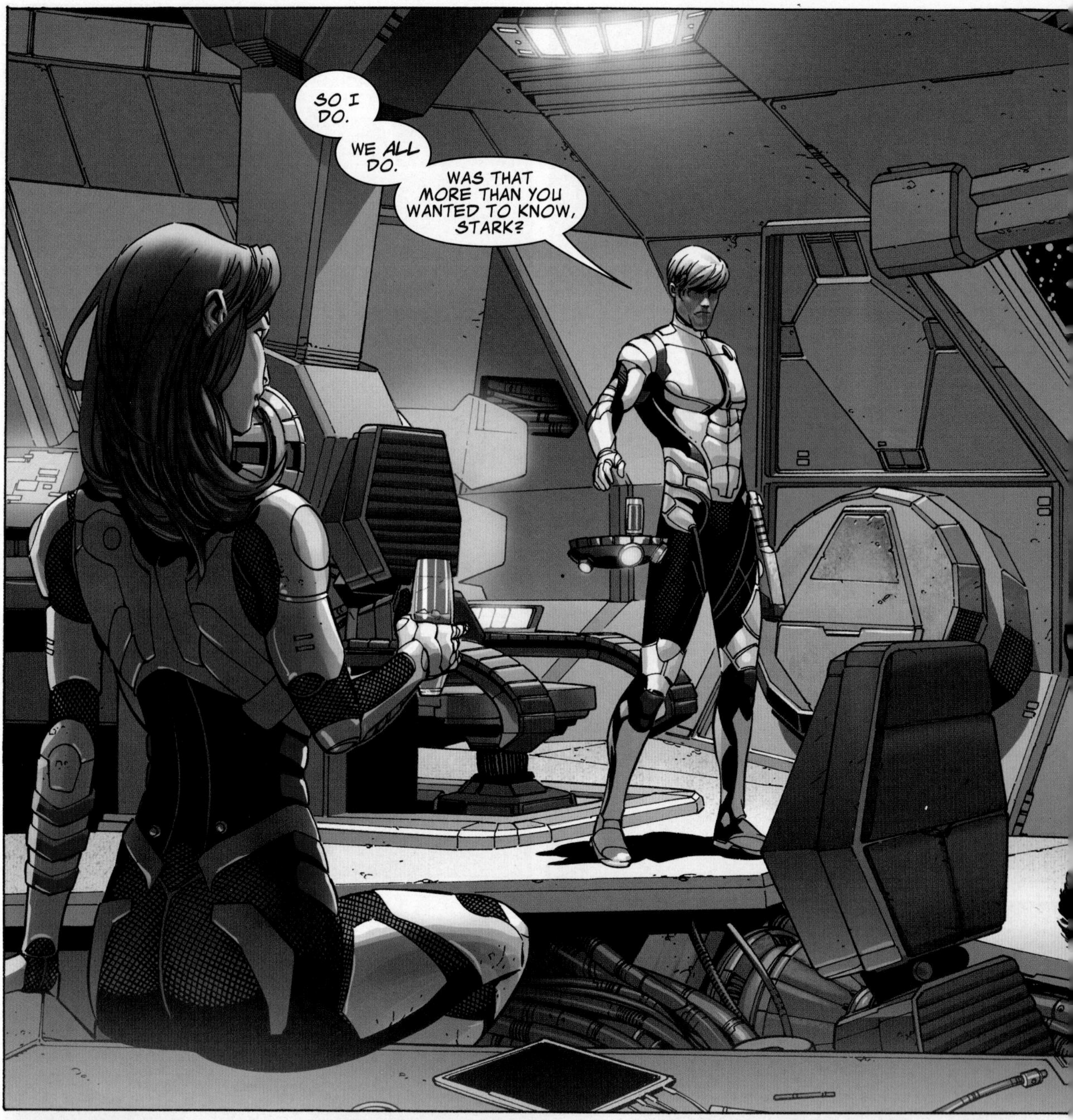
SO I DO.
WE ALL DO.
WAS THAT MORE THAN YOU WANTED TO KNOW, STARK?

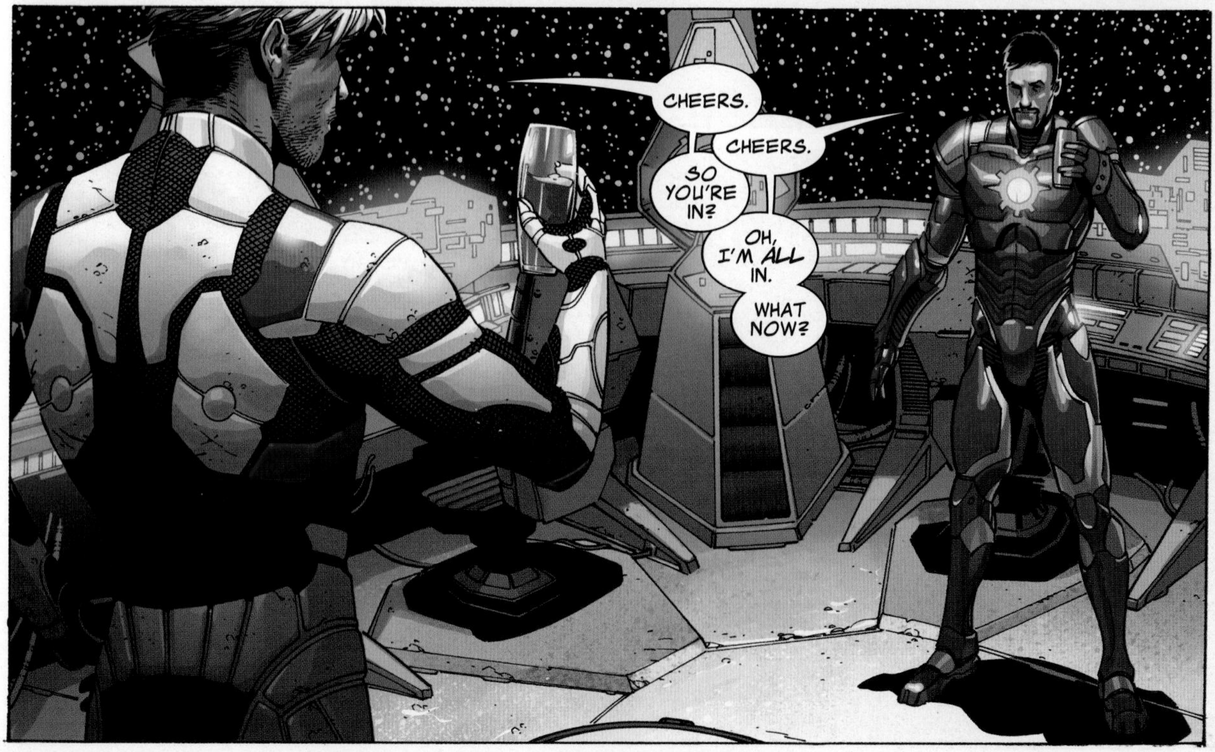
CHEERS.
CHEERS.
SO YOU'RE IN?
OH, I'M ALL IN.
WHAT NOW?

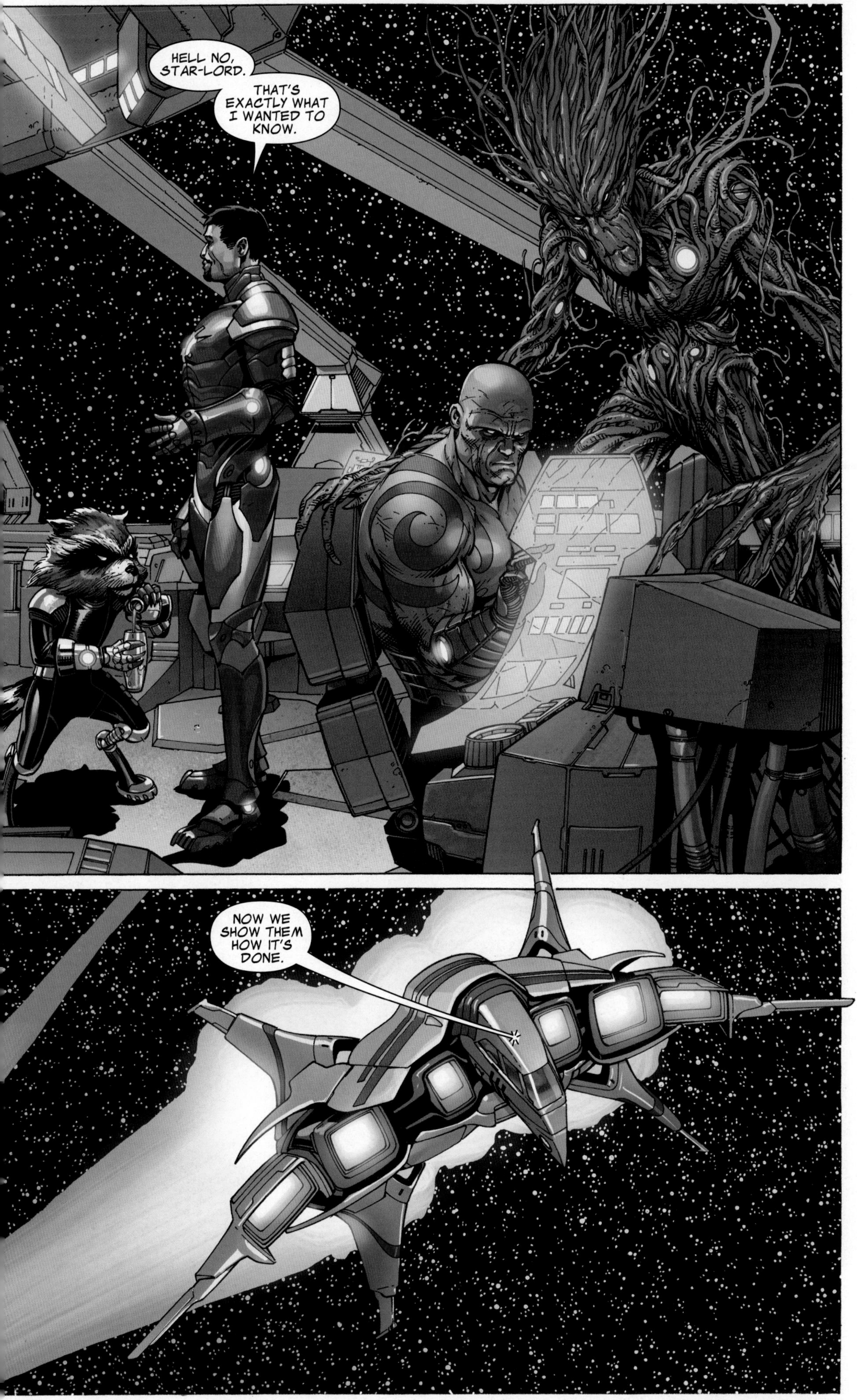
HELL NO, STAR-LORD.
THAT'S EXACTLY WHAT I WANTED TO KNOW.
NOW WE SHOW THEM HOW IT'S DONE.

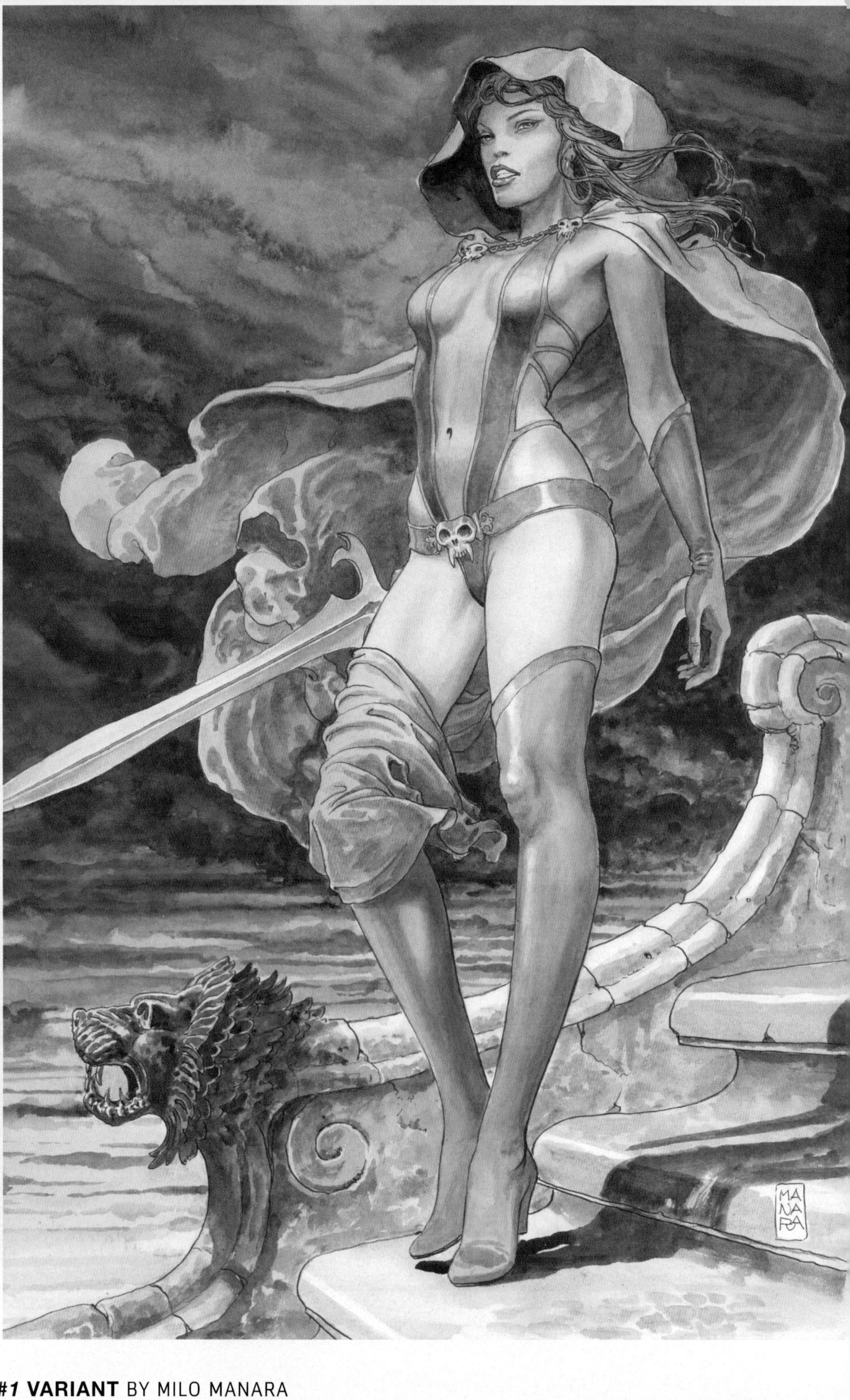
MANARA

***#1* VARIANT** BY MILO MANARA

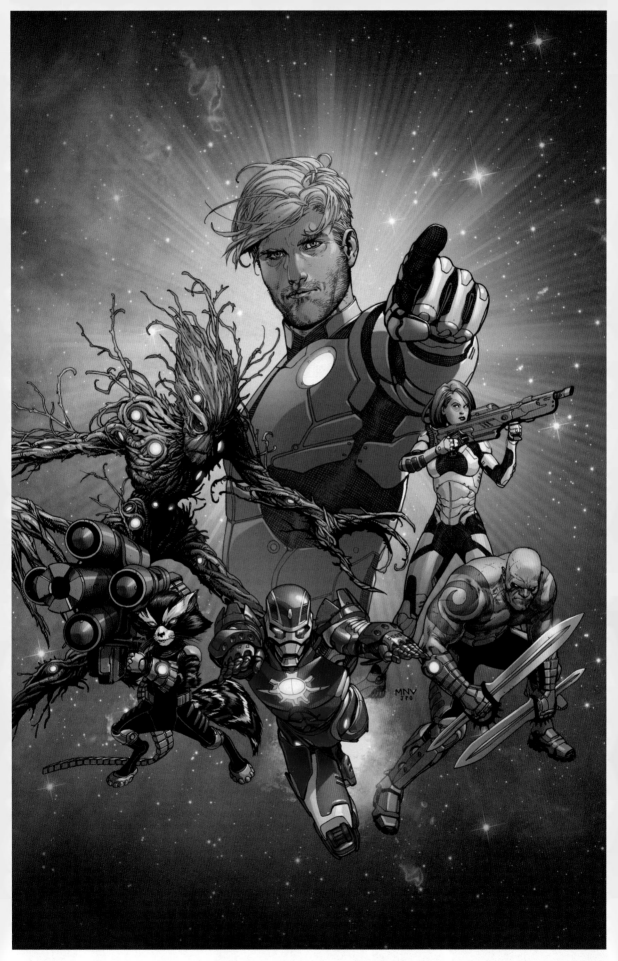

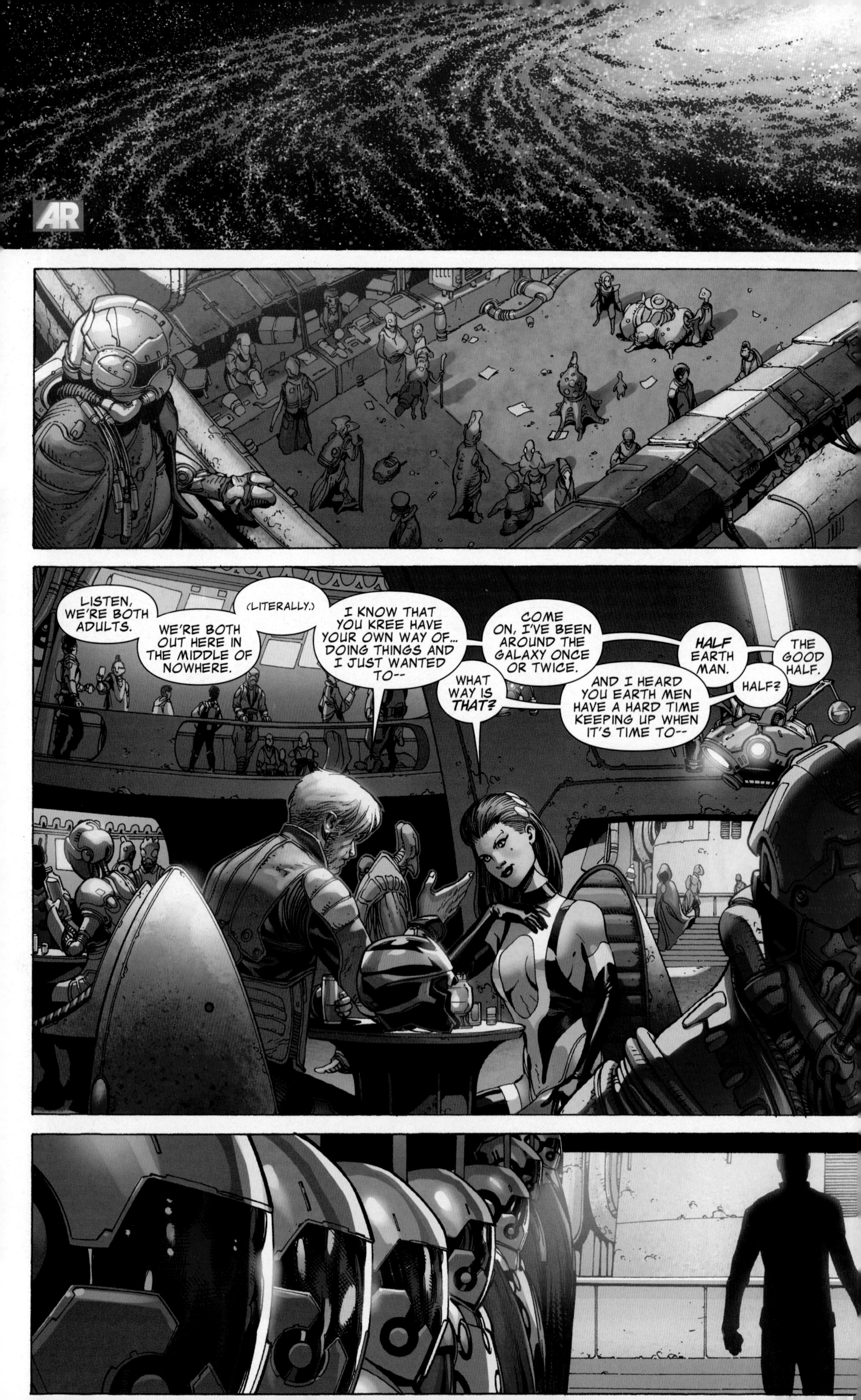
LISTEN, WE'RE BOTH ADULTS.
WE'RE BOTH OUT HERE IN THE MIDDLE OF NOWHERE.
(LITERALLY.)
I KNOW THAT YOU KREE HAVE YOUR OWN WAY OF... DOING THINGS AND I JUST WANTED TO--
WHAT WAY IS *THAT?*
COME ON, I'VE BEEN AROUND THE GALAXY ONCE OR TWICE.
AND I HEARD YOU EARTH MEN HAVE A HARD TIME KEEPING UP WHEN IT'S TIME TO--
HALF EARTH MAN.
HALF?
THE GOOD HALF.

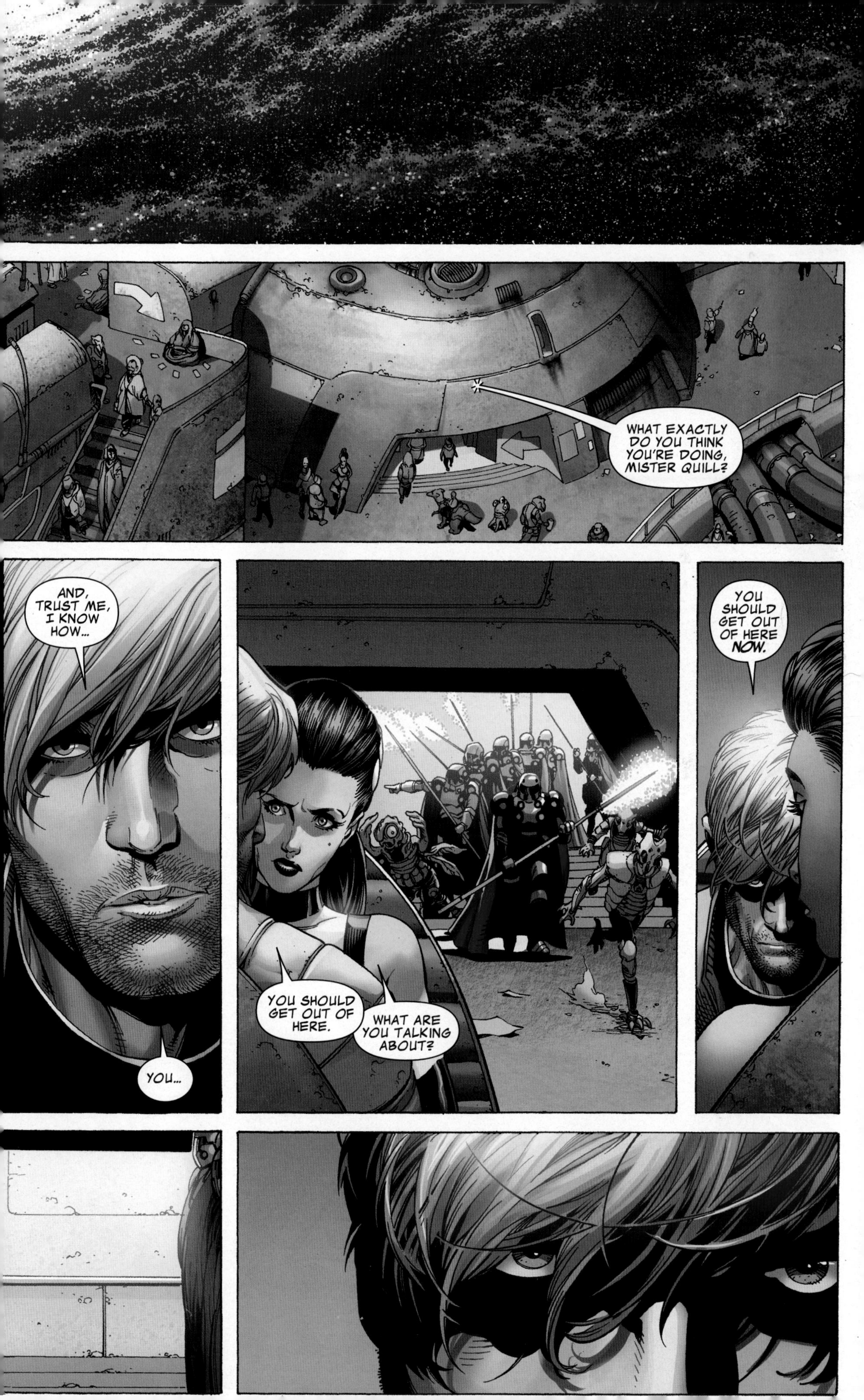
WHAT EXACTLY DO YOU THINK YOU'RE DOING, MISTER QUILL?
AND, TRUST ME, I KNOW HOW...
YOU...
YOU SHOULD GET OUT OF HERE.
WHAT ARE YOU TALKING ABOUT?
YOU SHOULD GET OUT OF HERE NOW.

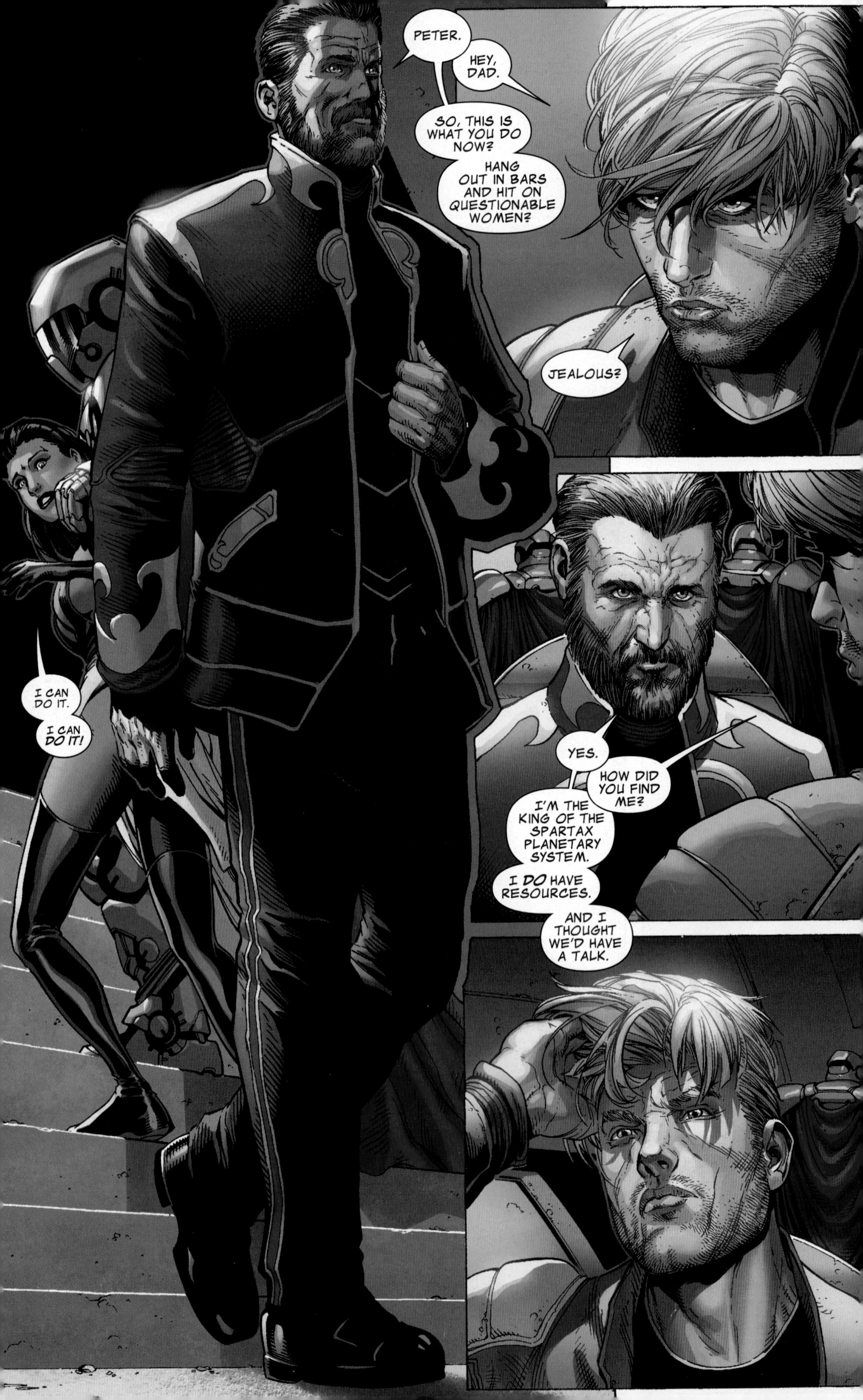
PETER.
HEY, DAD.
SO, THIS IS WHAT YOU DO NOW?
HANG OUT IN BARS AND HIT ON QUESTIONABLE WOMEN?
JEALOUS?
I CAN DO IT.
I CAN DO IT!
YES.
HOW DID YOU FIND ME?
I'M THE KING OF THE SPARTAX PLANETARY SYSTEM.
I DO HAVE RESOURCES.
AND I THOUGHT WE'D HAVE A TALK.

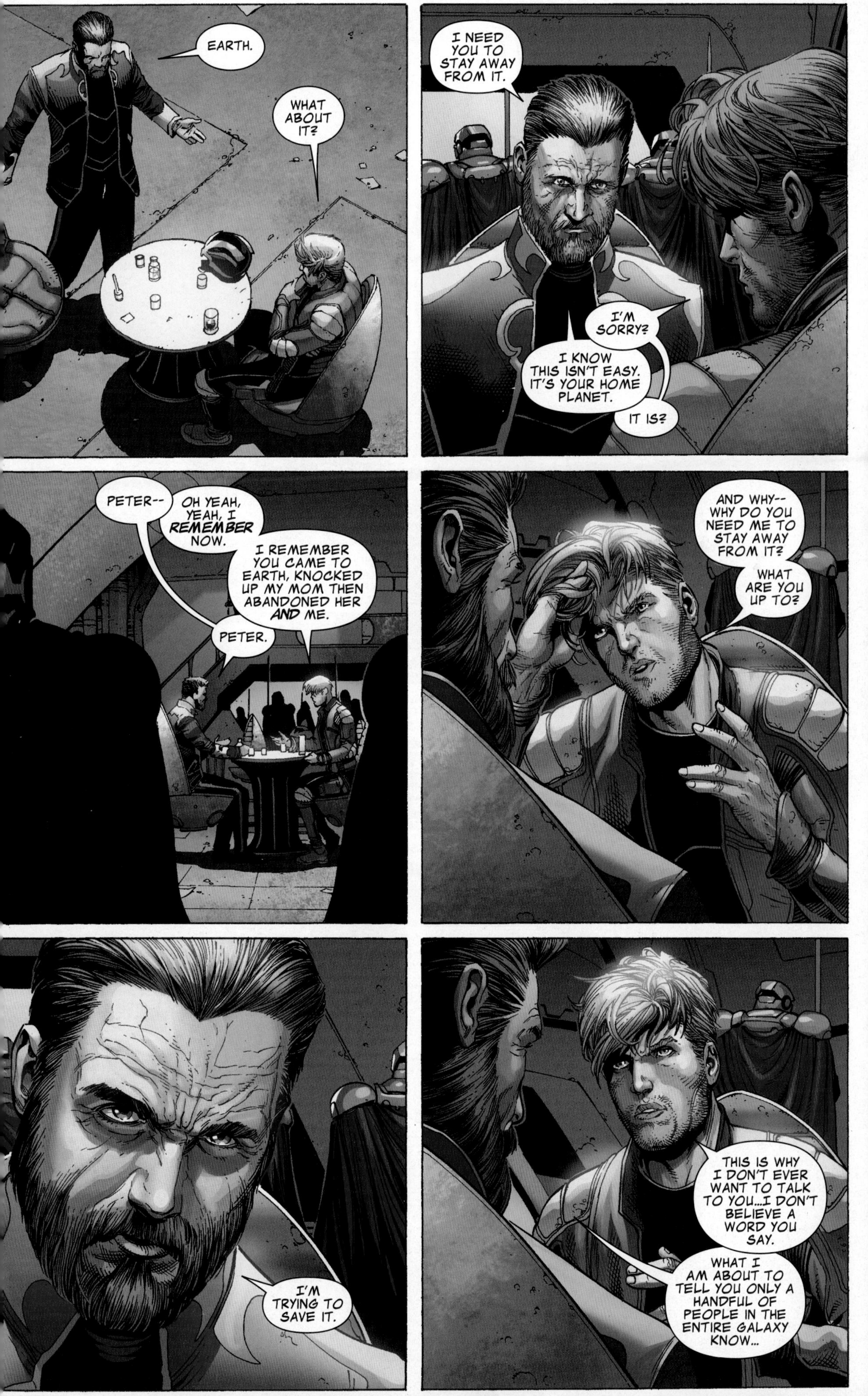

EARTH.
WHAT ABOUT IT?
I NEED YOU TO STAY AWAY FROM IT.
I'M SORRY?
I KNOW THIS ISN'T EASY. IT'S YOUR HOME PLANET.
IT IS?
PETER--
OH YEAH, YEAH, I REMEMBER NOW.
I REMEMBER YOU CAME TO EARTH, KNOCKED UP MY MOM THEN ABANDONED HER AND ME.
PETER.
AND WHY-- WHY DO YOU NEED ME TO STAY AWAY FROM IT?
WHAT ARE YOU UP TO?
I'M TRYING TO SAVE IT.
THIS IS WHY I DON'T EVER WANT TO TALK TO YOU...I DON'T BELIEVE A WORD YOU SAY.
WHAT I AM ABOUT TO TELL YOU ONLY A HANDFUL OF PEOPLE IN THE ENTIRE GALAXY KNOW...

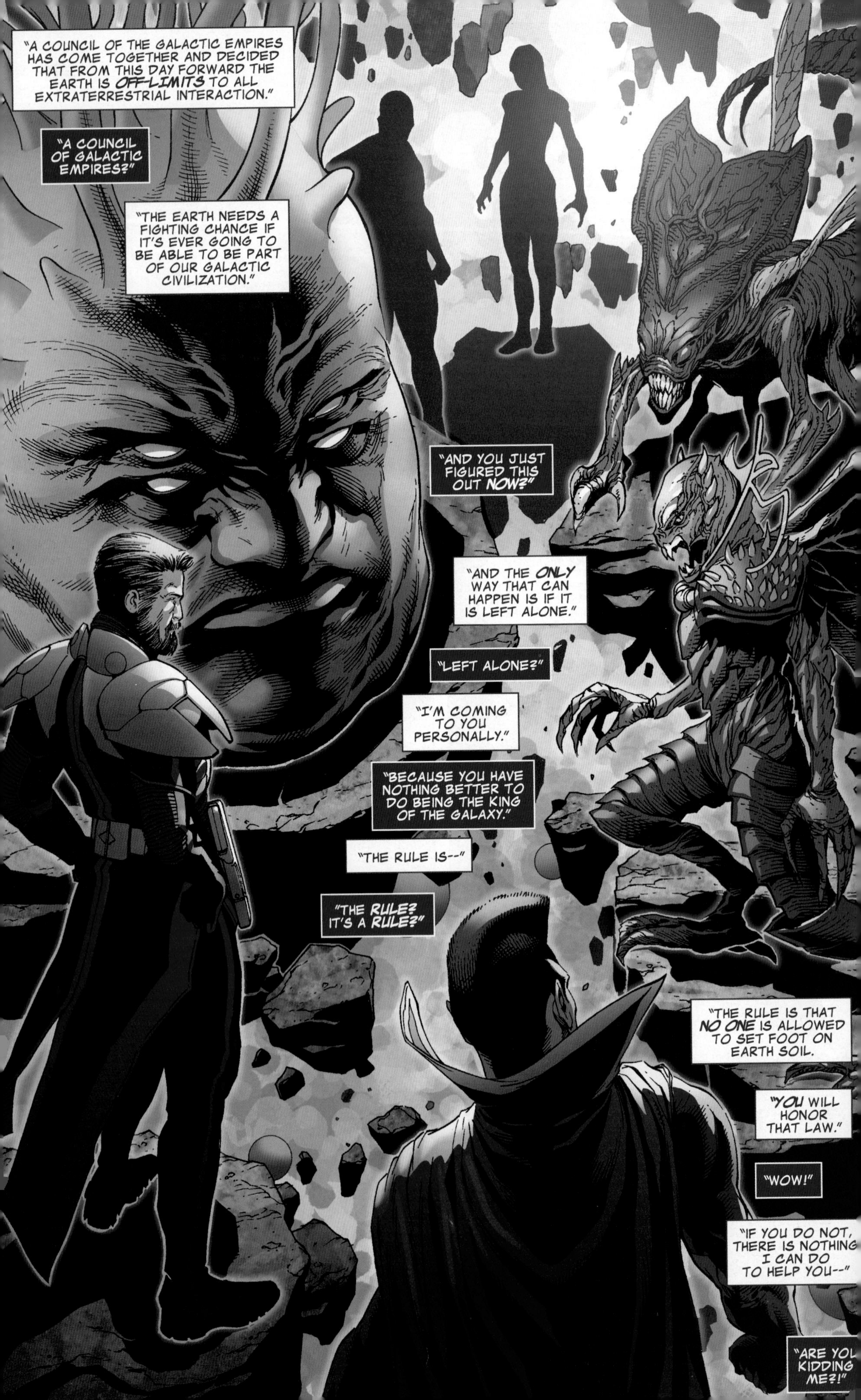
"A COUNCIL OF THE GALACTIC EMPIRES HAS COME TOGETHER AND DECIDED THAT FROM THIS DAY FORWARD THE EARTH IS OFF-LIMITS TO ALL EXTRATERRESTRIAL INTERACTION."
"A COUNCIL OF GALACTIC EMPIRES?"
"THE EARTH NEEDS A FIGHTING CHANCE IF IT'S EVER GOING TO BE ABLE TO BE PART OF OUR GALACTIC CIVILIZATION."
"AND YOU JUST FIGURED THIS OUT NOW?"
"AND THE ONLY WAY THAT CAN HAPPEN IS IF IT IS LEFT ALONE."
"LEFT ALONE?"
"I'M COMING TO YOU PERSONALLY."
"BECAUSE YOU HAVE NOTHING BETTER TO DO BEING THE KING OF THE GALAXY."
"THE RULE IS--"
"THE RULE? IT'S A RULE?"
"THE RULE IS THAT NO ONE IS ALLOWED TO SET FOOT ON EARTH SOIL.
"YOU WILL HONOR THAT LAW."
"WOW!"
"IF YOU DO NOT, THERE IS NOTHING I CAN DO TO HELP YOU--"
"ARE YOU KIDDING ME?!"

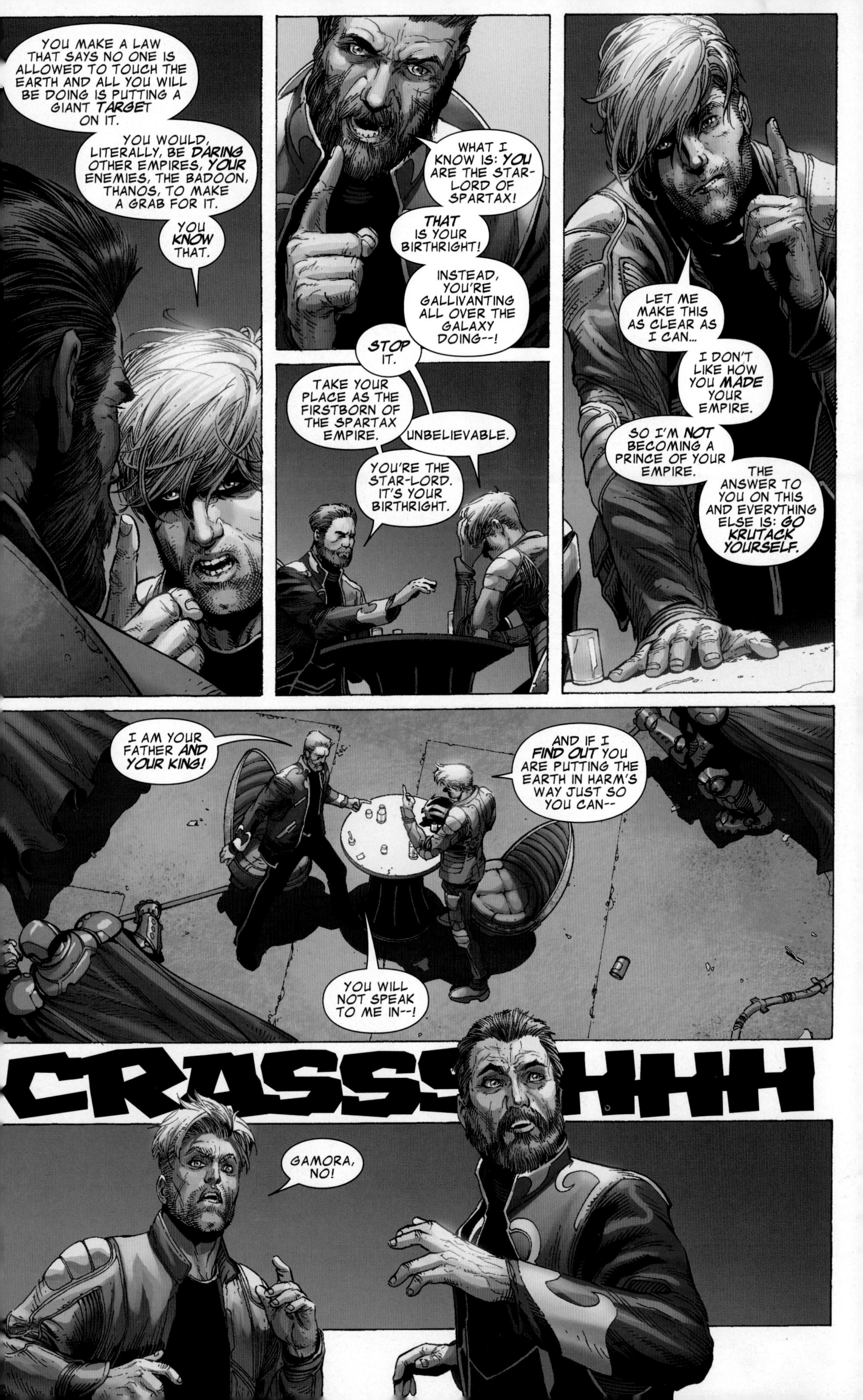

YOU MAKE A LAW THAT SAYS NO ONE IS ALLOWED TO TOUCH THE EARTH AND ALL YOU WILL BE DOING IS PUTTING A GIANT TARGET ON IT.
YOU WOULD, LITERALLY, BE DARING OTHER EMPIRES, YOUR ENEMIES, THE BADOON, THANOS, TO MAKE A GRAB FOR IT.
YOU KNOW THAT.
WHAT I KNOW IS: YOU ARE THE STAR-LORD OF SPARTAX!
THAT IS YOUR BIRTHRIGHT!
INSTEAD, YOU'RE GALLIVANTING ALL OVER THE GALAXY DOING--!
STOP IT.
TAKE YOUR PLACE AS THE FIRSTBORN OF THE SPARTAX EMPIRE.
UNBELIEVABLE.
YOU'RE THE STAR-LORD. IT'S YOUR BIRTHRIGHT.
LET ME MAKE THIS AS CLEAR AS I CAN...
I DON'T LIKE HOW YOU MADE YOUR EMPIRE.
SO I'M NOT BECOMING A PRINCE OF YOUR EMPIRE.
THE ANSWER TO YOU ON THIS AND EVERYTHING ELSE IS: GO KRUTACK YOURSELF.
I AM YOUR FATHER AND YOUR KING!
AND IF I FIND OUT YOU ARE PUTTING THE EARTH IN HARM'S WAY JUST SO YOU CAN--
YOU WILL NOT SPEAK TO ME IN--!
CRASSSHHHH
GAMORA, NO!

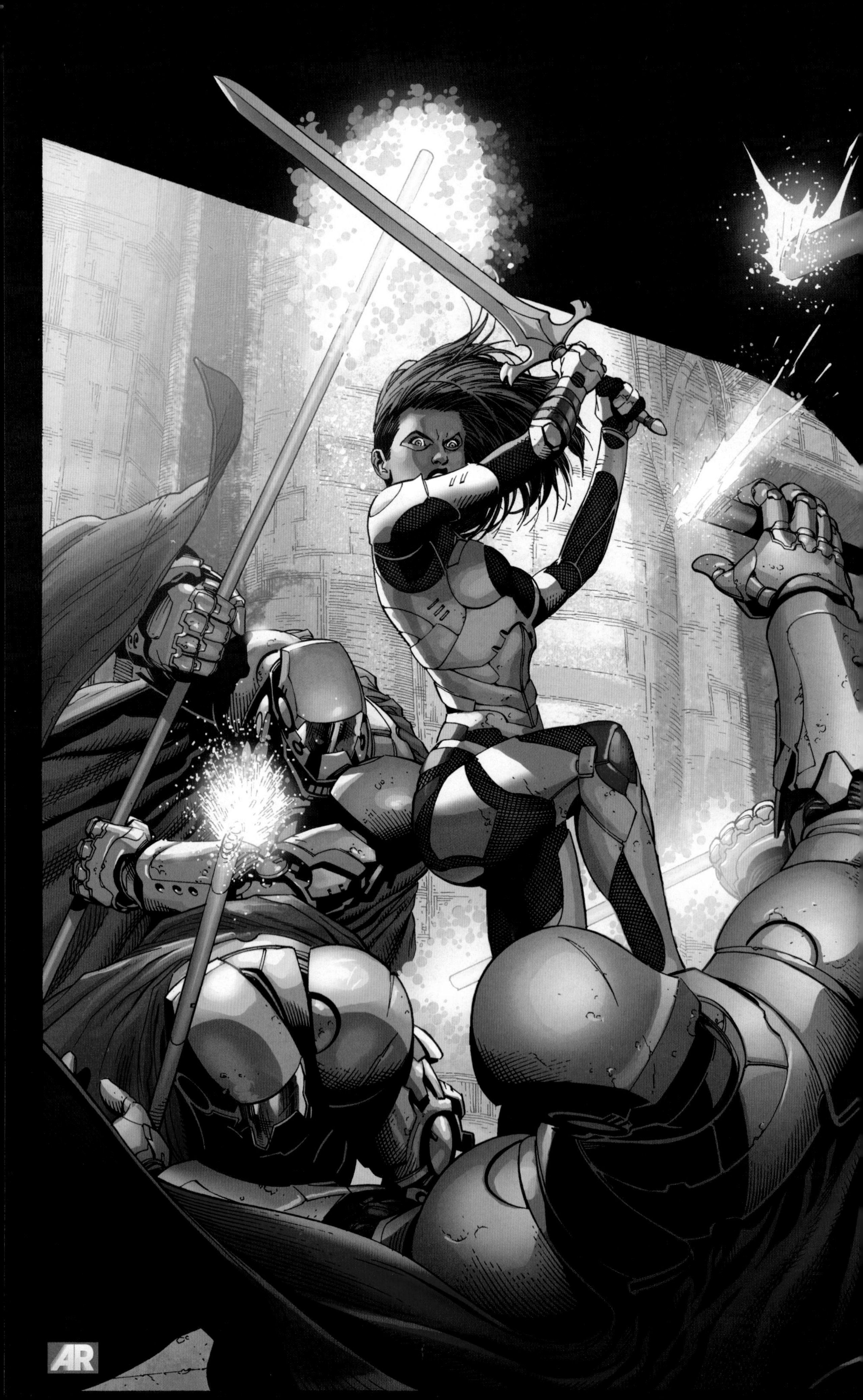

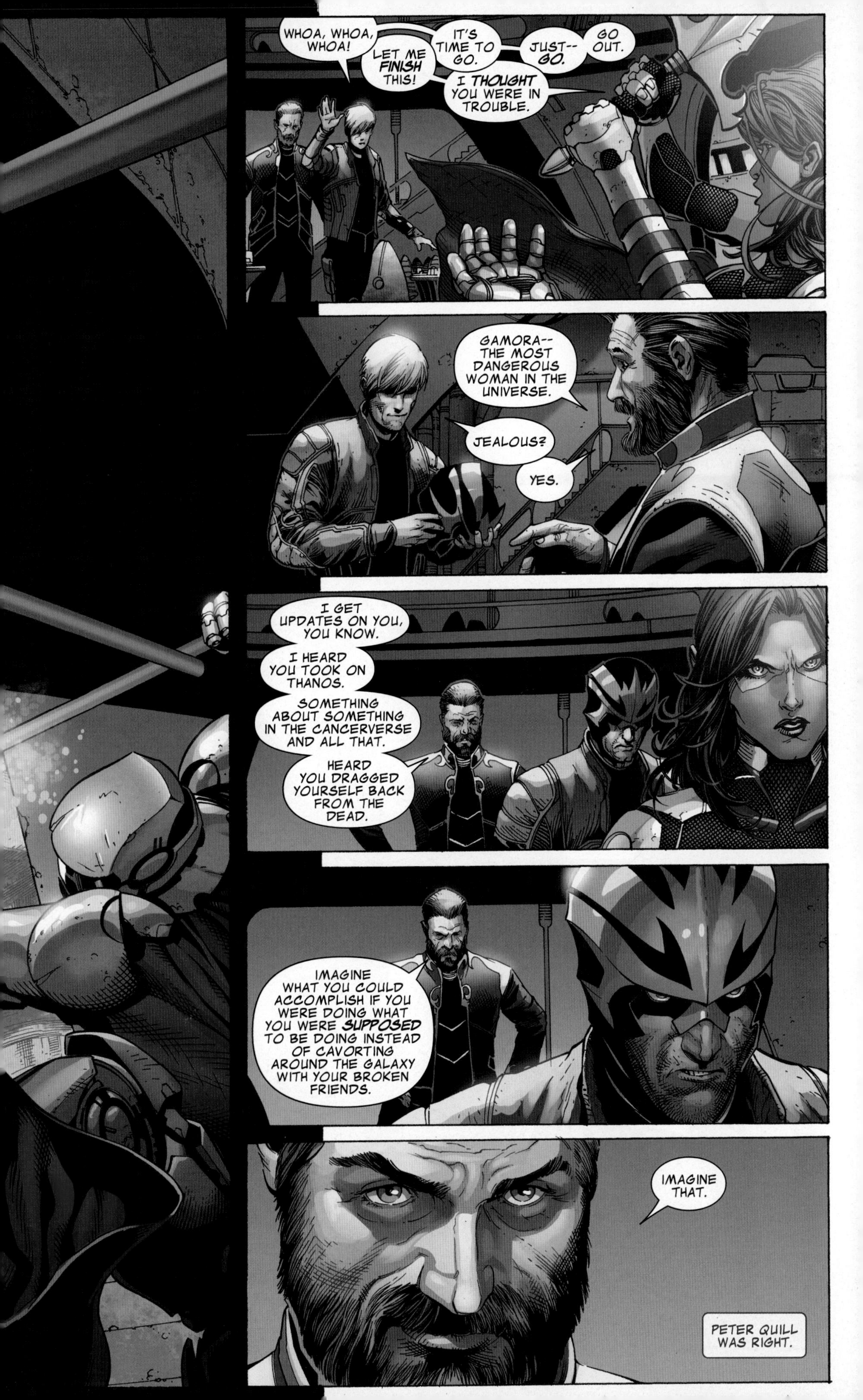
WHOA, WHOA, WHOA!
LET ME FINISH THIS!
IT'S TIME TO GO.
JUST-- GO.
GO OUT.
I THOUGHT YOU WERE IN TROUBLE.
GAMORA-- THE MOST DANGEROUS WOMAN IN THE UNIVERSE.
JEALOUS?
YES.
I GET UPDATES ON YOU, YOU KNOW.
I HEARD YOU TOOK ON THANOS.
SOMETHING ABOUT SOMETHING IN THE CANCERVERSE AND ALL THAT.
HEARD YOU DRAGGED YOURSELF BACK FROM THE DEAD.
IMAGINE WHAT YOU COULD ACCOMPLISH IF YOU WERE DOING WHAT YOU WERE SUPPOSED TO BE DOING INSTEAD OF CAVORTING AROUND THE GALAXY WITH YOUR BROKEN FRIENDS.
IMAGINE THAT.
PETER QUILL WAS RIGHT.

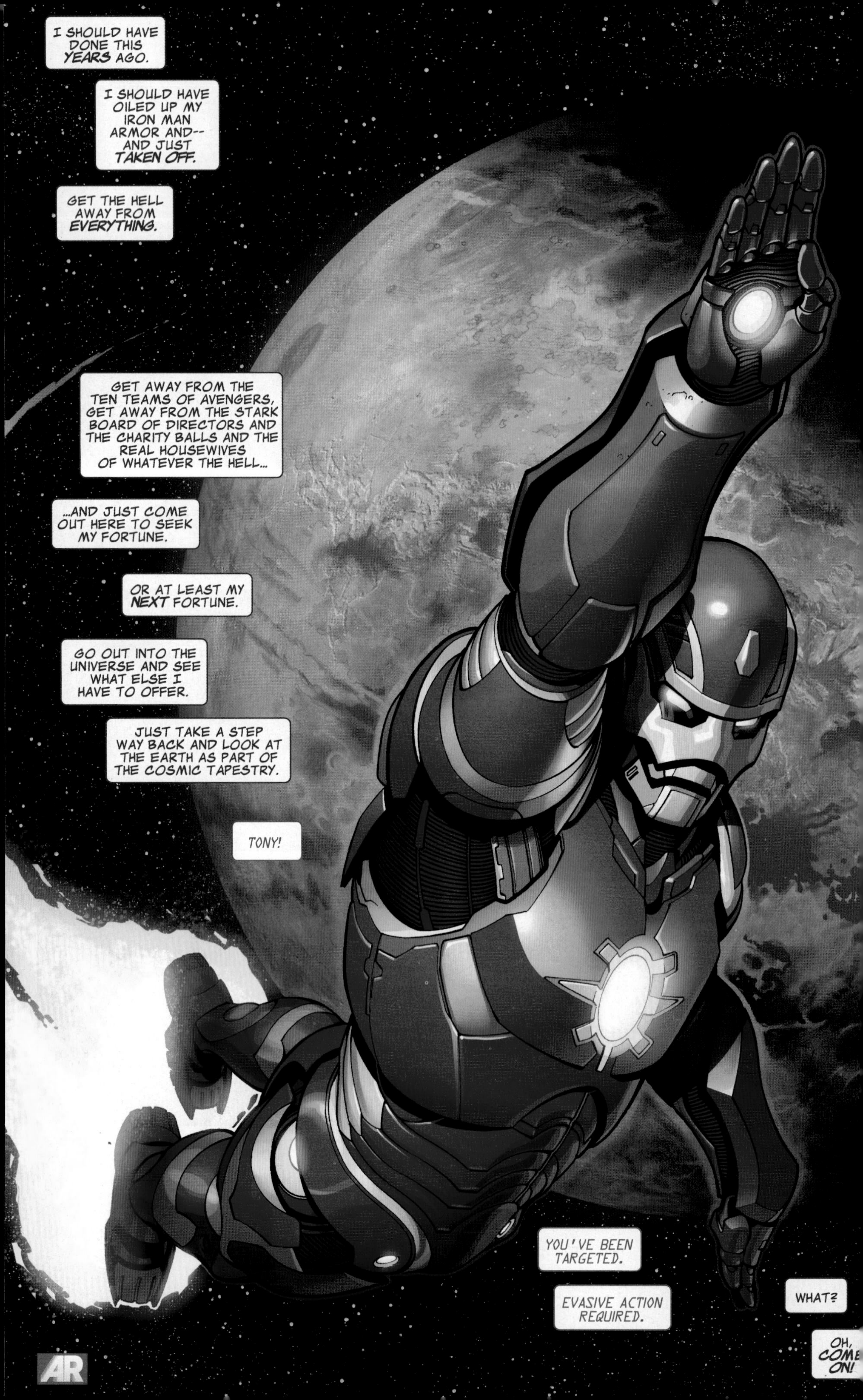
I SHOULD HAVE DONE THIS YEARS AGO.
I SHOULD HAVE OILED UP MY IRON MAN ARMOR AND-- AND JUST TAKEN OFF.
GET THE HELL AWAY FROM EVERYTHING.
GET AWAY FROM THE TEN TEAMS OF AVENGERS, GET AWAY FROM THE STARK BOARD OF DIRECTORS AND THE CHARITY BALLS AND THE REAL HOUSEWIVES OF WHATEVER THE HELL...
...AND JUST COME OUT HERE TO SEEK MY FORTUNE.
OR AT LEAST MY NEXT FORTUNE.
GO OUT INTO THE UNIVERSE AND SEE WHAT ELSE I HAVE TO OFFER.
JUST TAKE A STEP WAY BACK AND LOOK AT THE EARTH AS PART OF THE COSMIC TAPESTRY.
TONY!
YOU'VE BEEN TARGETED.
EVASIVE ACTION REQUIRED.
WHAT?
OH, COME ON!

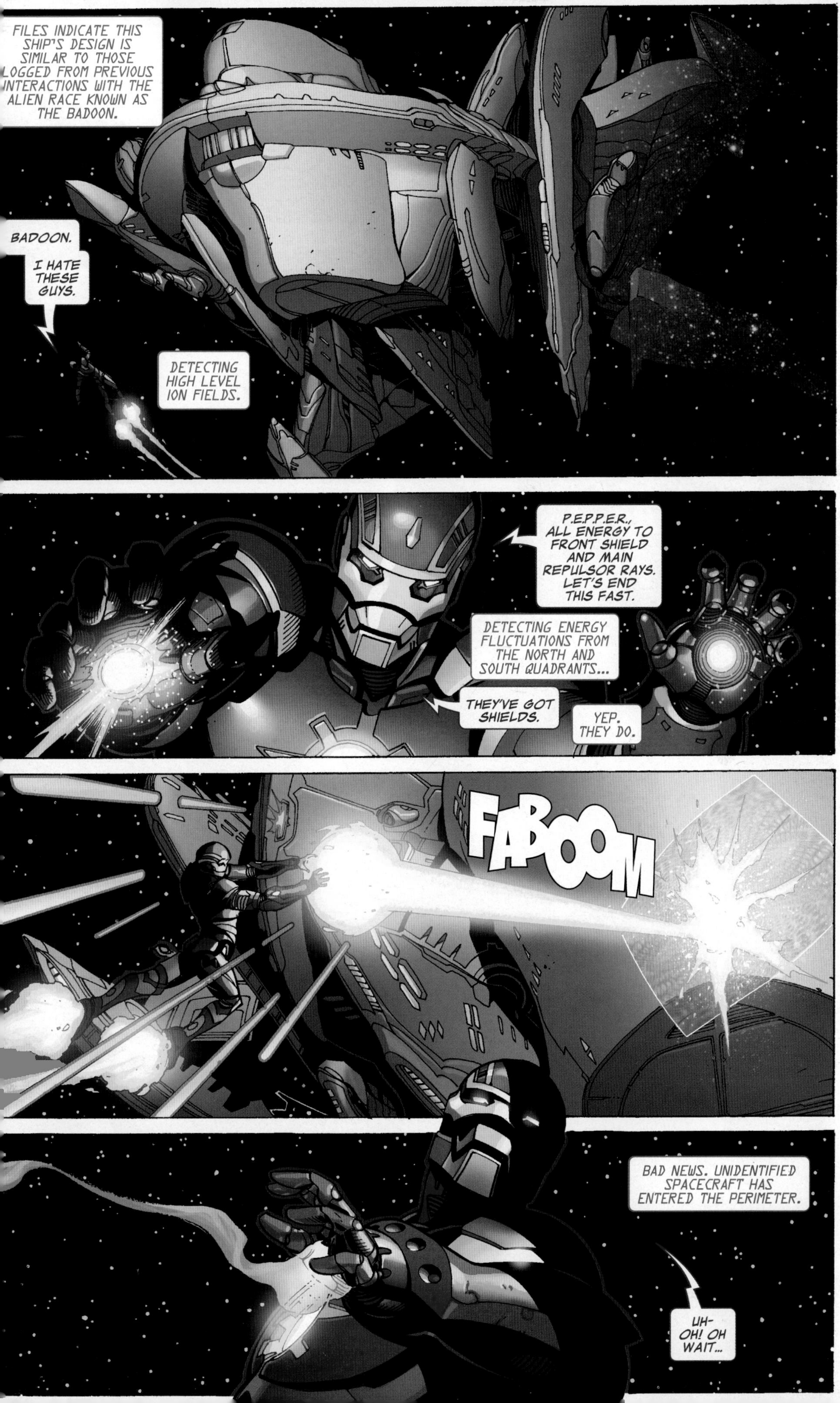
FILES INDICATE THIS SHIP'S DESIGN IS SIMILAR TO THOSE LOGGED FROM PREVIOUS INTERACTIONS WITH THE ALIEN RACE KNOWN AS THE BADOON.
BADOON.
I HATE THESE GUYS.
DETECTING HIGH LEVEL ION FIELDS.
P.E.P.P.E.R., ALL ENERGY TO FRONT SHIELD AND MAIN REPULSOR RAYS. LET'S END THIS FAST.
DETECTING ENERGY FLUCTUATIONS FROM THE NORTH AND SOUTH QUADRANTS...
THEY'VE GOT SHIELDS.
YEP. THEY DO.
FABOOM
BAD NEWS. UNIDENTIFIED SPACECRAFT HAS ENTERED THE PERIMETER.
UH-OH! OH WAIT...

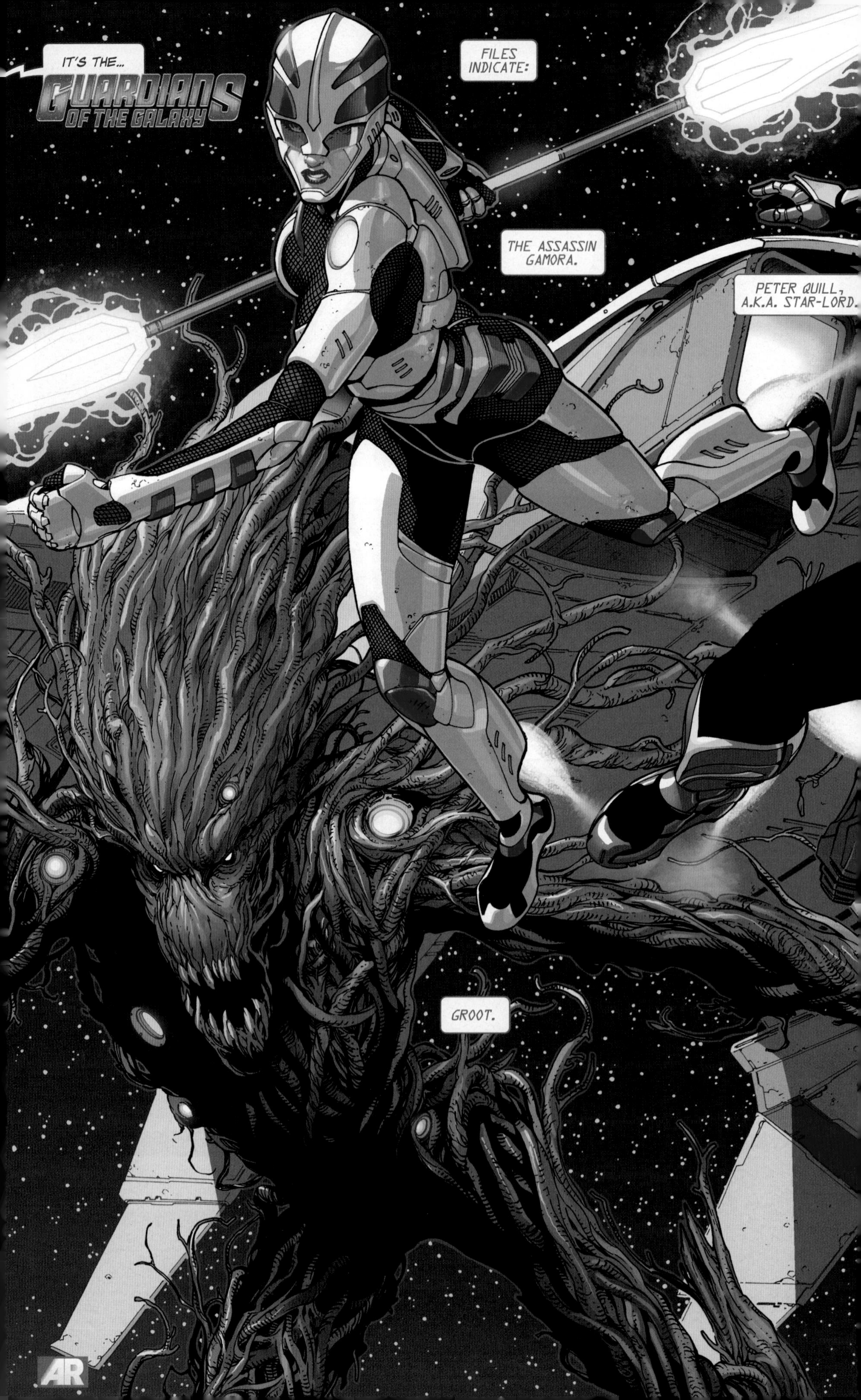
IT'S THE...
GUARDIANS OF THE GALAXY
FILES INDICATE:
THE ASSASSIN GAMORA.
PETER QUILL, A.K.A. STAR-LORD.
GROOT.

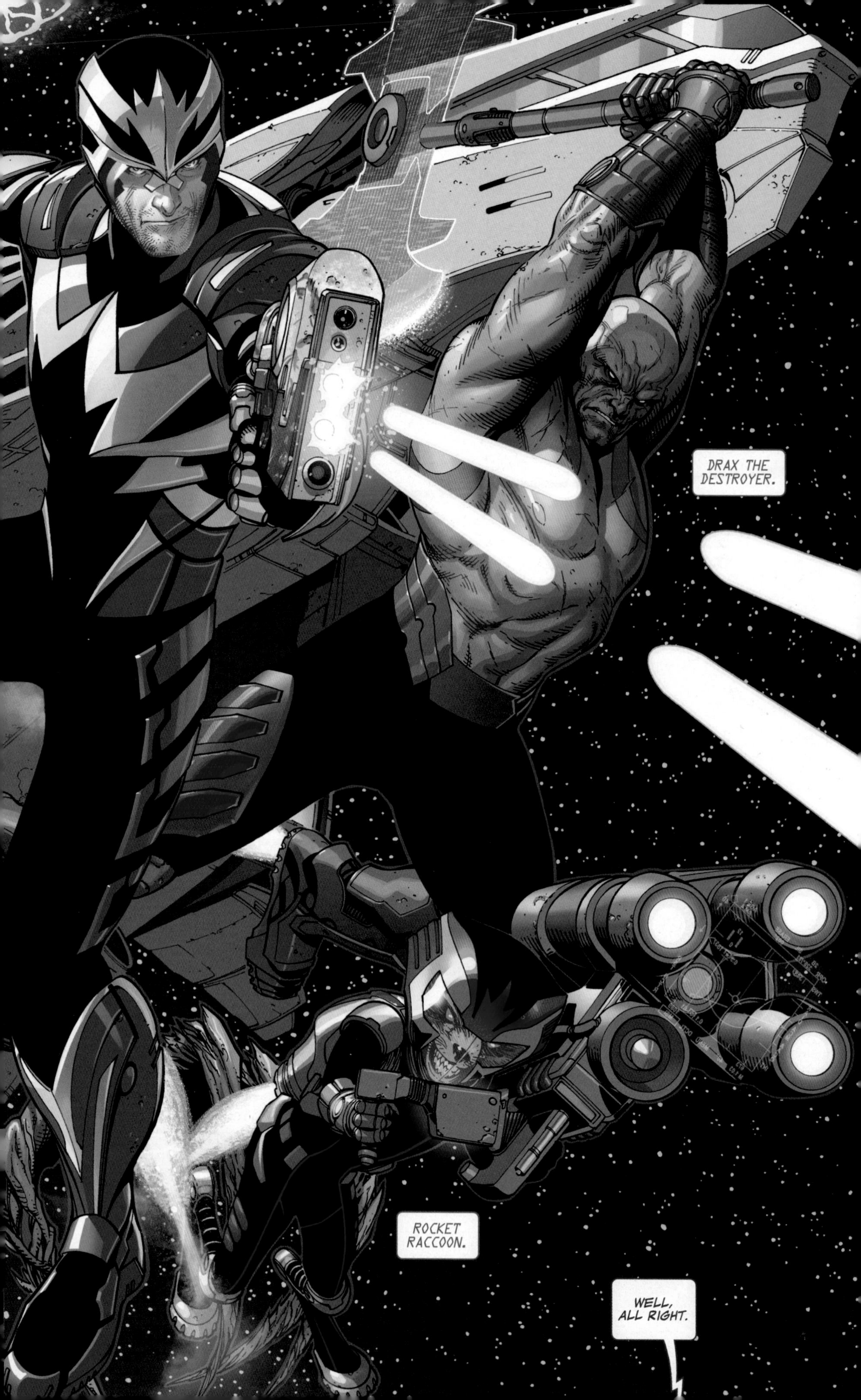
DRAX THE DESTROYER.
ROCKET RACCOON.
WELL, ALL RIGHT.

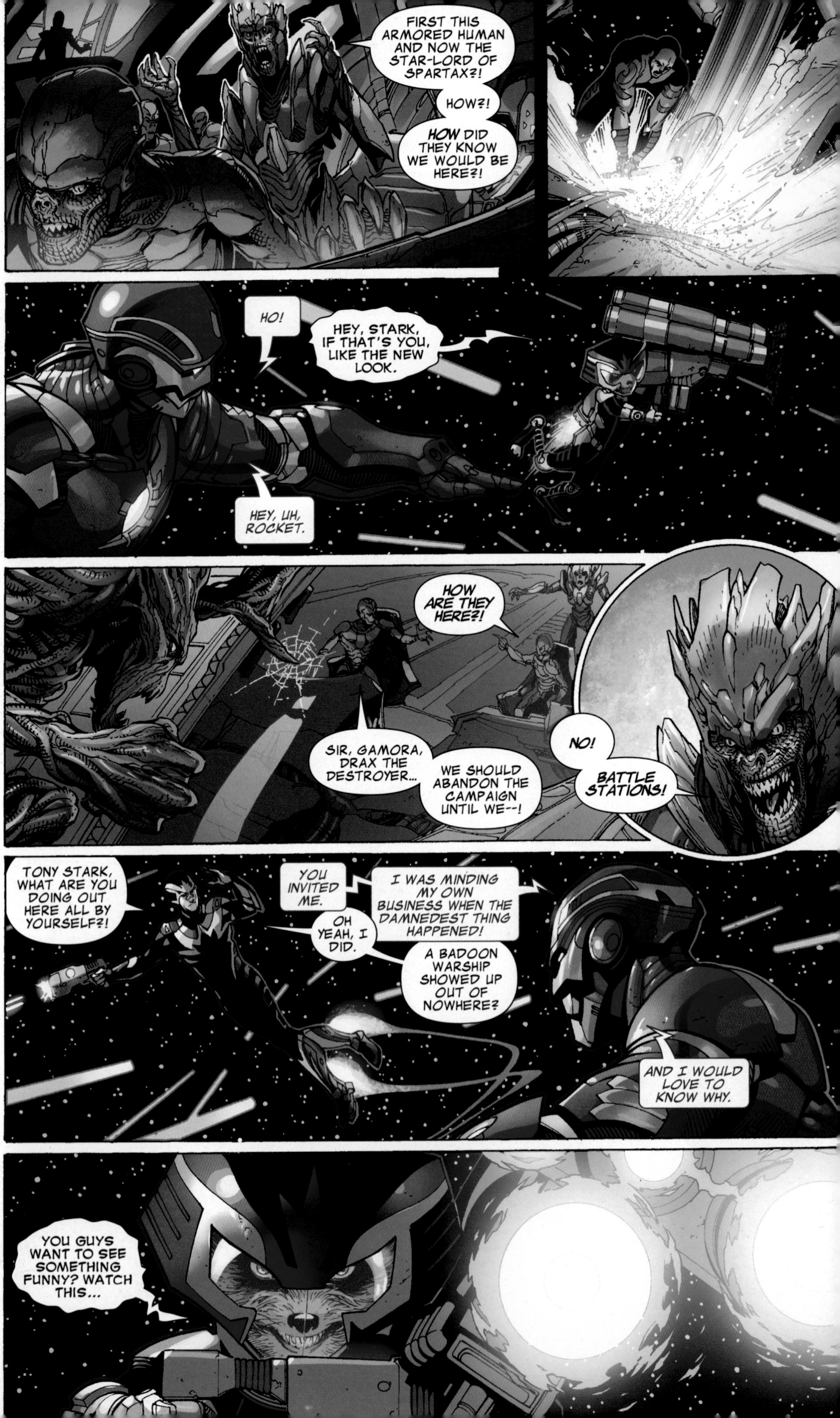
FIRST THIS ARMORED HUMAN AND NOW THE STAR-LORD OF SPARTAX?!
HOW?!
HOW DID THEY KNOW WE WOULD BE HERE?!
HO!
HEY, STARK, IF THAT'S YOU, LIKE THE NEW LOOK.
HEY, UH, ROCKET.
HOW ARE THEY HERE?!
SIR, GAMORA, DRAX THE DESTROYER...
WE SHOULD ABANDON THE CAMPAIGN UNTIL WE--!
NO!
BATTLE STATIONS!
TONY STARK, WHAT ARE YOU DOING OUT HERE ALL BY YOURSELF?!
YOU INVITED ME.
OH YEAH, I DID.
I WAS MINDING MY OWN BUSINESS WHEN THE DAMNEDEST THING HAPPENED!
A BADOON WARSHIP SHOWED UP OUT OF NOWHERE?
AND I WOULD LOVE TO KNOW WHY.
YOU GUYS WANT TO SEE SOMETHING FUNNY? WATCH THIS...

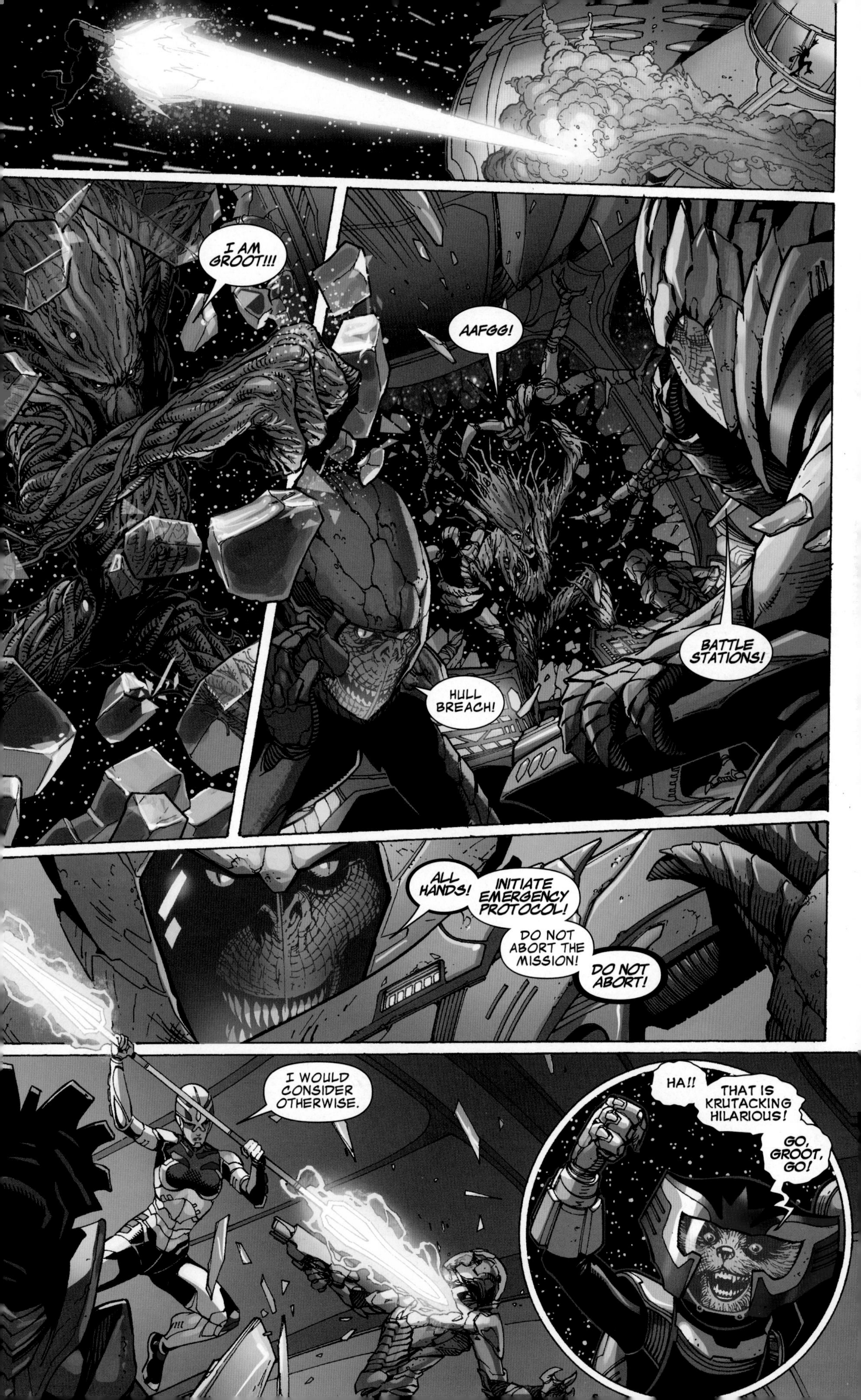
I AM GROOT!!!
AAFGG!
BATTLE STATIONS!
HULL BREACH!
ALL HANDS!
INITIATE EMERGENCY PROTOCOL!
DO NOT ABORT THE MISSION!
DO NOT ABORT!
I WOULD CONSIDER OTHERWISE.
HA!!
THAT IS KRUTACKING HILARIOUS!
GO, GROOT, GO!

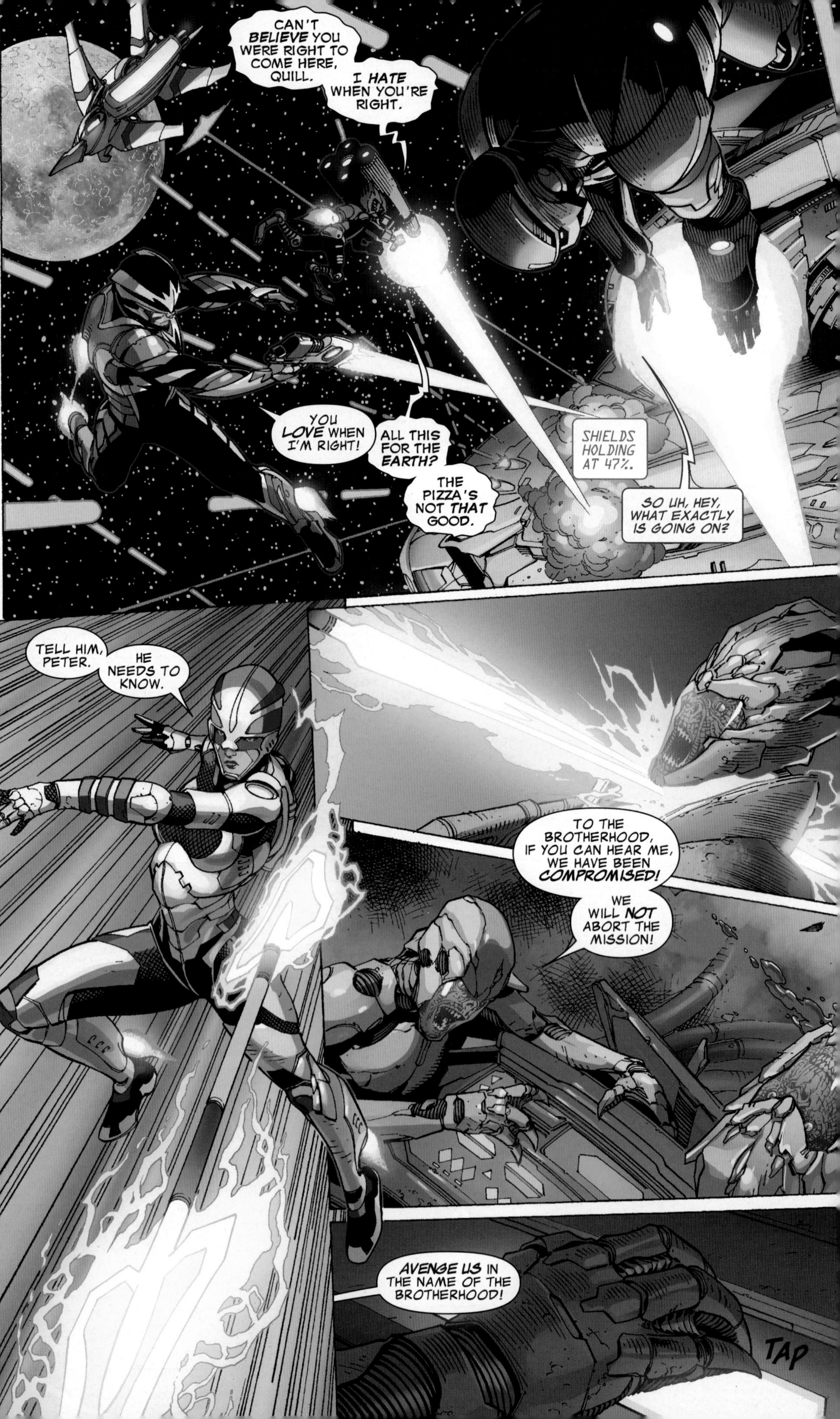
CAN'T BELIEVE YOU WERE RIGHT TO COME HERE, QUILL.
I HATE WHEN YOU'RE RIGHT.
YOU LOVE WHEN I'M RIGHT!
ALL THIS FOR THE EARTH?
THE PIZZA'S NOT THAT GOOD.
SHIELDS HOLDING AT 47%.
SO UH, HEY, WHAT EXACTLY IS GOING ON?
TELL HIM, PETER.
HE NEEDS TO KNOW.
TO THE BROTHERHOOD, IF YOU CAN HEAR ME, WE HAVE BEEN COMPROMISED!
WE WILL NOT ABORT THE MISSION!
AVENGE US IN THE NAME OF THE BROTHERHOOD!
TAP

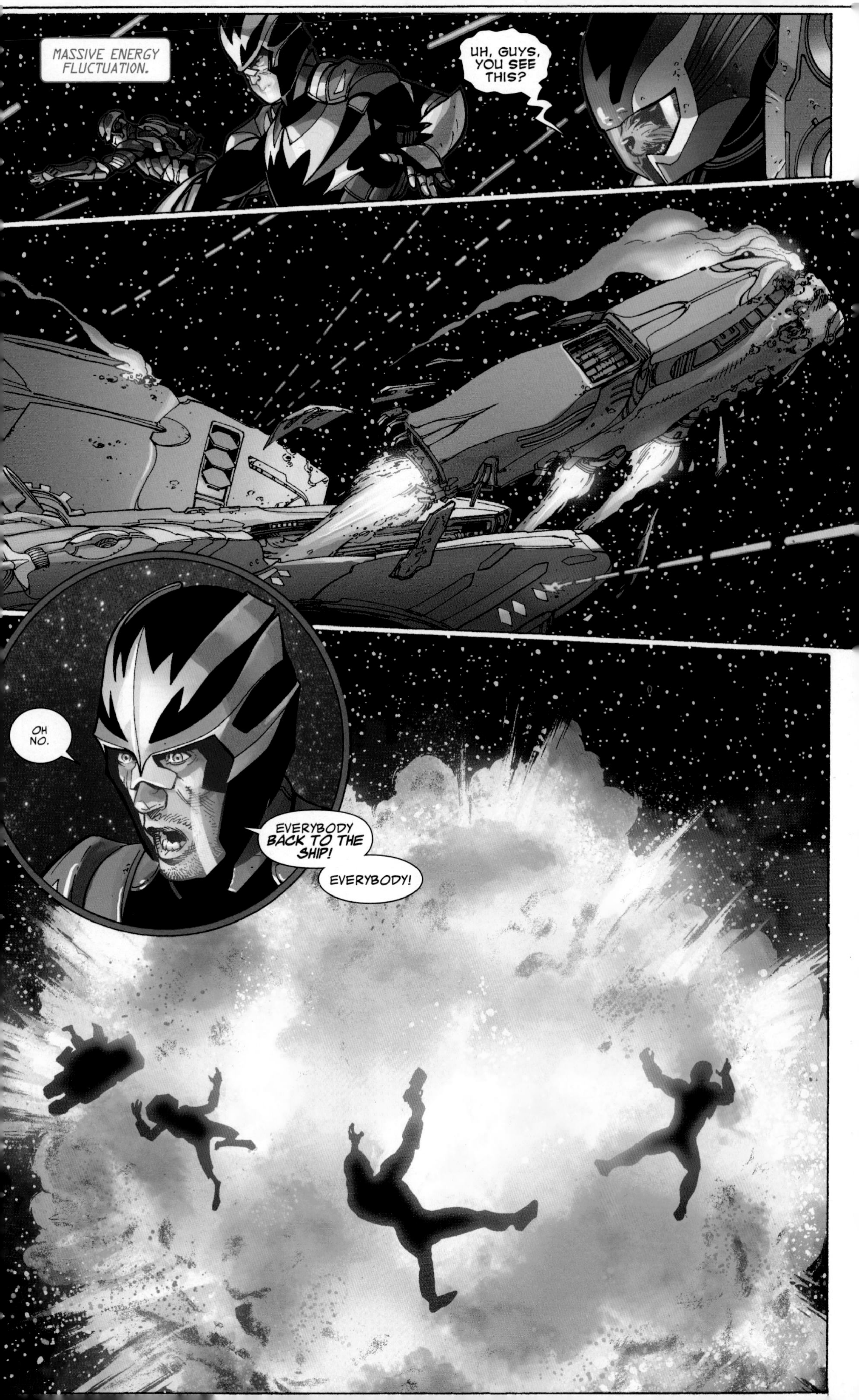
MASSIVE ENERGY FLUCTUATION.
UH, GUYS, YOU SEE THIS?
OH NO.
EVERYBODY BACK TO THE SHIP!
EVERYBODY!

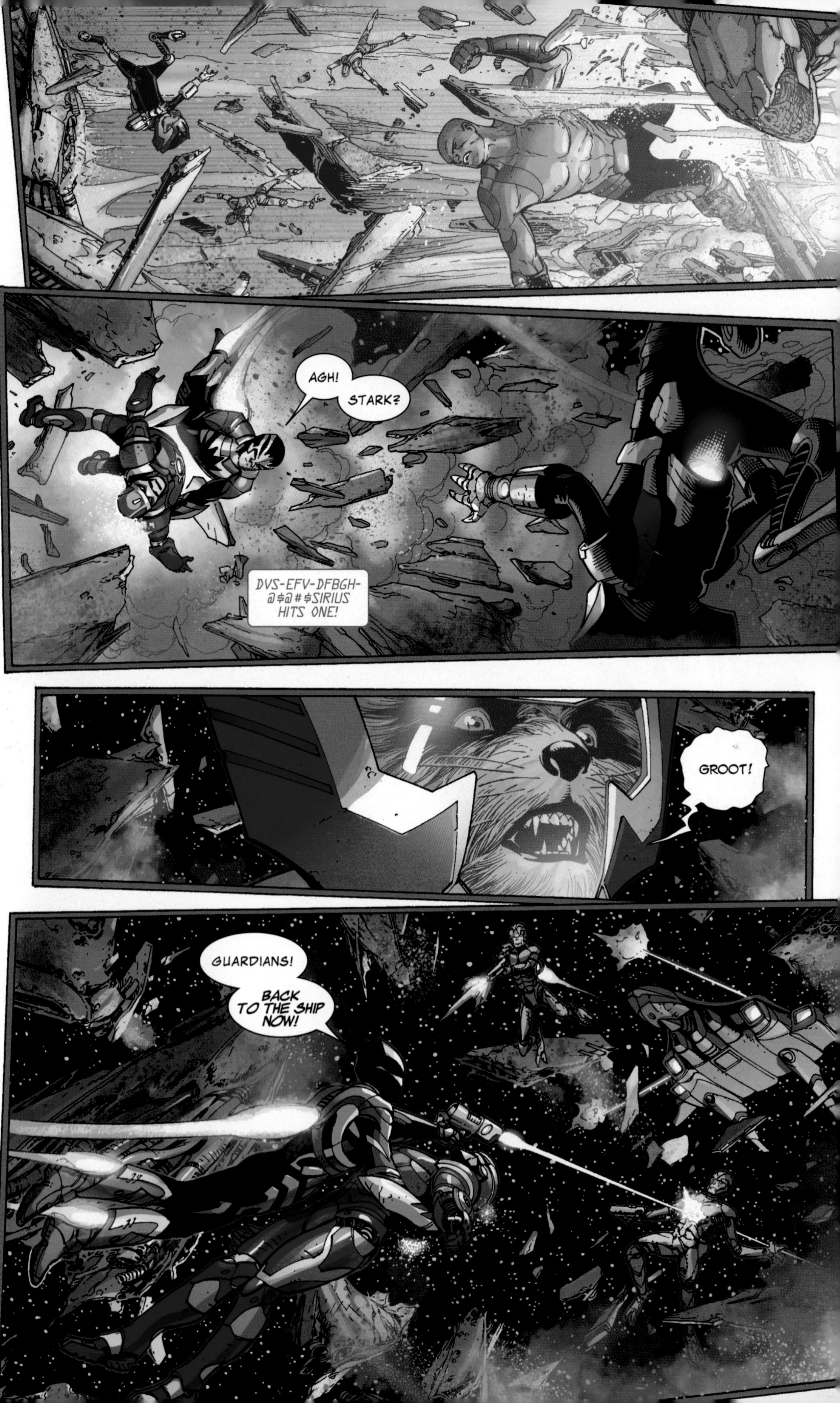
AGH!
STARK?
DVS-EFV-DFBGH-@$@#$SIRIUS HITS ONE!
GROOT!
GUARDIANS!
BACK TO THE SHIP NOW!

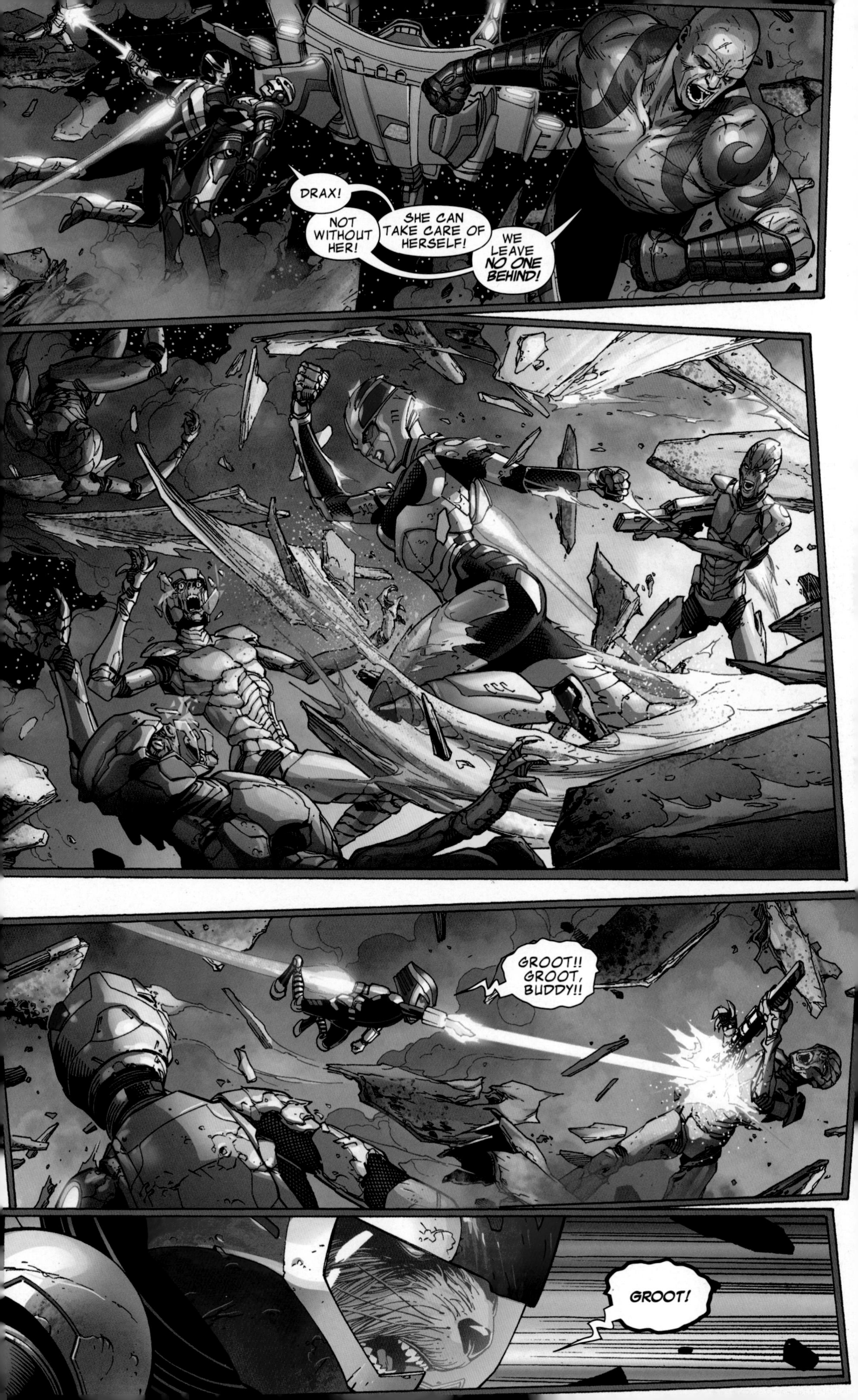
DRAX!
NOT WITHOUT HER!
SHE CAN TAKE CARE OF HERSELF!
WE LEAVE NO ONE BEHIND!
GROOT!! GROOT, BUDDY!!
GROOT!

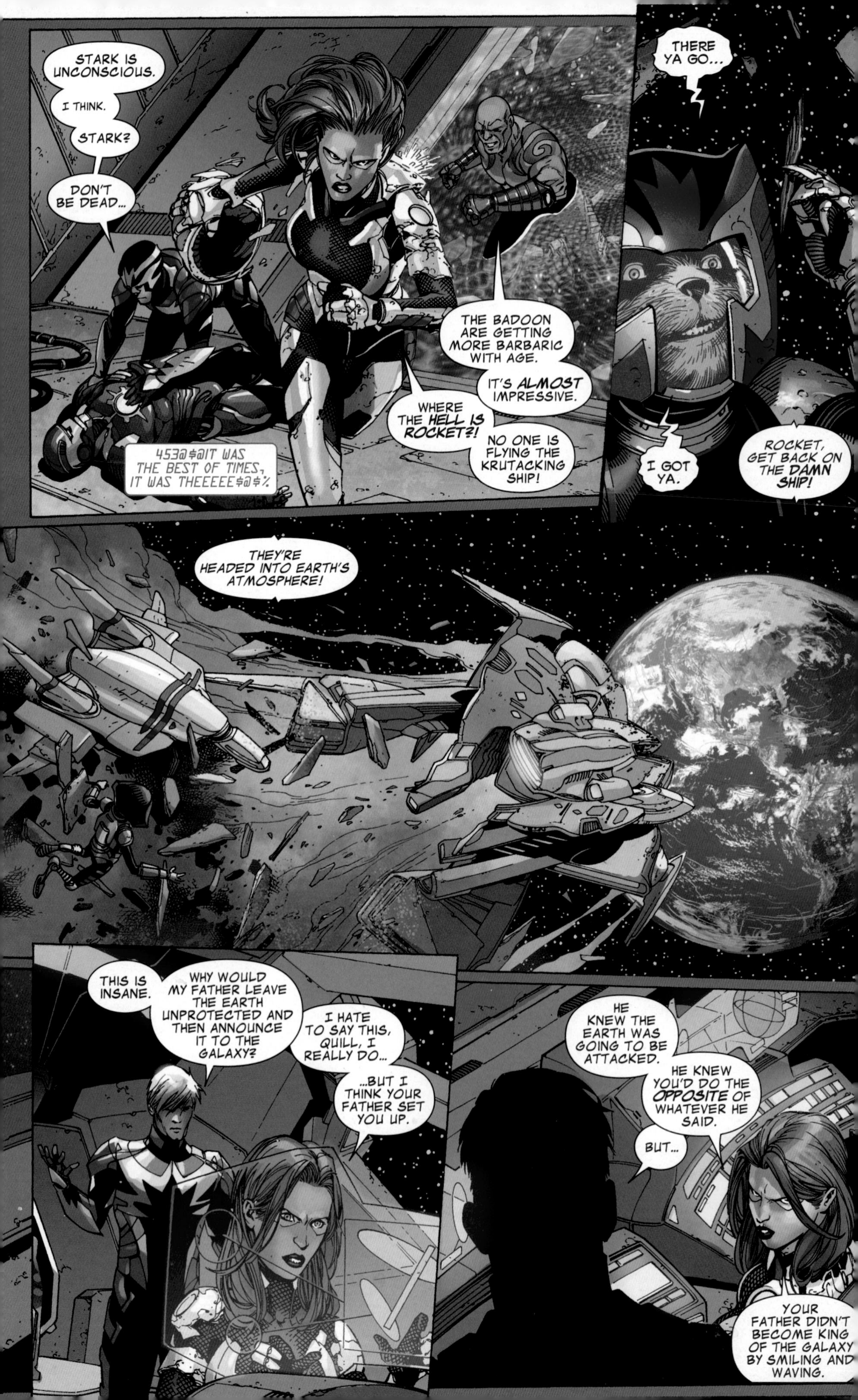
STARK IS UNCONSCIOUS.
I THINK.
STARK?
DON'T BE DEAD...
THE BADOON ARE GETTING MORE BARBARIC WITH AGE.
IT'S ALMOST IMPRESSIVE.
WHERE THE HELL IS ROCKET?!
NO ONE IS FLYING THE KRUTACKING SHIP!
453@$@IT WAS THE BEST OF TIMES, IT WAS THEEEEE$@$%
THERE YA GO...
I GOT YA.
ROCKET, GET BACK ON THE DAMN SHIP!
THEY'RE HEADED INTO EARTH'S ATMOSPHERE!
THIS IS INSANE.
WHY WOULD MY FATHER LEAVE THE EARTH UNPROTECTED AND THEN ANNOUNCE IT TO THE GALAXY?
I HATE TO SAY THIS, QUILL, I REALLY DO...
...BUT I THINK YOUR FATHER SET YOU UP.
HE KNEW THE EARTH WAS GOING TO BE ATTACKED.
HE KNEW YOU'D DO THE OPPOSITE OF WHATEVER HE SAID.
BUT...
YOUR FATHER DIDN'T BECOME KING OF THE GALAXY BY SMILING AND WAVING.

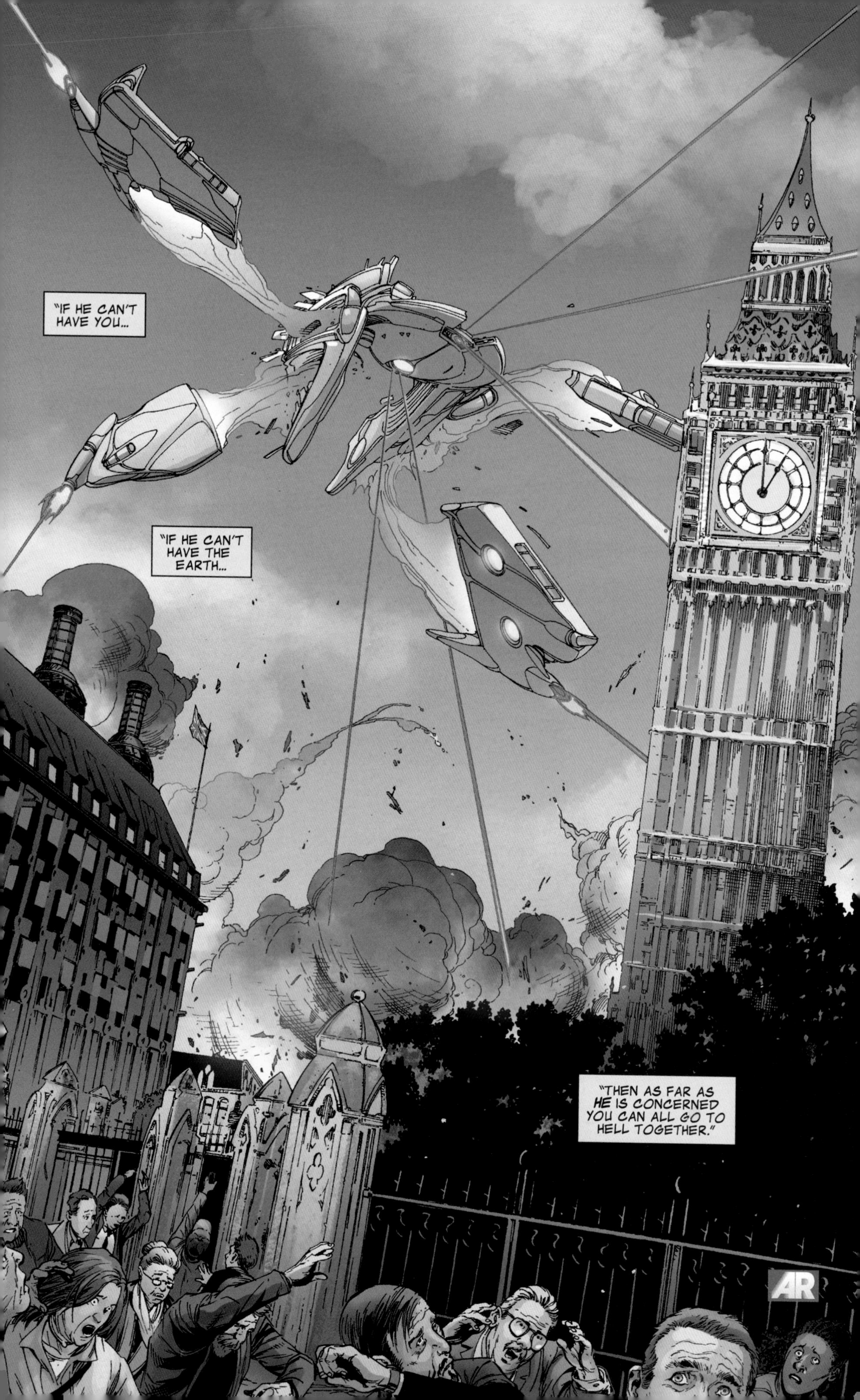
"IF HE CAN'T HAVE YOU...
"IF HE CAN'T HAVE THE EARTH...
"THEN AS FAR AS HE IS CONCERNED YOU CAN ALL GO TO HELL TOGETHER."

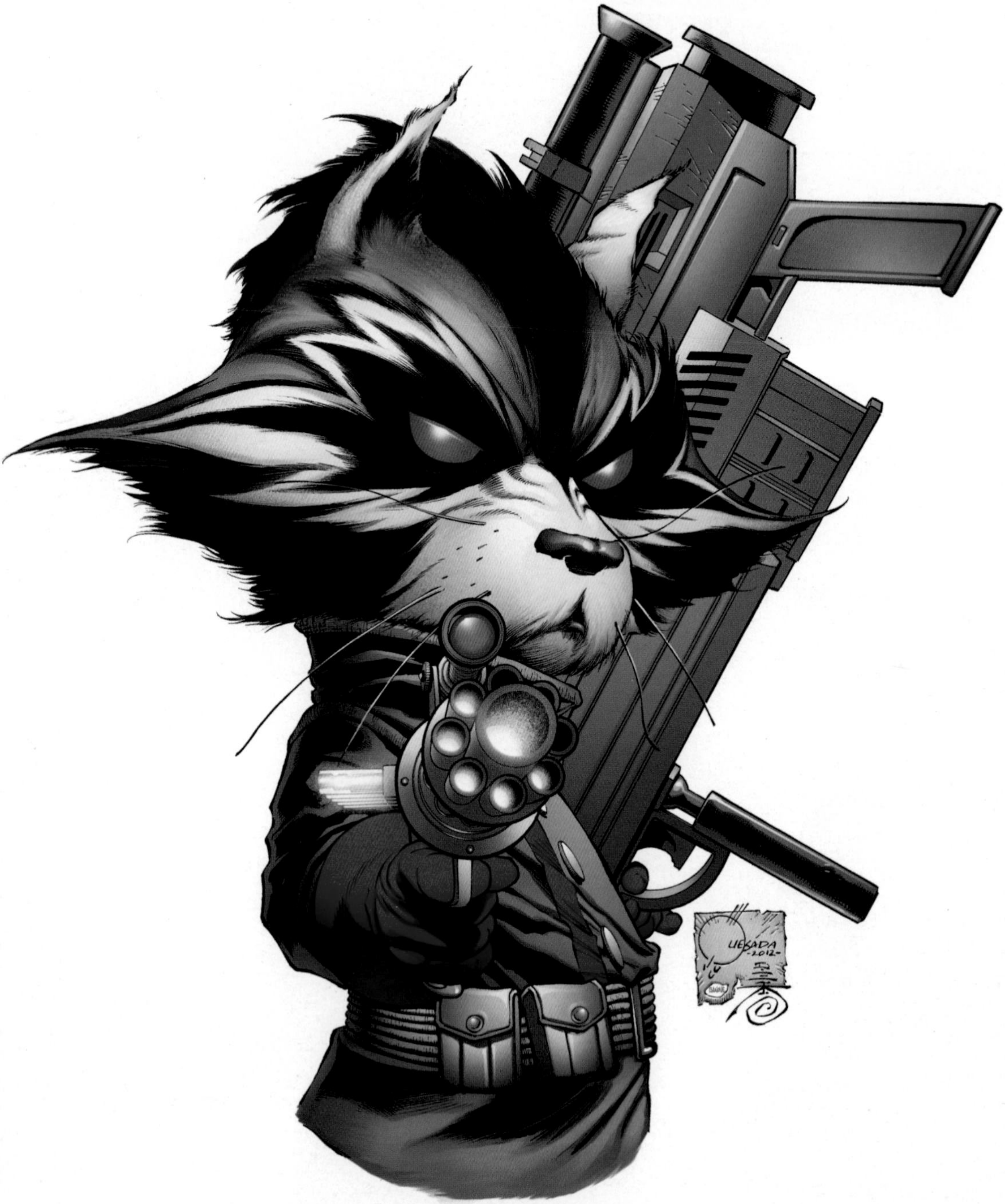

#2 VARIANT BY JOE QUESADA, DANNY MIKI & RICHARD ISANOVE

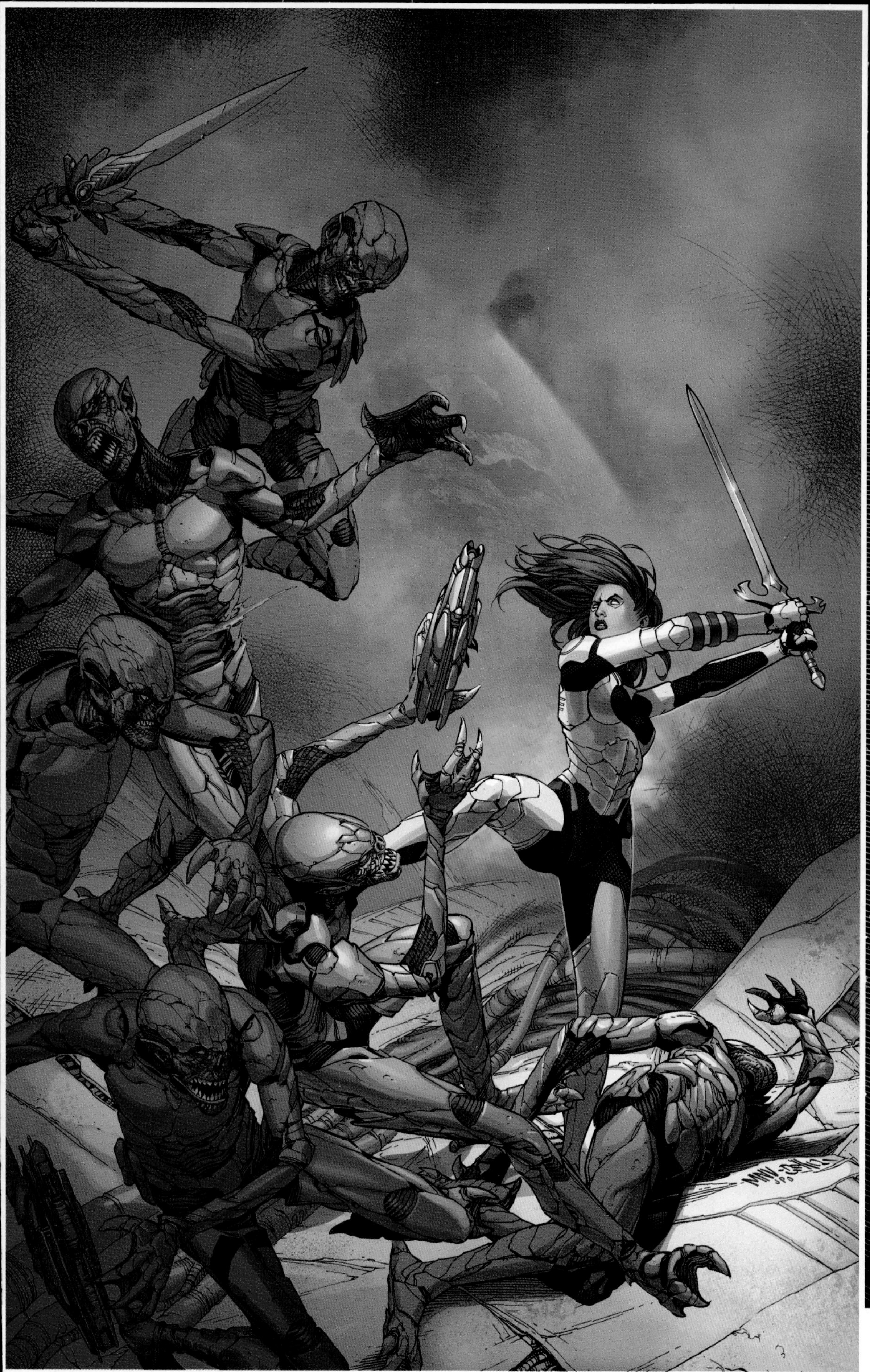

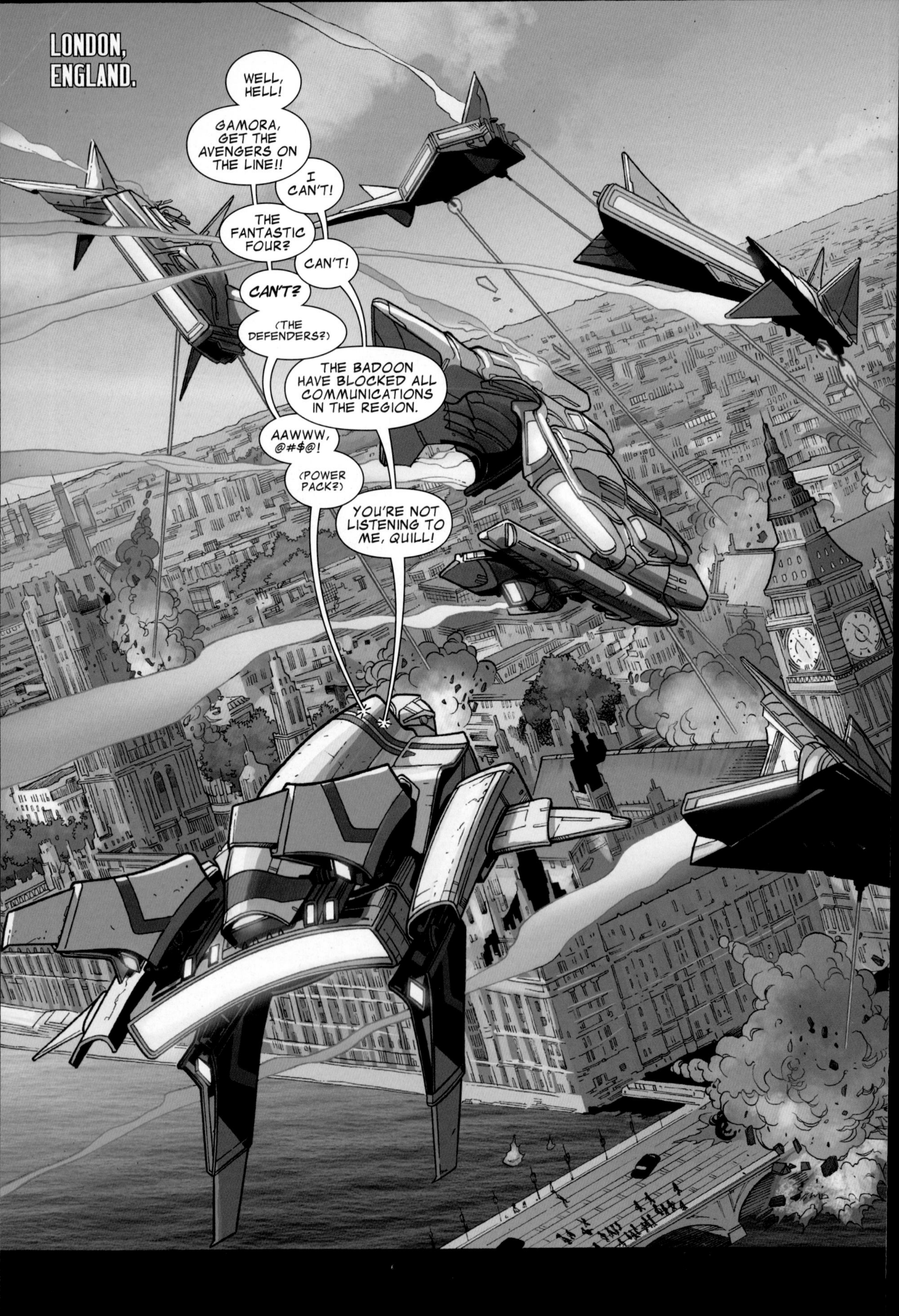
LONDON, ENGLAND.
WELL, HELL!
GAMORA, GET THE AVENGERS ON THE LINE!!
I CAN'T!
THE FANTASTIC FOUR?
CAN'T!
CAN'T?
(THE DEFENDERS?)
THE BADOON HAVE BLOCKED ALL COMMUNICATIONS IN THE REGION.
AAWWW, @#$@!
(POWER PACK?)
YOU'RE NOT LISTENING TO ME, QUILL!

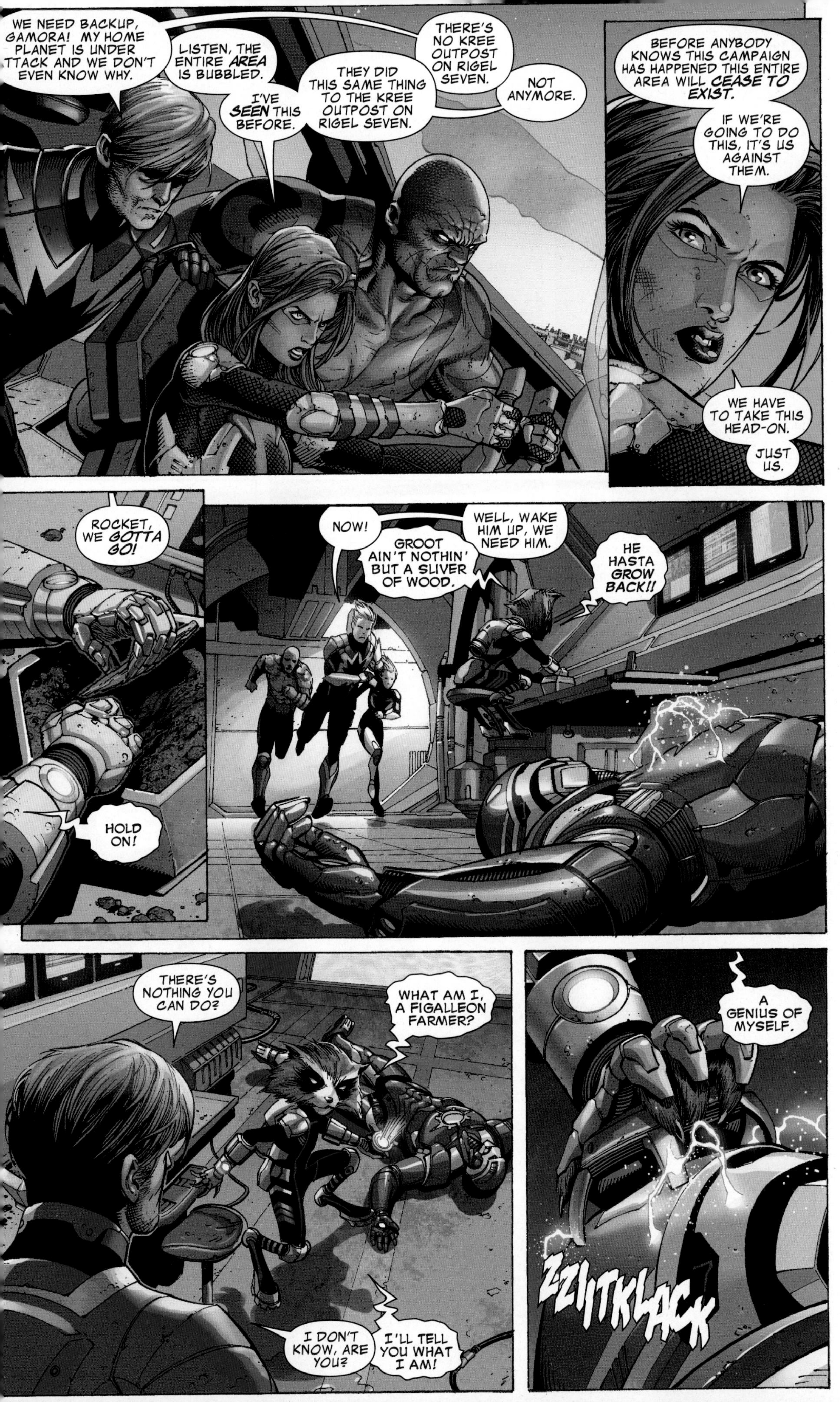

WE NEED BACKUP, GAMORA! MY HOME PLANET IS UNDER ATTACK AND WE DON'T EVEN KNOW WHY.
LISTEN, THE ENTIRE AREA IS BUBBLED.
I'VE SEEN THIS BEFORE.
THEY DID THIS SAME THING TO THE KREE OUTPOST ON RIGEL SEVEN.
THERE'S NO KREE OUTPOST ON RIGEL SEVEN.
NOT ANYMORE.
BEFORE ANYBODY KNOWS THIS CAMPAIGN HAS HAPPENED THIS ENTIRE AREA WILL CEASE TO EXIST.
IF WE'RE GOING TO DO THIS, IT'S US AGAINST THEM.
WE HAVE TO TAKE THIS HEAD-ON.
JUST US.
ROCKET, WE GOTTA GO!
HOLD ON!
NOW!
GROOT AIN'T NOTHIN' BUT A SLIVER OF WOOD.
WELL, WAKE HIM UP, WE NEED HIM.
HE HASTA GROW BACK!!
THERE'S NOTHING YOU CAN DO?
WHAT AM I, A FIGALLEON FARMER?
I DON'T KNOW, ARE YOU?
I'LL TELL YOU WHAT I AM!
A GENIUS OF MYSELF.
ZZIITKLACK

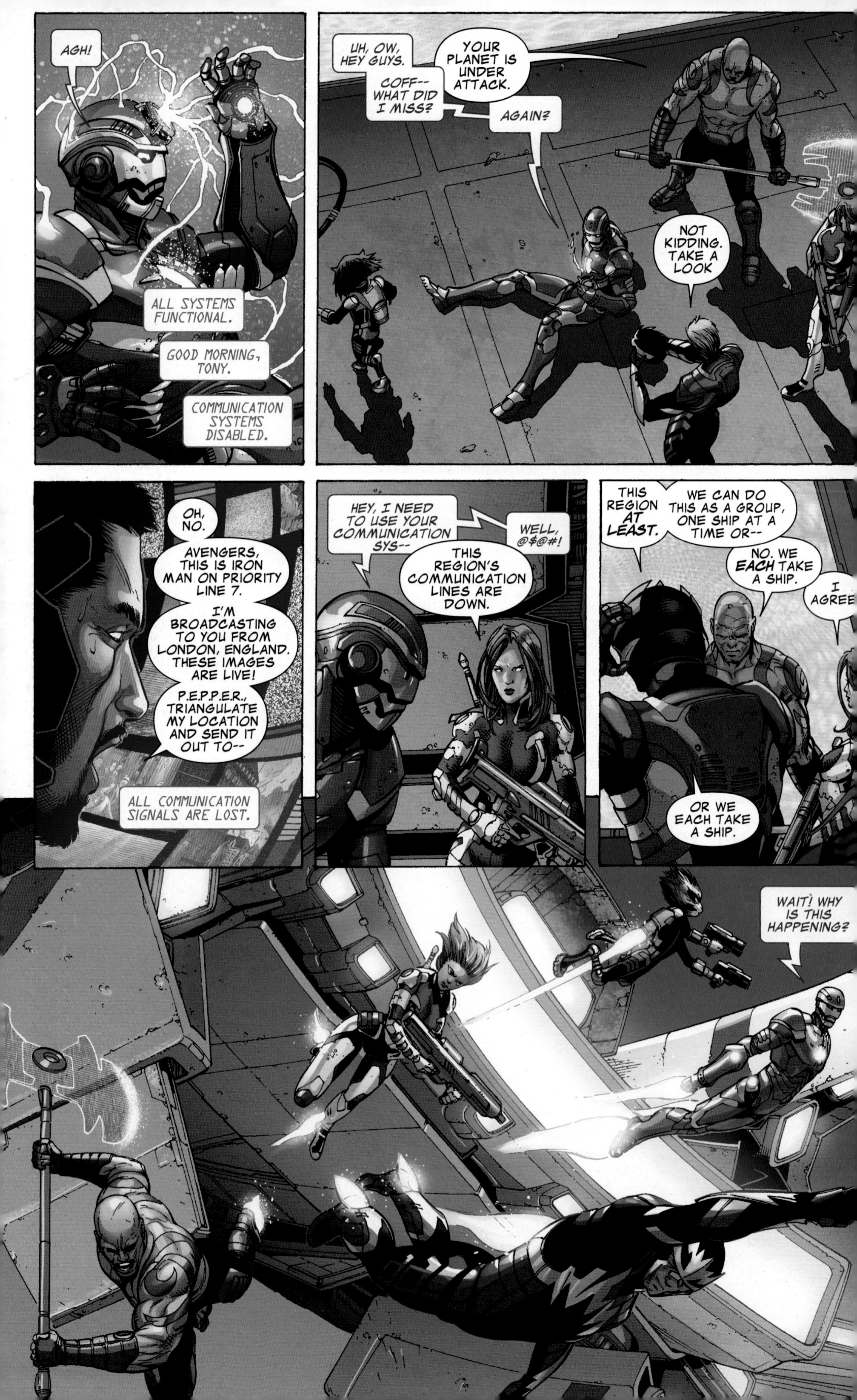
AGH!
ALL SYSTEMS FUNCTIONAL.
GOOD MORNING, TONY.
COMMUNICATION SYSTEMS DISABLED.
UH, OW, HEY GUYS.
COFF-- WHAT DID I MISS?
YOUR PLANET IS UNDER ATTACK.
AGAIN?
NOT KIDDING. TAKE A LOOK
OH, NO.
AVENGERS, THIS IS IRON MAN ON PRIORITY LINE 7.
I'M BROADCASTING TO YOU FROM LONDON, ENGLAND. THESE IMAGES ARE LIVE!
P.E.P.P.E.R., TRIANGULATE MY LOCATION AND SEND IT OUT TO--
ALL COMMUNICATION SIGNALS ARE LOST.
HEY, I NEED TO USE YOUR COMMUNICATION SYS--
WELL, @$@#!
THIS REGION'S COMMUNICATION LINES ARE DOWN.
THIS REGION AT LEAST.
WE CAN DO THIS AS A GROUP, ONE SHIP AT A TIME OR--
NO. WE EACH TAKE A SHIP.
I AGREE
OR WE EACH TAKE A SHIP.
WAIT! WHY IS THIS HAPPENING?

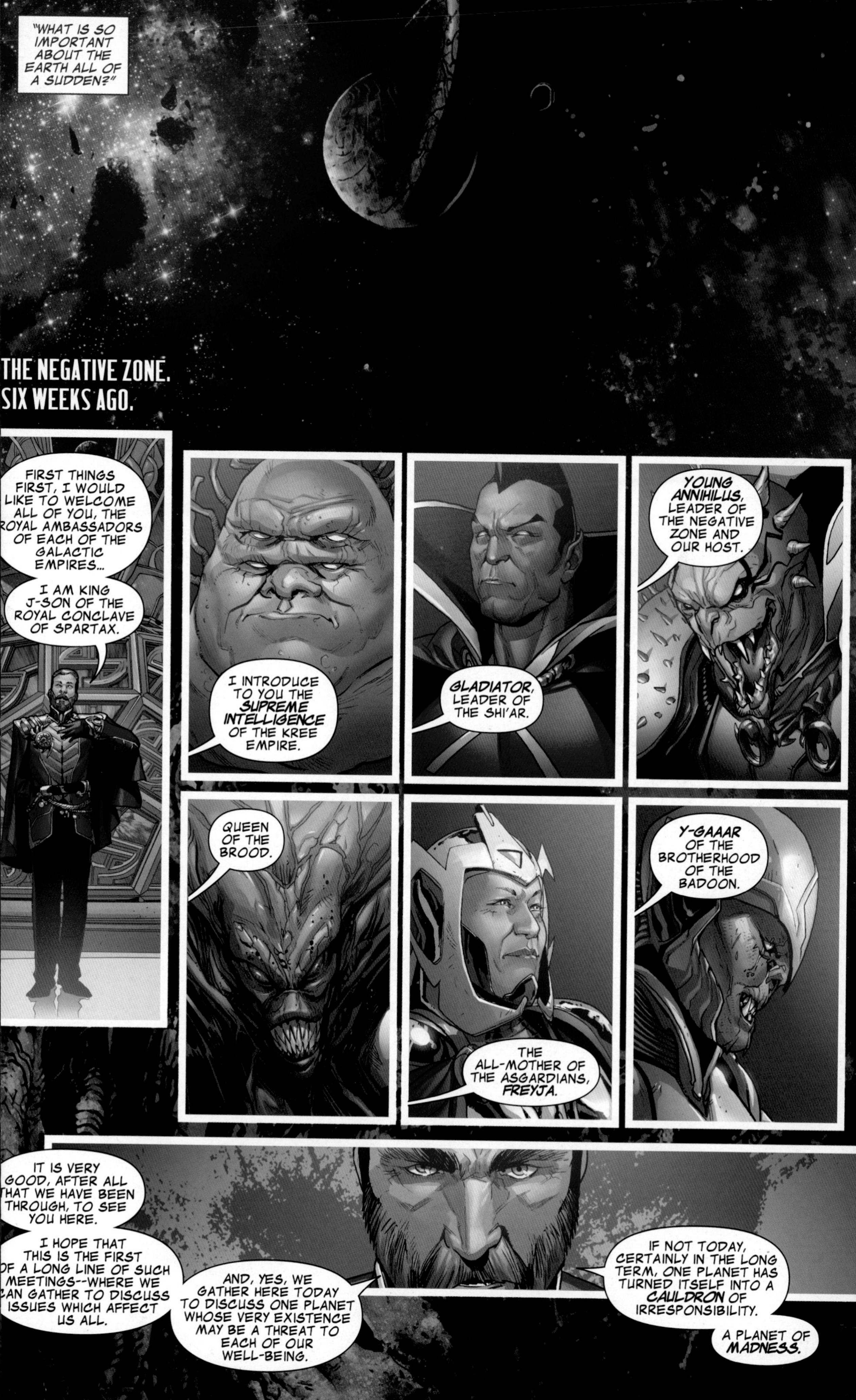
"WHAT IS SO IMPORTANT ABOUT THE EARTH ALL OF A SUDDEN?"
THE NEGATIVE ZONE. SIX WEEKS AGO.
FIRST THINGS FIRST, I WOULD LIKE TO WELCOME ALL OF YOU, THE ROYAL AMBASSADORS OF EACH OF THE GALACTIC EMPIRES...
I AM KING J-SON OF THE ROYAL CONCLAVE OF SPARTAX.
I INTRODUCE TO YOU THE SUPREME INTELLIGENCE OF THE KREE EMPIRE.
GLADIATOR, LEADER OF THE SHI'AR.
YOUNG ANNIHILUS, LEADER OF THE NEGATIVE ZONE AND OUR HOST.
QUEEN OF THE BROOD.
THE ALL-MOTHER OF THE ASGARDIANS, FREYJA.
Y-GAAAR OF THE BROTHERHOOD OF THE BADOON.
IT IS VERY GOOD, AFTER ALL THAT WE HAVE BEEN THROUGH, TO SEE YOU HERE.
I HOPE THAT THIS IS THE FIRST OF A LONG LINE OF SUCH MEETINGS--WHERE WE CAN GATHER TO DISCUSS ISSUES WHICH AFFECT US ALL.
AND, YES, WE GATHER HERE TODAY TO DISCUSS ONE PLANET WHOSE VERY EXISTENCE MAY BE A THREAT TO EACH OF OUR WELL-BEING.
IF NOT TODAY, CERTAINLY IN THE LONG TERM, ONE PLANET HAS TURNED ITSELF INTO A CAULDRON OF IRRESPONSIBILITY.
A PLANET OF MADNESS.

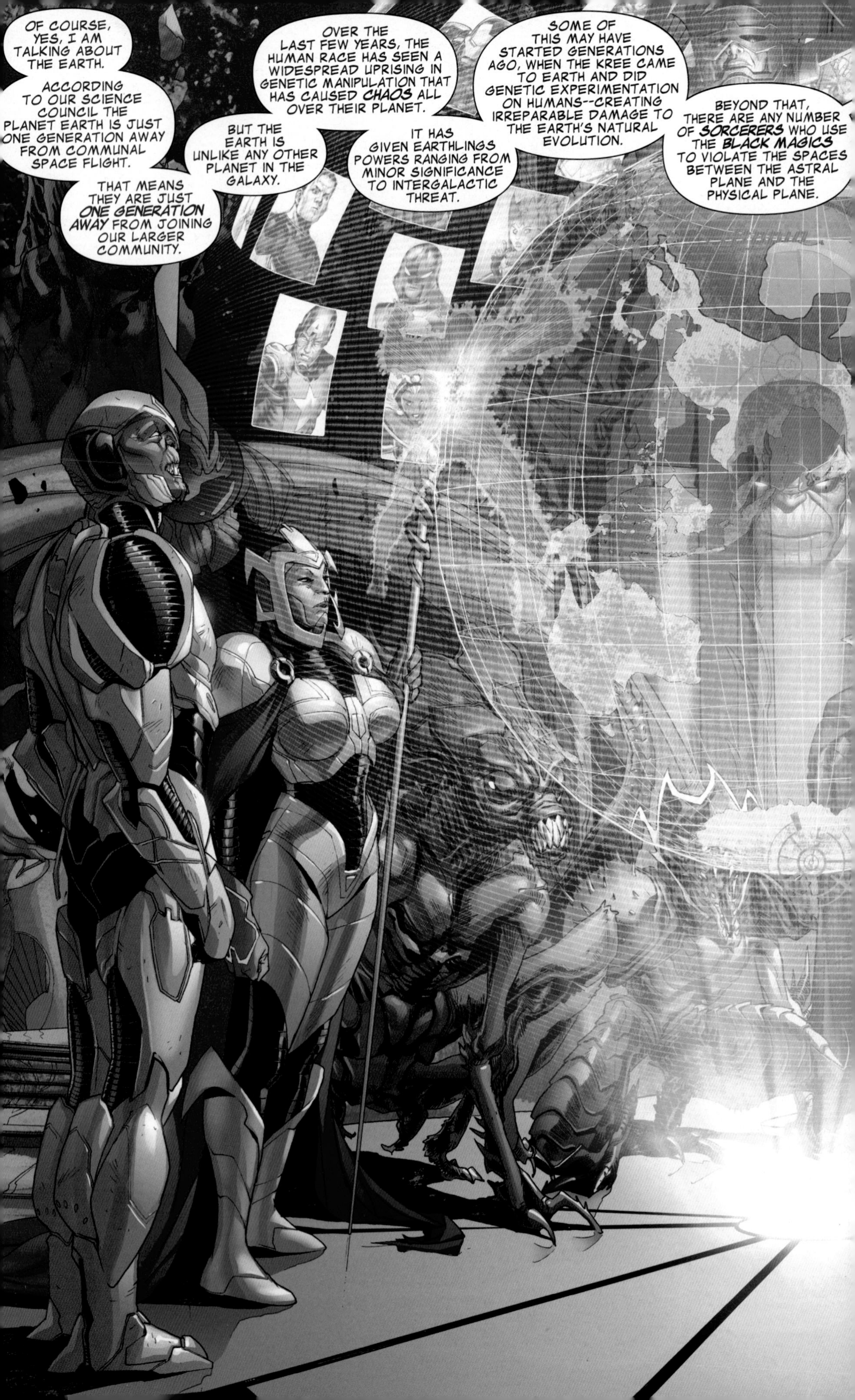
OF COURSE, YES, I AM TALKING ABOUT THE EARTH.
ACCORDING TO OUR SCIENCE COUNCIL THE PLANET EARTH IS JUST ONE GENERATION AWAY FROM COMMUNAL SPACE FLIGHT.
THAT MEANS THEY ARE JUST ONE GENERATION AWAY FROM JOINING OUR LARGER COMMUNITY.
BUT THE EARTH IS UNLIKE ANY OTHER PLANET IN THE GALAXY.
OVER THE LAST FEW YEARS, THE HUMAN RACE HAS SEEN A WIDESPREAD UPRISING IN GENETIC MANIPULATION THAT HAS CAUSED CHAOS ALL OVER THEIR PLANET.
IT HAS GIVEN EARTHLINGS POWERS RANGING FROM MINOR SIGNIFICANCE TO INTERGALACTIC THREAT.
SOME OF THIS MAY HAVE STARTED GENERATIONS AGO, WHEN THE KREE CAME TO EARTH AND DID GENETIC EXPERIMENTATION ON HUMANS--CREATING IRREPARABLE DAMAGE TO THE EARTH'S NATURAL EVOLUTION.
BEYOND THAT, THERE ARE ANY NUMBER OF SORCERERS WHO USE THE BLACK MAGICS TO VIOLATE THE SPACES BETWEEN THE ASTRAL PLANE AND THE PHYSICAL PLANE.

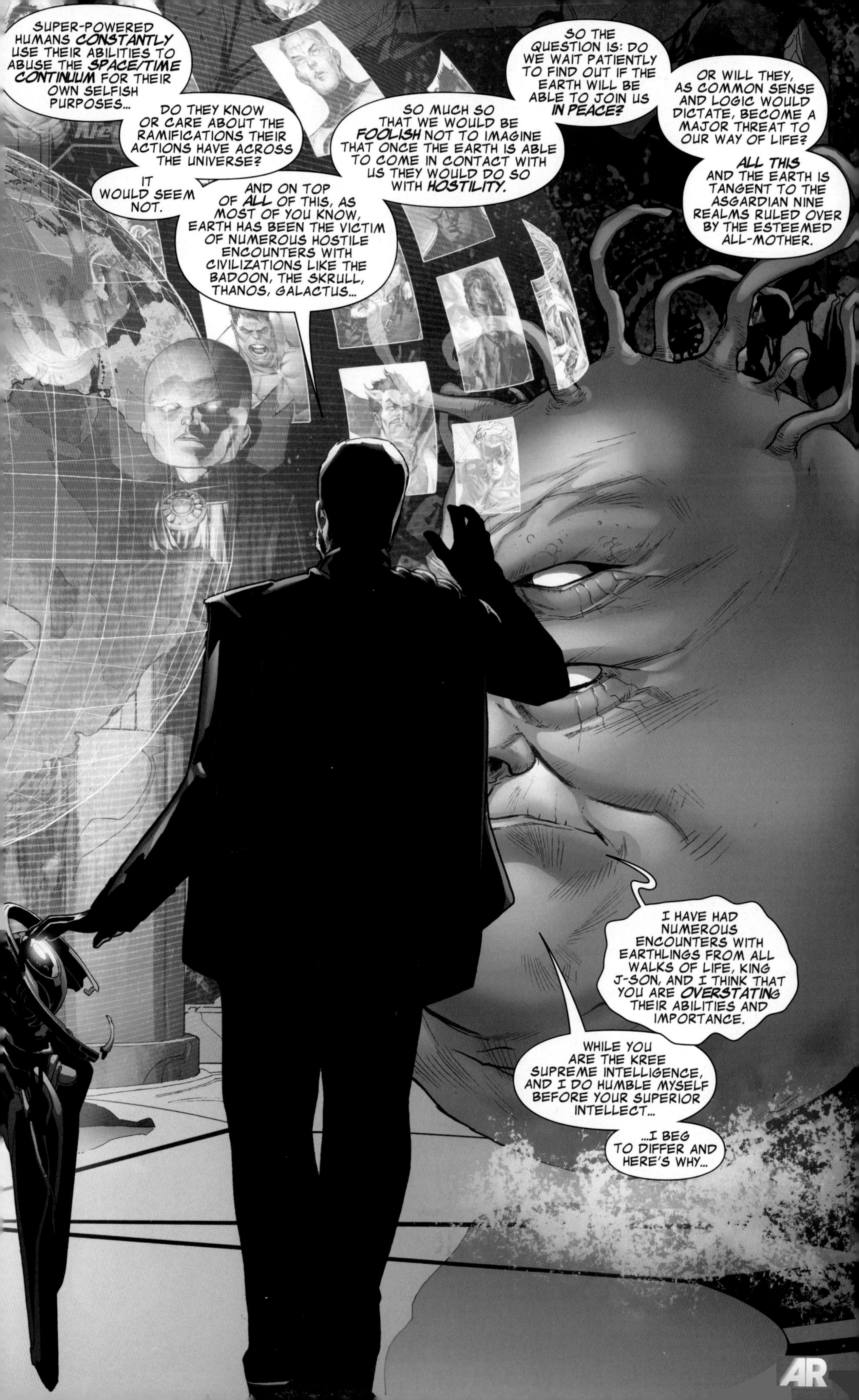
SUPER-POWERED HUMANS CONSTANTLY USE THEIR ABILITIES TO ABUSE THE SPACE/TIME CONTINUUM FOR THEIR OWN SELFISH PURPOSES...
DO THEY KNOW OR CARE ABOUT THE RAMIFICATIONS THEIR ACTIONS HAVE ACROSS THE UNIVERSE?
IT WOULD SEEM NOT.
AND ON TOP OF ALL OF THIS, AS MOST OF YOU KNOW, EARTH HAS BEEN THE VICTIM OF NUMEROUS HOSTILE ENCOUNTERS WITH CIVILIZATIONS LIKE THE BADOON, THE SKRULL, THANOS, GALACTUS...
SO MUCH SO THAT WE WOULD BE FOOLISH NOT TO IMAGINE THAT ONCE THE EARTH IS ABLE TO COME IN CONTACT WITH US THEY WOULD DO SO WITH HOSTILITY.
SO THE QUESTION IS: DO WE WAIT PATIENTLY TO FIND OUT IF THE EARTH WILL BE ABLE TO JOIN US IN PEACE?
OR WILL THEY, AS COMMON SENSE AND LOGIC WOULD DICTATE, BECOME A MAJOR THREAT TO OUR WAY OF LIFE?
ALL THIS AND THE EARTH IS TANGENT TO THE ASGARDIAN NINE REALMS RULED OVER BY THE ESTEEMED ALL-MOTHER.
I HAVE HAD NUMEROUS ENCOUNTERS WITH EARTHLINGS FROM ALL WALKS OF LIFE, KING J-SON, AND I THINK THAT YOU ARE OVERSTATING THEIR ABILITIES AND IMPORTANCE.
WHILE YOU ARE THE KREE SUPREME INTELLIGENCE, AND I DO HUMBLE MYSELF BEFORE YOUR SUPERIOR INTELLECT...
...I BEG TO DIFFER AND HERE'S WHY...

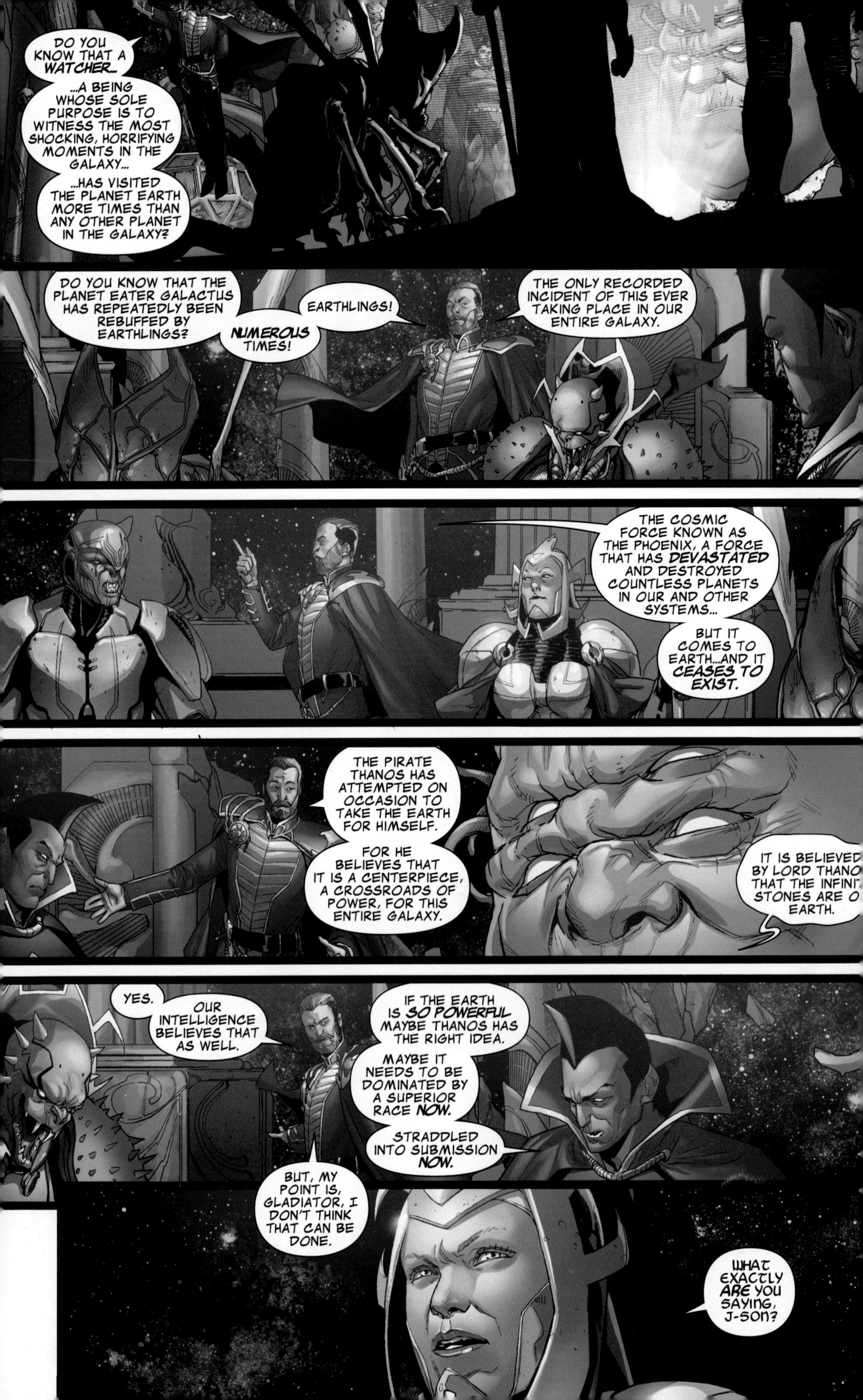
DO YOU KNOW THAT A WATCHER...
...A BEING WHOSE SOLE PURPOSE IS TO WITNESS THE MOST SHOCKING, HORRIFYING MOMENTS IN THE GALAXY...
...HAS VISITED THE PLANET EARTH MORE TIMES THAN ANY OTHER PLANET IN THE GALAXY?
DO YOU KNOW THAT THE PLANET EATER GALACTUS HAS REPEATEDLY BEEN REBUFFED BY EARTHLINGS?
EARTHLINGS!
NUMEROUS TIMES!
THE ONLY RECORDED INCIDENT OF THIS EVER TAKING PLACE IN OUR ENTIRE GALAXY.
THE COSMIC FORCE KNOWN AS THE PHOENIX, A FORCE THAT HAS DEVASTATED AND DESTROYED COUNTLESS PLANETS IN OUR AND OTHER SYSTEMS...
BUT IT COMES TO EARTH...AND IT CEASES TO EXIST.
THE PIRATE THANOS HAS ATTEMPTED ON OCCASION TO TAKE THE EARTH FOR HIMSELF.
FOR HE BELIEVES THAT IT IS A CENTERPIECE, A CROSSROADS OF POWER, FOR THIS ENTIRE GALAXY.
IT IS BELIEVED BY LORD THANO THAT THE INFINIT STONES ARE O EARTH.
YES.
OUR INTELLIGENCE BELIEVES THAT AS WELL.
IF THE EARTH IS SO POWERFUL MAYBE THANOS HAS THE RIGHT IDEA.
MAYBE IT NEEDS TO BE DOMINATED BY A SUPERIOR RACE NOW.
STRADDLED INTO SUBMISSION NOW.
BUT, MY POINT IS, GLADIATOR, I DON'T THINK THAT CAN BE DONE.
WHAT EXACTLY ARE YOU SAYING, J-SON?

LONDON, ENGLAND.

GUYS, FAST AND FURIOUS AND STAY IN CONTACT.

I HAVE THE SHOT.

IF YOU DON'T THINK YOU HAVE THE SHOT, DON'T TAKE IT.

SYNCHRONIZED ATTACK ON TARGET.

STAY WITH THE OTHER SHIPS. WE OUTNUMBER THEM.

BY YOUR COMMAND.

BUT THE GUARDIANS?

THE STARLORD IS BUT ONE SHIP.

MOTHER COMMAND WILL TAKE CARE OF THEM.

BOOM

AGH!

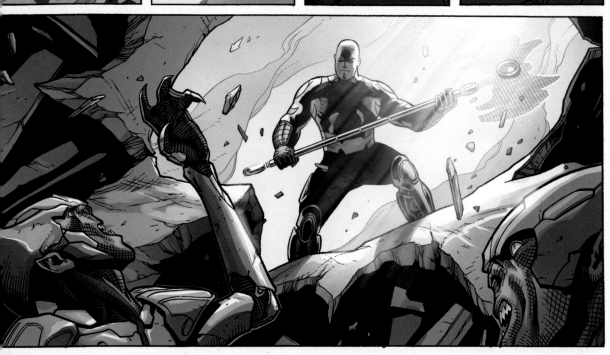

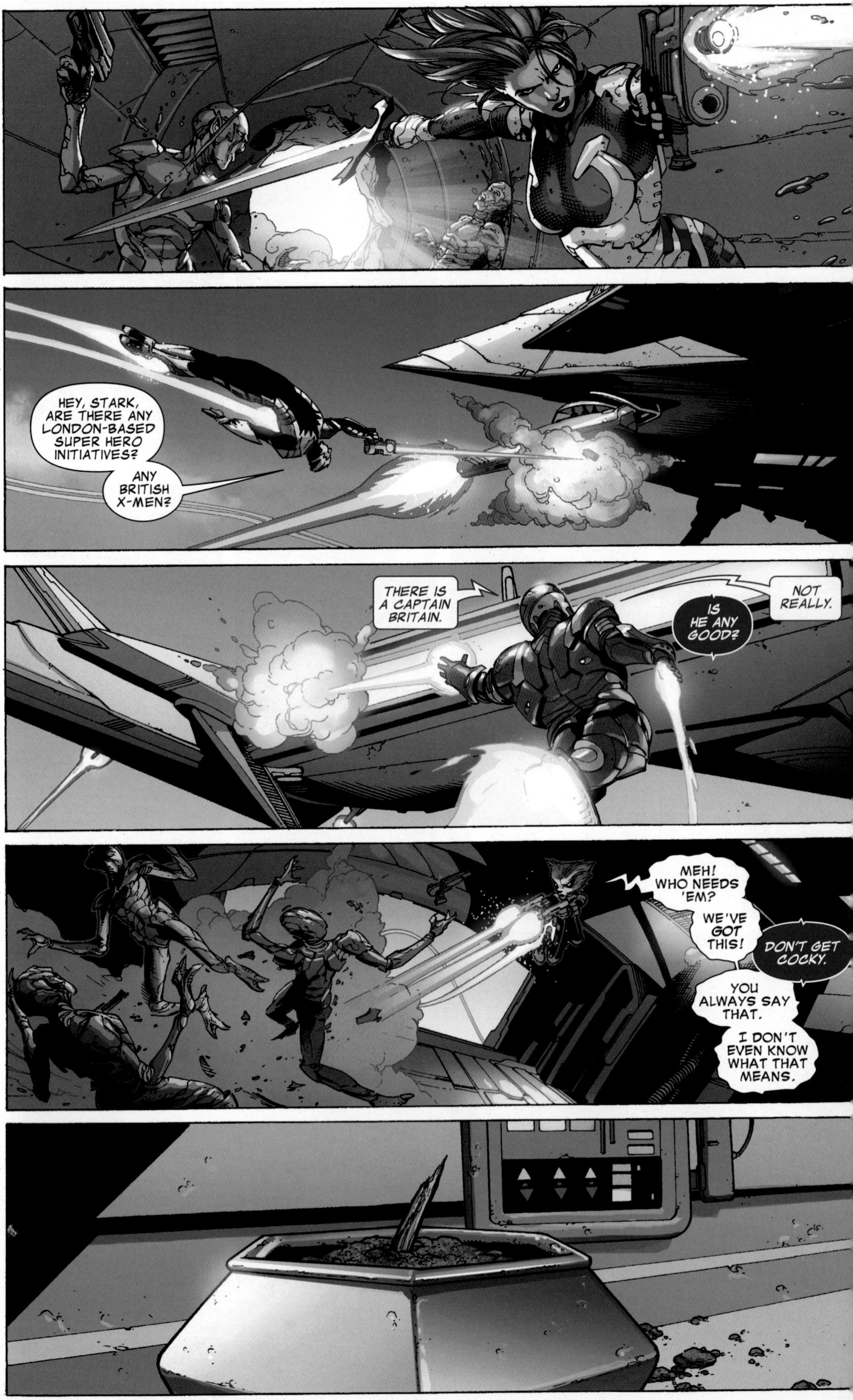
HEY, STARK, ARE THERE ANY LONDON-BASED SUPER HERO INITIATIVES?
ANY BRITISH X-MEN?
THERE IS A CAPTAIN BRITAIN.
IS HE ANY GOOD?
NOT REALLY.
MEH! WHO NEEDS 'EM?
WE'VE GOT THIS!
DON'T GET COCKY.
YOU ALWAYS SAY THAT.
I DON'T EVEN KNOW WHAT THAT MEANS.

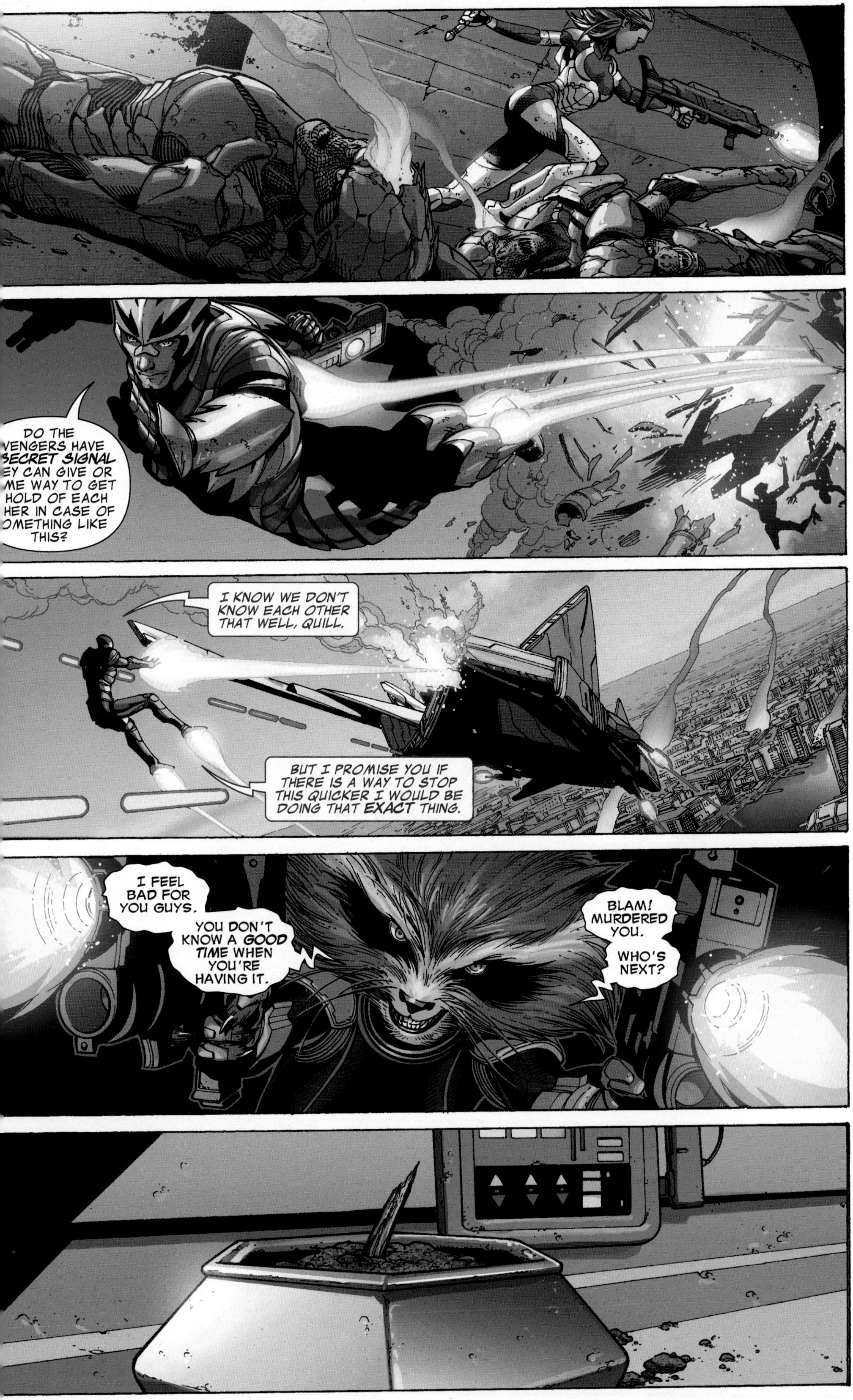
DO THE VENGERS HAVE SECRET SIGNAL EY CAN GIVE OR ME WAY TO GET HOLD OF EACH HER IN CASE OF OMETHING LIKE THIS?
I KNOW WE DON'T KNOW EACH OTHER THAT WELL, QUILL.
BUT I PROMISE YOU IF THERE IS A WAY TO STOP THIS QUICKER I WOULD BE DOING THAT EXACT THING.
I FEEL BAD FOR YOU GUYS.
YOU DON'T KNOW A GOOD TIME WHEN YOU'RE HAVING IT.
BLAM! MURDERED YOU.
WHO'S NEXT?

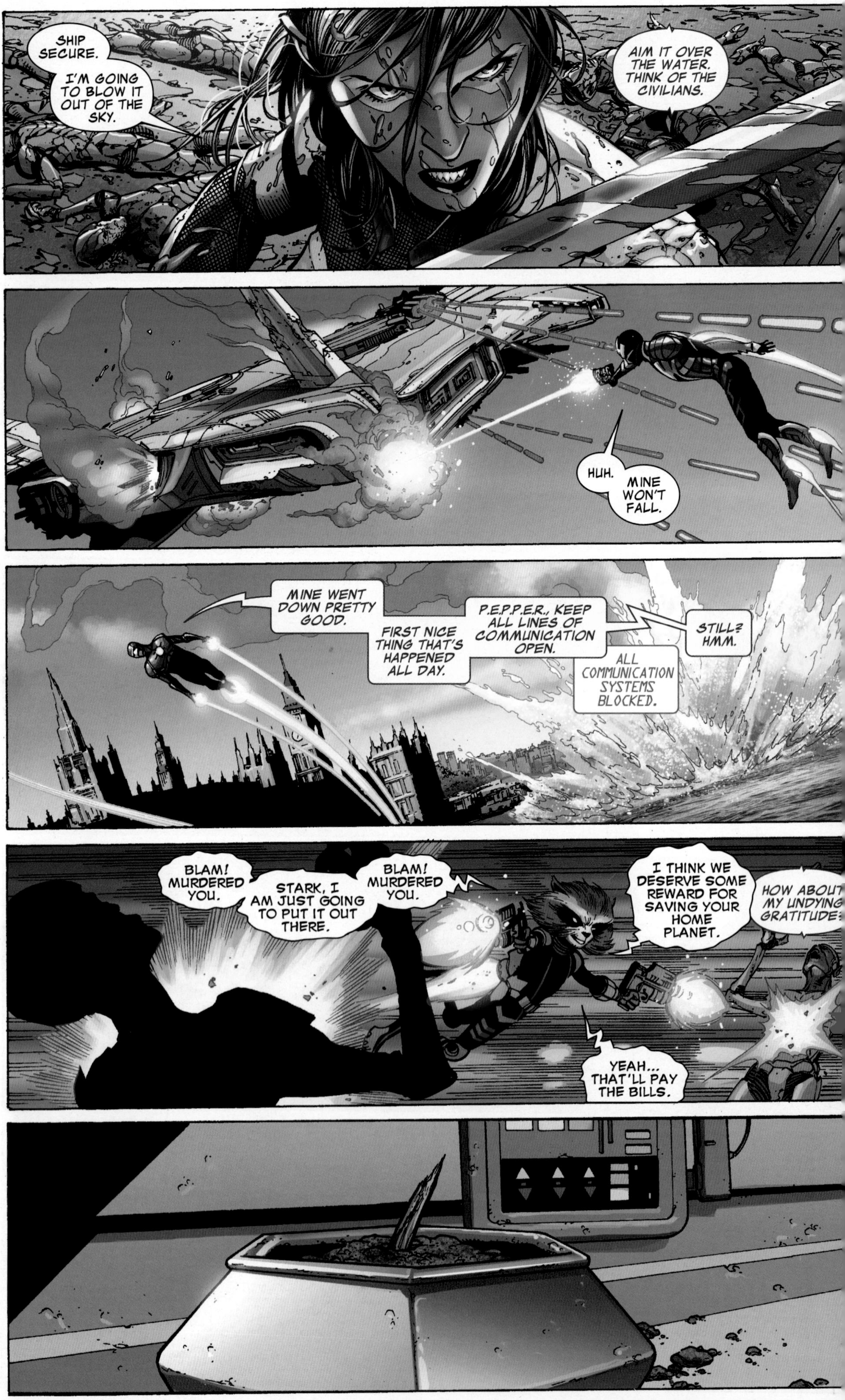
SHIP SECURE.
I'M GOING TO BLOW IT OUT OF THE SKY.
AIM IT OVER THE WATER. THINK OF THE CIVILIANS.
HUH.
MINE WON'T FALL.
MINE WENT DOWN PRETTY GOOD.
FIRST NICE THING THAT'S HAPPENED ALL DAY.
P.E.P.P.E.R., KEEP ALL LINES OF COMMUNICATION OPEN.
ALL COMMUNICATION SYSTEMS BLOCKED.
STILL? HMM.
BLAM! MURDERED YOU.
STARK, I AM JUST GOING TO PUT IT OUT THERE.
BLAM! MURDERED YOU.
I THINK WE DESERVE SOME REWARD FOR SAVING YOUR HOME PLANET.
HOW ABOUT MY UNDYING GRATITUDE?
YEAH... THAT'LL PAY THE BILLS.

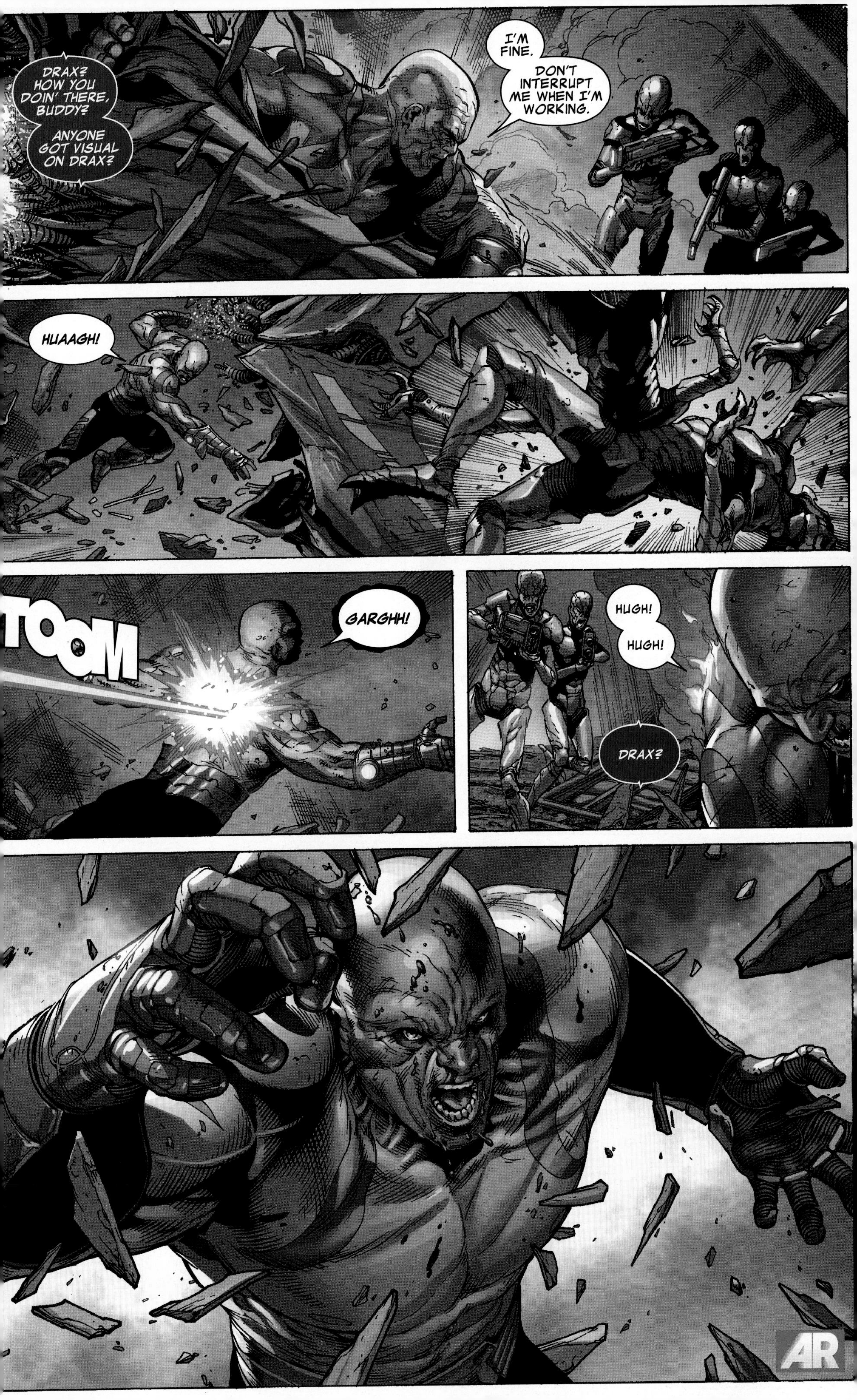
DRAX? HOW YOU DOIN' THERE, BUDDY?
ANYONE GOT VISUAL ON DRAX?
I'M FINE.
DON'T INTERRUPT ME WHEN I'M WORKING.
HUAAGH!
TOOM
GARGHH!
HUGH!
HUGH!
DRAX?
AR

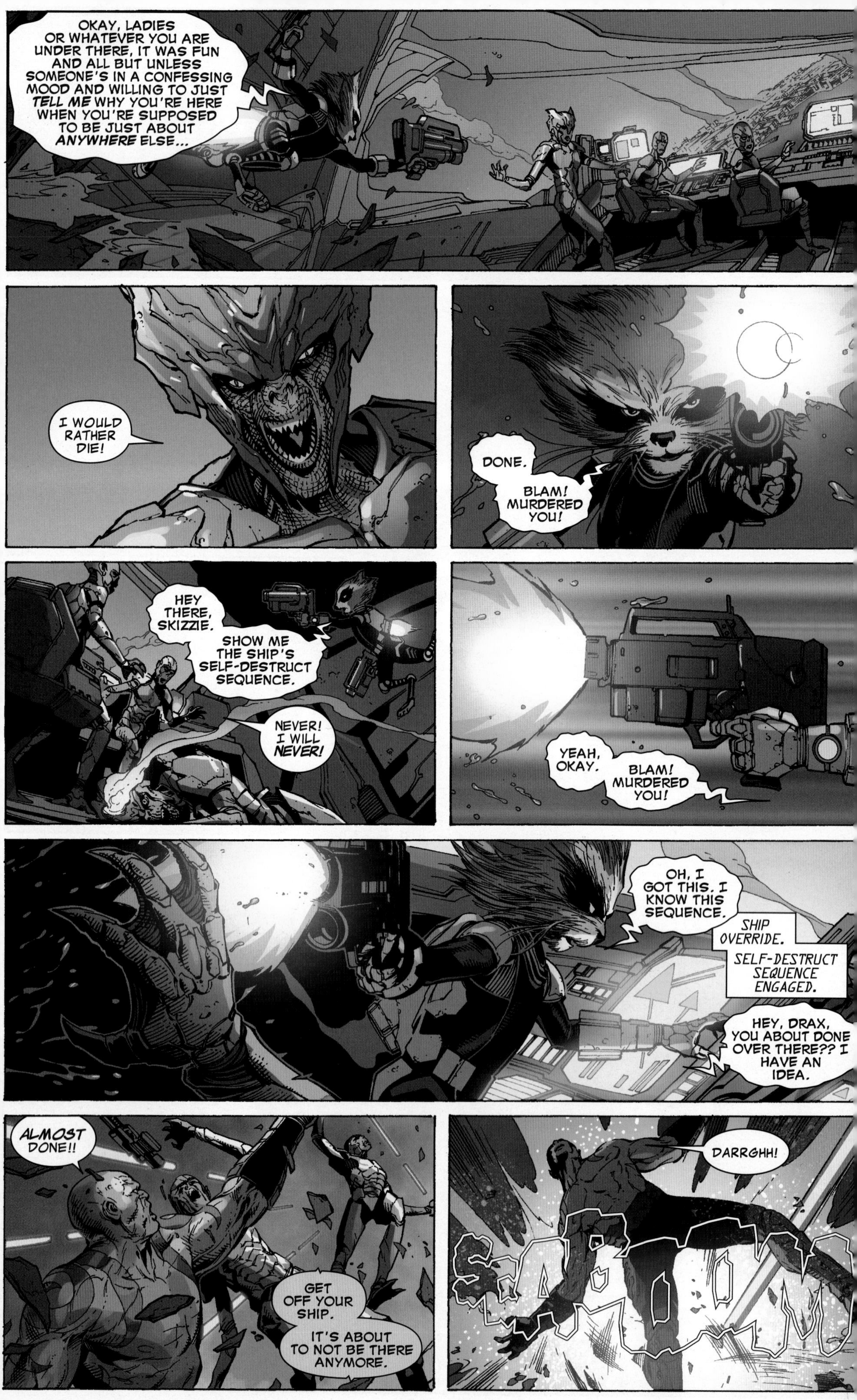
OKAY, LADIES OR WHATEVER YOU ARE UNDER THERE, IT WAS FUN AND ALL BUT UNLESS SOMEONE'S IN A CONFESSING MOOD AND WILLING TO JUST TELL ME WHY YOU'RE HERE WHEN YOU'RE SUPPOSED TO BE JUST ABOUT ANYWHERE ELSE...
I WOULD RATHER DIE!
DONE.
BLAM! MURDERED YOU!
HEY THERE, SKIZZIE.
SHOW ME THE SHIP'S SELF-DESTRUCT SEQUENCE.
NEVER! I WILL NEVER!
YEAH, OKAY.
BLAM! MURDERED YOU!
OH, I GOT THIS. I KNOW THIS SEQUENCE.
SHIP OVERRIDE.
SELF-DESTRUCT SEQUENCE ENGAGED.
HEY, DRAX, YOU ABOUT DONE OVER THERE?? I HAVE AN IDEA.
ALMOST DONE!!
GET OFF YOUR SHIP.
IT'S ABOUT TO NOT BE THERE ANYMORE.
DARRGHH!
SKA-BOOOM

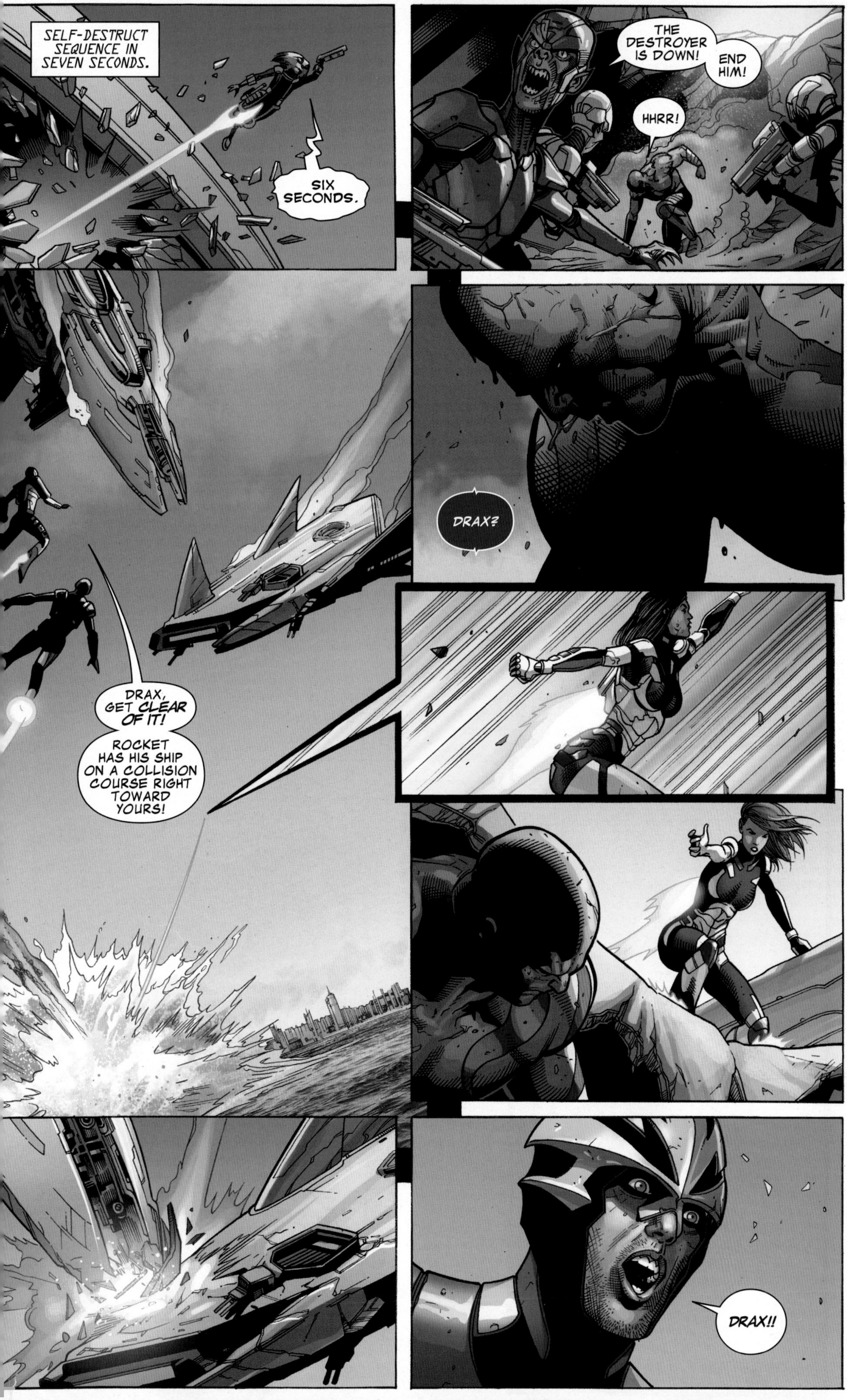
SELF-DESTRUCT SEQUENCE IN SEVEN SECONDS.
SIX SECONDS.
THE DESTROYER IS DOWN!
END HIM!
HHRR!
DRAX?
DRAX, GET CLEAR OF IT!
ROCKET HAS HIS SHIP ON A COLLISION COURSE RIGHT TOWARD YOURS!
DRAX!!

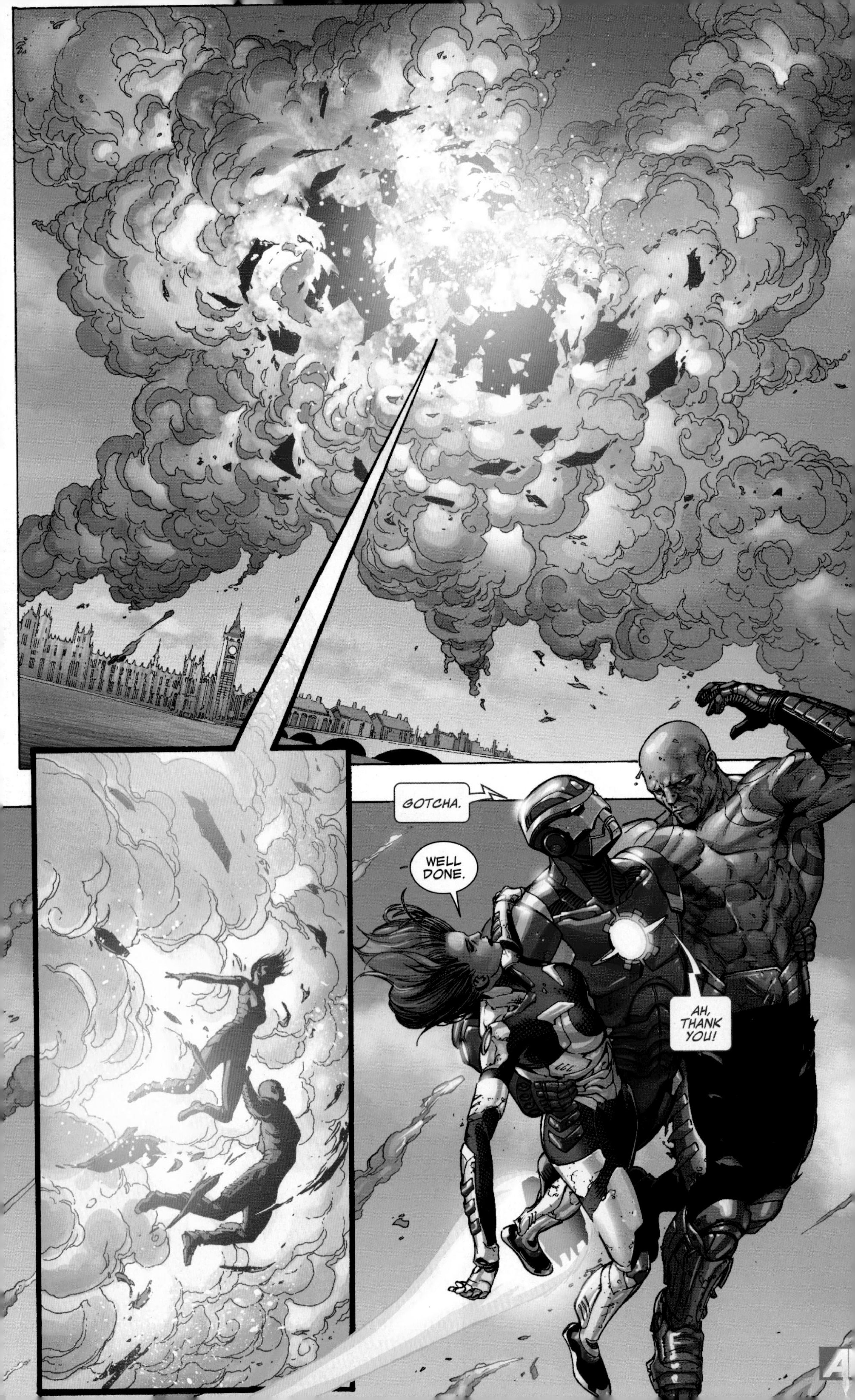
GOTCHA.
WELL DONE.
AH, THANK YOU!

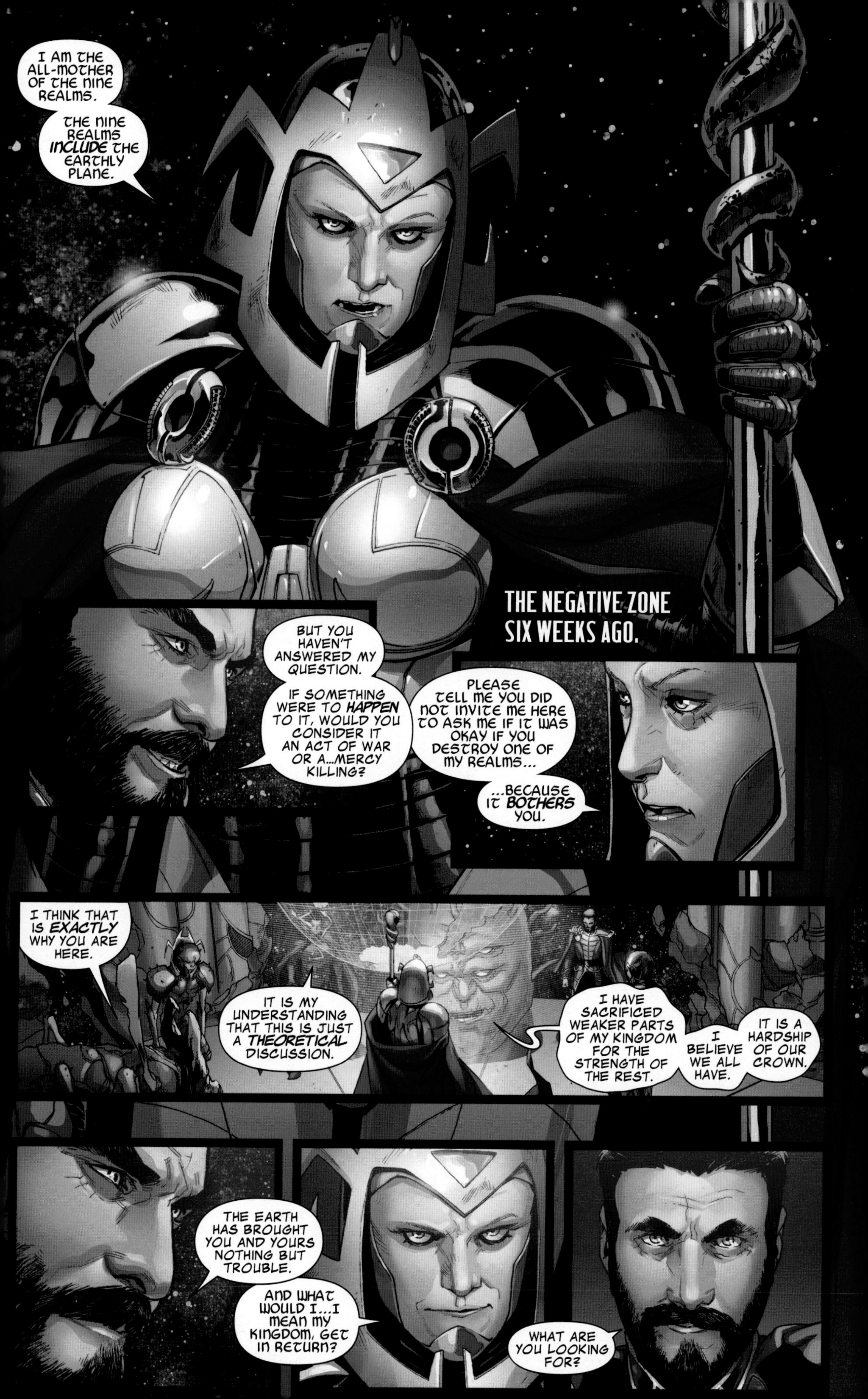
I AM THE ALL-MOTHER OF THE NINE REALMS.
THE NINE REALMS *INCLUDE* THE EARTHLY PLANE.
THE NEGATIVE ZONE SIX WEEKS AGO.
BUT YOU HAVEN'T ANSWERED MY QUESTION.
IF SOMETHING WERE TO *HAPPEN* TO IT, WOULD YOU CONSIDER IT AN ACT OF WAR OR A...MERCY KILLING?
PLEASE TELL ME YOU DID NOT INVITE ME HERE TO ASK ME IF IT WAS OKAY IF YOU DESTROY ONE OF MY REALMS...
...BECAUSE IT *BOTHERS* YOU.
I THINK THAT IS *EXACTLY* WHY YOU ARE HERE.
IT IS MY UNDERSTANDING THAT THIS IS JUST A *THEORETICAL* DISCUSSION.
I HAVE SACRIFICED WEAKER PARTS OF MY KINGDOM FOR THE STRENGTH OF THE REST.
I BELIEVE WE ALL HAVE.
IT IS A HARDSHIP OF OUR CROWN.
THE EARTH HAS BROUGHT YOU AND YOURS NOTHING BUT TROUBLE.
AND WHAT WOULD I...I MEAN MY KINGDOM, GET IN RETURN?
WHAT ARE YOU LOOKING FOR?

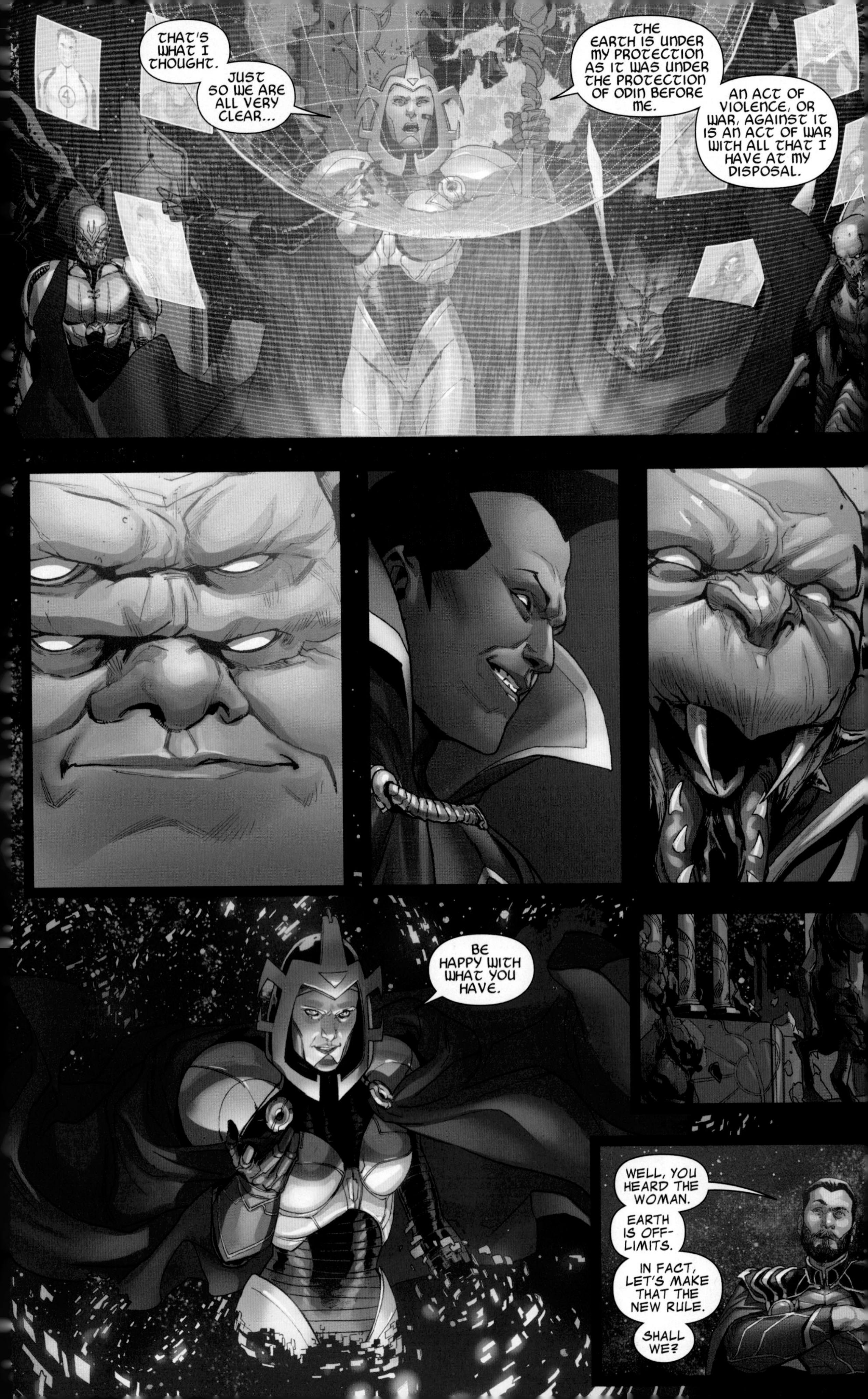

THAT'S WHAT I THOUGHT.
JUST SO WE ARE ALL VERY CLEAR...
THE EARTH IS UNDER MY PROTECTION AS IT WAS UNDER THE PROTECTION OF ODIN BEFORE ME.
AN ACT OF VIOLENCE, OR WAR, AGAINST IT IS AN ACT OF WAR WITH ALL THAT I HAVE AT MY DISPOSAL.
BE HAPPY WITH WHAT YOU HAVE.
WELL, YOU HEARD THE WOMAN.
EARTH IS OFF-LIMITS.
IN FACT, LET'S MAKE THAT THE NEW RULE.
SHALL WE?

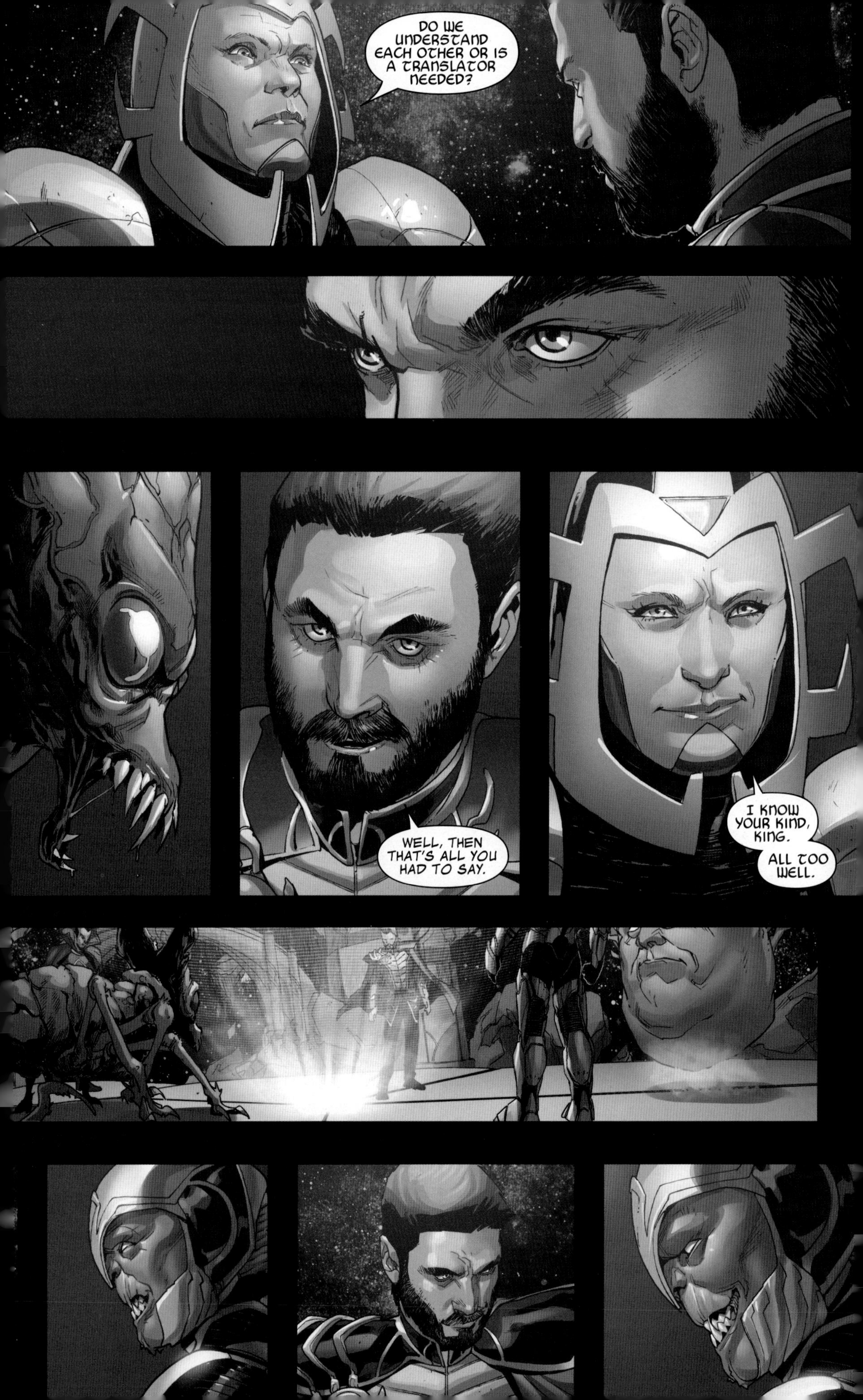
DO WE UNDERSTAND EACH OTHER OR IS A TRANSLATOR NEEDED?
WELL, THEN THAT'S ALL YOU HAD TO SAY.
I KNOW YOUR KIND, KING.
ALL TOO WELL.

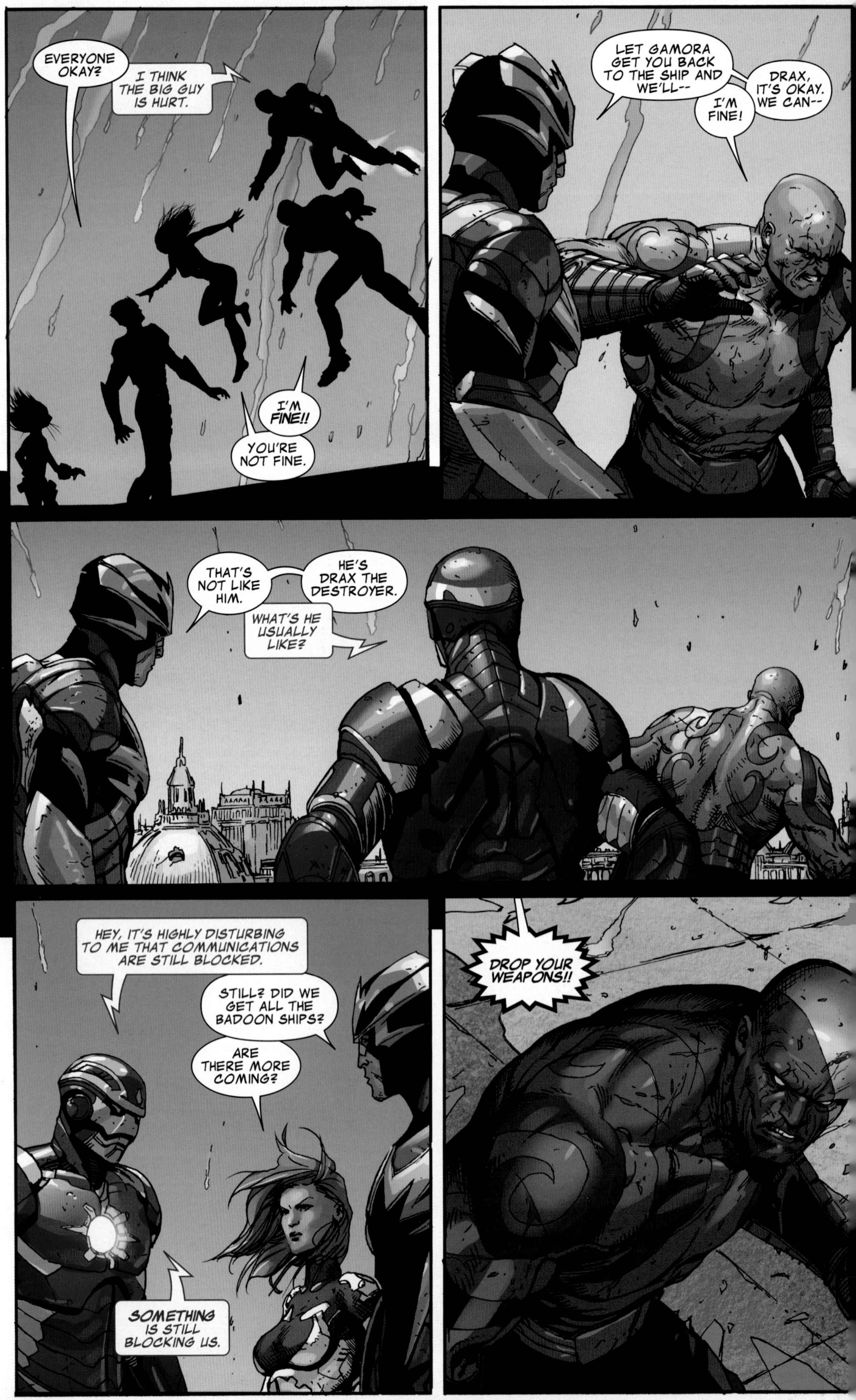
EVERYONE OKAY?
I THINK THE BIG GUY IS HURT.
I'M FINE!!
YOU'RE NOT FINE.
LET GAMORA GET YOU BACK TO THE SHIP AND WE'LL--
I'M FINE!
DRAX, IT'S OKAY. WE CAN--
THAT'S NOT LIKE HIM.
HE'S DRAX THE DESTROYER.
WHAT'S HE USUALLY LIKE?
HEY, IT'S HIGHLY DISTURBING TO ME THAT COMMUNICATIONS ARE STILL BLOCKED.
STILL? DID WE GET ALL THE BADOON SHIPS?
ARE THERE MORE COMING?
SOMETHING IS STILL BLOCKING US.
DROP YOUR WEAPONS!!

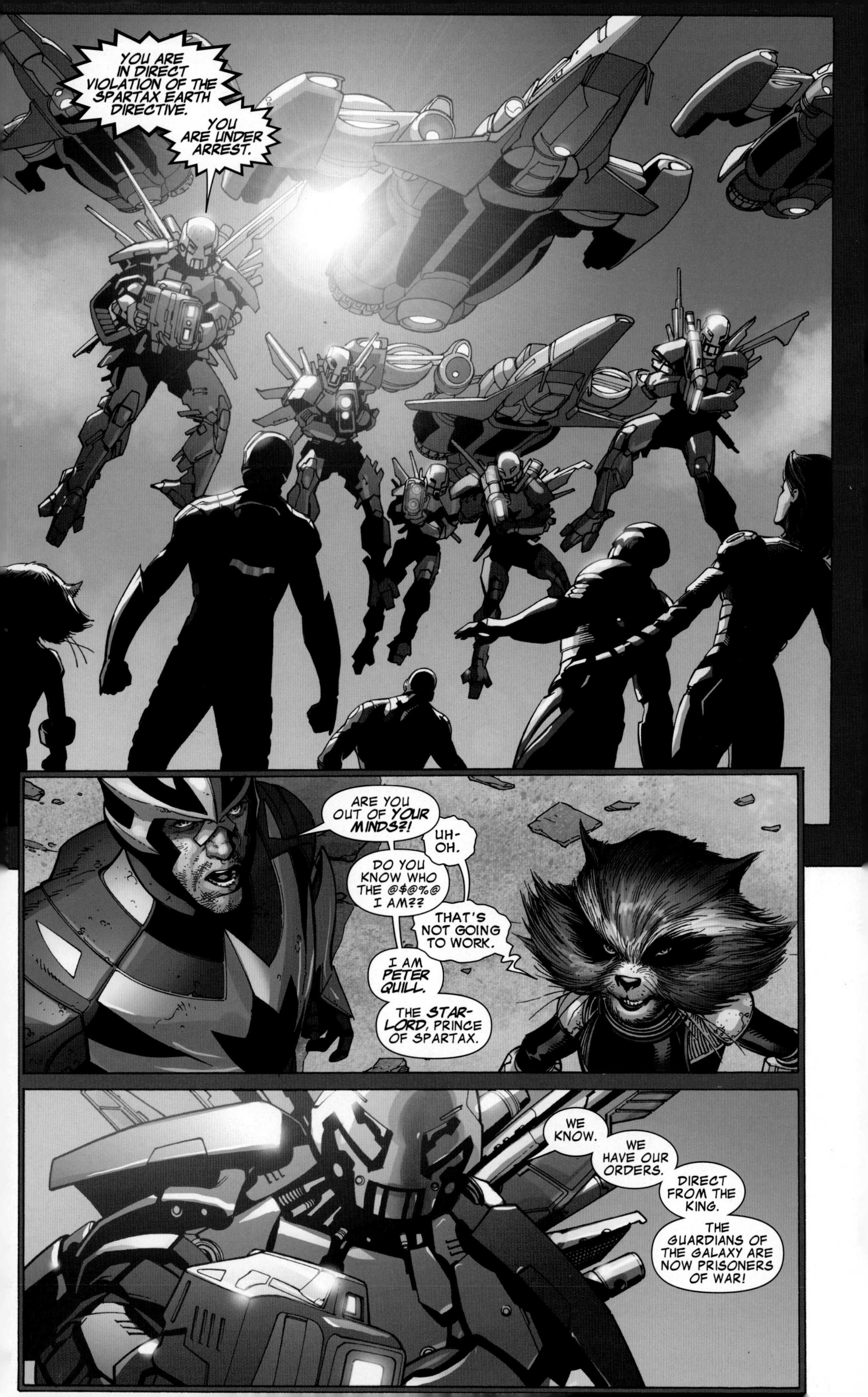
YOU ARE IN DIRECT VIOLATION OF THE SPARTAX EARTH DIRECTIVE.
YOU ARE UNDER ARREST.
ARE YOU OUT OF YOUR MINDS?!
UH-OH.
DO YOU KNOW WHO THE @$@%@ I AM??
THAT'S NOT GOING TO WORK.
I AM PETER QUILL.
THE STAR-LORD, PRINCE OF SPARTAX.
WE KNOW.
WE HAVE OUR ORDERS.
DIRECT FROM THE KING.
THE GUARDIANS OF THE GALAXY ARE NOW PRISONERS OF WAR!

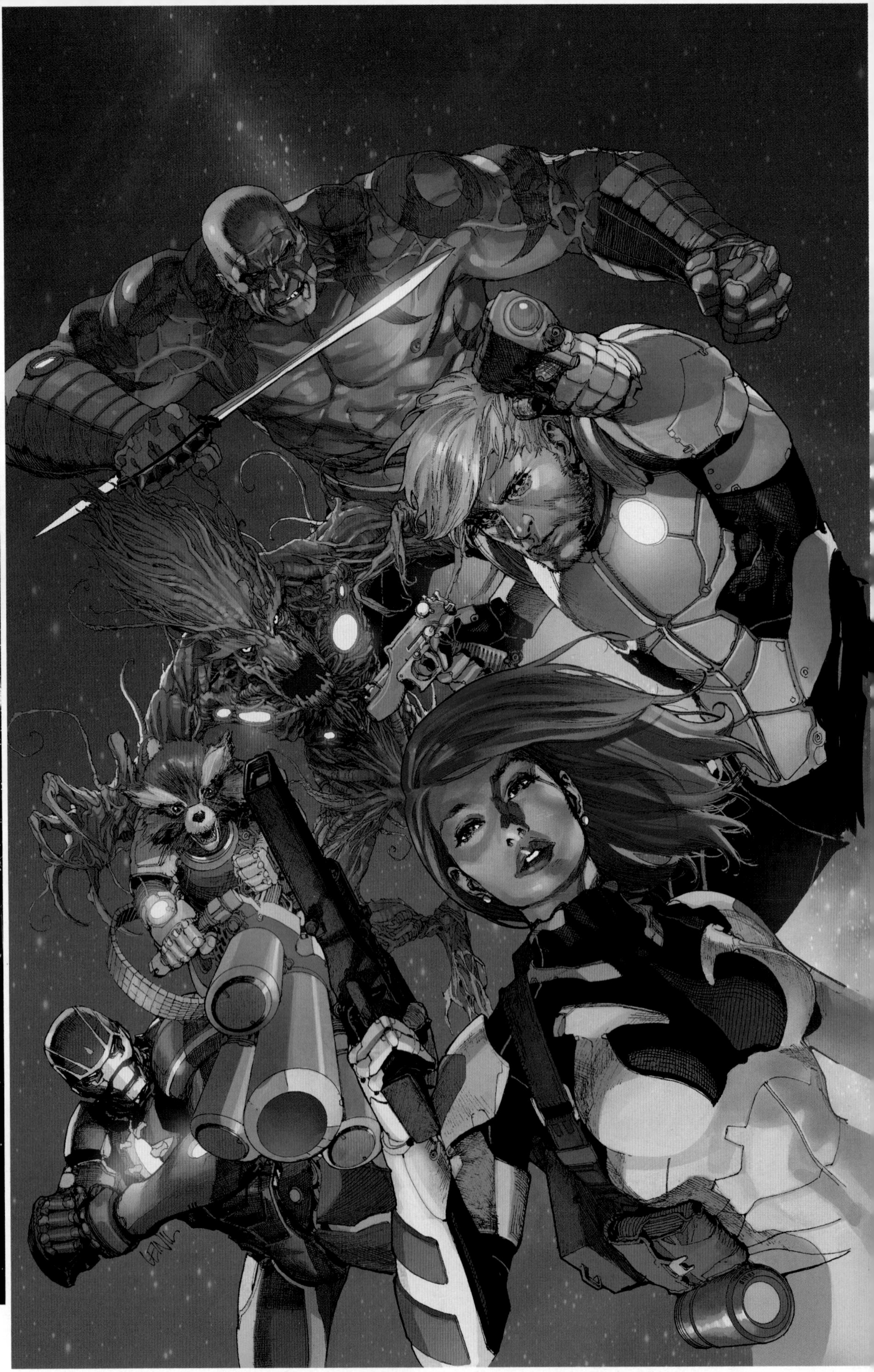

#3 VARIANT BY LEINIL YU & SUNNY GHO

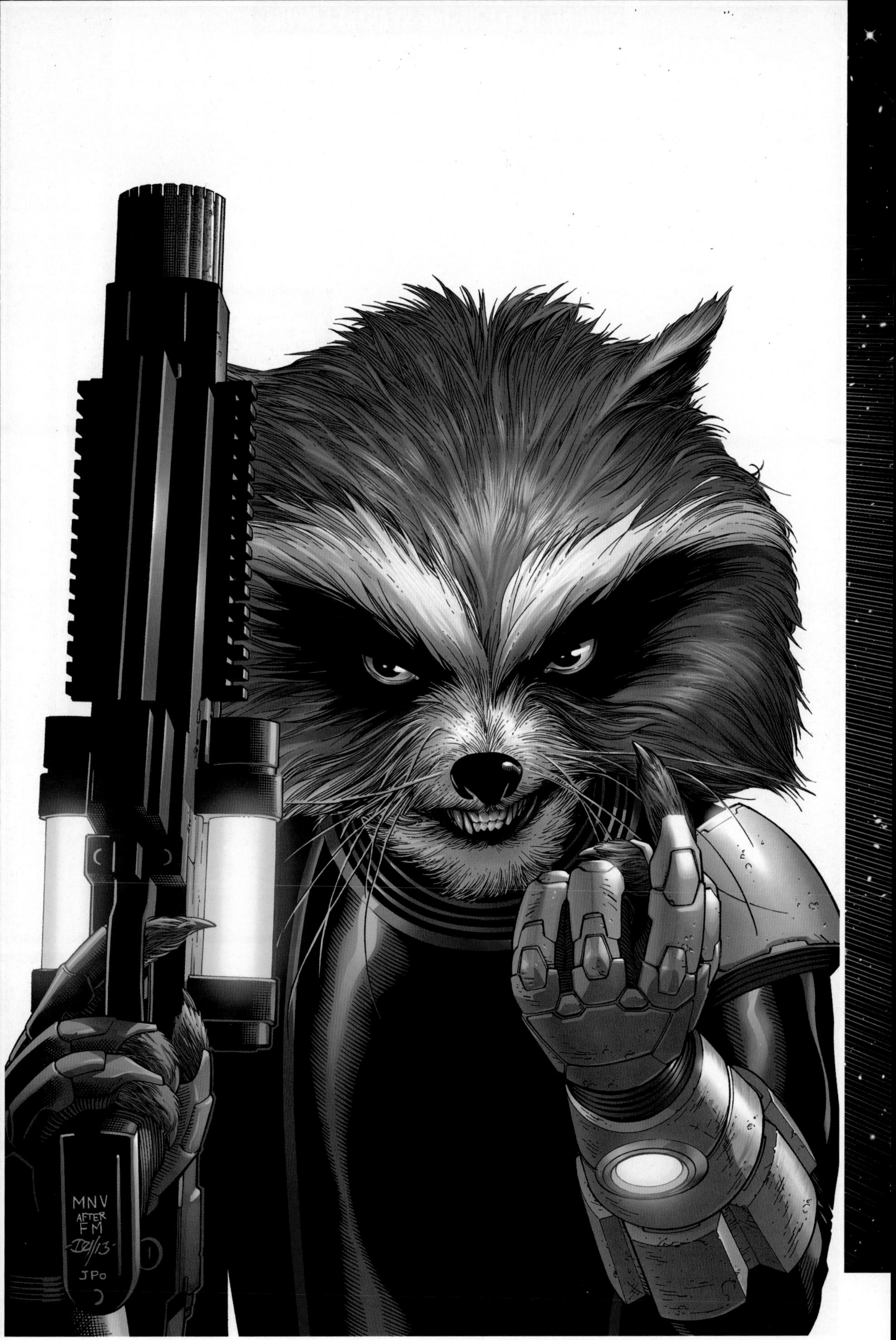
MNV
AFTER
FM
JPo

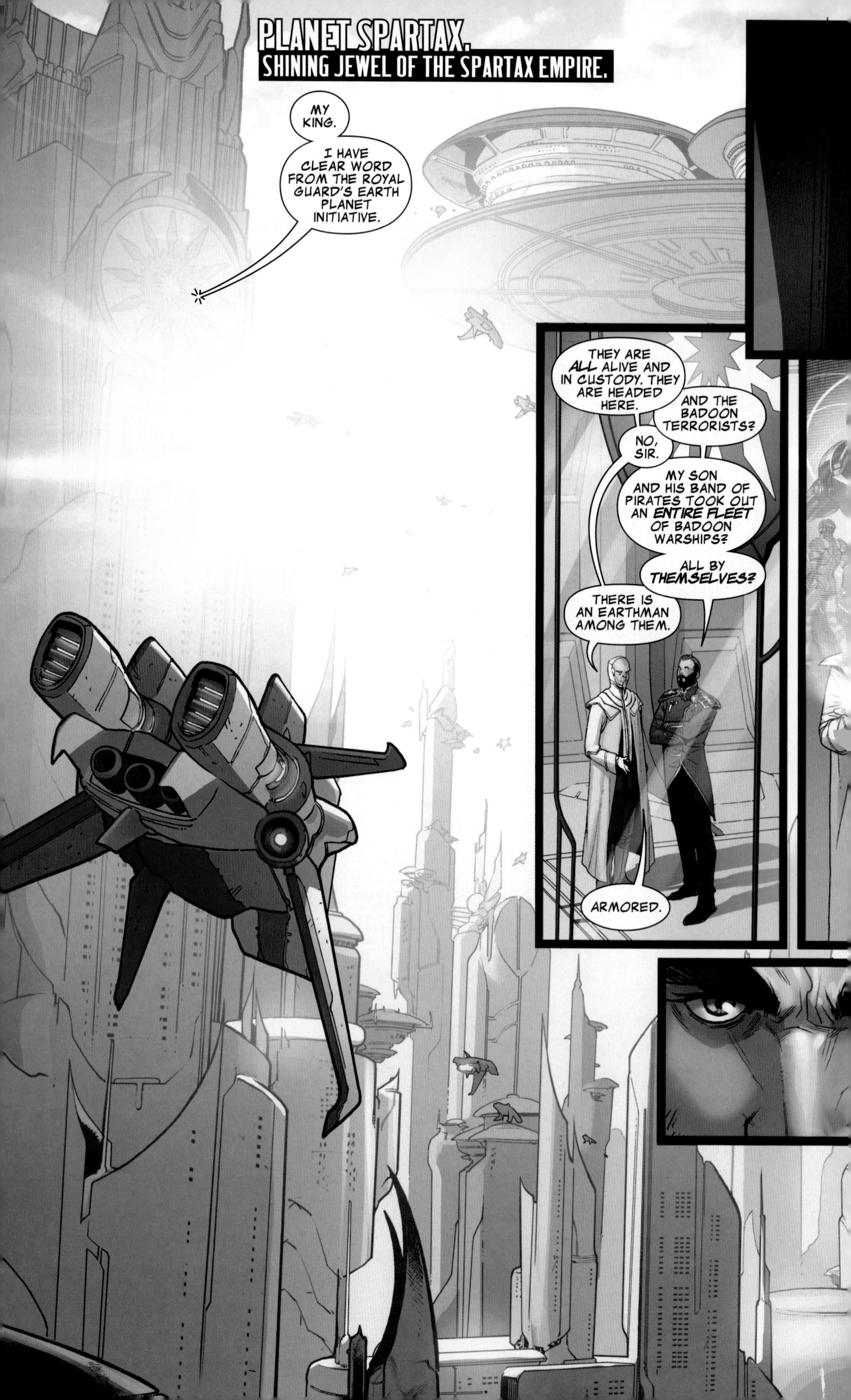
PLANET SPARTAX.
SHINING JEWEL OF THE SPARTAX EMPIRE.
MY KING.
I HAVE CLEAR WORD FROM THE ROYAL GUARD'S EARTH PLANET INITIATIVE.
THEY ARE ALL ALIVE AND IN CUSTODY. THEY ARE HEADED HERE.
AND THE BADOON TERRORISTS?
NO, SIR.
MY SON AND HIS BAND OF PIRATES TOOK OUT AN ENTIRE FLEET OF BADOON WARSHIPS?
ALL BY THEMSELVES?
THERE IS AN EARTHMAN AMONG THEM.
ARMORED.

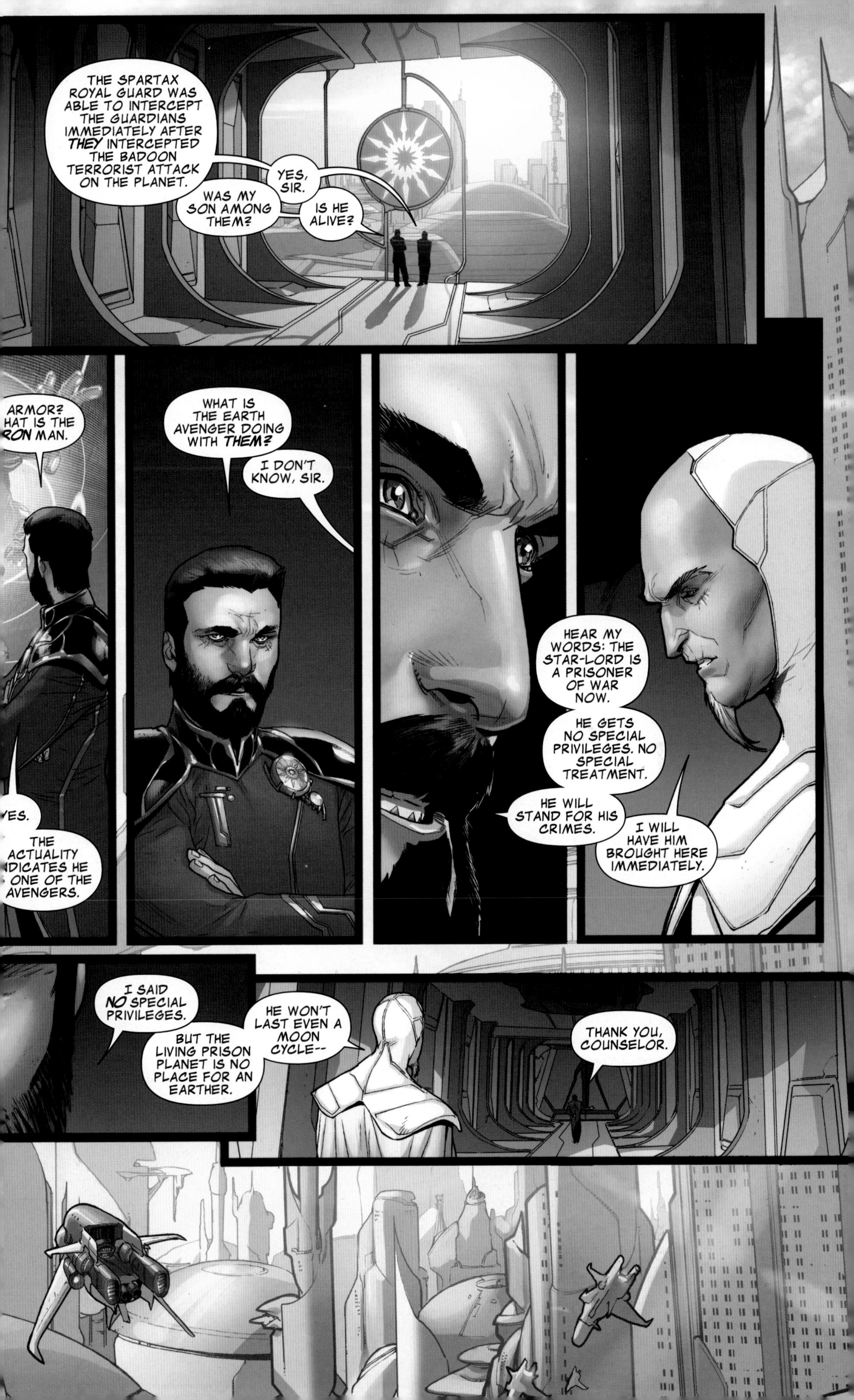

THE SPARTAX ROYAL GUARD WAS ABLE TO INTERCEPT THE GUARDIANS IMMEDIATELY AFTER THEY INTERCEPTED THE BADOON TERRORIST ATTACK ON THE PLANET.
WAS MY SON AMONG THEM?
YES, SIR.
IS HE ALIVE?
ARMOR? HAT IS THE RON MAN.
YES.
THE ACTUALITY NDICATES HE ONE OF THE AVENGERS.
WHAT IS THE EARTH AVENGER DOING WITH THEM?
I DON'T KNOW, SIR.
HEAR MY WORDS: THE STAR-LORD IS A PRISONER OF WAR NOW.
HE GETS NO SPECIAL PRIVILEGES. NO SPECIAL TREATMENT.
HE WILL STAND FOR HIS CRIMES.
I WILL HAVE HIM BROUGHT HERE IMMEDIATELY.
I SAID NO SPECIAL PRIVILEGES.
BUT THE LIVING PRISON PLANET IS NO PLACE FOR AN EARTHER.
HE WON'T LAST EVEN A MOON CYCLE--
THANK YOU, COUNSELOR.

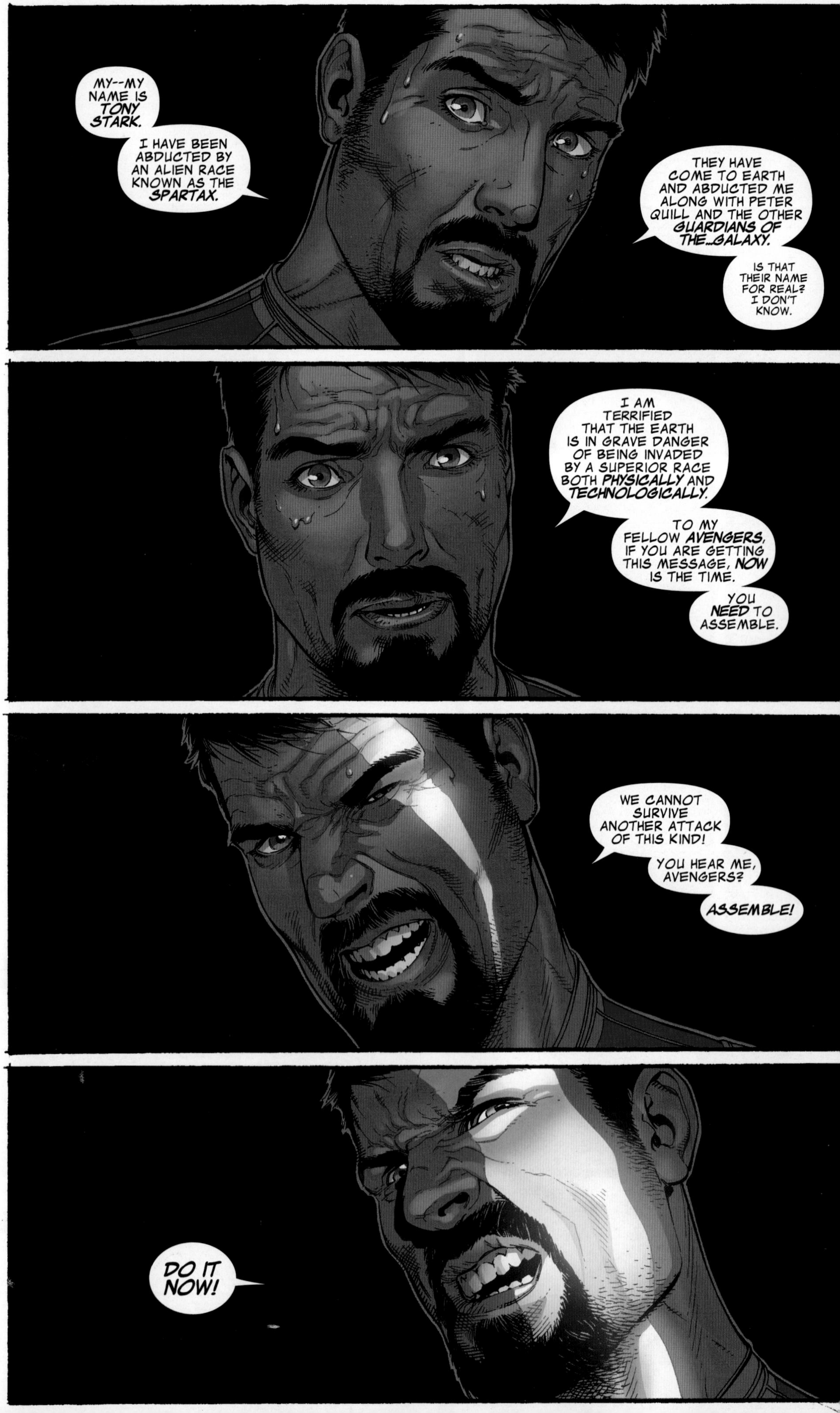
MY--MY NAME IS TONY STARK.
I HAVE BEEN ABDUCTED BY AN ALIEN RACE KNOWN AS THE SPARTAX.
THEY HAVE COME TO EARTH AND ABDUCTED ME ALONG WITH PETER QUILL AND THE OTHER GUARDIANS OF THE...GALAXY.
IS THAT THEIR NAME FOR REAL? I DON'T KNOW.
I AM TERRIFIED THAT THE EARTH IS IN GRAVE DANGER OF BEING INVADED BY A SUPERIOR RACE BOTH PHYSICALLY AND TECHNOLOGICALLY.
TO MY FELLOW AVENGERS, IF YOU ARE GETTING THIS MESSAGE, NOW IS THE TIME.
YOU NEED TO ASSEMBLE.
WE CANNOT SURVIVE ANOTHER ATTACK OF THIS KIND!
YOU HEAR ME, AVENGERS?
ASSEMBLE!
DO IT NOW!

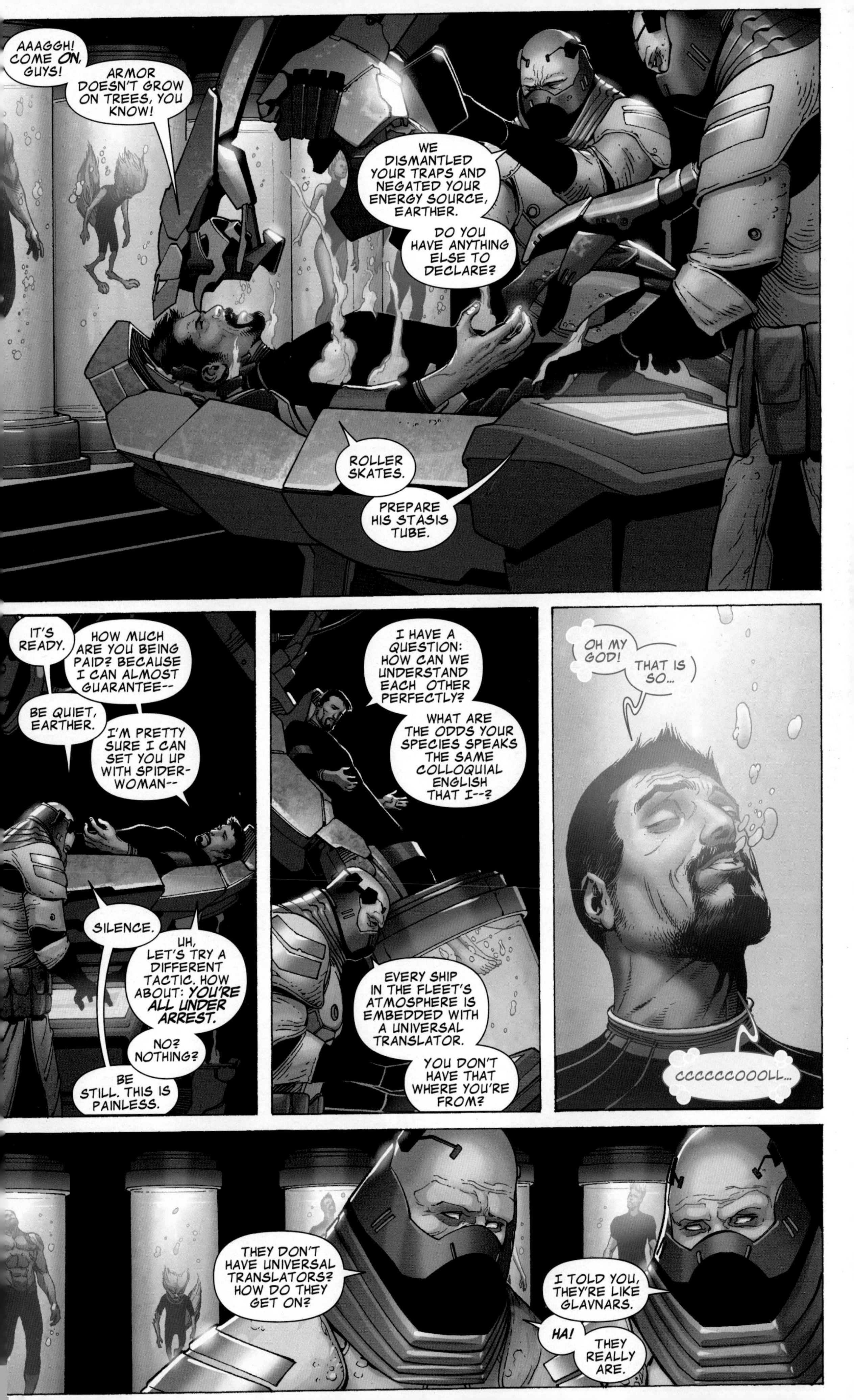
AAAGGH! COME ON, GUYS!
ARMOR DOESN'T GROW ON TREES, YOU KNOW!
WE DISMANTLED YOUR TRAPS AND NEGATED YOUR ENERGY SOURCE, EARTHER.
DO YOU HAVE ANYTHING ELSE TO DECLARE?
ROLLER SKATES.
PREPARE HIS STASIS TUBE.
IT'S READY.
HOW MUCH ARE YOU BEING PAID? BECAUSE I CAN ALMOST GUARANTEE--
BE QUIET, EARTHER.
I'M PRETTY SURE I CAN SET YOU UP WITH SPIDER-WOMAN--
SILENCE.
UH, LET'S TRY A DIFFERENT TACTIC. HOW ABOUT: YOU'RE ALL UNDER ARREST.
NO? NOTHING?
BE STILL. THIS IS PAINLESS.
I HAVE A QUESTION: HOW CAN WE UNDERSTAND EACH OTHER PERFECTLY?
WHAT ARE THE ODDS YOUR SPECIES SPEAKS THE SAME COLLOQUIAL ENGLISH THAT I--?
EVERY SHIP IN THE FLEET'S ATMOSPHERE IS EMBEDDED WITH A UNIVERSAL TRANSLATOR.
YOU DON'T HAVE THAT WHERE YOU'RE FROM?
OH MY GOD!
THAT IS SO...
CCCCCCOOOLL...
THEY DON'T HAVE UNIVERSAL TRANSLATORS? HOW DO THEY GET ON?
I TOLD YOU, THEY'RE LIKE GLAVNARS.
HA!
THEY REALLY ARE.

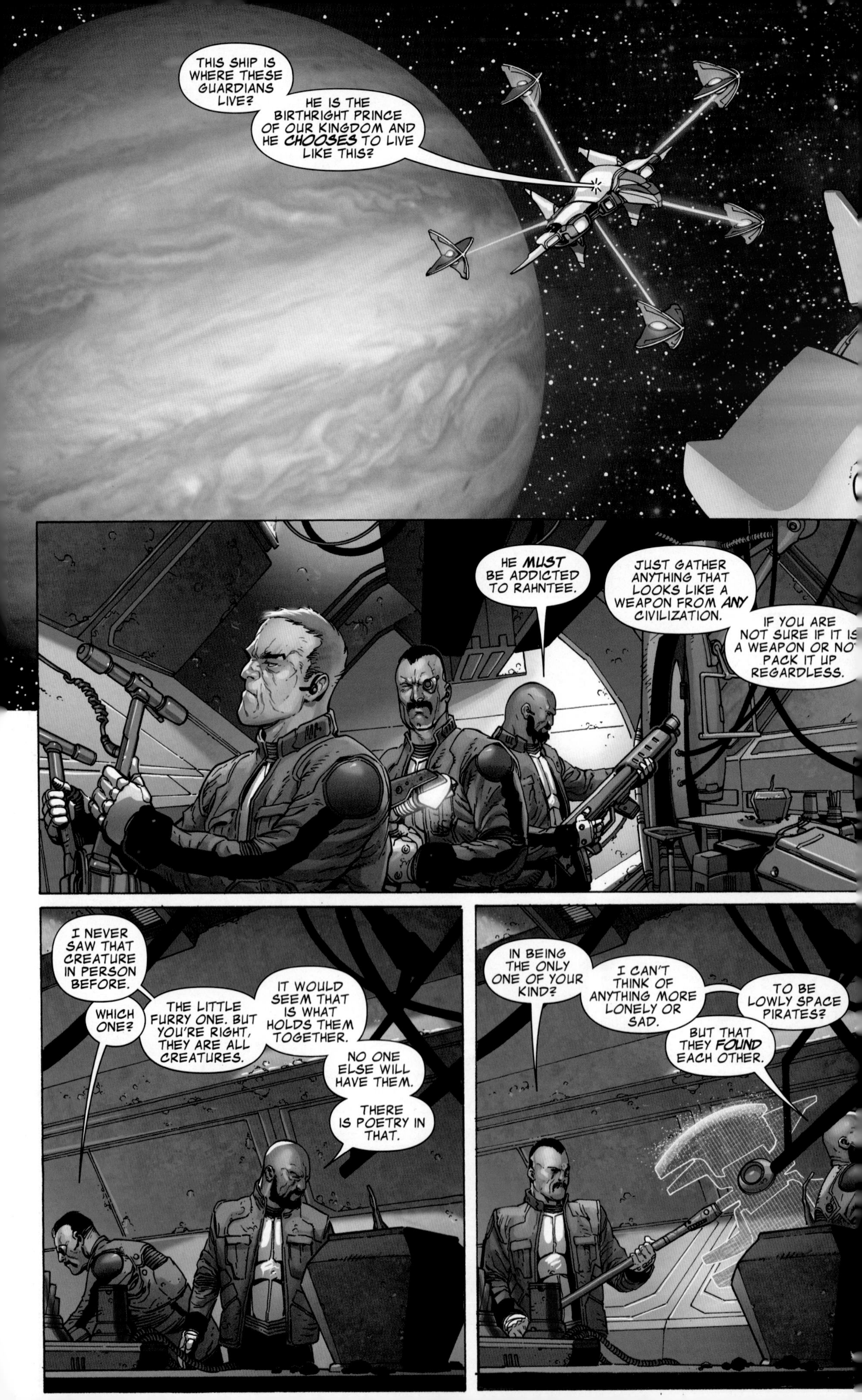
THIS SHIP IS WHERE THESE GUARDIANS LIVE?
HE IS THE BIRTHRIGHT PRINCE OF OUR KINGDOM AND HE CHOOSES TO LIVE LIKE THIS?
HE MUST BE ADDICTED TO RAHNTEE.
JUST GATHER ANYTHING THAT LOOKS LIKE A WEAPON FROM ANY CIVILIZATION.
IF YOU ARE NOT SURE IF IT IS A WEAPON OR NOT PACK IT UP REGARDLESS.
I NEVER SAW THAT CREATURE IN PERSON BEFORE.
WHICH ONE?
THE LITTLE FURRY ONE. BUT YOU'RE RIGHT, THEY ARE ALL CREATURES.
IT WOULD SEEM THAT IS WHAT HOLDS THEM TOGETHER.
NO ONE ELSE WILL HAVE THEM.
THERE IS POETRY IN THAT.
IN BEING THE ONLY ONE OF YOUR KIND?
I CAN'T THINK OF ANYTHING MORE LONELY OR SAD.
TO BE LOWLY SPACE PIRATES?
BUT THAT THEY FOUND EACH OTHER.

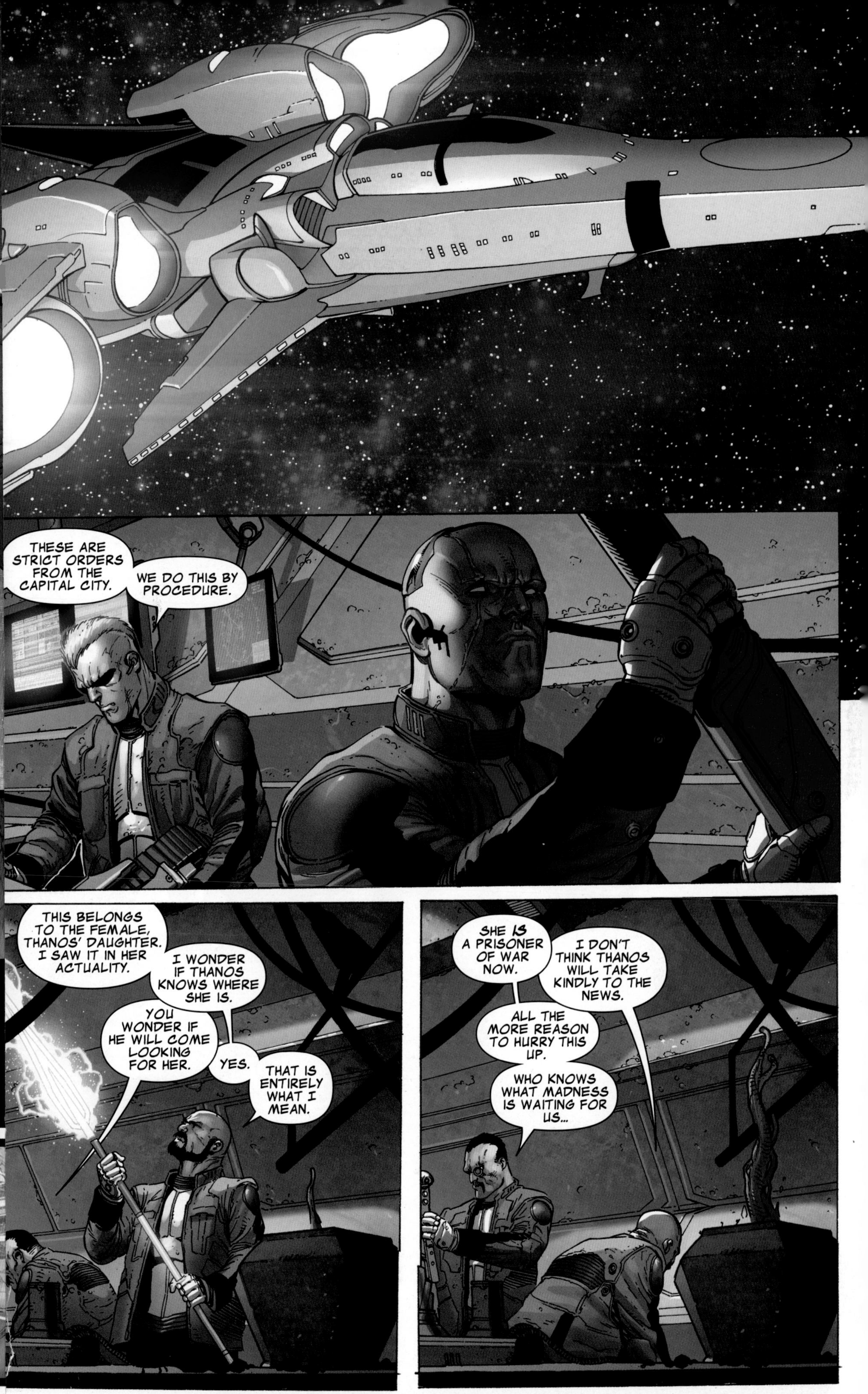
THESE ARE STRICT ORDERS FROM THE CAPITAL CITY.
WE DO THIS BY PROCEDURE.
THIS BELONGS TO THE FEMALE, THANOS' DAUGHTER. I SAW IT IN HER ACTUALITY.
I WONDER IF THANOS KNOWS WHERE SHE IS.
YOU WONDER IF HE WILL COME LOOKING FOR HER.
YES.
THAT IS ENTIRELY WHAT I MEAN.
SHE IS A PRISONER OF WAR NOW.
I DON'T THINK THANOS WILL TAKE KINDLY TO THE NEWS.
ALL THE MORE REASON TO HURRY THIS UP.
WHO KNOWS WHAT MADNESS IS WAITING FOR US...

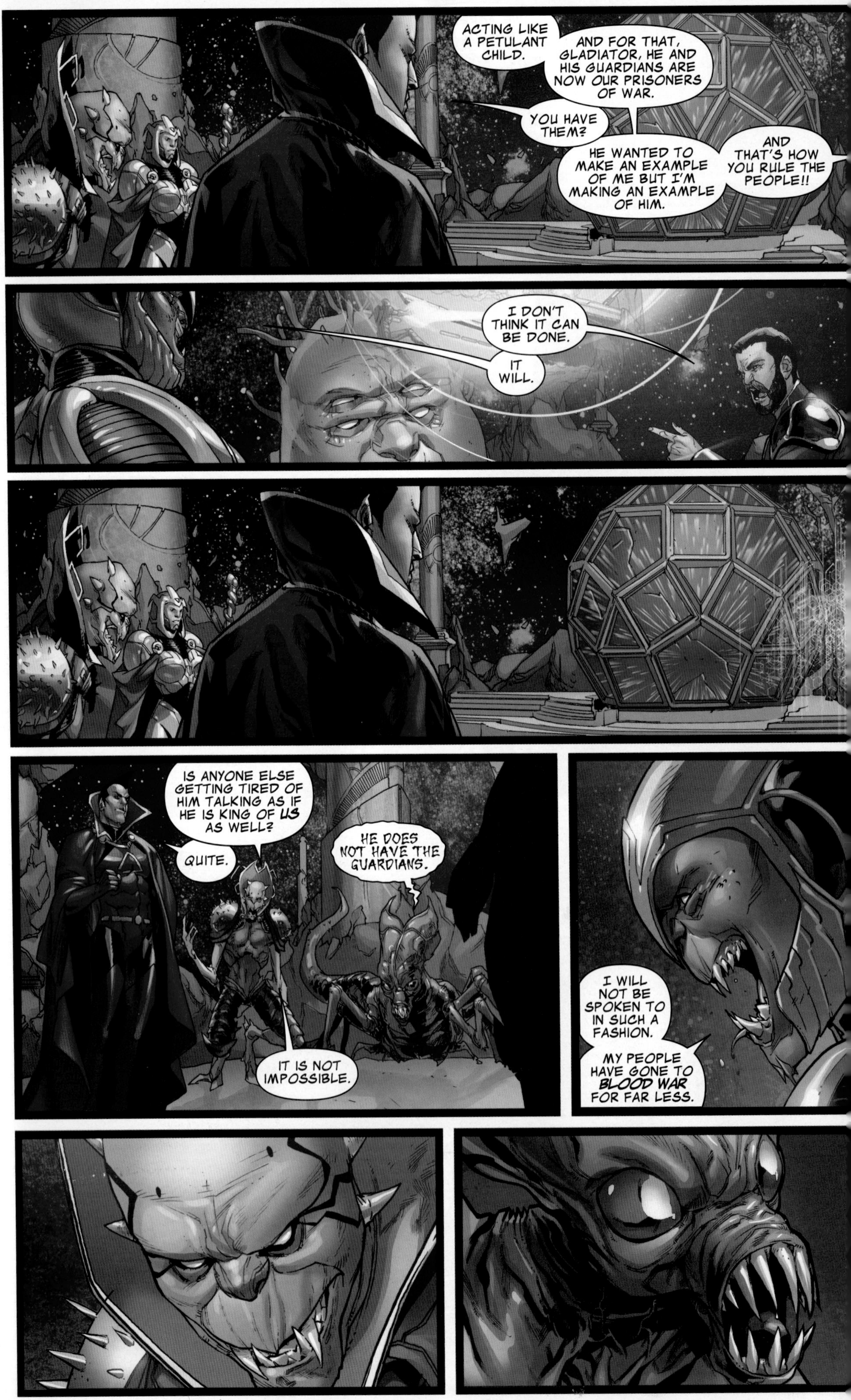
ACTING LIKE A PETULANT CHILD.
AND FOR THAT, GLADIATOR, HE AND HIS GUARDIANS ARE NOW OUR PRISONERS OF WAR.
YOU HAVE THEM?
HE WANTED TO MAKE AN EXAMPLE OF ME BUT I'M MAKING AN EXAMPLE OF HIM.
AND THAT'S HOW YOU RULE THE PEOPLE!!
I DON'T THINK IT CAN BE DONE.
IT WILL.
IS ANYONE ELSE GETTING TIRED OF HIM TALKING AS IF HE IS KING OF US AS WELL?
QUITE.
HE DOES NOT HAVE THE GUARDIANS.
IT IS NOT IMPOSSIBLE.
I WILL NOT BE SPOKEN TO IN SUCH A FASHION.
MY PEOPLE HAVE GONE TO BLOOD WAR FOR FAR LESS.

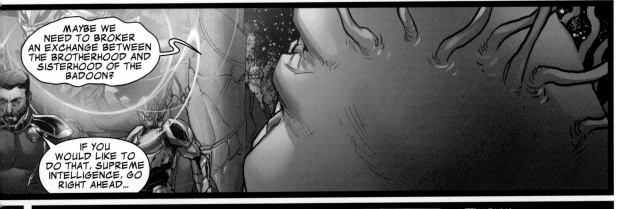

MAYBE WE NEED TO BROKER AN EXCHANGE BETWEEN THE BROTHERHOOD AND SISTERHOOD OF THE BADOON?

IF YOU WOULD LIKE TO DO THAT, SUPREME INTELLIGENCE, GO RIGHT AHEAD...

I WILL TAKE THAT AS A PROMISE.

AND THE NEXT TIME WE MEET, THAT PROMISE *WILL* BE KEPT.

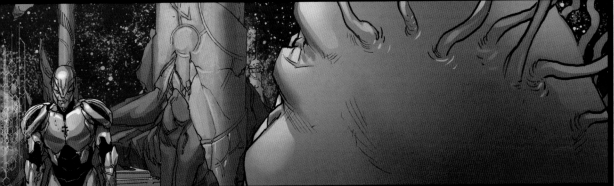

'ROVE URSELF, GAAAR.

AND VE J-SON WRONG...

...AND YOU WILL HAVE *ALL* OUR RESPECT.

I BELIEVE KING J-SON IS PLAYING A MORE COMPLICATED GAME THAN WE FIRST REALIZED.

I AM ALMOST CERTAIN OF IT.

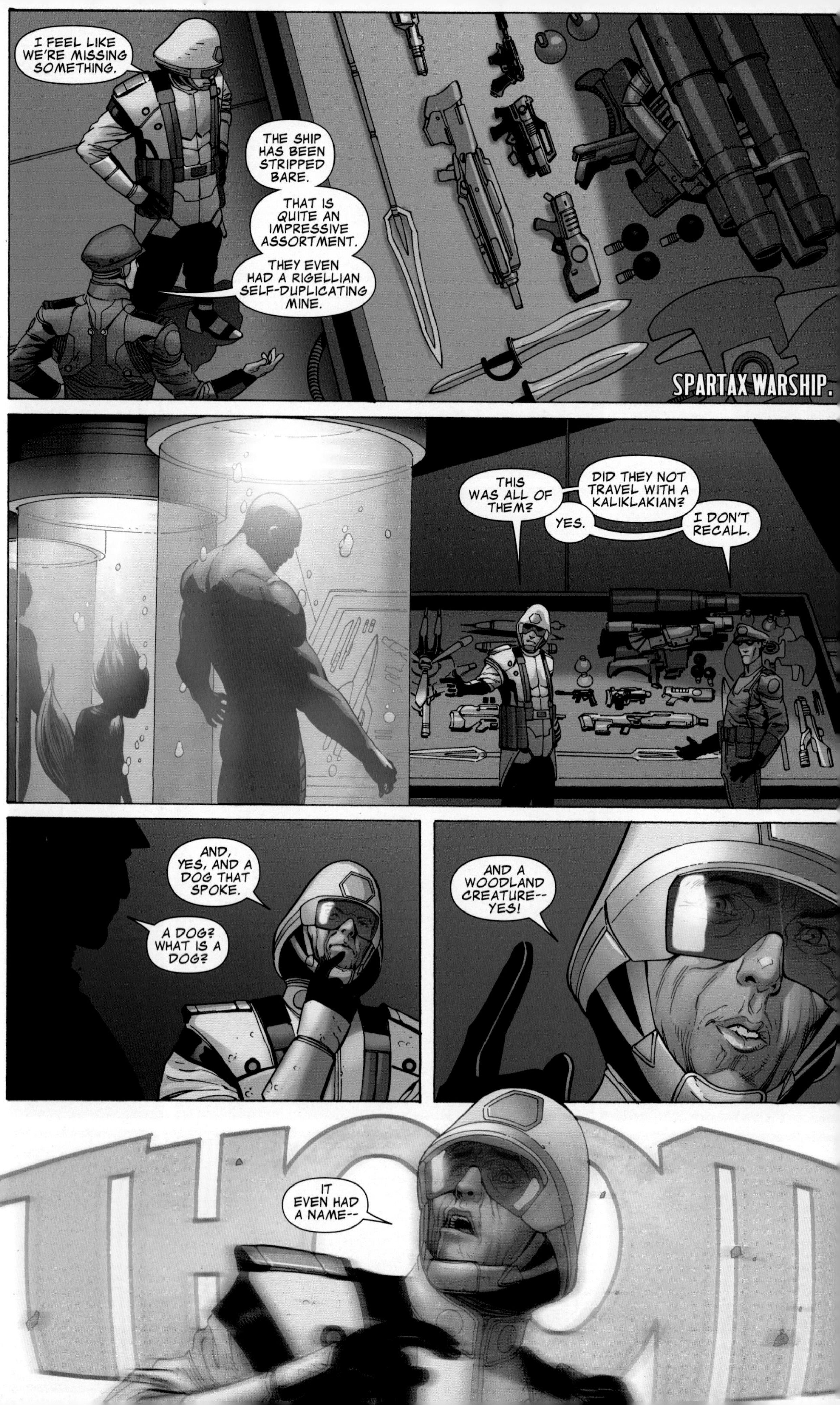
I FEEL LIKE WE'RE MISSING SOMETHING.
THE SHIP HAS BEEN STRIPPED BARE.
THAT IS QUITE AN IMPRESSIVE ASSORTMENT.
THEY EVEN HAD A RIGELLIAN SELF-DUPLICATING MINE.
SPARTAX WARSHIP.
THIS WAS ALL OF THEM?
DID THEY NOT TRAVEL WITH A KALIKLAKIAN?
YES.
I DON'T RECALL.
AND, YES, AND A DOG THAT SPOKE.
A DOG? WHAT IS A DOG?
AND A WOODLAND CREATURE-- YES!
IT EVEN HAD A NAME--

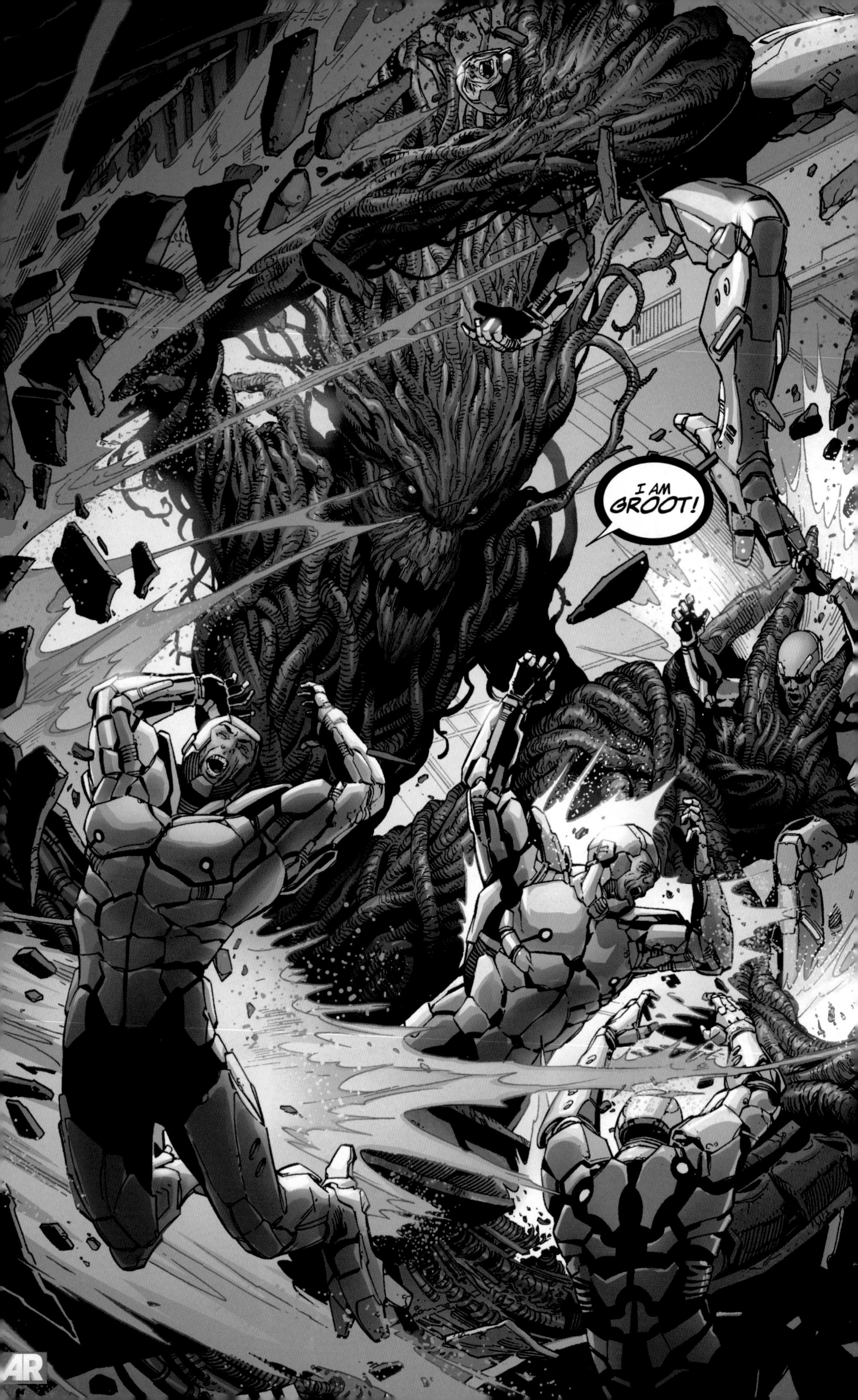
I AM GROOT!

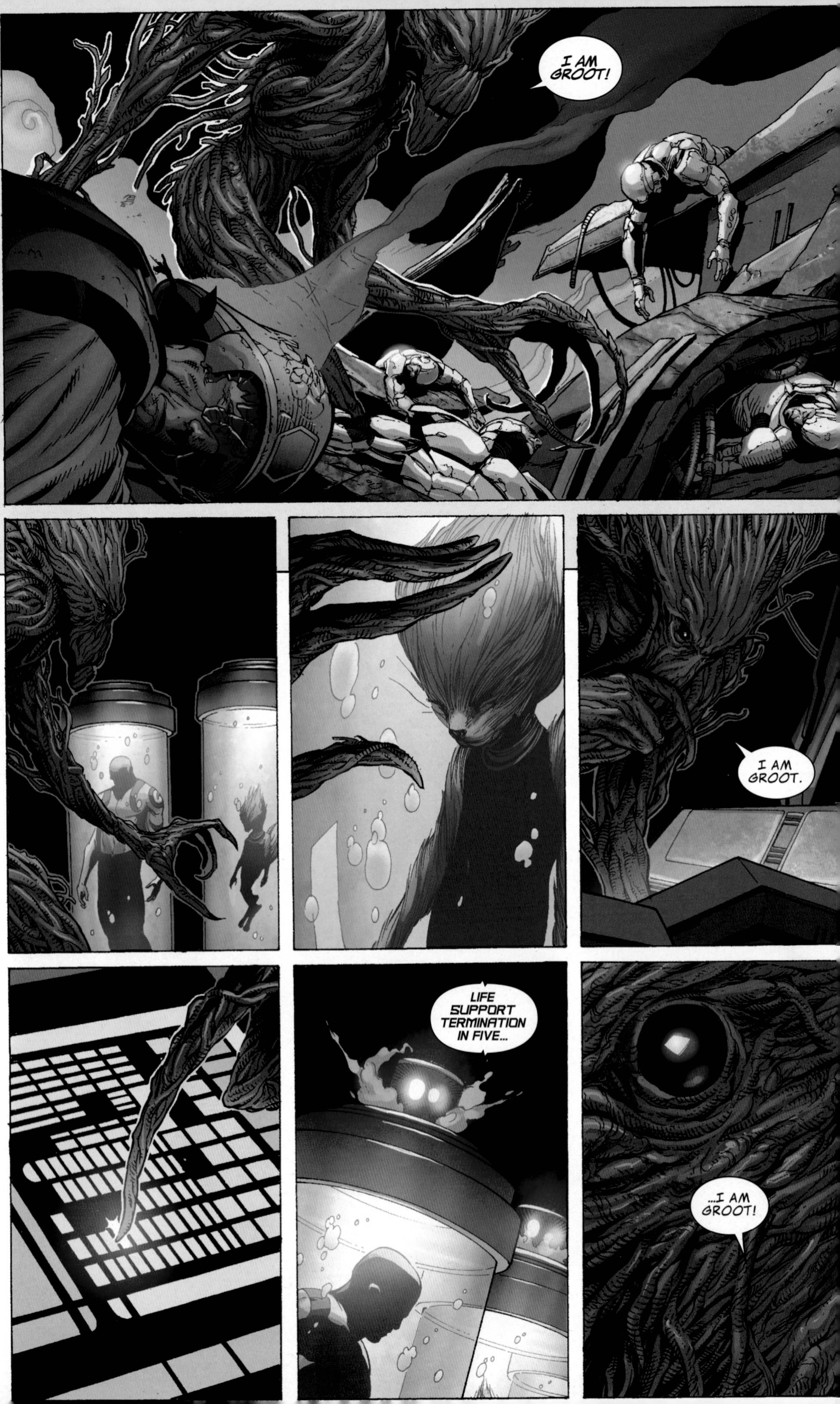
I AM GROOT!
I AM GROOT.
LIFE SUPPORT TERMINATION IN FIVE...
...I AM GROOT!

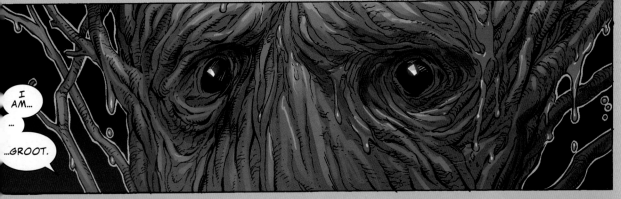

I AM...

....

...GROOT.

YES, YOU ARE.

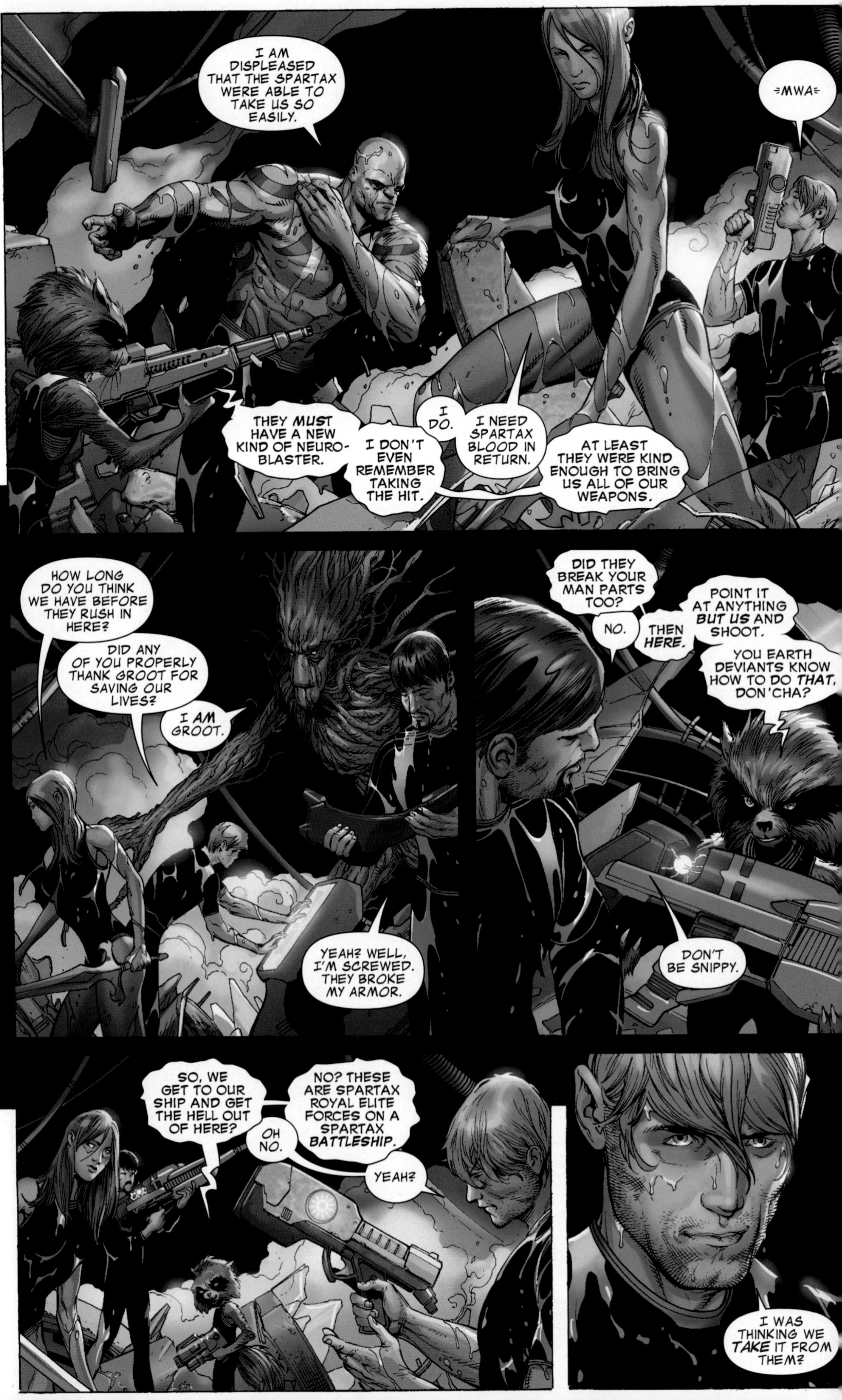
I AM DISPLEASED THAT THE SPARTAX WERE ABLE TO TAKE US SO EASILY.
=MWA=
THEY MUST HAVE A NEW KIND OF NEURO-BLASTER.
I DON'T EVEN REMEMBER TAKING THE HIT.
I DO.
I NEED SPARTAX BLOOD IN RETURN.
AT LEAST THEY WERE KIND ENOUGH TO BRING US ALL OF OUR WEAPONS.
HOW LONG DO YOU THINK WE HAVE BEFORE THEY RUSH IN HERE?
DID ANY OF YOU PROPERLY THANK GROOT FOR SAVING OUR LIVES?
I AM GROOT.
YEAH? WELL, I'M SCREWED. THEY BROKE MY ARMOR.
DID THEY BREAK YOUR MAN PARTS TOO?
NO.
THEN HERE.
POINT IT AT ANYTHING BUT US AND SHOOT.
YOU EARTH DEVIANTS KNOW HOW TO DO THAT, DON'CHA?
DON'T BE SNIPPY.
SO, WE GET TO OUR SHIP AND GET THE HELL OUT OF HERE?
NO? THESE ARE SPARTAX ROYAL ELITE FORCES ON A SPARTAX BATTLESHIP.
OH NO.
YEAH?
I WAS THINKING WE TAKE IT FROM THEM?

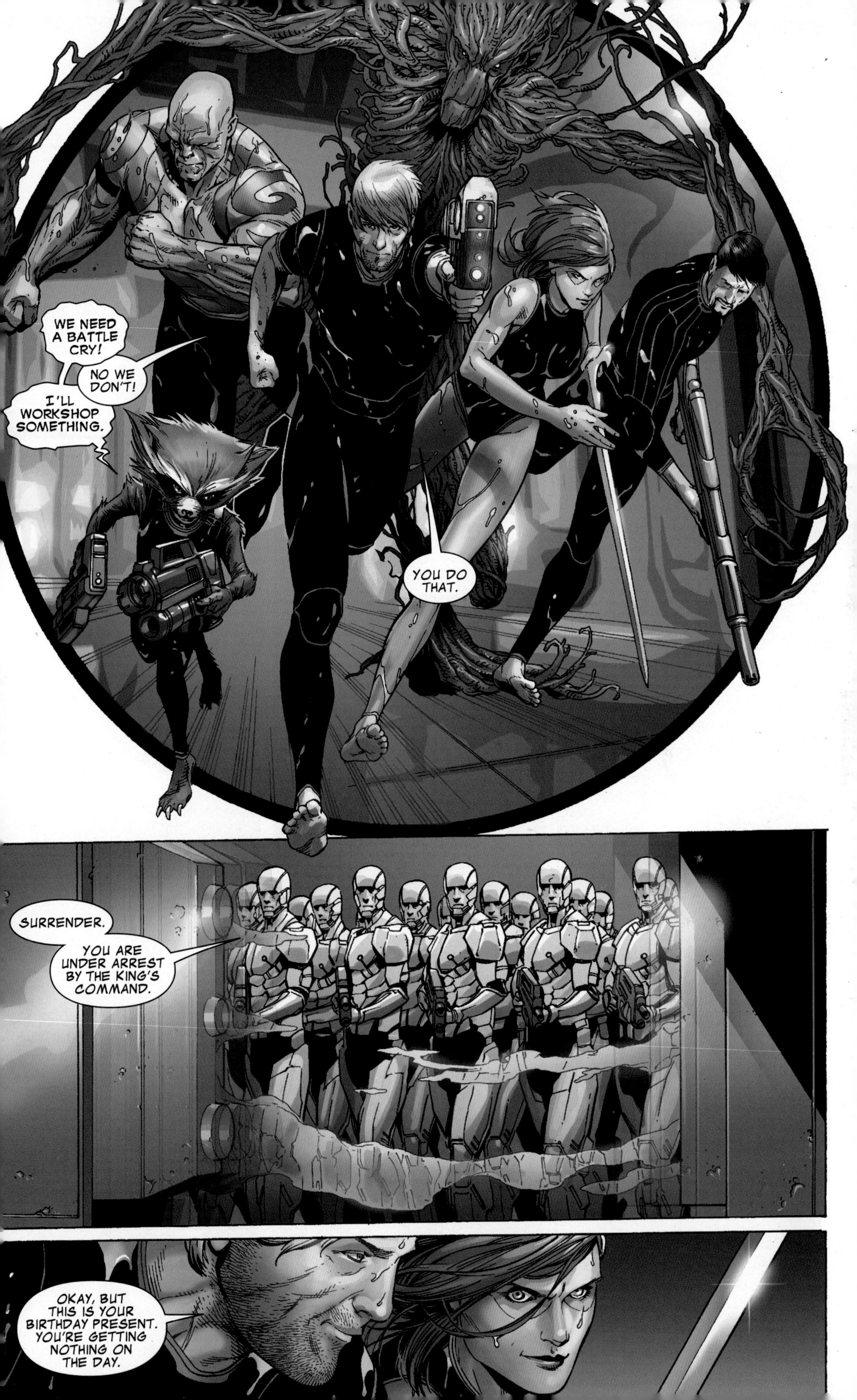
WE NEED A BATTLE CRY!
NO WE DON'T!
I'LL WORKSHOP SOMETHING.
YOU DO THAT.
SURRENDER.
YOU ARE UNDER ARREST BY THE KING'S COMMAND.
OKAY, BUT THIS IS YOUR BIRTHDAY PRESENT. YOU'RE GETTING NOTHING ON THE DAY.

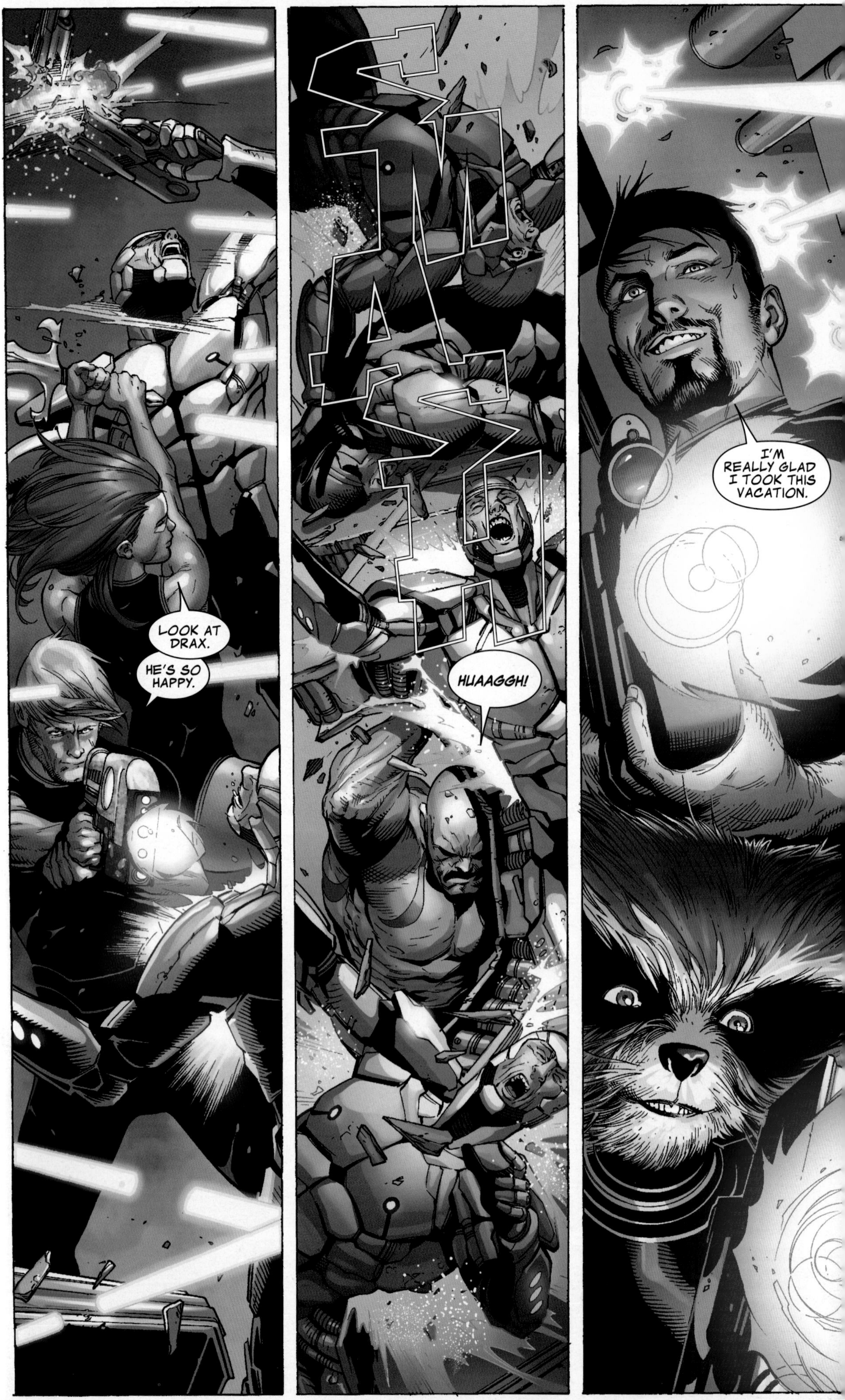
LOOK AT DRAX.
HE'S SO HAPPY.
SMASH
HUAAGGH!
I'M REALLY GLAD I TOOK THIS VACATION.

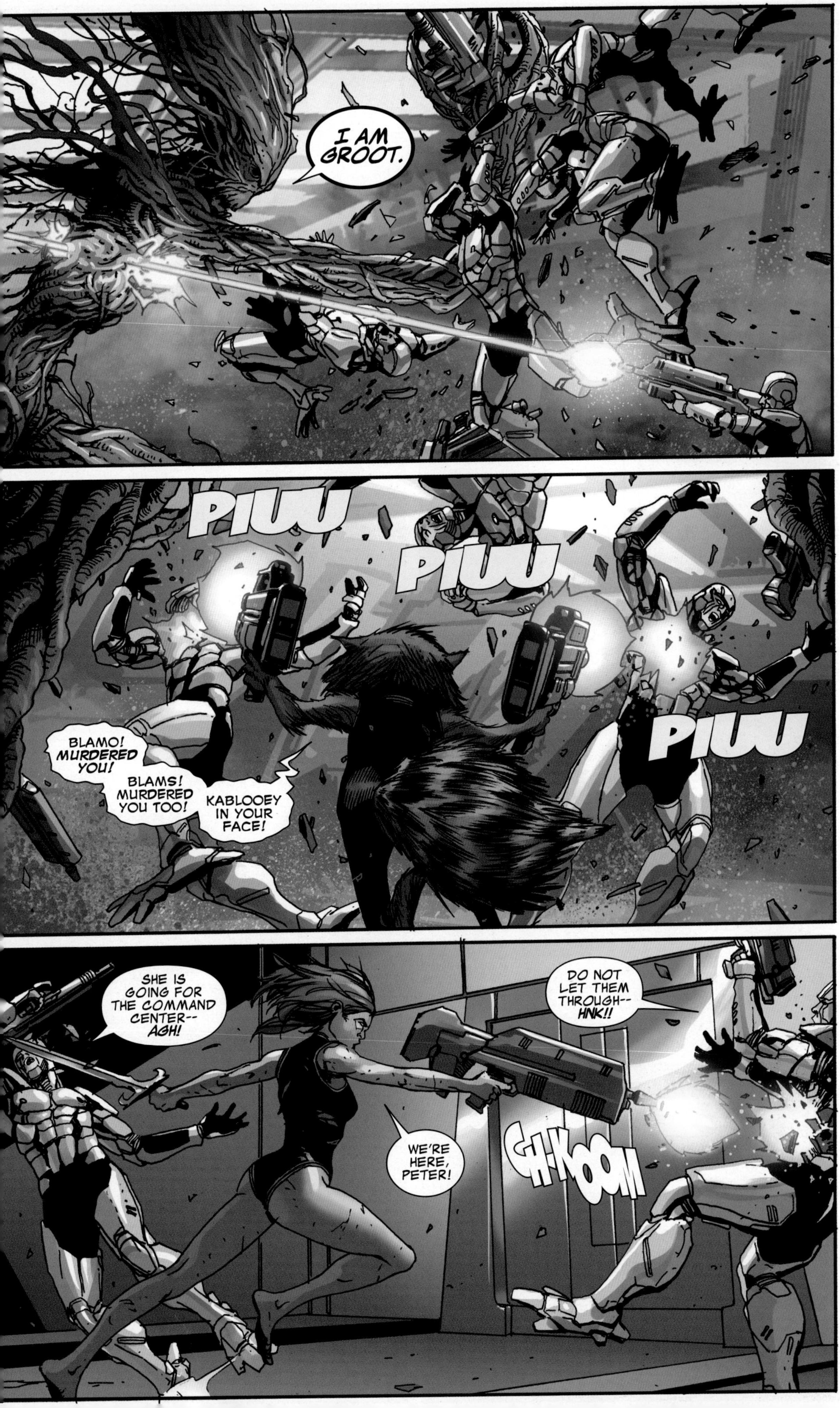
I AM GROOT.
PIUU
PIUU
PIUU
BLAMO! MURDERED YOU!
BLAMS! MURDERED YOU TOO!
KABLOOEY IN YOUR FACE!
SHE IS GOING FOR THE COMMAND CENTER-- AGH!
DO NOT LET THEM THROUGH-- HNK!!
WE'RE HERE, PETER!
CHKOOM

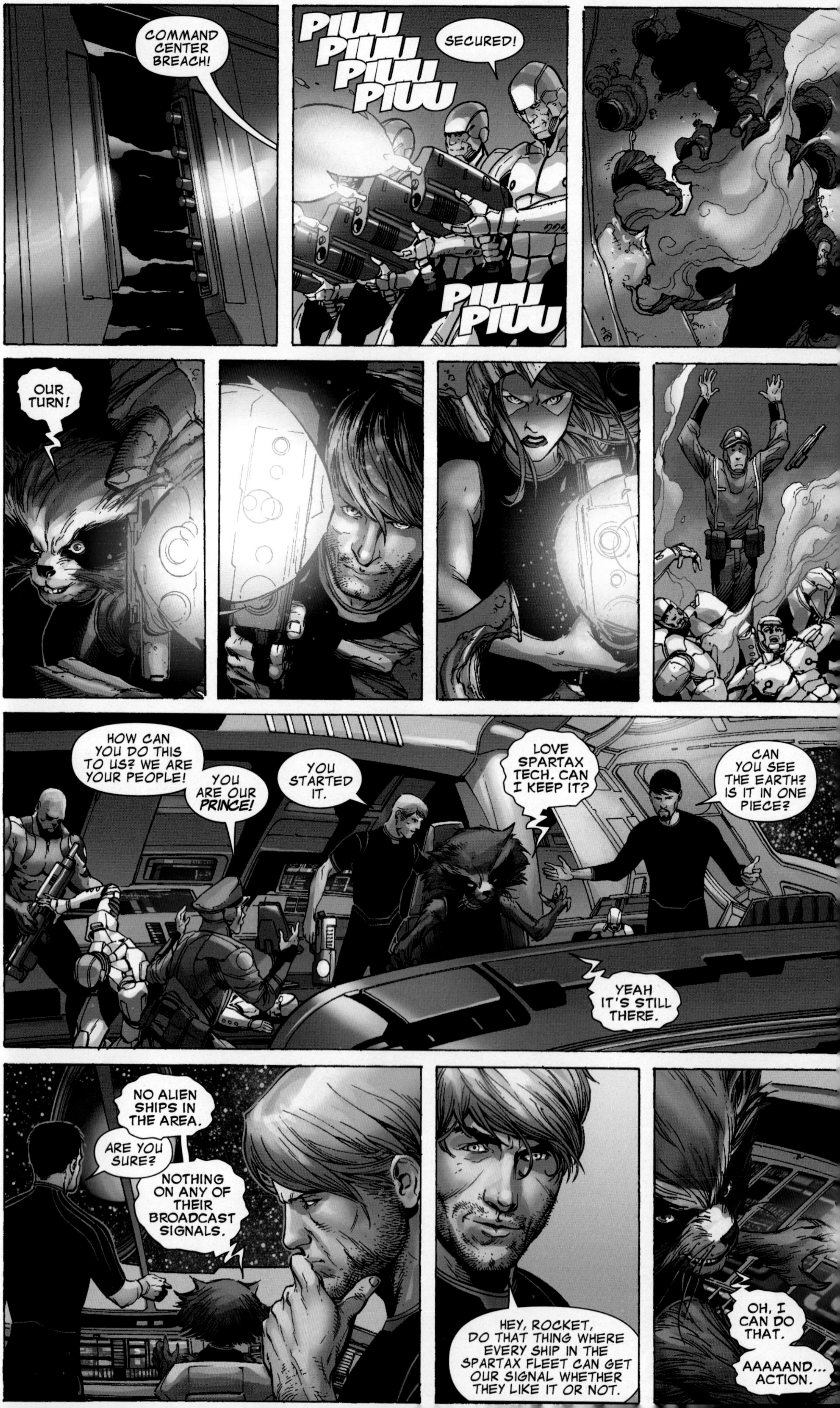
COMMAND CENTER BREACH!
PIUU PIUU PIUU PIUU
SECURED!
PIUU PIUU
OUR TURN!
HOW CAN YOU DO THIS TO US? WE ARE YOUR PEOPLE!
YOU ARE OUR *PRINCE!*
YOU STARTED IT.
LOVE SPARTAX TECH. CAN I KEEP IT?
CAN YOU SEE THE EARTH? IS IT IN ONE PIECE?
YEAH IT'S STILL THERE.
NO ALIEN SHIPS IN THE AREA.
ARE YOU SURE?
NOTHING ON ANY OF THEIR BROADCAST SIGNALS.
HEY, ROCKET, DO THAT THING WHERE EVERY SHIP IN THE SPARTAX FLEET CAN GET OUR SIGNAL WHETHER THEY LIKE IT OR NOT.
OH, I CAN DO THAT.
AAAAAND... ACTION.

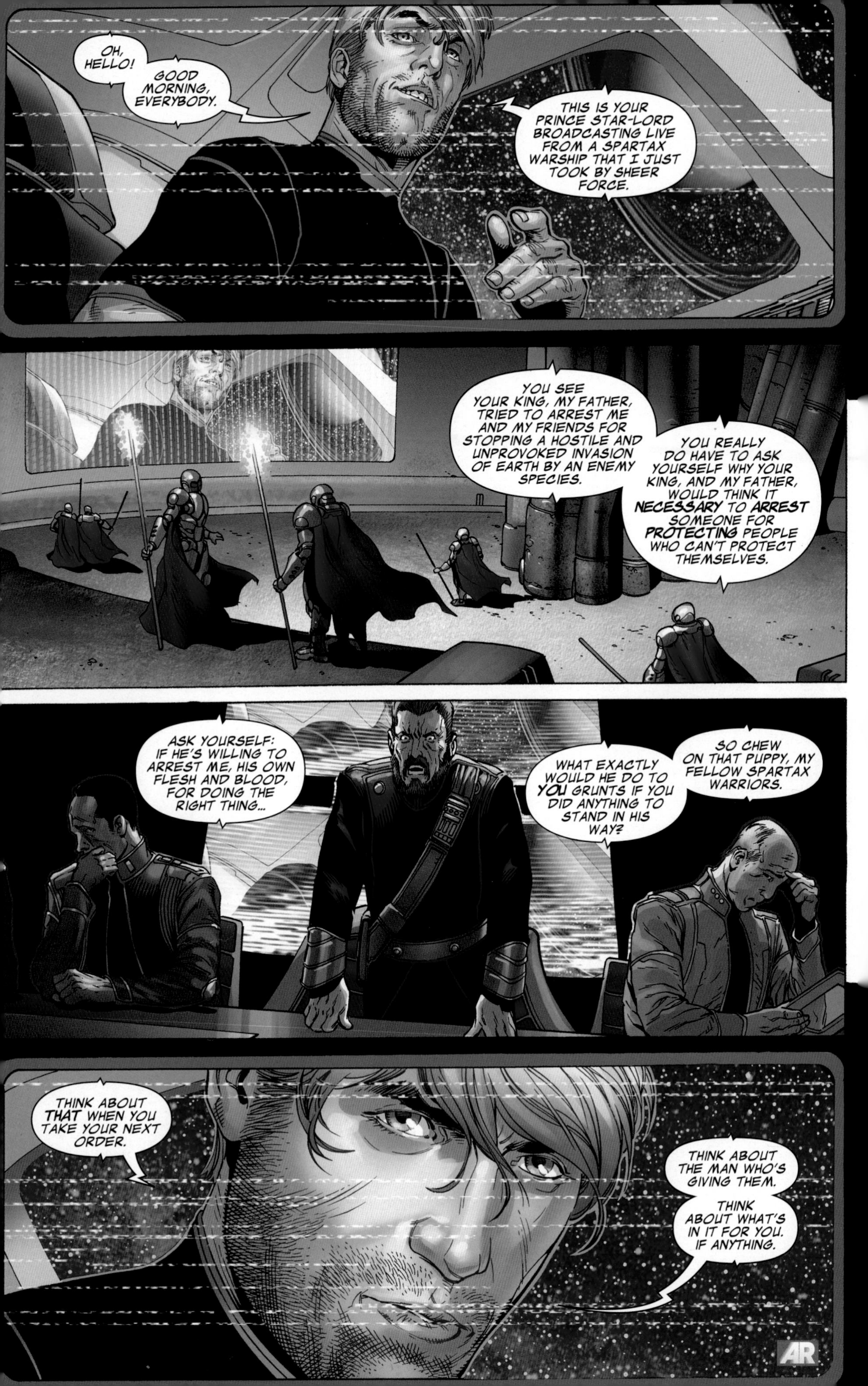
OH, HELLO!
GOOD MORNING, EVERYBODY.
THIS IS YOUR PRINCE STAR-LORD BROADCASTING LIVE FROM A SPARTAX WARSHIP THAT I JUST TOOK BY SHEER FORCE.
YOU SEE YOUR KING, MY FATHER, TRIED TO ARREST ME AND MY FRIENDS FOR STOPPING A HOSTILE AND UNPROVOKED INVASION OF EARTH BY AN ENEMY SPECIES.
YOU REALLY DO HAVE TO ASK YOURSELF WHY YOUR KING, AND MY FATHER, WOULD THINK IT NECESSARY TO ARREST SOMEONE FOR PROTECTING PEOPLE WHO CAN'T PROTECT THEMSELVES.
ASK YOURSELF: IF HE'S WILLING TO ARREST ME, HIS OWN FLESH AND BLOOD, FOR DOING THE RIGHT THING...
WHAT EXACTLY WOULD HE DO TO YOU GRUNTS IF YOU DID ANYTHING TO STAND IN HIS WAY?
SO CHEW ON THAT PUPPY, MY FELLOW SPARTAX WARRIORS.
THINK ABOUT THAT WHEN YOU TAKE YOUR NEXT ORDER.
THINK ABOUT THE MAN WHO'S GIVING THEM.
THINK ABOUT WHAT'S IN IT FOR YOU. IF ANYTHING.

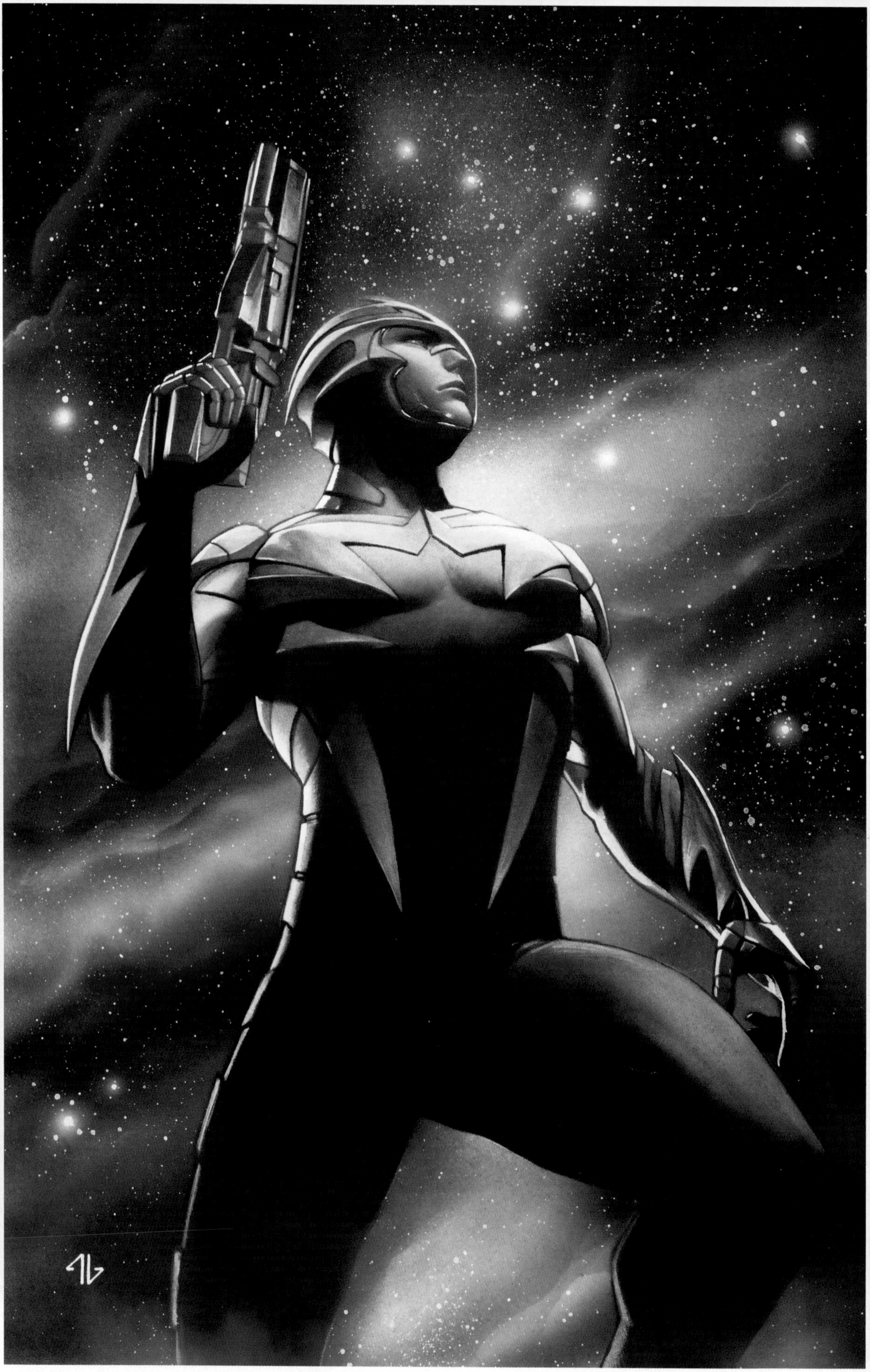

#4 VARIANT BY ADI GRANOV

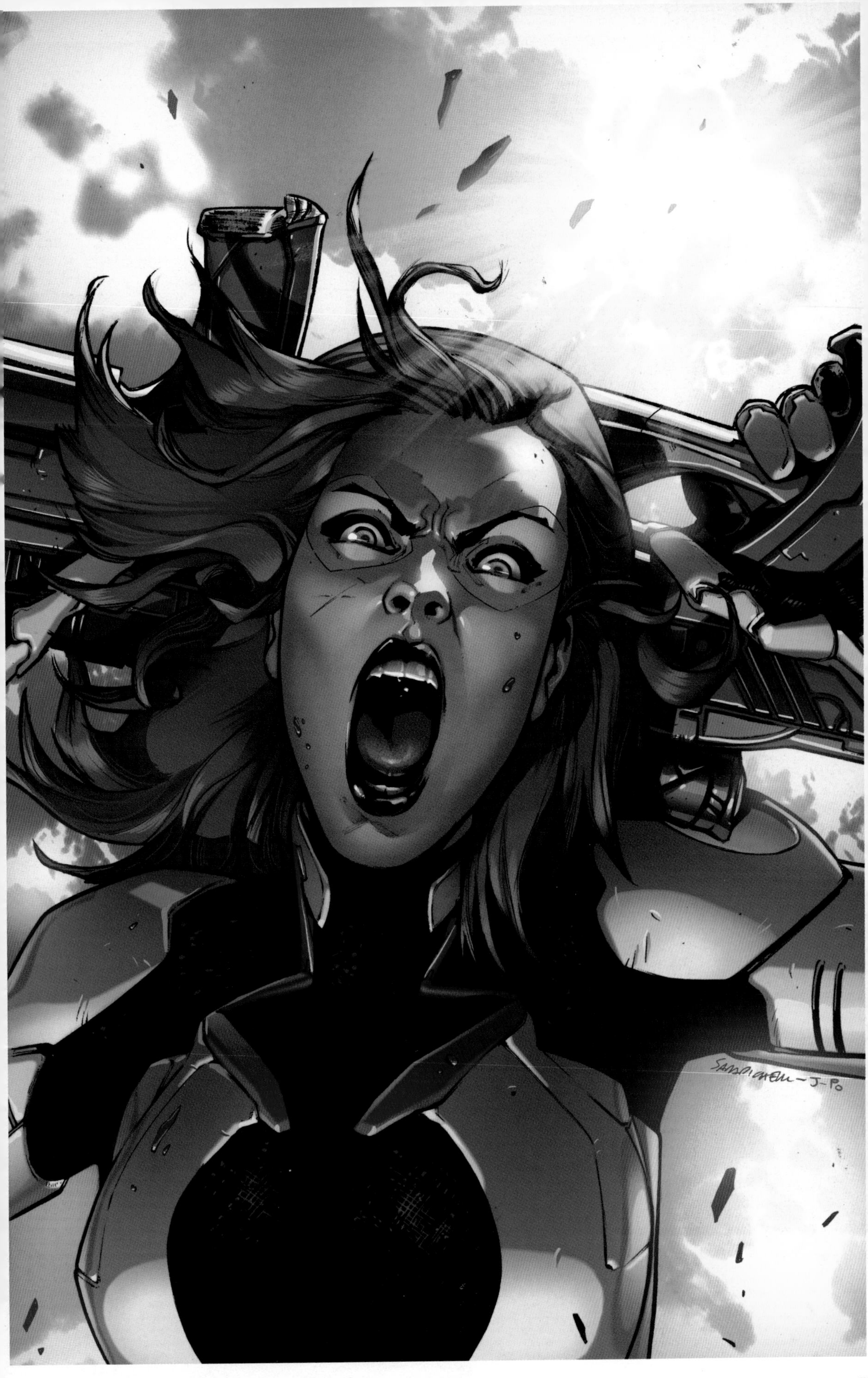

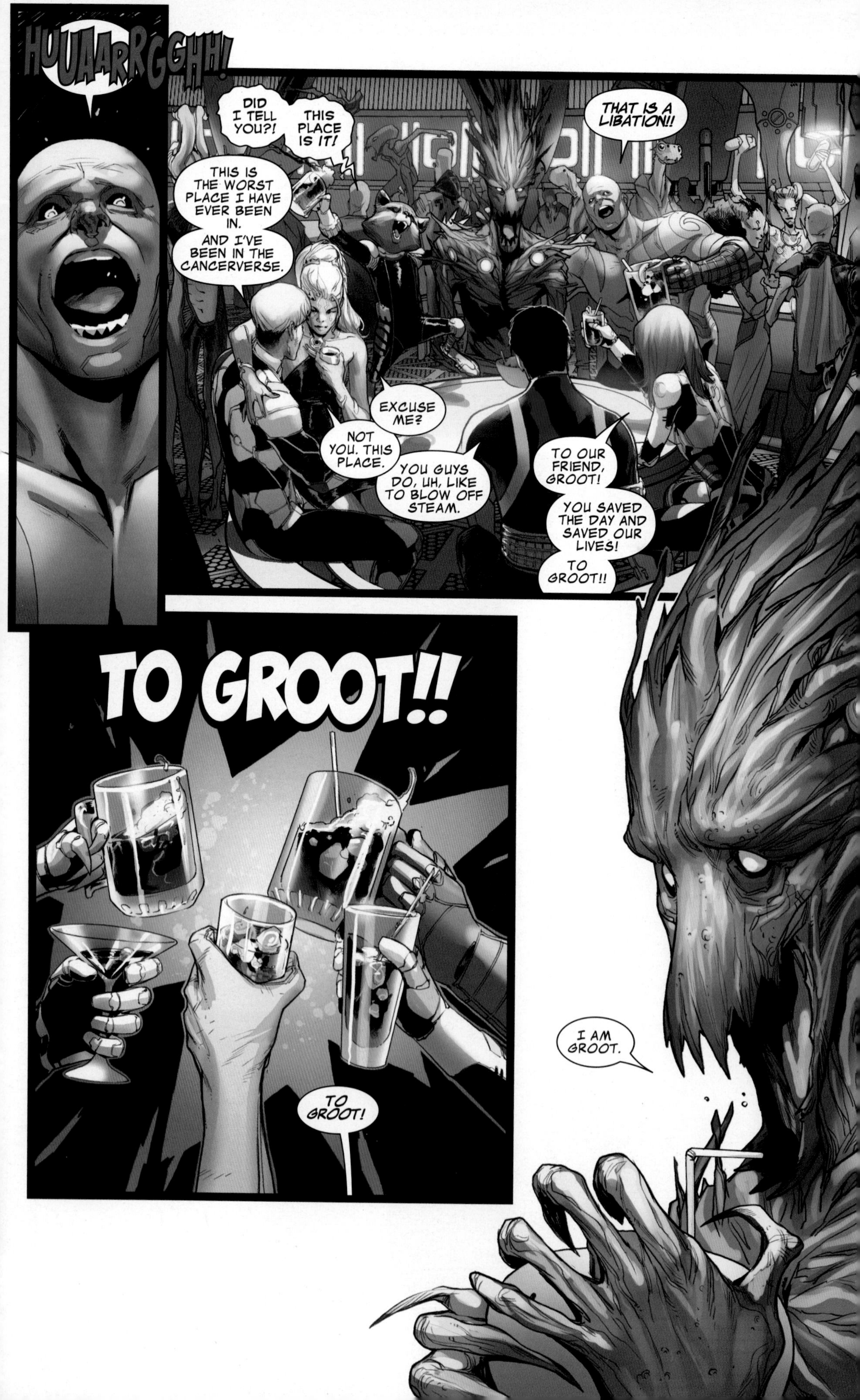
HUUAARRGGHH!
DID I TELL YOU?!
THIS PLACE IS IT!
THIS IS THE WORST PLACE I HAVE EVER BEEN IN.
AND I'VE BEEN IN THE CANCERVERSE.
THAT IS A LIBATION!!
EXCUSE ME?
NOT YOU. THIS PLACE.
YOU GUYS DO, UH, LIKE TO BLOW OFF STEAM.
TO OUR FRIEND, GROOT!
YOU SAVED THE DAY AND SAVED OUR LIVES!
TO GROOT!!
TO GROOT!!
TO GROOT!
I AM GROOT.

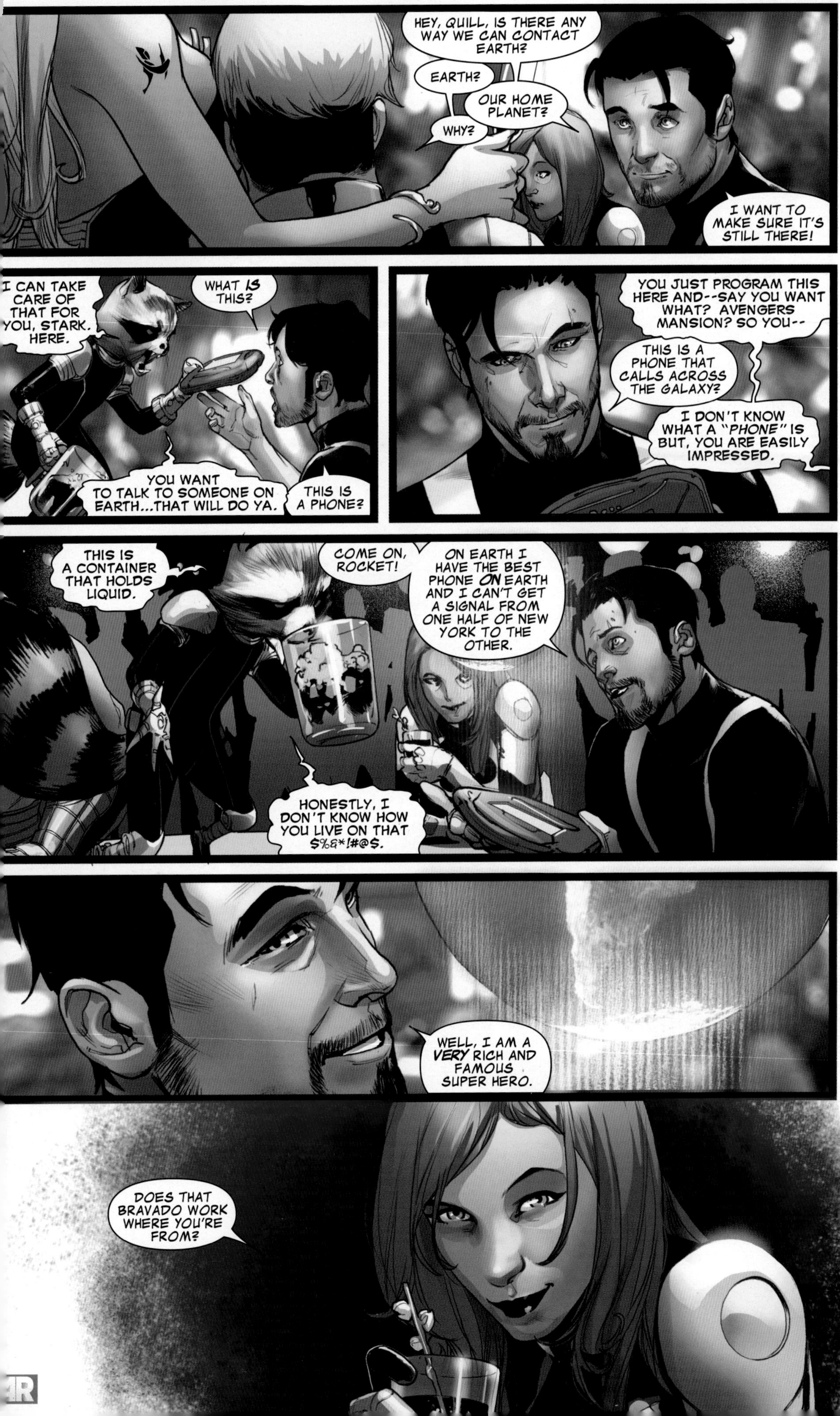
HEY, QUILL, IS THERE ANY WAY WE CAN CONTACT EARTH?
EARTH?
OUR HOME PLANET?
WHY?
I WANT TO MAKE SURE IT'S STILL THERE!
I CAN TAKE CARE OF THAT FOR YOU, STARK. HERE.
WHAT IS THIS?
YOU WANT TO TALK TO SOMEONE ON EARTH...THAT WILL DO YA.
THIS IS A PHONE?
YOU JUST PROGRAM THIS HERE AND--SAY YOU WANT WHAT? AVENGERS MANSION? SO YOU--
THIS IS A PHONE THAT CALLS ACROSS THE GALAXY?
I DON'T KNOW WHAT A "PHONE" IS BUT, YOU ARE EASILY IMPRESSED.
THIS IS A CONTAINER THAT HOLDS LIQUID.
COME ON, ROCKET!
ON EARTH I HAVE THE BEST PHONE ON EARTH AND I CAN'T GET A SIGNAL FROM ONE HALF OF NEW YORK TO THE OTHER.
HONESTLY, I DON'T KNOW HOW YOU LIVE ON THAT $%&*!#@$.
WELL, I AM A VERY RICH AND FAMOUS SUPER HERO.
DOES THAT BRAVADO WORK WHERE YOU'RE FROM?

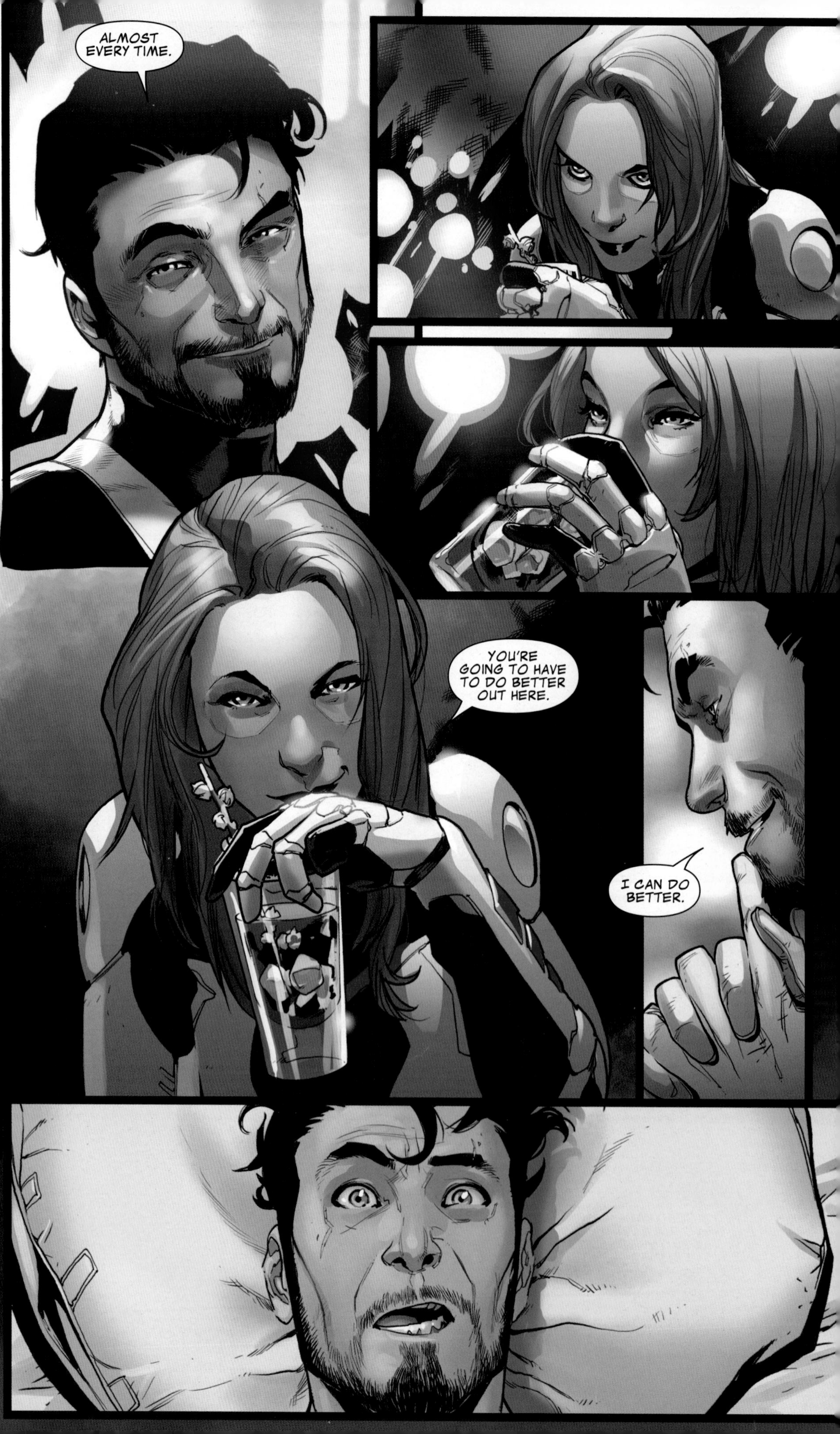
ALMOST EVERY TIME.
YOU'RE GOING TO HAVE TO DO BETTER OUT HERE.
I CAN DO BETTER.

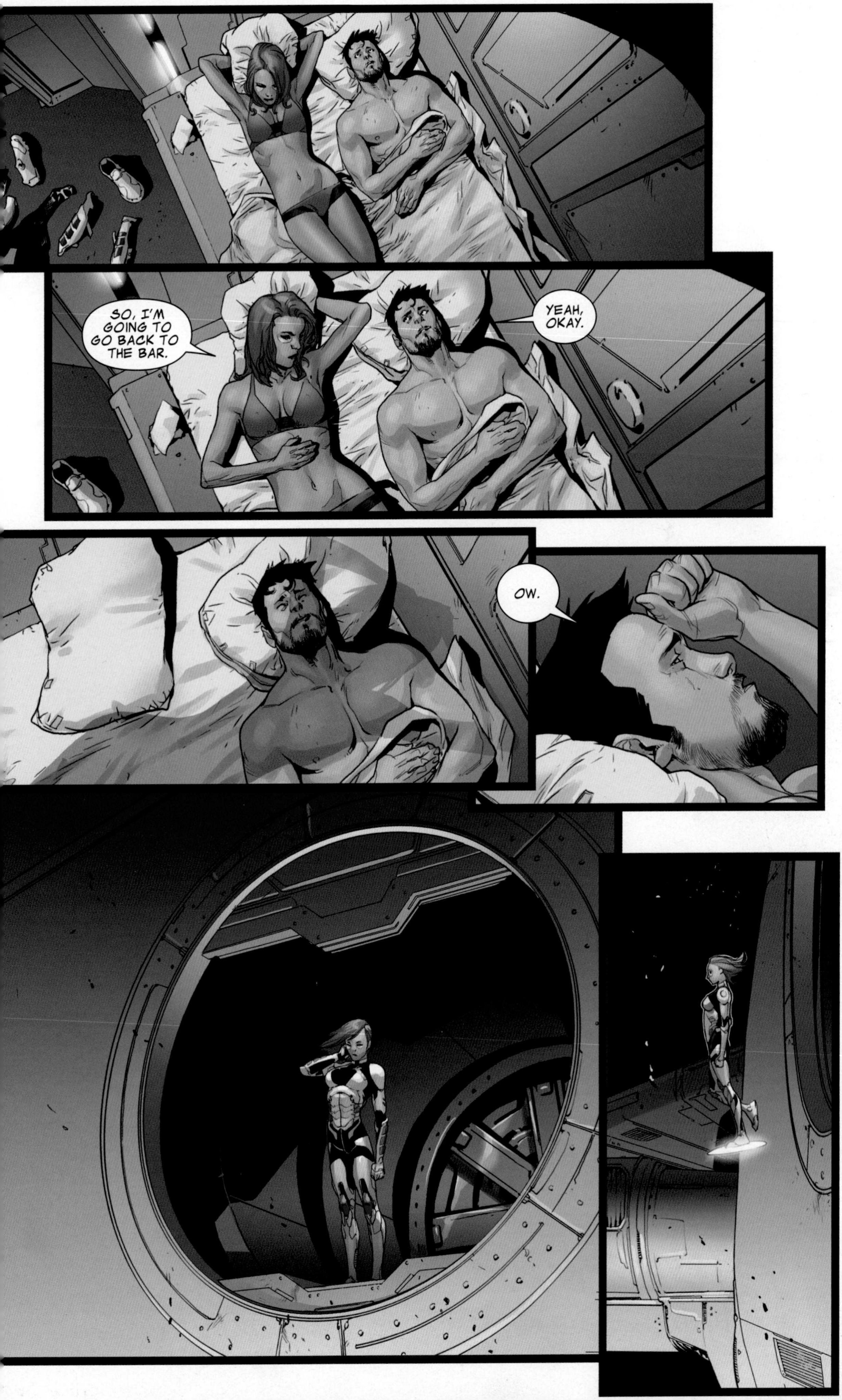
SO, I'M GOING TO GO BACK TO THE BAR.
YEAH, OKAY.
OW.

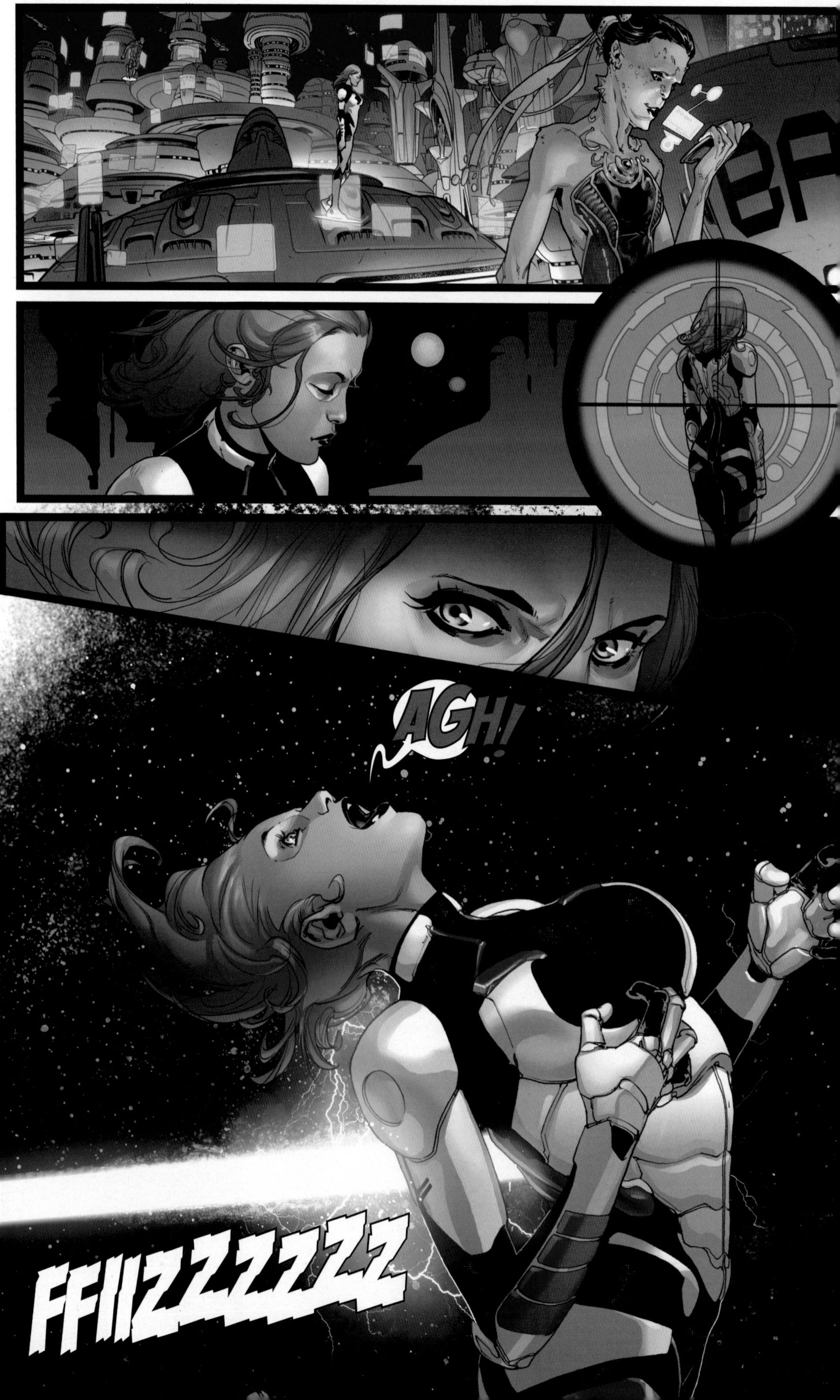
AGH!
FFIIZZZZZZ

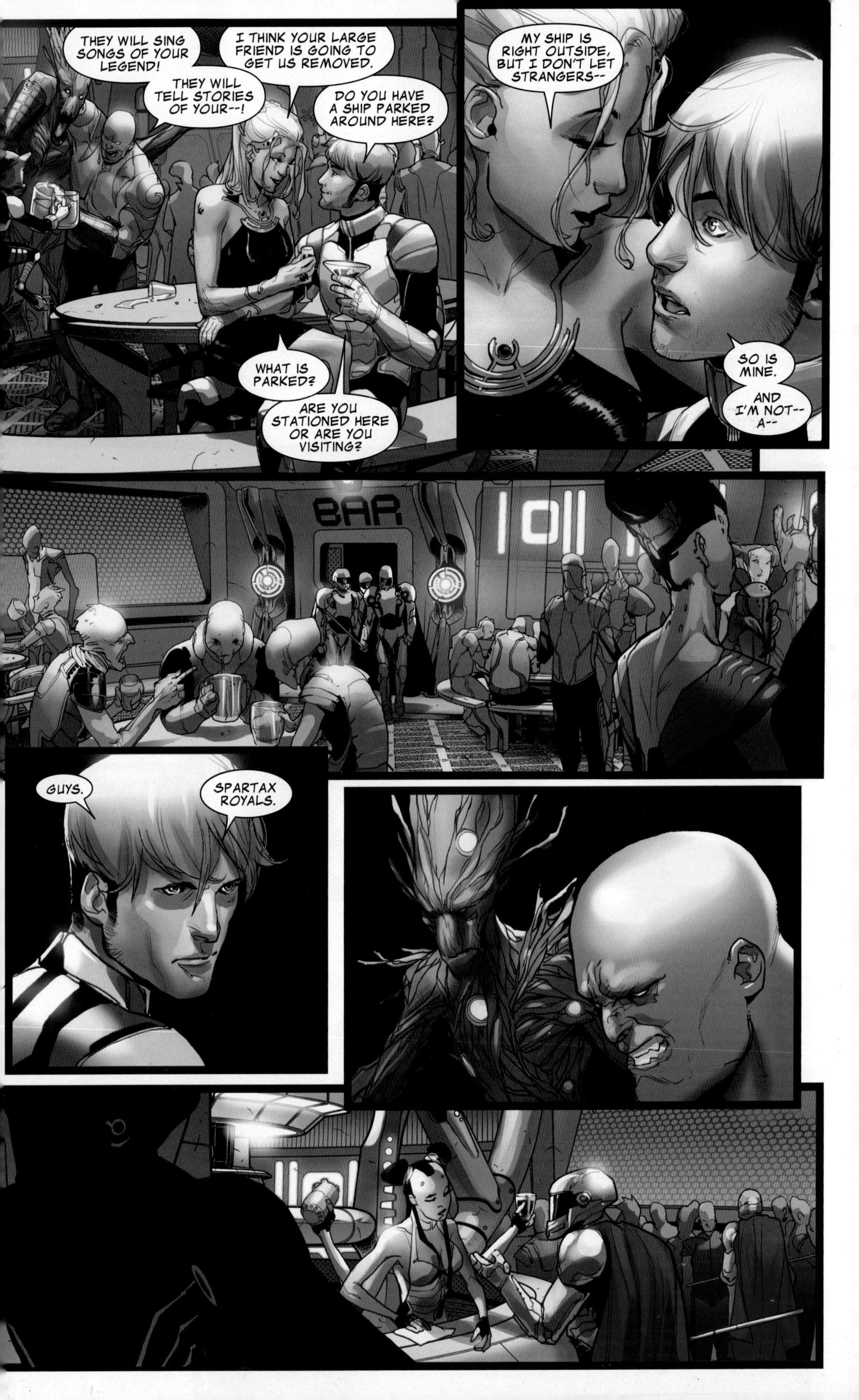
THEY WILL SING SONGS OF YOUR LEGEND!
THEY WILL TELL STORIES OF YOUR--!
I THINK YOUR LARGE FRIEND IS GOING TO GET US REMOVED.
DO YOU HAVE A SHIP PARKED AROUND HERE?
WHAT IS PARKED?
ARE YOU STATIONED HERE OR ARE YOU VISITING?
MY SHIP IS RIGHT OUTSIDE, BUT I DON'T LET STRANGERS--
SO IS MINE.
AND I'M NOT-- A--
BAR
GUYS.
SPARTAX ROYALS.

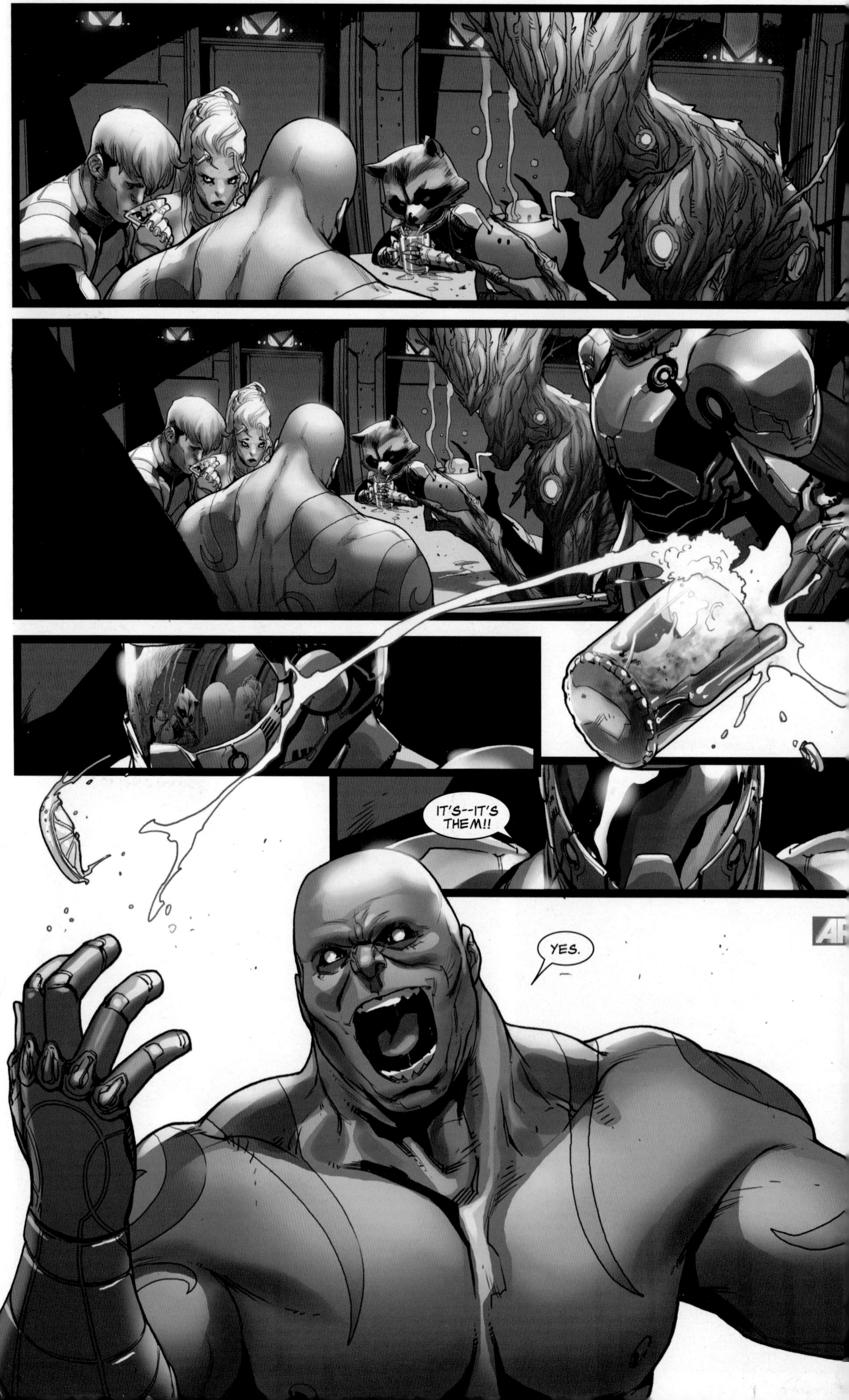
IT'S--IT'S THEM!!
YES.

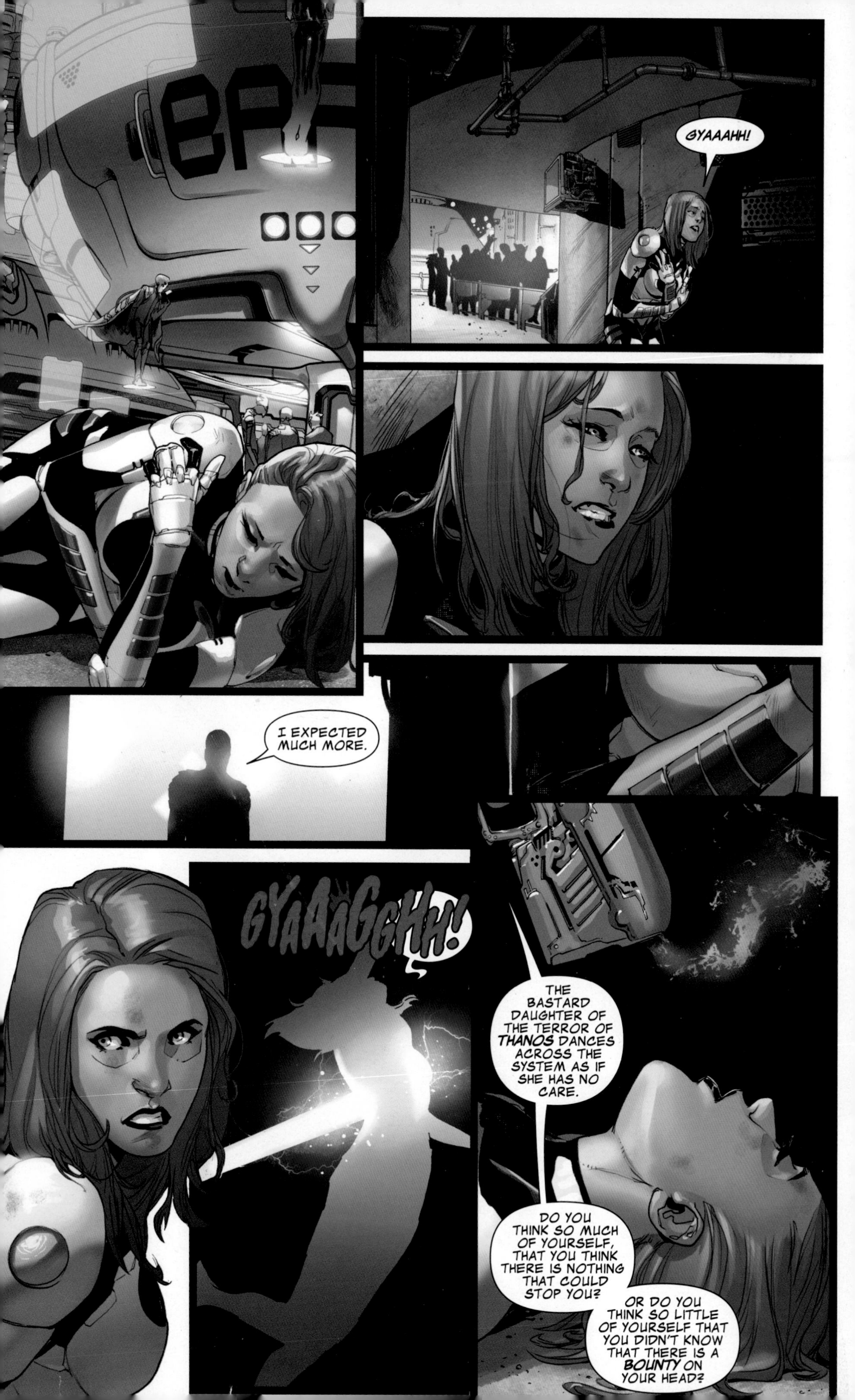
GYAAAHH!
I EXPECTED MUCH MORE.
GYAAAGGHH!
THE BASTARD DAUGHTER OF THE TERROR OF THANOS DANCES ACROSS THE SYSTEM AS IF SHE HAS NO CARE.
DO YOU THINK SO MUCH OF YOURSELF, THAT YOU THINK THERE IS NOTHING THAT COULD STOP YOU?
OR DO YOU THINK SO LITTLE OF YOURSELF THAT YOU DIDN'T KNOW THAT THERE IS A BOUNTY ON YOUR HEAD?

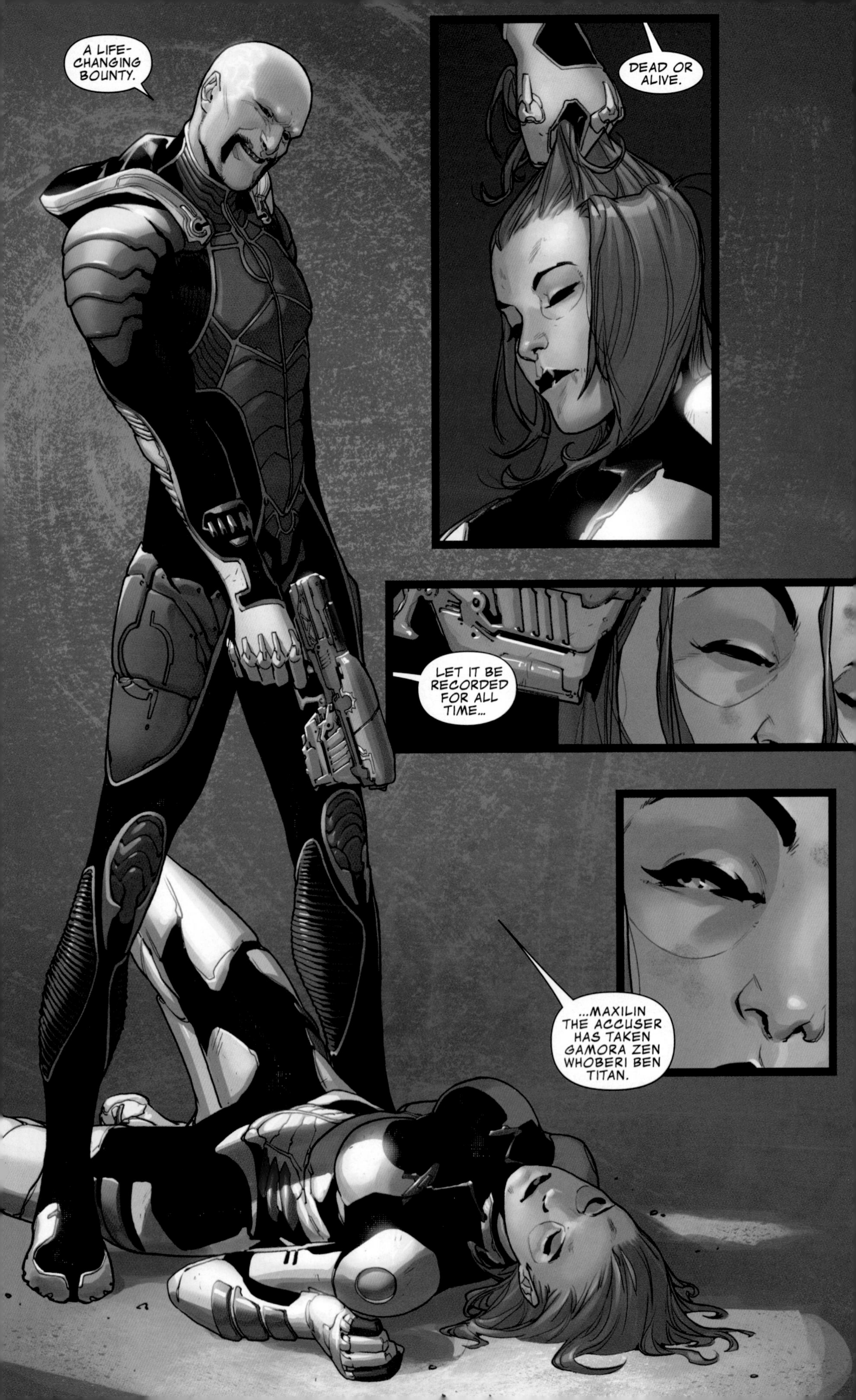
A LIFE-CHANGING BOUNTY.
DEAD OR ALIVE.
LET IT BE RECORDED FOR ALL TIME...
...MAXILIN THE ACCUSER HAS TAKEN GAMORA ZEN WHOBERI BEN TITAN.

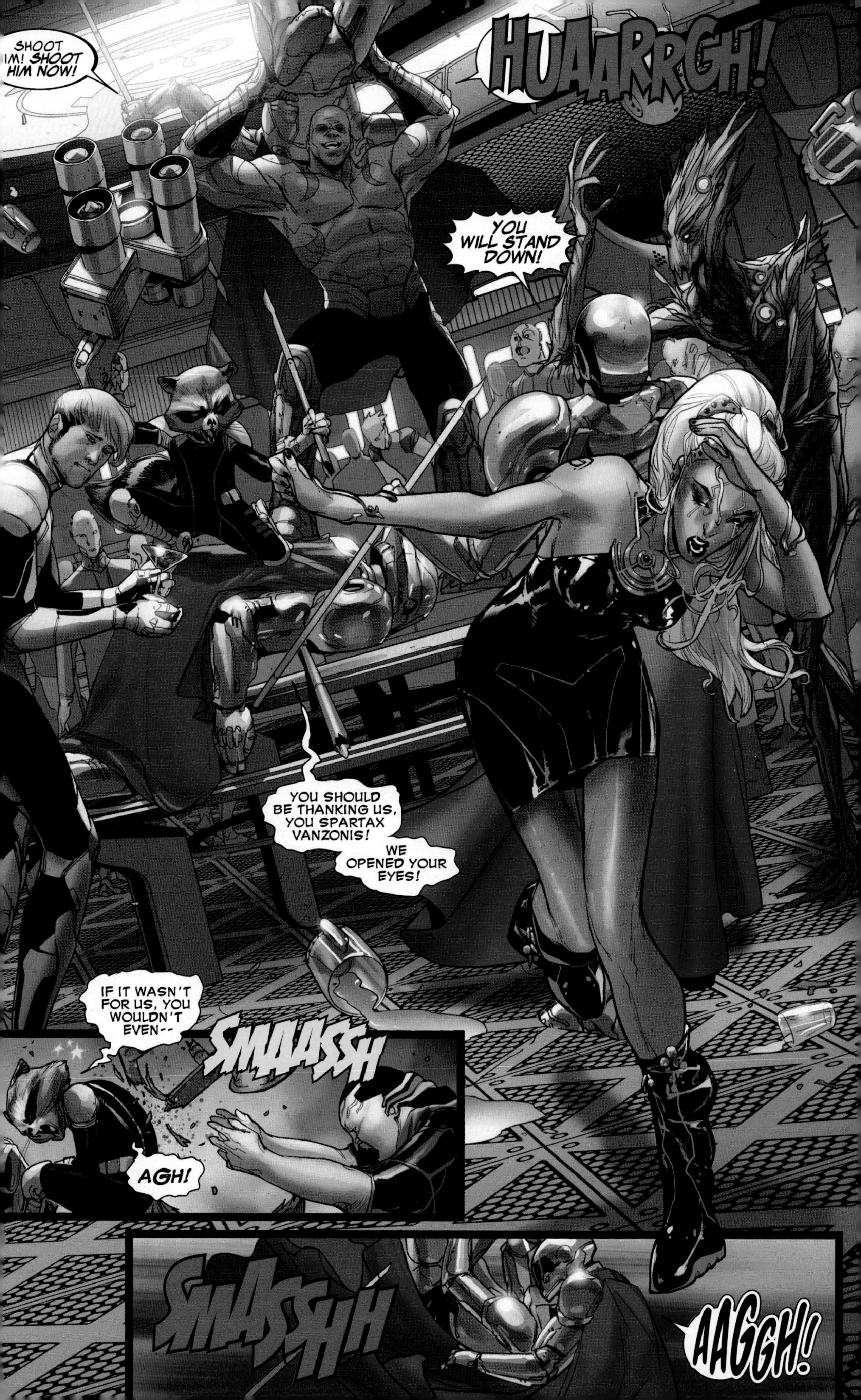
SHOOT IM! SHOOT HIM NOW!
HUAARRGH!
YOU WILL STAND DOWN!
YOU SHOULD BE THANKING US, YOU SPARTAX VANZONIS!
WE OPENED YOUR EYES!
IF IT WASN'T FOR US, YOU WOULDN'T EVEN--
SMAASSH
AGH!
SMASSHH
AAGGH!

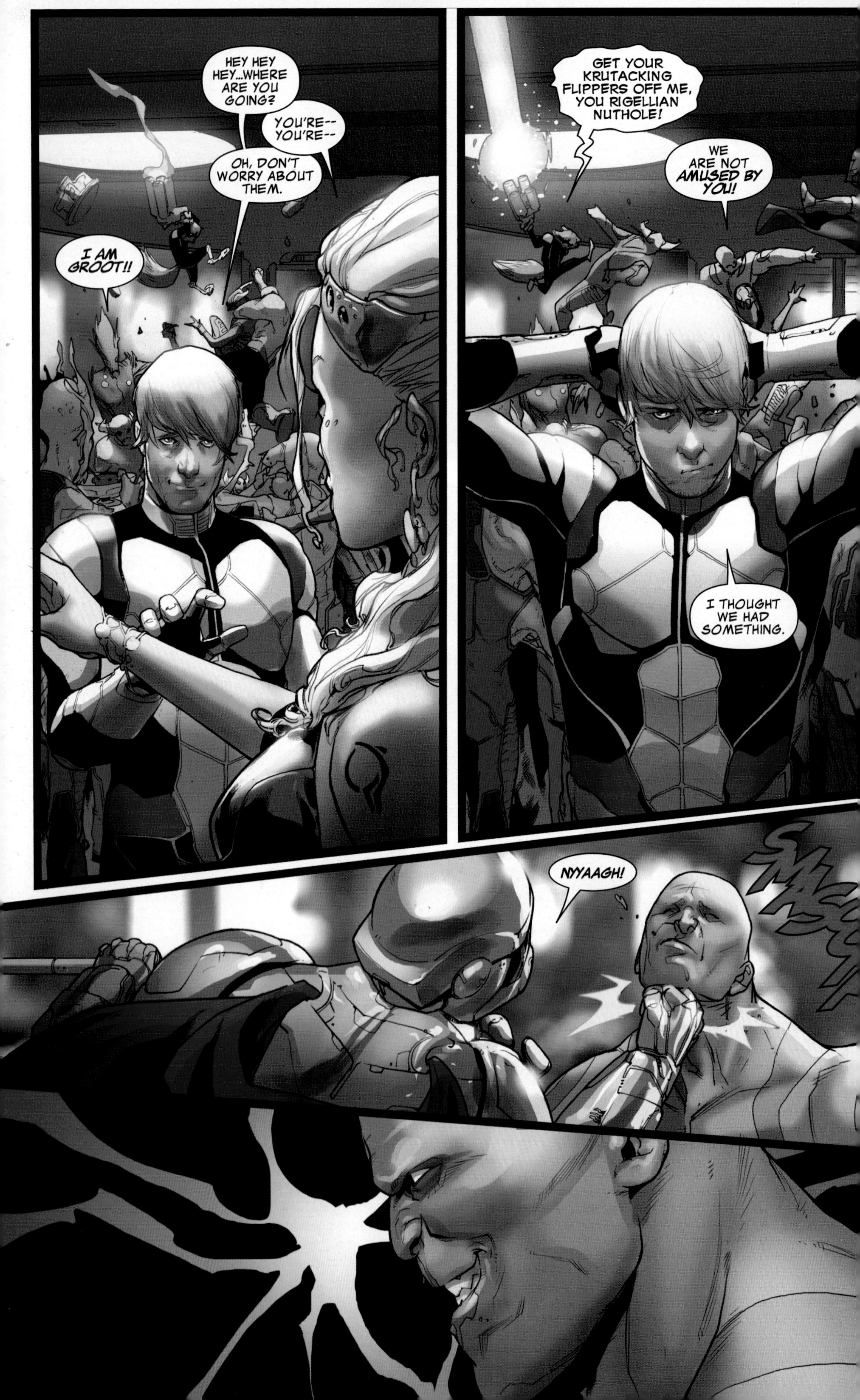
HEY HEY HEY...WHERE ARE YOU GOING?
YOU'RE-- YOU'RE--
OH, DON'T WORRY ABOUT THEM.
I AM GROOT!!
GET YOUR KRUTACKING FLIPPERS OFF ME, YOU RIGELLIAN NUTHOLE!
WE ARE NOT AMUSED BY YOU!
I THOUGHT WE HAD SOMETHING.
NYYAAGH!

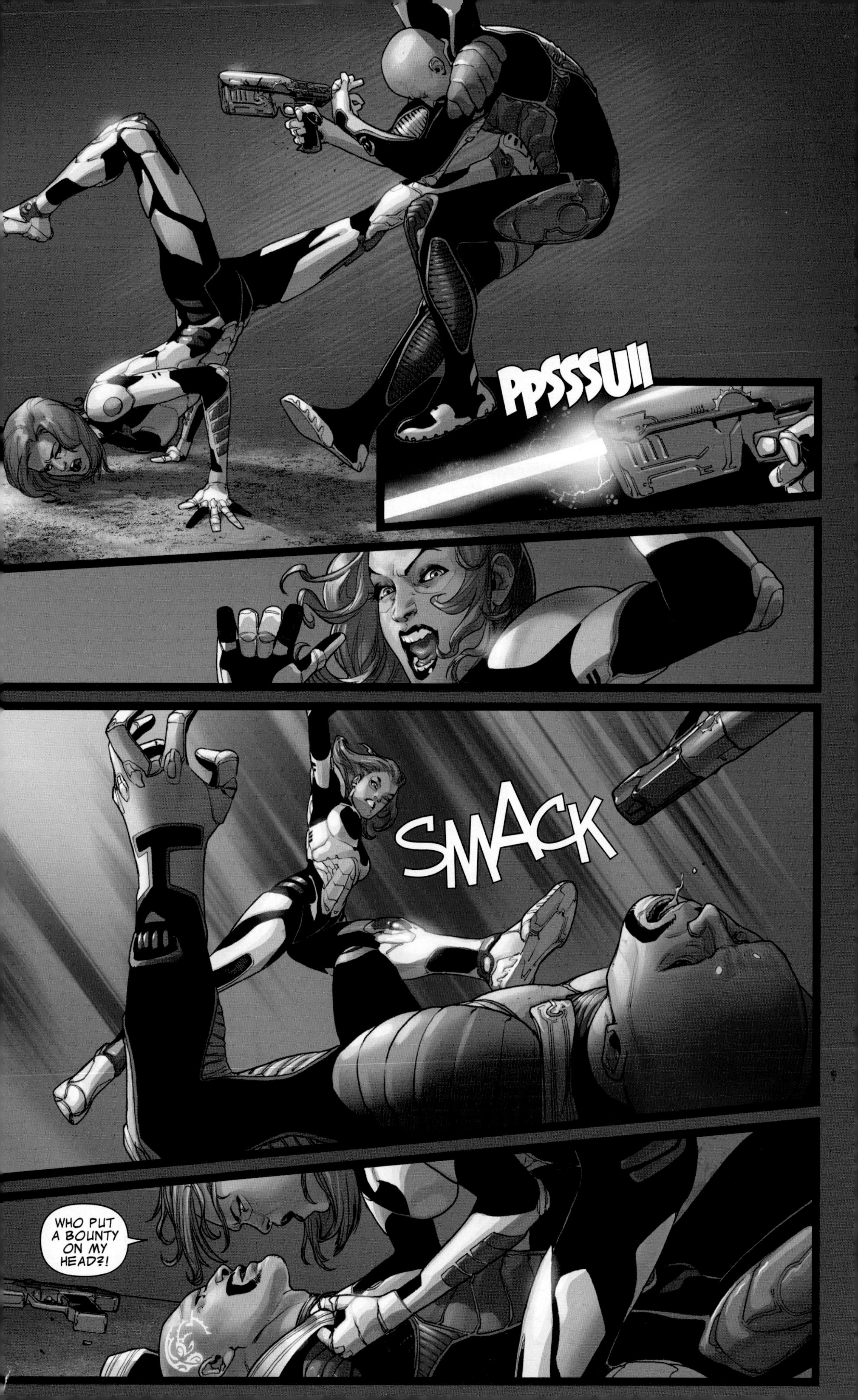
PPSSSUII
SMACK
WHO PUT A BOUNTY ON MY HEAD?!

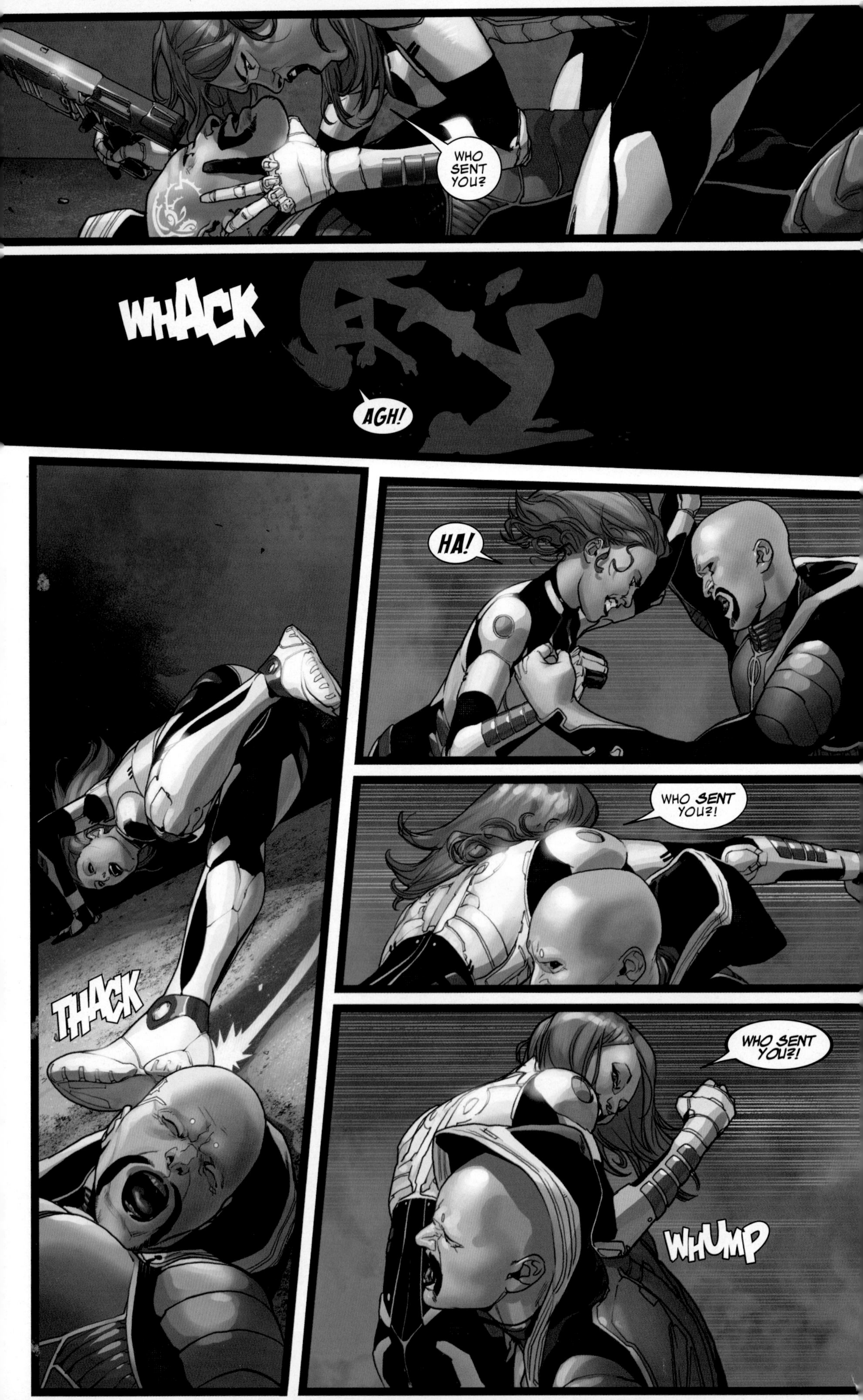
WHO SENT YOU?
WHACK
AGH!
THACK
HA!
WHO SENT YOU?!
WHO SENT YOU?!
WHUMP

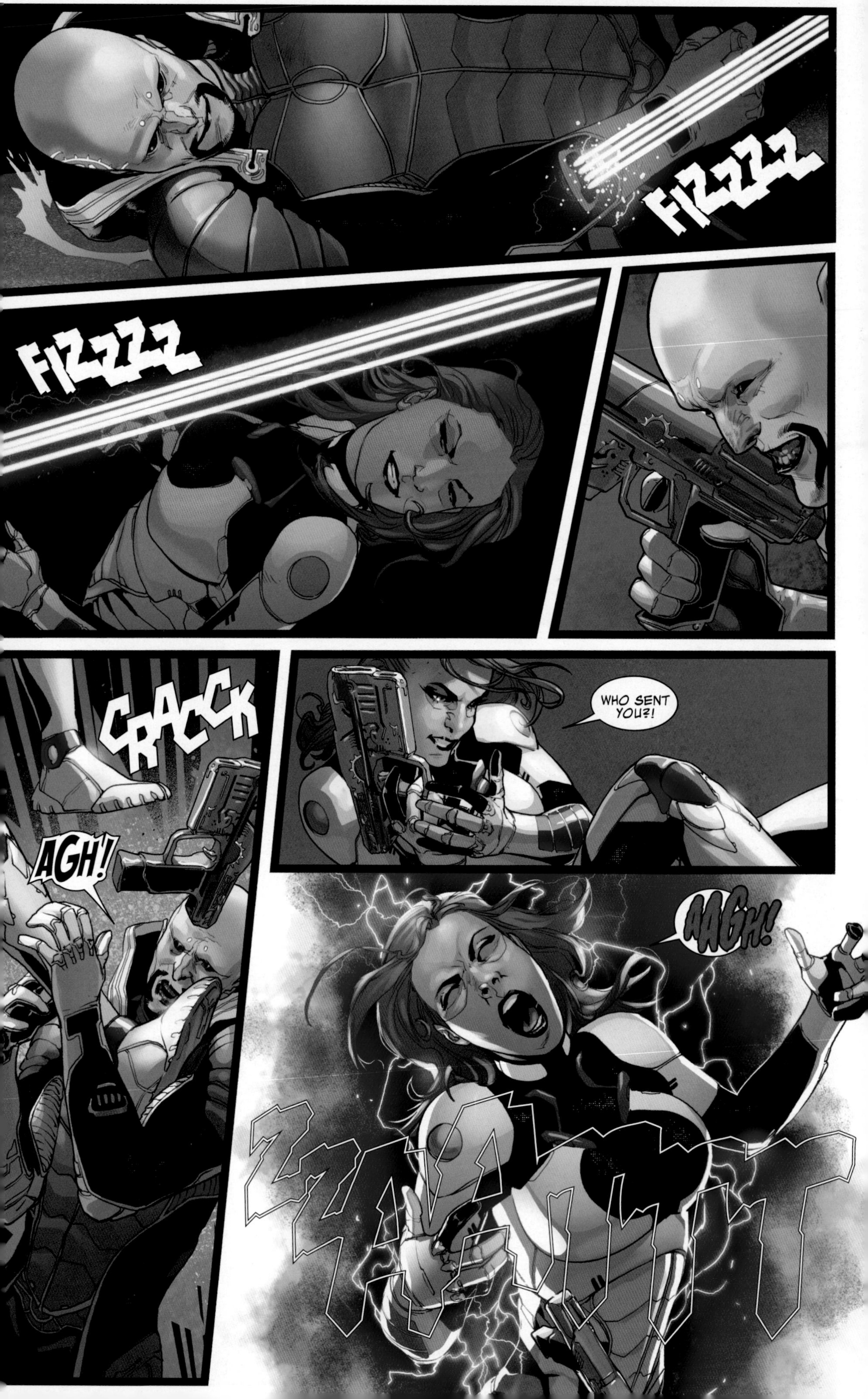
FIZZZZZ
FIZZZZ
CRACCK
WHO SENT YOU?!
AGH!
AAGH!
ZZAAAKT

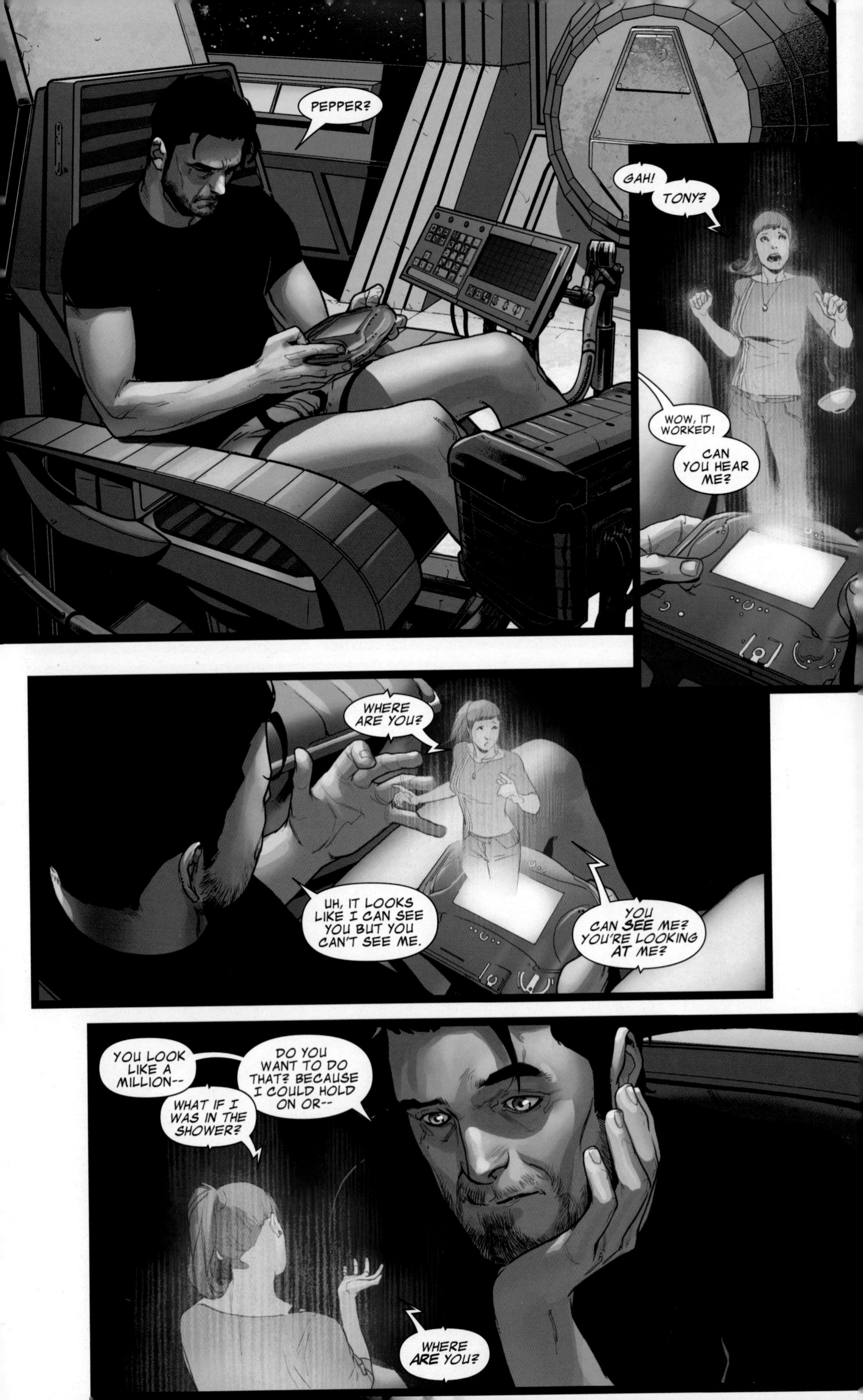
PEPPER?
GAH!
TONY?
WOW, IT WORKED!
CAN YOU HEAR ME?
WHERE ARE YOU?
UH, IT LOOKS LIKE I CAN SEE YOU BUT YOU CAN'T SEE ME.
YOU CAN SEE ME? YOU'RE LOOKING AT ME?
YOU LOOK LIKE A MILLION--
DO YOU WANT TO DO THAT? BECAUSE I COULD HOLD ON OR--
WHAT IF I WAS IN THE SHOWER?
WHERE ARE YOU?

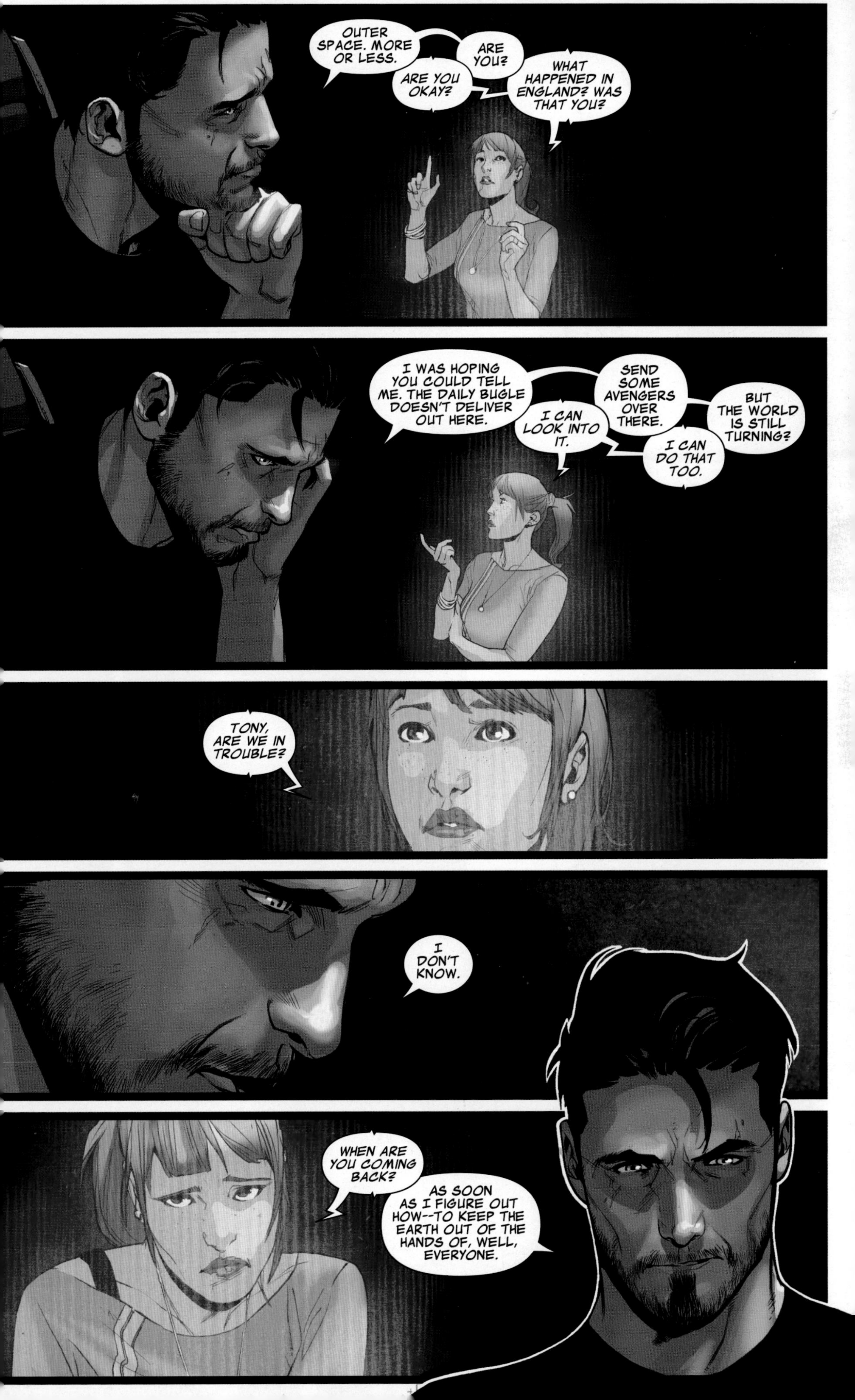
OUTER SPACE. MORE OR LESS.
ARE YOU OKAY?
ARE YOU?
WHAT HAPPENED IN ENGLAND? WAS THAT YOU?
I WAS HOPING YOU COULD TELL ME. THE DAILY BUGLE DOESN'T DELIVER OUT HERE.
I CAN LOOK INTO IT.
SEND SOME AVENGERS OVER THERE.
I CAN DO THAT TOO.
BUT THE WORLD IS STILL TURNING?
TONY, ARE WE IN TROUBLE?
I DON'T KNOW.
WHEN ARE YOU COMING BACK?
AS SOON AS I FIGURE OUT HOW--TO KEEP THE EARTH OUT OF THE HANDS OF, WELL, EVERYONE.

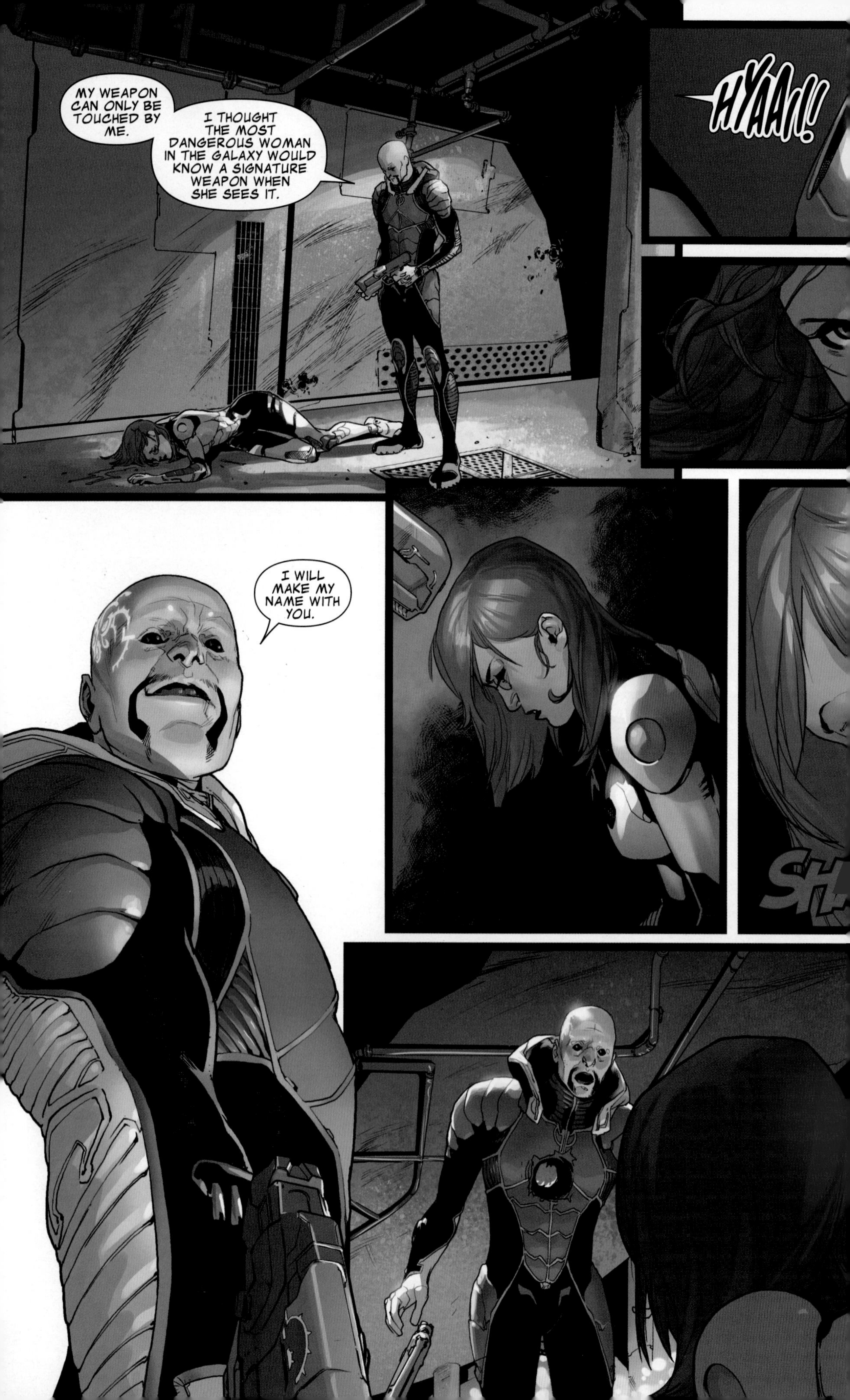
MY WEAPON CAN ONLY BE TOUCHED BY ME.
I THOUGHT THE MOST DANGEROUS WOMAN IN THE GALAXY WOULD KNOW A SIGNATURE WEAPON WHEN SHE SEES IT.
HYAAA!!
I WILL MAKE MY NAME WITH YOU.

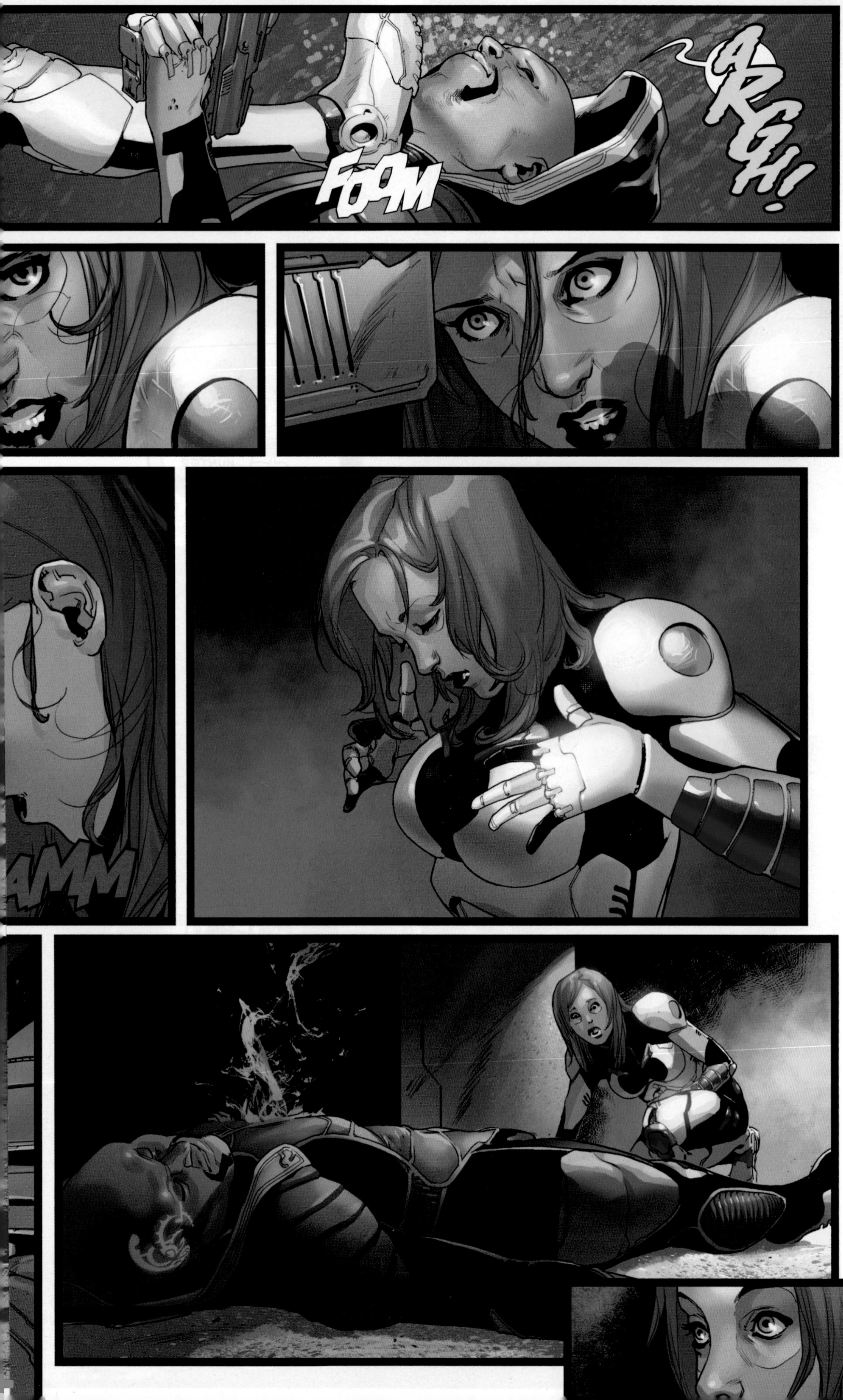

FOOM
ARGH!
AMM

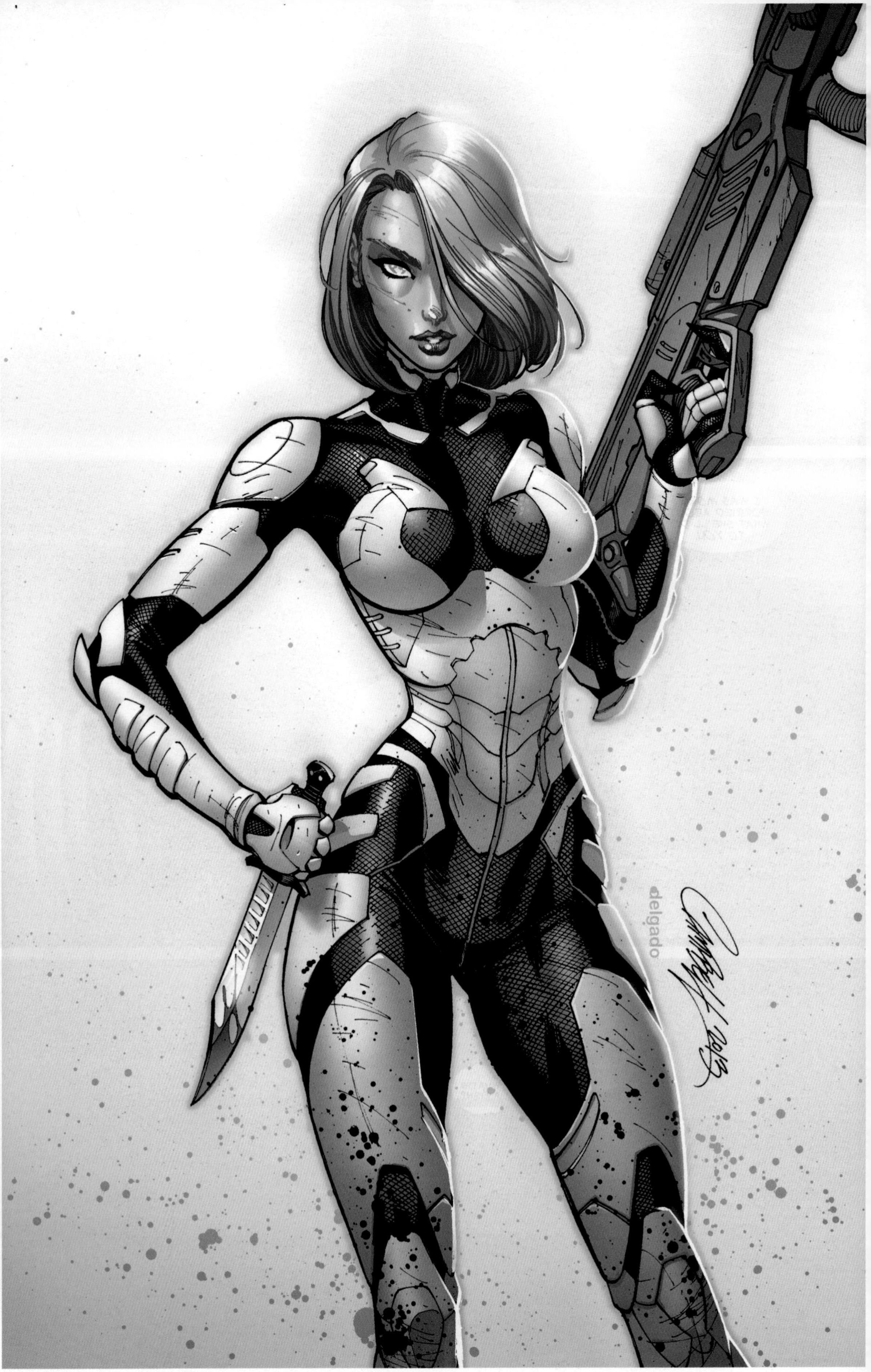
delgado

#4 VARIANT BY J. SCOTT CAMPBELL & EDGAR DELGADO

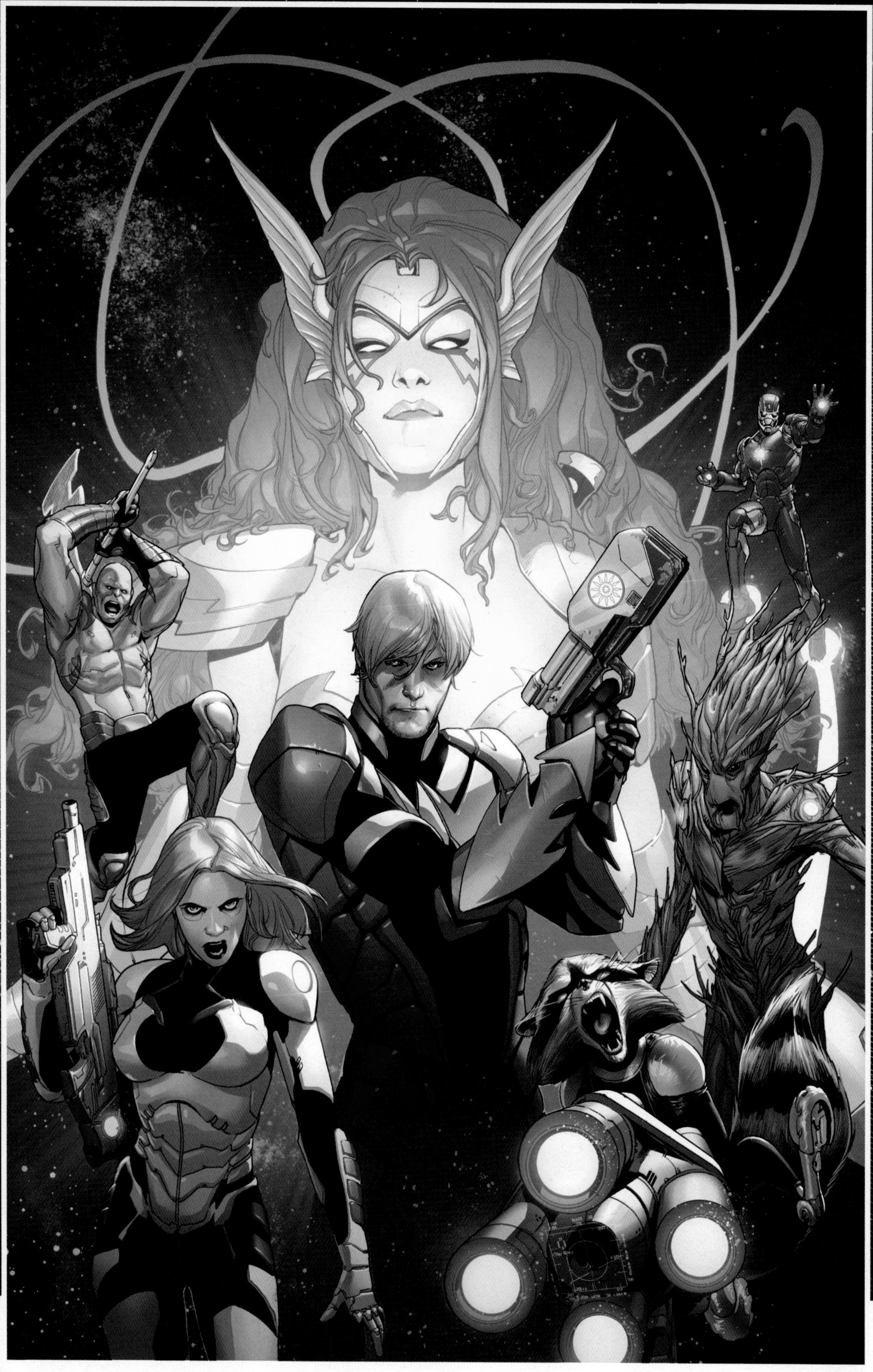

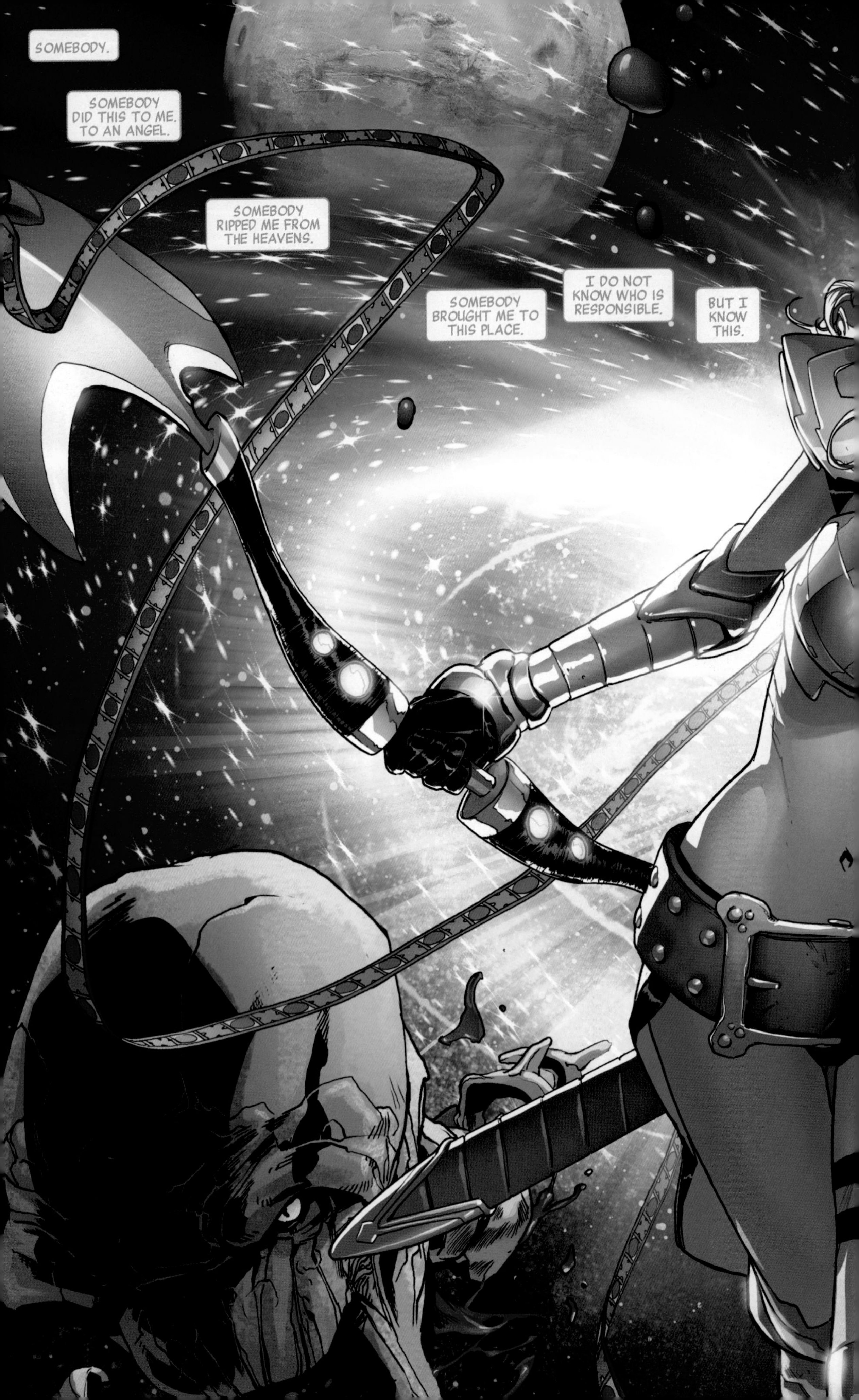
SOMEBODY.
SOMEBODY DID THIS TO ME. TO AN ANGEL.
SOMEBODY RIPPED ME FROM THE HEAVENS.
SOMEBODY BROUGHT ME TO THIS PLACE.
I DO NOT KNOW WHO IS RESPONSIBLE.
BUT I KNOW THIS.

WHOEVER YOU ARE...
WHATEVER YOU ARE...
I AM
ANGELA
I AM A HUNTER OF THE HEAVENS. AND I WANT TWO THINGS.
I WANT ANSWERS.
AND I WANT YOUR HEAD ON MY WALL.

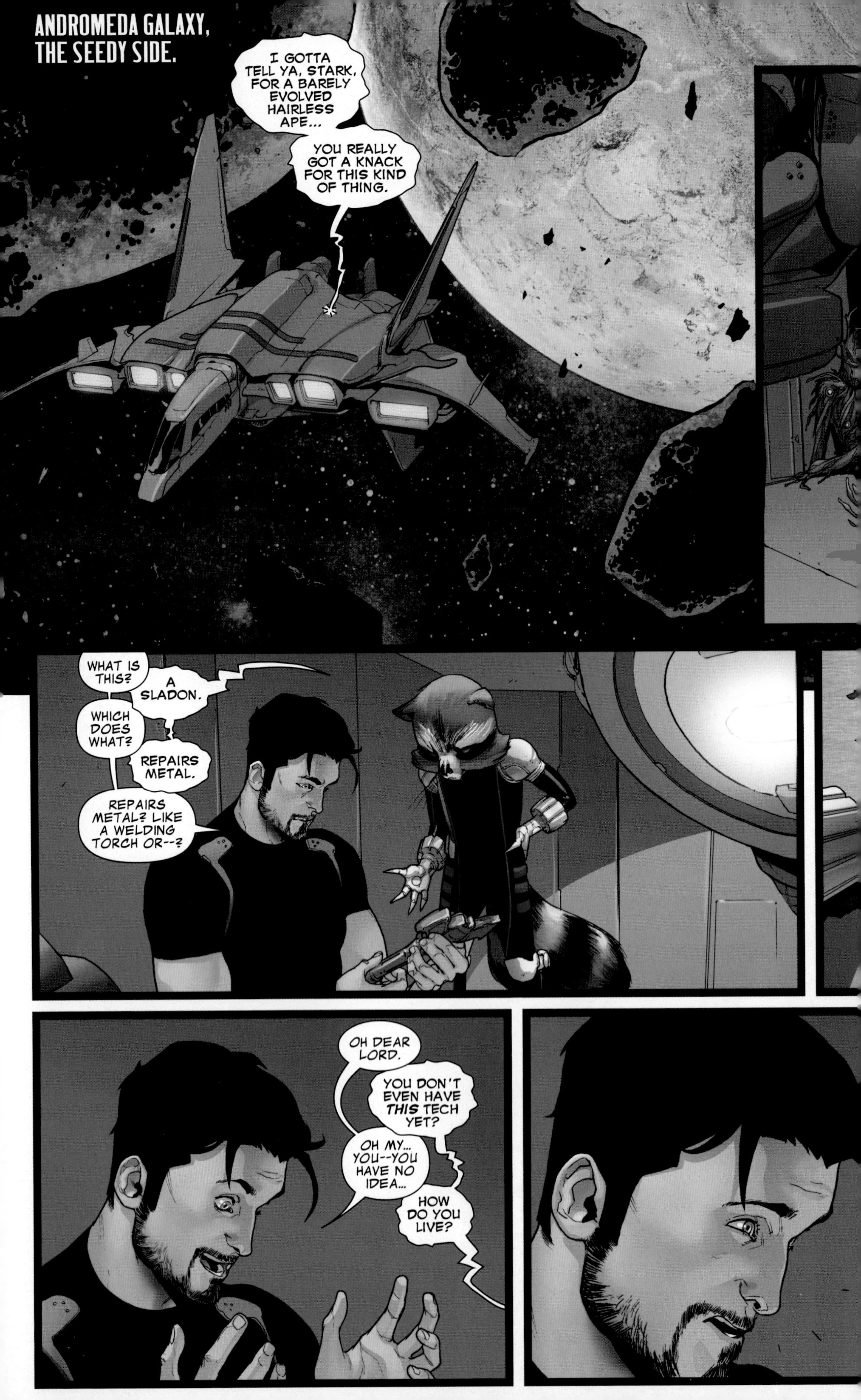
ANDROMEDA GALAXY, THE SEEDY SIDE.
I GOTTA TELL YA, STARK, FOR A BARELY EVOLVED HAIRLESS APE...
YOU REALLY GOT A KNACK FOR THIS KIND OF THING.
WHAT IS THIS?
A SLADON.
WHICH DOES WHAT?
REPAIRS METAL.
REPAIRS METAL? LIKE A WELDING TORCH OR--?
OH DEAR LORD.
YOU DON'T EVEN HAVE THIS TECH YET?
OH MY... YOU--YOU HAVE NO IDEA...
HOW DO YOU LIVE?

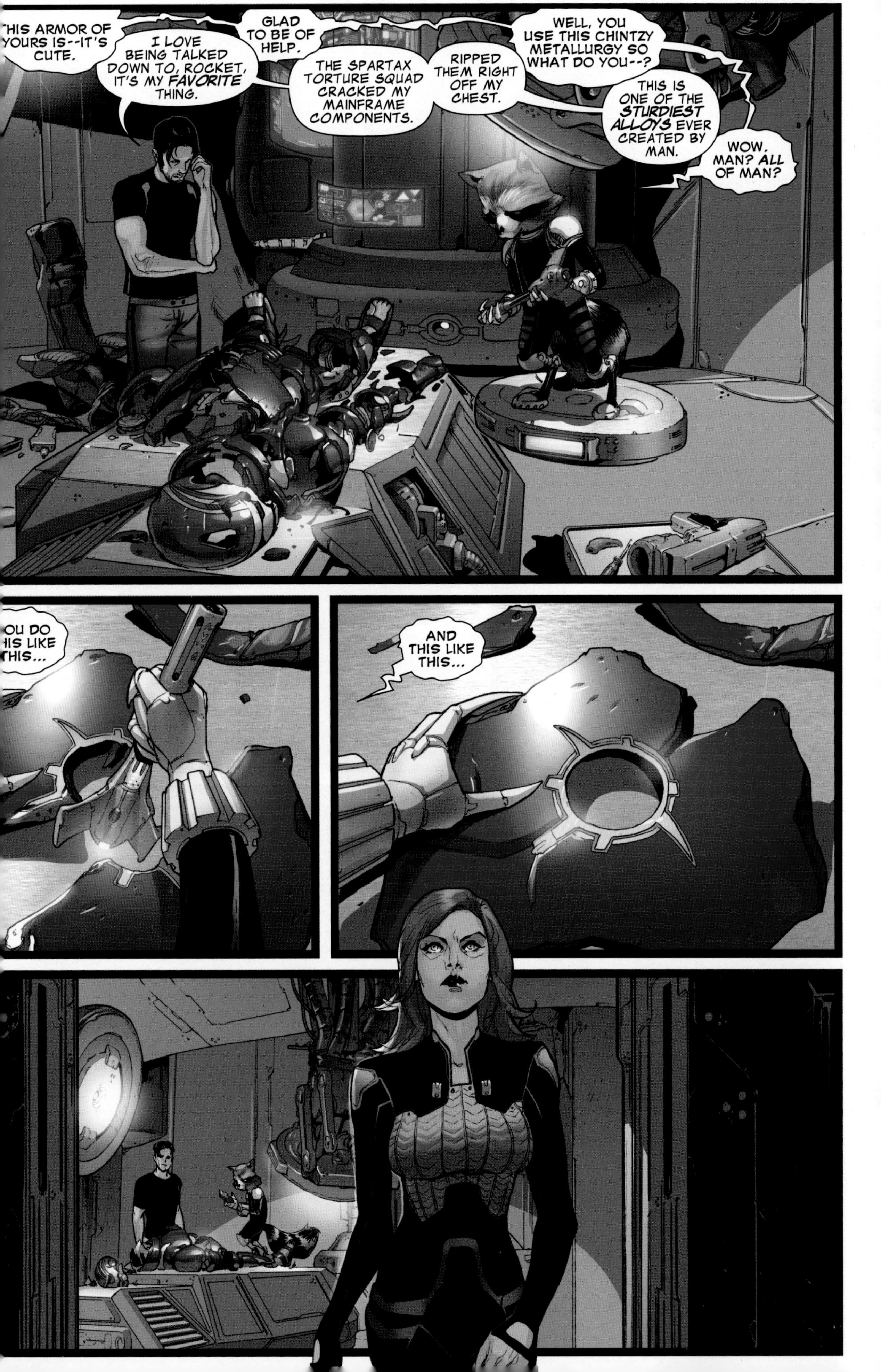
THIS ARMOR OF YOURS IS--IT'S CUTE.
I LOVE BEING TALKED DOWN TO, ROCKET, IT'S MY FAVORITE THING.
GLAD TO BE OF HELP.
THE SPARTAX TORTURE SQUAD CRACKED MY MAINFRAME COMPONENTS.
RIPPED THEM RIGHT OFF MY CHEST.
WELL, YOU USE THIS CHINTZY METALLURGY SO WHAT DO YOU--?
THIS IS ONE OF THE STURDIEST ALLOYS EVER CREATED BY MAN.
WOW. MAN? ALL OF MAN?
OU DO HIS LIKE THIS...
AND THIS LIKE THIS...

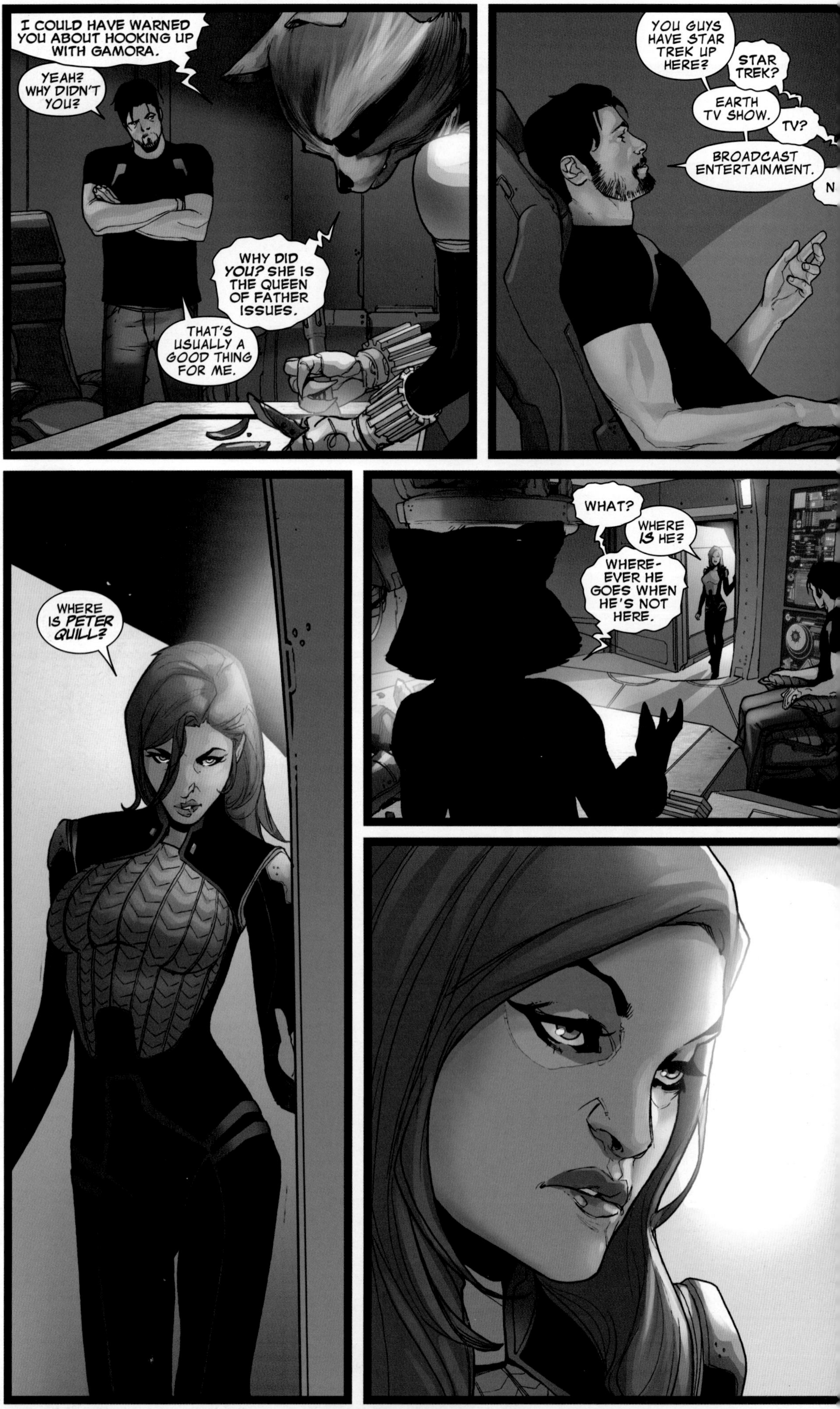
I COULD HAVE WARNED YOU ABOUT HOOKING UP WITH GAMORA.
YEAH? WHY DIDN'T YOU?
WHY DID *YOU?* SHE IS THE QUEEN OF FATHER ISSUES.
THAT'S USUALLY A GOOD THING FOR ME.
YOU GUYS HAVE STAR TREK UP HERE?
STAR TREK?
EARTH TV SHOW.
TV?
BROADCAST ENTERTAINMENT.
WHERE IS *PETER QUILL?*
WHAT?
WHERE *IS* HE?
WHERE-EVER HE GOES WHEN HE'S NOT HERE.

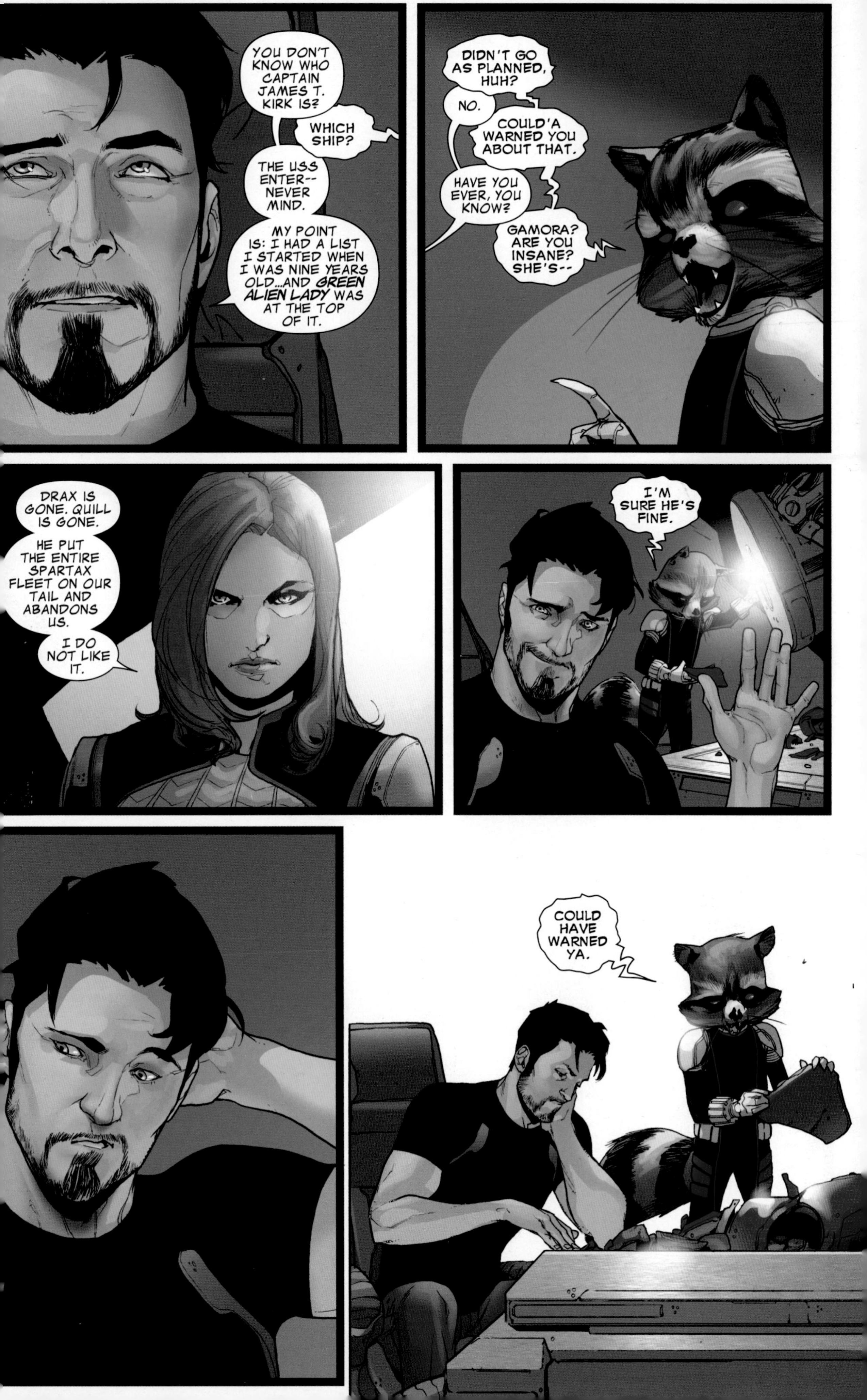
YOU DON'T KNOW WHO CAPTAIN JAMES T. KIRK IS?
WHICH SHIP?
THE USS ENTER-- NEVER MIND.
MY POINT IS: I HAD A LIST I STARTED WHEN I WAS NINE YEARS OLD...AND GREEN ALIEN LADY WAS AT THE TOP OF IT.
DIDN'T GO AS PLANNED, HUH?
NO.
COULD'A WARNED YOU ABOUT THAT.
HAVE YOU EVER, YOU KNOW?
GAMORA? ARE YOU INSANE? SHE'S--
DRAX IS GONE. QUILL IS GONE.
HE PUT THE ENTIRE SPARTAX FLEET ON OUR TAIL AND ABANDONS US.
I DO NOT LIKE IT.
I'M SURE HE'S FINE.
COULD HAVE WARNED YA.

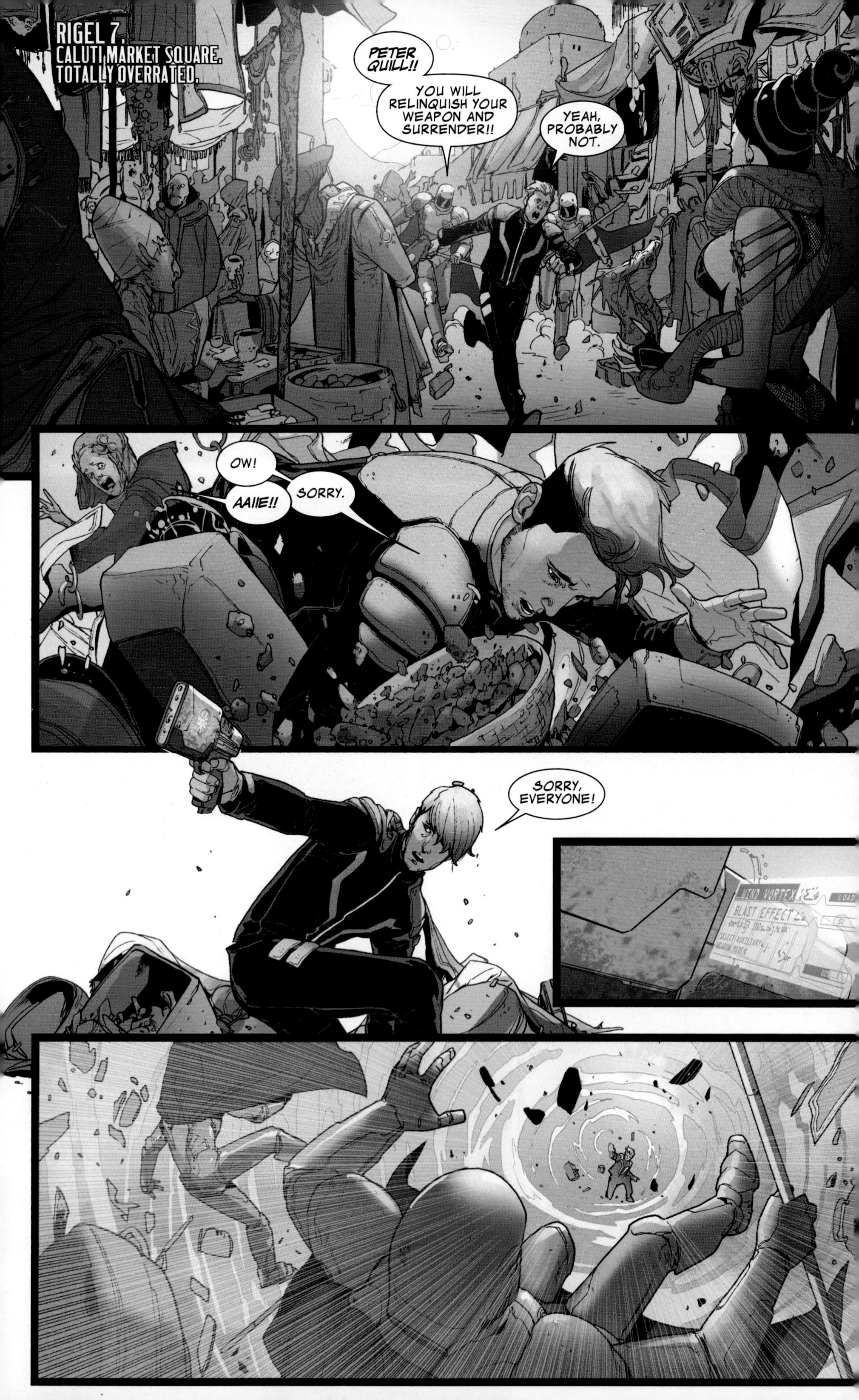
RIGEL 7.
CALUTI MARKET SQUARE.
TOTALLY OVERRATED.
PETER QUILL!!
YOU WILL RELINQUISH YOUR WEAPON AND SURRENDER!!
YEAH, PROBABLY NOT.
OW!
AAIIE!!
SORRY.
SORRY, EVERYONE!
WIND VORTEX
LOAD
BLAST EFFECT
SELECT AUXILIARY WEAPON MODE

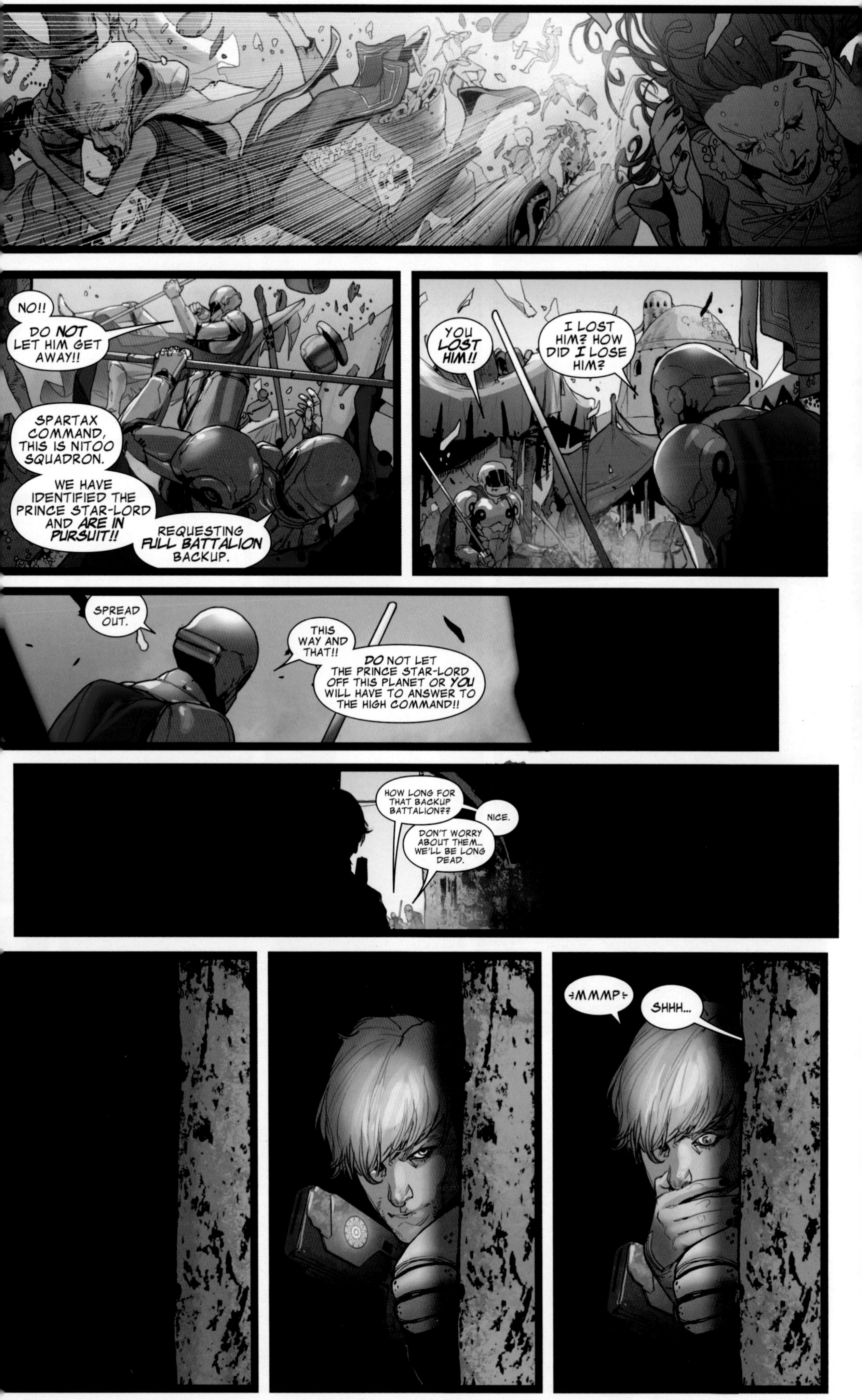
NO!!
DO NOT LET HIM GET AWAY!!
SPARTAX COMMAND, THIS IS NITOO SQUADRON.
WE HAVE IDENTIFIED THE PRINCE STAR-LORD AND ARE IN PURSUIT!!
REQUESTING FULL BATTALION BACKUP.
YOU LOST HIM!!
I LOST HIM? HOW DID I LOSE HIM?
SPREAD OUT.
THIS WAY AND THAT!!
DO NOT LET THE PRINCE STAR-LORD OFF THIS PLANET OR YOU WILL HAVE TO ANSWER TO THE HIGH COMMAND!!
HOW LONG FOR THAT BACKUP BATTALION??
NICE.
DON'T WORRY ABOUT THEM... WE'LL BE LONG DEAD.
MMMP
SHHH...

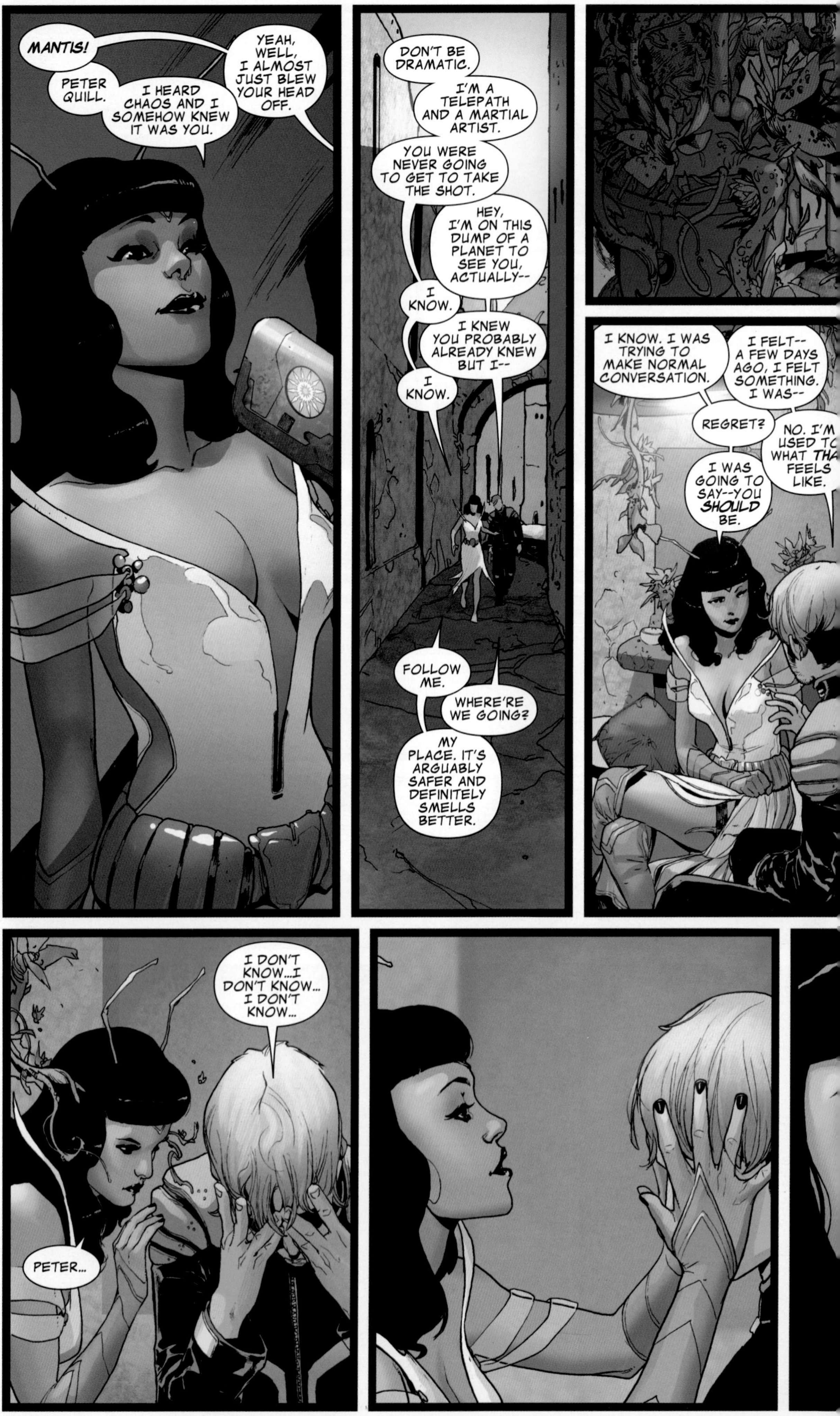
MANTIS!
PETER QUILL.
I HEARD CHAOS AND I SOMEHOW KNEW IT WAS YOU.
YEAH, WELL, I ALMOST JUST BLEW YOUR HEAD OFF.
DON'T BE DRAMATIC.
I'M A TELEPATH AND A MARTIAL ARTIST.
YOU WERE NEVER GOING TO GET TO TAKE THE SHOT.
HEY, I'M ON THIS DUMP OF A PLANET TO SEE YOU, ACTUALLY--
I KNOW.
I KNEW YOU PROBABLY ALREADY KNEW BUT I--
I KNOW.
FOLLOW ME.
WHERE'RE WE GOING?
MY PLACE. IT'S ARGUABLY SAFER AND DEFINITELY SMELLS BETTER.
I KNOW. I WAS TRYING TO MAKE NORMAL CONVERSATION.
I FELT-- A FEW DAYS AGO, I FELT SOMETHING. I WAS--
REGRET?
NO. I'M USED TO WHAT THA FEELS LIKE.
I WAS GOING TO SAY--YOU SHOULD BE.
I DON'T KNOW...I DON'T KNOW... I DON'T KNOW...
PETER...

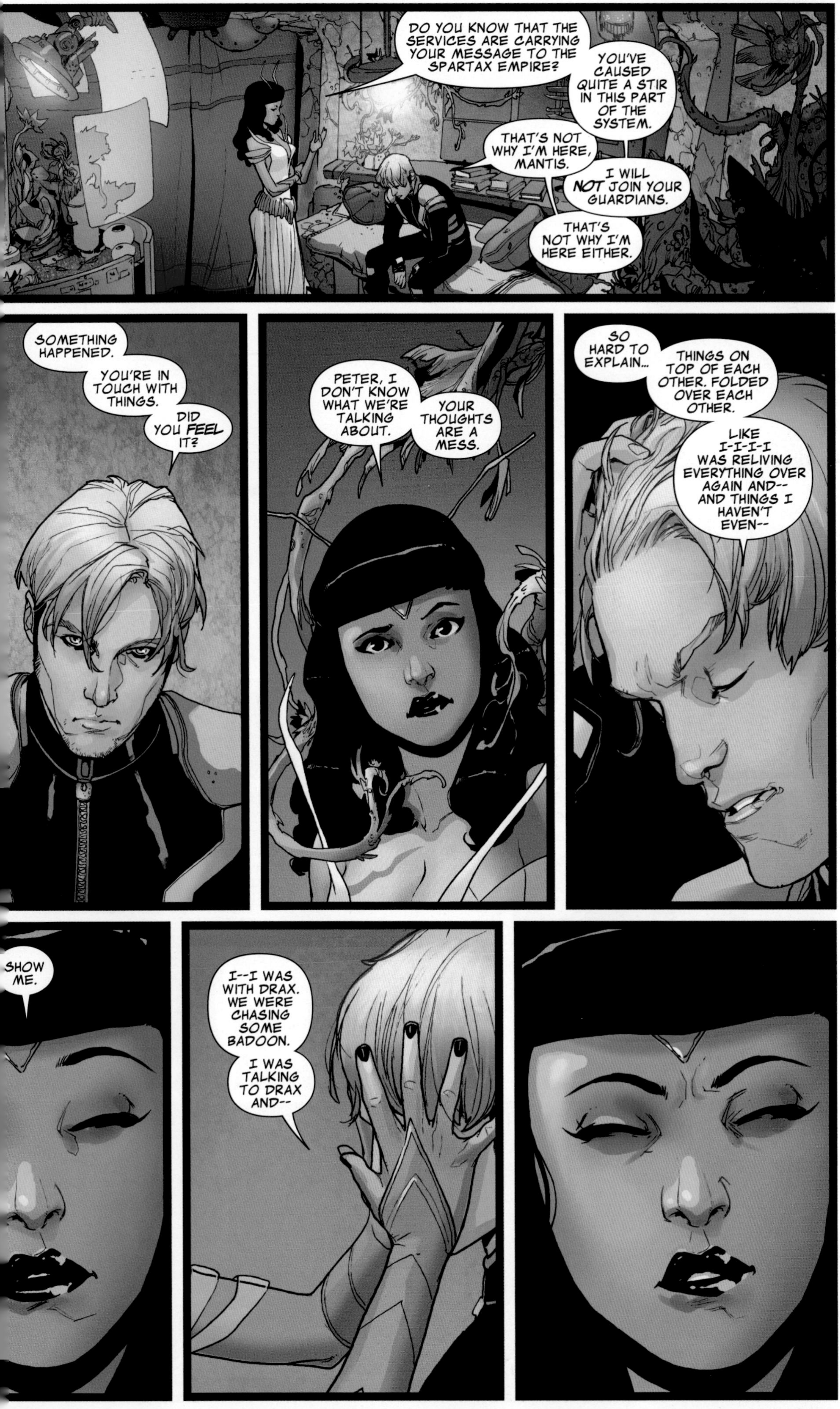
DO YOU KNOW THAT THE SERVICES ARE CARRYING YOUR MESSAGE TO THE SPARTAX EMPIRE?
YOU'VE CAUSED QUITE A STIR IN THIS PART OF THE SYSTEM.
THAT'S NOT WHY I'M HERE, MANTIS.
I WILL NOT JOIN YOUR GUARDIANS.
THAT'S NOT WHY I'M HERE EITHER.
SOMETHING HAPPENED.
YOU'RE IN TOUCH WITH THINGS.
DID YOU FEEL IT?
PETER, I DON'T KNOW WHAT WE'RE TALKING ABOUT.
YOUR THOUGHTS ARE A MESS.
SO HARD TO EXPLAIN...
THINGS ON TOP OF EACH OTHER. FOLDED OVER EACH OTHER.
LIKE I-I-I-I WAS RELIVING EVERYTHING OVER AGAIN AND-- AND THINGS I HAVEN'T EVEN--
SHOW ME.
I--I WAS WITH DRAX. WE WERE CHASING SOME BADOON.
I WAS TALKING TO DRAX AND--

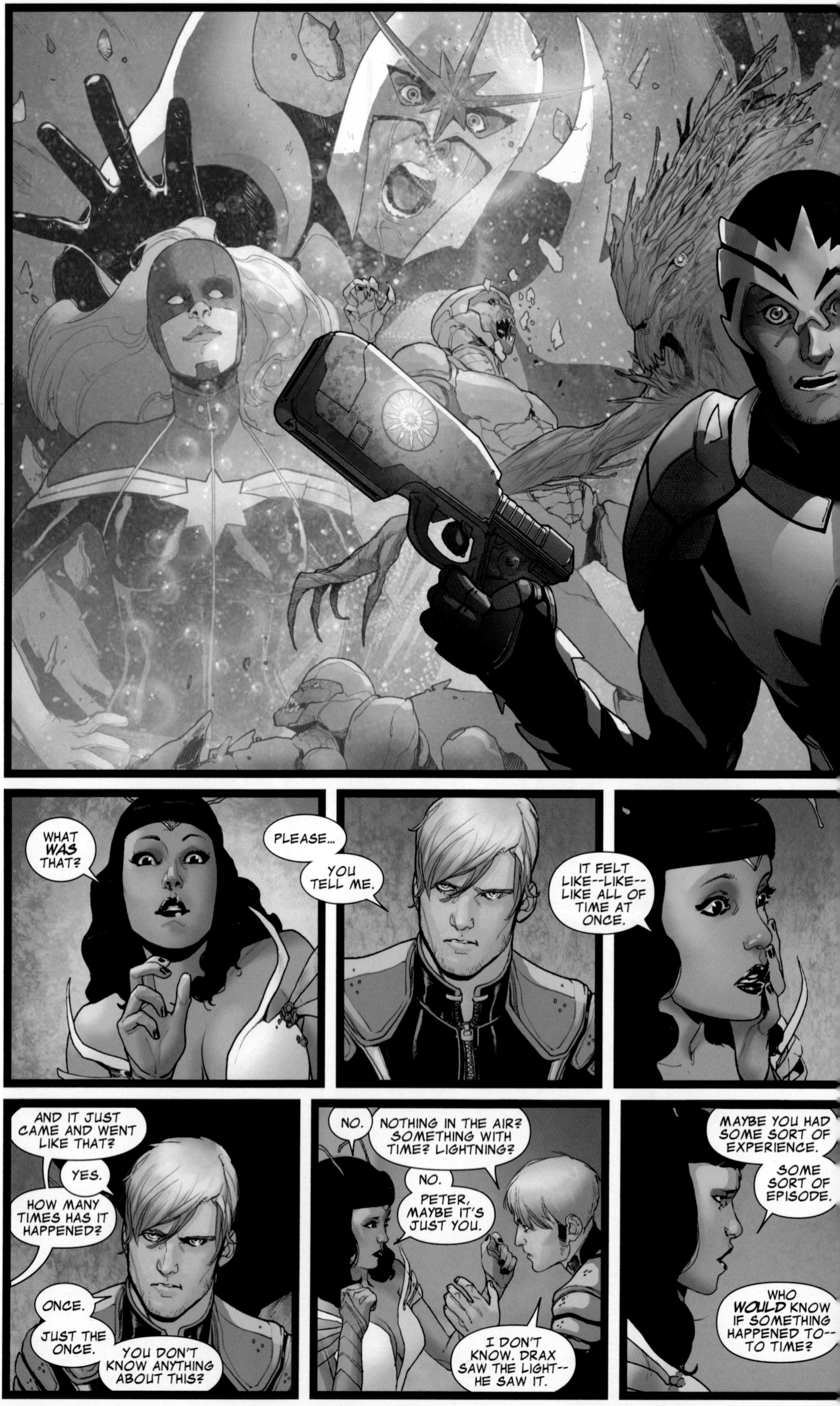
WHAT WAS THAT?
PLEASE...
YOU TELL ME.
IT FELT LIKE--LIKE--LIKE ALL OF TIME AT ONCE.
AND IT JUST CAME AND WENT LIKE THAT?
YES.
HOW MANY TIMES HAS IT HAPPENED?
ONCE.
JUST THE ONCE.
YOU DON'T KNOW ANYTHING ABOUT THIS?
NO.
NOTHING IN THE AIR? SOMETHING WITH TIME? LIGHTNING?
NO.
PETER, MAYBE IT'S JUST YOU.
I DON'T KNOW. DRAX SAW THE LIGHT--HE SAW IT.
MAYBE YOU HAD SOME SORT OF EXPERIENCE.
SOME SORT OF EPISODE.
WHO WOULD KNOW IF SOMETHING HAPPENED TO--TO TIME?

ALL TIME-- YES.

WHEN--**WHEN** DID THIS HAPPEN?

JUST, JUST A COUPLE OF DAYS AGO.

THERE WAS THIS--LIKE THIS LIGHTNING AND THEN--

THAT WAS THE ODDEST THING.

ODD??!!

IT'S FREAKING ME OUT.

AND--AND IT DIDN'T HAPPEN TO ANYONE *BUT* ME!!

DRAX SAW THE--THE LIGHTNING BUT-- HE'S FINE.

WELL, FOR DRAX HE'S FINE.

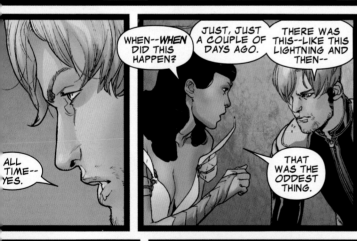

IF THE ACE-TIME NTINUUM R--OR IF METHING AS OFF.

WHO CAN I...?

OH.

IF YOU WANT TO OPEN THAT DOOR.

IF IT'S BOTHERING YOU *THAT* MUCH.

YOU KNOW EXACTLY WHO WOULD KNOW.

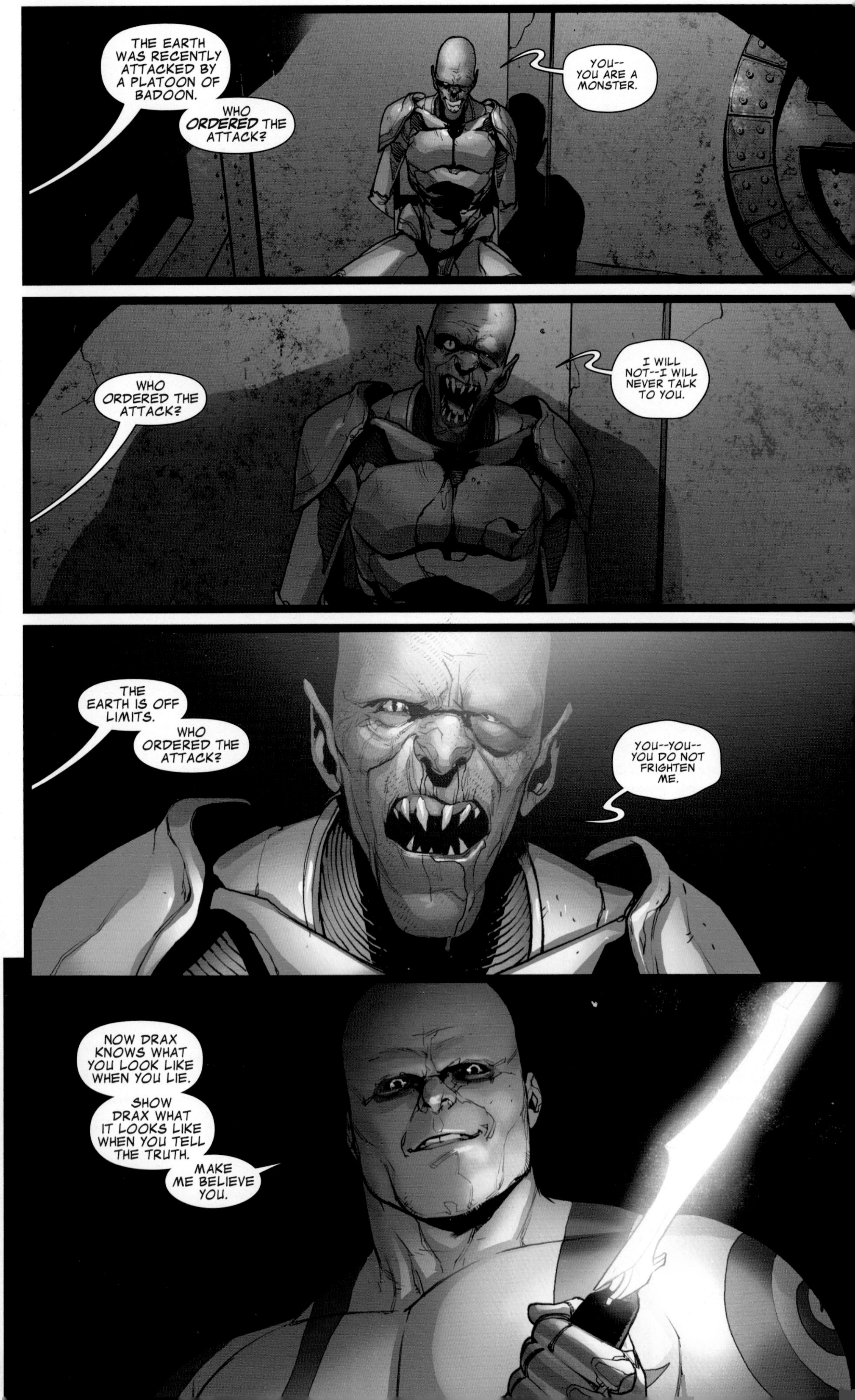
THE EARTH WAS RECENTLY ATTACKED BY A PLATOON OF BADOON.
WHO ORDERED THE ATTACK?
YOU-- YOU ARE A MONSTER.
WHO ORDERED THE ATTACK?
I WILL NOT--I WILL NEVER TALK TO YOU.
THE EARTH IS OFF LIMITS.
WHO ORDERED THE ATTACK?
YOU--YOU-- YOU DO NOT FRIGHTEN ME.
NOW DRAX KNOWS WHAT YOU LOOK LIKE WHEN YOU LIE.
SHOW DRAX WHAT IT LOOKS LIKE WHEN YOU TELL THE TRUTH.
MAKE ME BELIEVE YOU.

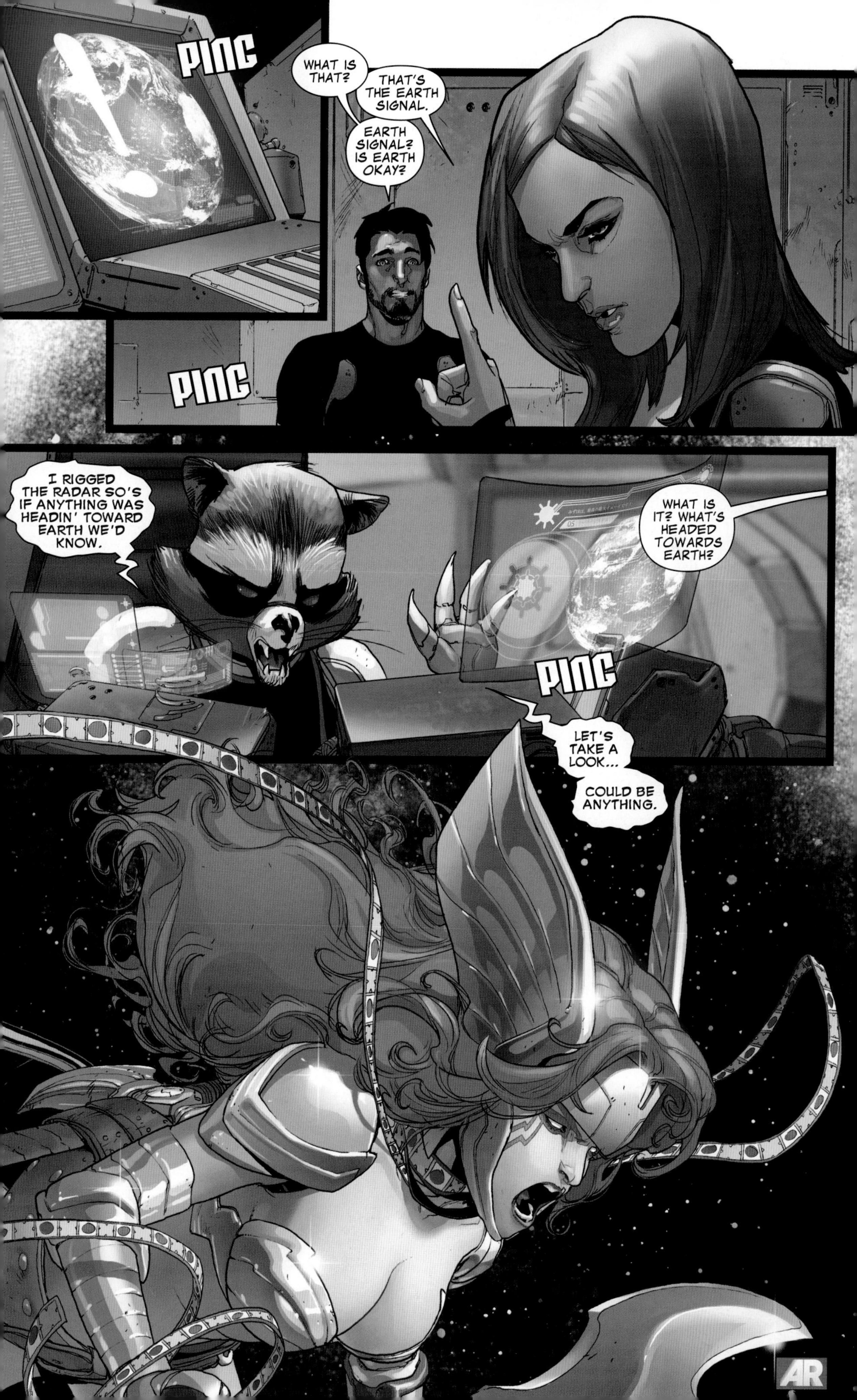
PING
WHAT IS THAT?
THAT'S THE EARTH SIGNAL.
EARTH SIGNAL? IS EARTH OKAY?
PING
I RIGGED THE RADAR SO'S IF ANYTHING WAS HEADIN' TOWARD EARTH WE'D KNOW.
WHAT IS IT? WHAT'S HEADED TOWARDS EARTH?
PING
LET'S TAKE A LOOK...
COULD BE ANYTHING.
AR

GIVE ME THAT LONG RANGE COMMUNICATION THINGY OF YOURS, I'LL CALL THE AVENGERS.
WHAT THE HELL ARE THEY GONNA DO?
WE GOT THIS.
GOT THIS? WE'RE HALF A GALAXY AWAY!
YOU'RE FUNNY.
BUCKLE UP, BUTTERCUP.

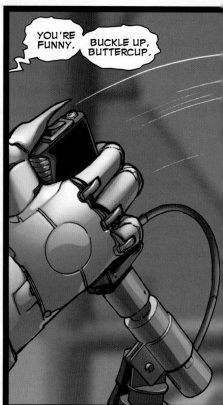

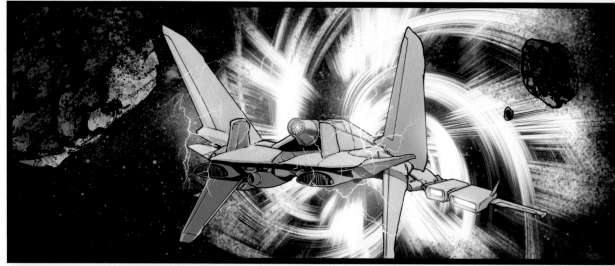

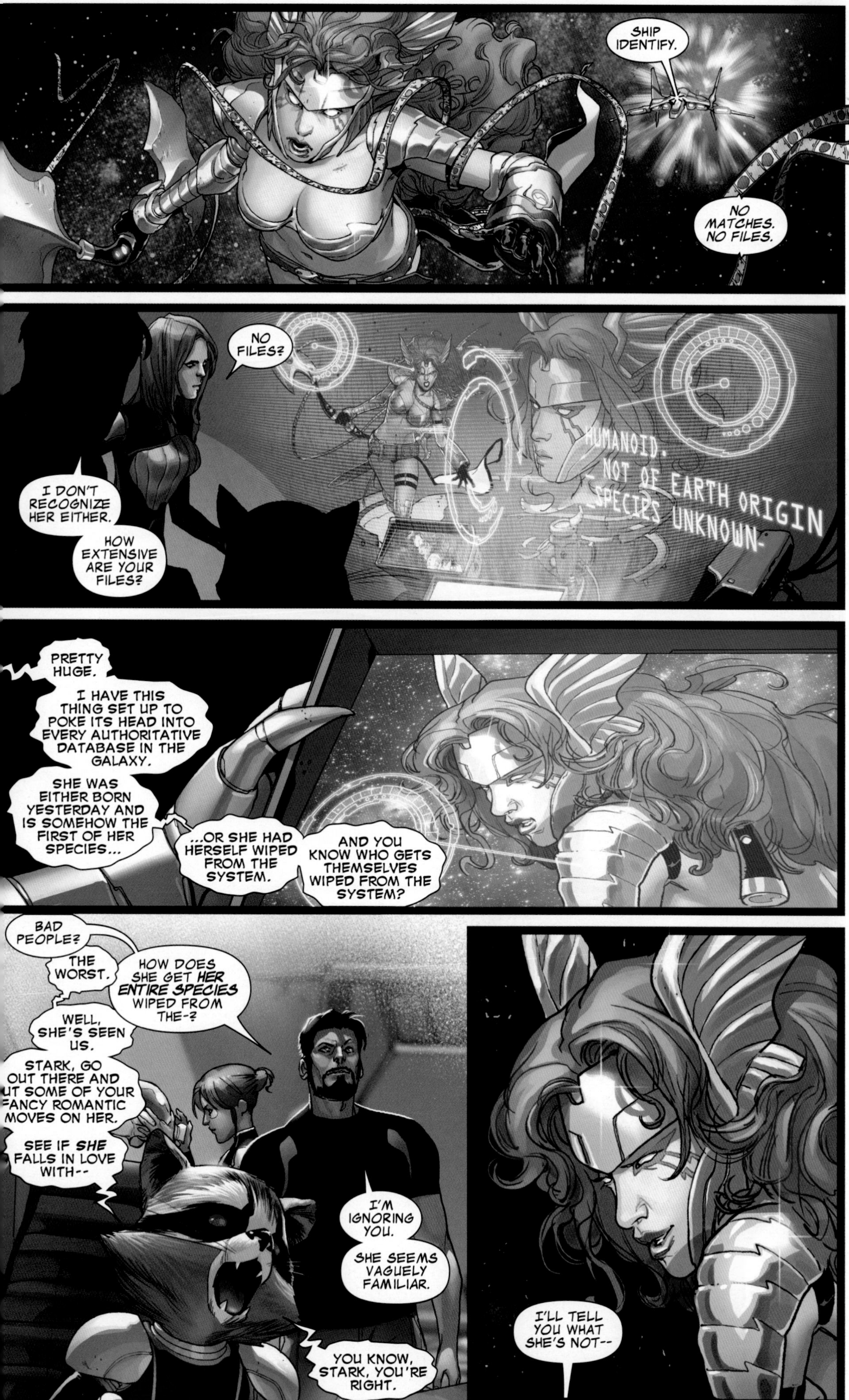
SHIP IDENTIFY.
NO MATCHES. NO FILES.
NO FILES?
HUMANOID.
-NOT OF EARTH ORIGIN
-SPECIES UNKNOWN-
I DON'T RECOGNIZE HER EITHER.
HOW EXTENSIVE ARE YOUR FILES?
PRETTY HUGE.
I HAVE THIS THING SET UP TO POKE ITS HEAD INTO EVERY AUTHORITATIVE DATABASE IN THE GALAXY.
SHE WAS EITHER BORN YESTERDAY AND IS SOMEHOW THE FIRST OF HER SPECIES...
...OR SHE HAD HERSELF WIPED FROM THE SYSTEM.
AND YOU KNOW WHO GETS THEMSELVES WIPED FROM THE SYSTEM?
BAD PEOPLE?
THE WORST.
HOW DOES SHE GET HER ENTIRE SPECIES WIPED FROM THE-?
WELL, SHE'S SEEN US.
STARK, GO OUT THERE AND UT SOME OF YOUR ANCY ROMANTIC MOVES ON HER.
SEE IF SHE FALLS IN LOVE WITH--
I'M IGNORING YOU.
SHE SEEMS VAGUELY FAMILIAR.
YOU KNOW, STARK, YOU'RE RIGHT.
I'LL TELL YOU WHAT SHE'S NOT--

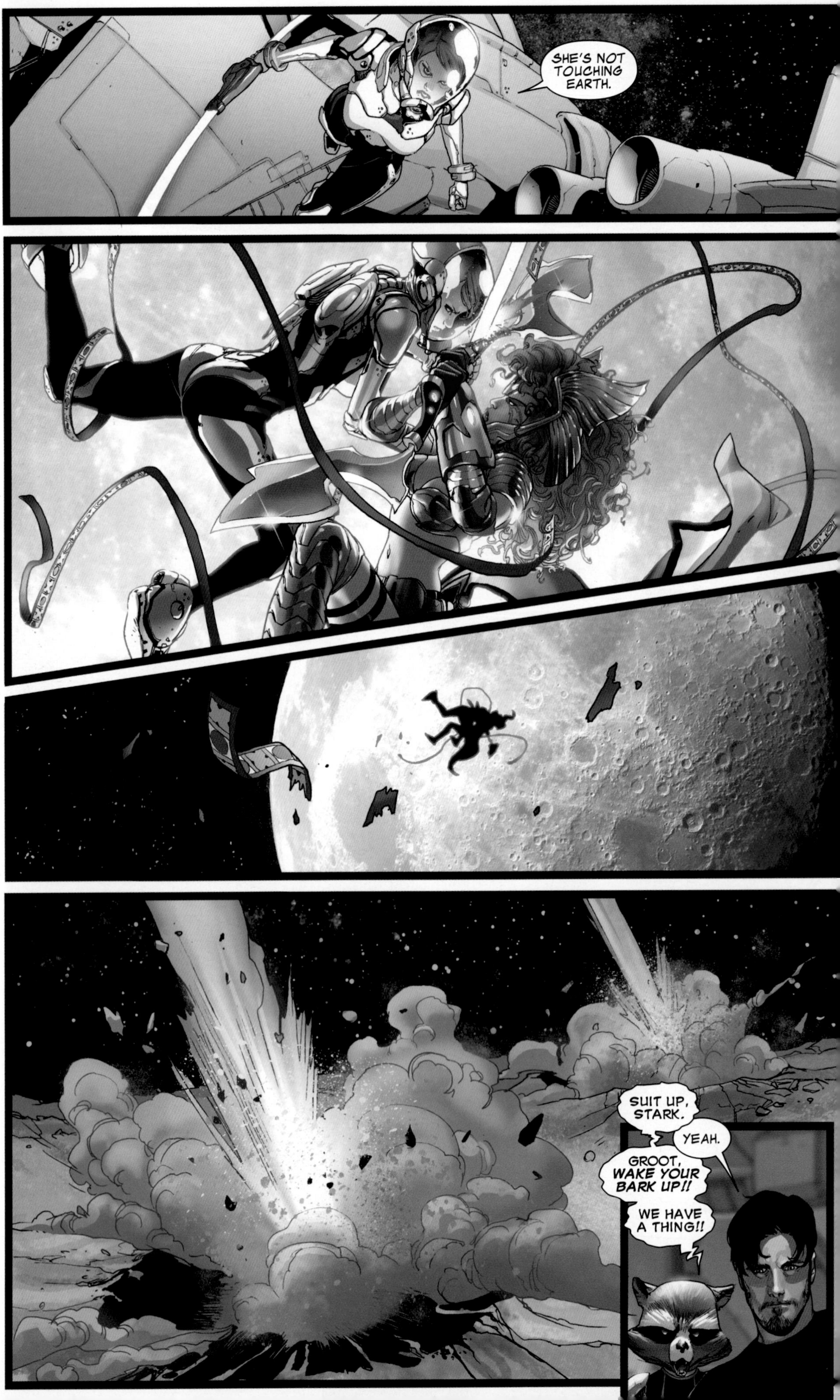
SHE'S NOT TOUCHING EARTH.
SUIT UP, STARK.
YEAH.
GROOT, WAKE YOUR BARK UP!!
WE HAVE A THING!!

THIS *IS* A SURPRISE, PETER QUILL.

YEAH, WELL, YOU KNOW YOU'RE ALWAYS FIRST ON MY LIST WHEN I NEED HELP...

I WONDER IF ANYONE ACTUALLY FINDS YOU AS HUMOROUS AS YOU THINK YOU ARE.

YEAH, I SUDDENLY REALIZE I SHOULDN'T HAVE COME HERE.

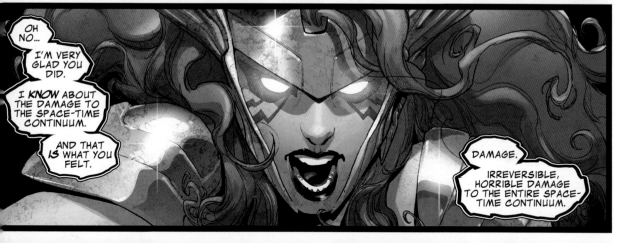

OH NO...

I'M VERY GLAD YOU DID.

I *KNOW* ABOUT THE DAMAGE TO THE SPACE-TIME CONTINUUM.

AND THAT *IS* WHAT YOU FELT.

DAMAGE.

IRREVERSIBLE, HORRIBLE DAMAGE TO THE ENTIRE SPACE-TIME CONTINUUM.

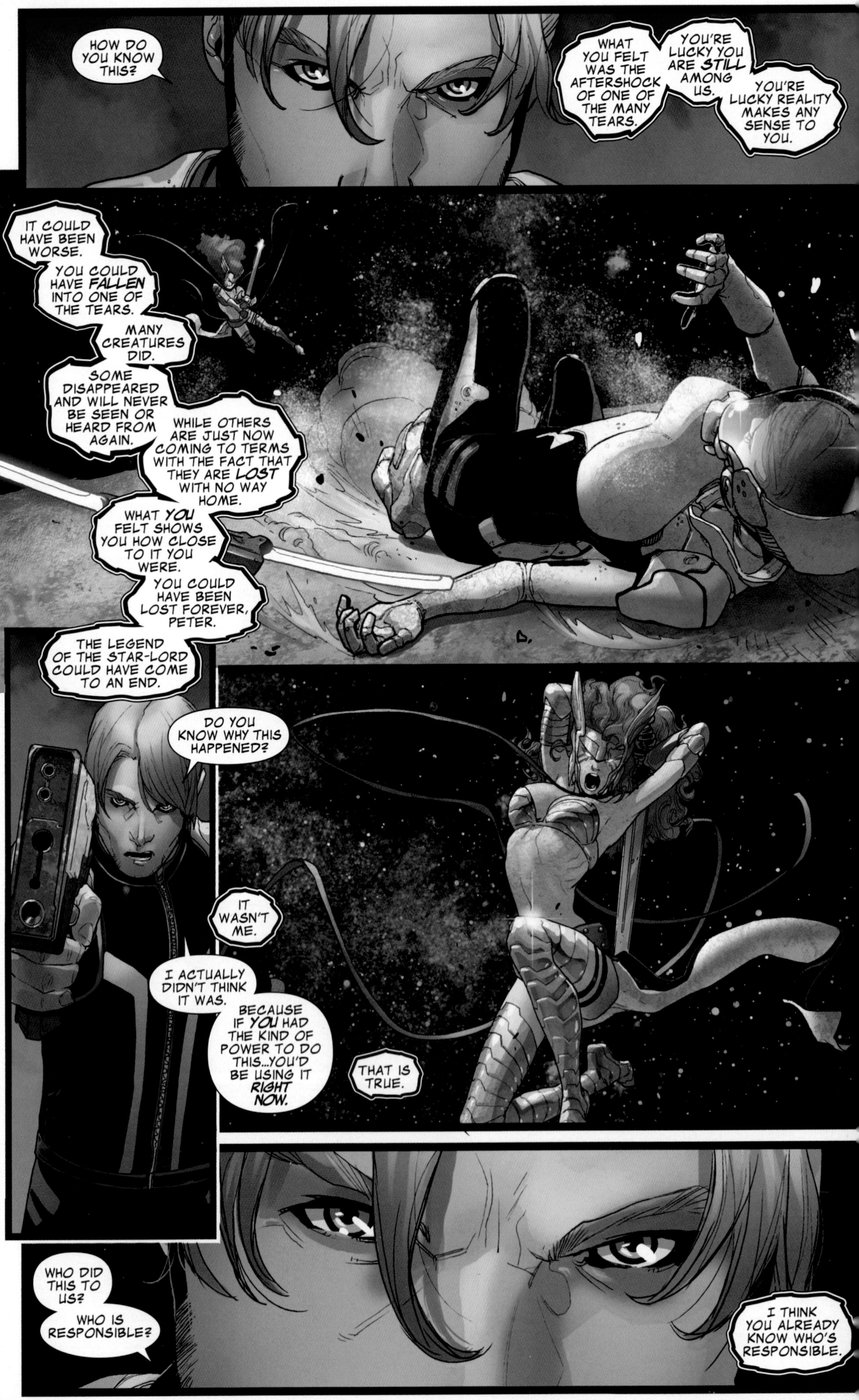
HOW DO YOU KNOW THIS?
WHAT YOU FELT WAS THE AFTERSHOCK OF ONE OF THE MANY TEARS.
YOU'RE LUCKY YOU ARE STILL AMONG US.
YOU'RE LUCKY REALITY MAKES ANY SENSE TO YOU.
IT COULD HAVE BEEN WORSE.
YOU COULD HAVE FALLEN INTO ONE OF THE TEARS.
MANY CREATURES DID.
SOME DISAPPEARED AND WILL NEVER BE SEEN OR HEARD FROM AGAIN.
WHILE OTHERS ARE JUST NOW COMING TO TERMS WITH THE FACT THAT THEY ARE LOST WITH NO WAY HOME.
WHAT YOU FELT SHOWS YOU HOW CLOSE TO IT YOU WERE.
YOU COULD HAVE BEEN LOST FOREVER, PETER.
THE LEGEND OF THE STAR-LORD COULD HAVE COME TO AN END.
DO YOU KNOW WHY THIS HAPPENED?
IT WASN'T ME.
I ACTUALLY DIDN'T THINK IT WAS.
BECAUSE IF YOU HAD THE KIND OF POWER TO DO THIS...YOU'D BE USING IT RIGHT NOW.
THAT IS TRUE.
WHO DID THIS TO US?
WHO IS RESPONSIBLE?
I THINK YOU ALREADY KNOW WHO'S RESPONSIBLE.

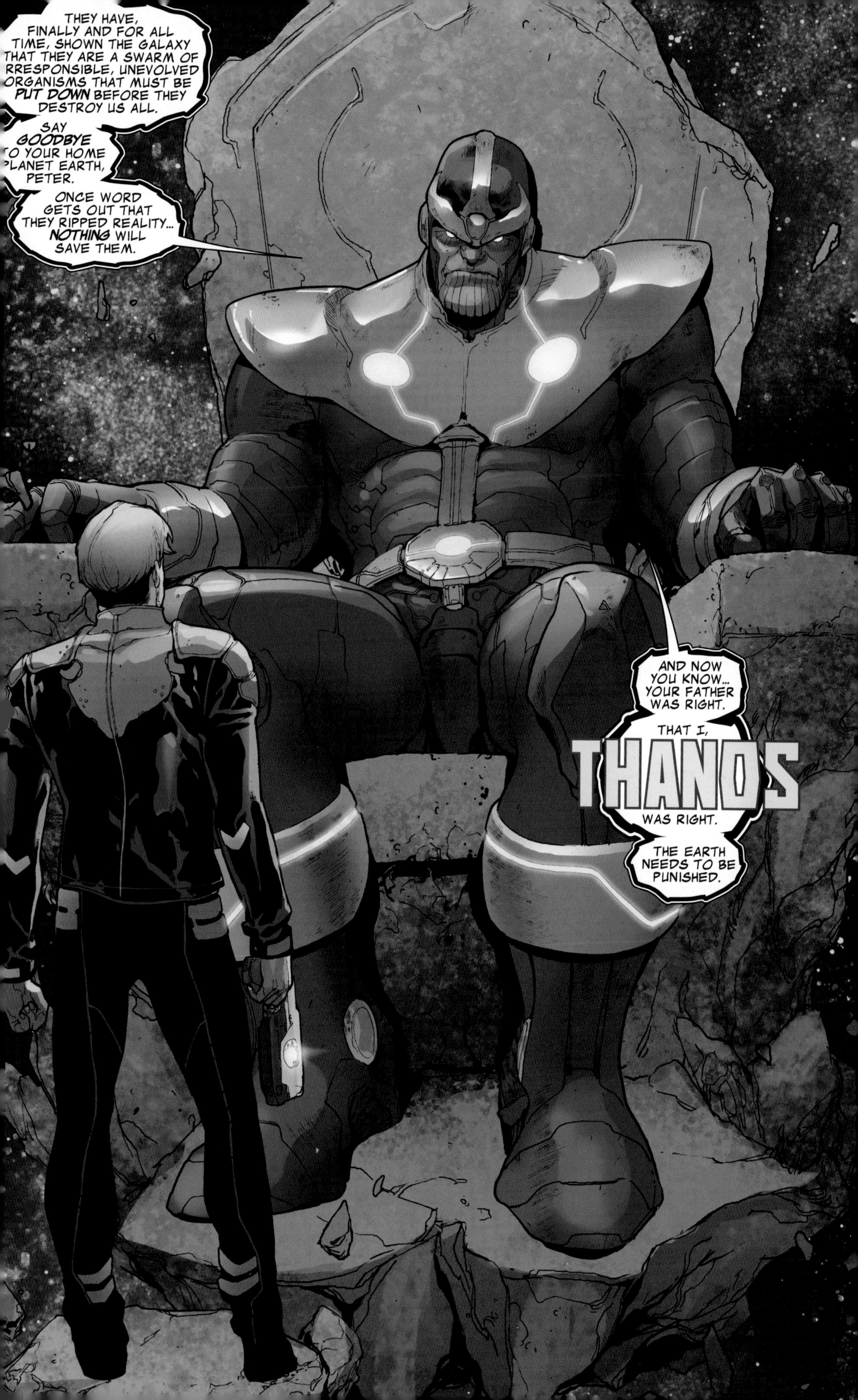
THEY HAVE, FINALLY AND FOR ALL TIME, SHOWN THE GALAXY THAT THEY ARE A SWARM OF RRESPONSIBLE, UNEVOLVED ORGANISMS THAT MUST BE PUT DOWN BEFORE THEY DESTROY US ALL.
SAY GOODBYE TO YOUR HOME PLANET EARTH, PETER.
ONCE WORD GETS OUT THAT THEY RIPPED REALITY... NOTHING WILL SAVE THEM.
AND NOW YOU KNOW... YOUR FATHER WAS RIGHT.
THAT I, THANOS WAS RIGHT.
THE EARTH NEEDS TO BE PUNISHED.

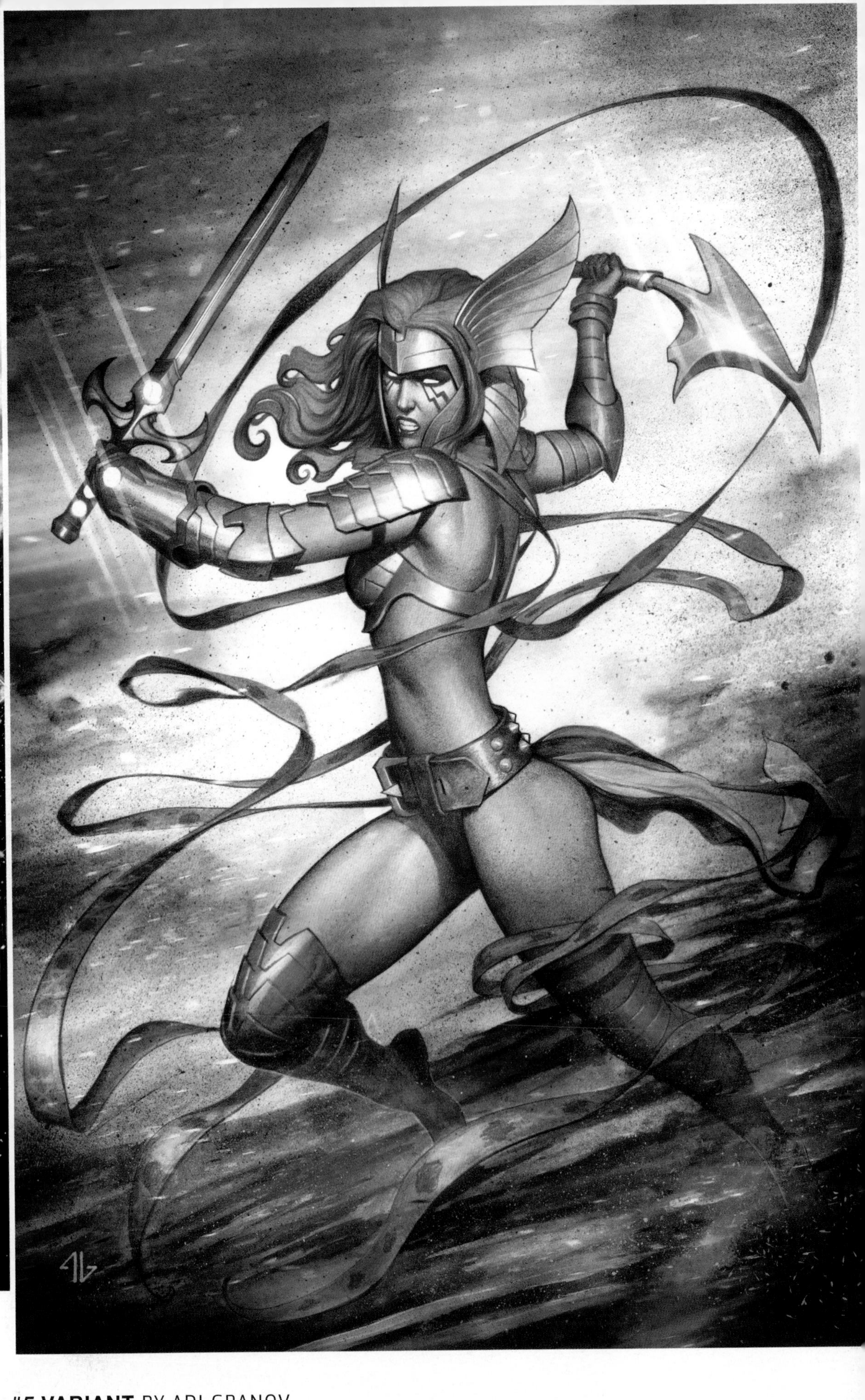

#5 VARIANT BY ADI GRANOV

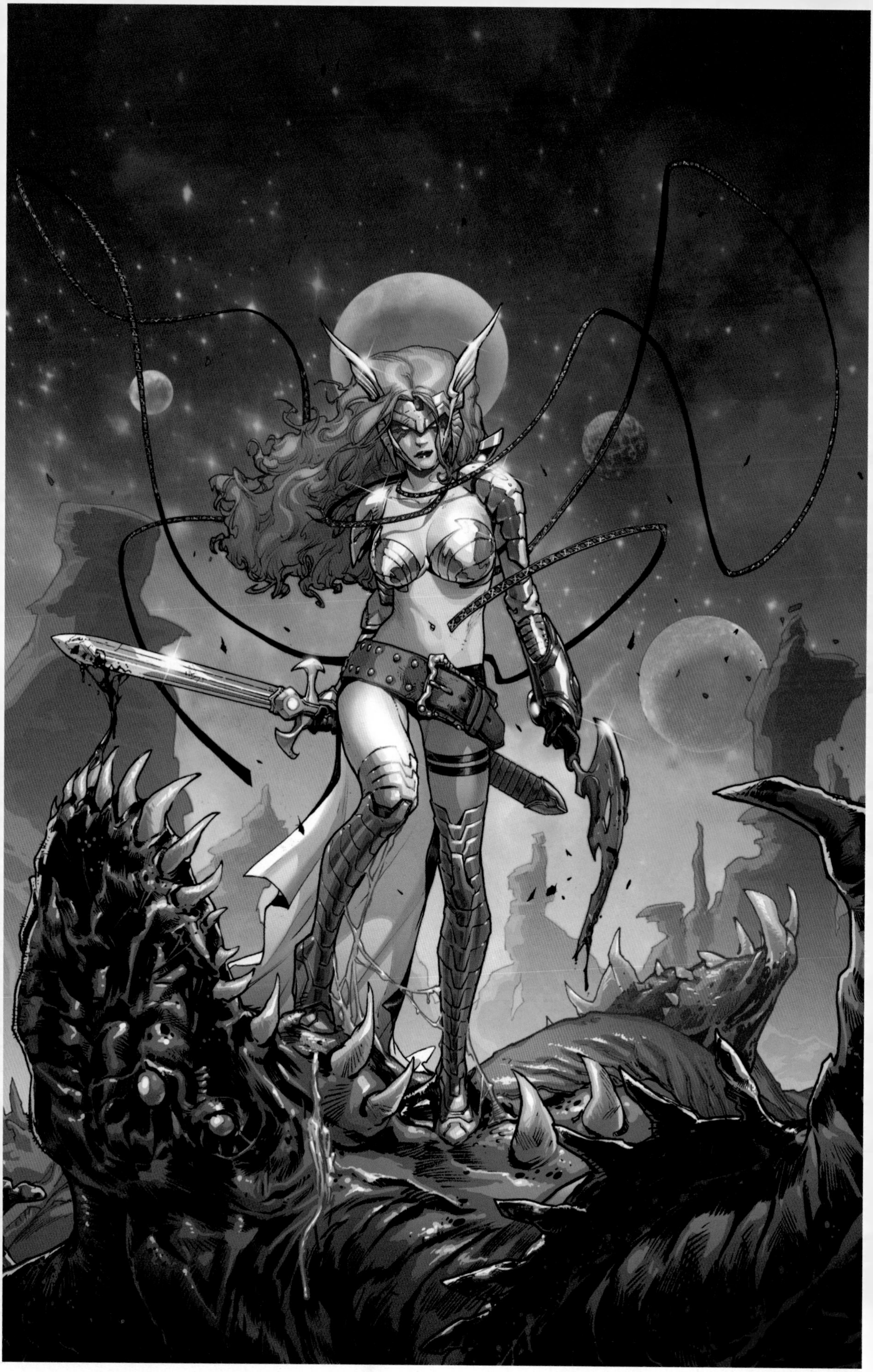

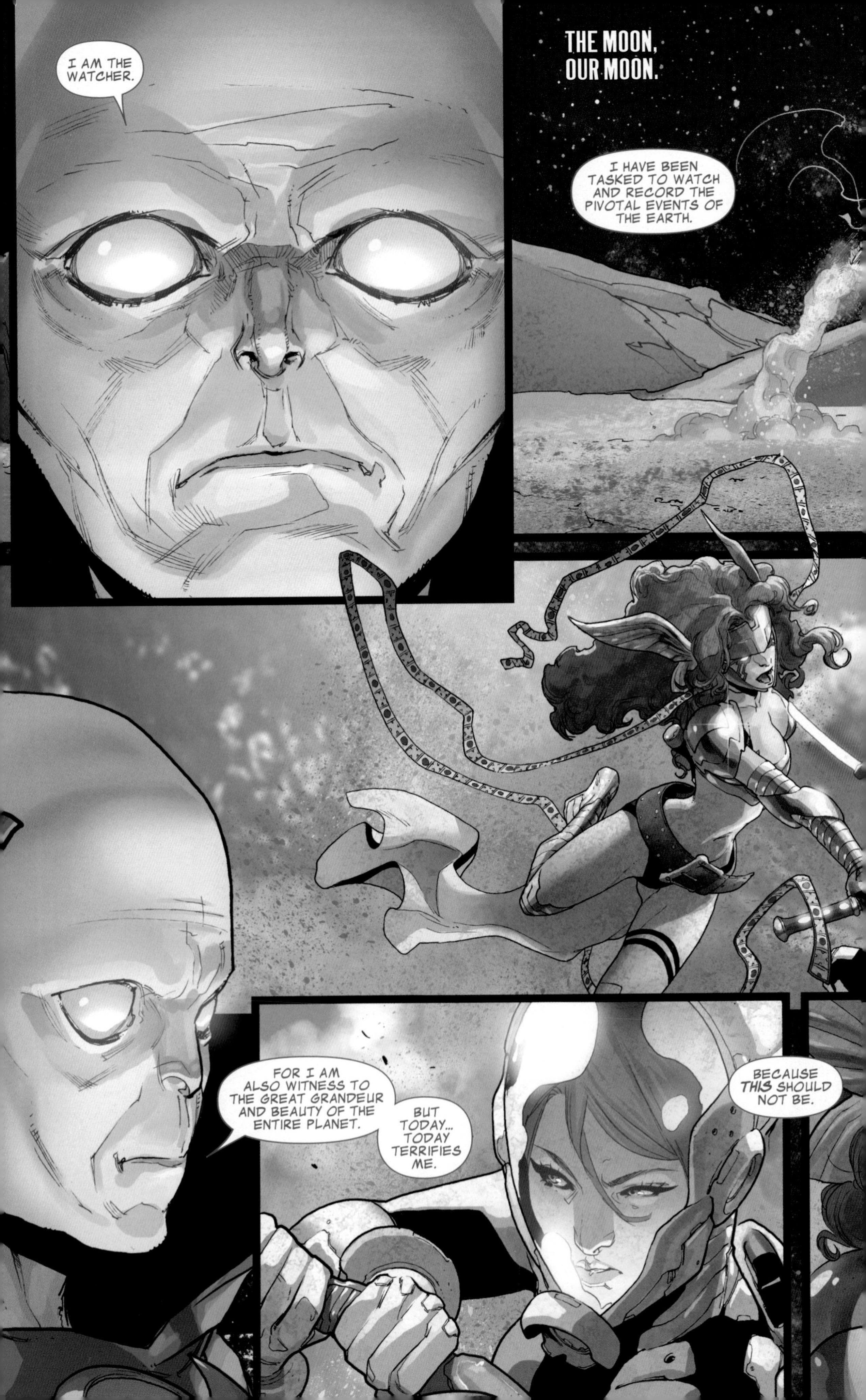
I AM THE WATCHER.
THE MOON, OUR MOON.
I HAVE BEEN TASKED TO WATCH AND RECORD THE PIVOTAL EVENTS OF THE EARTH.
FOR I AM ALSO WITNESS TO THE GREAT GRANDEUR AND BEAUTY OF THE ENTIRE PLANET.
BUT TODAY... TODAY TERRIFIES ME.
BECAUSE THIS SHOULD NOT BE.

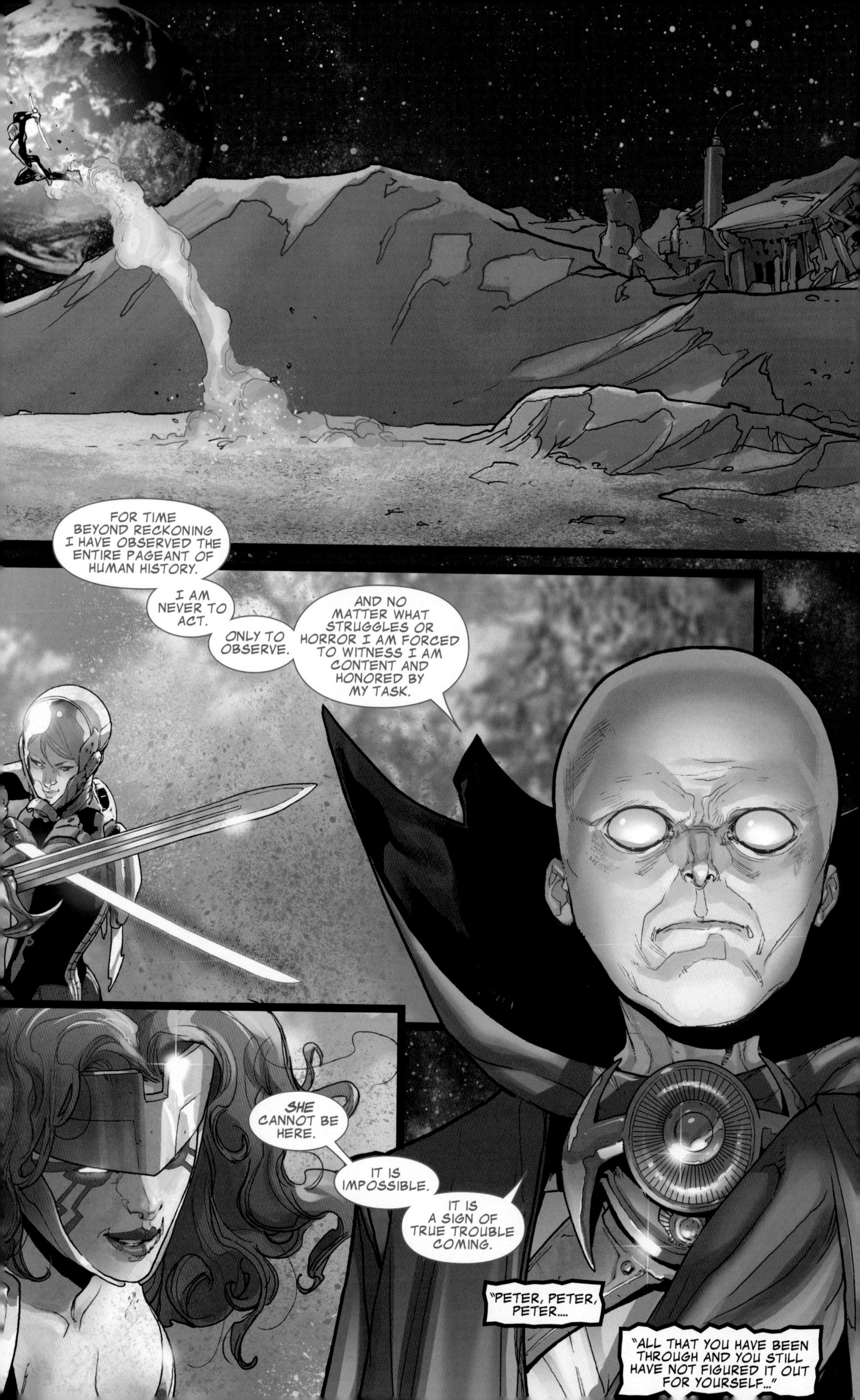
FOR TIME BEYOND RECKONING I HAVE OBSERVED THE ENTIRE PAGEANT OF HUMAN HISTORY.
I AM NEVER TO ACT.
ONLY TO OBSERVE.
AND NO MATTER WHAT STRUGGLES OR HORROR I AM FORCED TO WITNESS I AM CONTENT AND HONORED BY MY TASK.
SHE CANNOT BE HERE.
IT IS IMPOSSIBLE.
IT IS A SIGN OF TRUE TROUBLE COMING.
"PETER, PETER, PETER....
"ALL THAT YOU HAVE BEEN THROUGH AND YOU STILL HAVE NOT FIGURED IT OUT FOR YOURSELF..."

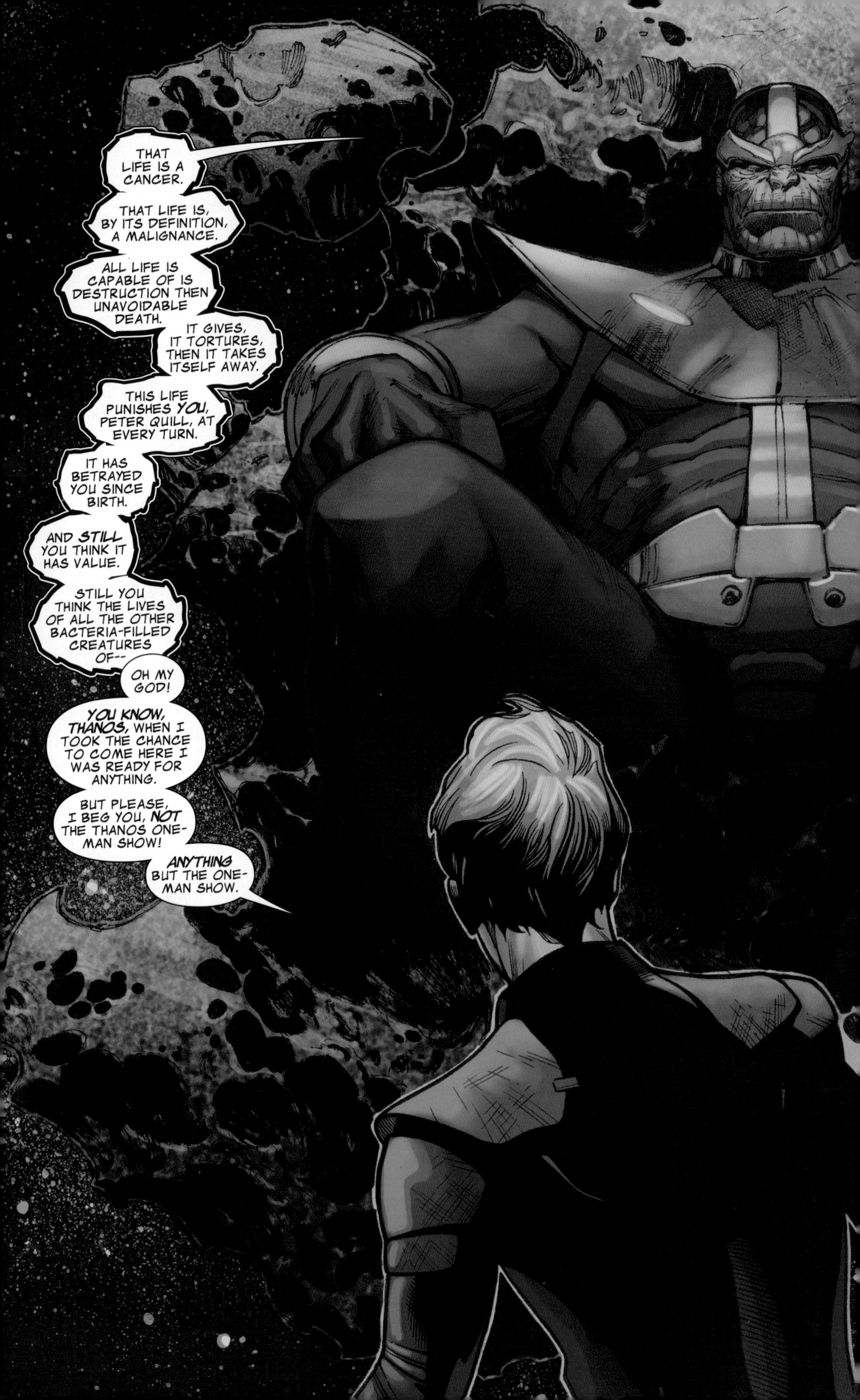
THAT LIFE IS A CANCER.
THAT LIFE IS, BY ITS DEFINITION, A MALIGNANCE.
ALL LIFE IS CAPABLE OF IS DESTRUCTION THEN UNAVOIDABLE DEATH.
IT GIVES, IT TORTURES, THEN IT TAKES ITSELF AWAY.
THIS LIFE PUNISHES YOU, PETER QUILL, AT EVERY TURN.
IT HAS BETRAYED YOU SINCE BIRTH.
AND STILL YOU THINK IT HAS VALUE.
STILL YOU THINK THE LIVES OF ALL THE OTHER BACTERIA-FILLED CREATURES OF--
OH MY GOD!
YOU KNOW, THANOS, WHEN I TOOK THE CHANCE TO COME HERE I WAS READY FOR ANYTHING.
BUT PLEASE, I BEG YOU, NOT THE THANOS ONE-MAN SHOW!
ANYTHING BUT THE ONE-MAN SHOW.

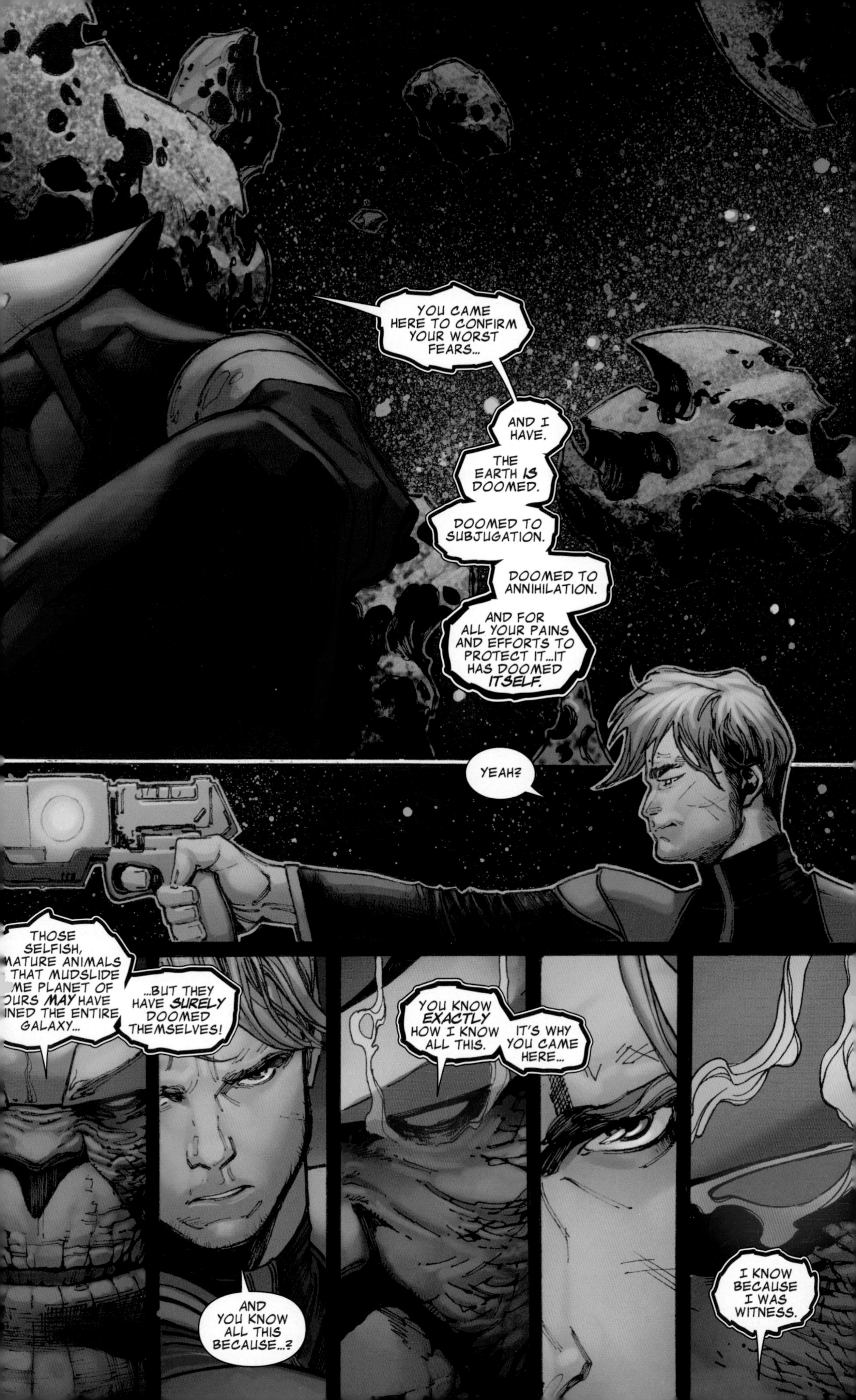
YOU CAME HERE TO CONFIRM YOUR WORST FEARS...
AND I HAVE.
THE EARTH **IS** DOOMED.
DOOMED TO SUBJUGATION.
DOOMED TO ANNIHILATION.
AND FOR ALL YOUR PAINS AND EFFORTS TO PROTECT IT...IT HAS DOOMED ***ITSELF.***
YEAH?
THOSE SELFISH, MATURE ANIMALS THAT MUDSLIDE ME PLANET OF OURS ***MAY*** HAVE INED THE ENTIRE GALAXY...
...BUT THEY HAVE ***SURELY*** DOOMED THEMSELVES!
AND YOU KNOW ALL THIS BECAUSE...?
YOU KNOW ***EXACTLY*** HOW I KNOW ALL THIS.
IT'S WHY YOU CAME HERE...
I KNOW BECAUSE I WAS WITNESS.

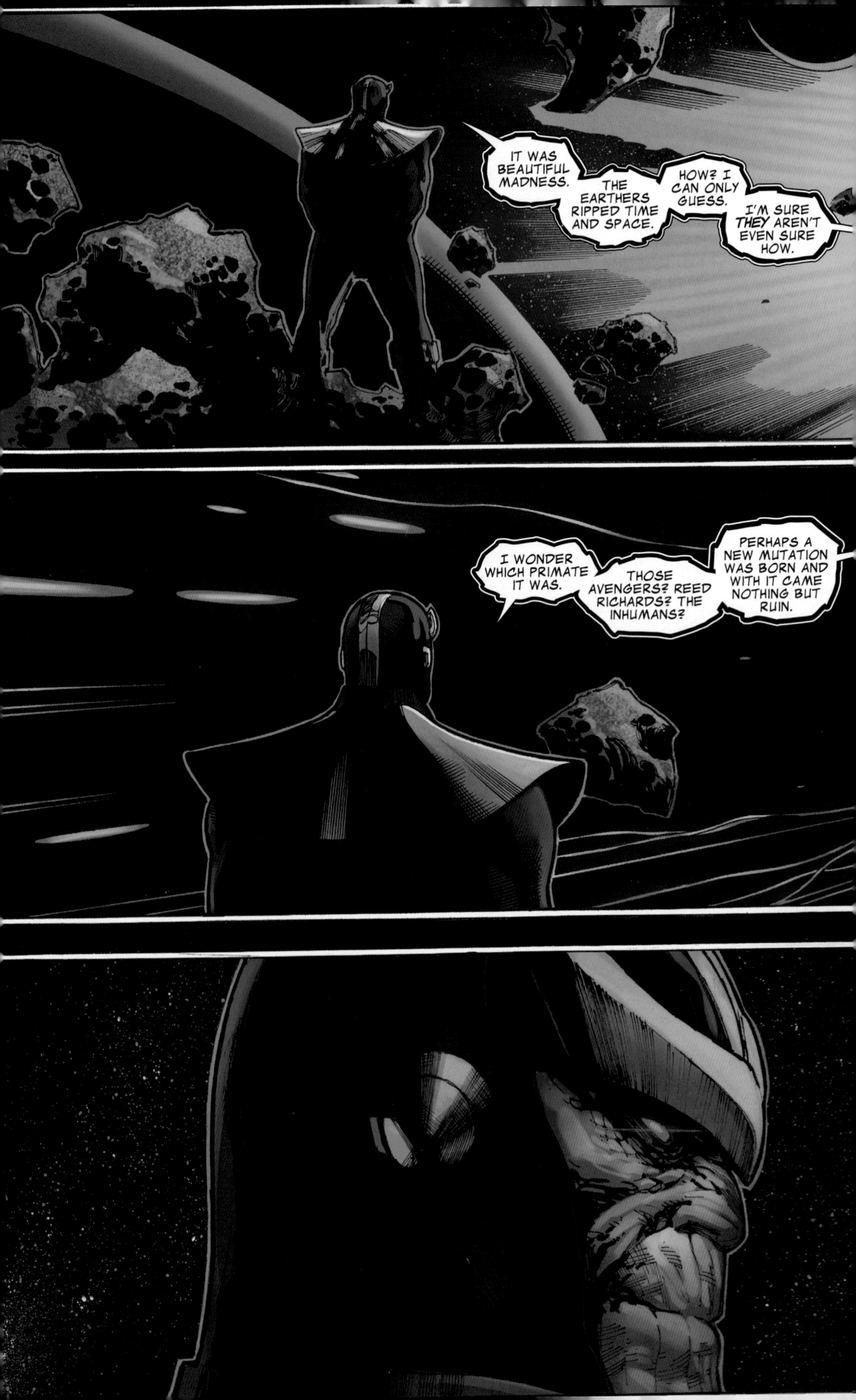
IT WAS BEAUTIFUL MADNESS.
THE EARTHERS RIPPED TIME AND SPACE.
HOW? I CAN ONLY GUESS.
I'M SURE *THEY* AREN'T EVEN SURE HOW.
I WONDER WHICH PRIMATE IT WAS.
THOSE AVENGERS? REED RICHARDS? THE INHUMANS?
PERHAPS A NEW MUTATION WAS BORN AND WITH IT CAME NOTHING BUT RUIN.

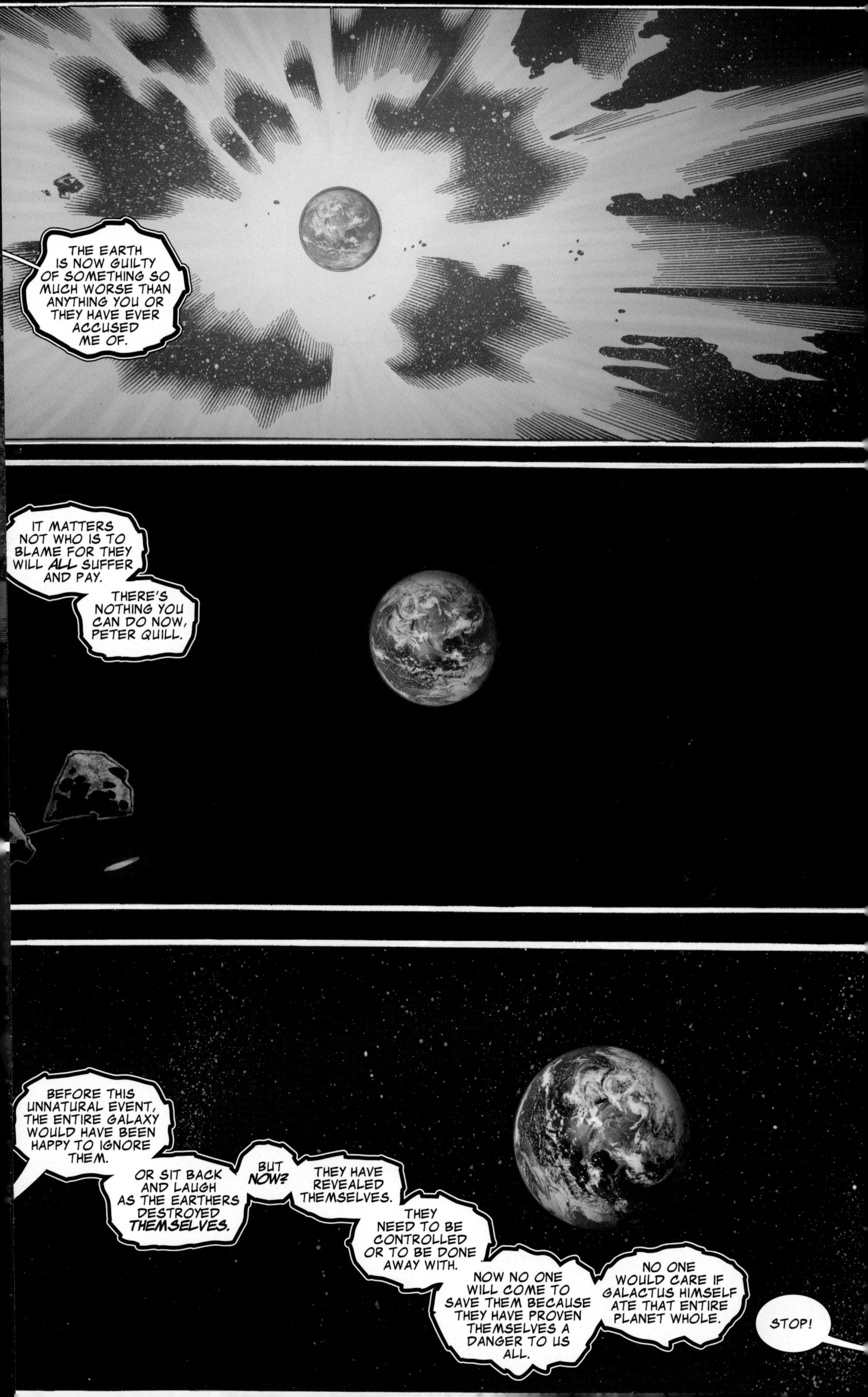
THE EARTH IS NOW GUILTY OF SOMETHING SO MUCH WORSE THAN ANYTHING YOU OR THEY HAVE EVER ACCUSED ME OF.
IT MATTERS NOT WHO IS TO BLAME FOR THEY WILL ALL SUFFER AND PAY.
THERE'S NOTHING YOU CAN DO NOW, PETER QUILL.
BEFORE THIS UNNATURAL EVENT, THE ENTIRE GALAXY WOULD HAVE BEEN HAPPY TO IGNORE THEM.
OR SIT BACK AND LAUGH AS THE EARTHERS DESTROYED THEMSELVES.
BUT NOW?
THEY HAVE REVEALED THEMSELVES.
THEY NEED TO BE CONTROLLED OR TO BE DONE AWAY WITH.
NOW NO ONE WILL COME TO SAVE THEM BECAUSE THEY HAVE PROVEN THEMSELVES A DANGER TO US ALL.
NO ONE WOULD CARE IF GALACTUS HIMSELF ATE THAT ENTIRE PLANET WHOLE.
STOP!

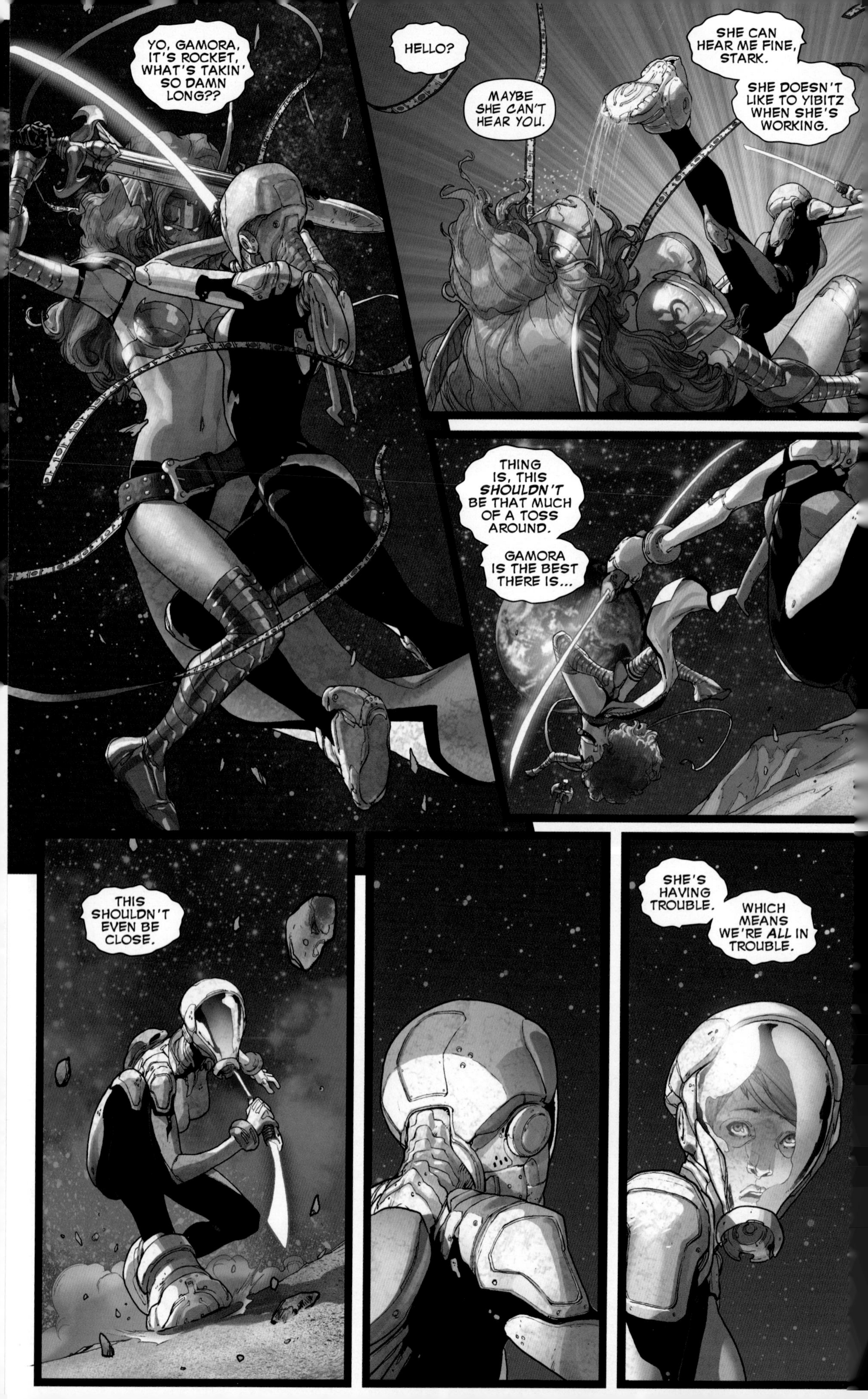

YO, GAMORA, IT'S ROCKET, WHAT'S TAKIN' SO DAMN LONG??
HELLO?
MAYBE SHE CAN'T HEAR YOU.
SHE CAN HEAR ME FINE, STARK.
SHE DOESN'T LIKE TO YIBITZ WHEN SHE'S WORKING.
THING IS, THIS SHOULDN'T BE THAT MUCH OF A TOSS AROUND.
GAMORA IS THE BEST THERE IS...
THIS SHOULDN'T EVEN BE CLOSE.
SHE'S HAVING TROUBLE.
WHICH MEANS WE'RE ALL IN TROUBLE.

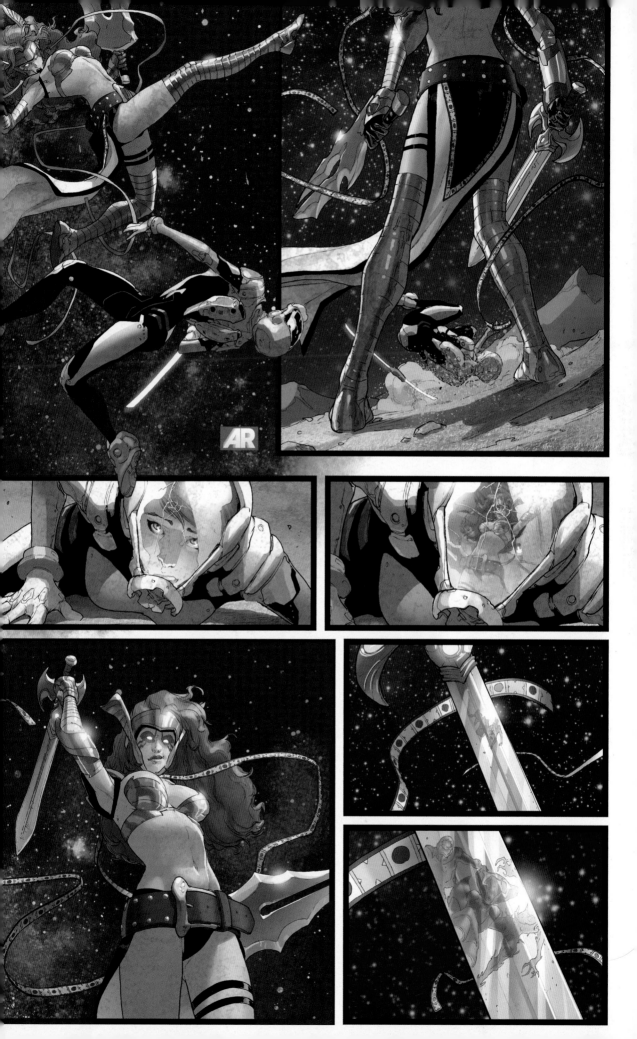

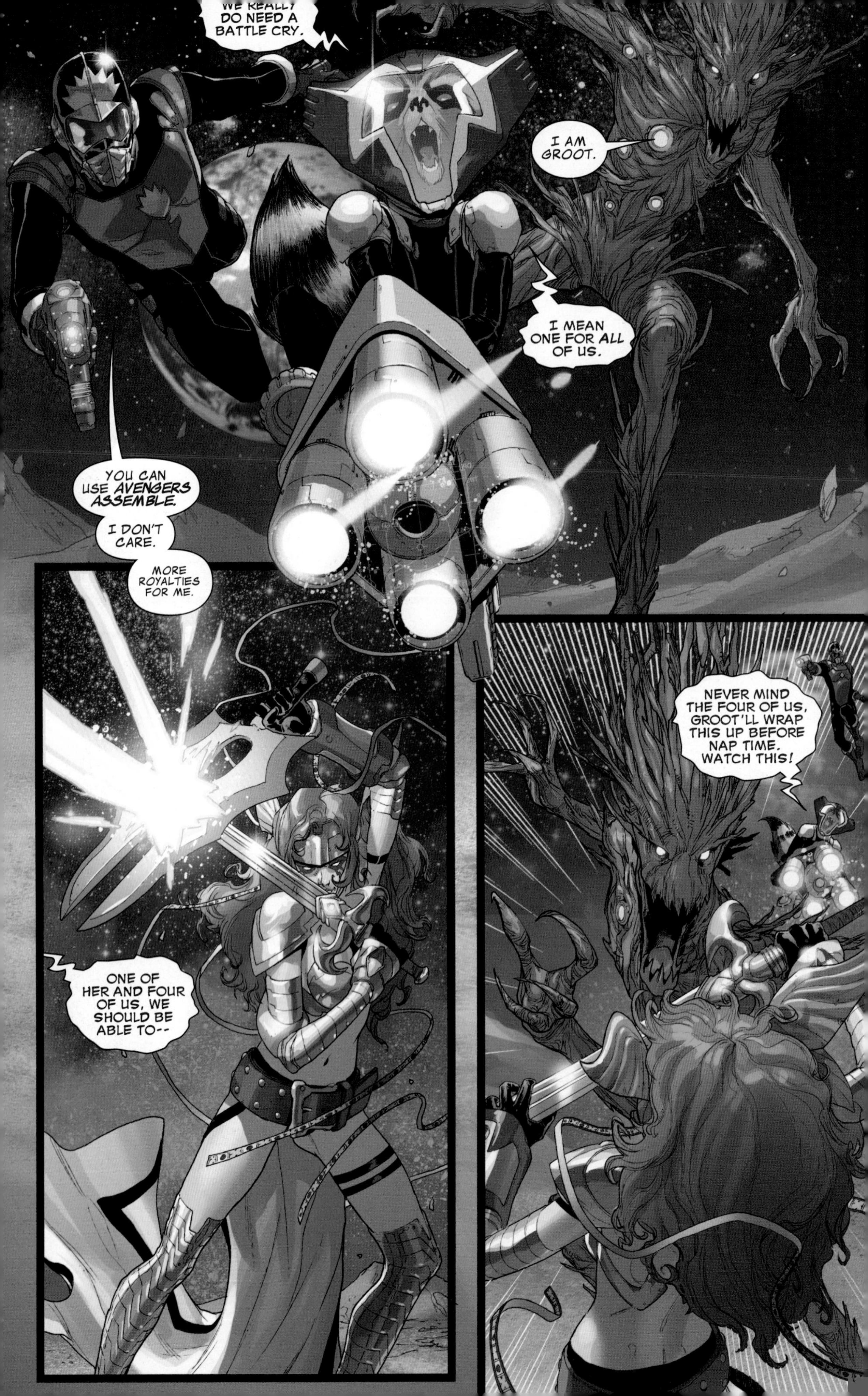
WE REALLY DO NEED A BATTLE CRY.
I AM GROOT.
I MEAN ONE FOR ALL OF US.
YOU CAN USE AVENGERS ASSEMBLE.
I DON'T CARE.
MORE ROYALTIES FOR ME.
ONE OF HER AND FOUR OF US, WE SHOULD BE ABLE TO--
NEVER MIND THE FOUR OF US, GROOT'LL WRAP THIS UP BEFORE NAP TIME. WATCH THIS!

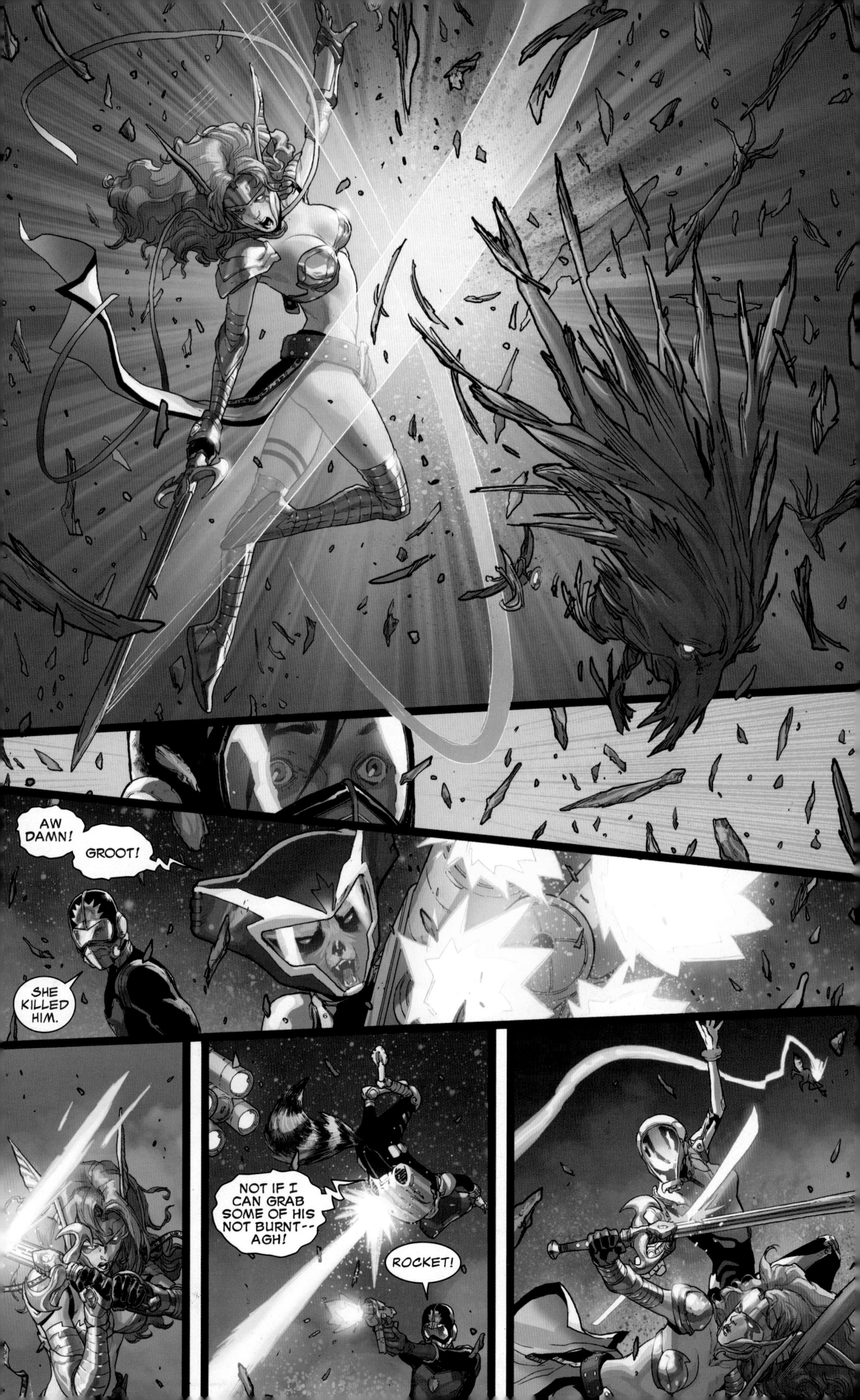
AW DAMN!
GROOT!
SHE KILLED HIM.
NOT IF I CAN GRAB SOME OF HIS NOT BURNT-- AGH!
ROCKET!

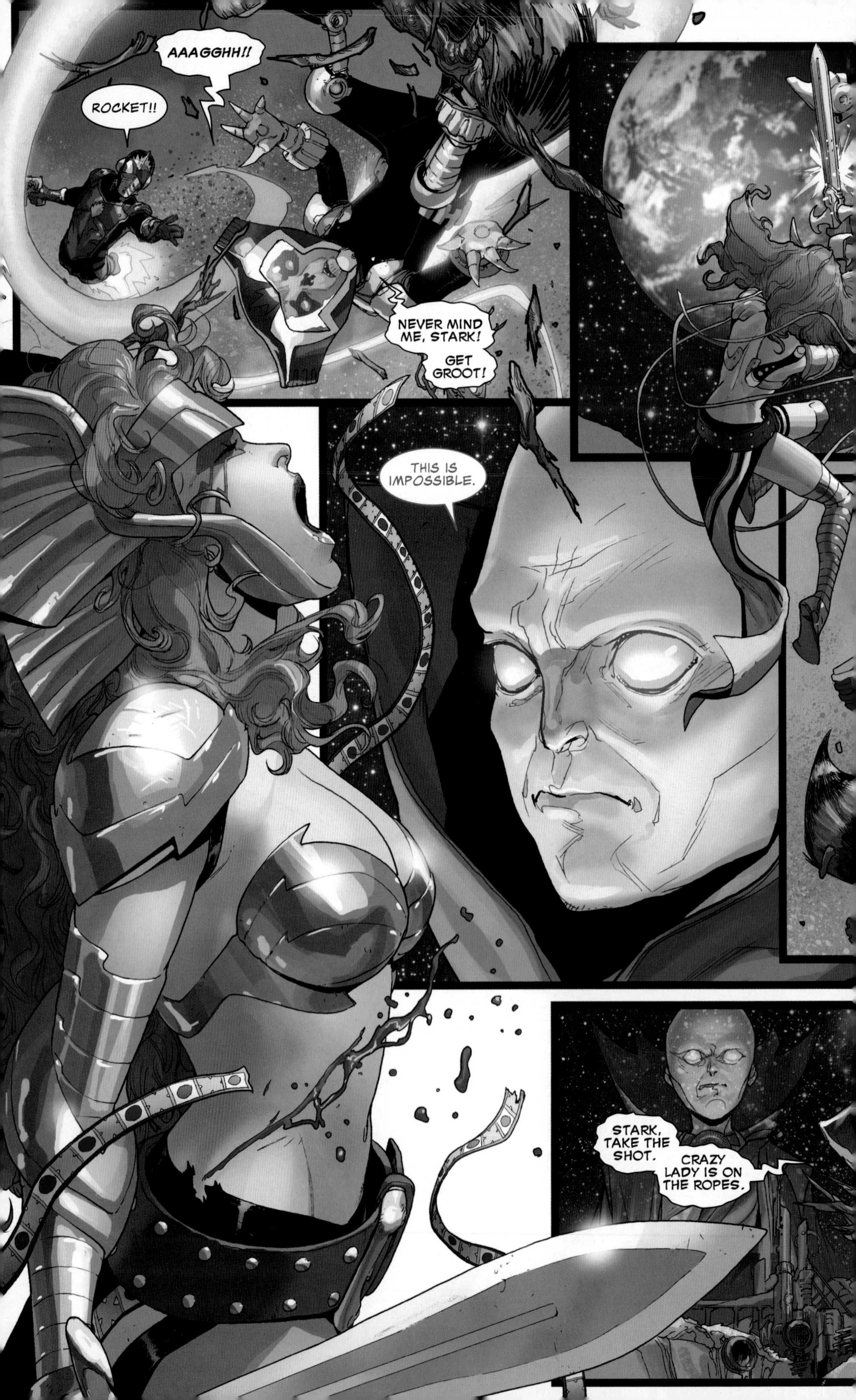
AAAGGHH!!
ROCKET!!
NEVER MIND ME, STARK!
GET GROOT!
THIS IS IMPOSSIBLE.
STARK, TAKE THE SHOT.
CRAZY LADY IS ON THE ROPES.

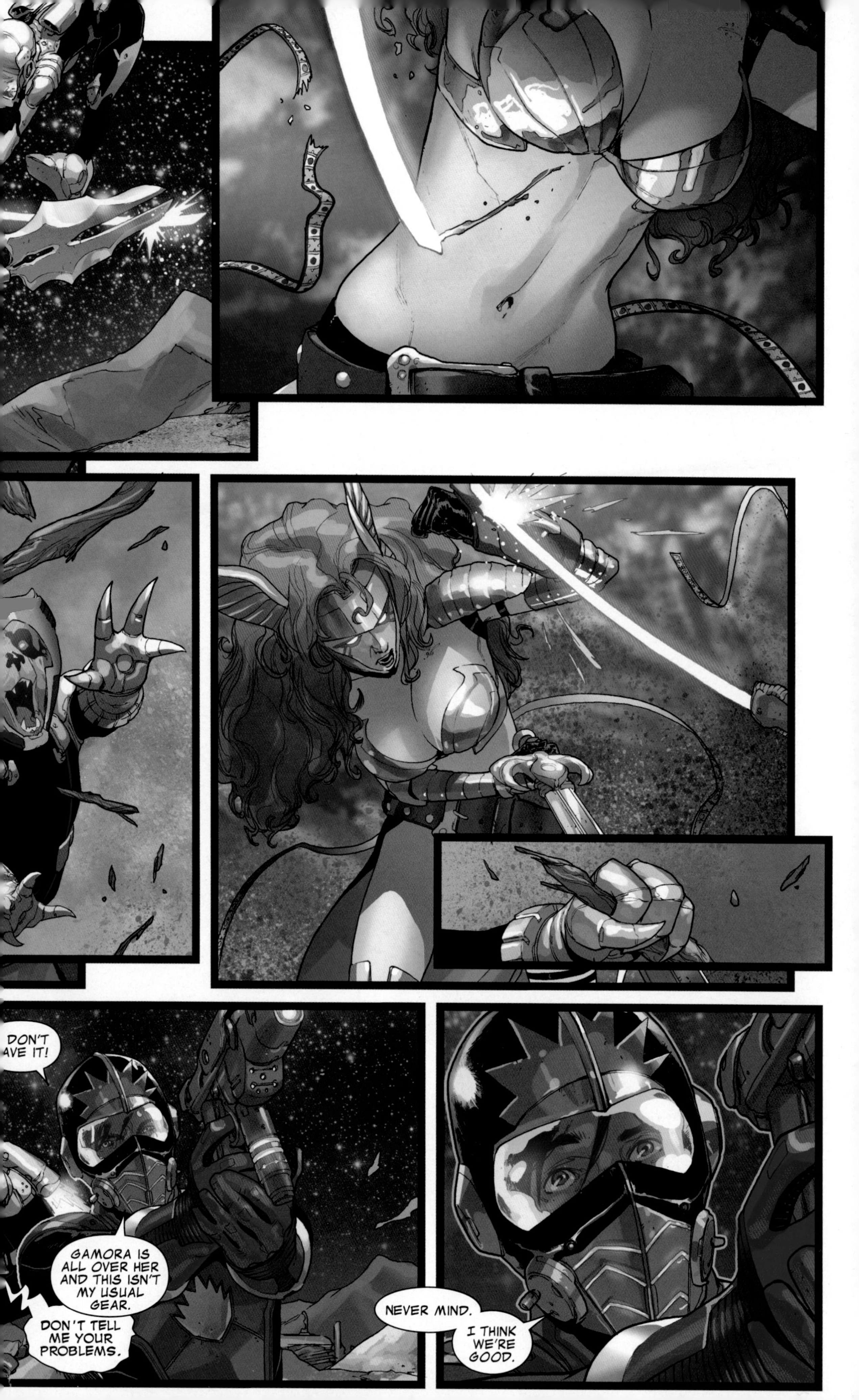
DON'T
AVE IT!
GAMORA IS ALL OVER HER AND THIS ISN'T MY USUAL GEAR.
DON'T TELL ME YOUR PROBLEMS.
NEVER MIND.
I THINK WE'RE GOOD.

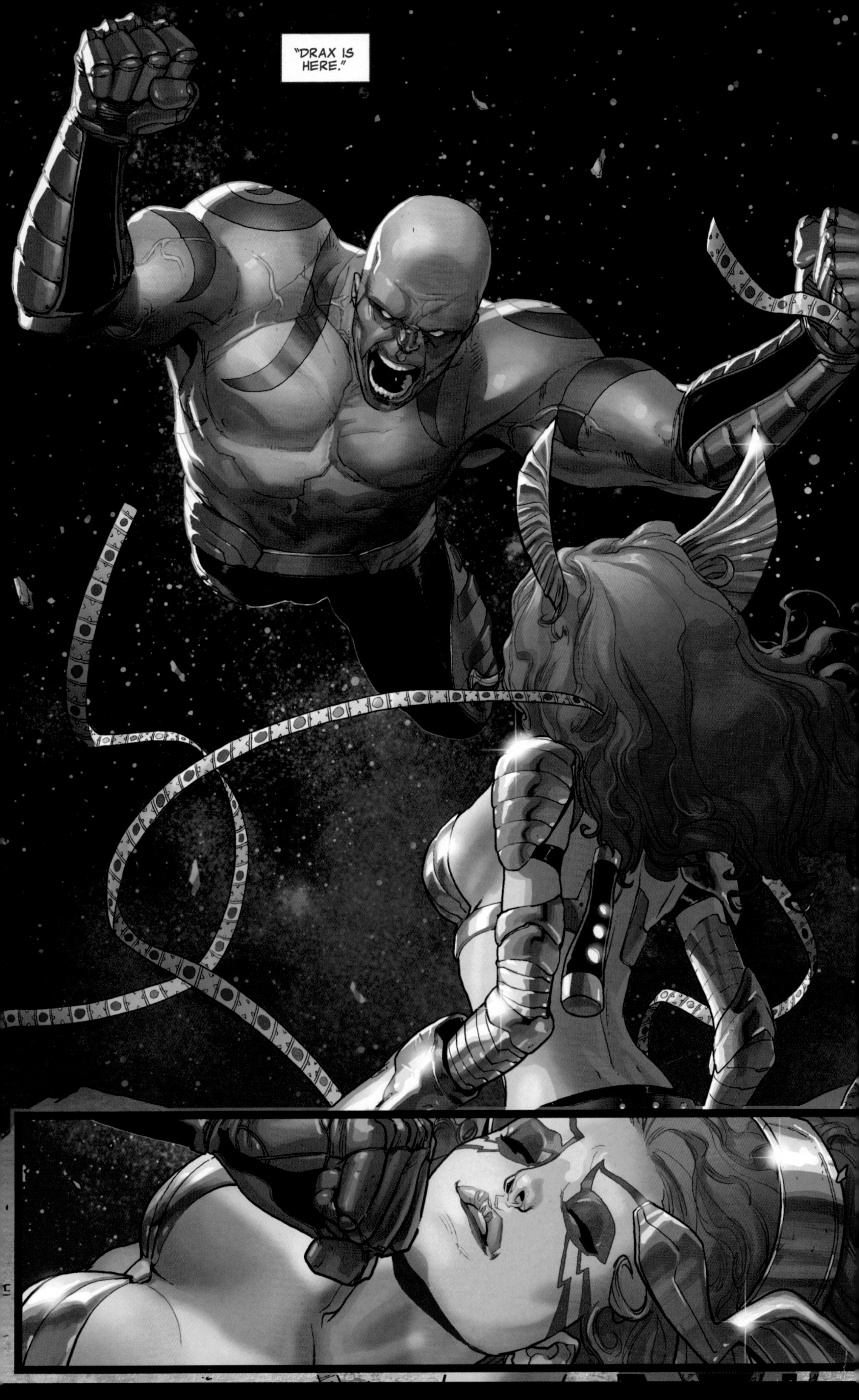
"DRAX IS HERE."

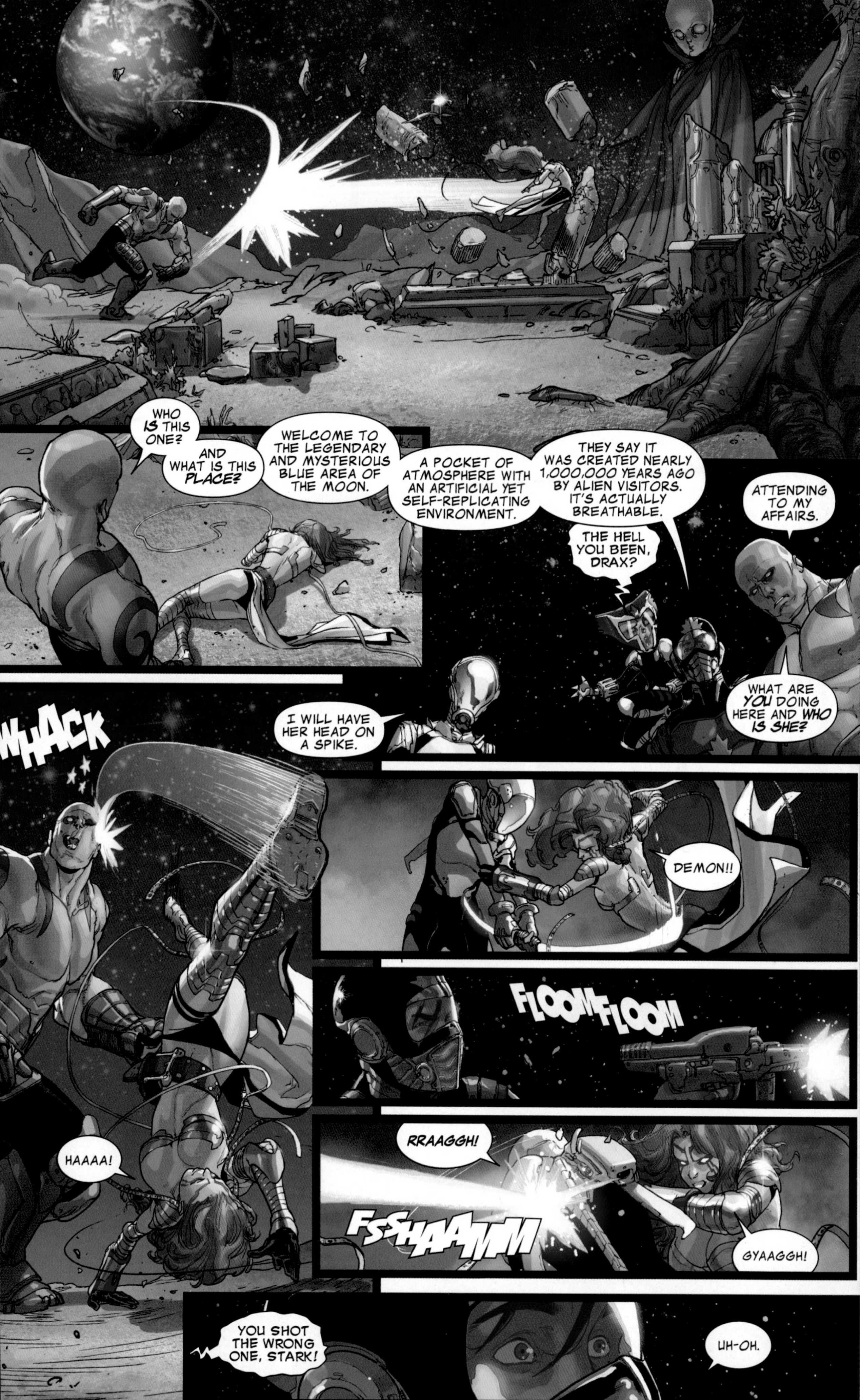

WHO IS THIS ONE?
AND WHAT IS THIS PLACE?
WELCOME TO THE LEGENDARY AND MYSTERIOUS BLUE AREA OF THE MOON.
A POCKET OF ATMOSPHERE WITH AN ARTIFICIAL YET SELF-REPLICATING ENVIRONMENT.
THEY SAY IT WAS CREATED NEARLY 1,000,000 YEARS AGO BY ALIEN VISITORS. IT'S ACTUALLY BREATHABLE.
THE HELL YOU BEEN, DRAX?
ATTENDING TO MY AFFAIRS.
WHAT ARE YOU DOING HERE AND WHO IS SHE?
I WILL HAVE HER HEAD ON A SPIKE.
WHACK
DEMON!!
FLOOM FLOOM
HAAAA!
RRAAGGH!
FSSHAAMM
GYAAGGH!
YOU SHOT THE WRONG ONE, STARK!
UH-OH.

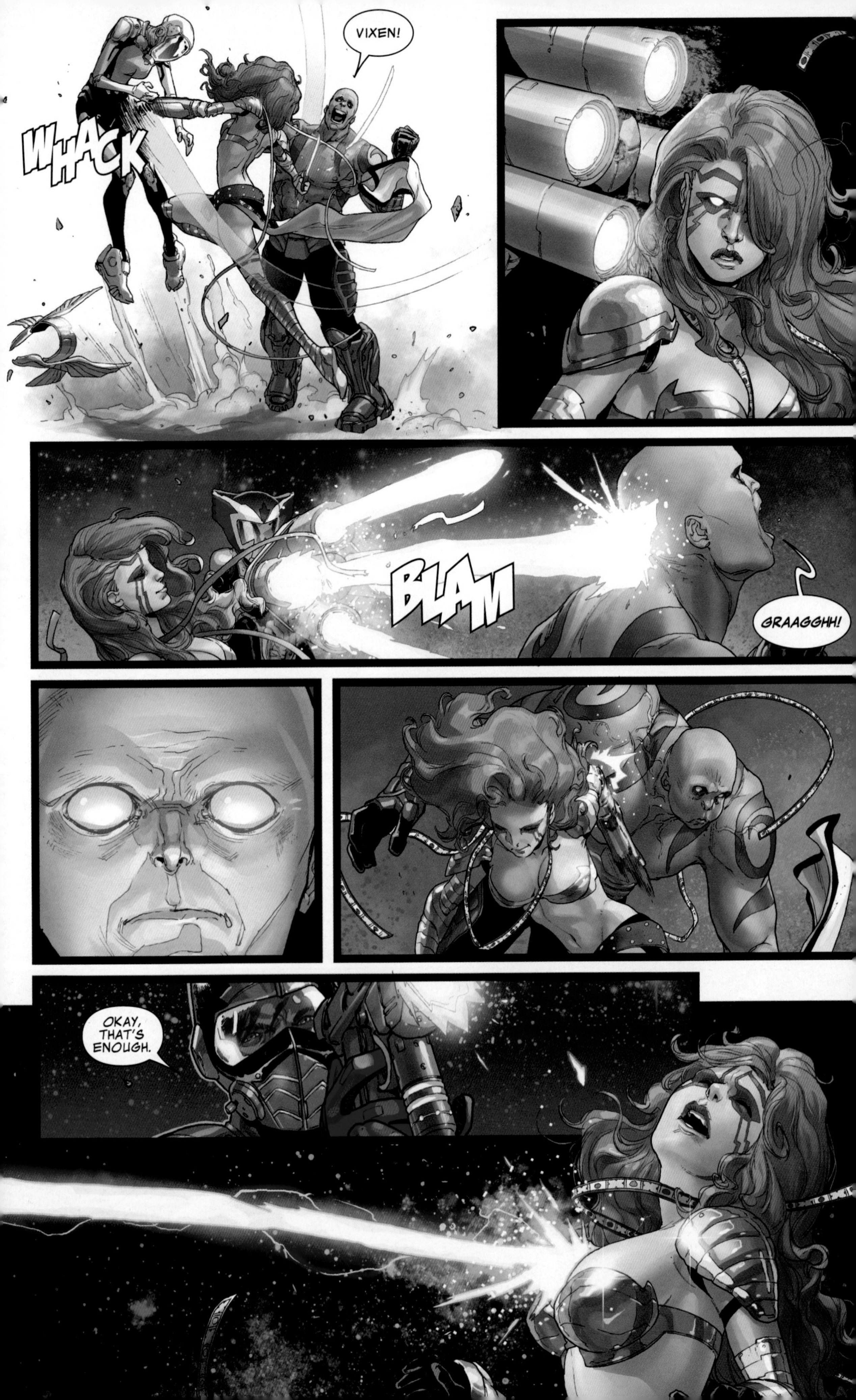
VIXEN!
WHACK
BLAM
GRAAGGHH!
OKAY, THAT'S ENOUGH.

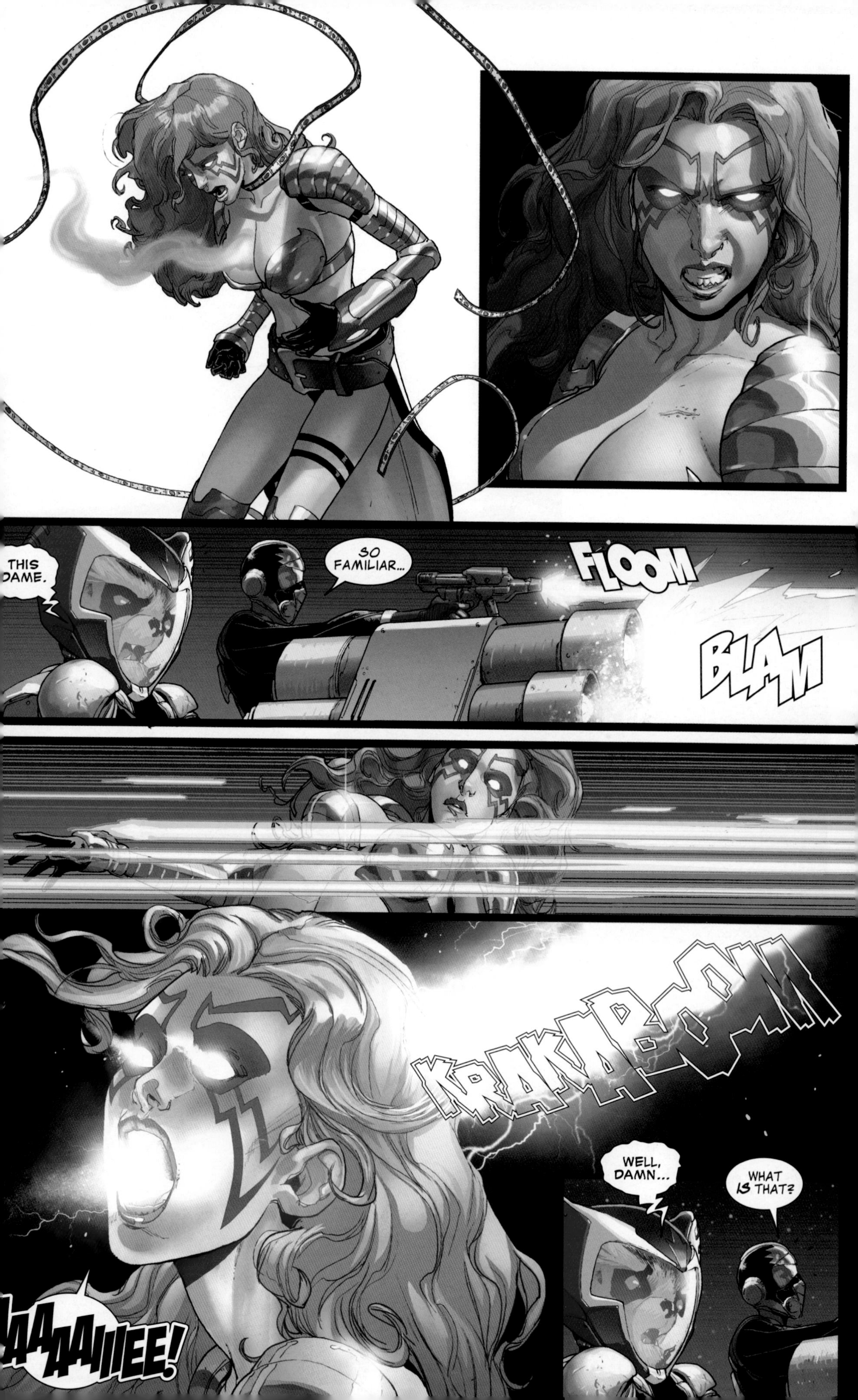
THIS DAME.
SO FAMILIAR...
FLOOM
BLAM
KRAKA-BOOM
AAAAAIIEEE!
WELL, DAMN...
WHAT IS THAT?

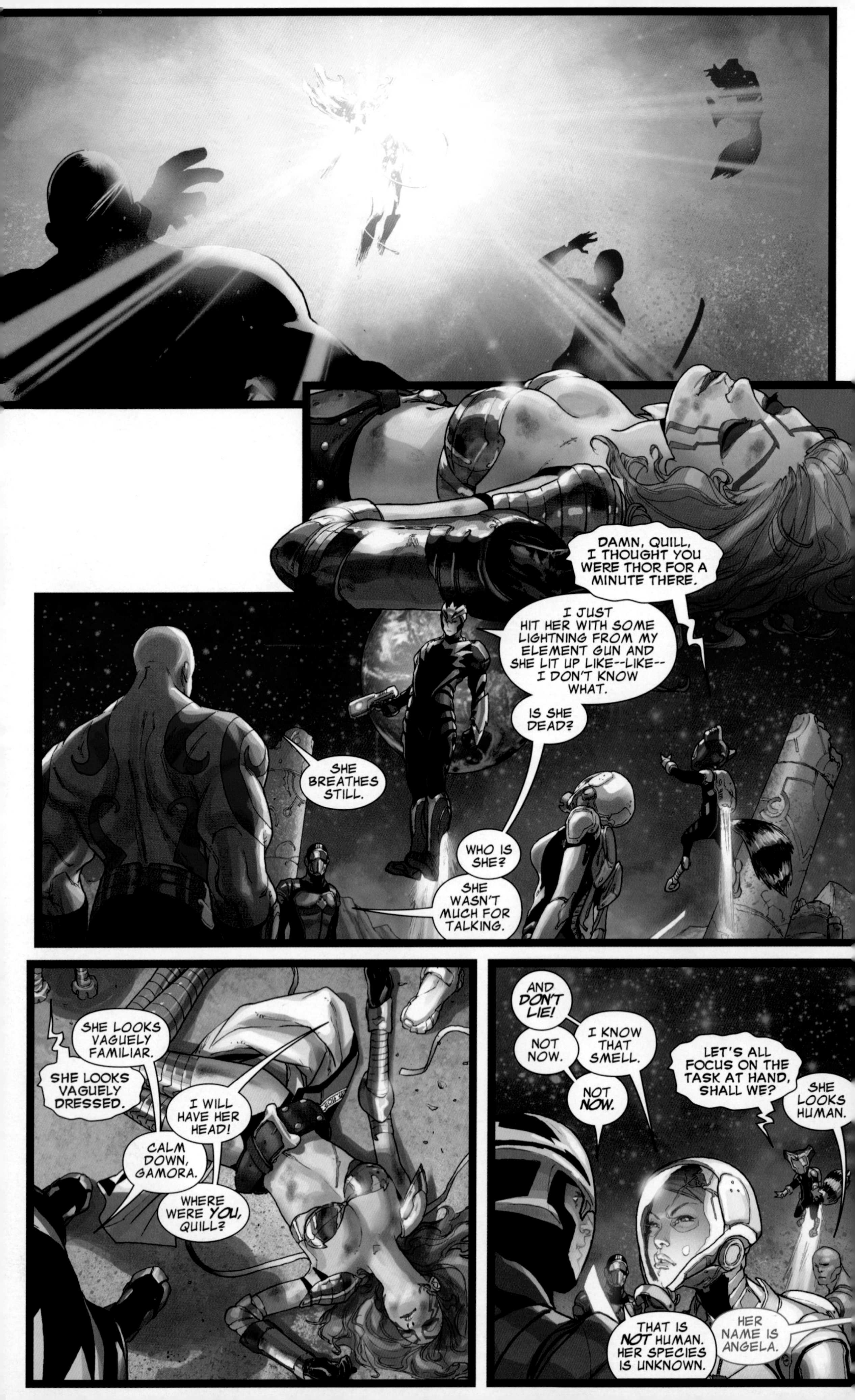
DAMN, QUILL, I THOUGHT YOU WERE THOR FOR A MINUTE THERE.
I JUST HIT HER WITH SOME LIGHTNING FROM MY ELEMENT GUN AND SHE LIT UP LIKE--LIKE-- I DON'T KNOW WHAT.
IS SHE DEAD?
SHE BREATHES STILL.
WHO IS SHE?
SHE WASN'T MUCH FOR TALKING.
SHE LOOKS VAGUELY FAMILIAR.
SHE LOOKS VAGUELY DRESSED.
I WILL HAVE HER HEAD!
CALM DOWN, GAMORA.
WHERE WERE YOU, QUILL?
AND DON'T LIE!
NOT NOW.
I KNOW THAT SMELL.
NOT NOW.
LET'S ALL FOCUS ON THE TASK AT HAND, SHALL WE?
SHE LOOKS HUMAN.
THAT IS NOT HUMAN. HER SPECIES IS UNKNOWN.
HER NAME IS ANGELA.

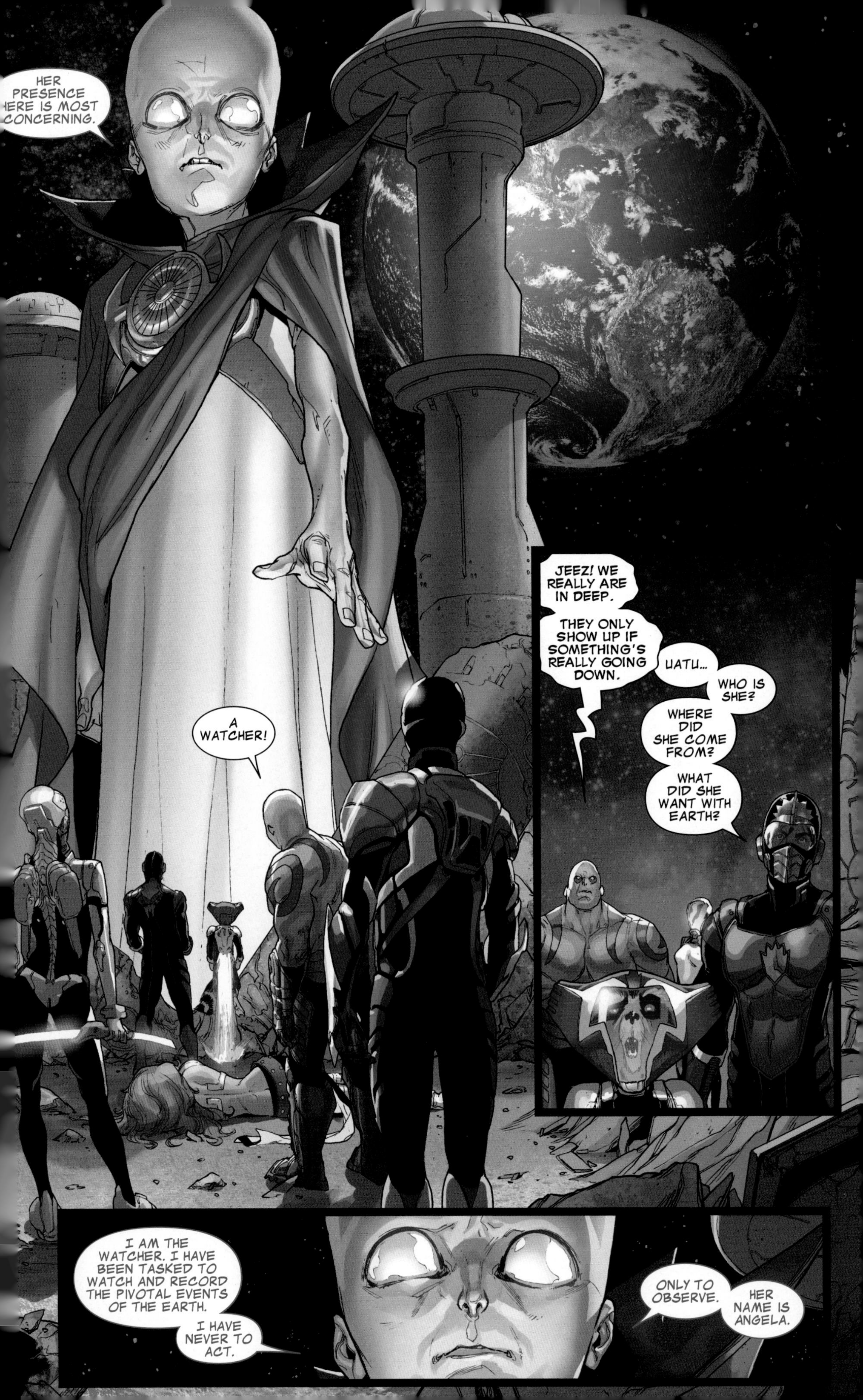
HER PRESENCE HERE IS MOST CONCERNING.
A WATCHER!
JEEZ! WE REALLY ARE IN DEEP.
THEY ONLY SHOW UP IF SOMETHING'S REALLY GOING DOWN.
UATU...
WHO IS SHE?
WHERE DID SHE COME FROM?
WHAT DID SHE WANT WITH EARTH?
I AM THE WATCHER. I HAVE BEEN TASKED TO WATCH AND RECORD THE PIVOTAL EVENTS OF THE EARTH.
I HAVE NEVER TO ACT.
ONLY TO OBSERVE.
HER NAME IS ANGELA.

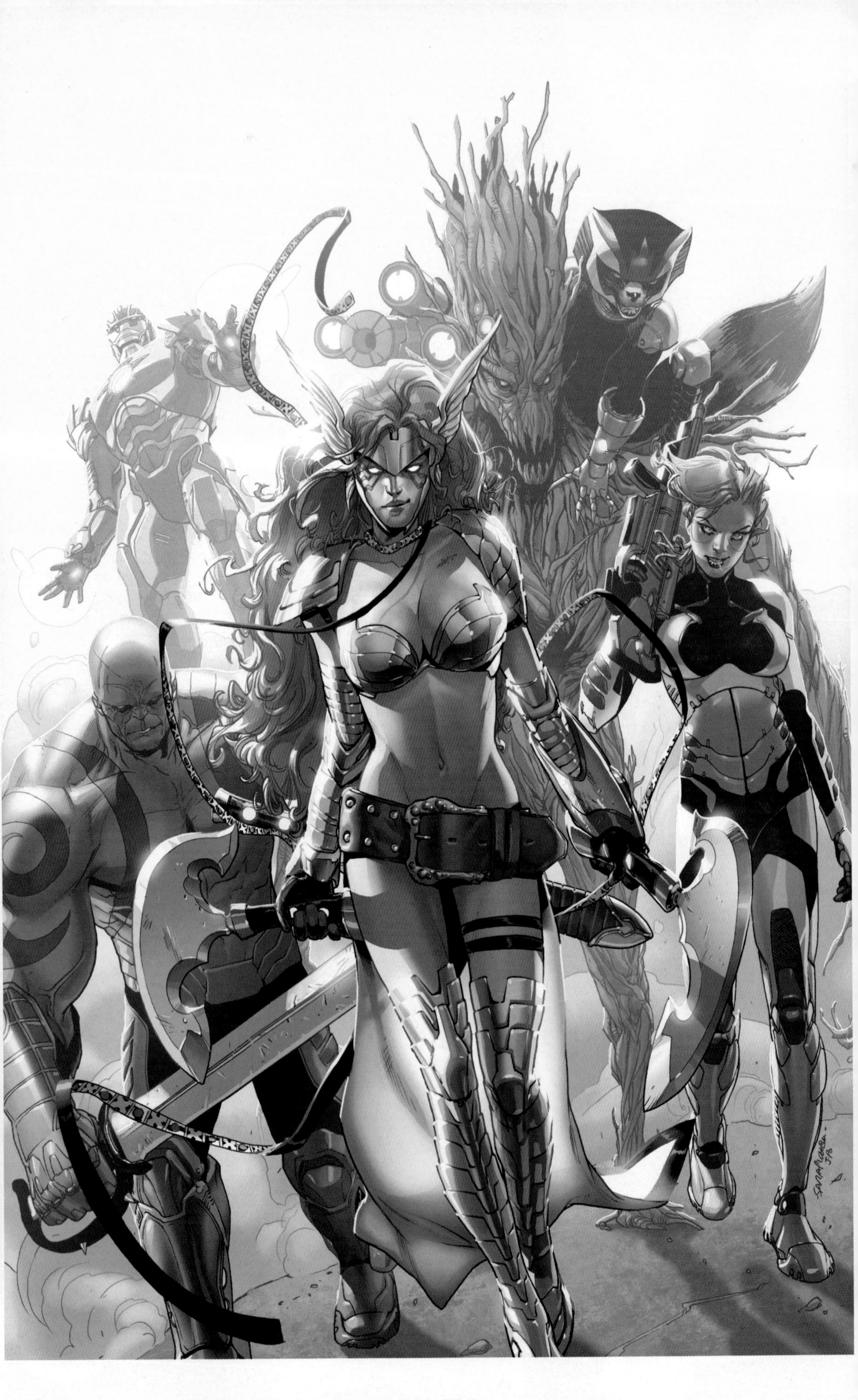

#7 VARIANT BY SARA PICHELLI & JUSTIN PONSOR

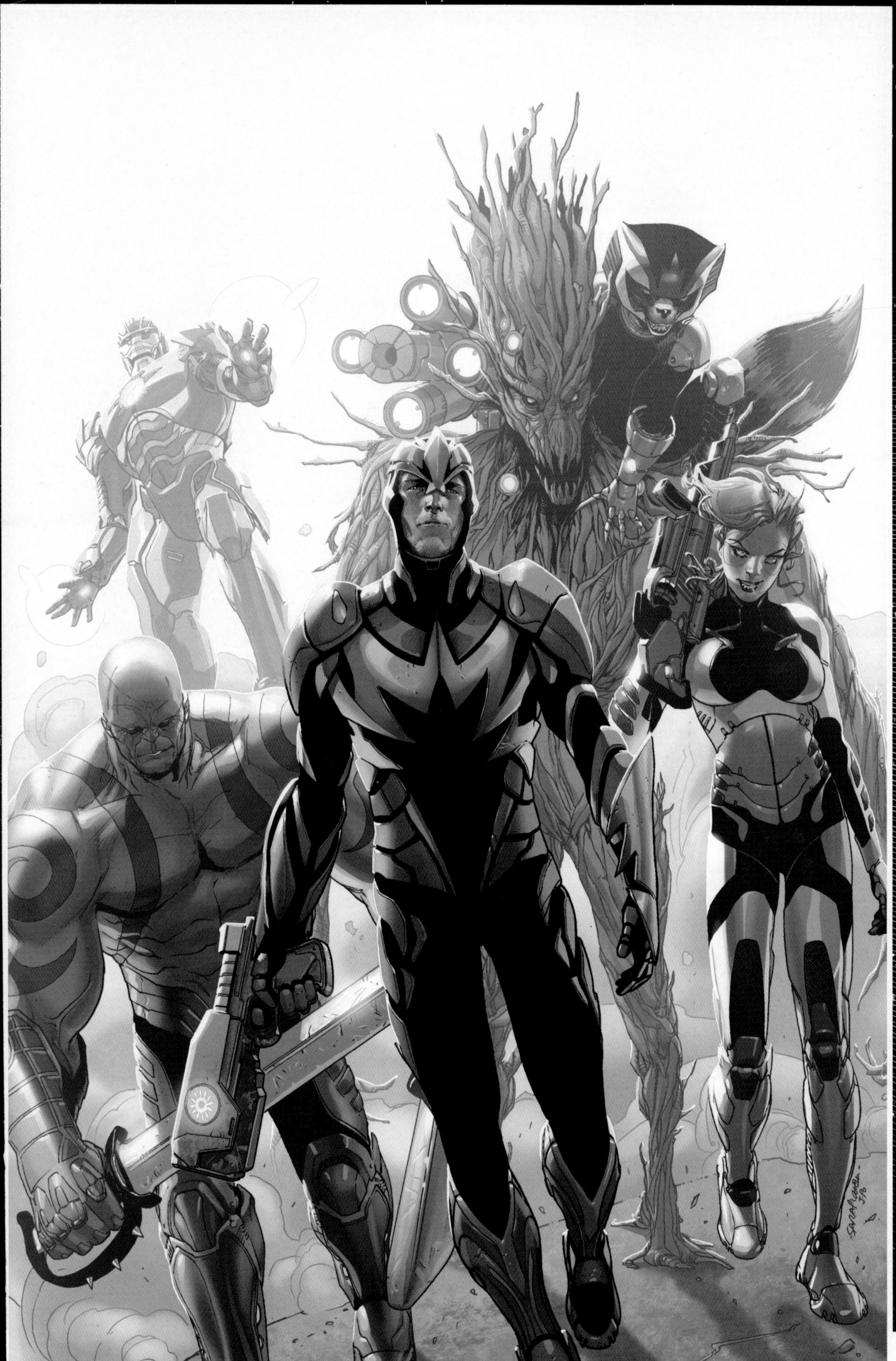

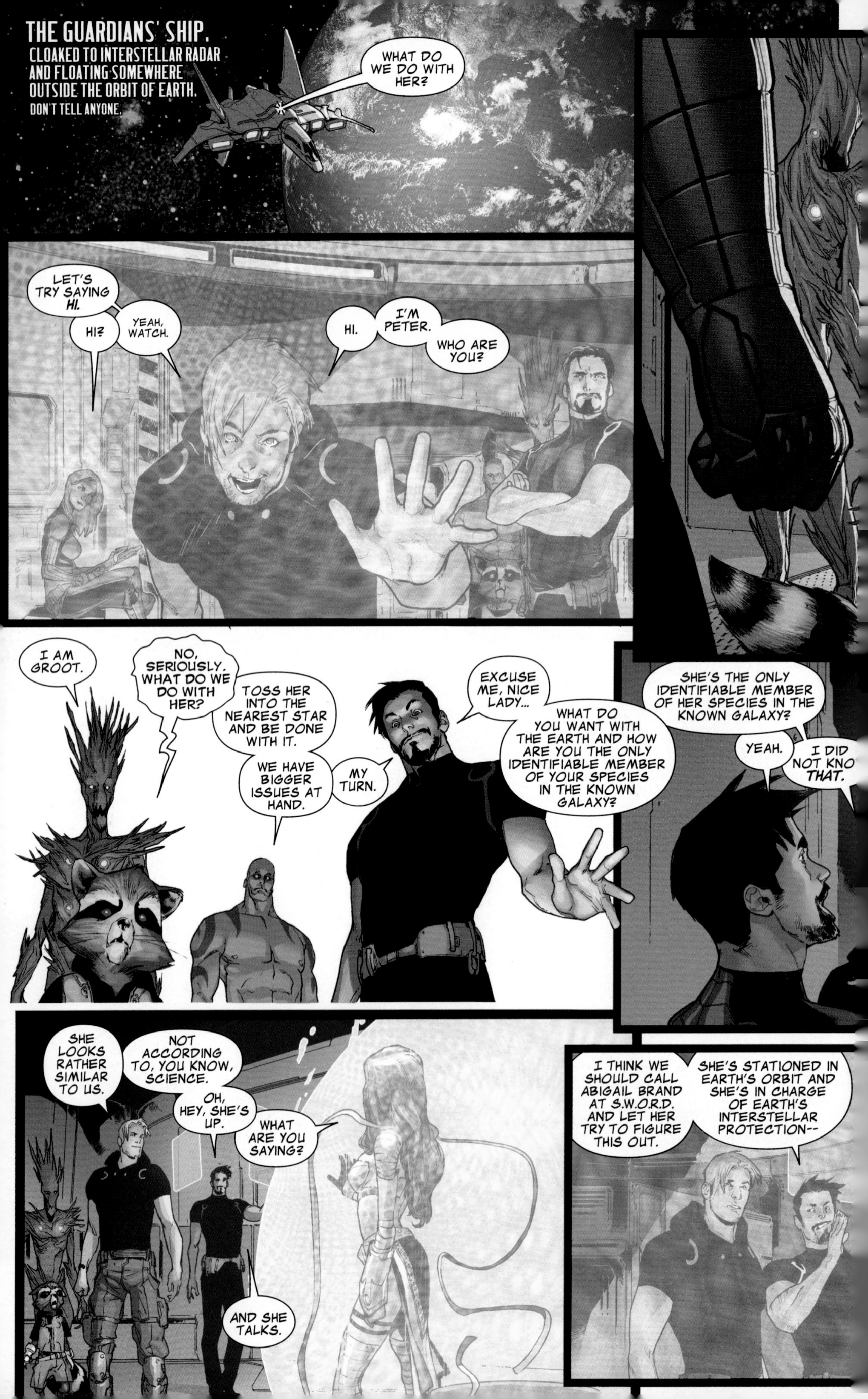
THE GUARDIANS' SHIP.
CLOAKED TO INTERSTELLAR RADAR AND FLOATING SOMEWHERE OUTSIDE THE ORBIT OF EARTH.
DON'T TELL ANYONE.
WHAT DO WE DO WITH HER?
LET'S TRY SAYING *HI.*
HI?
YEAH, WATCH.
HI.
I'M PETER.
WHO ARE YOU?
I AM GROOT.
NO, SERIOUSLY. WHAT DO WE DO WITH HER?
TOSS HER INTO THE NEAREST STAR AND BE DONE WITH IT.
WE HAVE BIGGER ISSUES AT HAND.
MY TURN.
EXCUSE ME, NICE LADY...
WHAT DO YOU WANT WITH THE EARTH AND HOW ARE YOU THE ONLY IDENTIFIABLE MEMBER OF YOUR SPECIES IN THE KNOWN GALAXY?
SHE'S THE ONLY IDENTIFIABLE MEMBER OF HER SPECIES IN THE KNOWN GALAXY?
YEAH.
I DID NOT KNO *THAT.*
SHE LOOKS RATHER SIMILAR TO US.
NOT ACCORDING TO, YOU KNOW, SCIENCE.
OH, HEY, SHE'S UP.
WHAT ARE YOU SAYING?
AND SHE TALKS.
I THINK WE SHOULD CALL ABIGAIL BRAND AT S.W.O.R.D. AND LET HER TRY TO FIGURE THIS OUT.
SHE'S STATIONED IN EARTH'S ORBIT AND SHE'S IN CHARGE OF EARTH'S INTERSTELLAR PROTECTION--

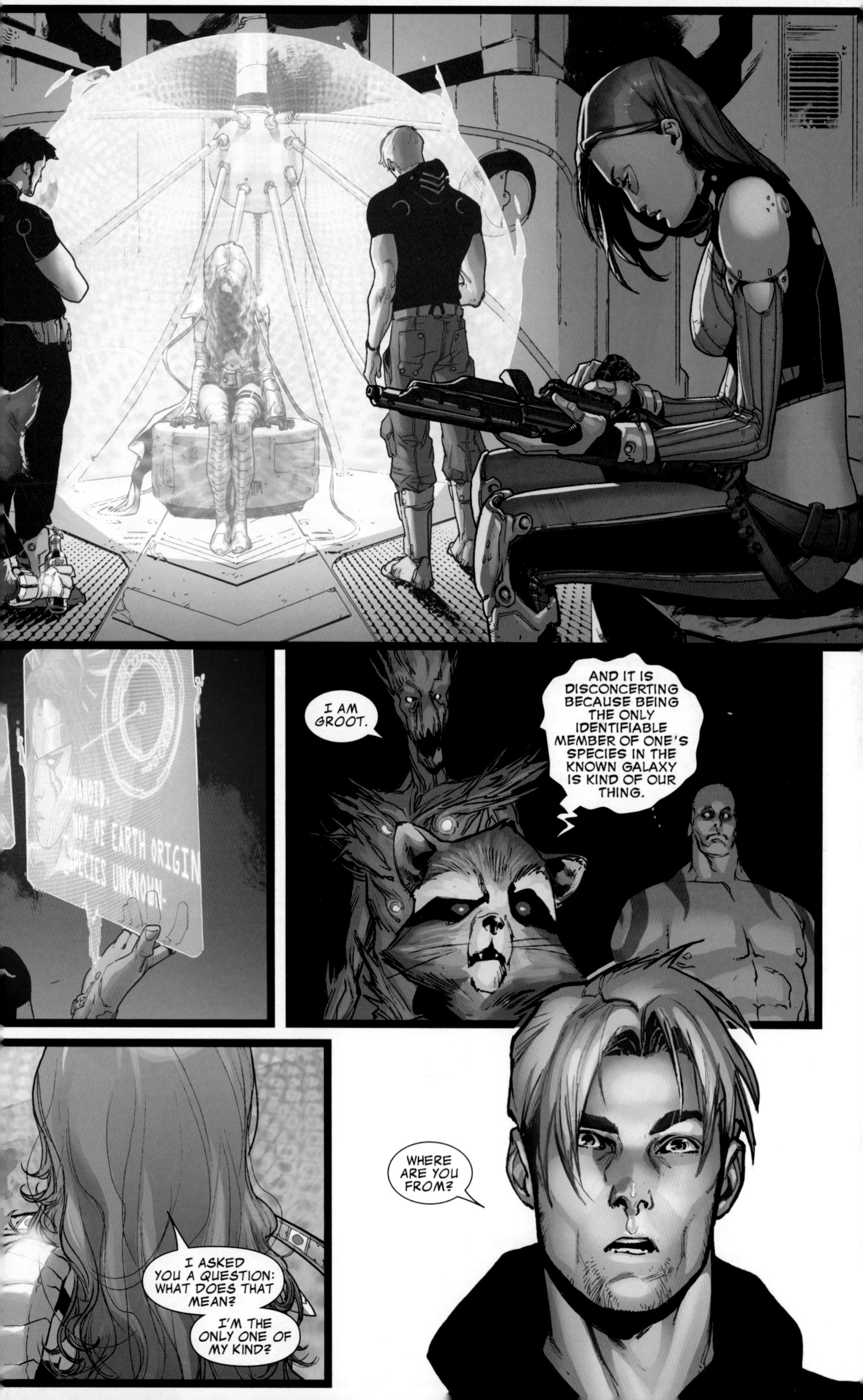
HUMANOID.
NOT OF EARTH ORIGIN
SPECIES UNKNOWN
I AM GROOT.
AND IT IS DISCONCERTING BECAUSE BEING THE ONLY IDENTIFIABLE MEMBER OF ONE'S SPECIES IN THE KNOWN GALAXY IS KIND OF OUR THING.
I ASKED YOU A QUESTION: WHAT DOES THAT MEAN?
I'M THE ONLY ONE OF MY KIND?
WHERE ARE YOU FROM?

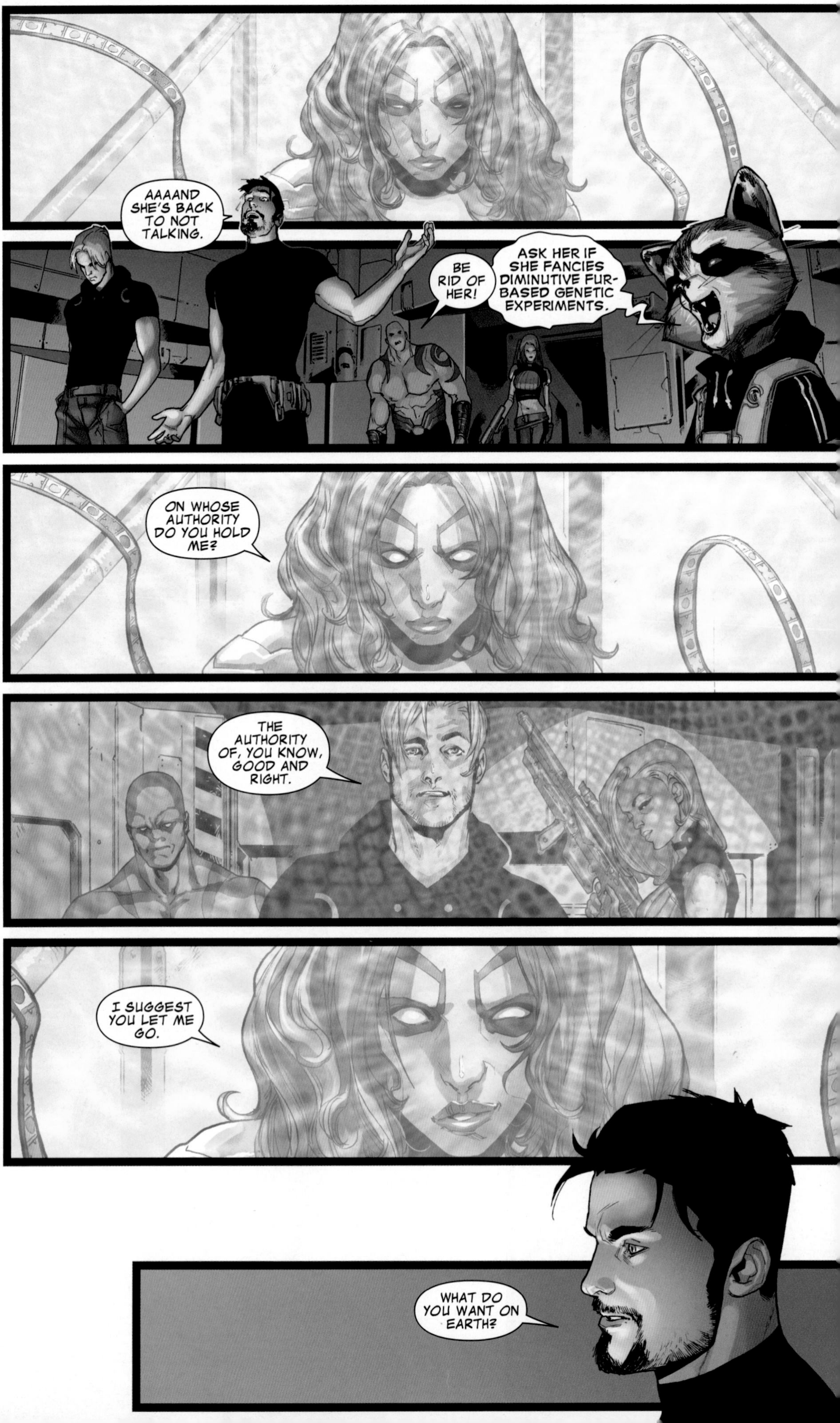

AAAAND SHE'S BACK TO NOT TALKING.
BE RID OF HER!
ASK HER IF SHE FANCIES DIMINUTIVE FUR-BASED GENETIC EXPERIMENTS.
ON WHOSE AUTHORITY DO YOU HOLD ME?
THE AUTHORITY OF, YOU KNOW, GOOD AND RIGHT.
I SUGGEST YOU LET ME GO.
WHAT DO YOU WANT ON EARTH?

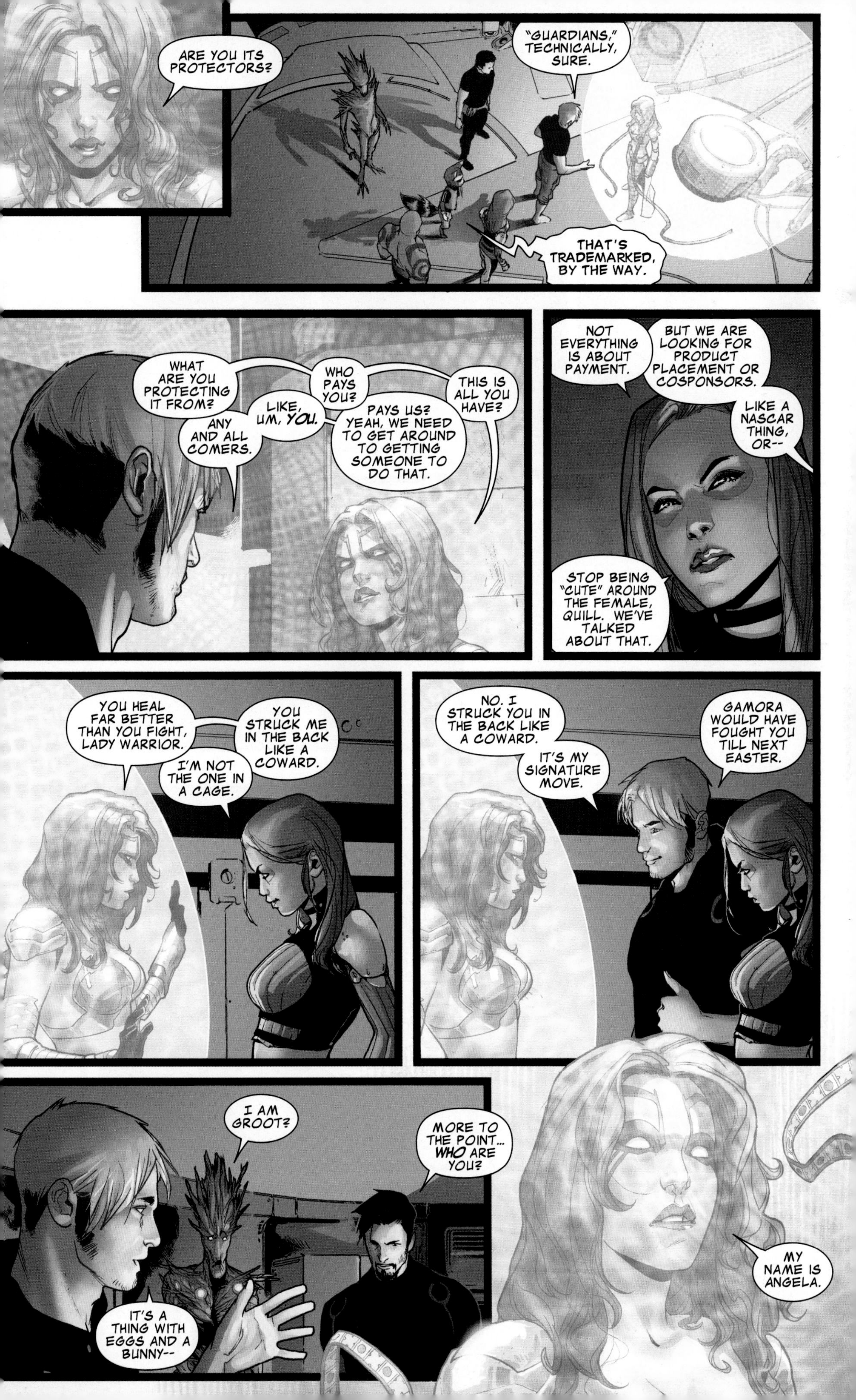
ARE YOU ITS PROTECTORS?
"GUARDIANS," TECHNICALLY, SURE.
THAT'S TRADEMARKED, BY THE WAY.
WHAT ARE YOU PROTECTING IT FROM?
ANY AND ALL COMERS.
WHO PAYS YOU?
LIKE, UM, YOU.
PAYS US? YEAH, WE NEED TO GET AROUND TO GETTING SOMEONE TO DO THAT.
THIS IS ALL YOU HAVE?
NOT EVERYTHING IS ABOUT PAYMENT.
BUT WE ARE LOOKING FOR PRODUCT PLACEMENT OR COSPONSORS.
LIKE A NASCAR THING, OR--
STOP BEING "CUTE" AROUND THE FEMALE, QUILL. WE'VE TALKED ABOUT THAT.
YOU HEAL FAR BETTER THAN YOU FIGHT, LADY WARRIOR.
YOU STRUCK ME IN THE BACK LIKE A COWARD.
I'M NOT THE ONE IN A CAGE.
NO. I STRUCK YOU IN THE BACK LIKE A COWARD.
IT'S MY SIGNATURE MOVE.
GAMORA WOULD HAVE FOUGHT YOU TILL NEXT EASTER.
I AM GROOT?
IT'S A THING WITH EGGS AND A BUNNY--
MORE TO THE POINT... WHO ARE YOU?
MY NAME IS ANGELA.

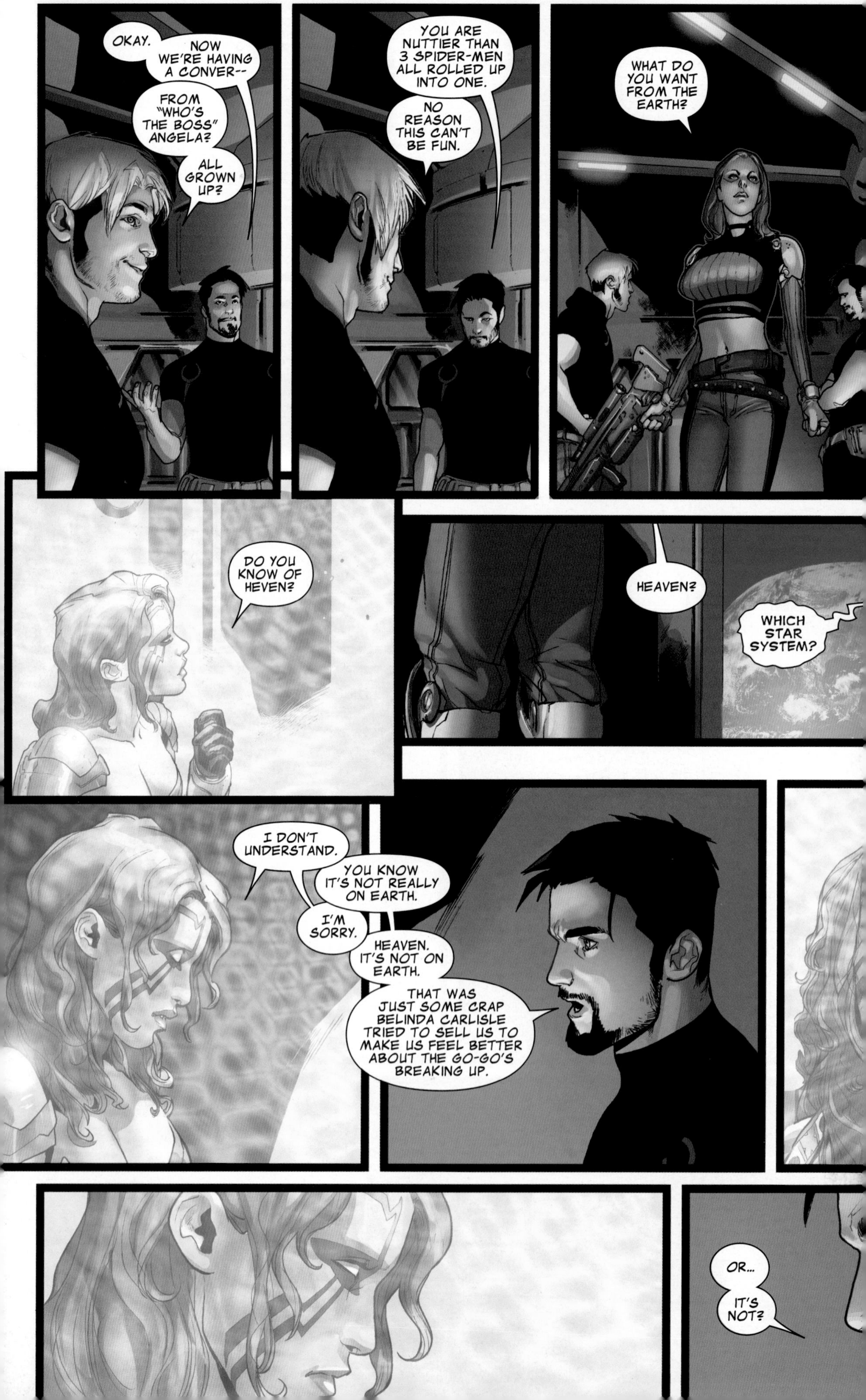
OKAY.
NOW WE'RE HAVING A CONVER--
FROM "WHO'S THE BOSS" ANGELA?
ALL GROWN UP?
YOU ARE NUTTIER THAN 3 SPIDER-MEN ALL ROLLED UP INTO ONE.
NO REASON THIS CAN'T BE FUN.
WHAT DO YOU WANT FROM THE EARTH?
DO YOU KNOW OF HEVEN?
HEAVEN?
WHICH STAR SYSTEM?
I DON'T UNDERSTAND.
YOU KNOW IT'S NOT REALLY ON EARTH.
I'M SORRY.
HEAVEN. IT'S NOT ON EARTH.
THAT WAS JUST SOME CRAP BELINDA CARLISLE TRIED TO SELL US TO MAKE US FEEL BETTER ABOUT THE GO-GO'S BREAKING UP.
OR...
IT'S NOT?

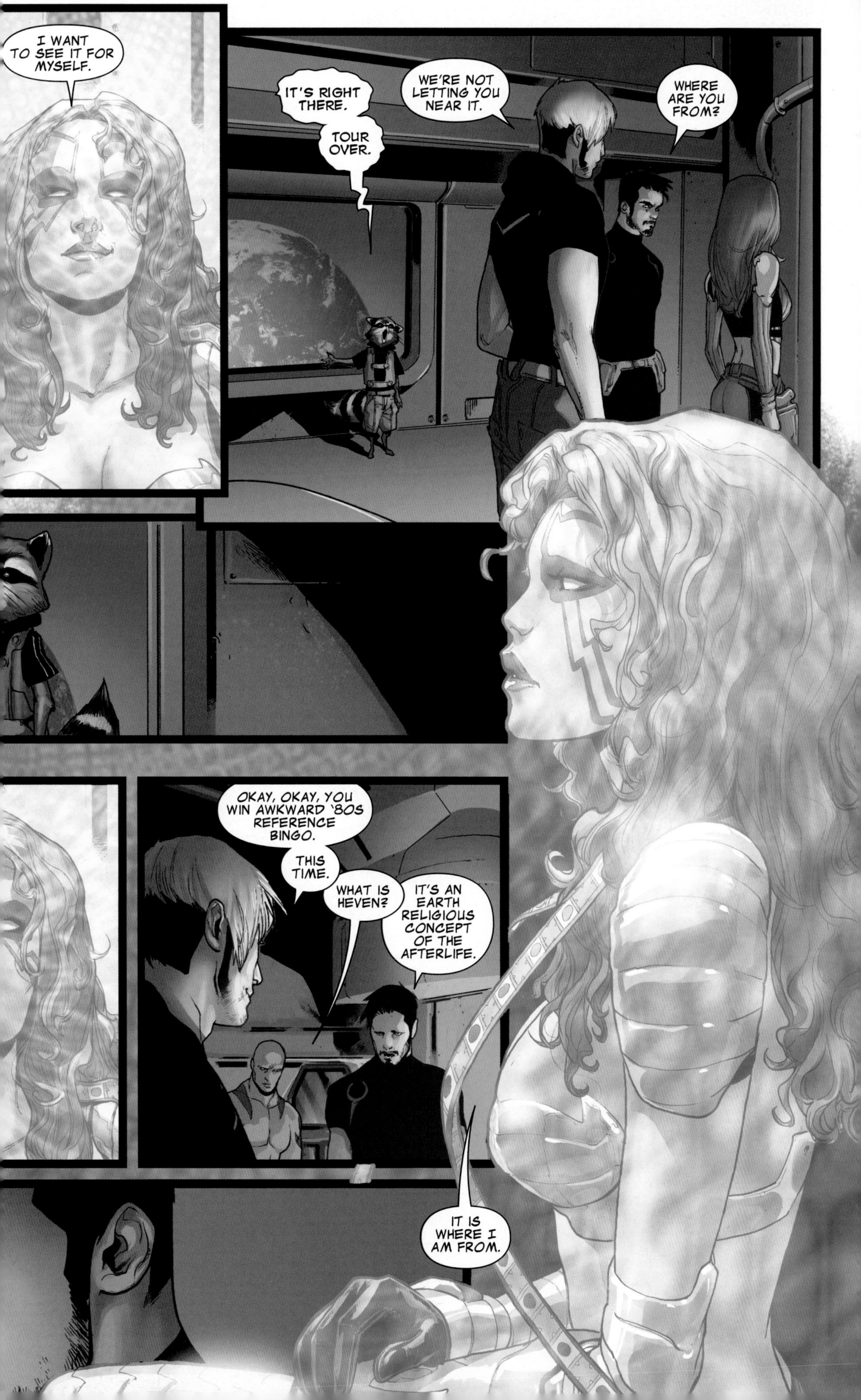
I WANT TO SEE IT FOR MYSELF.
IT'S RIGHT THERE.
TOUR OVER.
WE'RE NOT LETTING YOU NEAR IT.
WHERE ARE YOU FROM?
OKAY, OKAY, YOU WIN AWKWARD '80S REFERENCE BINGO.
THIS TIME.
WHAT IS HEVEN?
IT'S AN EARTH RELIGIOUS CONCEPT OF THE AFTERLIFE.
IT IS WHERE I AM FROM.

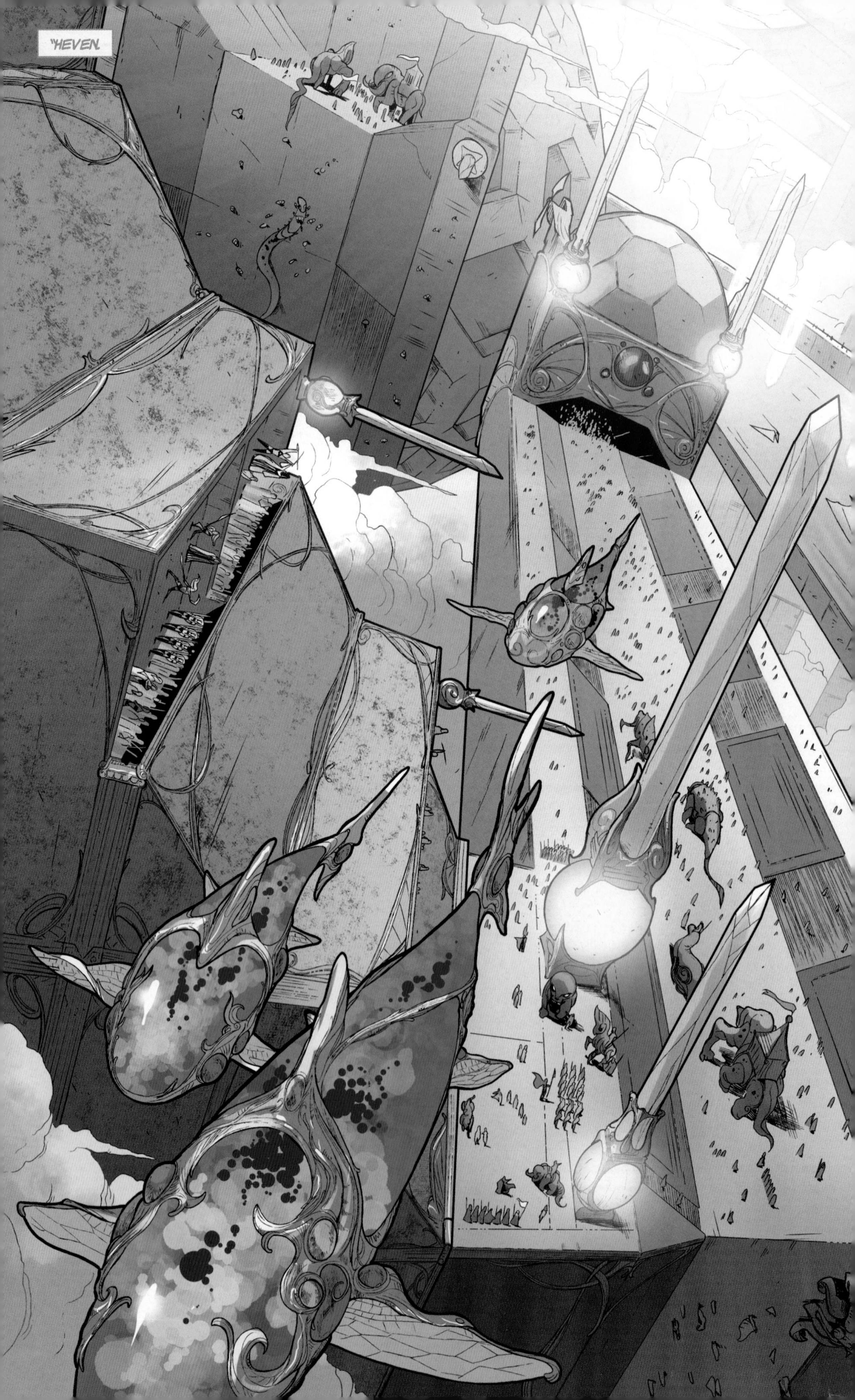
"HEVEN.

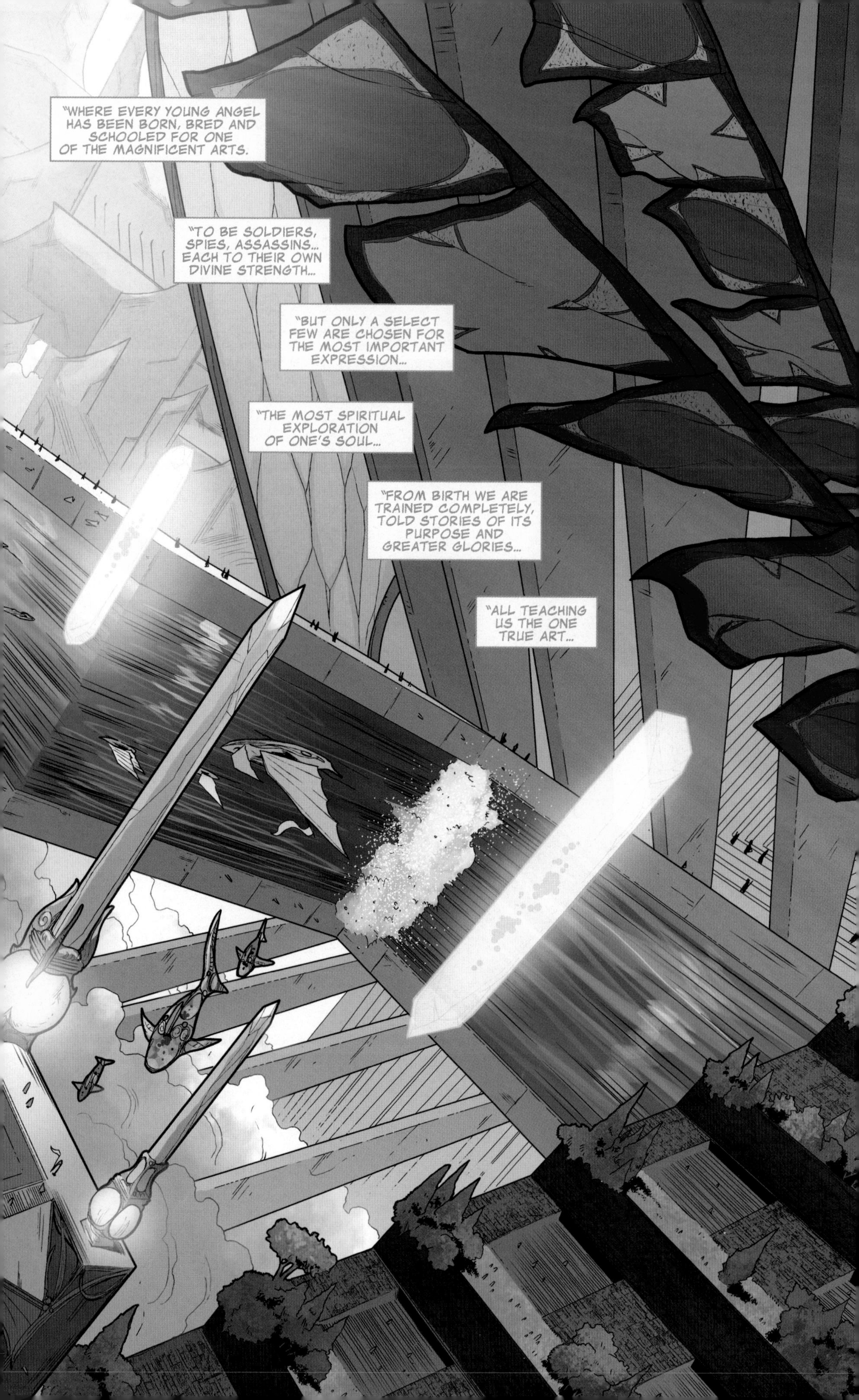
"WHERE EVERY YOUNG ANGEL HAS BEEN BORN, BRED AND SCHOOLED FOR ONE OF THE MAGNIFICENT ARTS.
"TO BE SOLDIERS, SPIES, ASSASSINS... EACH TO THEIR OWN DIVINE STRENGTH...
"BUT ONLY A SELECT FEW ARE CHOSEN FOR THE MOST IMPORTANT EXPRESSION...
"THE MOST SPIRITUAL EXPLORATION OF ONE'S SOUL...
"FROM BIRTH WE ARE TRAINED COMPLETELY, TOLD STORIES OF ITS PURPOSE AND GREATER GLORIES...
"ALL TEACHING US THE ONE TRUE ART...

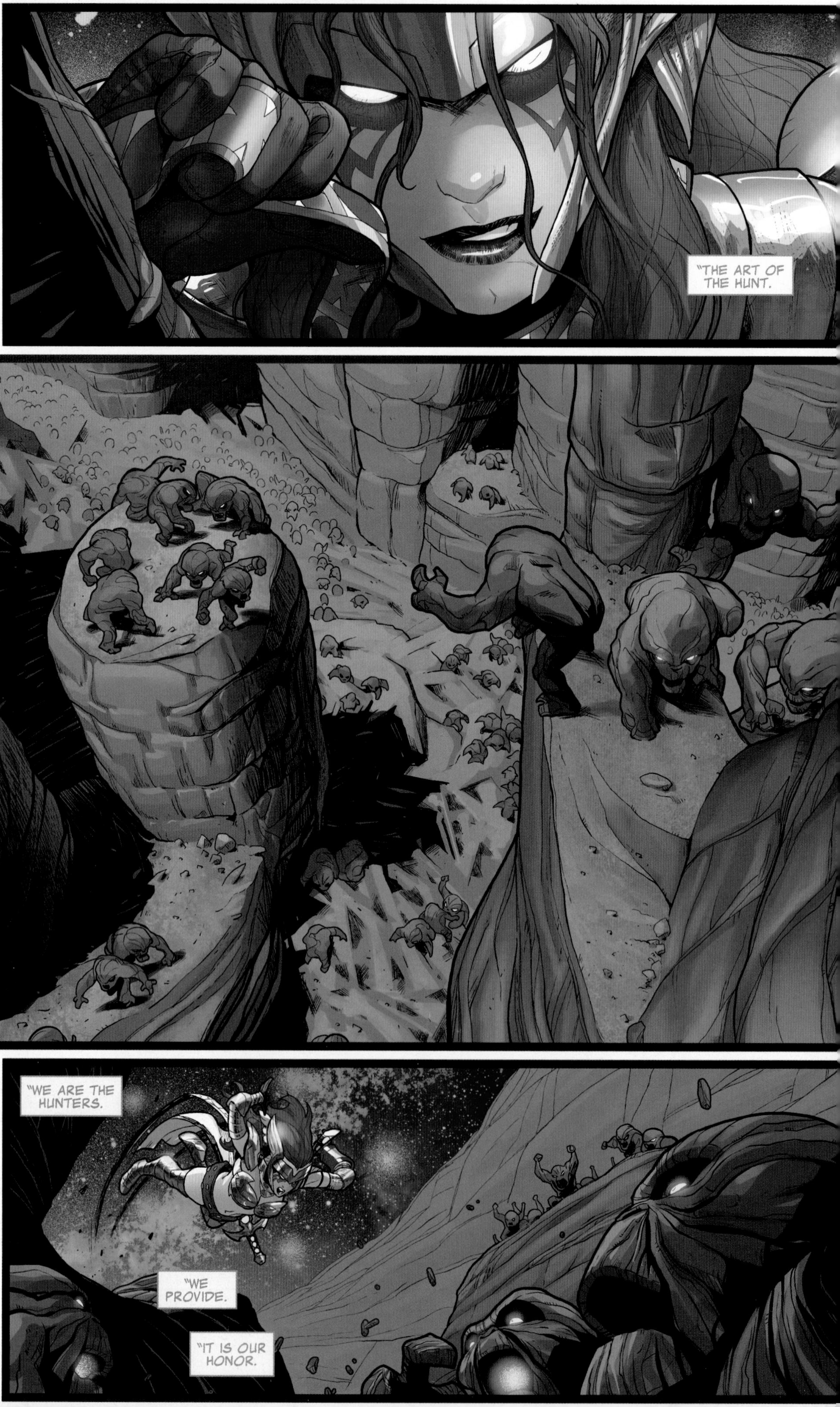
"THE ART OF THE HUNT.
"WE ARE THE HUNTERS.
"WE PROVIDE.
"IT IS OUR HONOR.

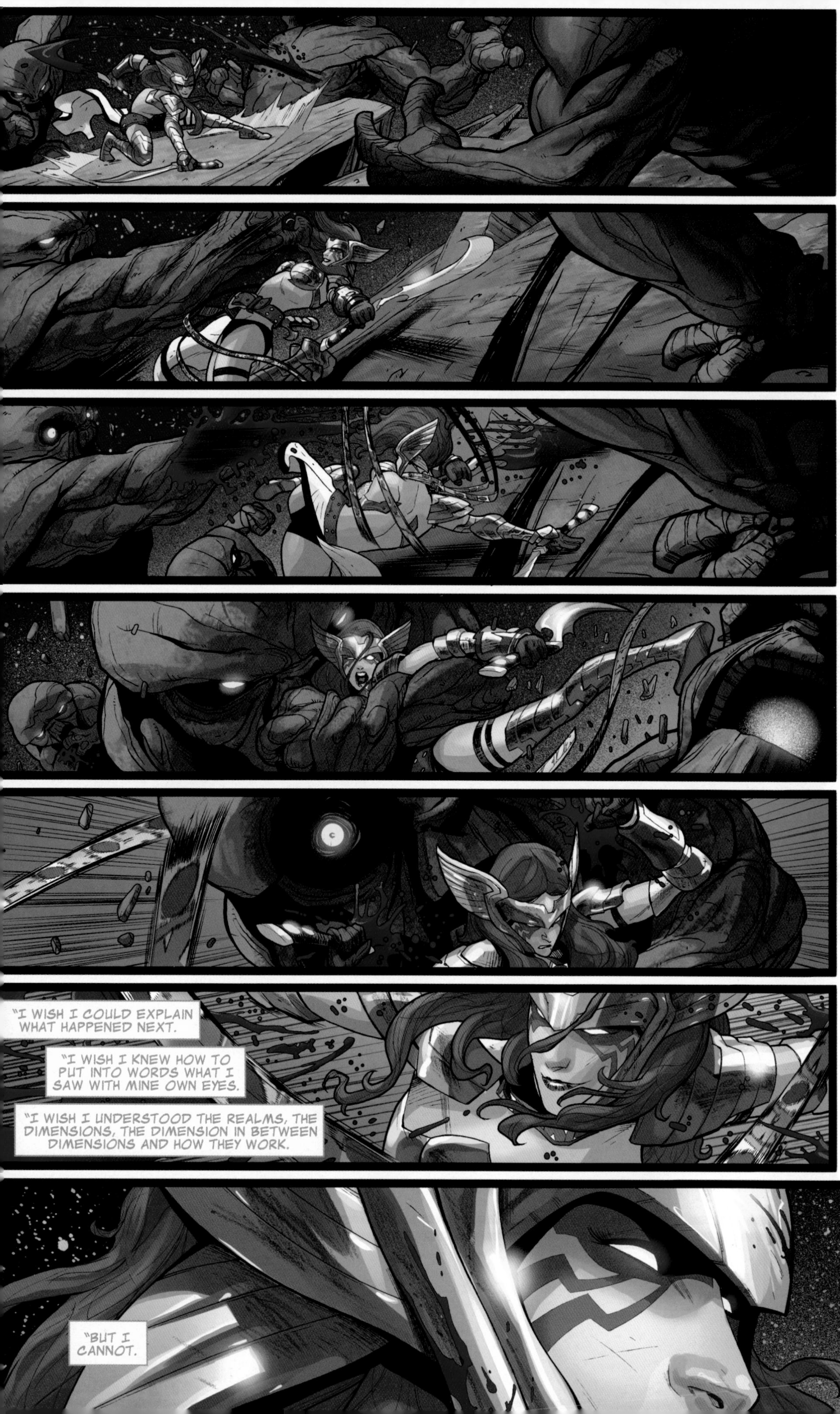
"I WISH I COULD EXPLAIN WHAT HAPPENED NEXT.
"I WISH I KNEW HOW TO PUT INTO WORDS WHAT I SAW WITH MINE OWN EYES.
"I WISH I UNDERSTOOD THE REALMS, THE DIMENSIONS, THE DIMENSION IN BETWEEN DIMENSIONS AND HOW THEY WORK.
"BUT I CANNOT.

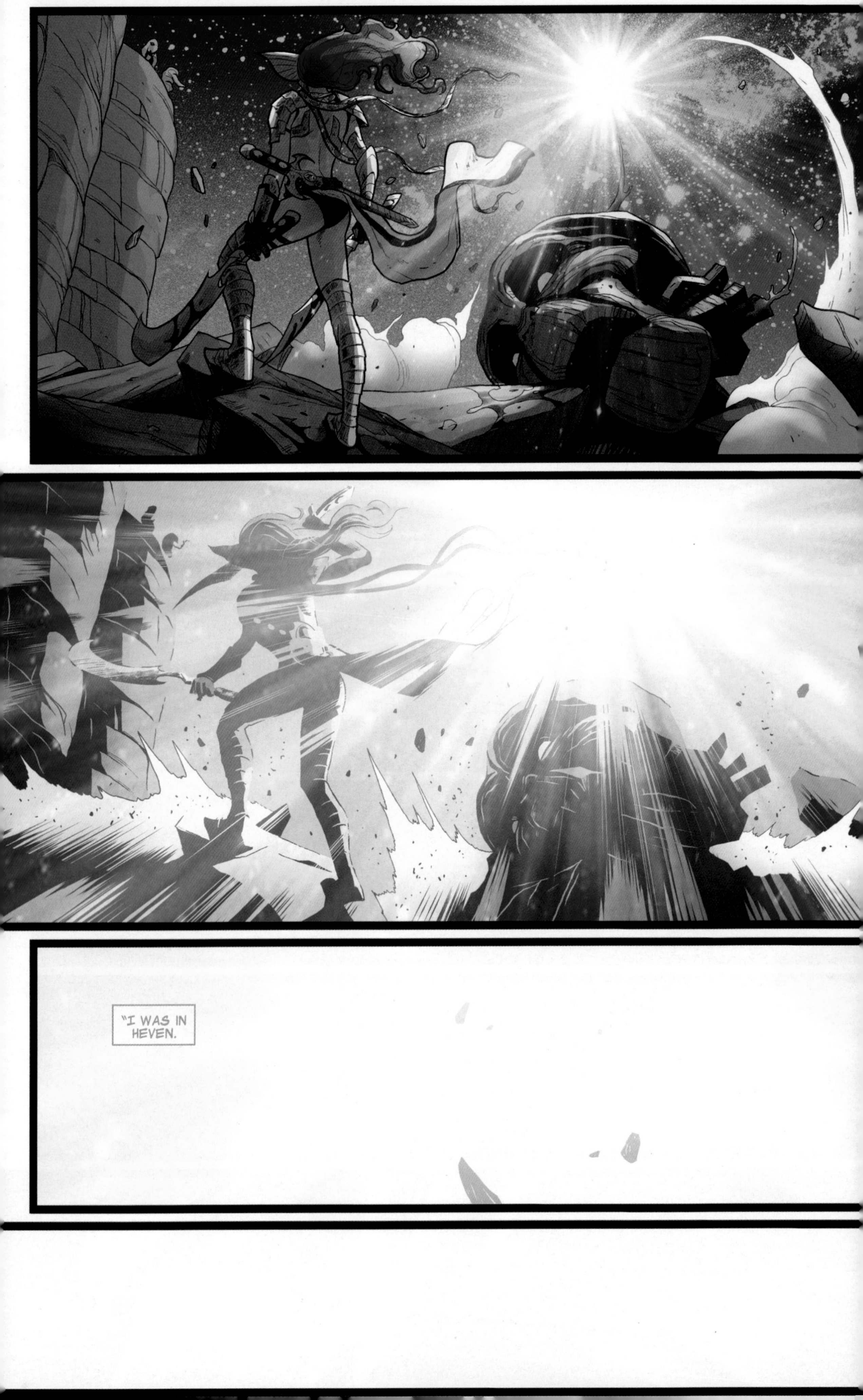
"I WAS IN HEVEN.

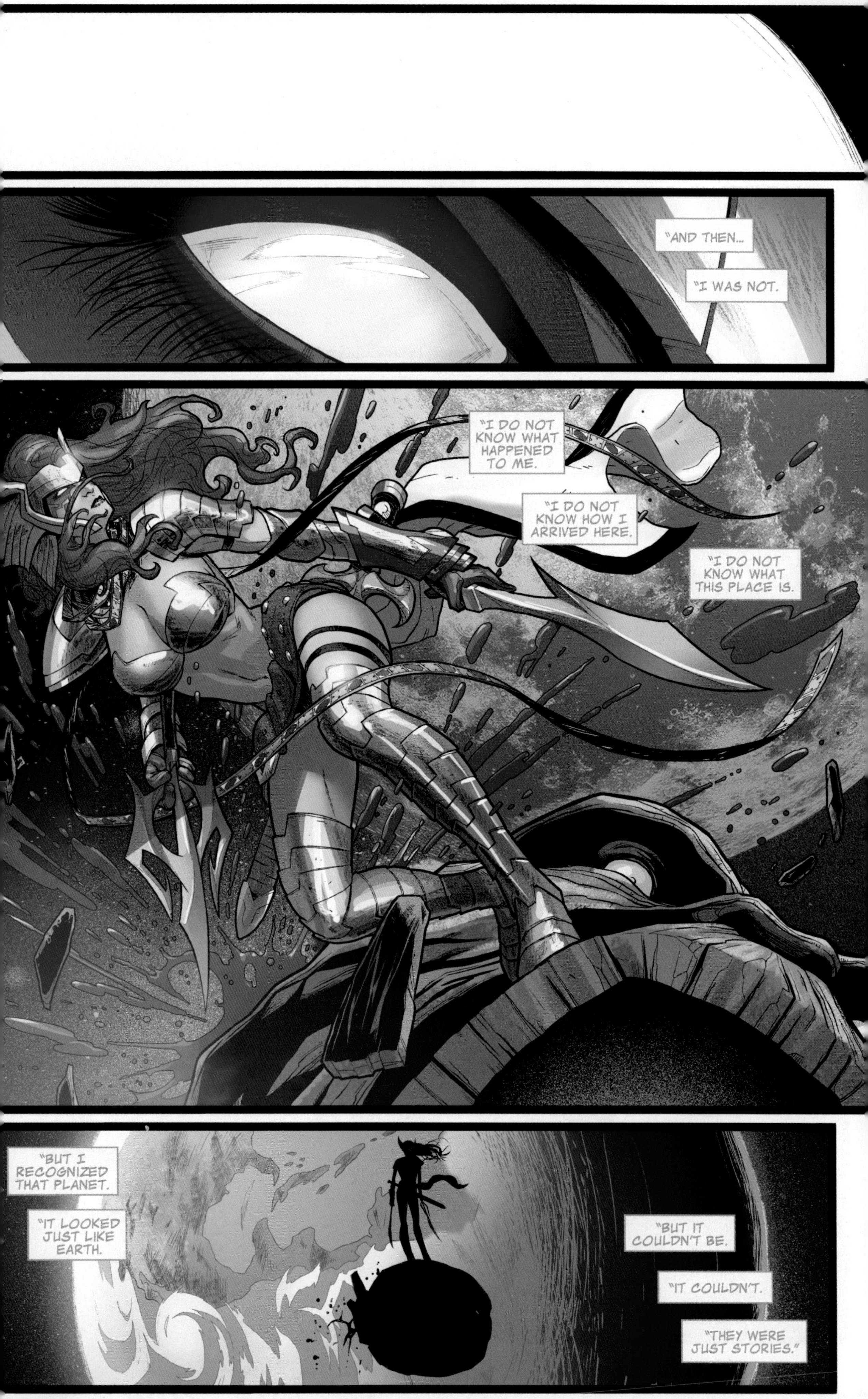
"AND THEN...
"I WAS NOT.
"I DO NOT KNOW WHAT HAPPENED TO ME.
"I DO NOT KNOW HOW I ARRIVED HERE.
"I DO NOT KNOW WHAT THIS PLACE IS.
"BUT I RECOGNIZED THAT PLANET.
"IT LOOKED JUST LIKE EARTH.
"BUT IT COULDN'T BE.
"IT COULDN'T.
"THEY WERE JUST STORIES."

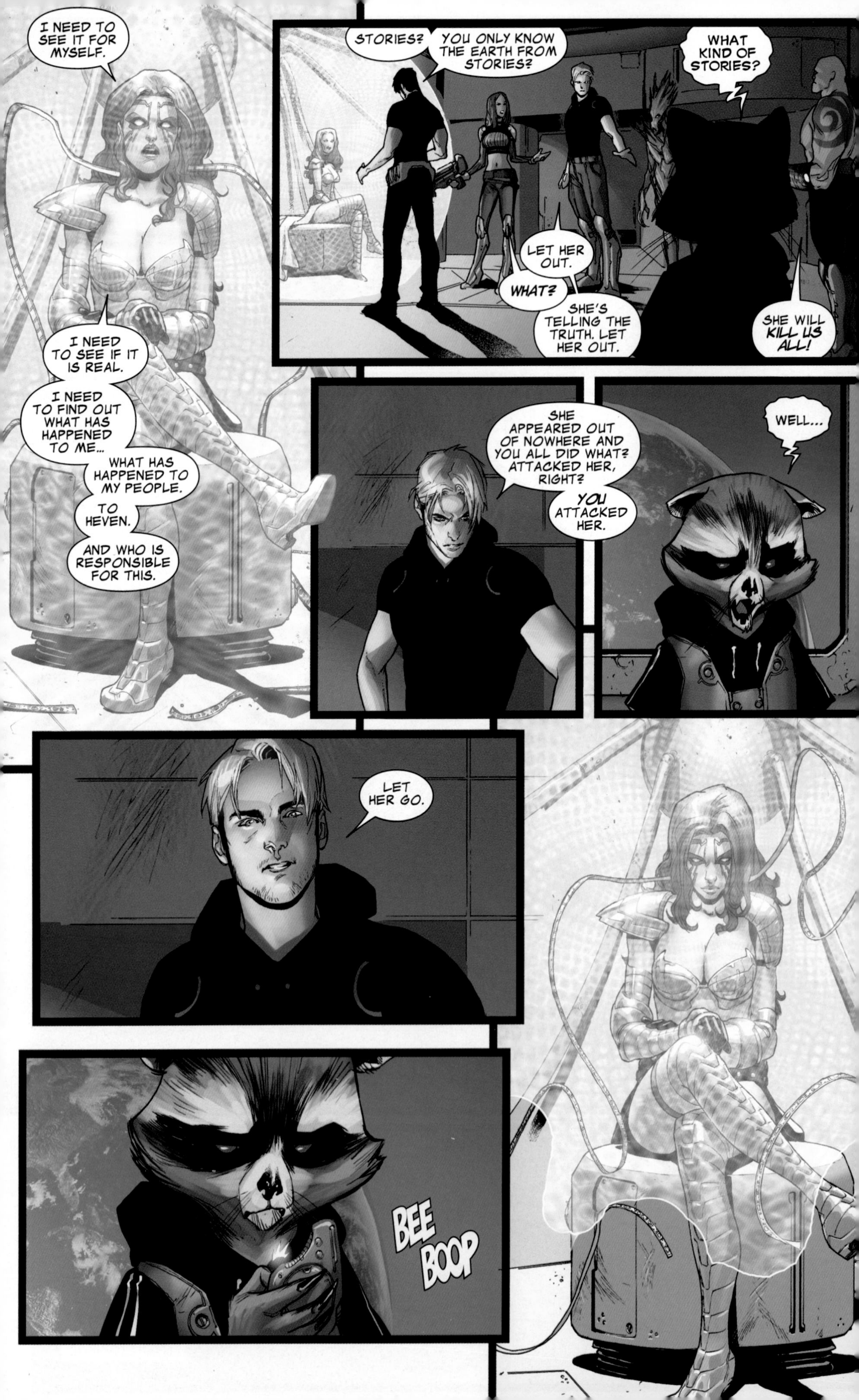
I NEED TO SEE IT FOR MYSELF.
STORIES?
YOU ONLY KNOW THE EARTH FROM STORIES?
WHAT KIND OF STORIES?
LET HER OUT.
WHAT?
SHE'S TELLING THE TRUTH. LET HER OUT.
SHE WILL KILL US ALL!
I NEED TO SEE IF IT IS REAL.
I NEED TO FIND OUT WHAT HAS HAPPENED TO ME...
WHAT HAS HAPPENED TO MY PEOPLE.
TO HEVEN.
AND WHO IS RESPONSIBLE FOR THIS.
SHE APPEARED OUT OF NOWHERE AND YOU ALL DID WHAT? ATTACKED HER, RIGHT?
YOU ATTACKED HER.
WELL...
LET HER GO.
BEE BOOP

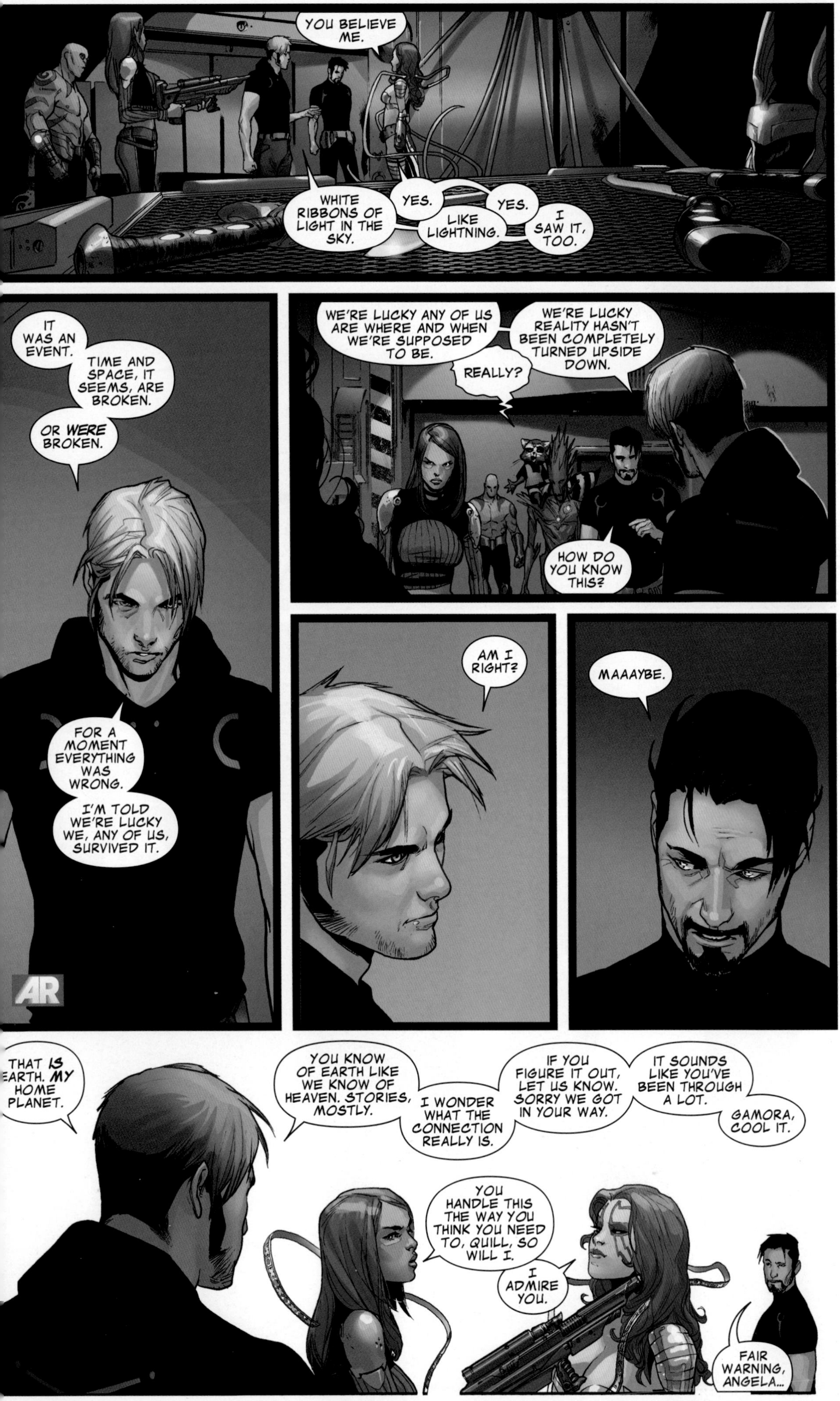
YOU BELIEVE ME.
WHITE RIBBONS OF LIGHT IN THE SKY.
YES.
LIKE LIGHTNING.
YES.
I SAW IT, TOO.
IT WAS AN EVENT.
TIME AND SPACE, IT SEEMS, ARE BROKEN.
OR WERE BROKEN.
FOR A MOMENT EVERYTHING WAS WRONG.
I'M TOLD WE'RE LUCKY WE, ANY OF US, SURVIVED IT.
WE'RE LUCKY ANY OF US ARE WHERE AND WHEN WE'RE SUPPOSED TO BE.
WE'RE LUCKY REALITY HASN'T BEEN COMPLETELY TURNED UPSIDE DOWN.
REALLY?
HOW DO YOU KNOW THIS?
AM I RIGHT?
MAAAYBE.
THAT IS EARTH. MY HOME PLANET.
YOU KNOW OF EARTH LIKE WE KNOW OF HEAVEN. STORIES, MOSTLY.
I WONDER WHAT THE CONNECTION REALLY IS.
IF YOU FIGURE IT OUT, LET US KNOW. SORRY WE GOT IN YOUR WAY.
IT SOUNDS LIKE YOU'VE BEEN THROUGH A LOT.
GAMORA, COOL IT.
YOU HANDLE THIS THE WAY YOU THINK YOU NEED TO, QUILL, SO WILL I.
I ADMIRE YOU.
FAIR WARNING, ANGELA...

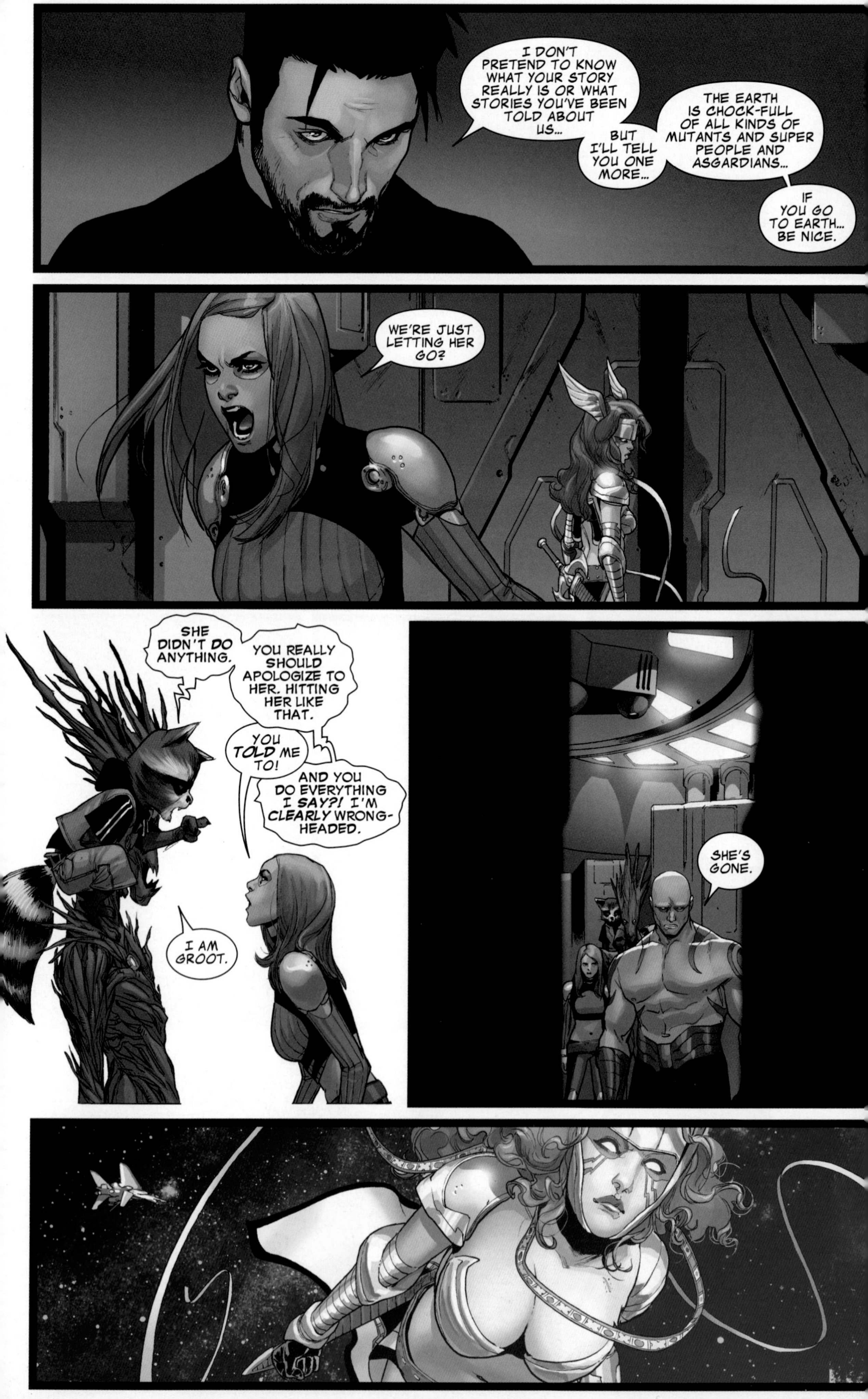
I DON'T PRETEND TO KNOW WHAT YOUR STORY REALLY IS OR WHAT STORIES YOU'VE BEEN TOLD ABOUT US...
BUT I'LL TELL YOU ONE MORE...
THE EARTH IS CHOCK-FULL OF ALL KINDS OF MUTANTS AND SUPER PEOPLE AND ASGARDIANS...
IF YOU GO TO EARTH... BE NICE.
WE'RE JUST LETTING HER GO?
SHE DIDN'T DO ANYTHING.
YOU REALLY SHOULD APOLOGIZE TO HER. HITTING HER LIKE THAT.
YOU TOLD ME TO!
AND YOU DO EVERYTHING I SAY?! I'M CLEARLY WRONG-HEADED.
I AM GROOT.
SHE'S GONE.

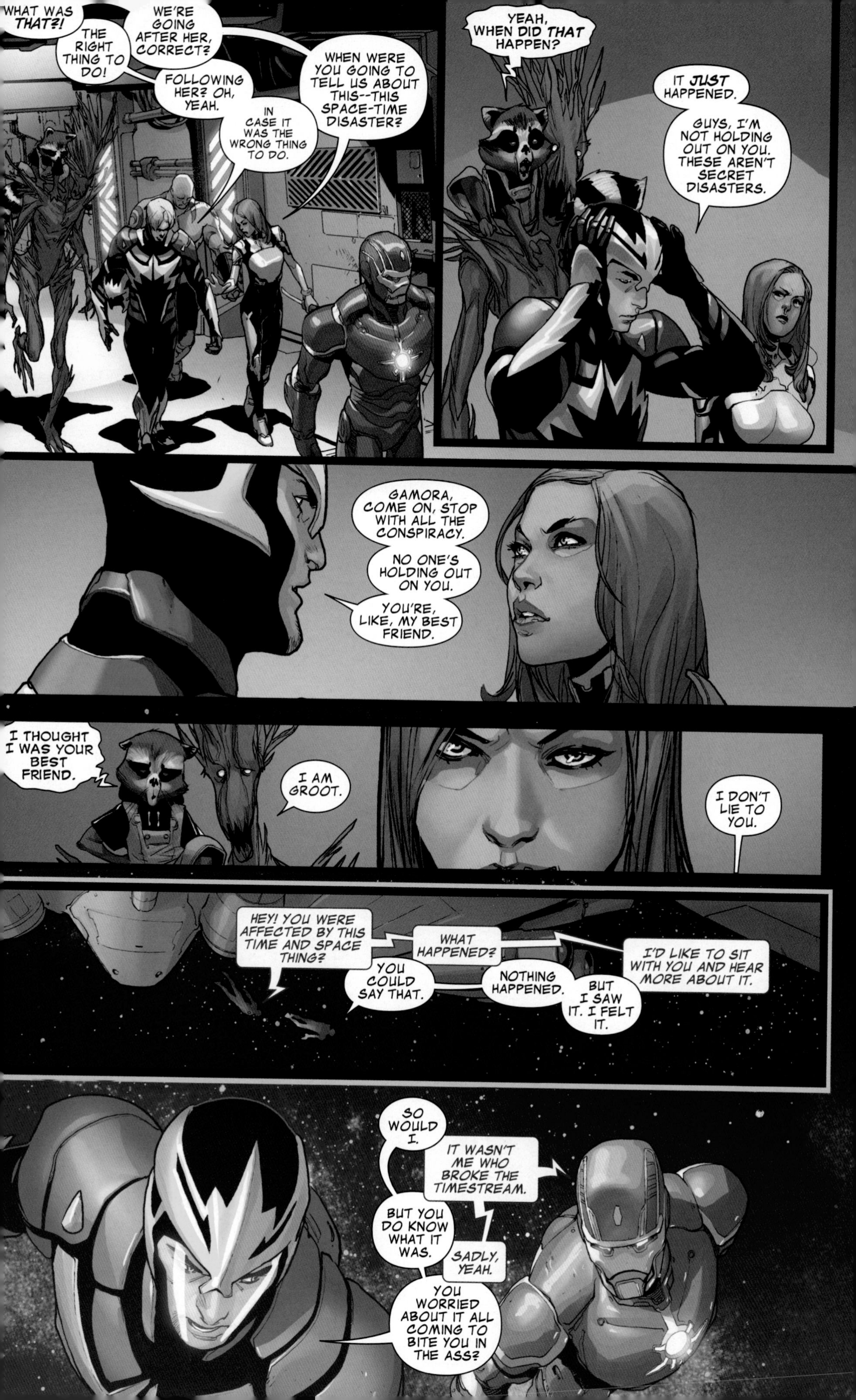
WHAT WAS THAT?!
THE RIGHT THING TO DO!
WE'RE GOING AFTER HER, CORRECT?
FOLLOWING HER? OH, YEAH.
IN CASE IT WAS THE WRONG THING TO DO.
WHEN WERE YOU GOING TO TELL US ABOUT THIS--THIS SPACE-TIME DISASTER?
YEAH, WHEN DID THAT HAPPEN?
IT JUST HAPPENED.
GUYS, I'M NOT HOLDING OUT ON YOU. THESE AREN'T SECRET DISASTERS.
GAMORA, COME ON, STOP WITH ALL THE CONSPIRACY.
NO ONE'S HOLDING OUT ON YOU.
YOU'RE, LIKE, MY BEST FRIEND.
I THOUGHT I WAS YOUR BEST FRIEND.
I AM GROOT.
I DON'T LIE TO YOU.
HEY! YOU WERE AFFECTED BY THIS TIME AND SPACE THING?
WHAT HAPPENED?
YOU COULD SAY THAT.
NOTHING HAPPENED.
BUT I SAW IT. I FELT IT.
I'D LIKE TO SIT WITH YOU AND HEAR MORE ABOUT IT.
SO WOULD I.
IT WASN'T ME WHO BROKE THE TIMESTREAM.
BUT YOU DO KNOW WHAT IT WAS.
SADLY, YEAH.
YOU WORRIED ABOUT IT ALL COMING TO BITE YOU IN THE ASS?

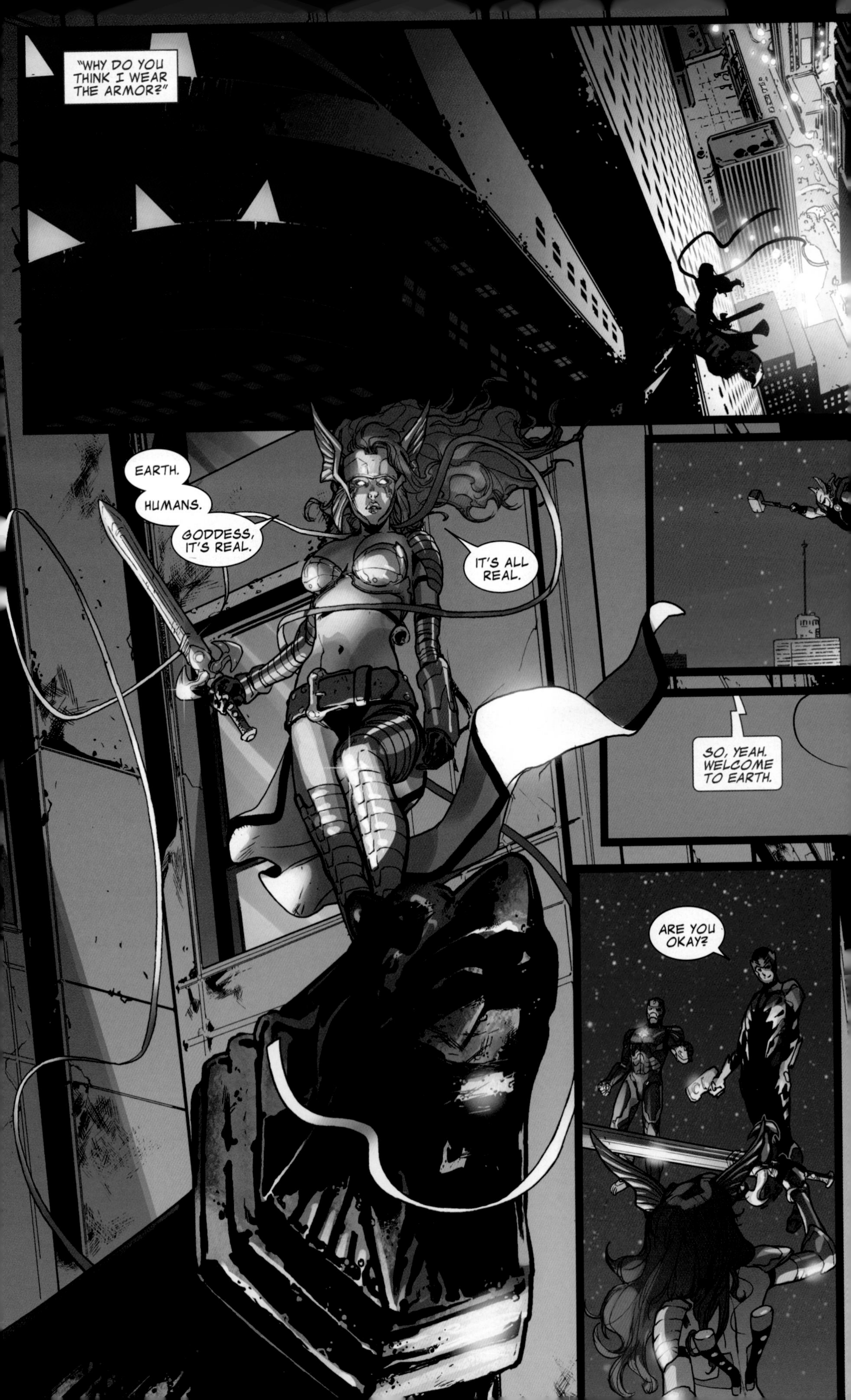
"WHY DO YOU THINK I WEAR THE ARMOR?"
EARTH.
HUMANS.
GODDESS, IT'S REAL.
IT'S ALL REAL.
SO, YEAH. WELCOME TO EARTH.
ARE YOU OKAY?

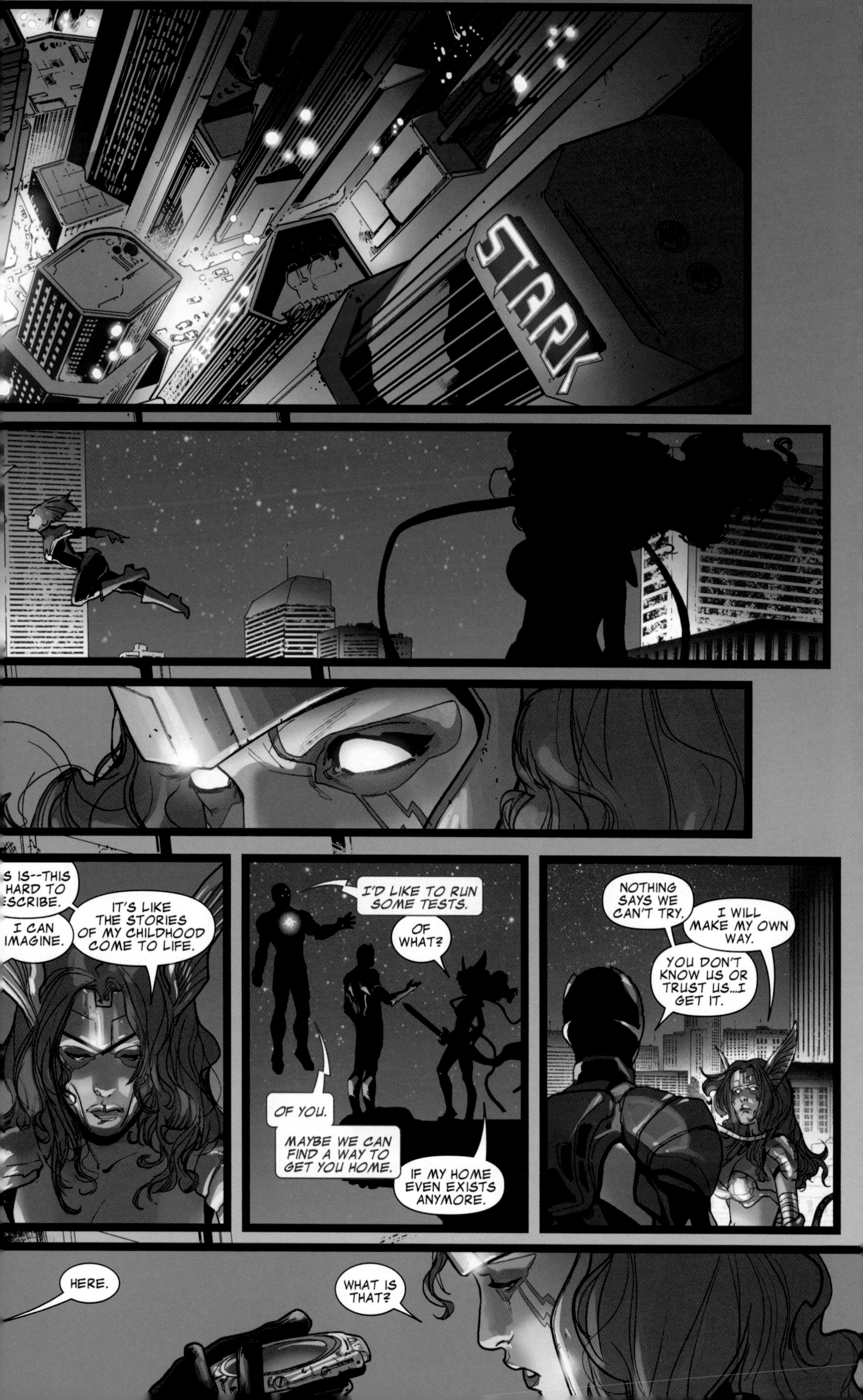

STARK
S IS--THIS HARD TO ESCRIBE.
I CAN IMAGINE.
IT'S LIKE THE STORIES OF MY CHILDHOOD COME TO LIFE.
I'D LIKE TO RUN SOME TESTS.
OF WHAT?
OF YOU.
MAYBE WE CAN FIND A WAY TO GET YOU HOME.
IF MY HOME EVEN EXISTS ANYMORE.
NOTHING SAYS WE CAN'T TRY.
I WILL MAKE MY OWN WAY.
YOU DON'T KNOW US OR TRUST US...I GET IT.
HERE.
WHAT IS THAT?

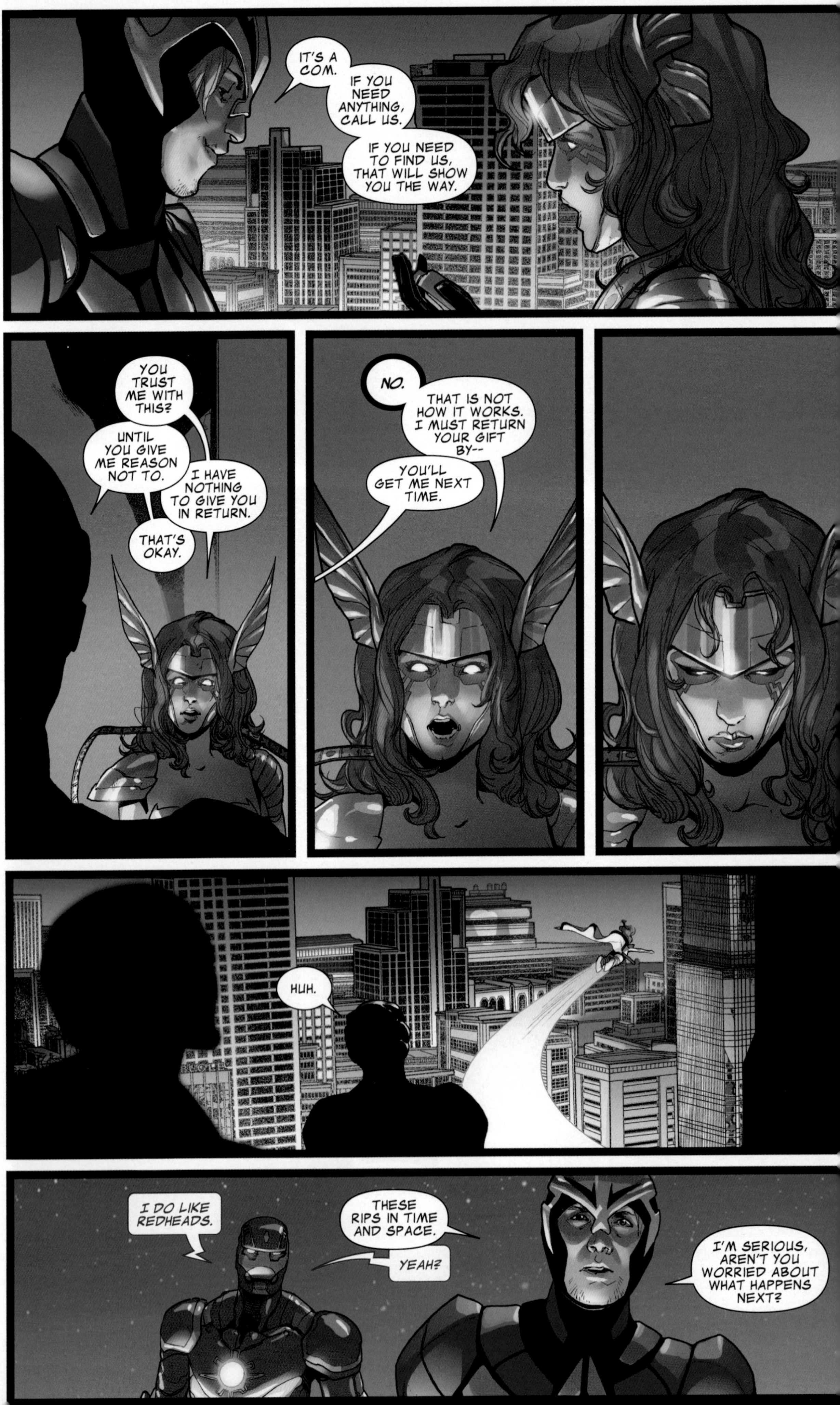
IT'S A COM.
IF YOU NEED ANYTHING, CALL US.
IF YOU NEED TO FIND US, THAT WILL SHOW YOU THE WAY.
YOU TRUST ME WITH THIS?
UNTIL YOU GIVE ME REASON NOT TO.
I HAVE NOTHING TO GIVE YOU IN RETURN.
THAT'S OKAY.
NO.
THAT IS NOT HOW IT WORKS. I MUST RETURN YOUR GIFT BY--
YOU'LL GET ME NEXT TIME.
HUH.
I DO LIKE REDHEADS.
THESE RIPS IN TIME AND SPACE.
YEAH?
I'M SERIOUS, AREN'T YOU WORRIED ABOUT WHAT HAPPENS NEXT?

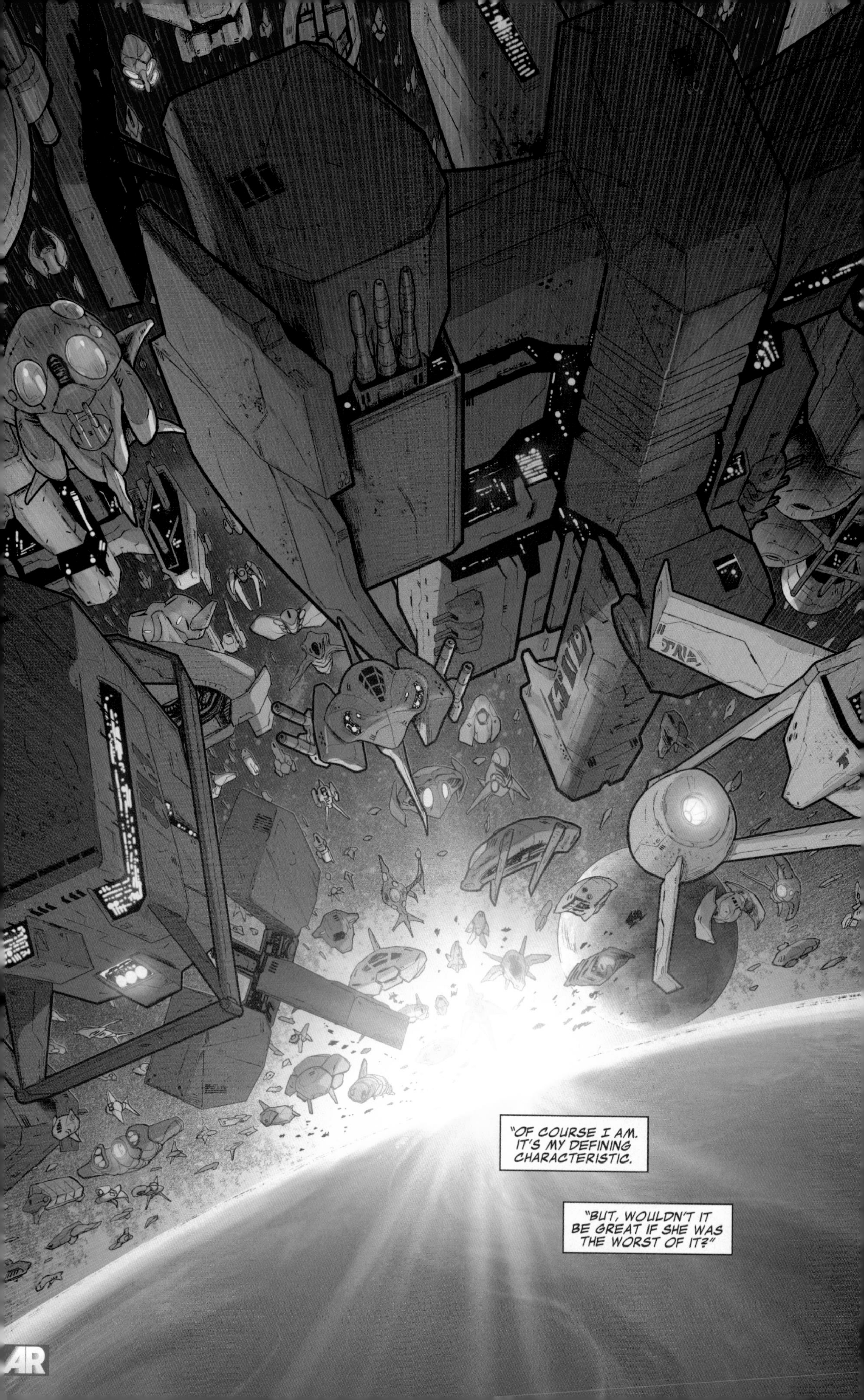
"OF COURSE I AM. IT'S MY DEFINING CHARACTERISTIC.
"BUT, WOULDN'T IT BE GREAT IF SHE WAS THE WORST OF IT?"

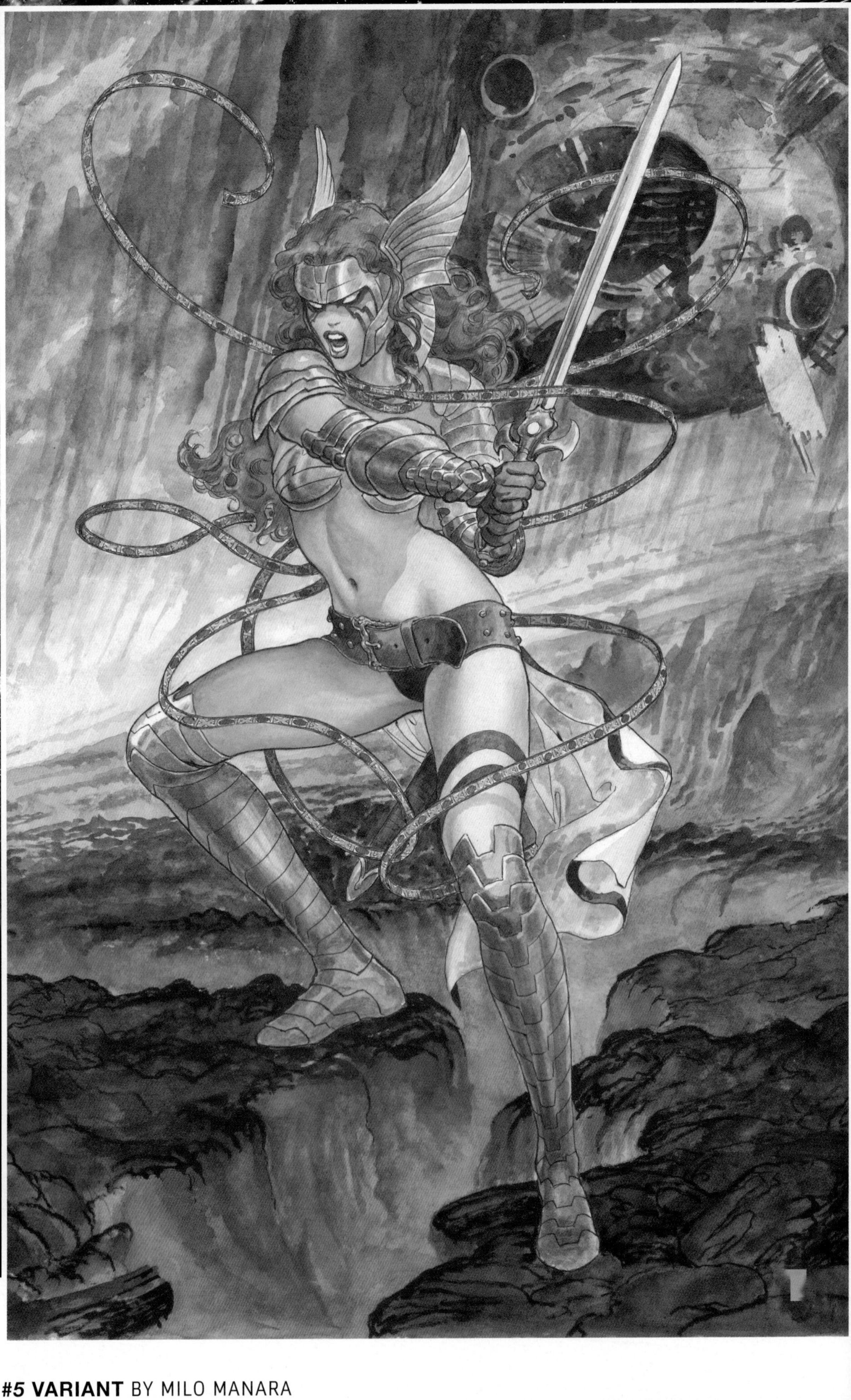

#5 VARIANT BY MILO MANARA

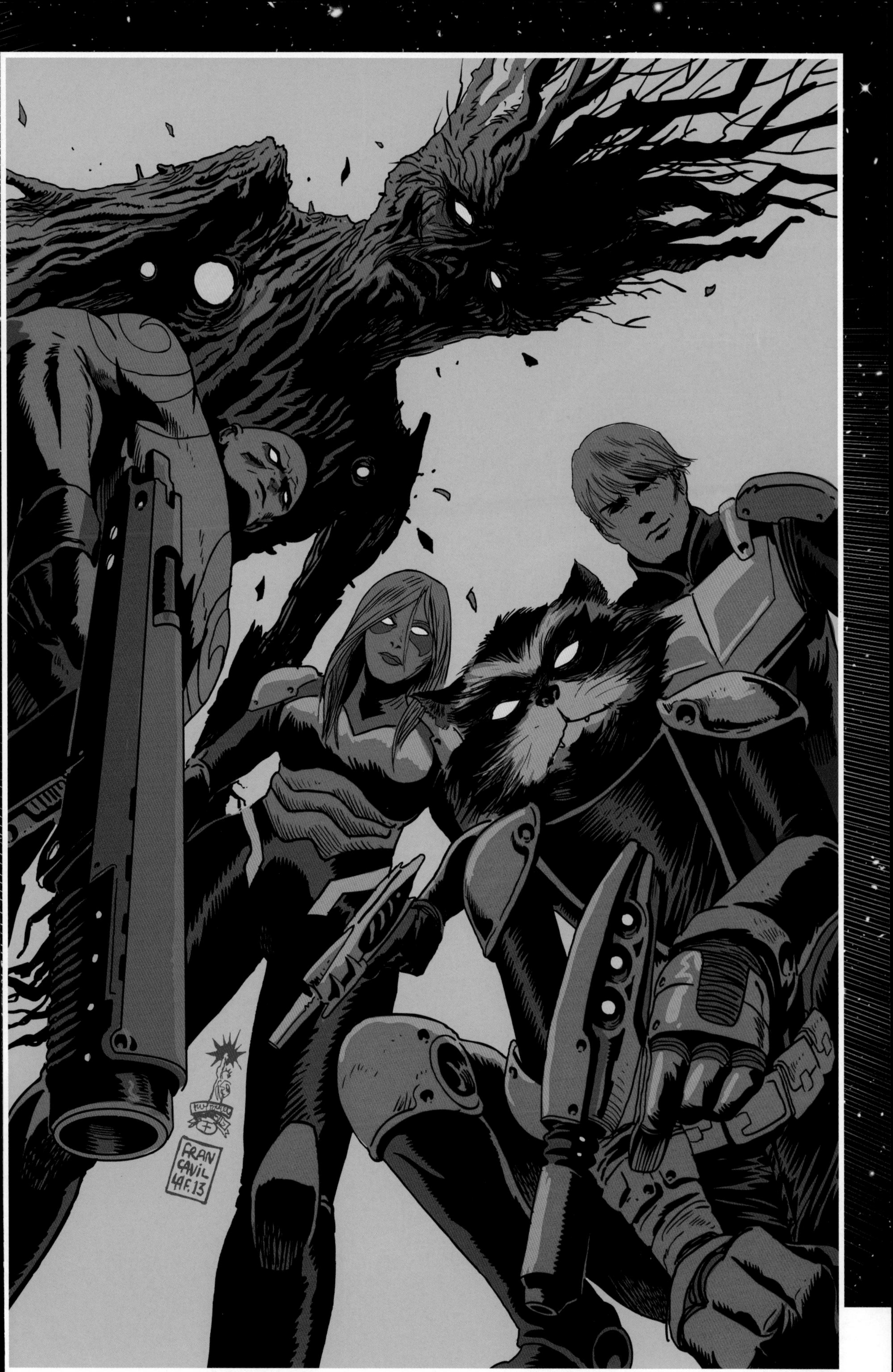

8

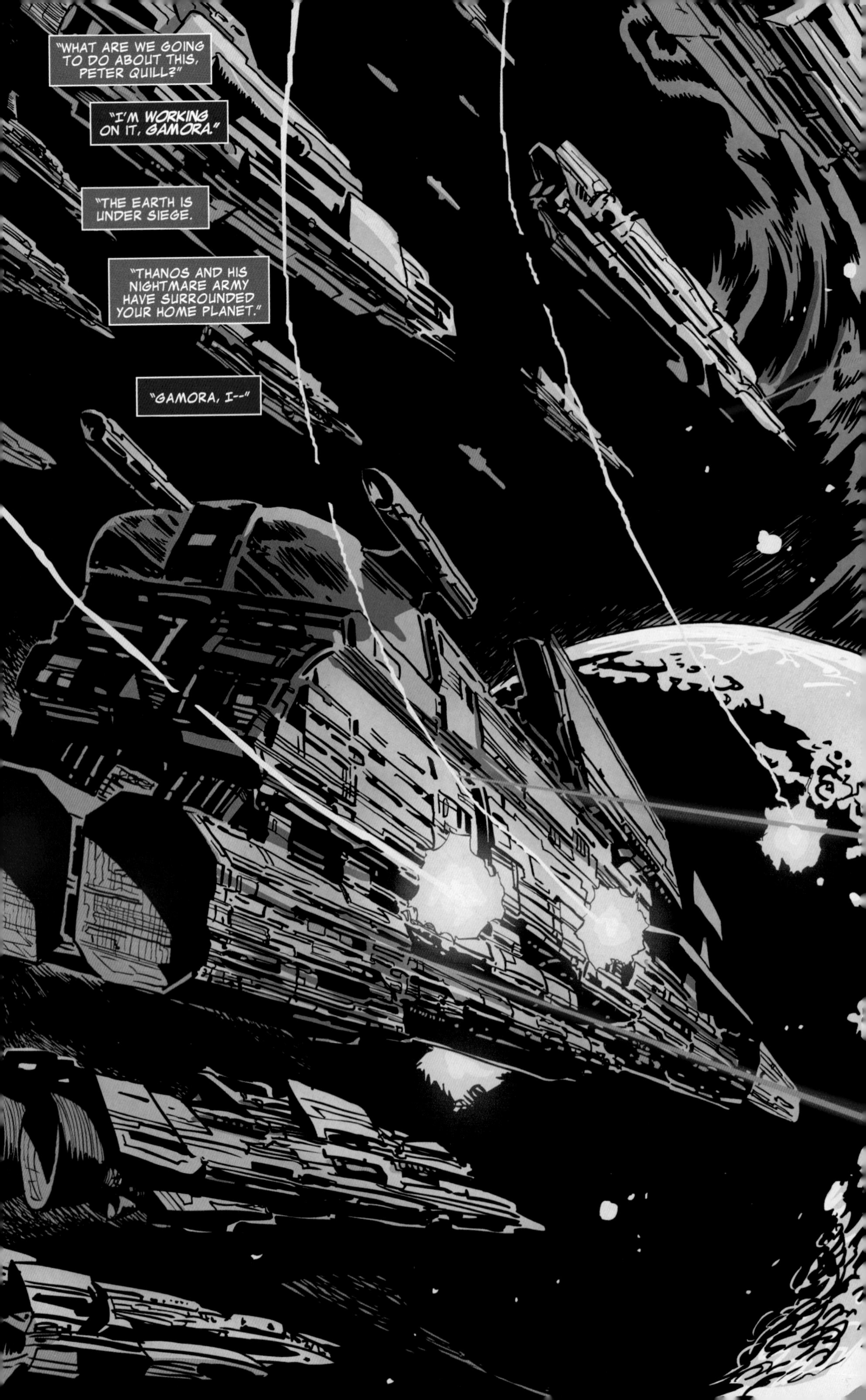
"WHAT ARE WE GOING TO DO ABOUT THIS, PETER QUILL?"
"I'M WORKING ON IT, GAMORA."
"THE EARTH IS UNDER SIEGE.
"THANOS AND HIS NIGHTMARE ARMY HAVE SURROUNDED YOUR HOME PLANET."
"GAMORA, I--"

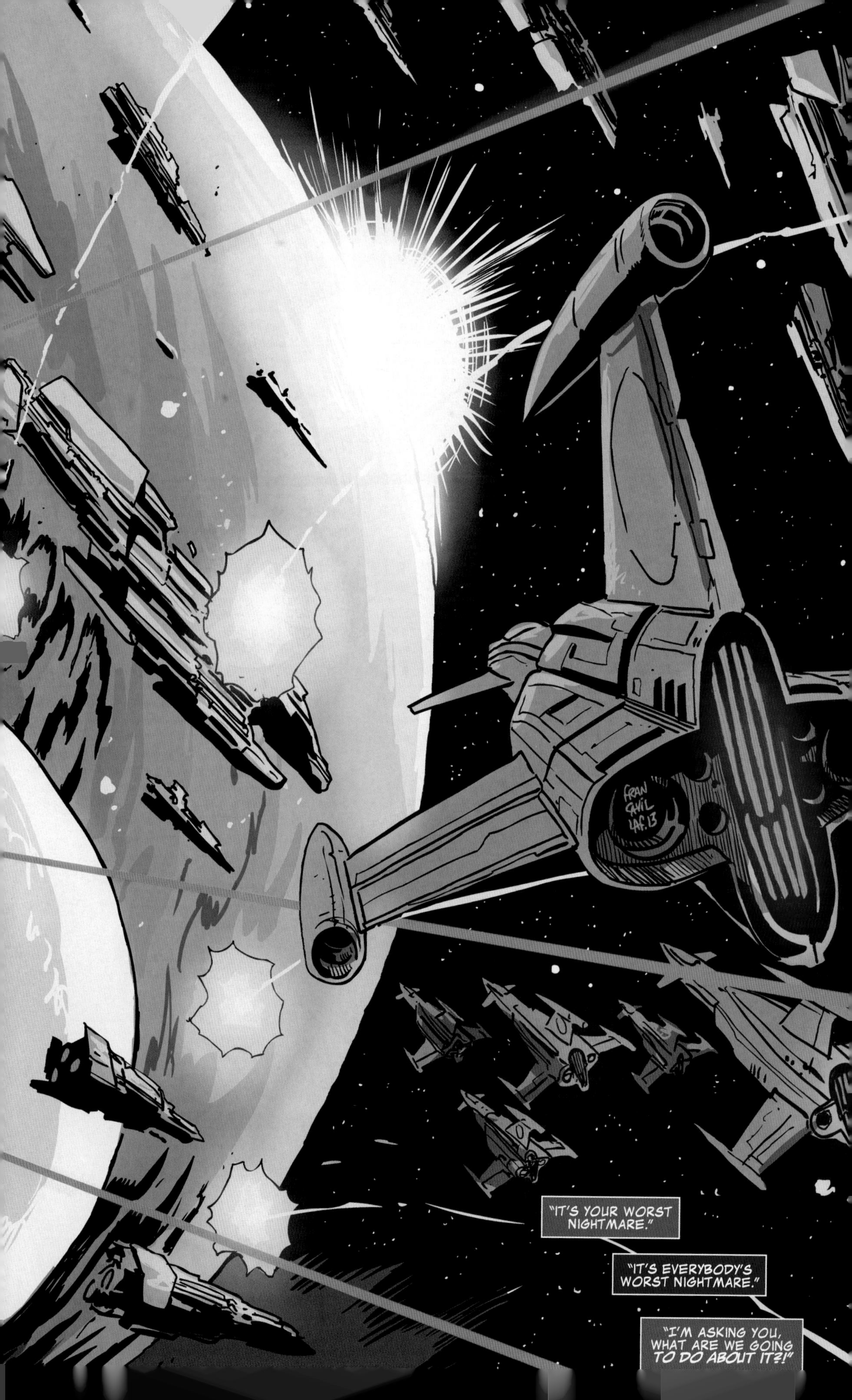
"IT'S YOUR WORST NIGHTMARE."
"IT'S EVERYBODY'S WORST NIGHTMARE."
"I'M ASKING YOU, WHAT ARE WE GOING TO DO ABOUT IT?!"

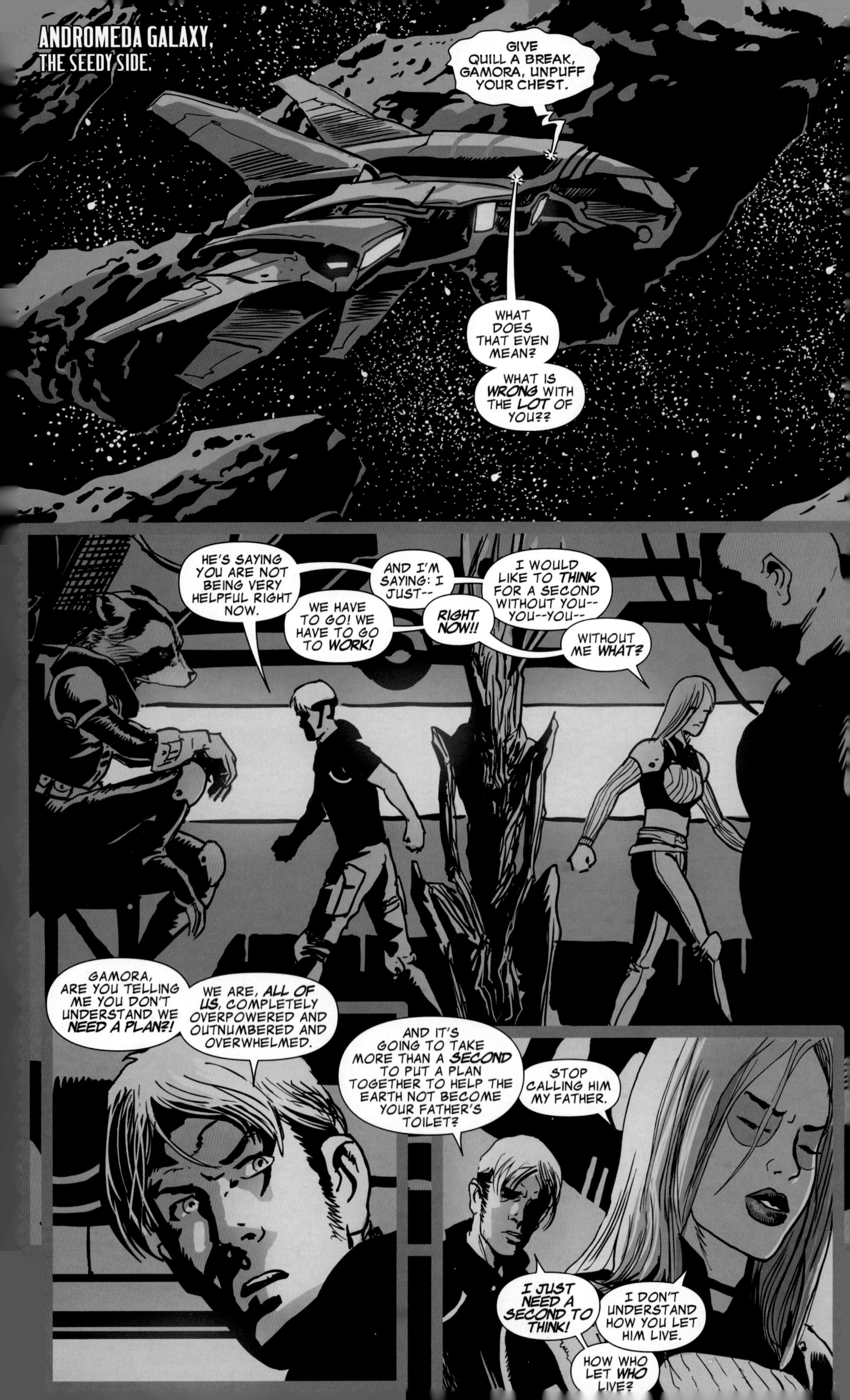

ANDROMEDA GALAXY, THE SEEDY SIDE.
GIVE QUILL A BREAK, GAMORA, UNPUFF YOUR CHEST.
WHAT DOES THAT EVEN MEAN?
WHAT IS WRONG WITH THE LOT OF YOU??
HE'S SAYING YOU ARE NOT BEING VERY HELPFUL RIGHT NOW.
AND I'M SAYING: I JUST--
I WOULD LIKE TO THINK FOR A SECOND WITHOUT YOU--YOU--YOU--
WE HAVE TO GO! WE HAVE TO GO TO WORK!
RIGHT NOW!!
WITHOUT ME WHAT?
GAMORA, ARE YOU TELLING ME YOU DON'T UNDERSTAND WE NEED A PLAN?!
WE ARE, ALL OF US, COMPLETELY OVERPOWERED AND OUTNUMBERED AND OVERWHELMED.
AND IT'S GOING TO TAKE MORE THAN A SECOND TO PUT A PLAN TOGETHER TO HELP THE EARTH NOT BECOME YOUR FATHER'S TOILET?
STOP CALLING HIM MY FATHER.
I JUST NEED A SECOND TO THINK!
I DON'T UNDERSTAND HOW YOU LET HIM LIVE.
HOW WHO LET WHO LIVE?

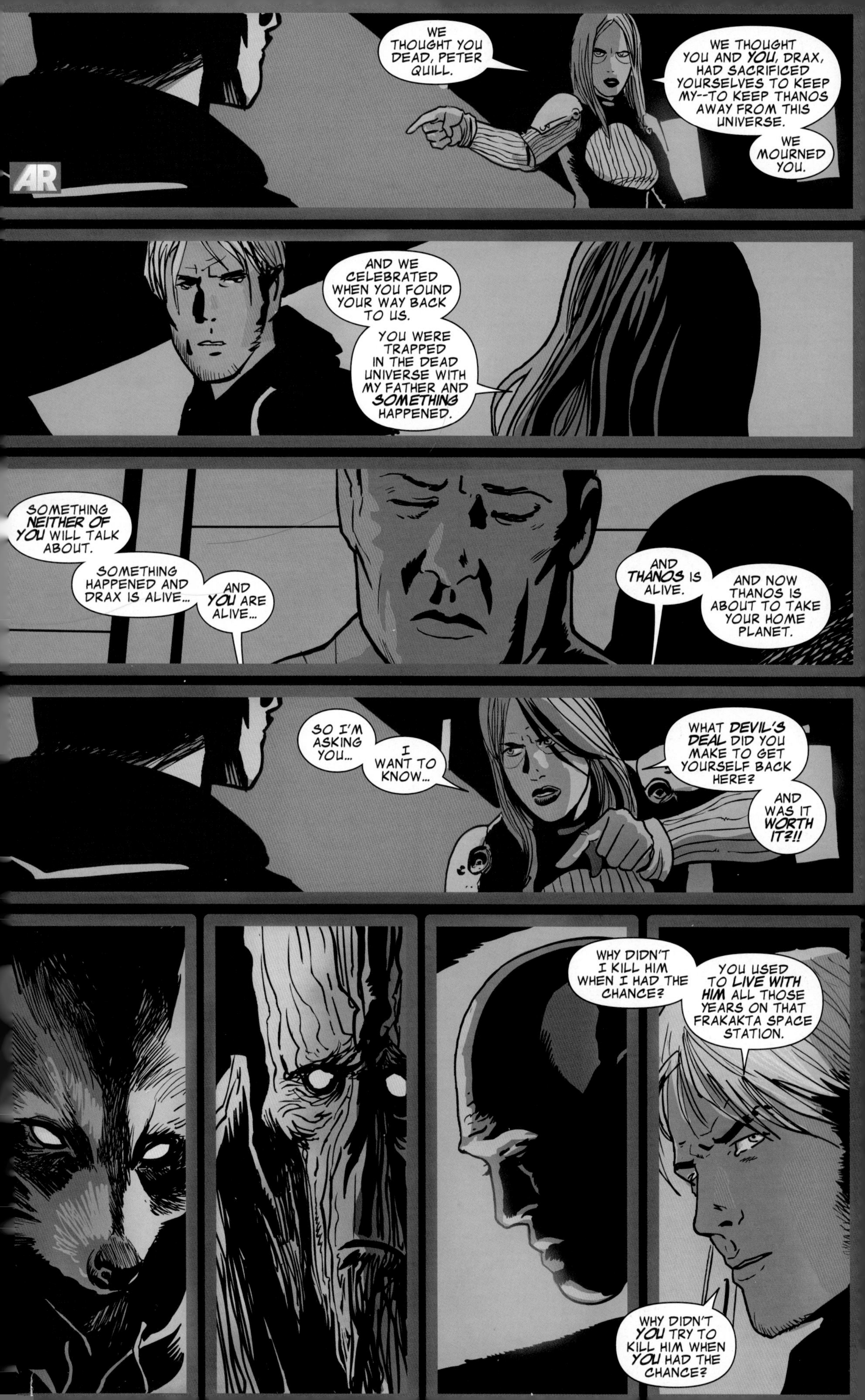
WE THOUGHT YOU DEAD, PETER QUILL.
WE THOUGHT YOU AND YOU, DRAX, HAD SACRIFICED YOURSELVES TO KEEP MY--TO KEEP THANOS AWAY FROM THIS UNIVERSE.
WE MOURNED YOU.
AND WE CELEBRATED WHEN YOU FOUND YOUR WAY BACK TO US.
YOU WERE TRAPPED IN THE DEAD UNIVERSE WITH MY FATHER AND SOMETHING HAPPENED.
SOMETHING NEITHER OF YOU WILL TALK ABOUT.
SOMETHING HAPPENED AND DRAX IS ALIVE...
AND YOU ARE ALIVE...
AND THANOS IS ALIVE.
AND NOW THANOS IS ABOUT TO TAKE YOUR HOME PLANET.
SO I'M ASKING YOU...
I WANT TO KNOW...
WHAT DEVIL'S DEAL DID YOU MAKE TO GET YOURSELF BACK HERE?
AND WAS IT WORTH IT?!!
WHY DIDN'T I KILL HIM WHEN I HAD THE CHANCE?
YOU USED TO LIVE WITH HIM ALL THOSE YEARS ON THAT FRAKAKTA SPACE STATION.
WHY DIDN'T YOU TRY TO KILL HIM WHEN YOU HAD THE CHANCE?

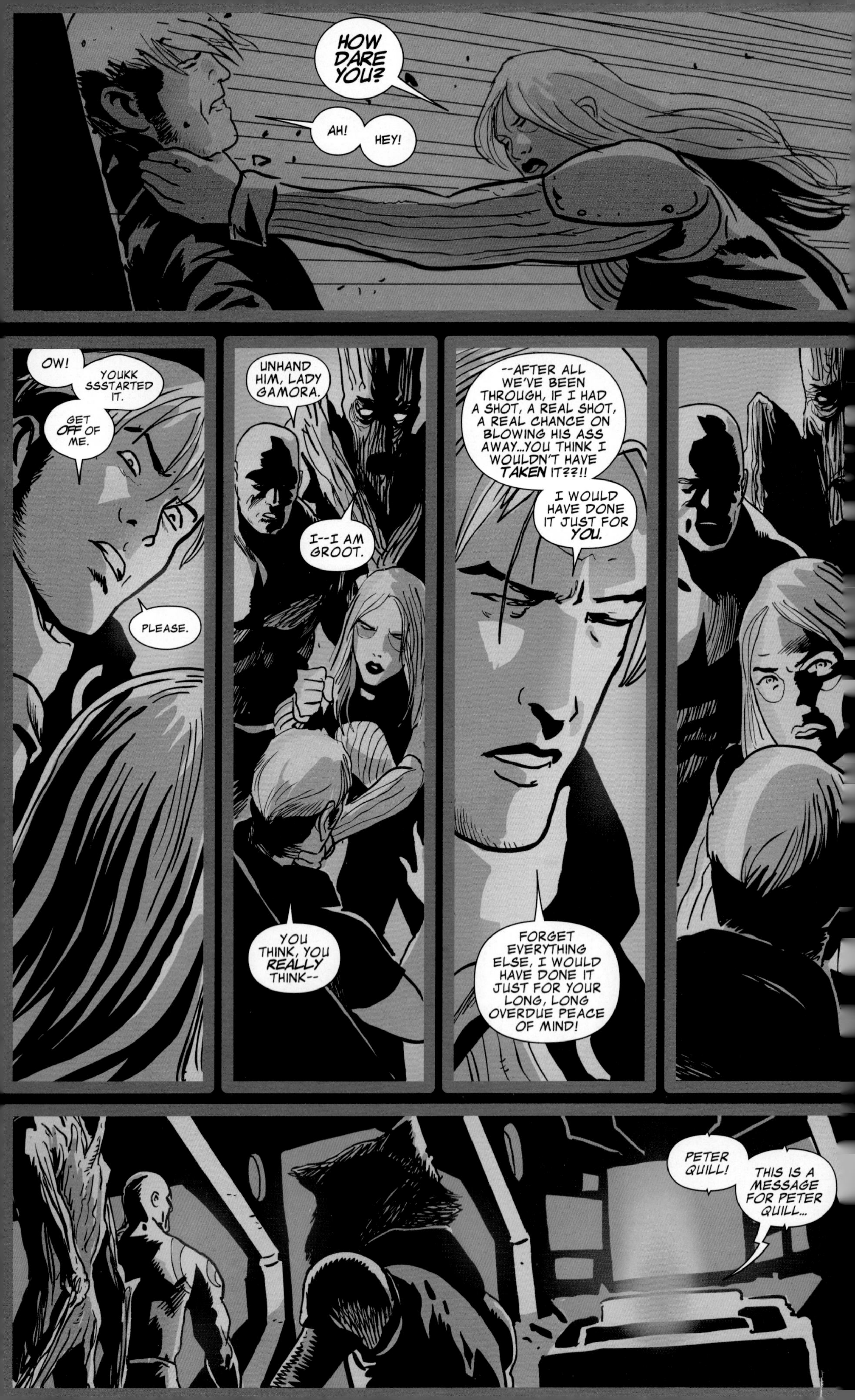
HOW DARE YOU?
AH!
HEY!
OW!
YOUKK SSSTARTED IT.
GET OFF OF ME.
PLEASE.
UNHAND HIM, LADY GAMORA.
I--I AM GROOT.
YOU THINK, YOU REALLY THINK--
--AFTER ALL WE'VE BEEN THROUGH, IF I HAD A SHOT, A REAL SHOT, A REAL CHANCE ON BLOWING HIS ASS AWAY...YOU THINK I WOULDN'T HAVE TAKEN IT??!!
I WOULD HAVE DONE IT JUST FOR YOU.
FORGET EVERYTHING ELSE, I WOULD HAVE DONE IT JUST FOR YOUR LONG, LONG OVERDUE PEACE OF MIND!
PETER QUILL!
THIS IS A MESSAGE FOR PETER QUILL...

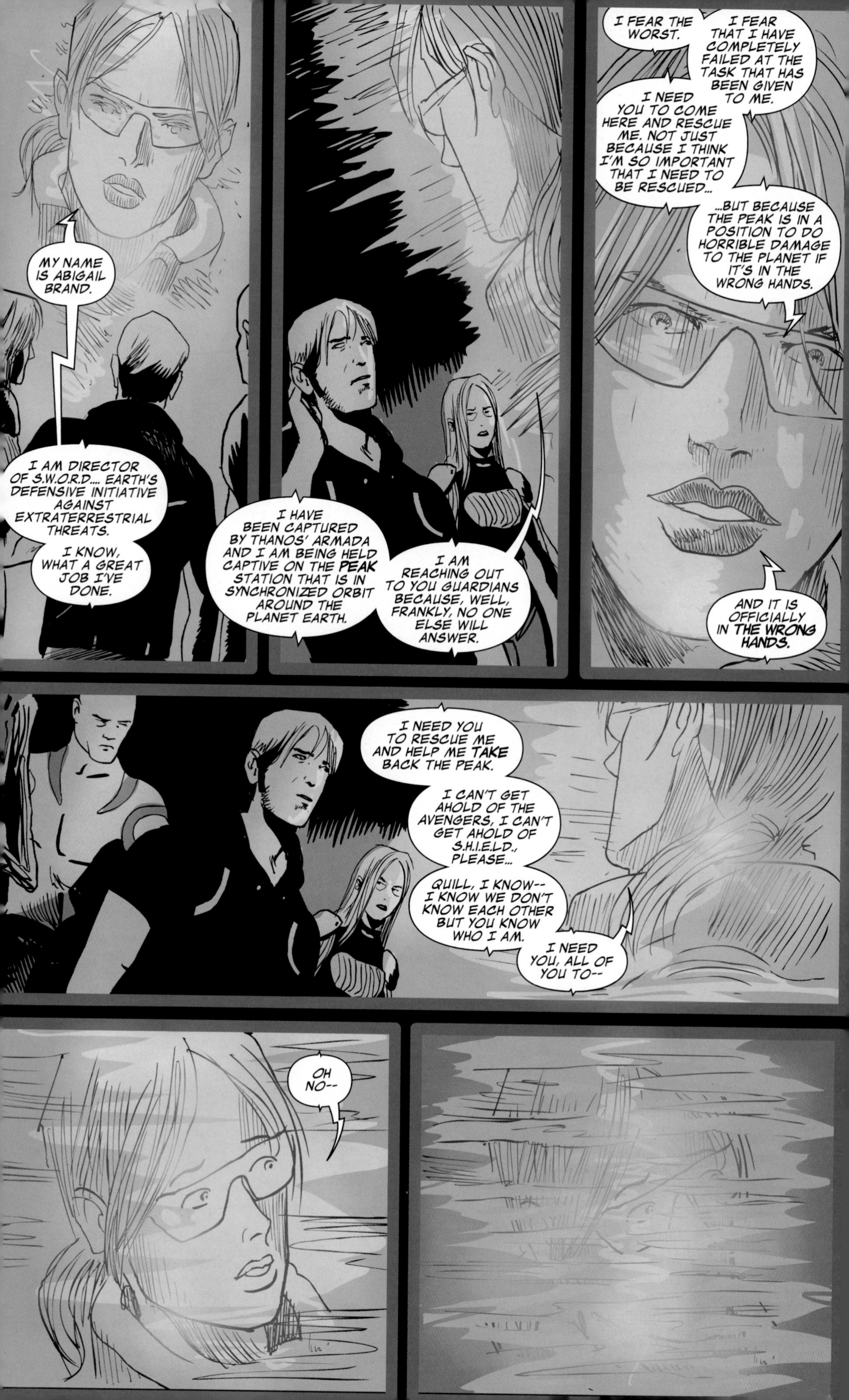
MY NAME IS ABIGAIL BRAND.
I AM DIRECTOR OF S.W.O.R.D.... EARTH'S DEFENSIVE INITIATIVE AGAINST EXTRATERRESTRIAL THREATS.
I KNOW, WHAT A GREAT JOB I'VE DONE.
I HAVE BEEN CAPTURED BY THANOS' ARMADA AND I AM BEING HELD CAPTIVE ON THE PEAK STATION THAT IS IN SYNCHRONIZED ORBIT AROUND THE PLANET EARTH.
I AM REACHING OUT TO YOU GUARDIANS BECAUSE, WELL, FRANKLY, NO ONE ELSE WILL ANSWER.
I FEAR THE WORST.
I FEAR THAT I HAVE COMPLETELY FAILED AT THE TASK THAT HAS BEEN GIVEN TO ME.
I NEED YOU TO COME HERE AND RESCUE ME. NOT JUST BECAUSE I THINK I'M SO IMPORTANT THAT I NEED TO BE RESCUED...
...BUT BECAUSE THE PEAK IS IN A POSITION TO DO HORRIBLE DAMAGE TO THE PLANET IF IT'S IN THE WRONG HANDS.
AND IT IS OFFICIALLY IN THE WRONG HANDS.
I NEED YOU TO RESCUE ME AND HELP ME TAKE BACK THE PEAK.
I CAN'T GET AHOLD OF THE AVENGERS, I CAN'T GET AHOLD OF S.H.I.E.L.D., PLEASE...
QUILL, I KNOW-- I KNOW WE DON'T KNOW EACH OTHER BUT YOU KNOW WHO I AM.
I NEED YOU, ALL OF YOU TO--
OH NO--

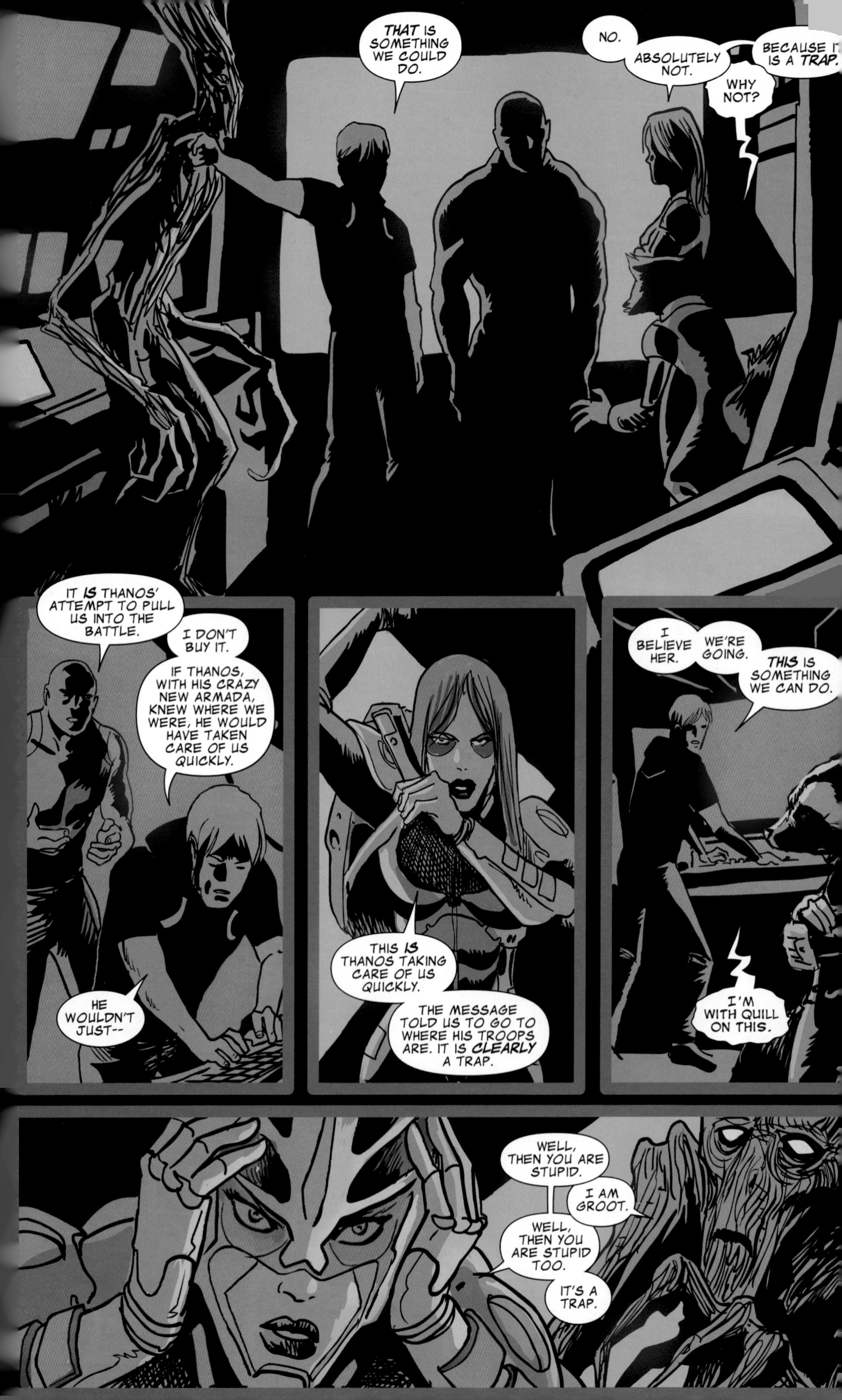
THAT IS SOMETHING WE COULD DO.
NO.
ABSOLUTELY NOT.
WHY NOT?
BECAUSE IT IS A TRAP.
IT IS THANOS' ATTEMPT TO PULL US INTO THE BATTLE.
I DON'T BUY IT.
IF THANOS, WITH HIS CRAZY NEW ARMADA, KNEW WHERE WE WERE, HE WOULD HAVE TAKEN CARE OF US QUICKLY.
HE WOULDN'T JUST--
THIS IS THANOS TAKING CARE OF US QUICKLY.
THE MESSAGE TOLD US TO GO TO WHERE HIS TROOPS ARE. IT IS CLEARLY A TRAP.
I BELIEVE HER.
WE'RE GOING.
THIS IS SOMETHING WE CAN DO.
I'M WITH QUILL ON THIS.
WELL, THEN YOU ARE STUPID.
I AM GROOT.
WELL, THEN YOU ARE STUPID TOO.
IT'S A TRAP.

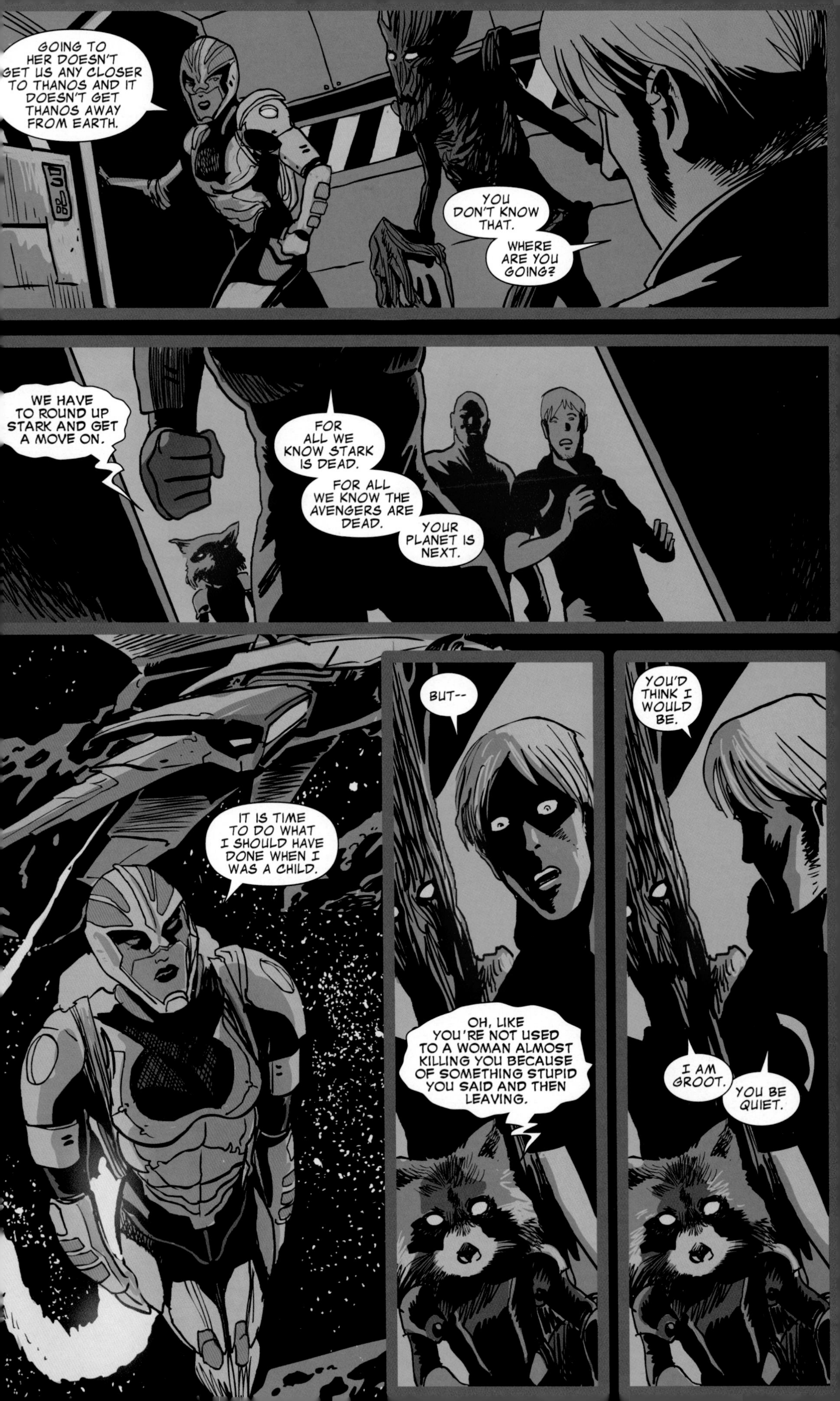
GOING TO HER DOESN'T GET US ANY CLOSER TO THANOS AND IT DOESN'T GET THANOS AWAY FROM EARTH.
YOU DON'T KNOW THAT.
WHERE ARE YOU GOING?
WE HAVE TO ROUND UP STARK AND GET A MOVE ON.
FOR ALL WE KNOW STARK IS DEAD.
FOR ALL WE KNOW THE AVENGERS ARE DEAD.
YOUR PLANET IS NEXT.
IT IS TIME TO DO WHAT I SHOULD HAVE DONE WHEN I WAS A CHILD.
BUT--
OH, LIKE YOU'RE NOT USED TO A WOMAN ALMOST KILLING YOU BECAUSE OF SOMETHING STUPID YOU SAID AND THEN LEAVING.
YOU'D THINK I WOULD BE.
I AM GROOT.
YOU BE QUIET.

THE PEAK.
ORBITAL HEADQUARTERS OF S.W.O.R.D.
Sentient World Observation and Response Department.

"THAT'S IT?"

"IT'S DECENT FO
EARTH PEOPLE."

"IT LOOKS LIKE
A SDORKTI PLAY
STRUCTURE.

"I CAN'T BE
EVERYON
CONSTANTLY F
OVER THIS
PLANET OF Y

"DUMB."

"WAIT, DO YOU
SEE THAT?"

"WHA
WHAT A
LOOKING

"THER

"T
G
C

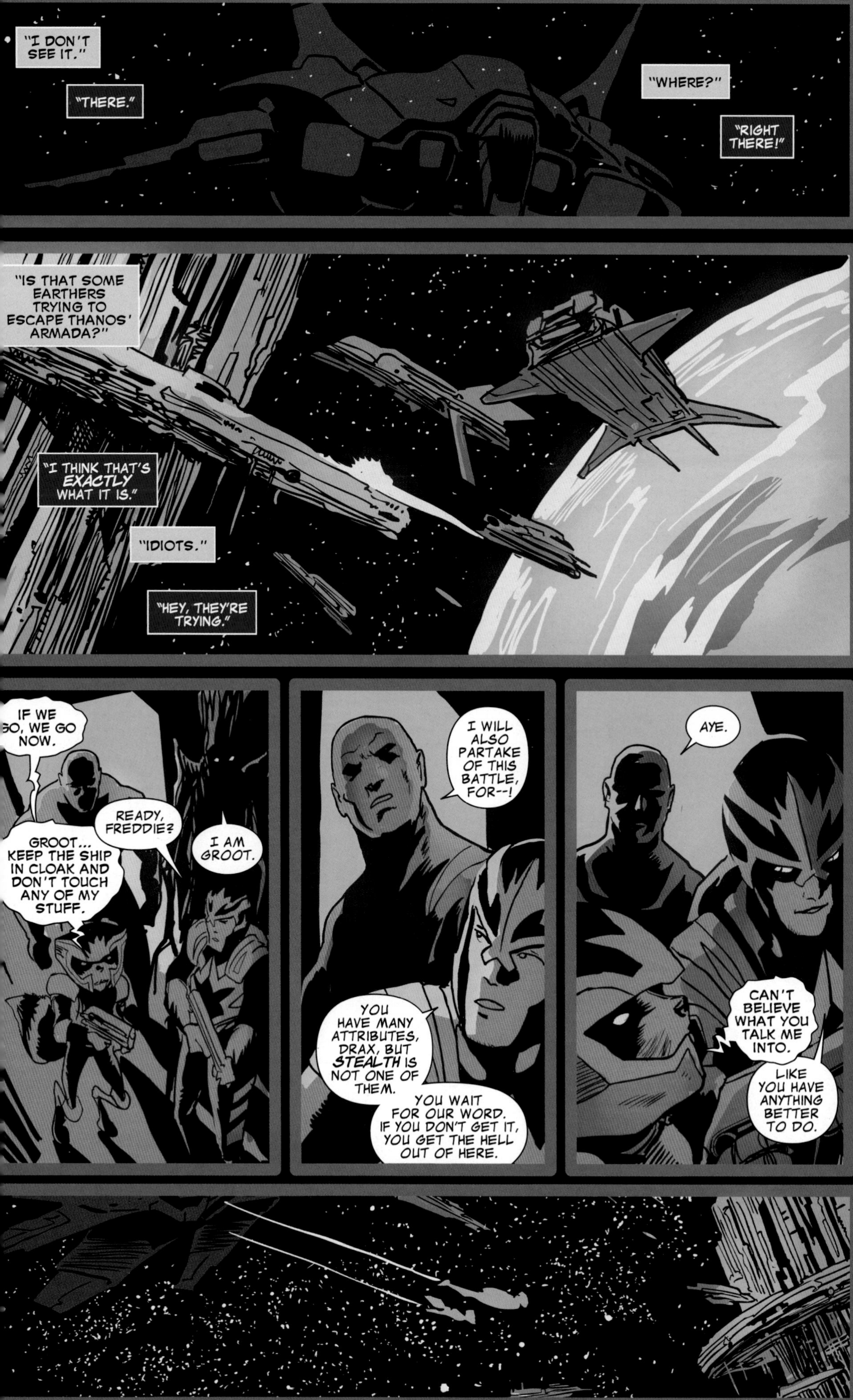
"I DON'T SEE IT."
"THERE."
"WHERE?"
"RIGHT THERE!"
"IS THAT SOME EARTHERS TRYING TO ESCAPE THANOS' ARMADA?"
"I THINK THAT'S *EXACTLY* WHAT IT IS."
"IDIOTS."
"HEY, THEY'RE TRYING."
IF WE GO, WE GO NOW.
GROOT... KEEP THE SHIP IN CLOAK AND DON'T TOUCH ANY OF MY STUFF.
READY, FREDDIE?
I AM GROOT.
I WILL ALSO PARTAKE OF THIS BATTLE, FOR--!
YOU HAVE MANY ATTRIBUTES, DRAX, BUT *STEALTH* IS NOT ONE OF THEM.
YOU WAIT FOR OUR WORD. IF YOU DON'T GET IT, YOU GET THE HELL OUT OF HERE.
AYE.
CAN'T BELIEVE WHAT YOU TALK ME INTO.
LIKE YOU HAVE ANYTHING BETTER TO DO.

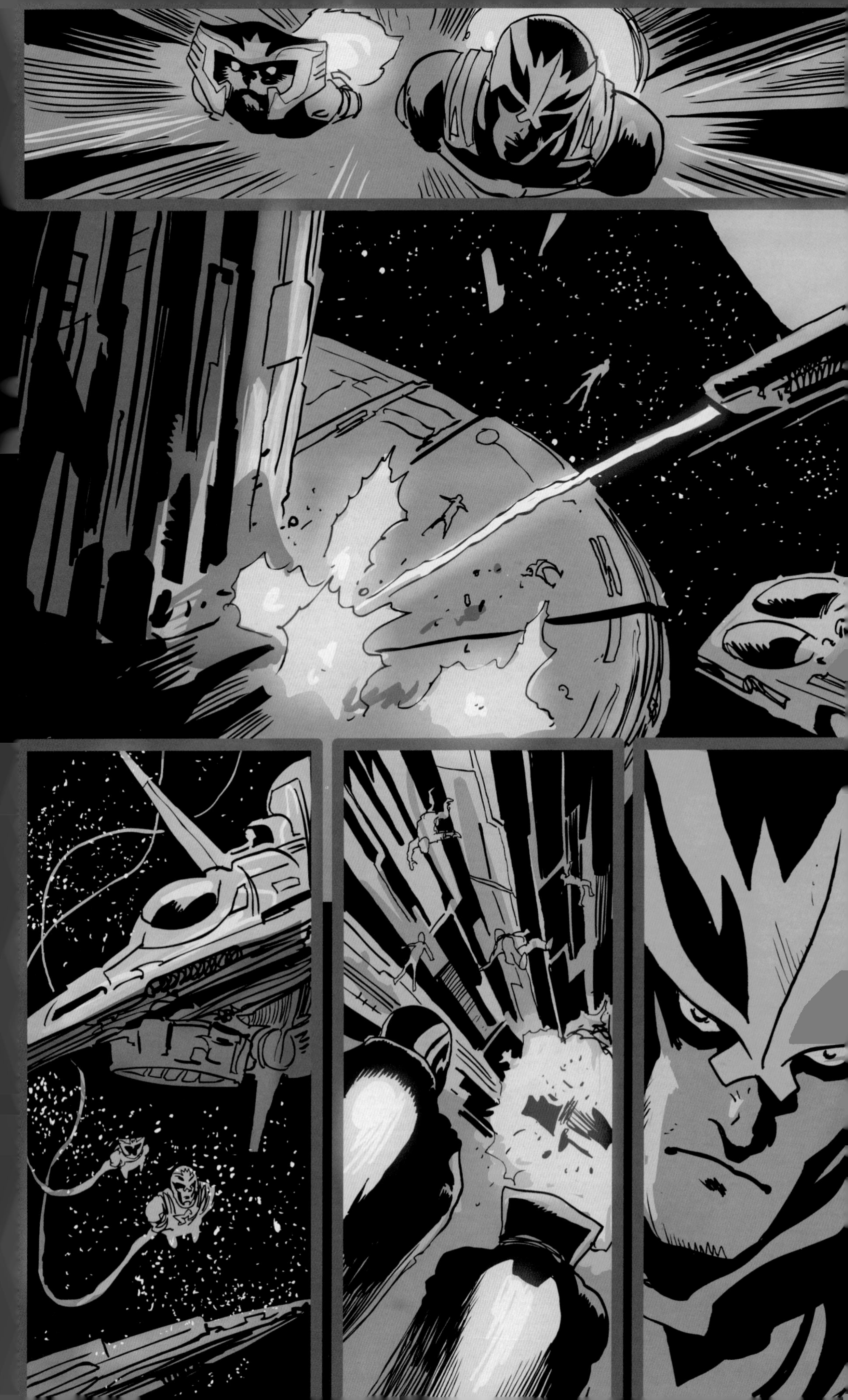

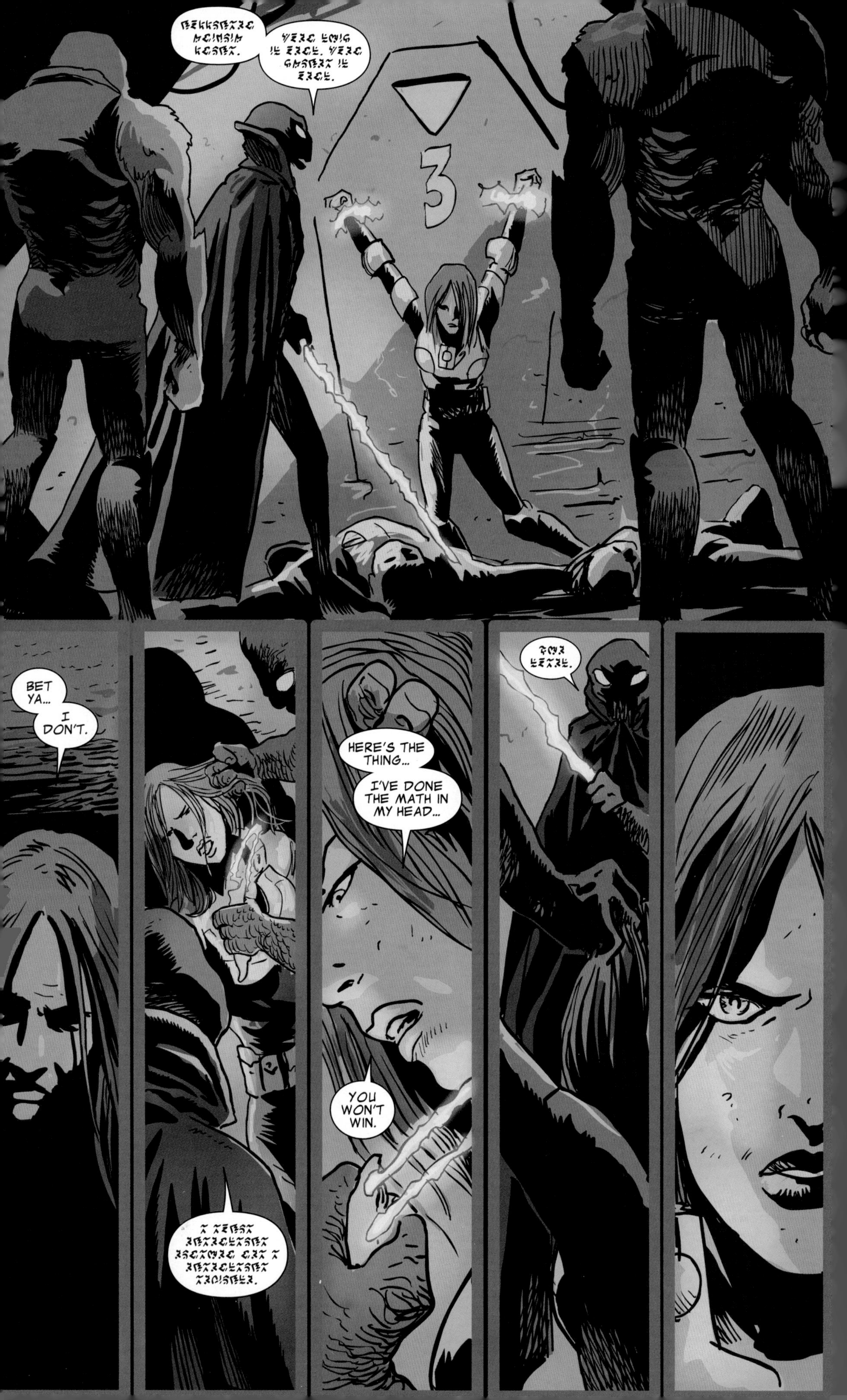
BET YA...
I DON'T.
HERE'S THE THING...
I'VE DONE THE MATH IN MY HEAD...
YOU WON'T WIN.

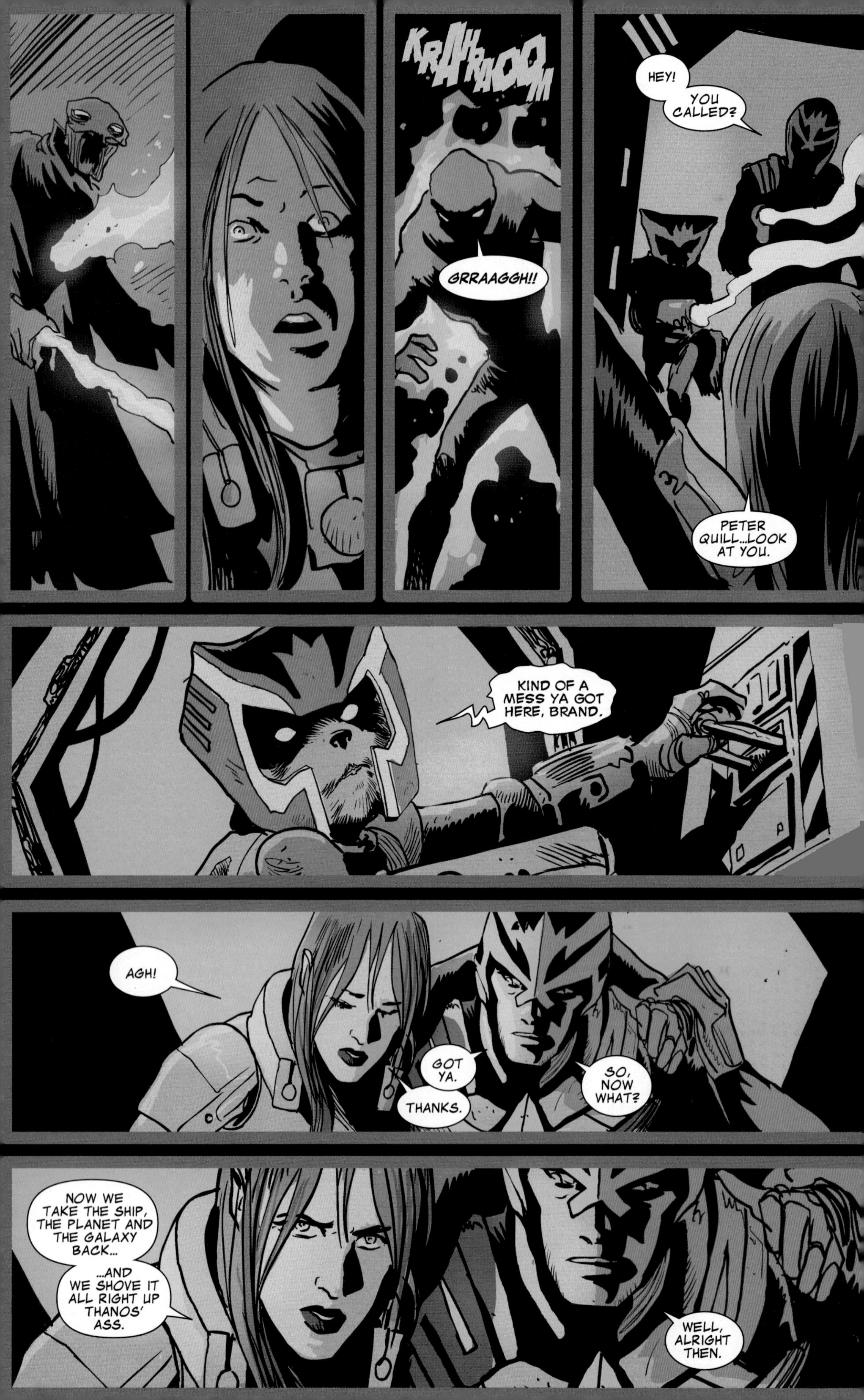
KRAHRAOOM
GRRAAGGH!!
HEY!
YOU CALLED?
PETER QUILL...LOOK AT YOU.
KIND OF A MESS YA GOT HERE, BRAND.
AGH!
GOT YA.
THANKS.
SO, NOW WHAT?
NOW WE TAKE THE SHIP, THE PLANET AND THE GALAXY BACK...
...AND WE SHOVE IT ALL RIGHT UP THANOS' ASS.
WELL, ALRIGHT THEN.

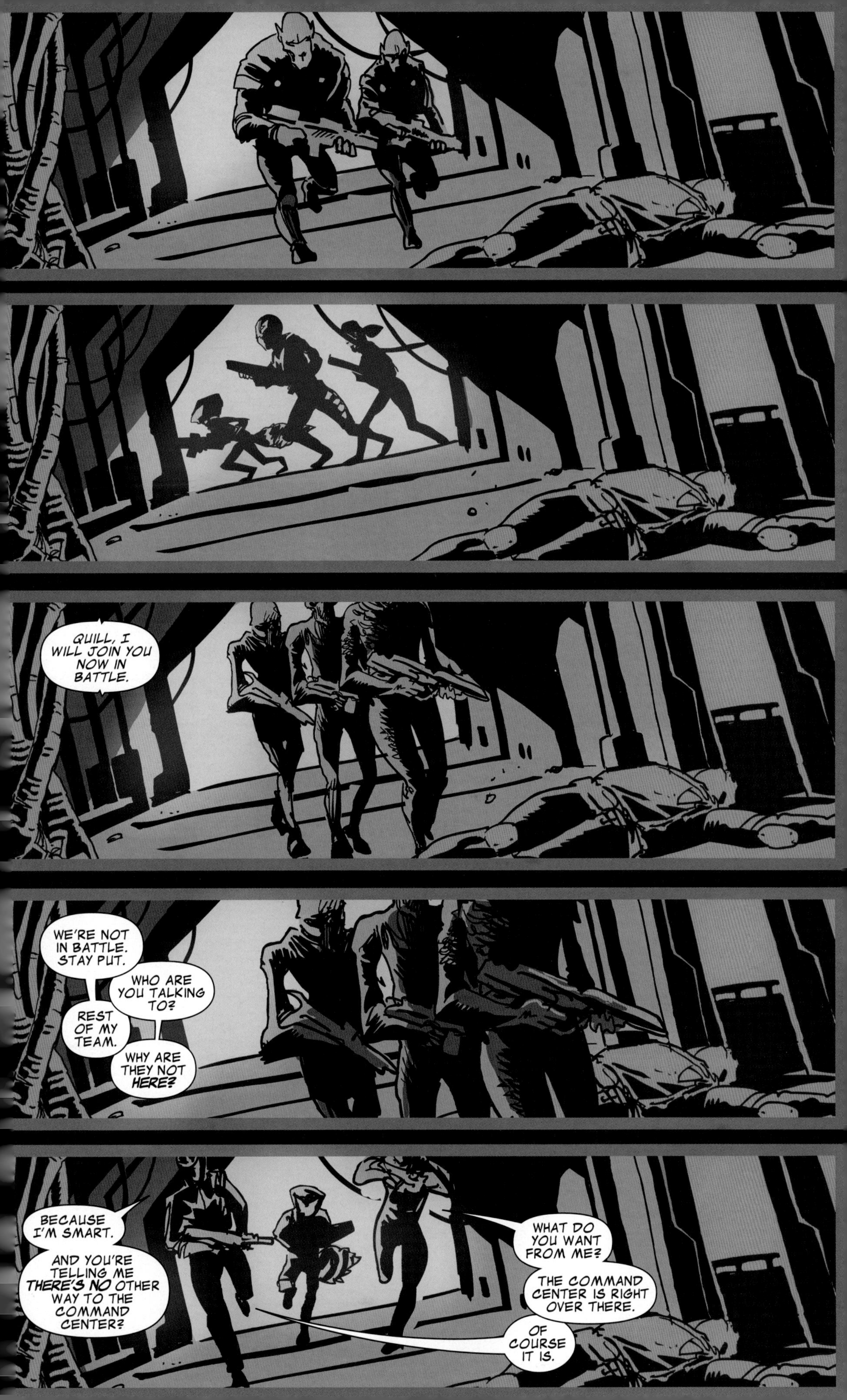
QUILL, I WILL JOIN YOU NOW IN BATTLE.
WE'RE NOT IN BATTLE. STAY PUT.
WHO ARE YOU TALKING TO?
REST OF MY TEAM.
WHY ARE THEY NOT HERE?
BECAUSE I'M SMART.
AND YOU'RE TELLING ME THERE'S NO OTHER WAY TO THE COMMAND CENTER?
WHAT DO YOU WANT FROM ME?
THE COMMAND CENTER IS RIGHT OVER THERE.
OF COURSE IT IS.

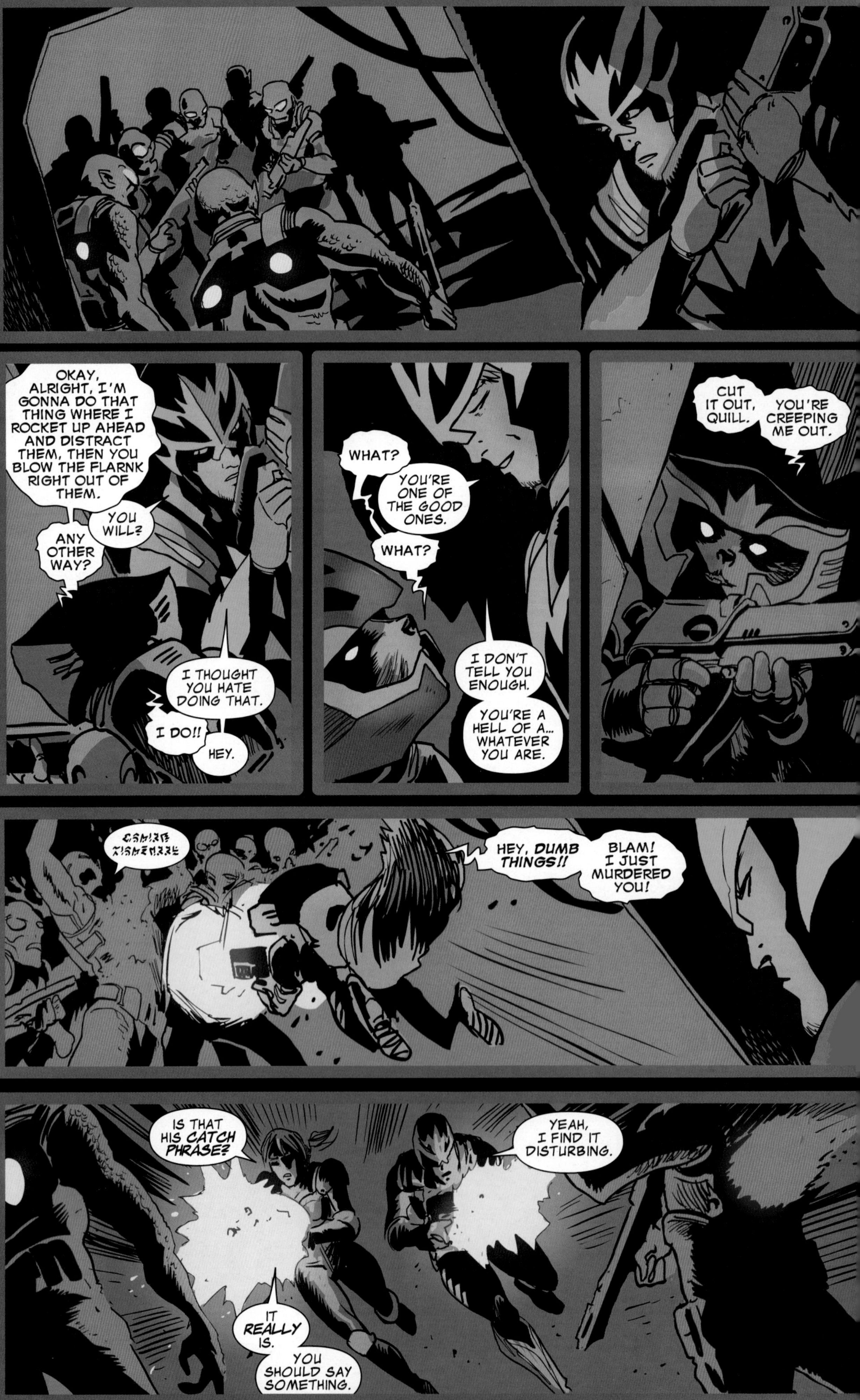
OKAY, ALRIGHT, I'M GONNA DO THAT THING WHERE I ROCKET UP AHEAD AND DISTRACT THEM, THEN YOU BLOW THE FLARNK RIGHT OUT OF THEM.
YOU WILL?
ANY OTHER WAY?
I THOUGHT YOU HATE DOING THAT.
I DO!!
HEY.
WHAT?
YOU'RE ONE OF THE GOOD ONES.
WHAT?
I DON'T TELL YOU ENOUGH.
YOU'RE A HELL OF A... WHATEVER YOU ARE.
CUT IT OUT, QUILL.
YOU'RE CREEPING ME OUT.
HEY, **DUMB THINGS!!**
BLAM! I JUST MURDERED YOU!
IS THAT HIS ***CATCH PHRASE?***
YEAH, I FIND IT DISTURBING.
IT ***REALLY*** IS.
YOU SHOULD SAY SOMETHING.

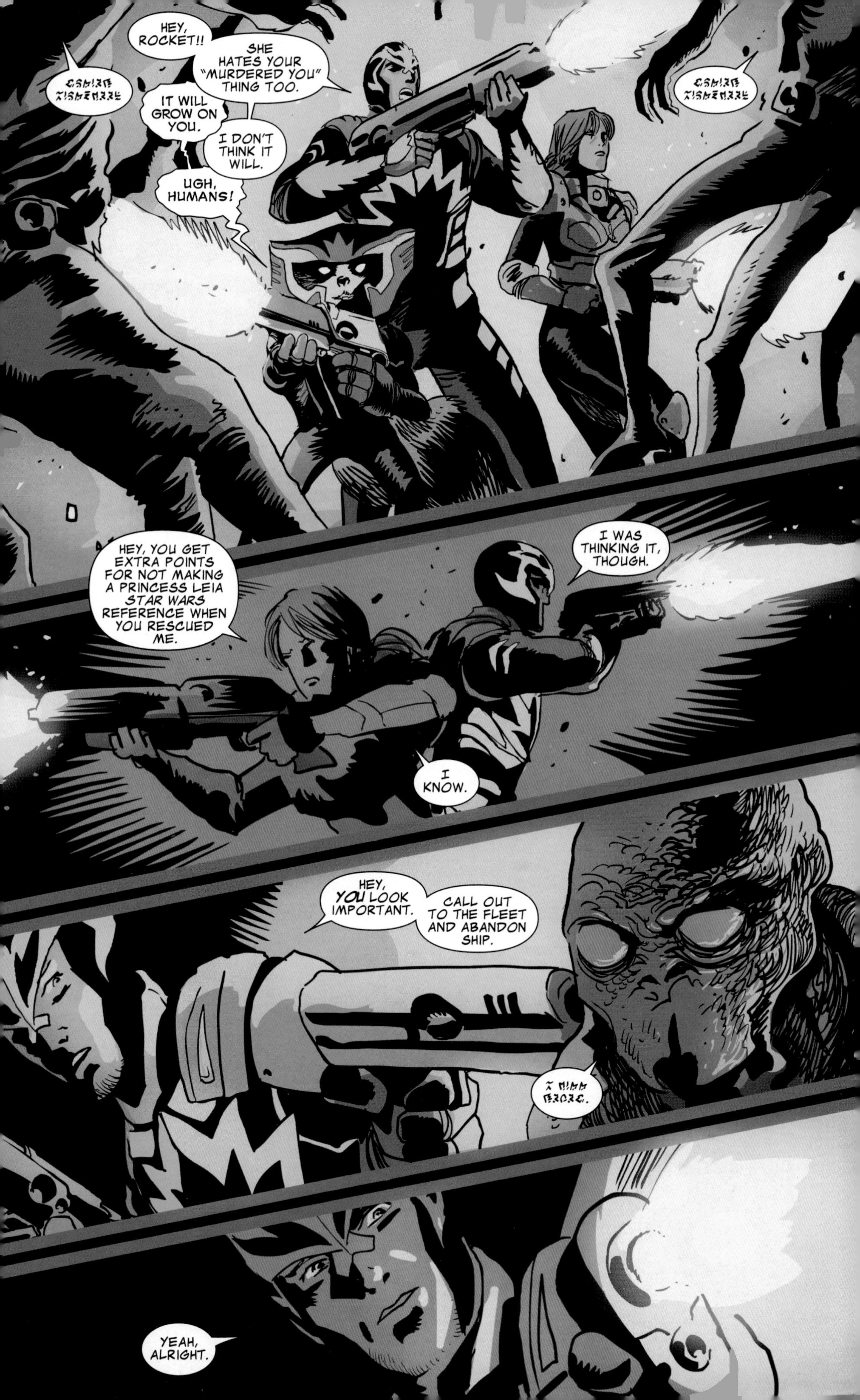
HEY, ROCKET!!
SHE HATES YOUR "MURDERED YOU" THING TOO.
IT WILL GROW ON YOU.
I DON'T THINK IT WILL.
UGH, HUMANS!
HEY, YOU GET EXTRA POINTS FOR NOT MAKING A PRINCESS LEIA STAR WARS REFERENCE WHEN YOU RESCUED ME.
I WAS THINKING IT, THOUGH.
I KNOW.
HEY, YOU LOOK IMPORTANT.
CALL OUT TO THE FLEET AND ABANDON SHIP.
YEAH, ALRIGHT.

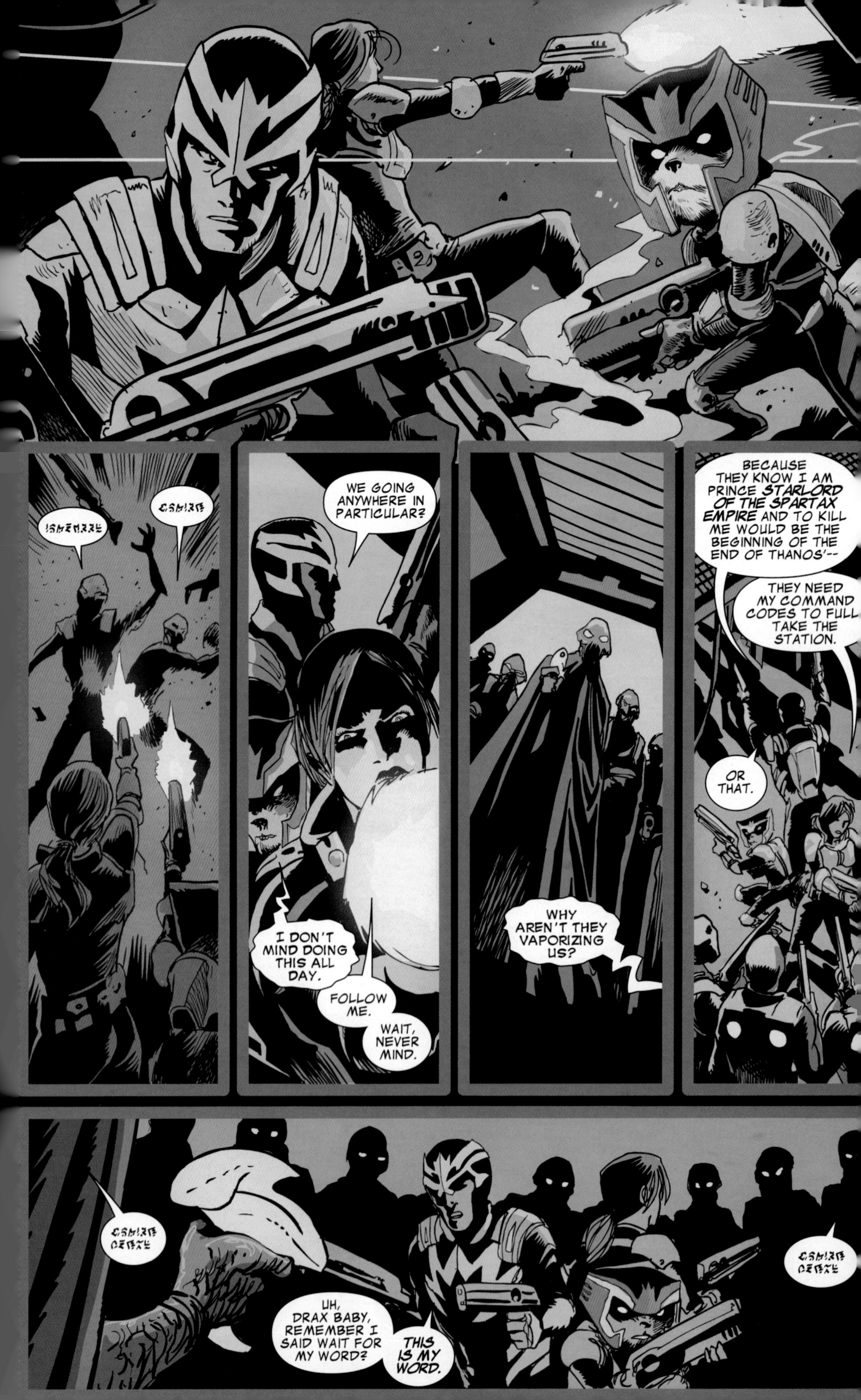
WE GOING ANYWHERE IN PARTICULAR?
I DON'T MIND DOING THIS ALL DAY.
FOLLOW ME.
WAIT, NEVER MIND.
WHY AREN'T THEY VAPORIZING US?
BECAUSE THEY KNOW I AM PRINCE STARLORD OF THE SPARTAX EMPIRE AND TO KILL ME WOULD BE THE BEGINNING OF THE END OF THANOS'--
THEY NEED MY COMMAND CODES TO FULL TAKE THE STATION.
OR THAT.
UH, DRAX BABY, REMEMBER I SAID WAIT FOR MY WORD?
THIS IS MY WORD.

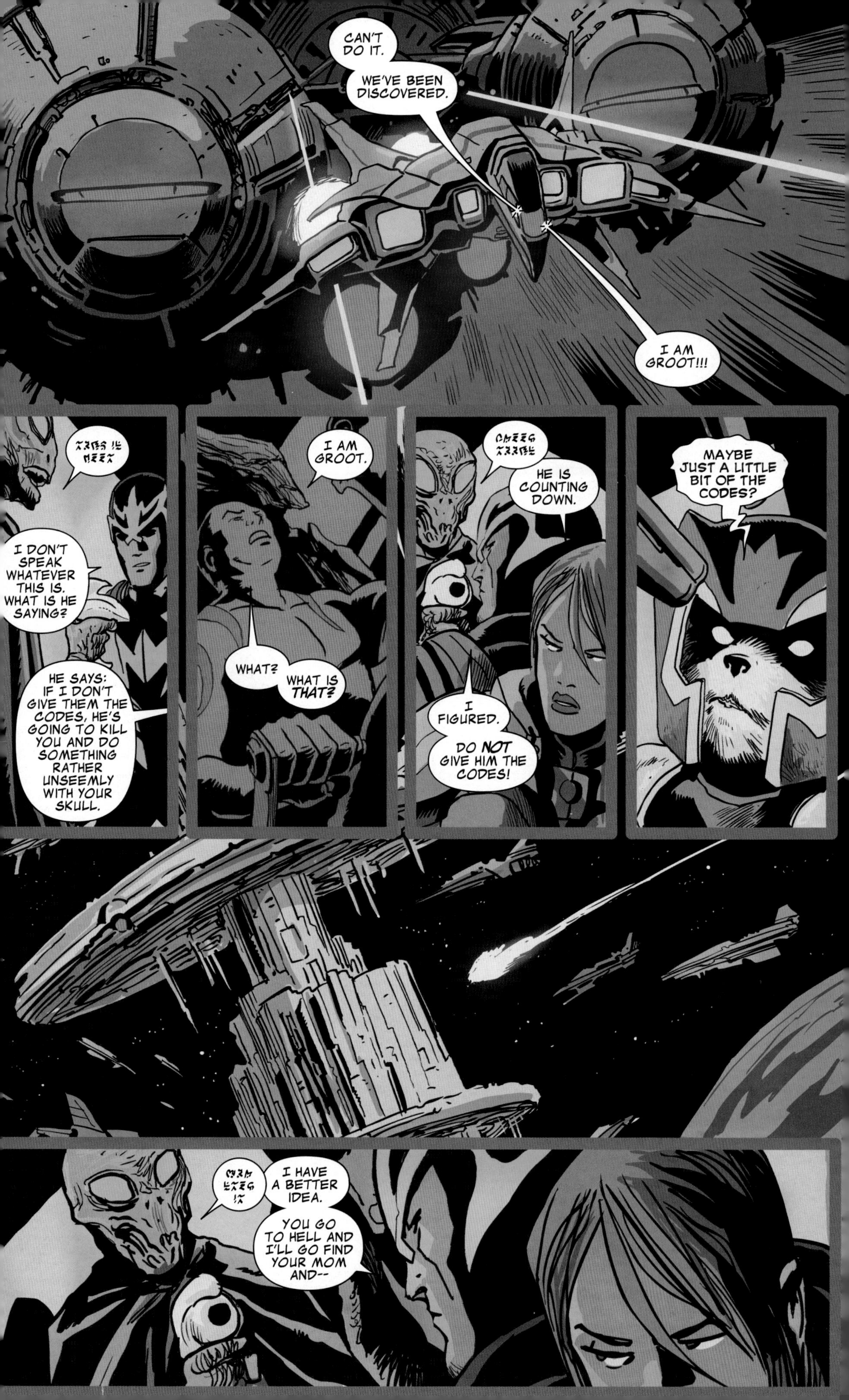

CAN'T DO IT.
WE'VE BEEN DISCOVERED.
I AM GROOT!!!
I DON'T SPEAK WHATEVER THIS IS. WHAT IS HE SAYING?
HE SAYS: IF I DON'T GIVE THEM THE CODES, HE'S GOING TO KILL YOU AND DO SOMETHING RATHER UNSEEMLY WITH YOUR SKULL.
I AM GROOT.
WHAT?
WHAT IS THAT?
HE IS COUNTING DOWN.
I FIGURED.
DO NOT GIVE HIM THE CODES!
MAYBE JUST A LITTLE BIT OF THE CODES?
I HAVE A BETTER IDEA.
YOU GO TO HELL AND I'LL GO FIND YOUR MOM AND--

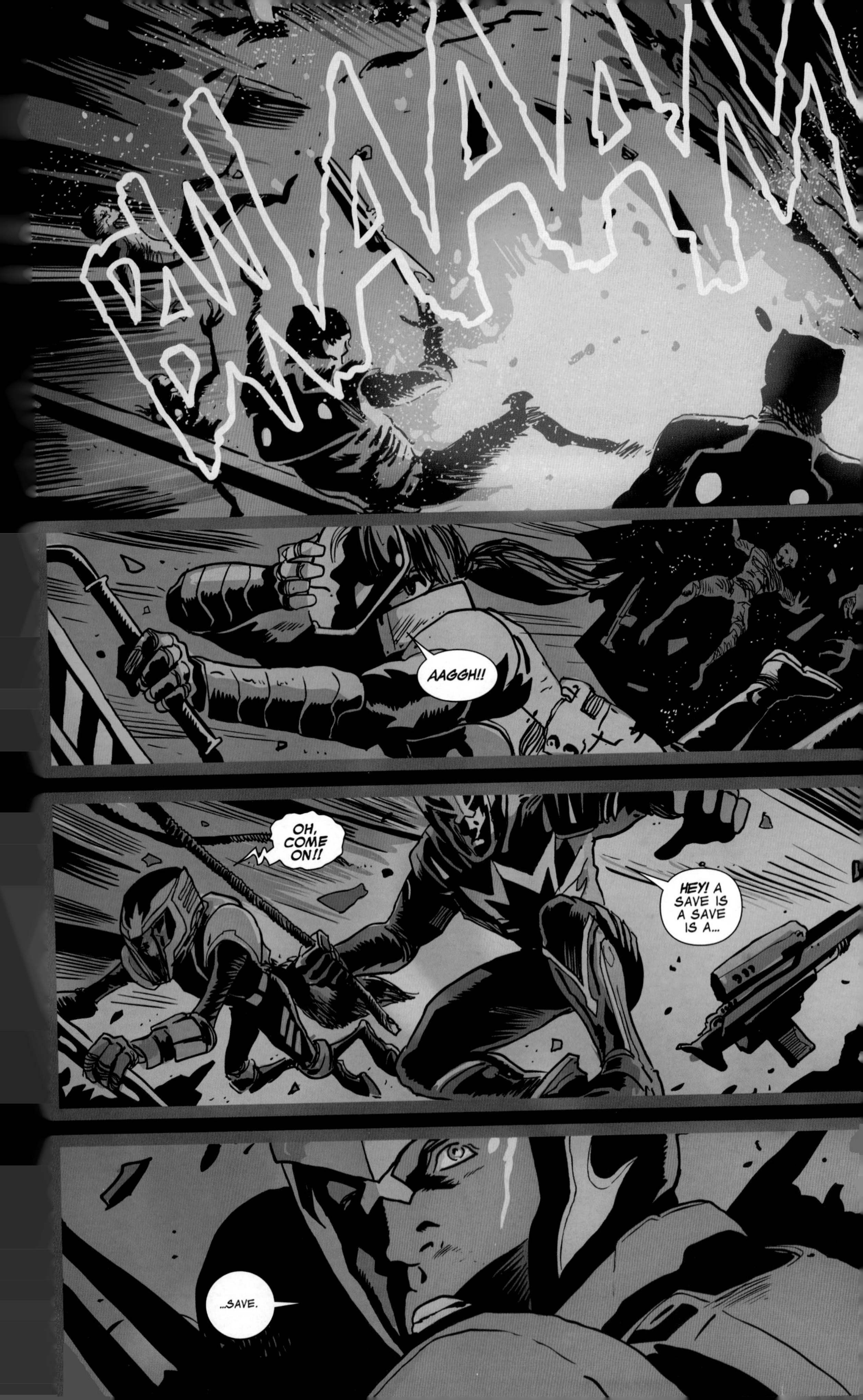
BHAAAAM
AAGGH!!
OH, COME ON!!
HEY! A SAVE IS A SAVE IS A...
...SAVE.

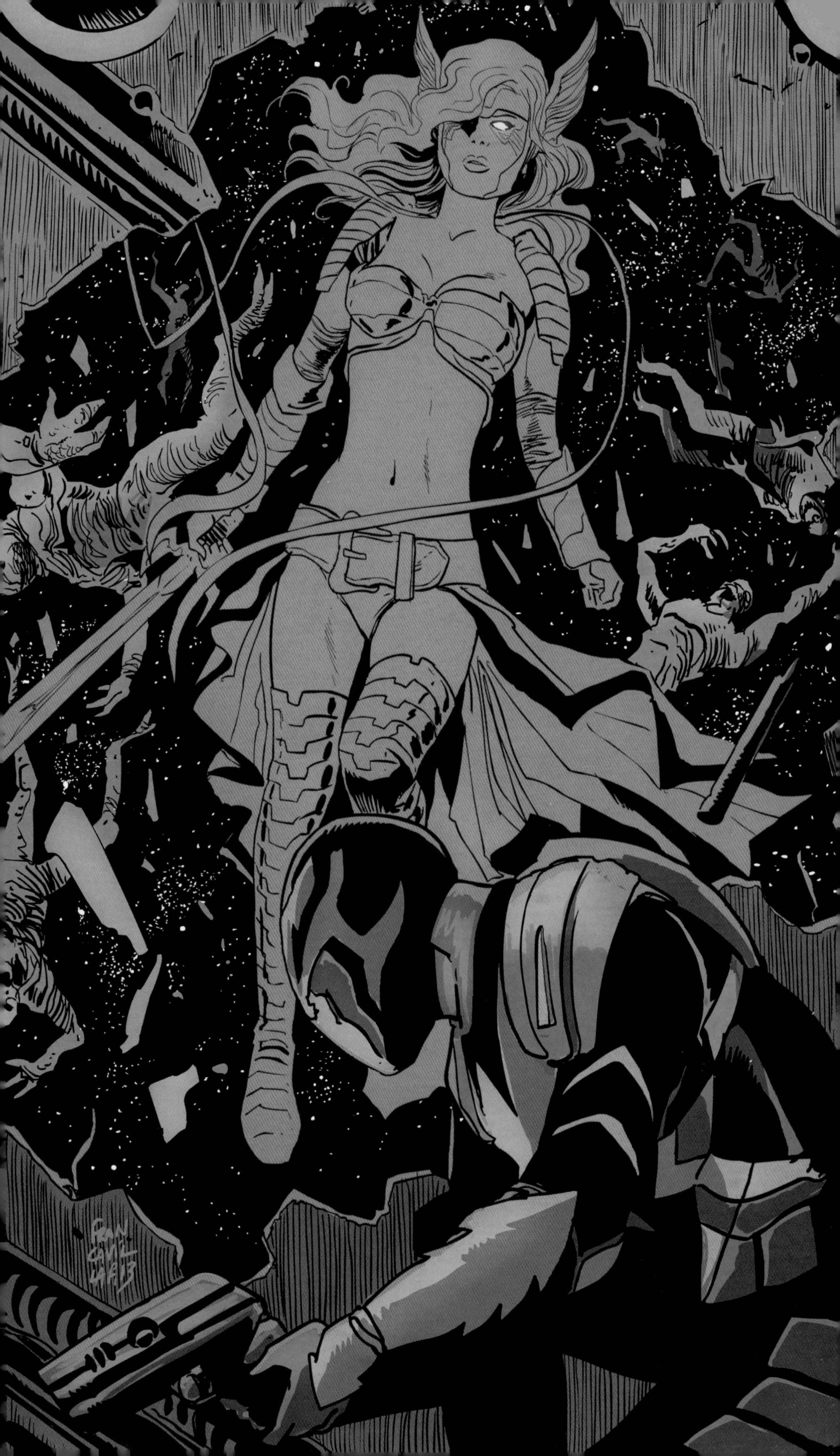

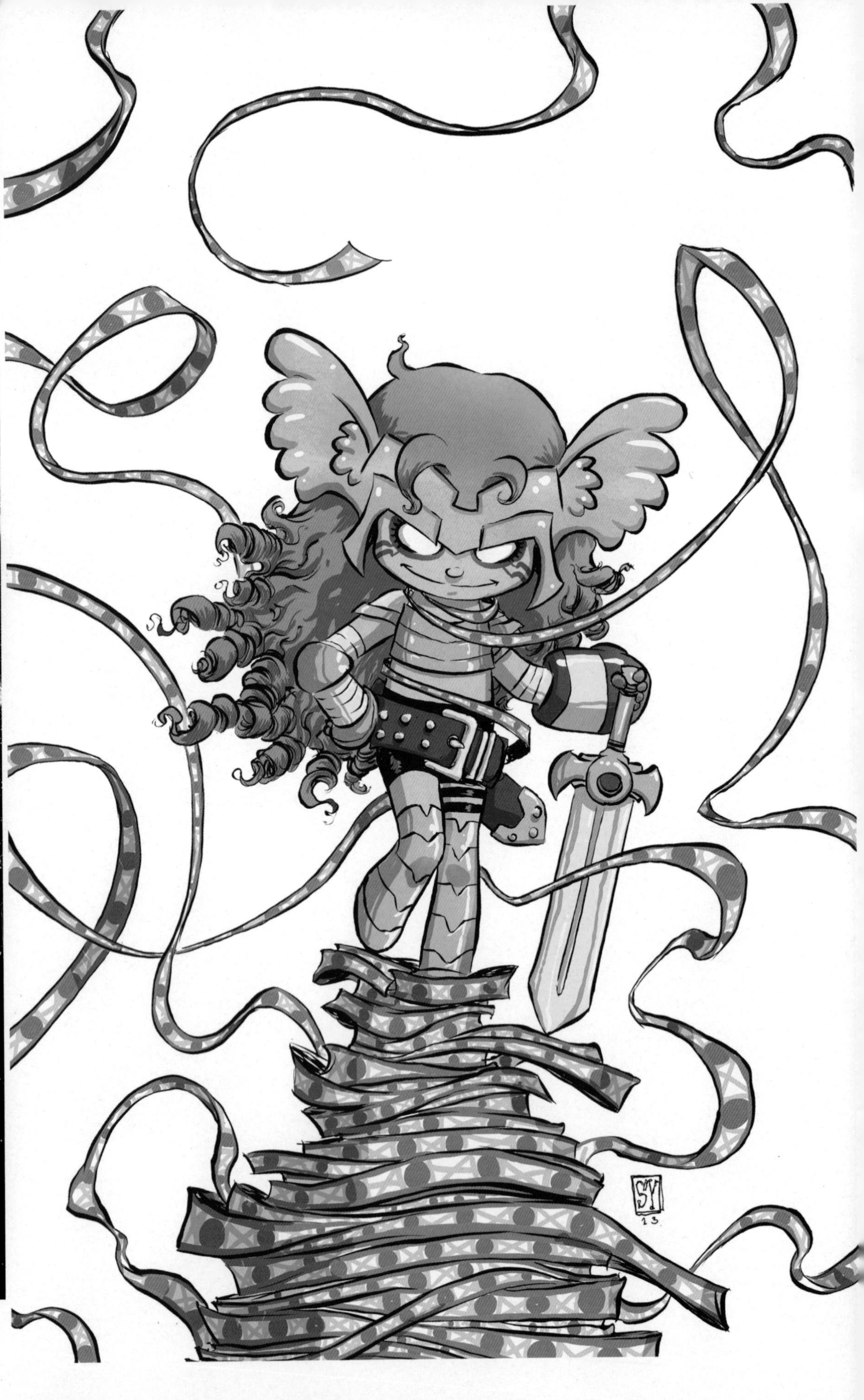
SY
13

#5 VARIANT BY SKOTTIE YOUNG

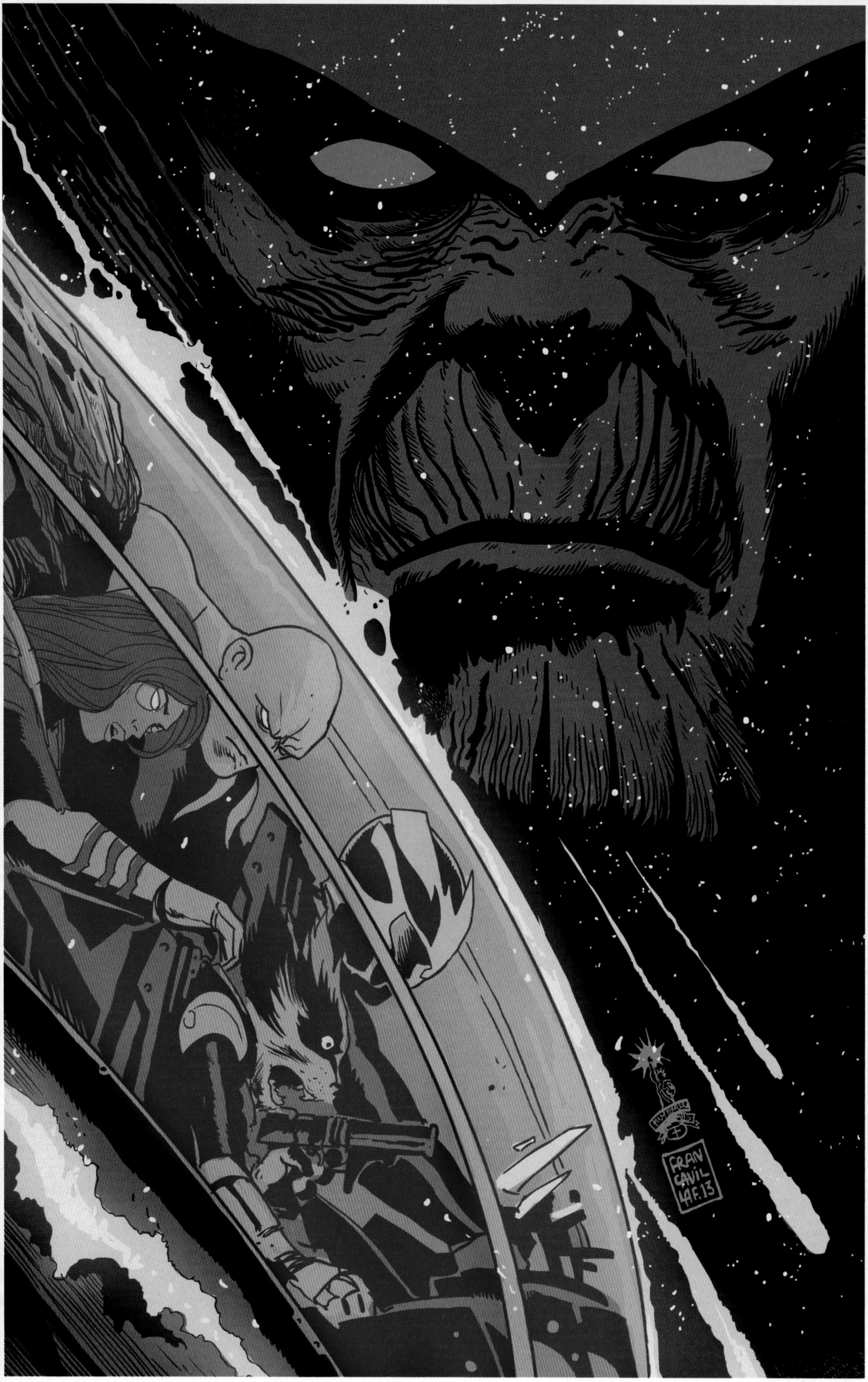

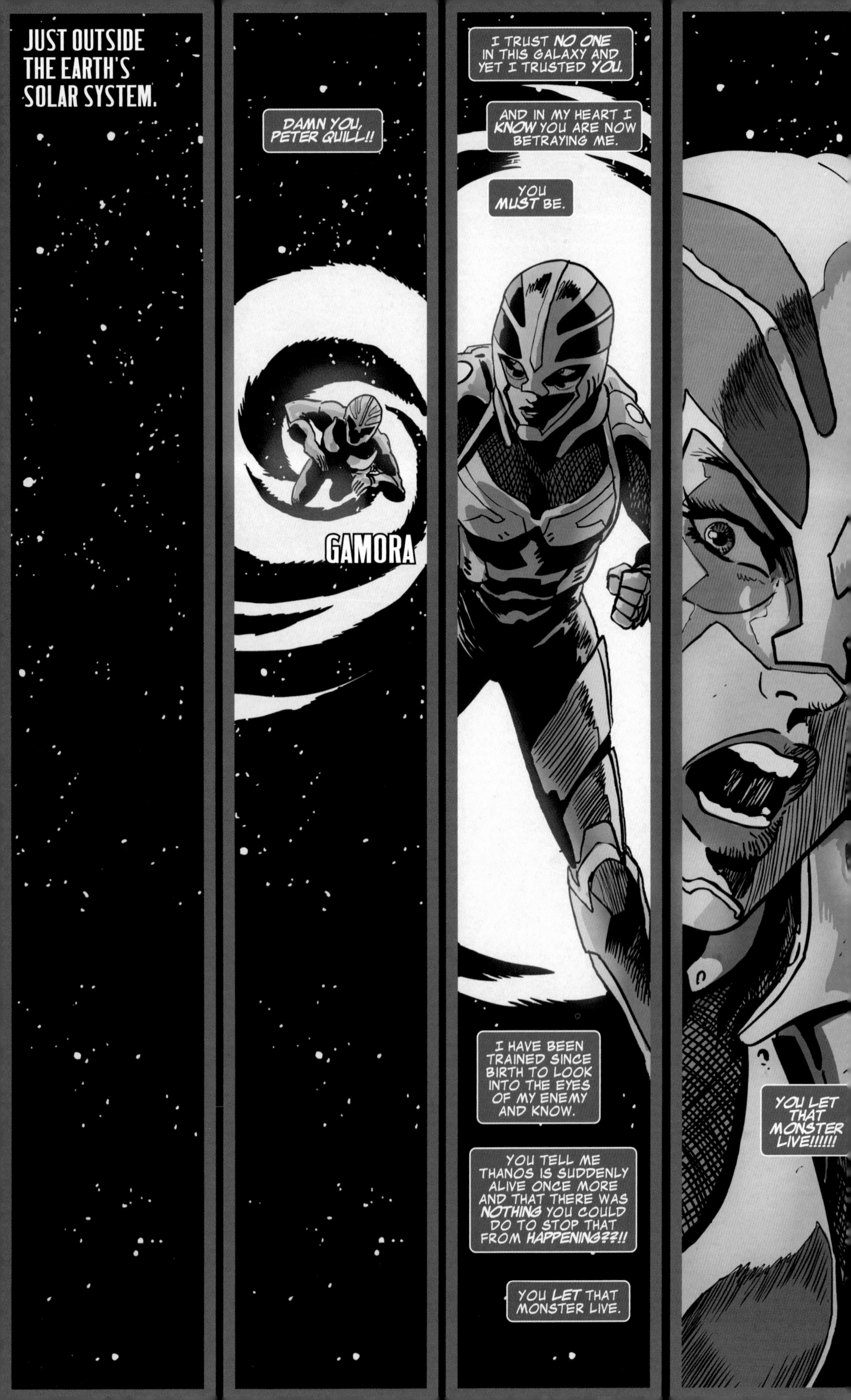
JUST OUTSIDE THE EARTH'S SOLAR SYSTEM.
DAMN YOU, PETER QUILL!!
GAMORA
I TRUST NO ONE IN THIS GALAXY AND YET I TRUSTED YOU.
AND IN MY HEART I KNOW YOU ARE NOW BETRAYING ME.
YOU MUST BE.
I HAVE BEEN TRAINED SINCE BIRTH TO LOOK INTO THE EYES OF MY ENEMY AND KNOW.
YOU TELL ME THANOS IS SUDDENLY ALIVE ONCE MORE AND THAT THERE WAS NOTHING YOU COULD DO TO STOP THAT FROM HAPPENING??!!
YOU LET THAT MONSTER LIVE.
YOU LET THAT MONSTER LIVE!!!!!!

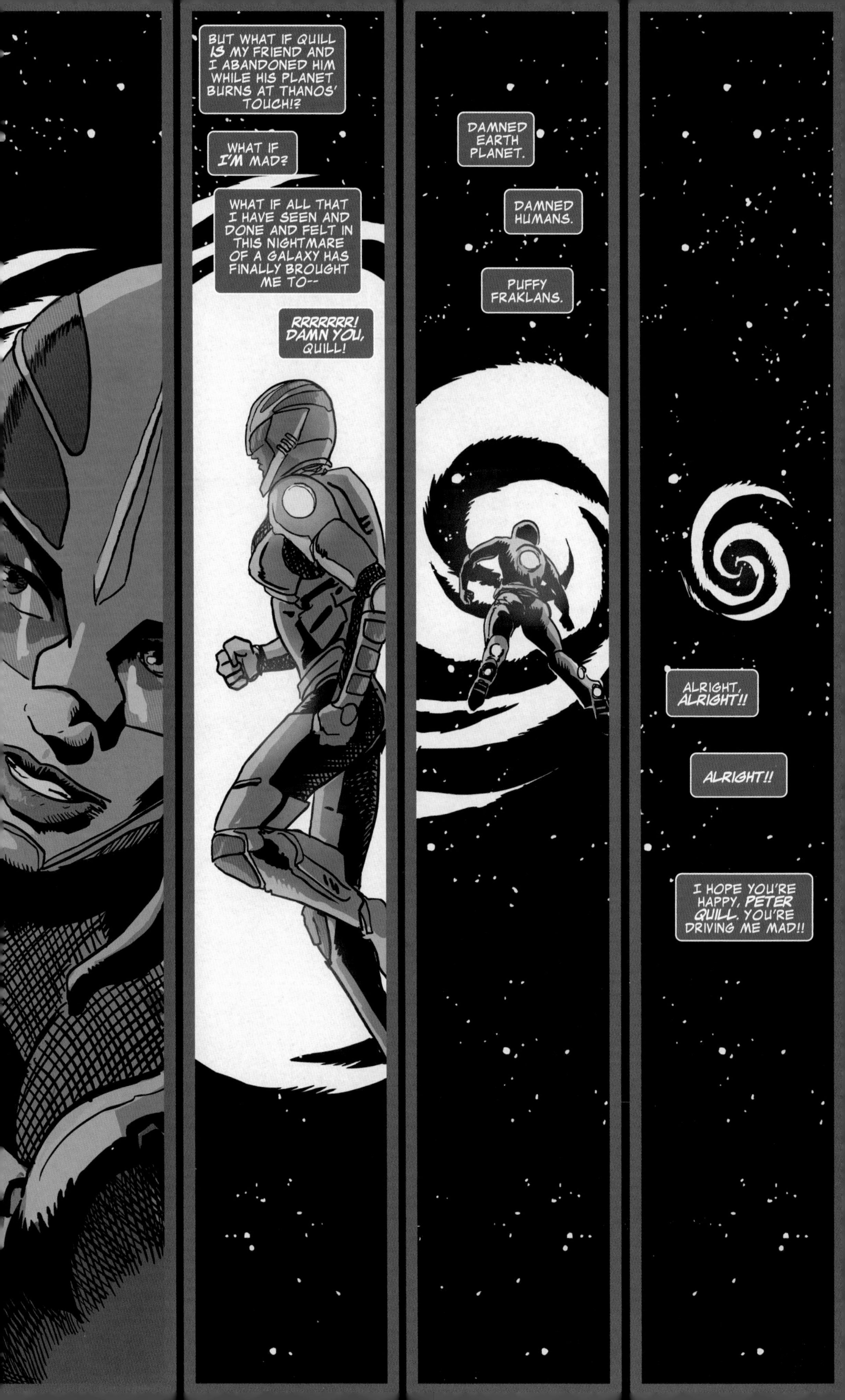
BUT WHAT IF QUILL IS MY FRIEND AND I ABANDONED HIM WHILE HIS PLANET BURNS AT THANOS' TOUCH!?
WHAT IF I'M MAD?
WHAT IF ALL THAT I HAVE SEEN AND DONE AND FELT IN THIS NIGHTMARE OF A GALAXY HAS FINALLY BROUGHT ME TO--
RRRRRRR! DAMN YOU, QUILL!
DAMNED EARTH PLANET.
DAMNED HUMANS.
PUFFY FRAKLANS.
ALRIGHT, ALRIGHT!!
ALRIGHT!!
I HOPE YOU'RE HAPPY, PETER QUILL. YOU'RE DRIVING ME MAD!!

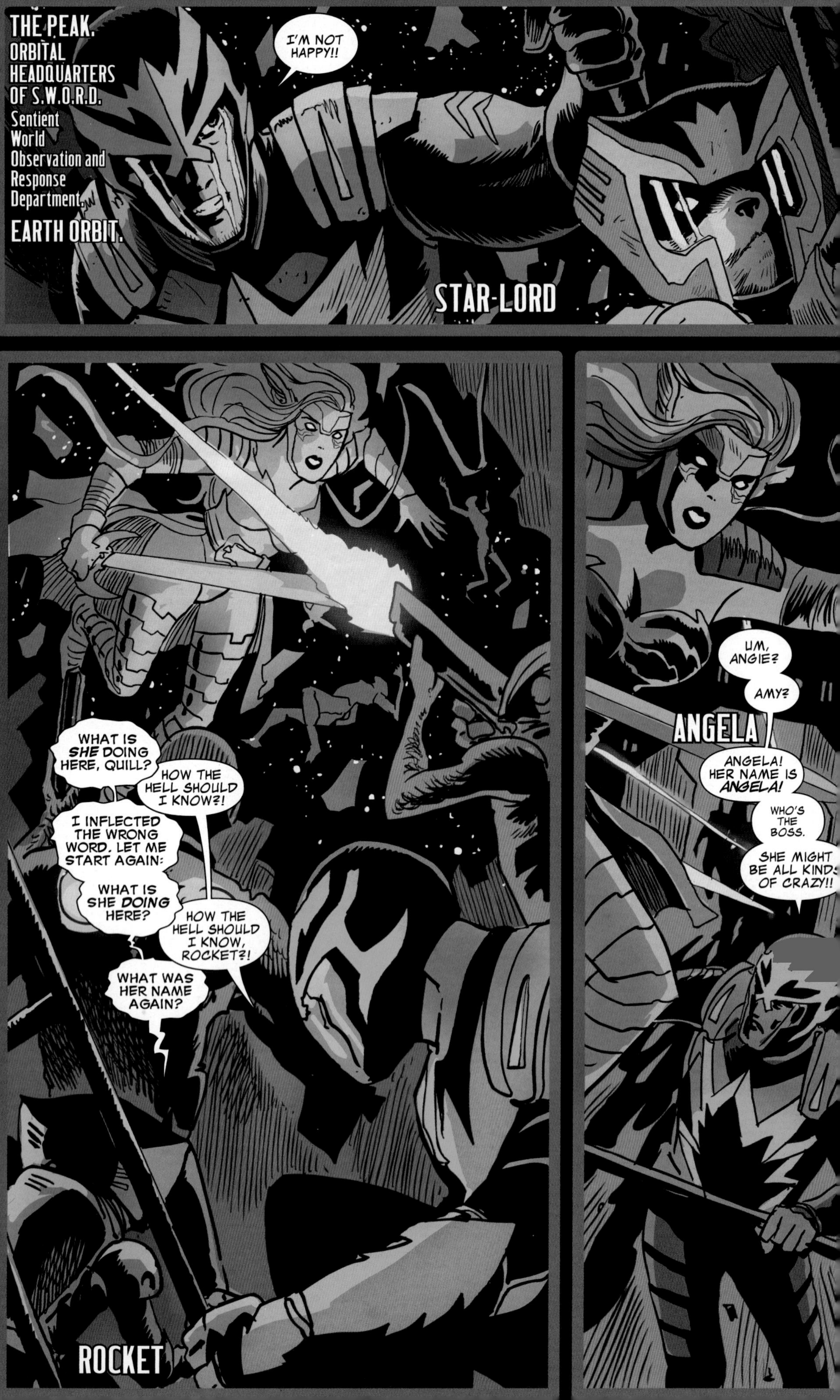
THE PEAK.
ORBITAL HEADQUARTERS OF S.W.O.R.D.
Sentient World Observation and Response Department.
EARTH ORBIT.
I'M NOT HAPPY!!
STAR-LORD
WHAT IS SHE DOING HERE, QUILL?
HOW THE HELL SHOULD I KNOW?!
I INFLECTED THE WRONG WORD. LET ME START AGAIN:
WHAT IS SHE DOING HERE?
HOW THE HELL SHOULD I KNOW, ROCKET?!
WHAT WAS HER NAME AGAIN?
ROCKET
UM, ANGIE?
AMY?
ANGELA
ANGELA! HER NAME IS ANGELA!
WHO'S THE BOSS.
SHE MIGHT BE ALL KINDS OF CRAZY!!

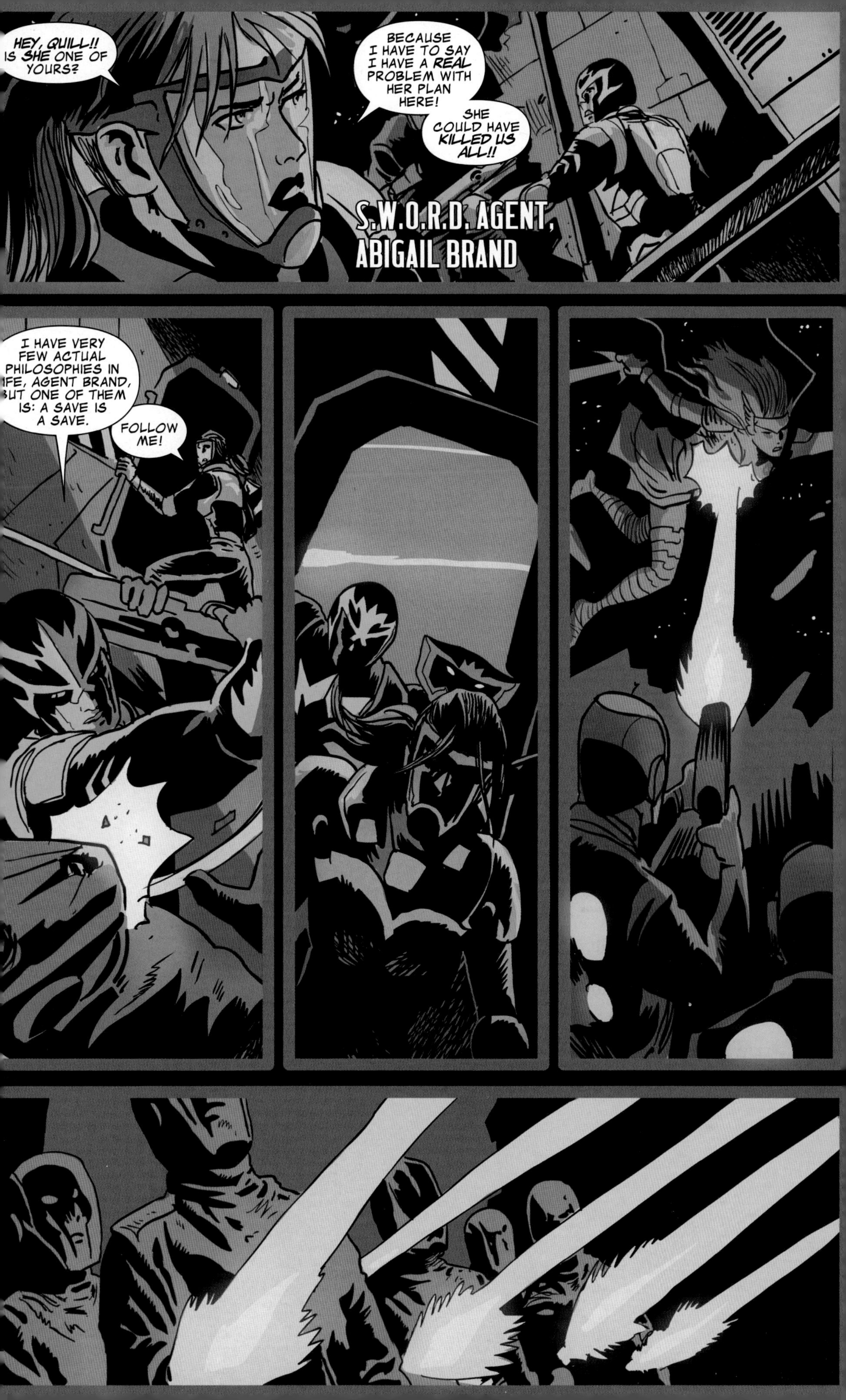
HEY, QUILL!! IS SHE ONE OF YOURS?
BECAUSE I HAVE TO SAY I HAVE A REAL PROBLEM WITH HER PLAN HERE!
SHE COULD HAVE KILLED US ALL!!
S.W.O.R.D. AGENT, ABIGAIL BRAND
I HAVE VERY FEW ACTUAL PHILOSOPHIES IN LIFE, AGENT BRAND, BUT ONE OF THEM IS: A SAVE IS A SAVE.
FOLLOW ME!

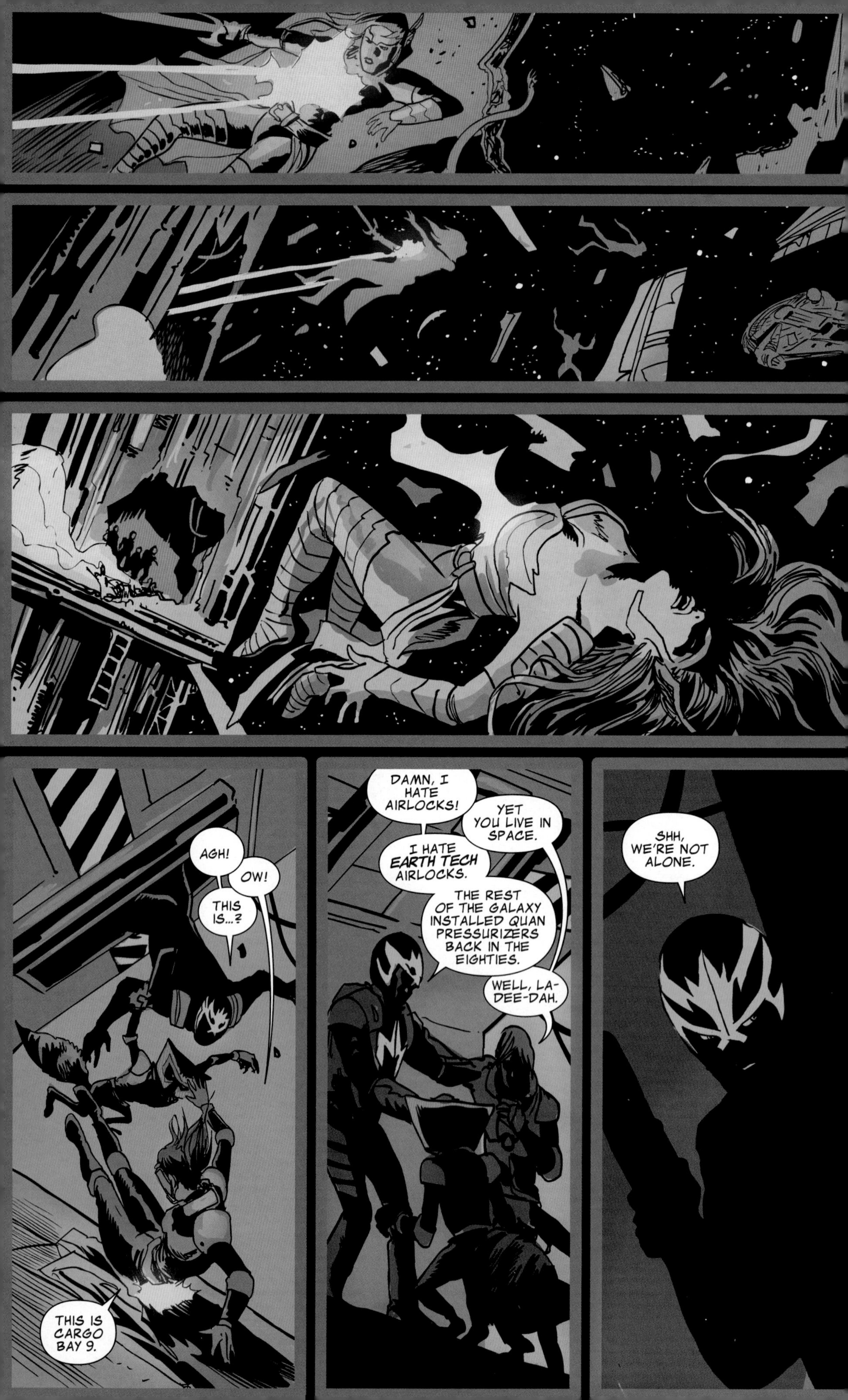
AGH!
OW!
THIS IS...?
THIS IS CARGO BAY 9.
DAMN, I HATE AIRLOCKS!
YET YOU LIVE IN SPACE.
I HATE ***EARTH TECH*** AIRLOCKS.
THE REST OF THE GALAXY INSTALLED QUAN PRESSURIZERS BACK IN THE EIGHTIES.
WELL, LA-DEE-DAH.
SHH, WE'RE NOT ALONE.

I CAN'T BELIEVE THAT CRAZY REDHEAD JUST DOVE IN OUT OF NOWHERE TO SAVE US.

THAT DOESN'T MEAN SHE'S GOING TO MARRY YOU, QUILL.

I THINK IT DOES.

SHH!! WE HAVE TO GET TO THE CONTROL ROOM.

WE HAVE TO LOWER THE EARTH DEFENSE SHIELDS SO THE AVENGERS CAN GET BACK TO EARTH.

IF THEY'RE STILL ALIVE. I HAVEN'T HEARD FROM THEM AND I'M--

ᛃᛗᛉᚾᚠ ᛉᛗᛃᚺ ᛋᚷᚿᛃ!!

HEY GUYS!

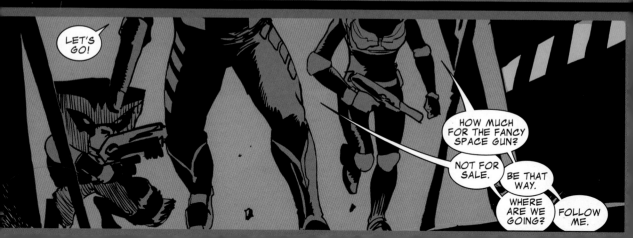

LET'S GO!

HOW MUCH FOR THE FANCY SPACE GUN?

NOT FOR SALE.

BE THAT WAY.

WHERE ARE WE GOING?

FOLLOW ME.

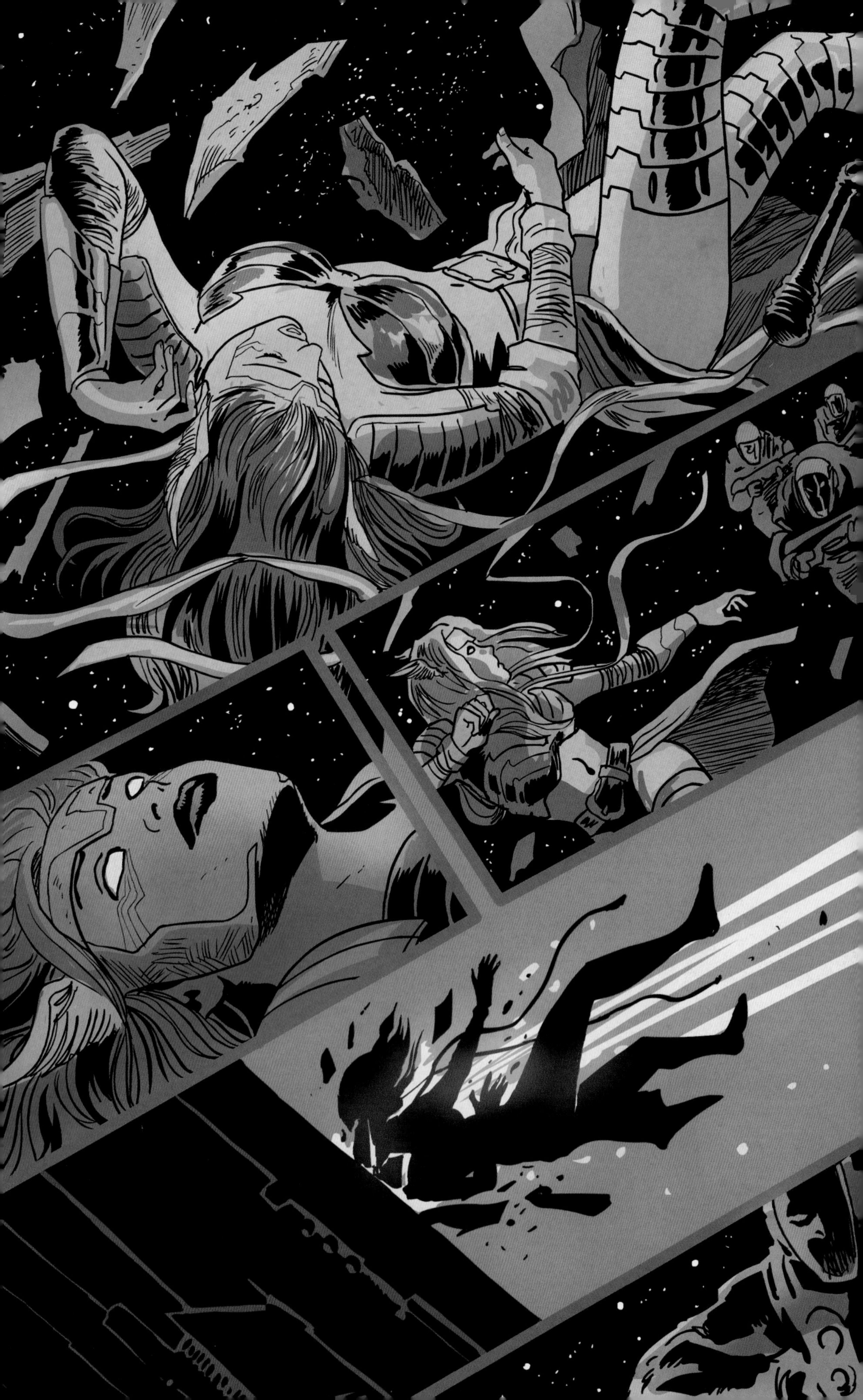

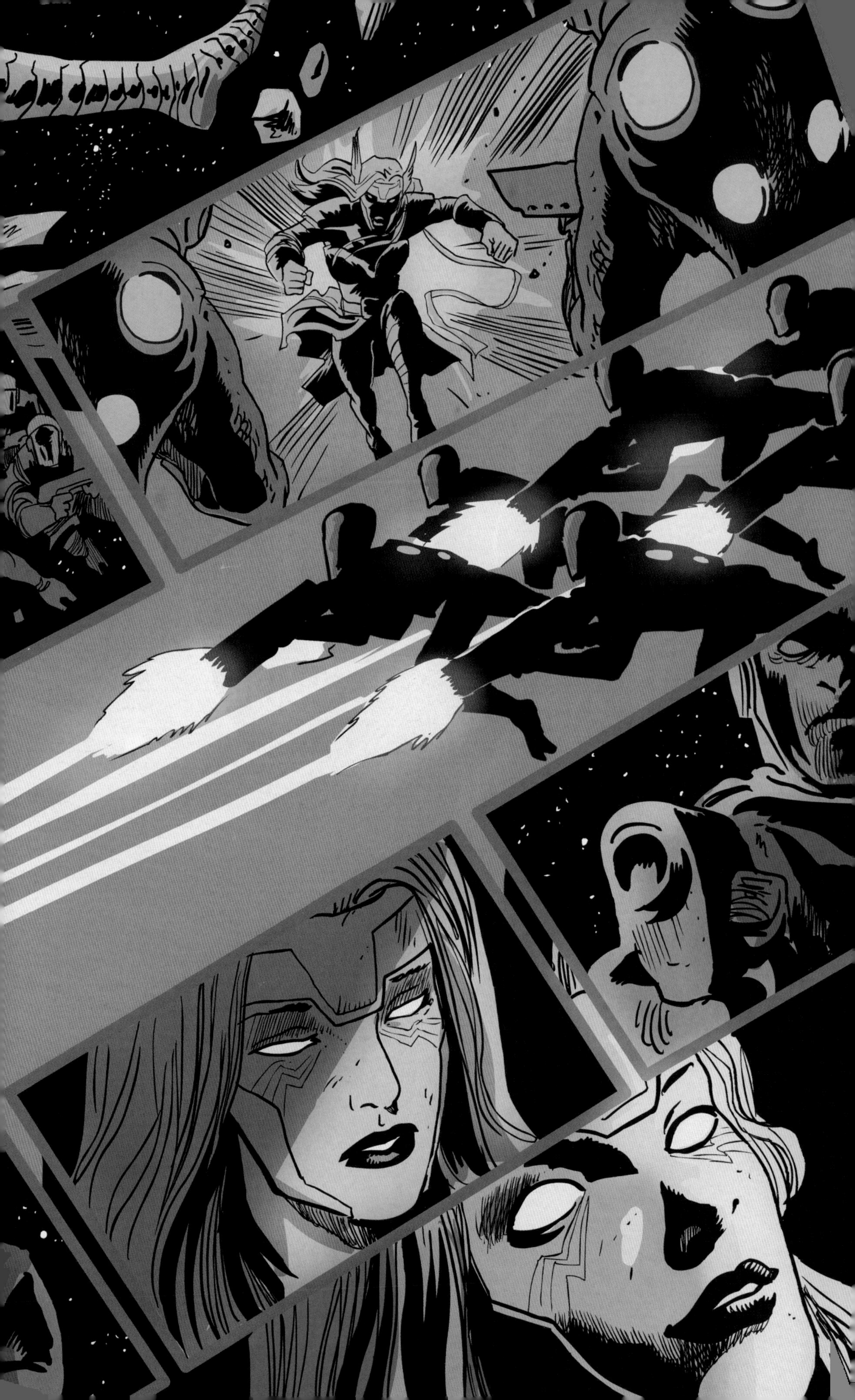

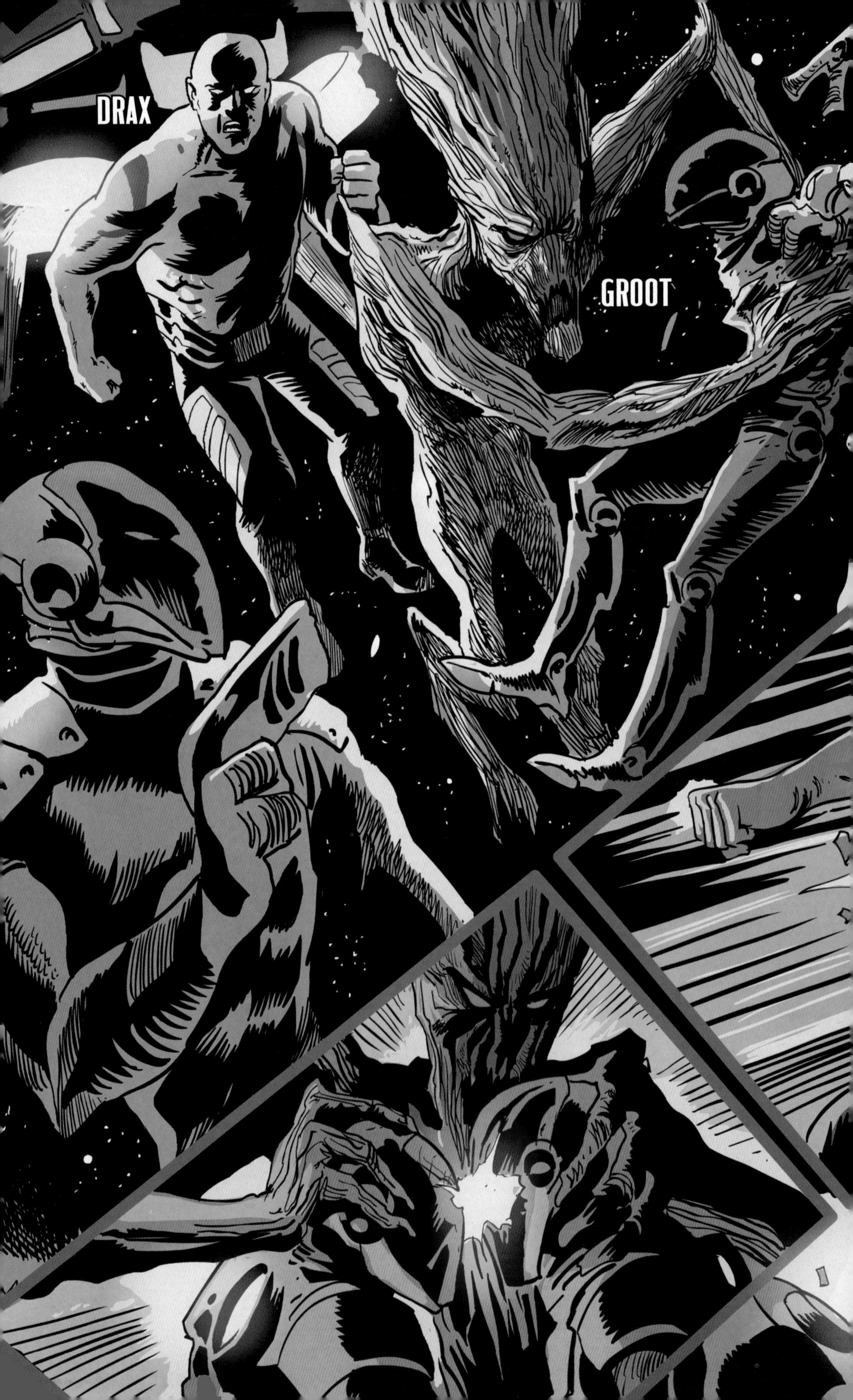
DRAX
GROOT

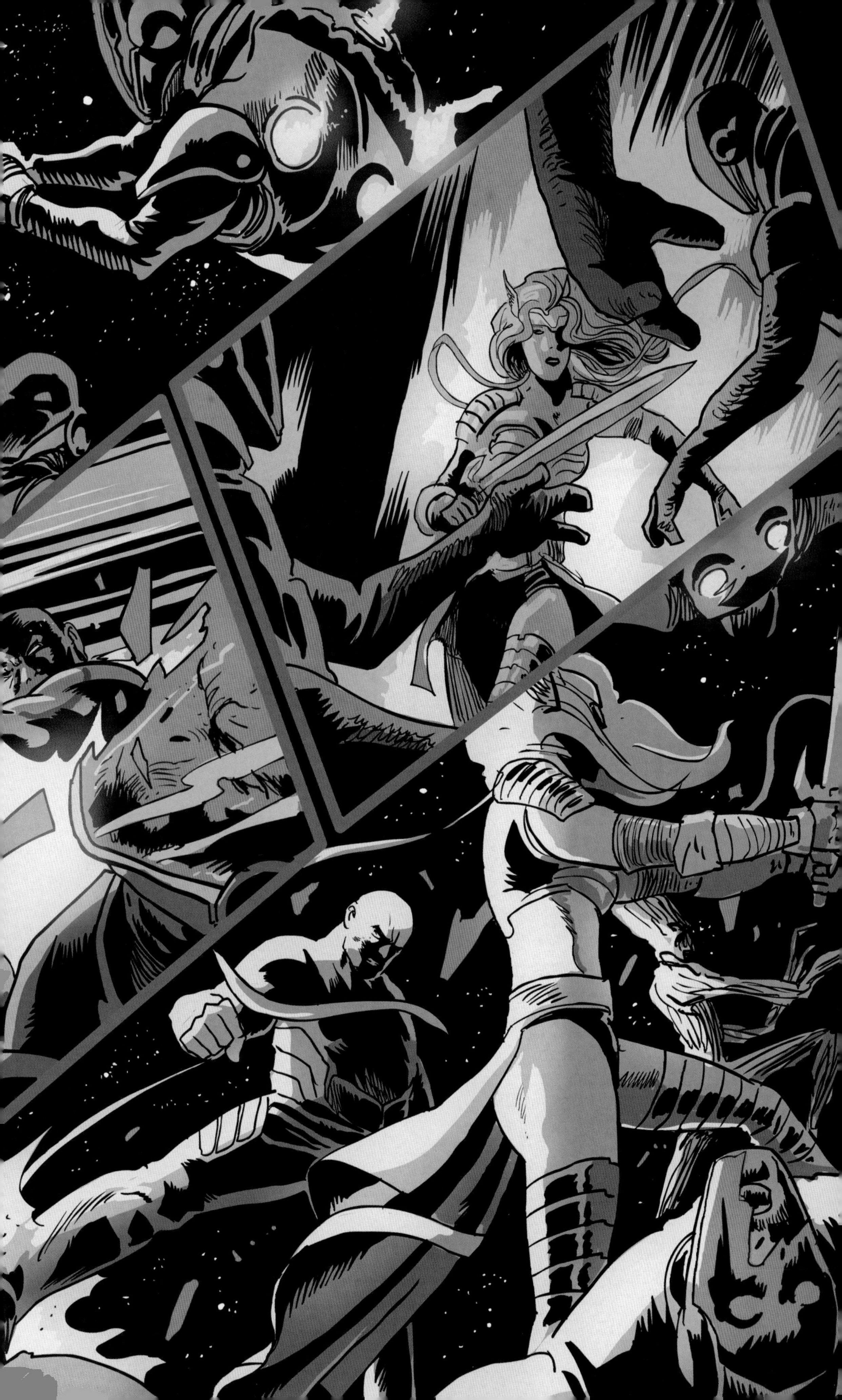

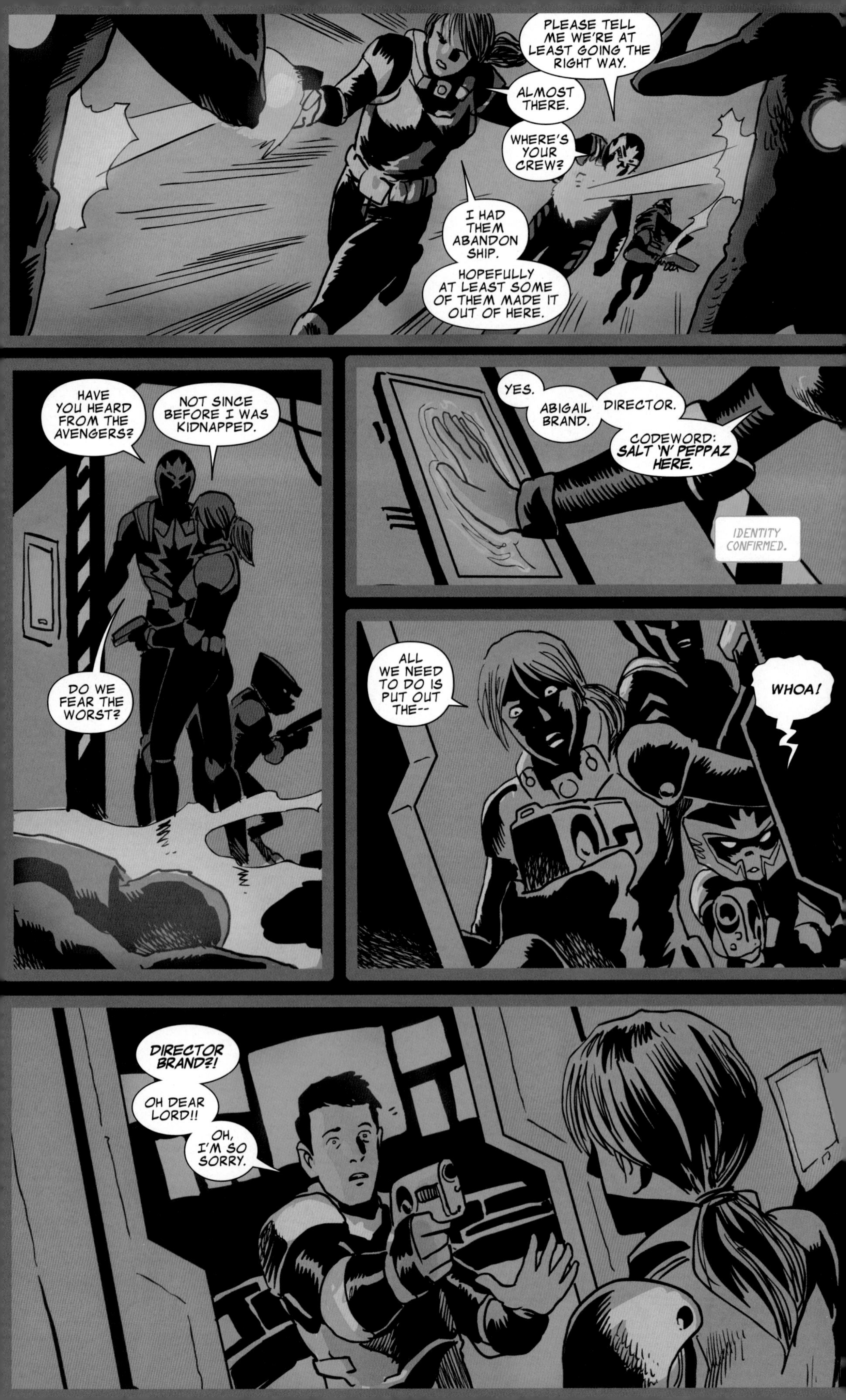
PLEASE TELL ME WE'RE AT LEAST GOING THE RIGHT WAY.
ALMOST THERE.
WHERE'S YOUR CREW?
I HAD THEM ABANDON SHIP.
HOPEFULLY AT LEAST SOME OF THEM MADE IT OUT OF HERE.
HAVE YOU HEARD FROM THE AVENGERS?
NOT SINCE BEFORE I WAS KIDNAPPED.
DO WE FEAR THE WORST?
YES.
ABIGAIL BRAND.
DIRECTOR.
CODEWORD: SALT 'N' PEPPAZ HERE.
IDENTITY CONFIRMED.
ALL WE NEED TO DO IS PUT OUT THE--
WHOA!
DIRECTOR BRAND?!
OH DEAR LORD!!
OH, I'M SO SORRY.

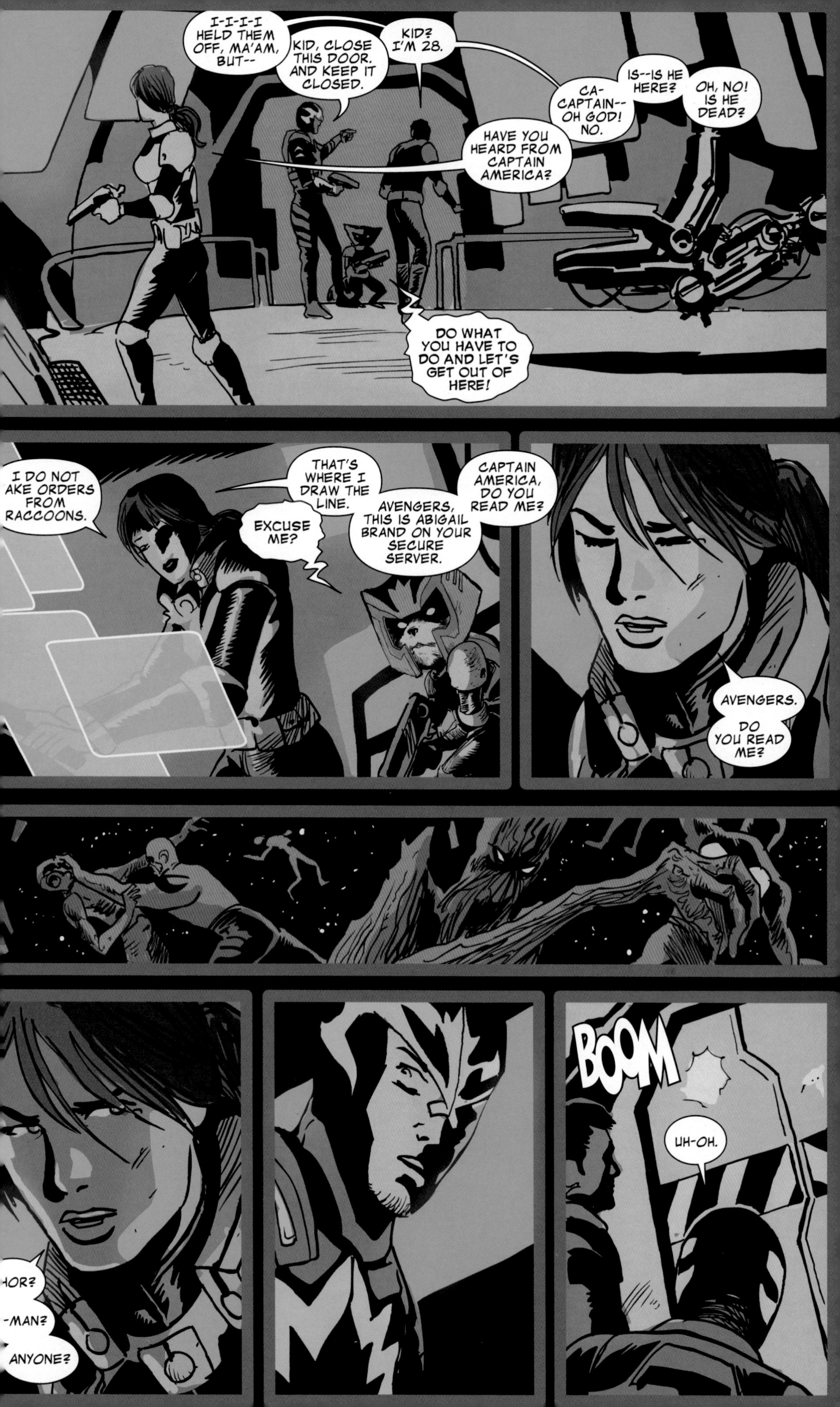
I-I-I-I HELD THEM OFF, MA'AM, BUT--
KID, CLOSE THIS DOOR. AND KEEP IT CLOSED.
KID? I'M 28.
HAVE YOU HEARD FROM CAPTAIN AMERICA?
CA-CAPTAIN--OH GOD! NO.
IS--IS HE HERE?
OH, NO! IS HE DEAD?
DO WHAT YOU HAVE TO DO AND LET'S GET OUT OF HERE!
I DO NOT AKE ORDERS FROM RACCOONS.
THAT'S WHERE I DRAW THE LINE.
EXCUSE ME?
AVENGERS, THIS IS ABIGAIL BRAND ON YOUR SECURE SERVER.
CAPTAIN AMERICA, DO YOU READ ME?
AVENGERS.
DO YOU READ ME?
HOR?
-MAN?
ANYONE?
BOOM
UH-OH.

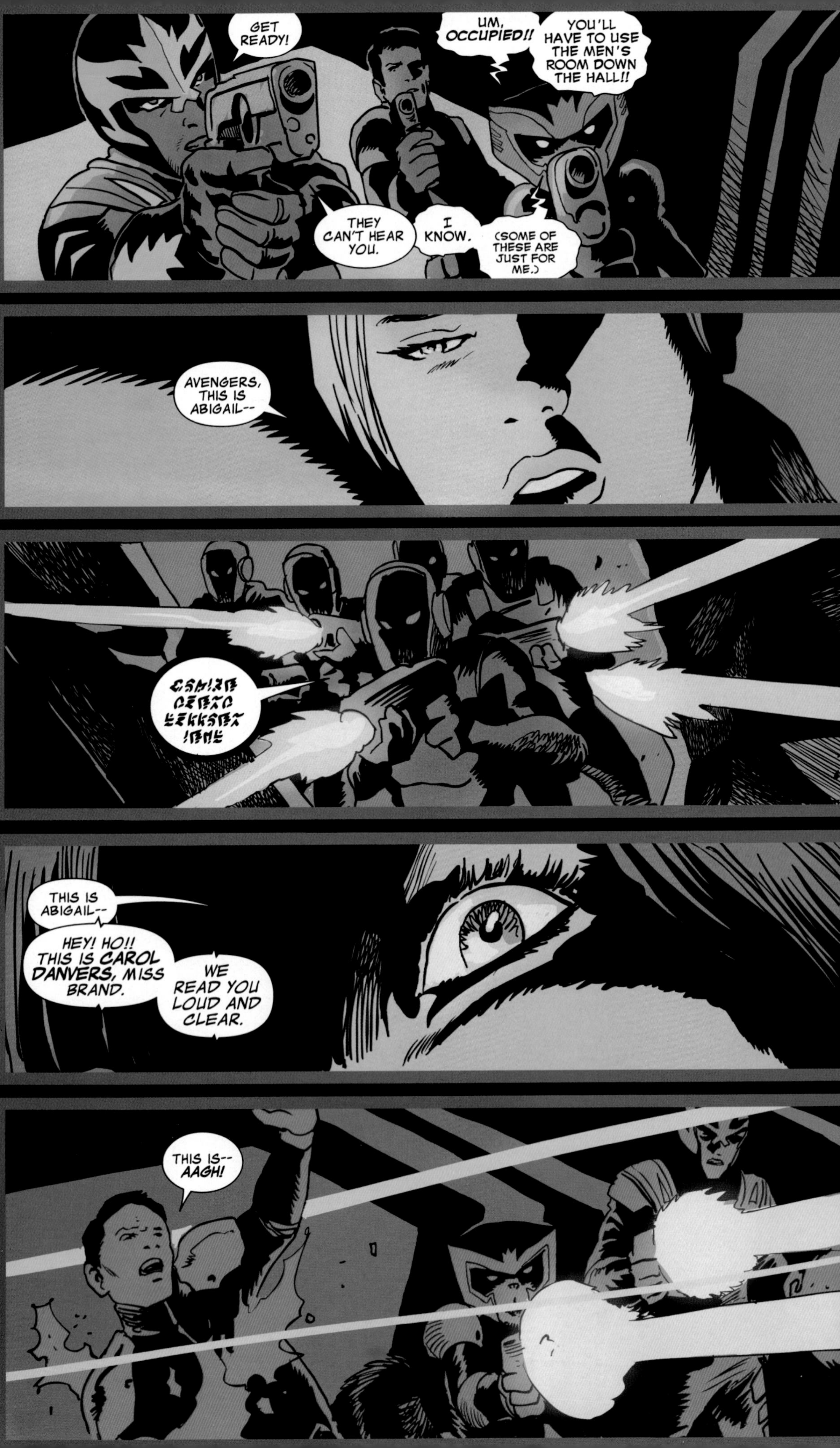
GET READY!
UM, OCCUPIED!!
YOU'LL HAVE TO USE THE MEN'S ROOM DOWN THE HALL!!
THEY CAN'T HEAR YOU.
I KNOW.
(SOME OF THESE ARE JUST FOR ME.)
AVENGERS, THIS IS ABIGAIL--
THIS IS ABIGAIL--
HEY! HO!! THIS IS CAROL DANVERS, MISS BRAND.
WE READ YOU LOUD AND CLEAR.
THIS IS-- AAGH!

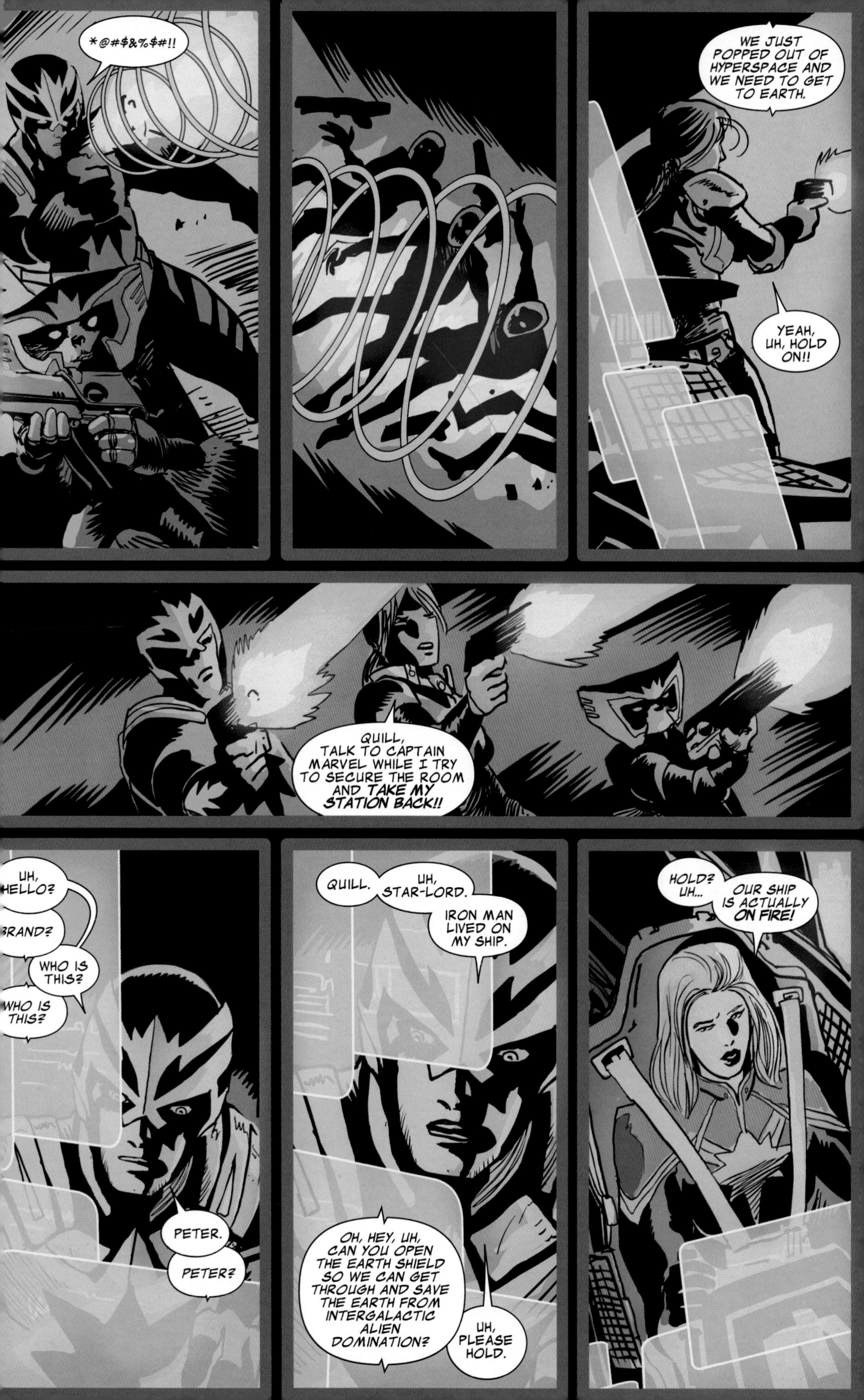
*@#$&%$#!!
WE JUST POPPED OUT OF HYPERSPACE AND WE NEED TO GET TO EARTH.
YEAH, UH, HOLD ON!!
QUILL, TALK TO CAPTAIN MARVEL WHILE I TRY TO SECURE THE ROOM AND *TAKE MY STATION BACK!!*
UH, HELLO?
BRAND?
WHO IS THIS?
WHO IS THIS?
PETER.
PETER?
QUILL.
UH, STAR-LORD.
IRON MAN LIVED ON MY SHIP.
OH, HEY, UH, CAN YOU OPEN THE EARTH SHIELD SO WE CAN GET THROUGH AND SAVE THE EARTH FROM INTERGALACTIC ALIEN DOMINATION?
UH, PLEASE HOLD.
HOLD? UH...
OUR SHIP IS ACTUALLY *ON FIRE!*

BRAND, WHAT DO I DO?!!

OPEN THE SHIELD!!

HIT THE BLUE BUTTON!

UM...

NO.

THE OTHER ONE.

THE OTHER BLUE ONE.

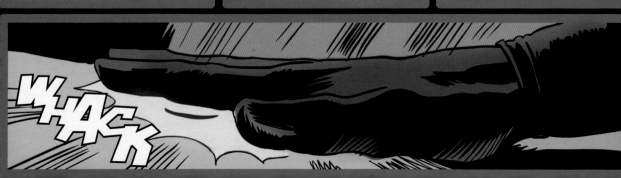

WHACK

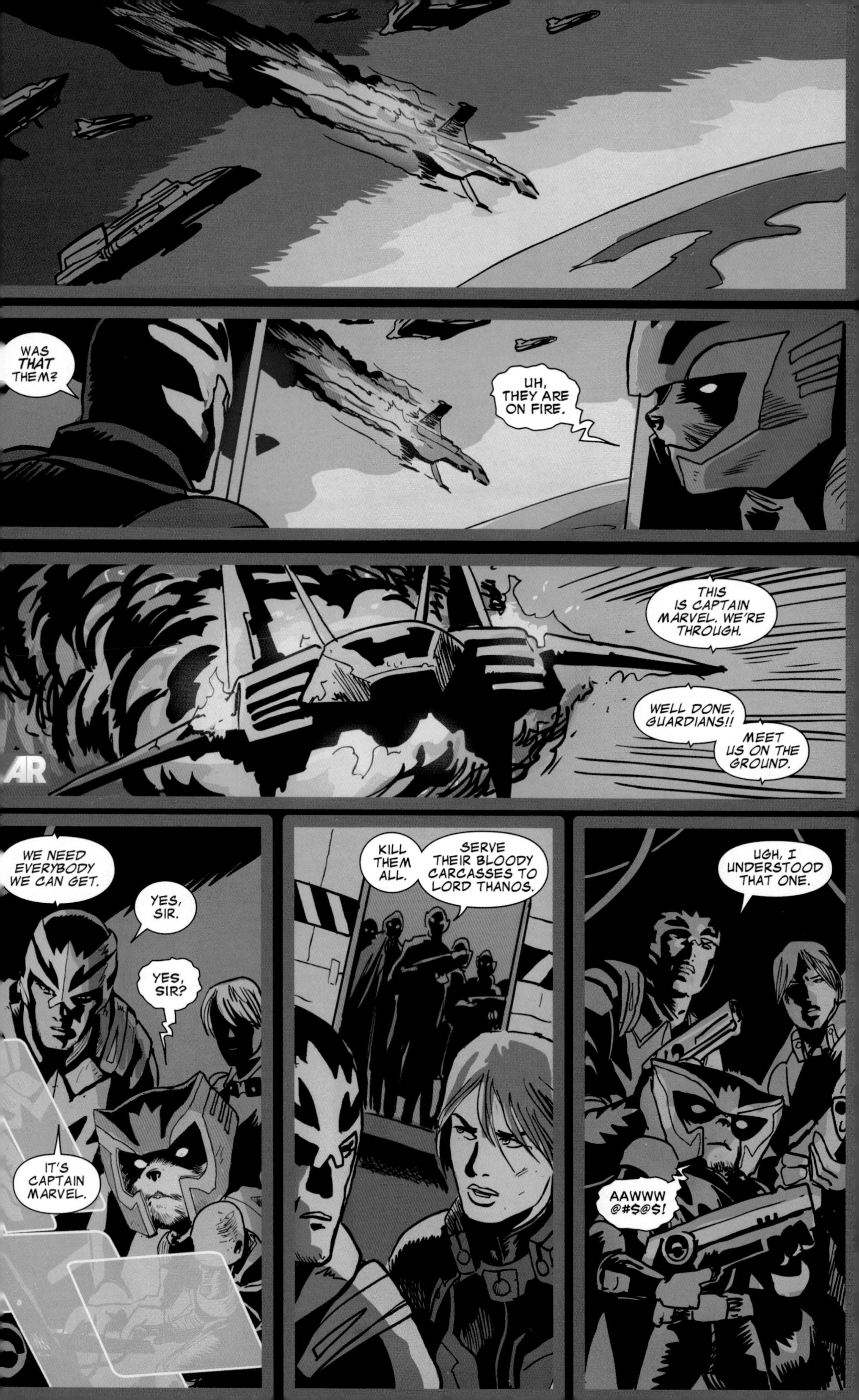
WAS THAT THEM?
UH, THEY ARE ON FIRE.
THIS IS CAPTAIN MARVEL. WE'RE THROUGH.
WELL DONE, GUARDIANS!!
MEET US ON THE GROUND.
AR
WE NEED EVERYBODY WE CAN GET.
YES, SIR.
YES, SIR?
IT'S CAPTAIN MARVEL.
KILL THEM ALL.
SERVE THEIR BLOODY CARCASSES TO LORD THANOS.
UGH, I UNDERSTOOD THAT ONE.
AAWWW @#$@$!

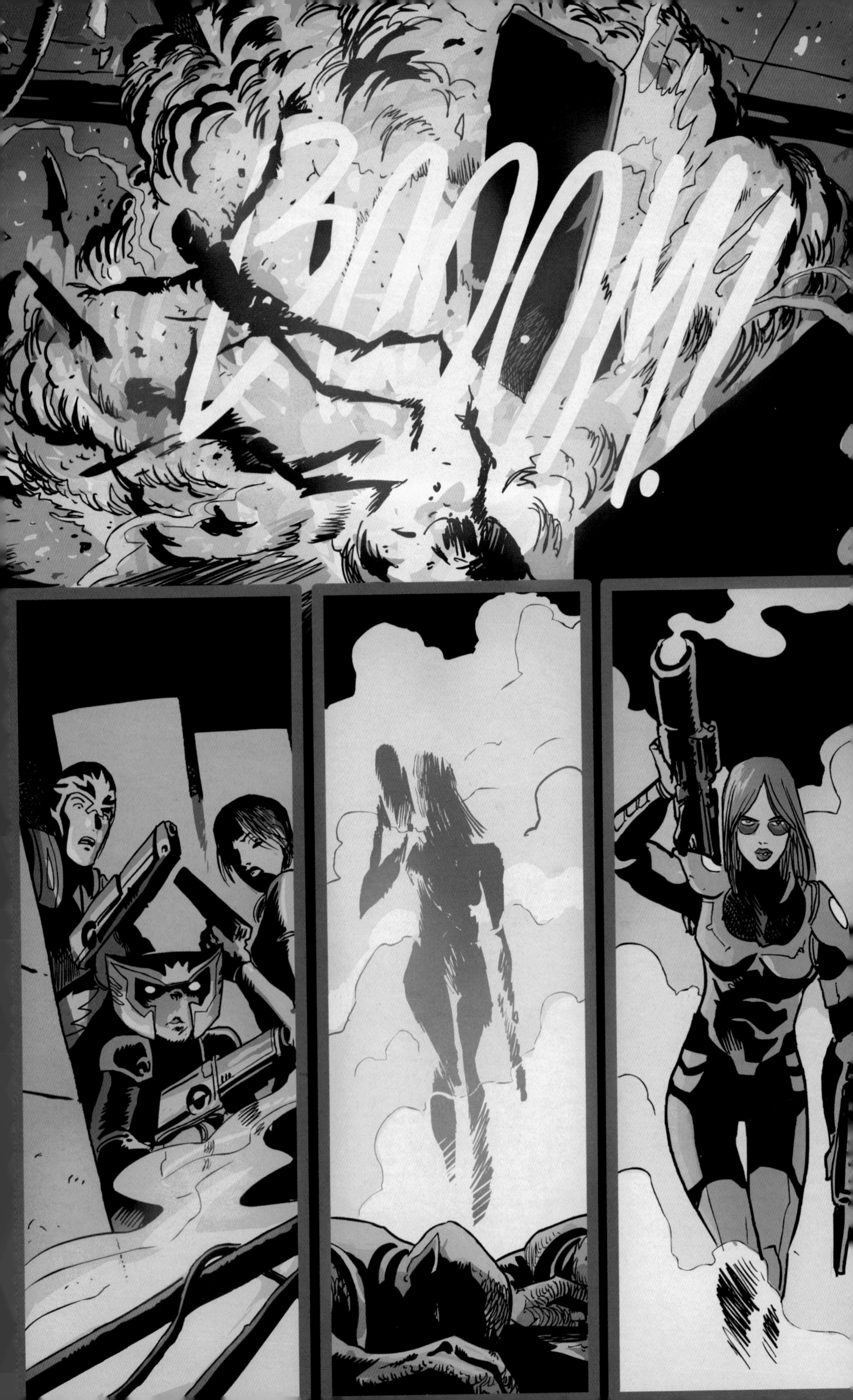
BOOOM!

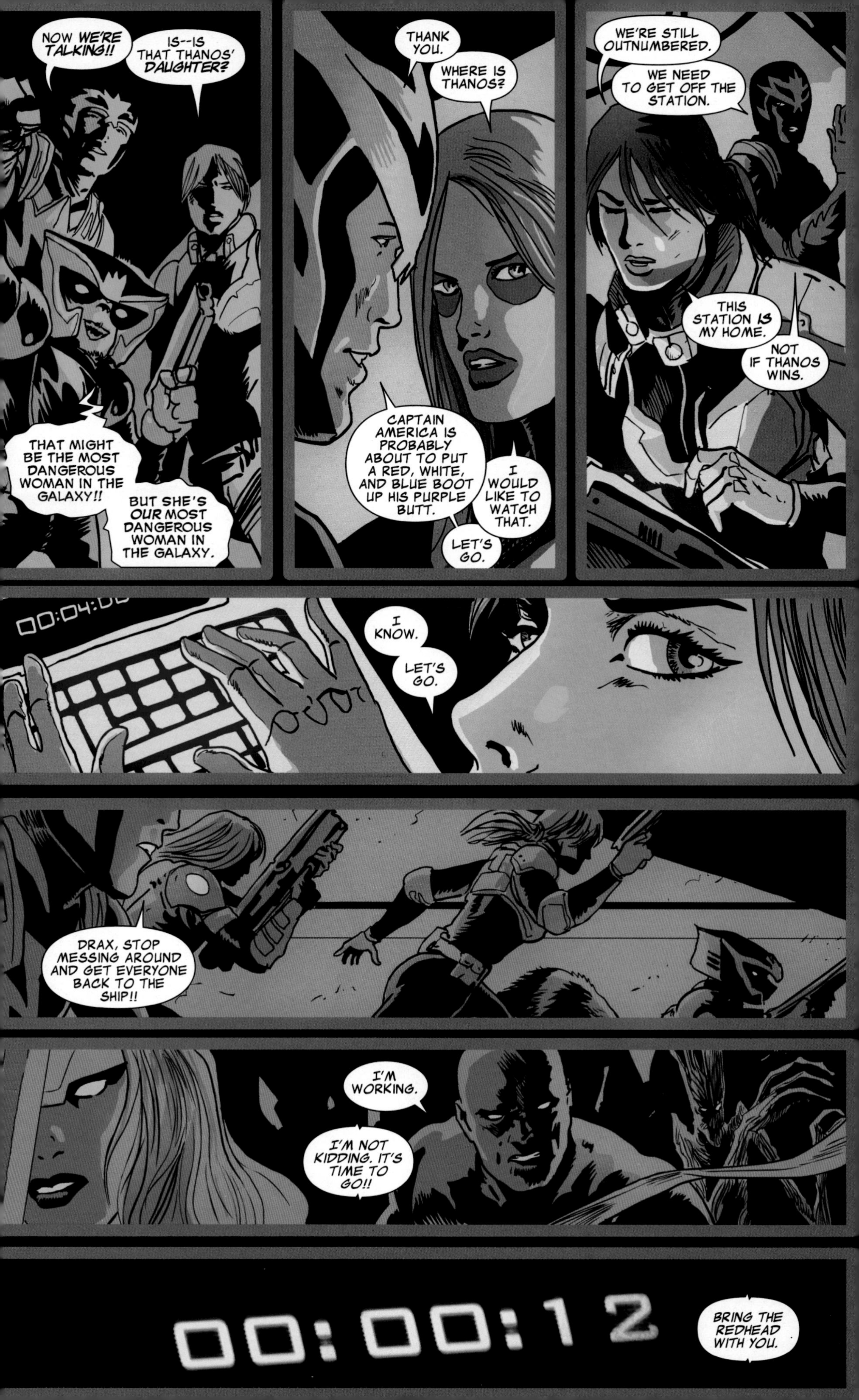
NOW WE'RE TALKING!!
IS--IS THAT THANOS' DAUGHTER?
THAT MIGHT BE THE MOST DANGEROUS WOMAN IN THE GALAXY!!
BUT SHE'S OUR MOST DANGEROUS WOMAN IN THE GALAXY.
THANK YOU.
WHERE IS THANOS?
CAPTAIN AMERICA IS PROBABLY ABOUT TO PUT A RED, WHITE, AND BLUE BOOT UP HIS PURPLE BUTT.
I WOULD LIKE TO WATCH THAT.
LET'S GO.
WE'RE STILL OUTNUMBERED.
WE NEED TO GET OFF THE STATION.
THIS STATION IS MY HOME.
NOT IF THANOS WINS.
I KNOW.
LET'S GO.
DRAX, STOP MESSING AROUND AND GET EVERYONE BACK TO THE SHIP!!
I'M WORKING.
I'M NOT KIDDING. IT'S TIME TO GO!!
00:00:12
BRING THE REDHEAD WITH YOU.

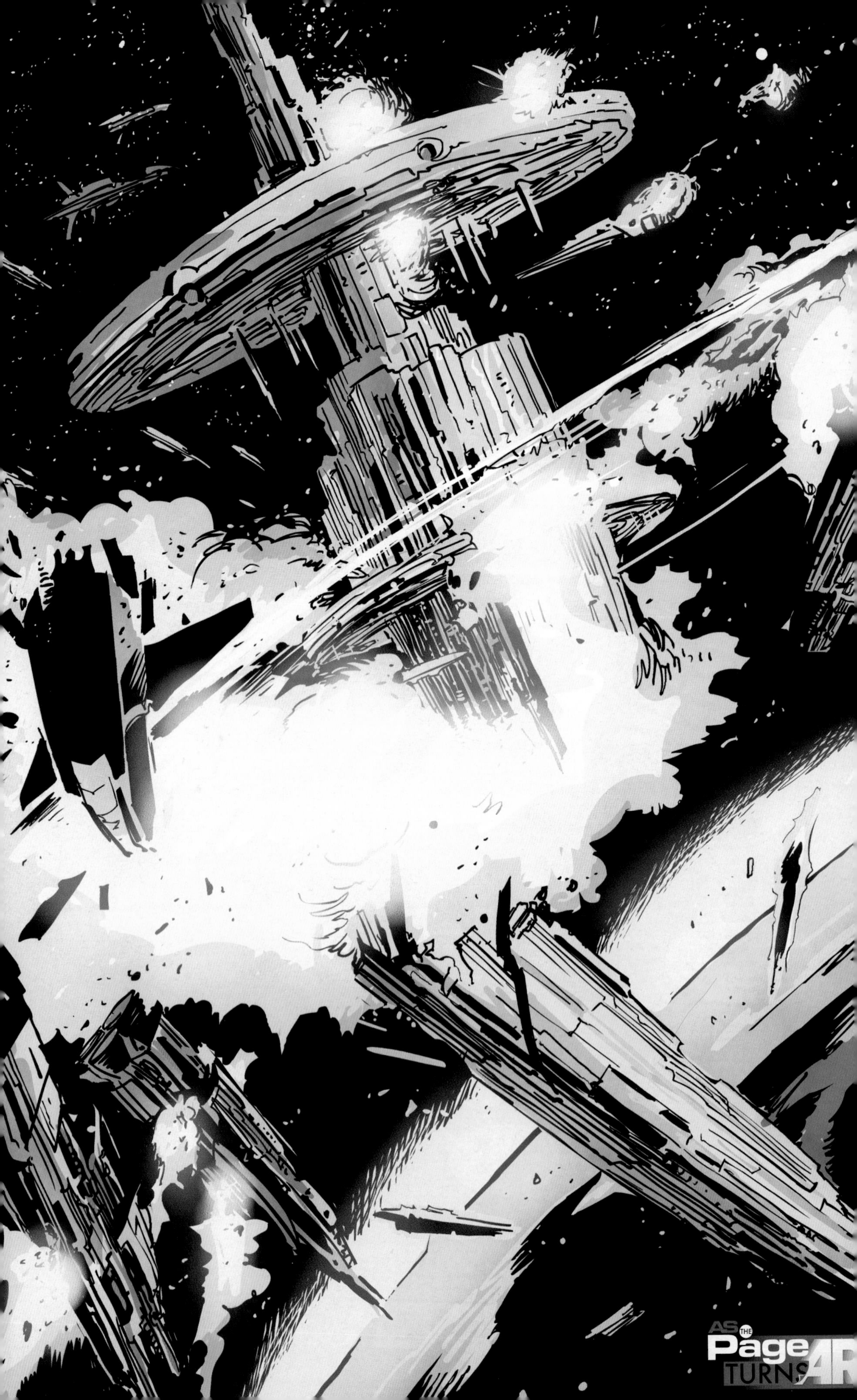

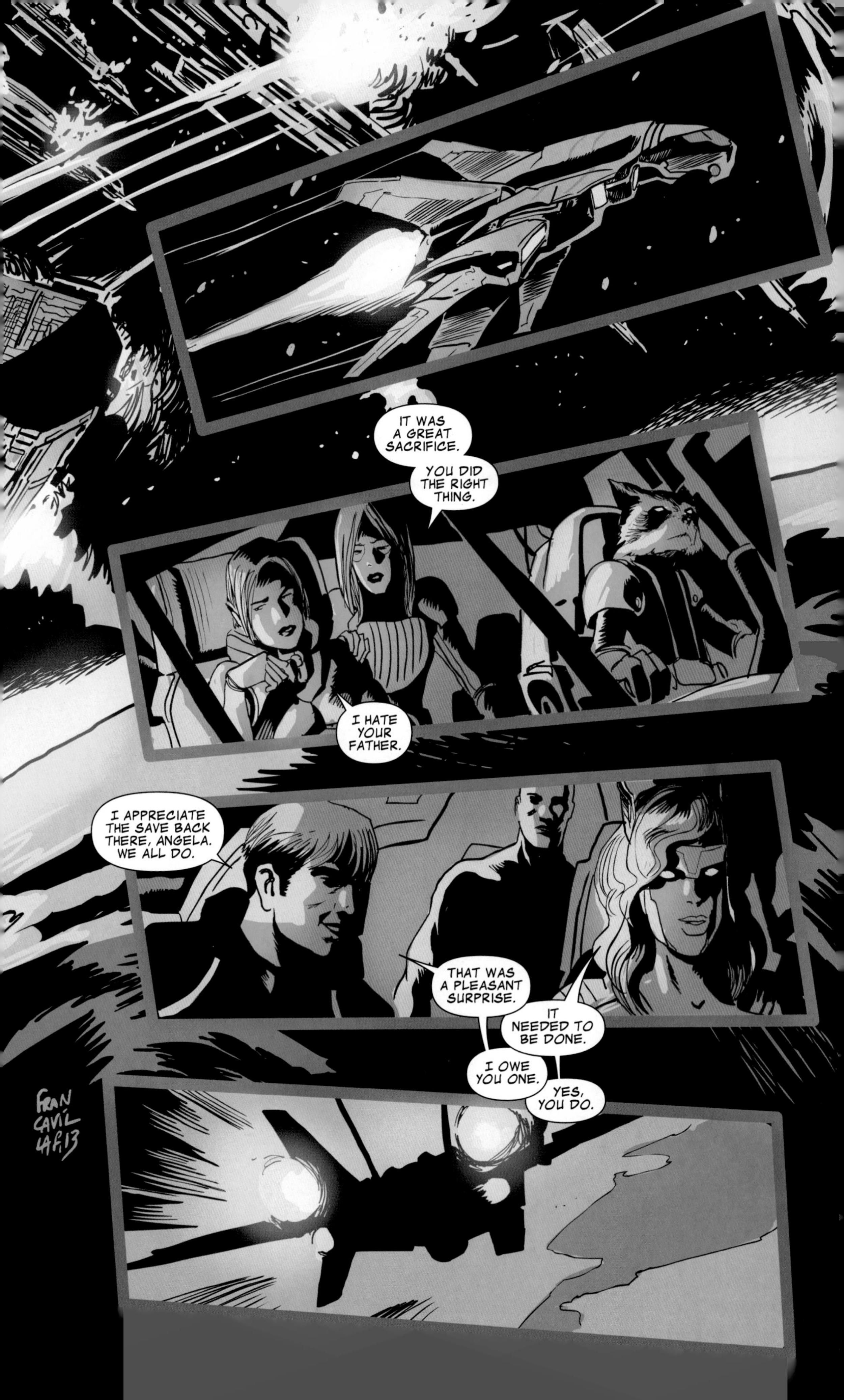
IT WAS A GREAT SACRIFICE.
YOU DID THE RIGHT THING.
I HATE YOUR FATHER.
I APPRECIATE THE SAVE BACK THERE, ANGELA. WE ALL DO.
THAT WAS A PLEASANT SURPRISE.
IT NEEDED TO BE DONE.
I OWE YOU ONE.
YES, YOU DO.
FRAN CAVIL

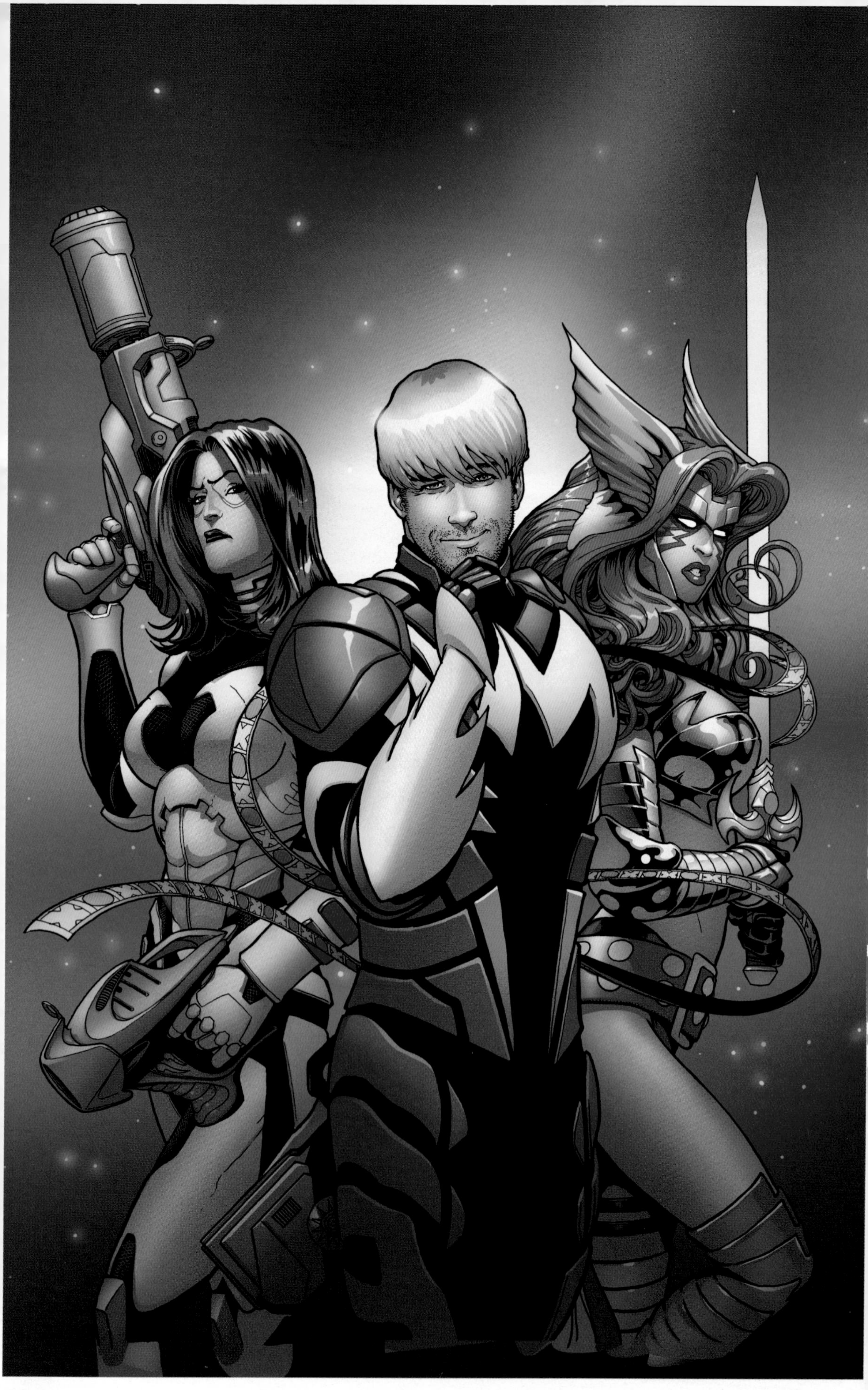

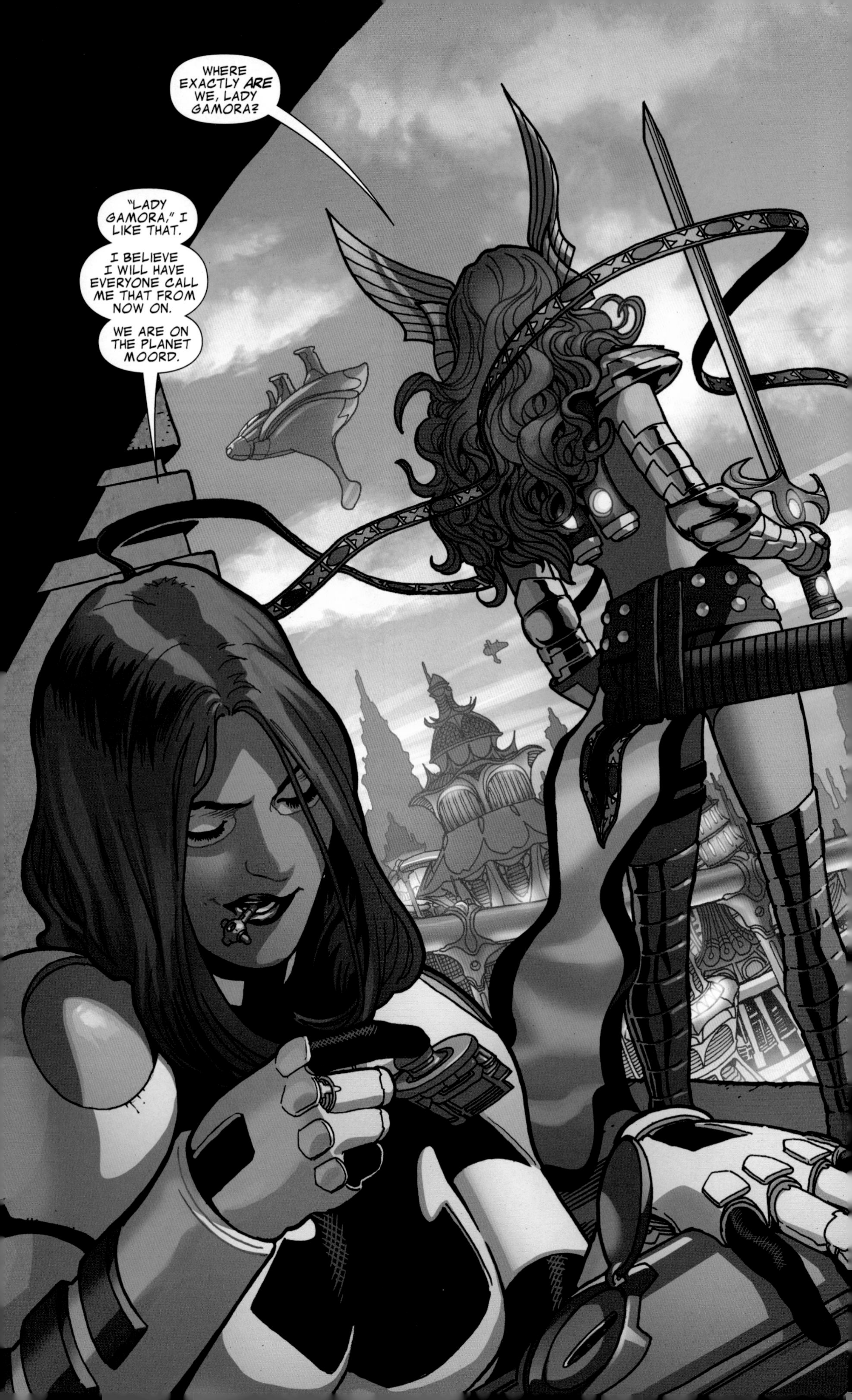
WHERE EXACTLY ARE WE, LADY GAMORA?
"LADY GAMORA," I LIKE THAT.
I BELIEVE I WILL HAVE EVERYONE CALL ME THAT FROM NOW ON.
WE ARE ON THE PLANET MOORD.

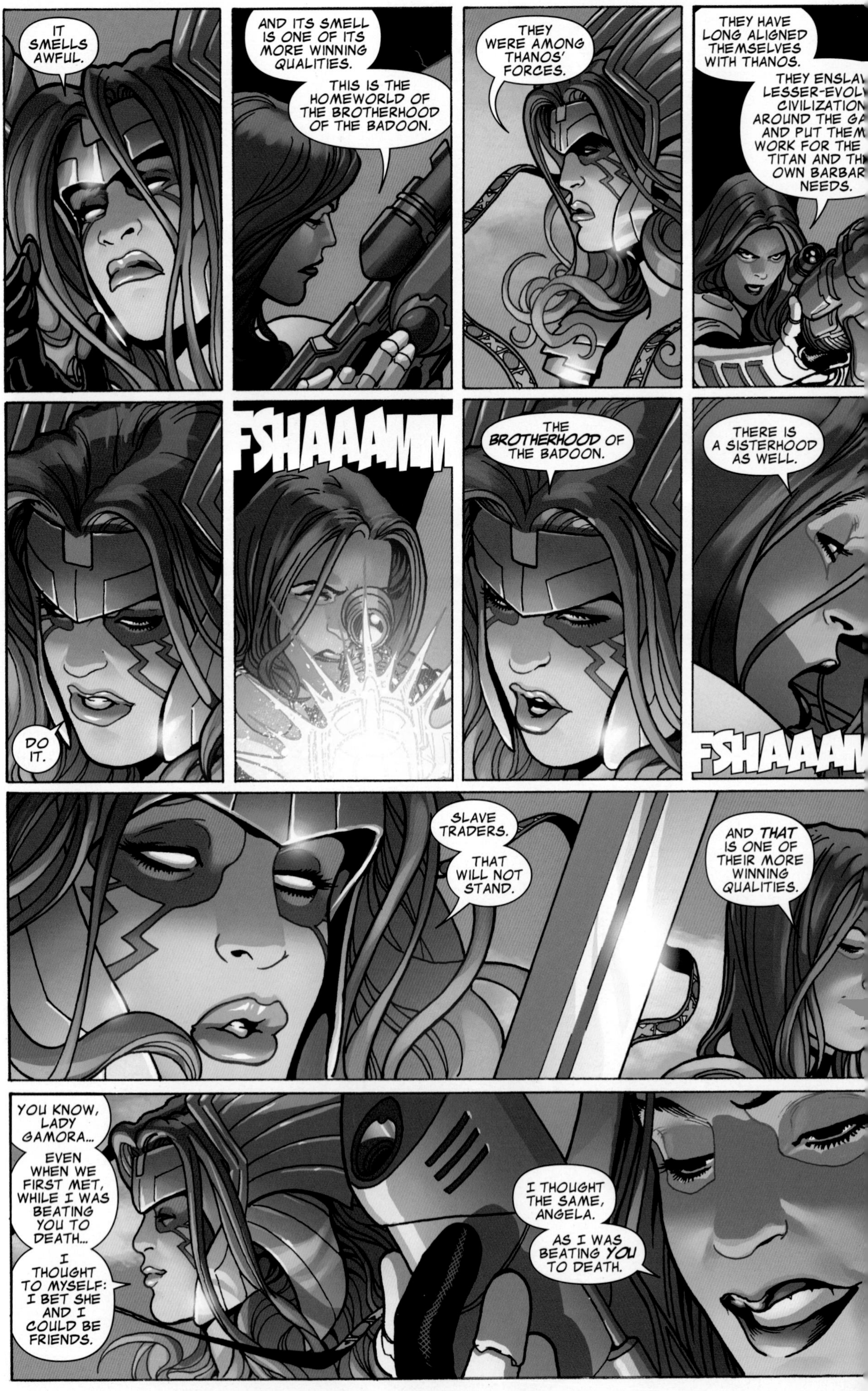
IT SMELLS AWFUL.
AND ITS SMELL IS ONE OF ITS MORE WINNING QUALITIES.
THIS IS THE HOMEWORLD OF THE BROTHERHOOD OF THE BADOON.
THEY WERE AMONG THANOS' FORCES.
THEY HAVE LONG ALIGNED THEMSELVES WITH THANOS.
THEY ENSLAV LESSER-EVOLV CIVILIZATION AROUND THE GA AND PUT THEM WORK FOR THE TITAN AND TH OWN BARBAR NEEDS.
DO IT.
FSHAAAMM
THE BROTHERHOOD OF THE BADOON.
THERE IS A SISTERHOOD AS WELL.
FSHAAAM
SLAVE TRADERS.
THAT WILL NOT STAND.
AND THAT IS ONE OF THEIR MORE WINNING QUALITIES.
YOU KNOW, LADY GAMORA...
EVEN WHEN WE FIRST MET, WHILE I WAS BEATING YOU TO DEATH...
I THOUGHT TO MYSELF: I BET SHE AND I COULD BE FRIENDS.
I THOUGHT THE SAME, ANGELA.
AS I WAS BEATING YOU TO DEATH.

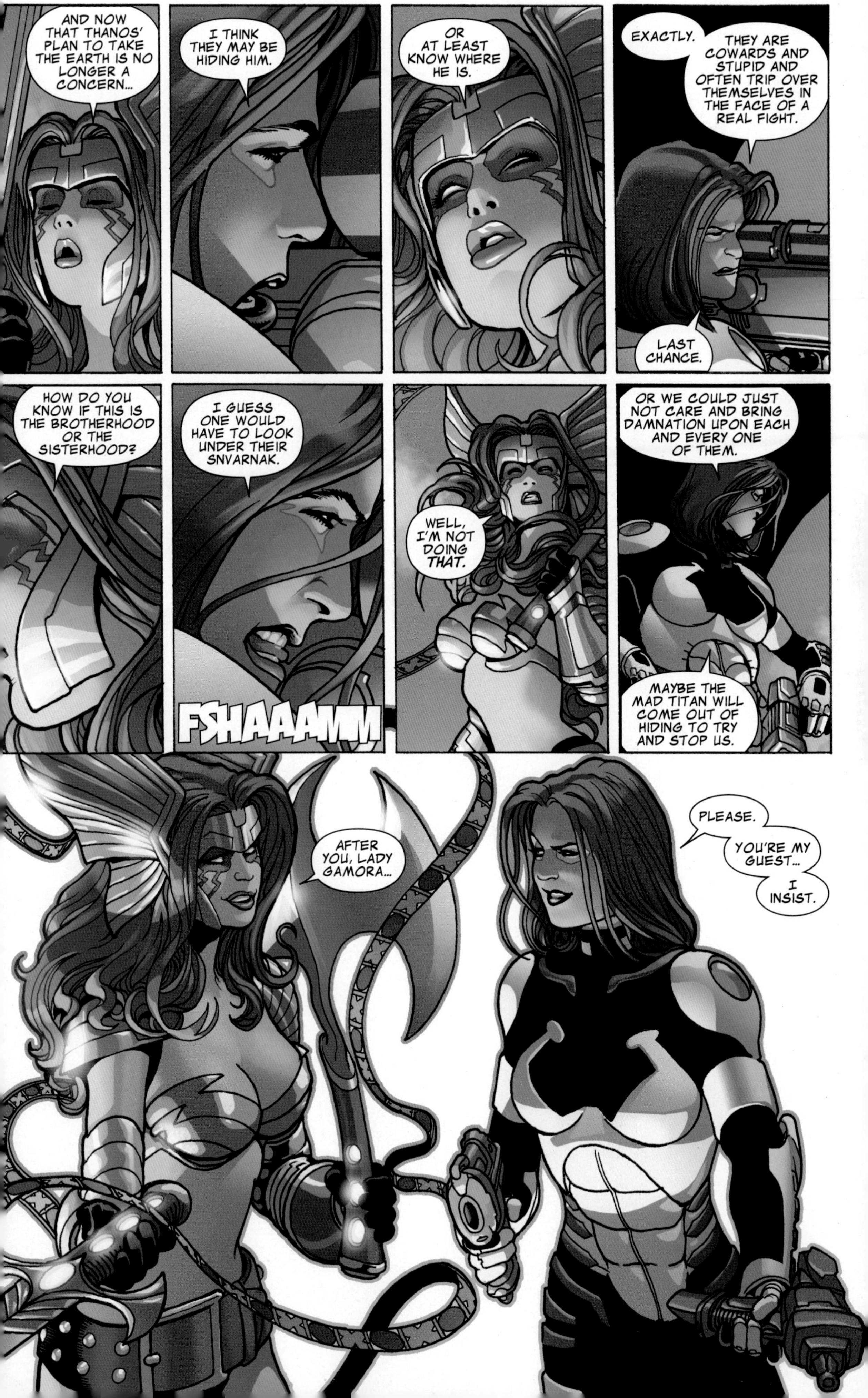

AND NOW THAT THANOS' PLAN TO TAKE THE EARTH IS NO LONGER A CONCERN...
I THINK THEY MAY BE HIDING HIM.
OR AT LEAST KNOW WHERE HE IS.
EXACTLY.
THEY ARE COWARDS AND STUPID AND OFTEN TRIP OVER THEMSELVES IN THE FACE OF A REAL FIGHT.
LAST CHANCE.
HOW DO YOU KNOW IF THIS IS THE BROTHERHOOD OR THE SISTERHOOD?
I GUESS ONE WOULD HAVE TO LOOK UNDER THEIR SNVARNAK.
FSHAAAMM
WELL, I'M NOT DOING THAT.
OR WE COULD JUST NOT CARE AND BRING DAMNATION UPON EACH AND EVERY ONE OF THEM.
MAYBE THE MAD TITAN WILL COME OUT OF HIDING TO TRY AND STOP US.
AFTER YOU, LADY GAMORA...
PLEASE.
YOU'RE MY GUEST...
I INSIST.

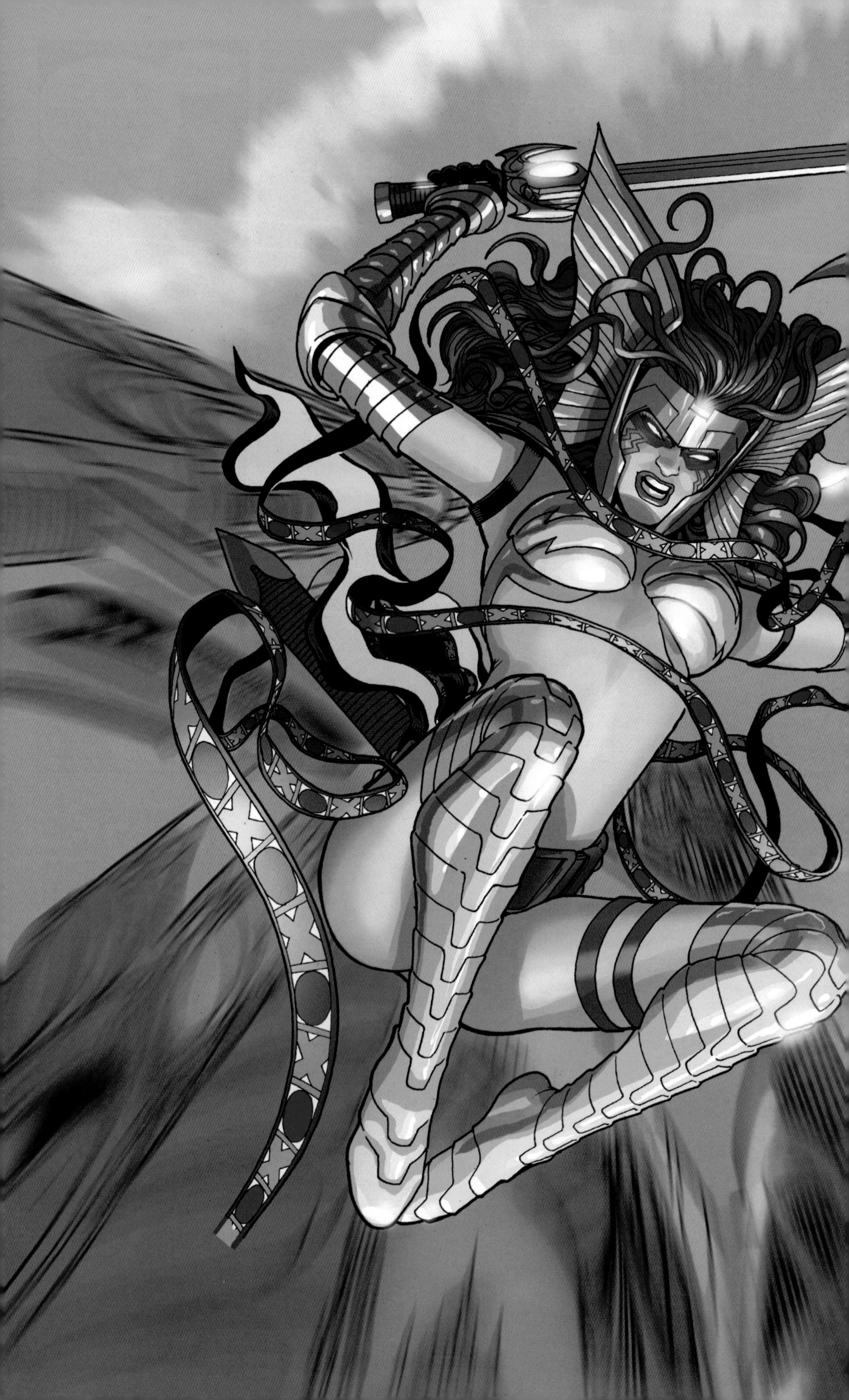

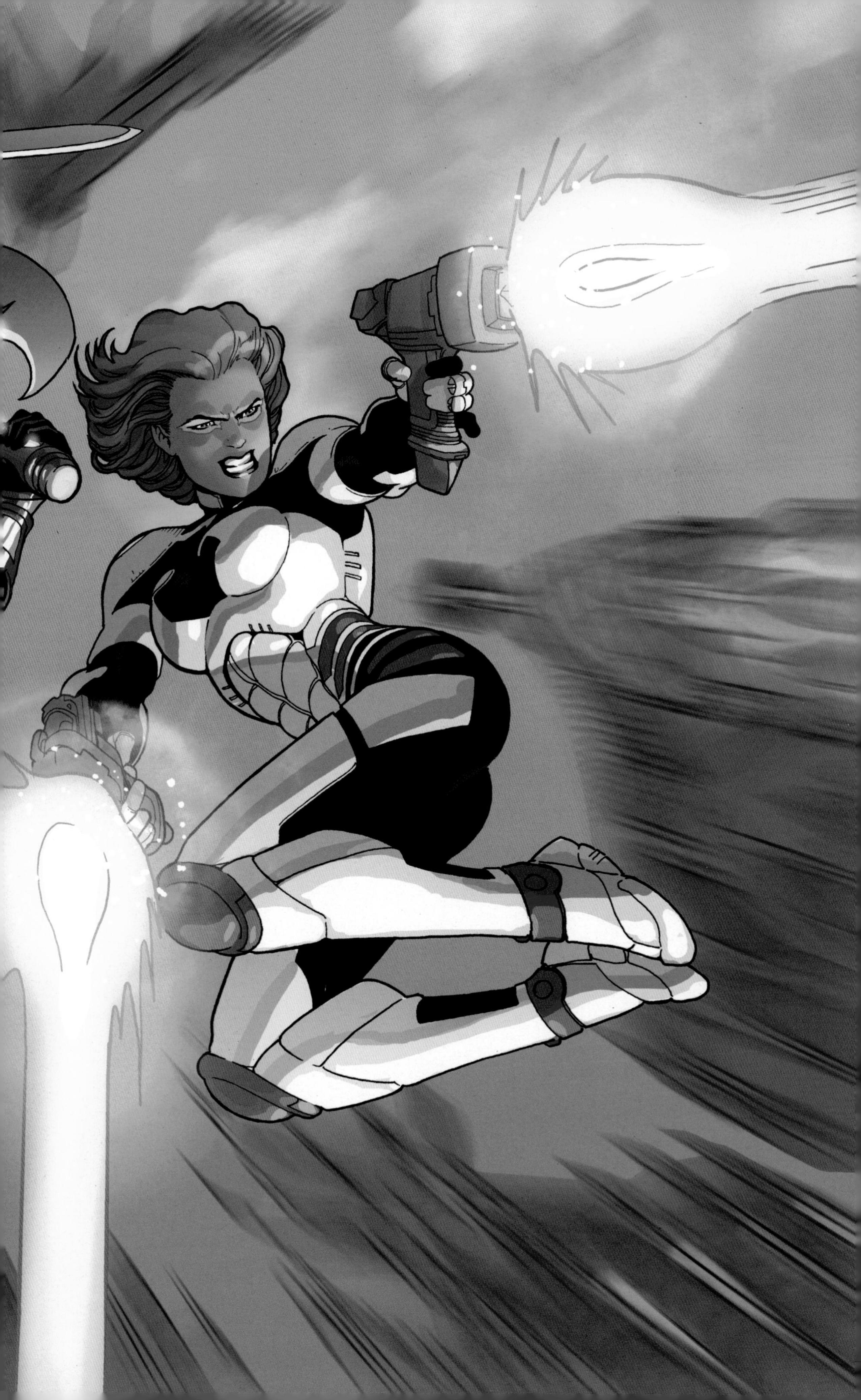

PREVIOUSLY IN *INFINITY:*
Thanos' army came very close to taking the Earth, but the Guardians helped save the planet. The Mad Titan has disappeared.

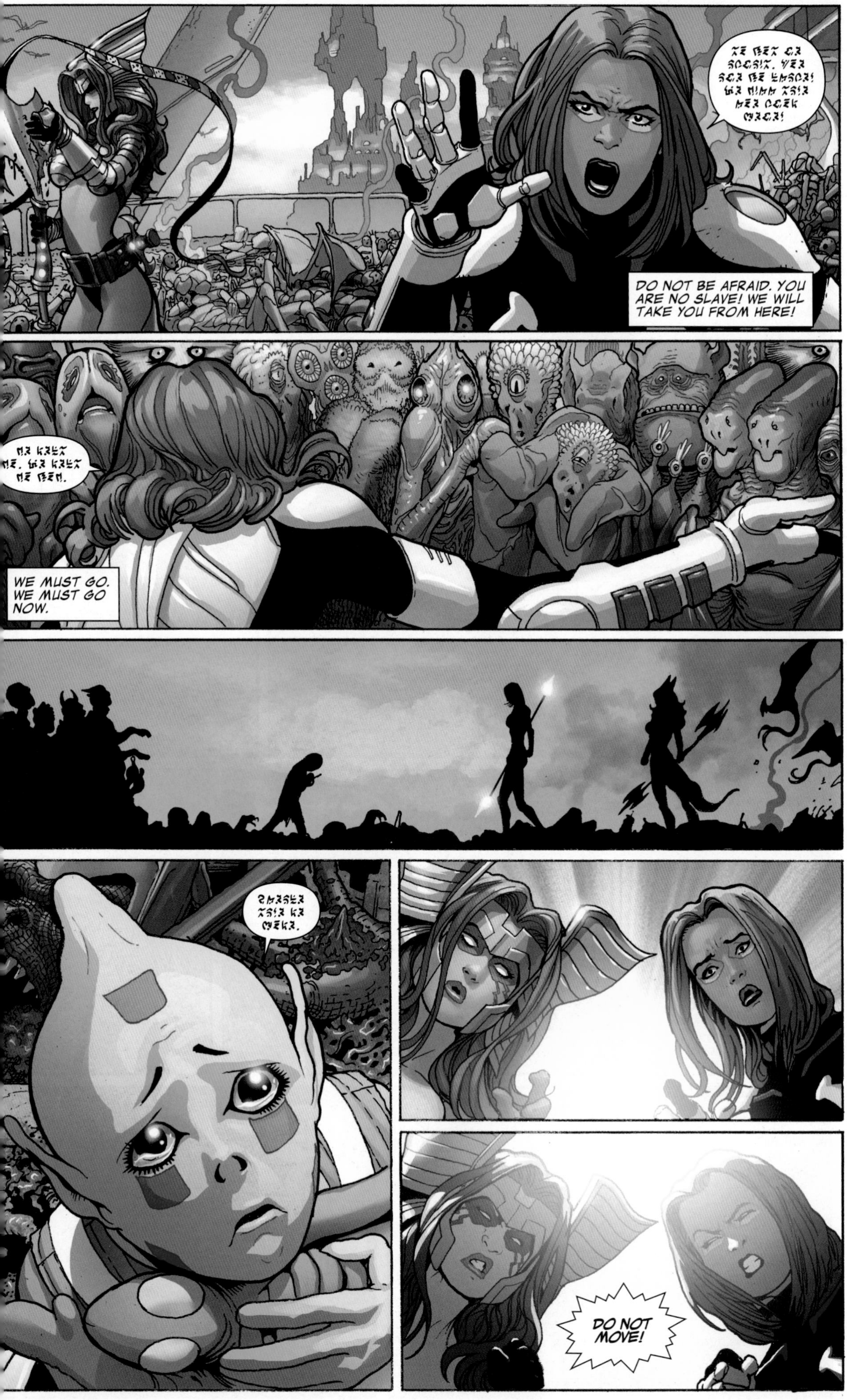
DO NOT BE AFRAID. YOU ARE NO SLAVE! WE WILL TAKE YOU FROM HERE!
WE MUST GO. WE MUST GO NOW.
DO NOT MOVE!

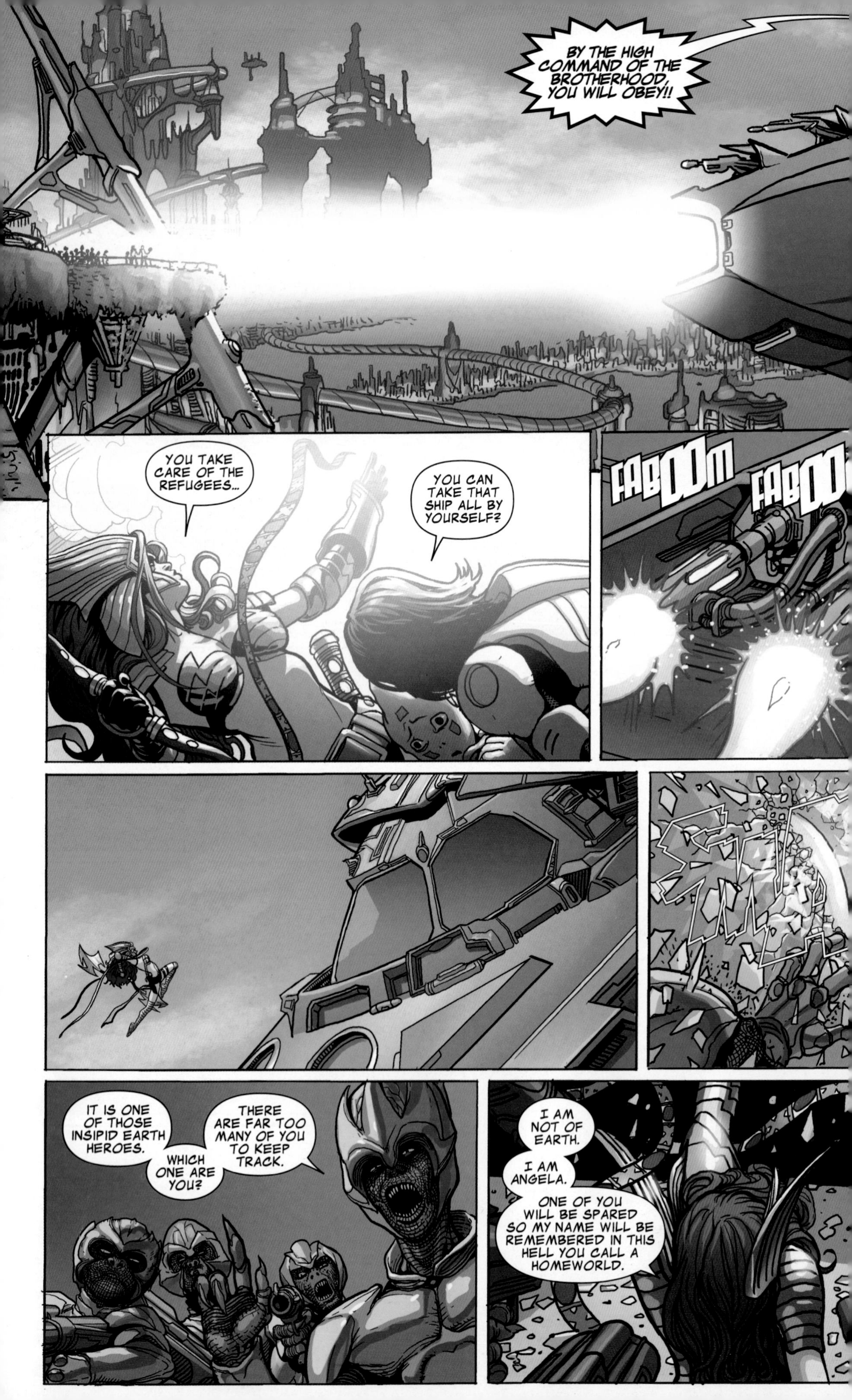
BY THE HIGH COMMAND OF THE BROTHERHOOD, YOU WILL OBEY!!
YOU TAKE CARE OF THE REFUGEES...
YOU CAN TAKE THAT SHIP ALL BY YOURSELF?
FABOOM
FABOO
IT IS ONE OF THOSE INSIPID EARTH HEROES.
WHICH ONE ARE YOU?
THERE ARE FAR TOO MANY OF YOU TO KEEP TRACK.
I AM NOT OF EARTH.
I AM ANGELA.
ONE OF YOU WILL BE SPARED SO MY NAME WILL BE REMEMBERED IN THIS HELL YOU CALL A HOMEWORLD.

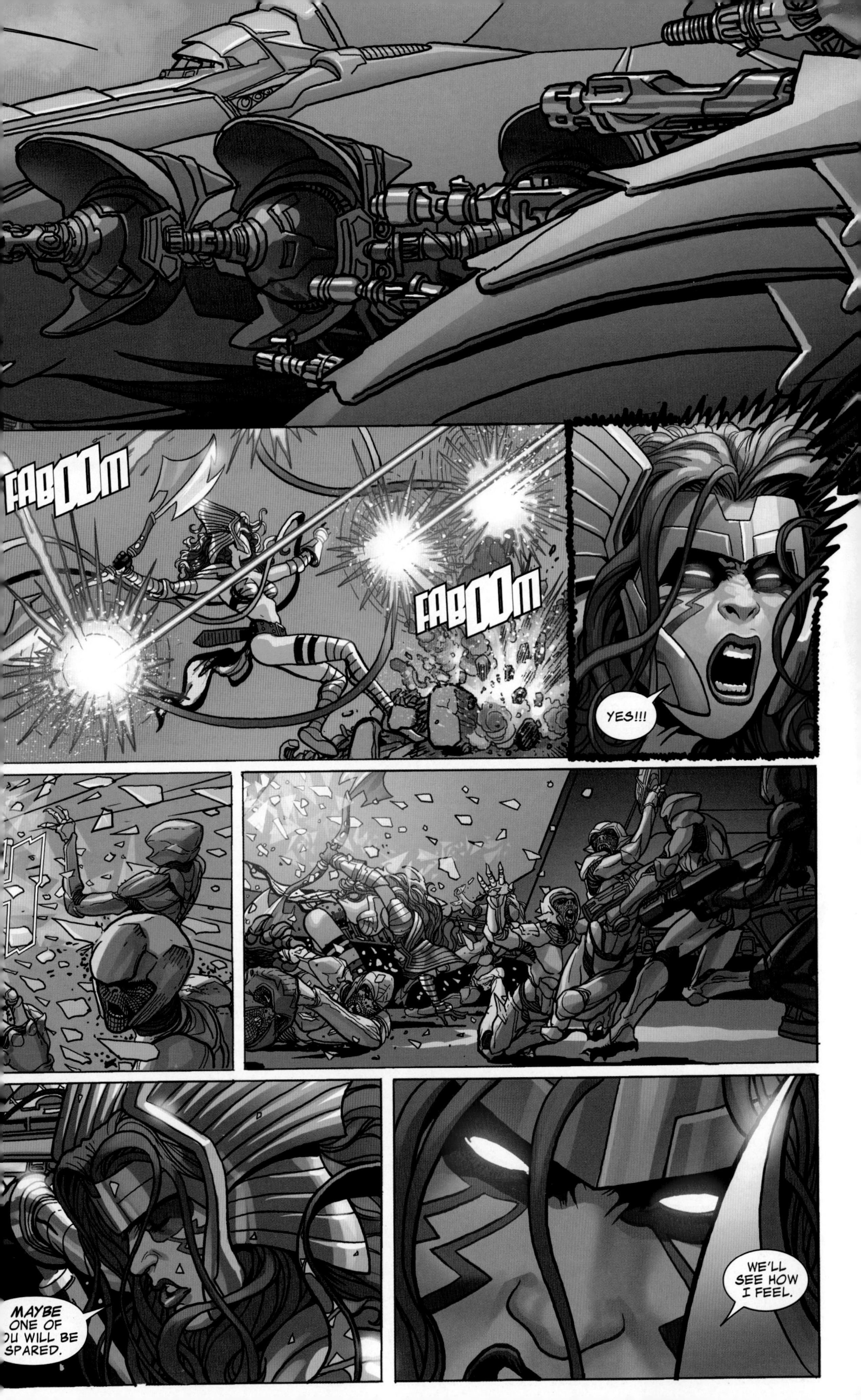
FABOOM
FABOOM
YES!!!
MAYBE ONE OF OU WILL BE SPARED.
WE'LL SEE HOW I FEEL.

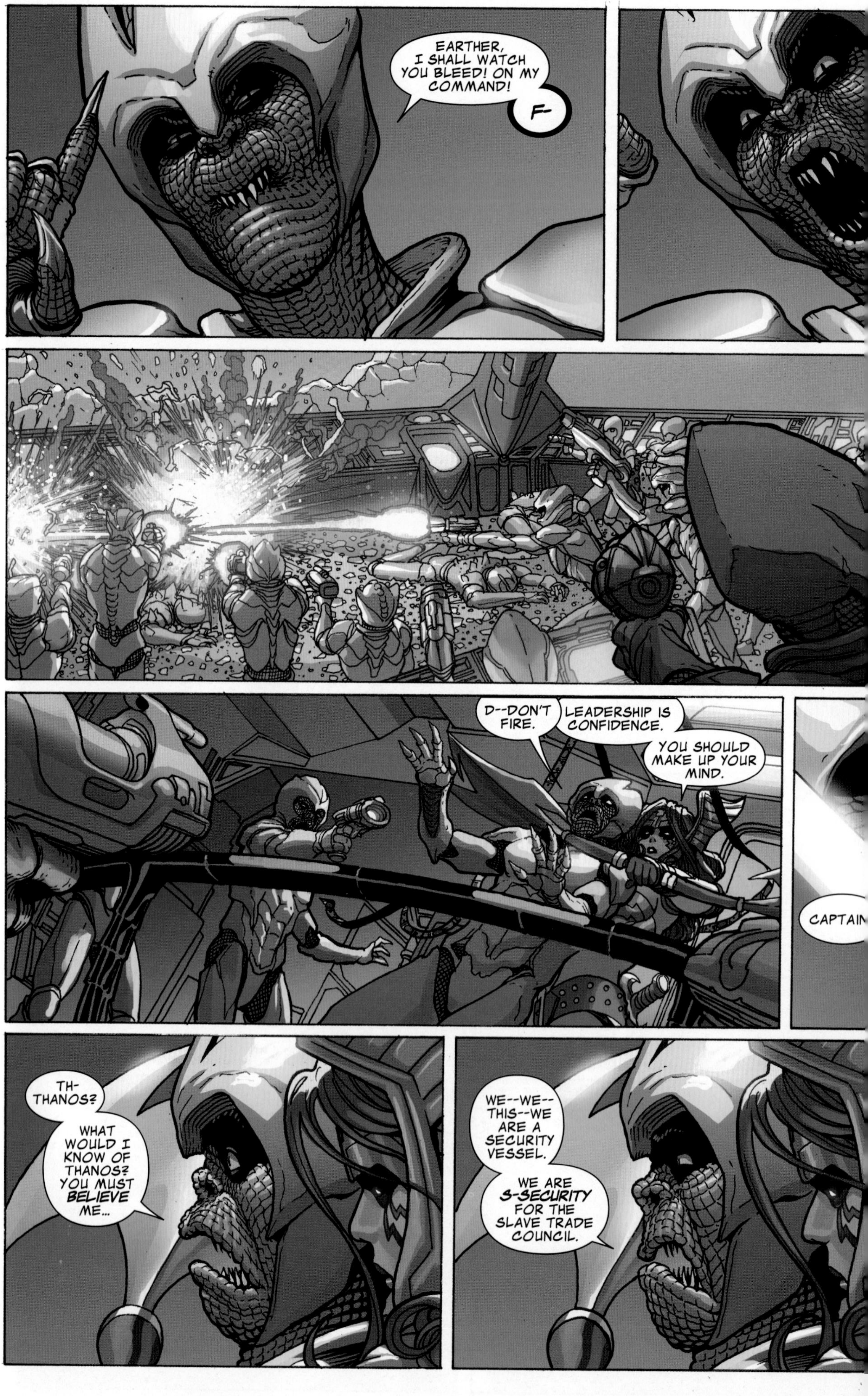
EARTHER, I SHALL WATCH YOU BLEED! ON MY COMMAND!
F-
D--DON'T FIRE.
LEADERSHIP IS CONFIDENCE.
YOU SHOULD MAKE UP YOUR MIND.
CAPTAIN
TH-THANOS?
WHAT WOULD I KNOW OF THANOS? YOU MUST BELIEVE ME...
WE--WE--THIS--WE ARE A SECURITY VESSEL.
WE ARE S-SECURITY FOR THE SLAVE TRADE COUNCIL.

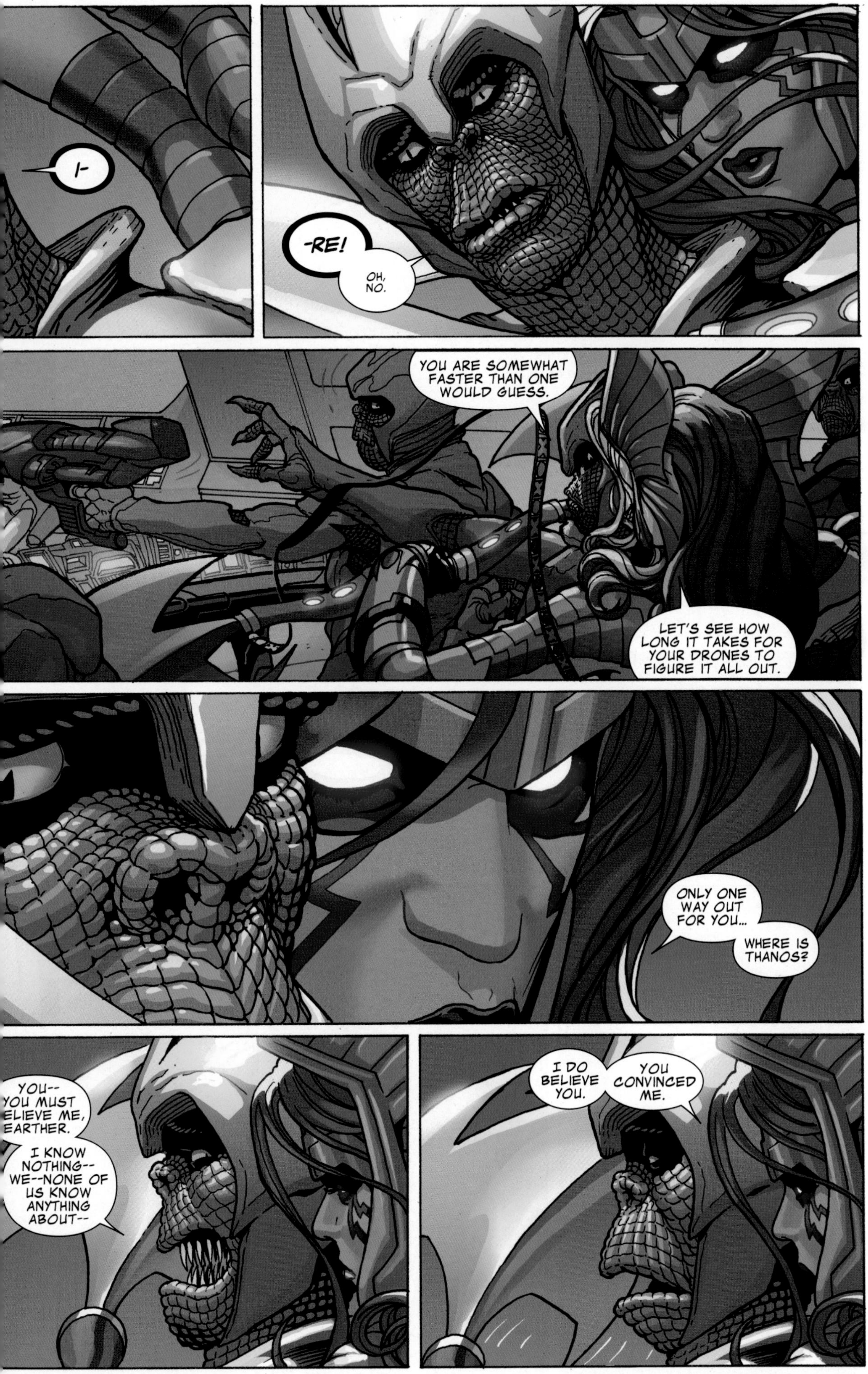
I-
-RE!
OH, NO.
YOU ARE SOMEWHAT FASTER THAN ONE WOULD GUESS.
LET'S SEE HOW LONG IT TAKES FOR YOUR DRONES TO FIGURE IT ALL OUT.
ONLY ONE WAY OUT FOR YOU...
WHERE IS THANOS?
YOU-- YOU MUST BELIEVE ME, EARTHER.
I KNOW NOTHING-- WE--NONE OF US KNOW ANYTHING ABOUT--
I DO BELIEVE YOU.
YOU CONVINCED ME.

SCHIK!

KCBCK

CHBCB

FASSOOMMM

ALL OF YOU!! SEEK SHELTER!! RUN!! GO!!

WHERE? WHERE DO WE GO??

I'M NOT YOUR MOTHER!! YOU NEED TO FIND TRANS--

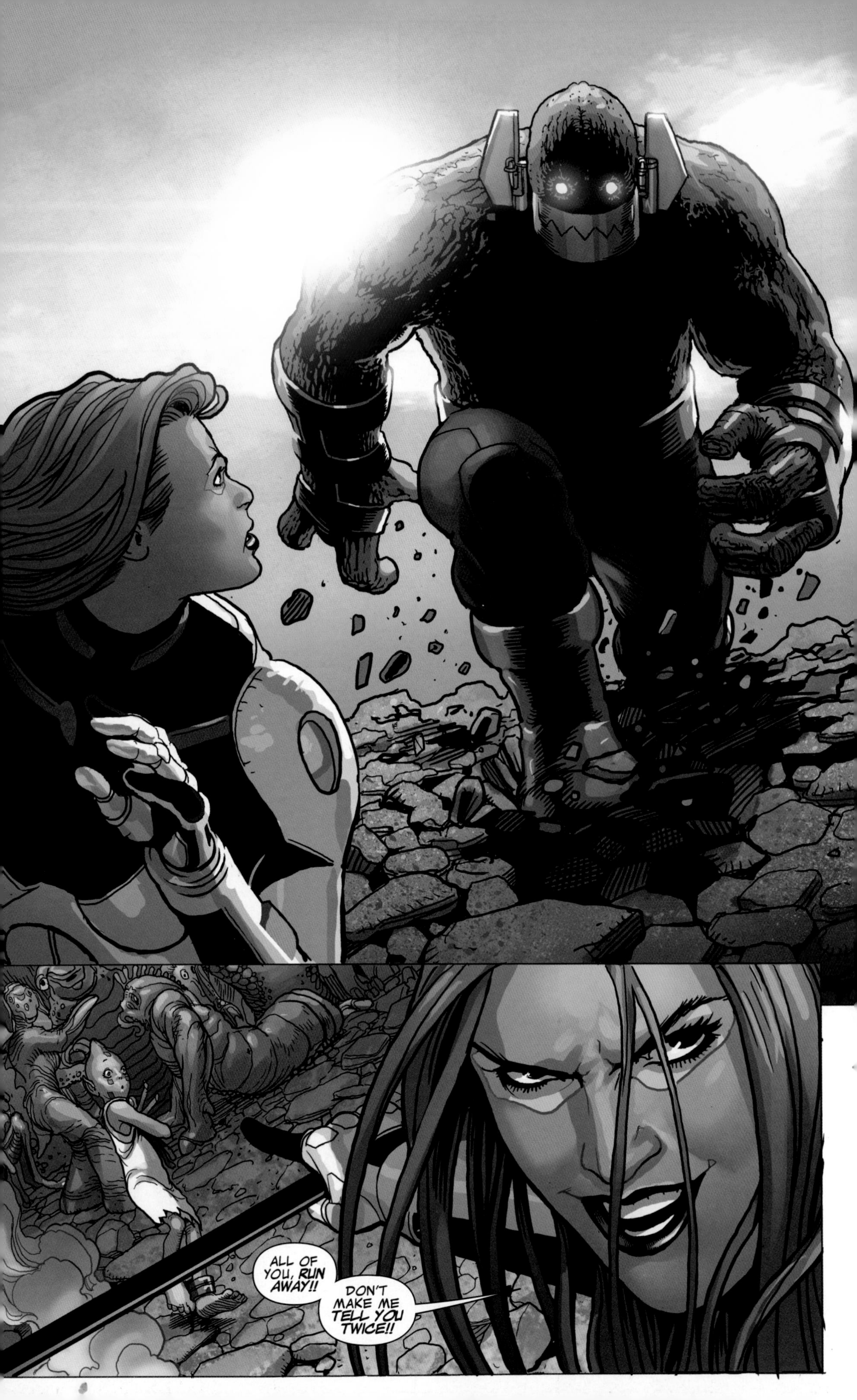
ALL OF YOU, RUN AWAY!!
DON'T MAKE ME TELL YOU TWICE!!

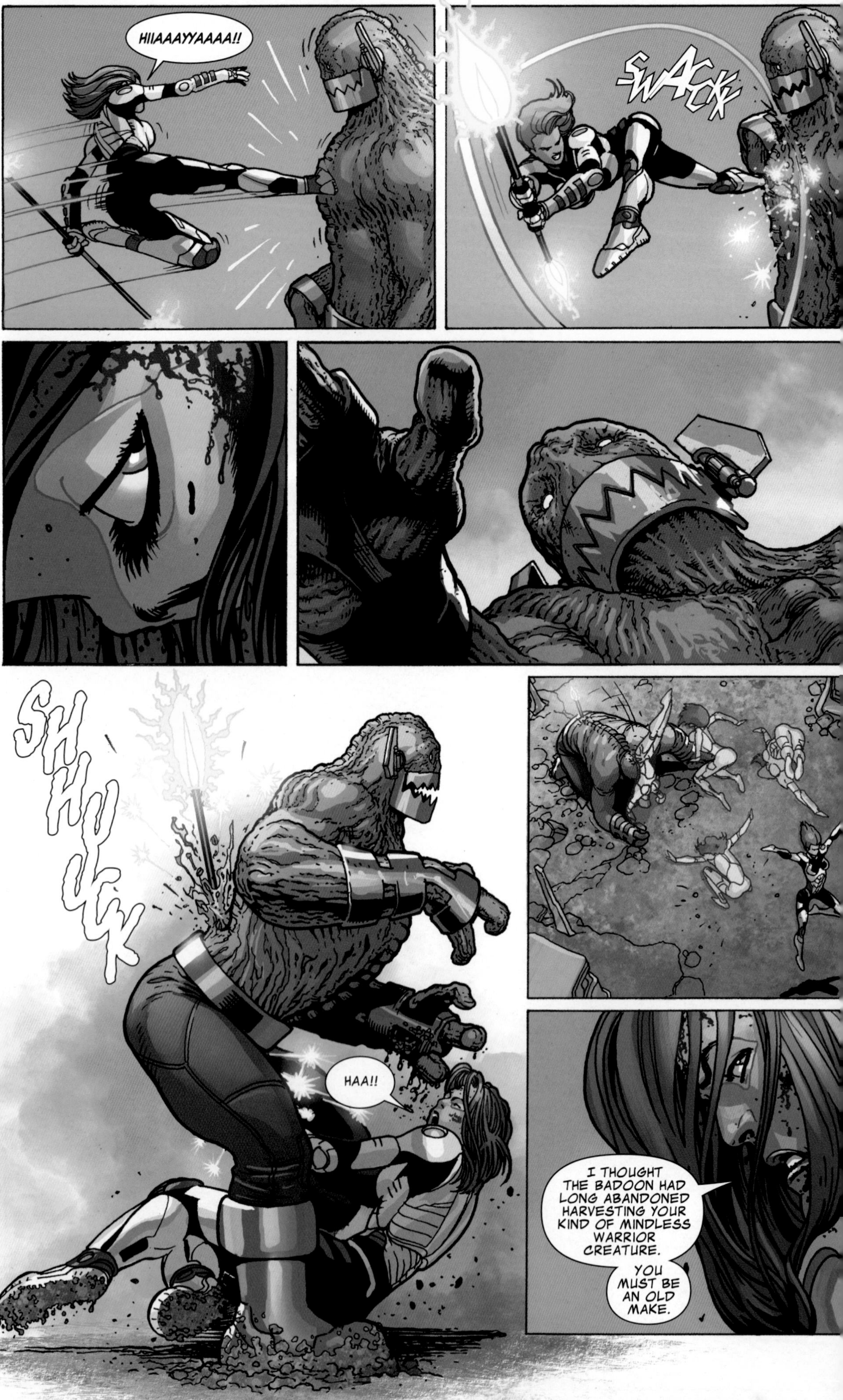
HIIAAAYYAAAA!!
SWACKK
SHHUCK
HAA!!
I THOUGHT THE BADOON HAD LONG ABANDONED HARVESTING YOUR KIND OF MINDLESS WARRIOR CREATURE.
YOU MUST BE AN OLD MAKE.

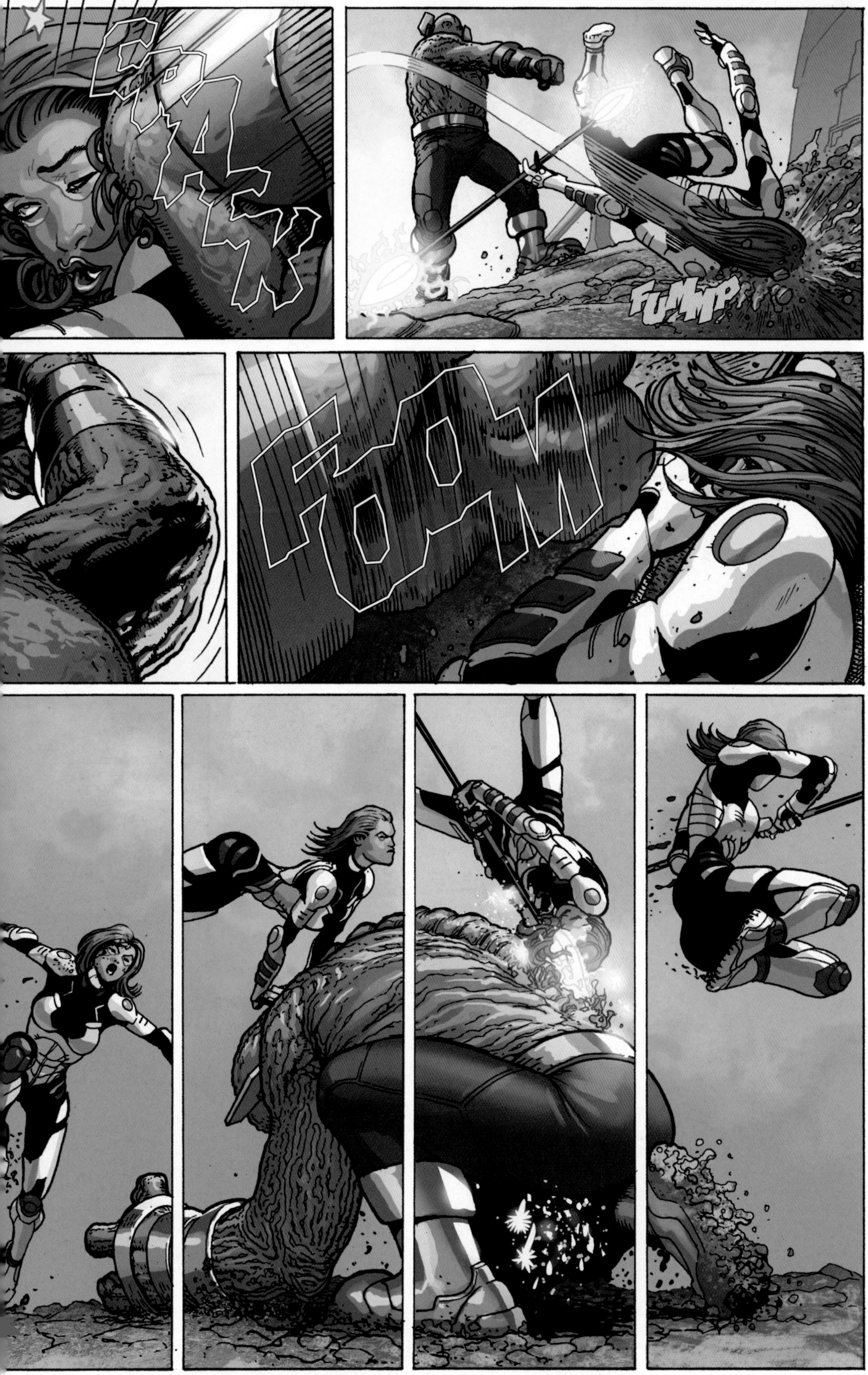
CRACK
FUMMP
FOOM

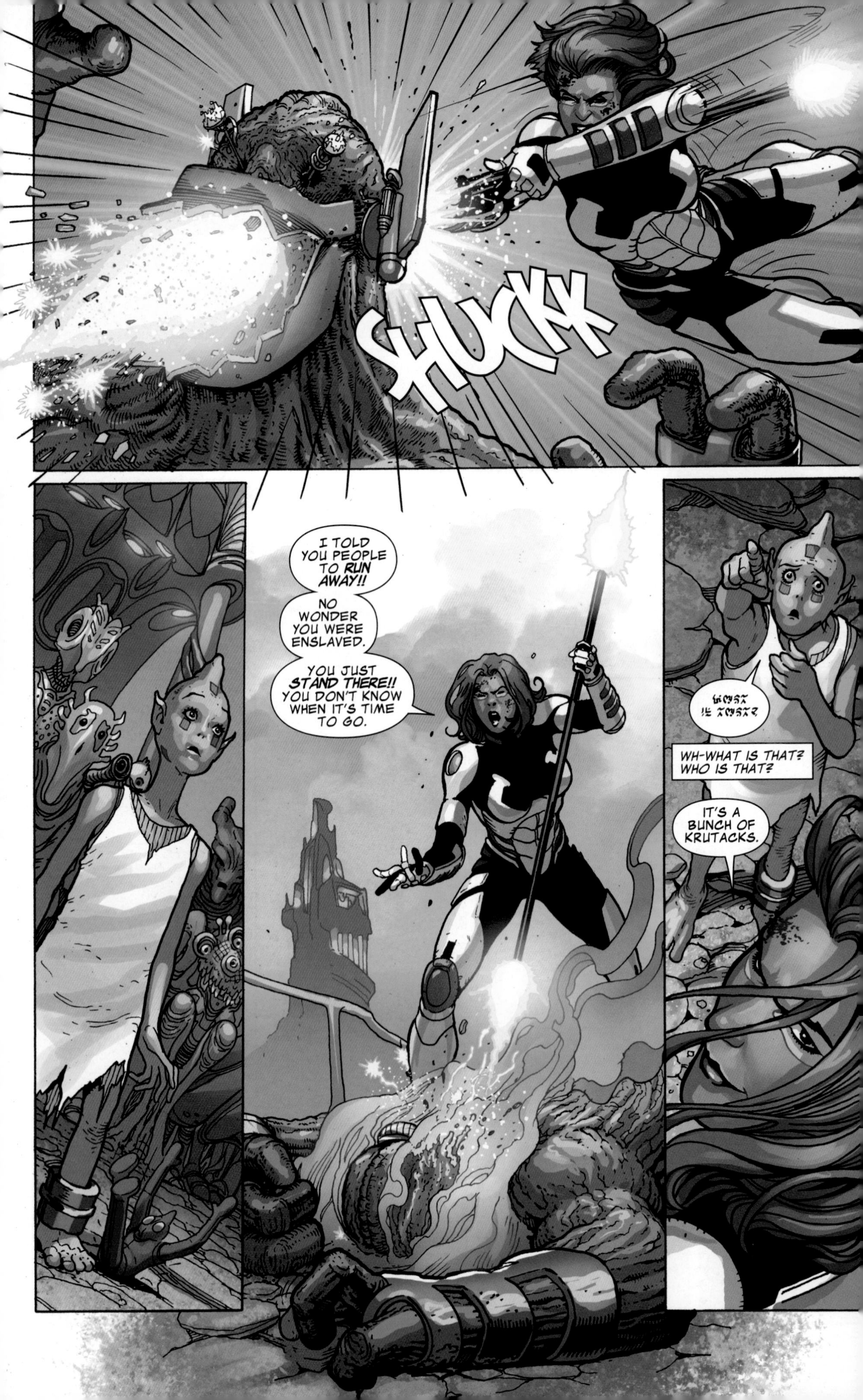
SHUCKK
I TOLD YOU PEOPLE TO **RUN AWAY!!**
NO WONDER YOU WERE ENSLAVED.
YOU JUST **STAND THERE!!** YOU DON'T KNOW WHEN IT'S TIME TO GO.
WH-WHAT IS THAT? WHO IS THAT?
IT'S A BUNCH OF KRUTACKS.

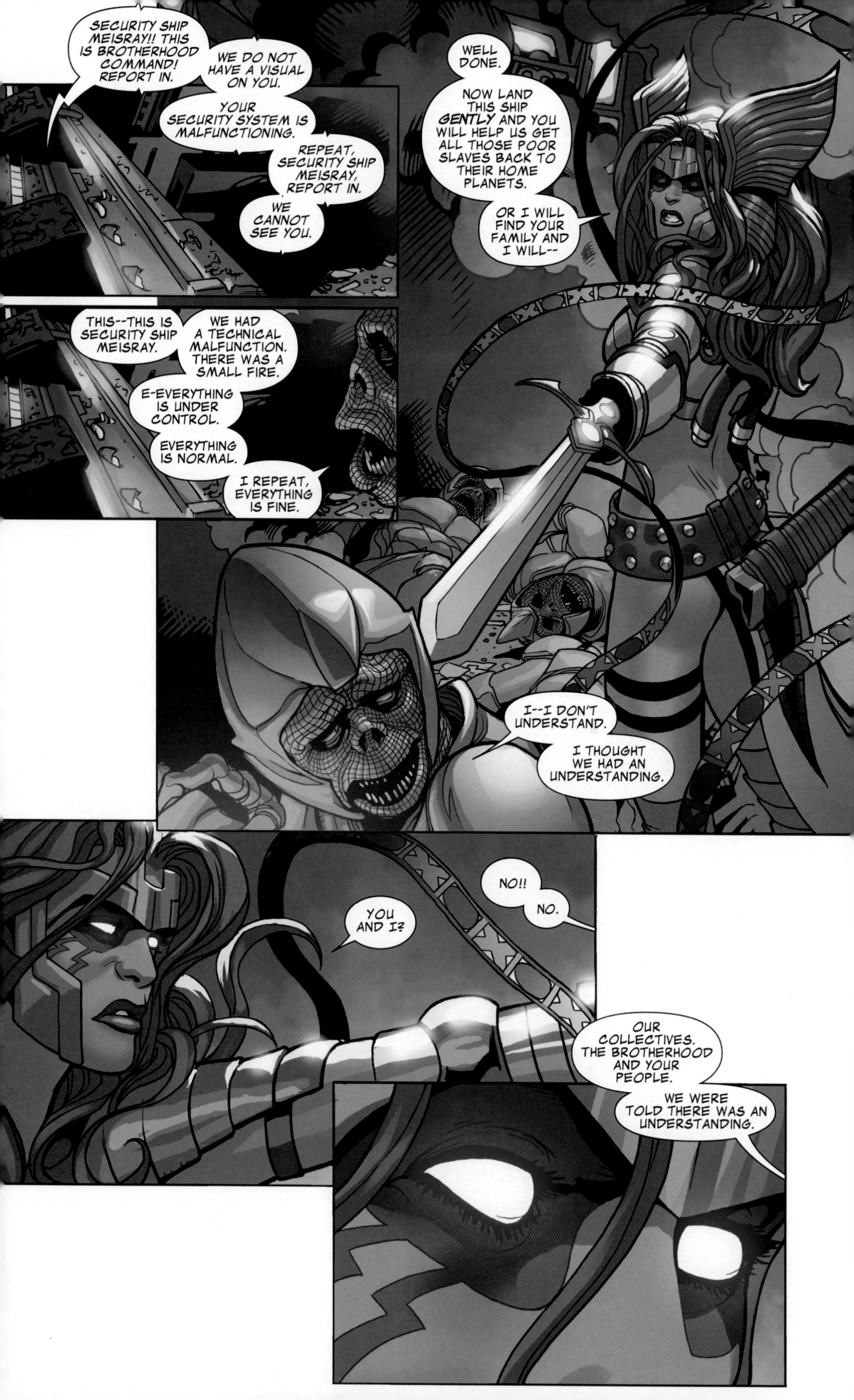

SECURITY SHIP MEISRAY!! THIS IS BROTHERHOOD COMMAND! REPORT IN.
WE DO NOT HAVE A VISUAL ON YOU.
YOUR SECURITY SYSTEM IS MALFUNCTIONING.
REPEAT, SECURITY SHIP MEISRAY, REPORT IN.
WE CANNOT SEE YOU.
WELL DONE.
NOW LAND THIS SHIP GENTLY AND YOU WILL HELP US GET ALL THOSE POOR SLAVES BACK TO THEIR HOME PLANETS.
OR I WILL FIND YOUR FAMILY AND I WILL--
THIS--THIS IS SECURITY SHIP MEISRAY.
WE HAD A TECHNICAL MALFUNCTION. THERE WAS A SMALL FIRE.
E-EVERYTHING IS UNDER CONTROL.
EVERYTHING IS NORMAL.
I REPEAT, EVERYTHING IS FINE.
I--I DON'T UNDERSTAND.
I THOUGHT WE HAD AN UNDERSTANDING.
YOU AND I?
NO!!
NO.
OUR COLLECTIVES. THE BROTHERHOOD AND YOUR PEOPLE.
WE WERE TOLD THERE WAS AN UNDERSTANDING.

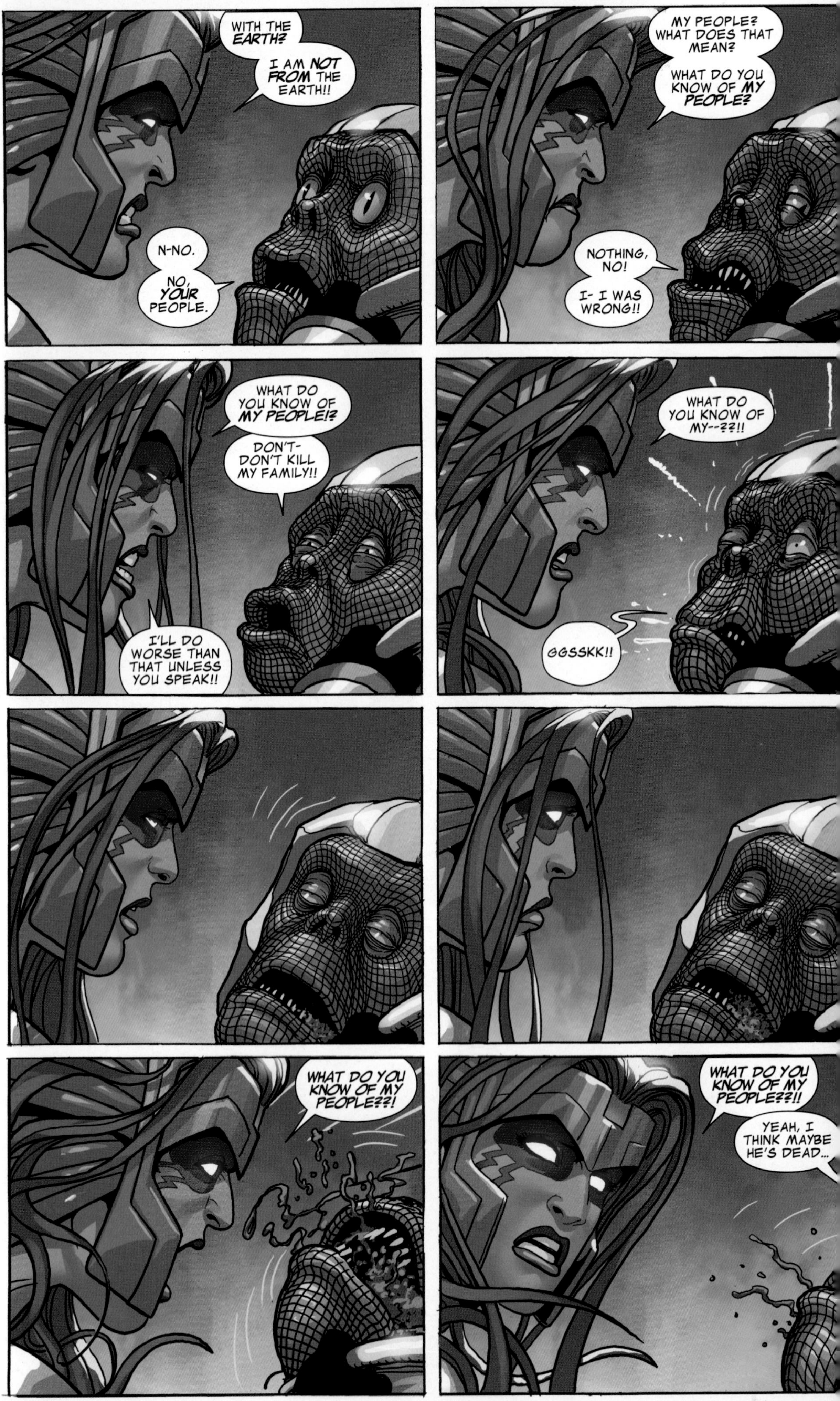
WITH THE EARTH?
I AM NOT FROM THE EARTH!!
N-NO.
NO, YOUR PEOPLE.
MY PEOPLE? WHAT DOES THAT MEAN?
WHAT DO YOU KNOW OF MY PEOPLE?
NOTHING, NO!
I- I WAS WRONG!!
WHAT DO YOU KNOW OF MY PEOPLE!?
DON'T- DON'T KILL MY FAMILY!!
I'LL DO WORSE THAN THAT UNLESS YOU SPEAK!!
WHAT DO YOU KNOW OF MY--??!!
GGSSKK!!
WHAT DO YOU KNOW OF MY PEOPLE??!
WHAT DO YOU KNOW OF MY PEOPLE??!!
YEAH, I THINK MAYBE HE'S DEAD...

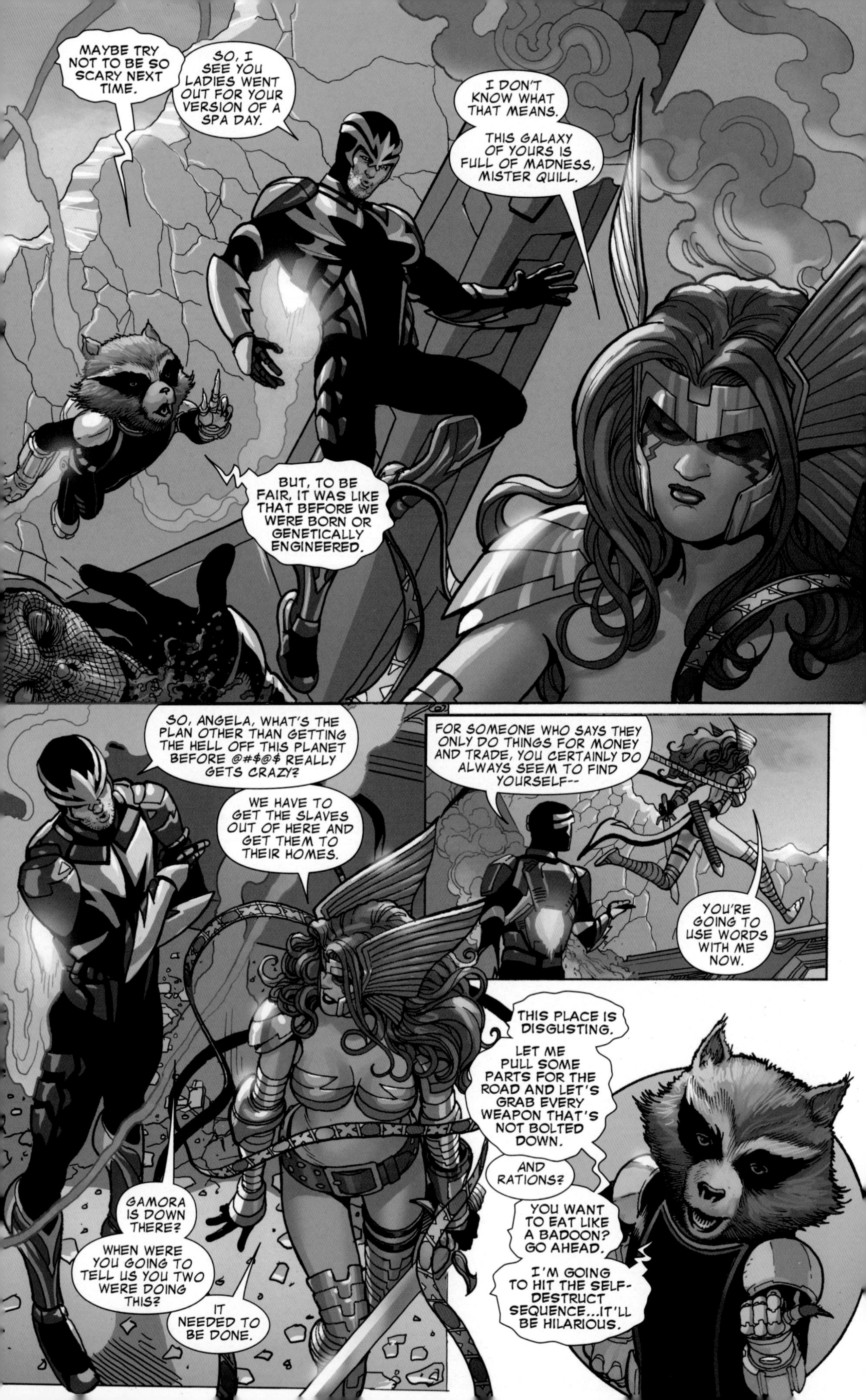
MAYBE TRY NOT TO BE SO SCARY NEXT TIME.
SO, I SEE YOU LADIES WENT OUT FOR YOUR VERSION OF A SPA DAY.
I DON'T KNOW WHAT THAT MEANS.
THIS GALAXY OF YOURS IS FULL OF MADNESS, MISTER QUILL.
BUT, TO BE FAIR, IT WAS LIKE THAT BEFORE WE WERE BORN OR GENETICALLY ENGINEERED.
SO, ANGELA, WHAT'S THE PLAN OTHER THAN GETTING THE HELL OFF THIS PLANET BEFORE @#$@$ REALLY GETS CRAZY?
WE HAVE TO GET THE SLAVES OUT OF HERE AND GET THEM TO THEIR HOMES.
FOR SOMEONE WHO SAYS THEY ONLY DO THINGS FOR MONEY AND TRADE, YOU CERTAINLY DO ALWAYS SEEM TO FIND YOURSELF--
YOU'RE GOING TO USE WORDS WITH ME NOW.
GAMORA IS DOWN THERE?
WHEN WERE YOU GOING TO TELL US YOU TWO WERE DOING THIS?
IT NEEDED TO BE DONE.
THIS PLACE IS DISGUSTING.
LET ME PULL SOME PARTS FOR THE ROAD AND LET'S GRAB EVERY WEAPON THAT'S NOT BOLTED DOWN.
AND RATIONS?
YOU WANT TO EAT LIKE A BADOON? GO AHEAD.
I'M GOING TO HIT THE SELF-DESTRUCT SEQUENCE...IT'LL BE HILARIOUS.

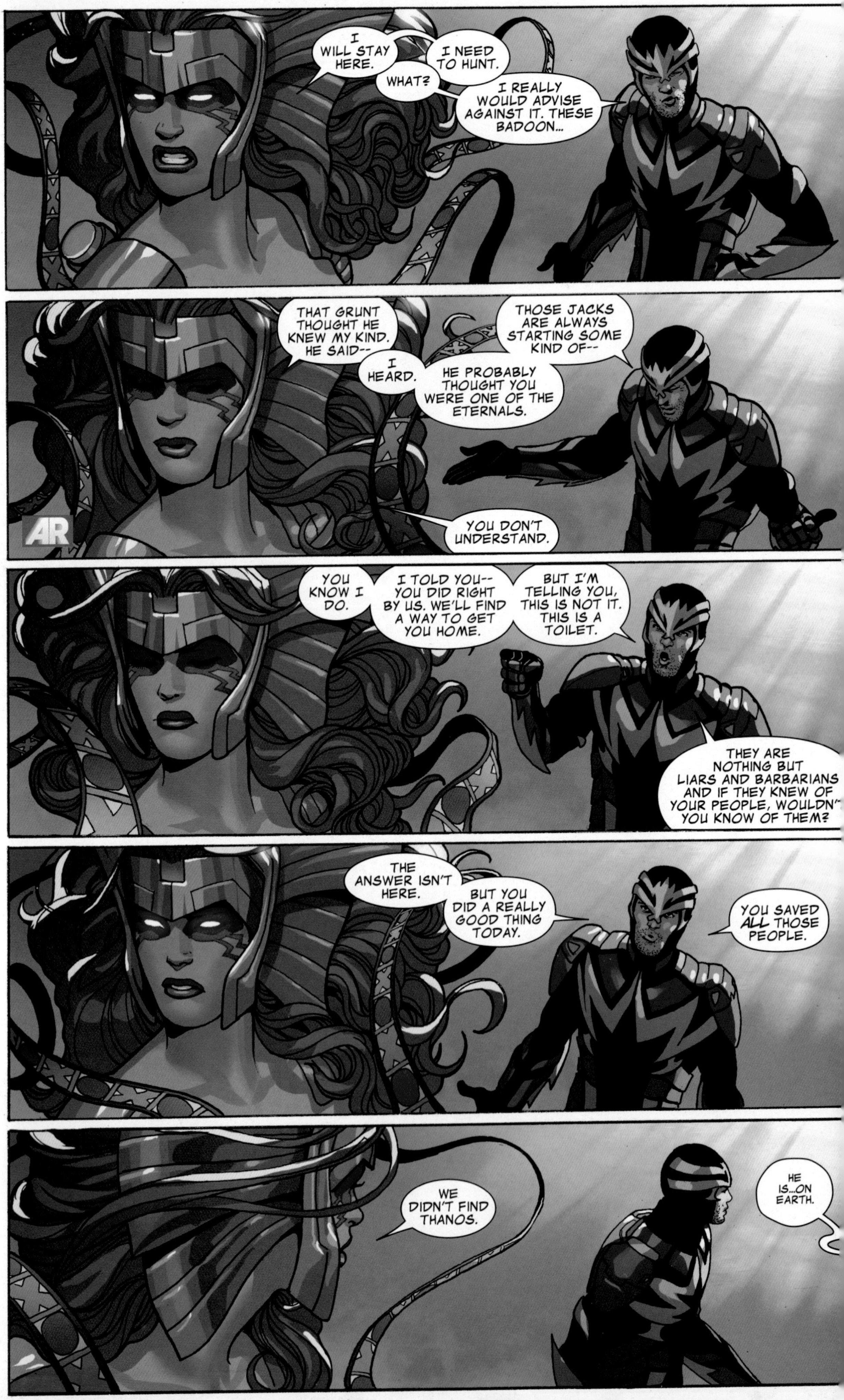
I WILL STAY HERE.
I NEED TO HUNT.
WHAT?
I REALLY WOULD ADVISE AGAINST IT. THESE BADOON...
THAT GRUNT THOUGHT HE KNEW MY KIND. HE SAID--
THOSE JACKS ARE ALWAYS STARTING SOME KIND OF--
I HEARD.
HE PROBABLY THOUGHT YOU WERE ONE OF THE ETERNALS.
YOU DON'T UNDERSTAND.
YOU KNOW I DO.
I TOLD YOU-- YOU DID RIGHT BY US. WE'LL FIND A WAY TO GET YOU HOME.
BUT I'M TELLING YOU, THIS IS NOT IT. THIS IS A TOILET.
THEY ARE NOTHING BUT LIARS AND BARBARIANS AND IF THEY KNEW OF YOUR PEOPLE, WOULDN'T YOU KNOW OF THEM?
THE ANSWER ISN'T HERE.
BUT YOU DID A REALLY GOOD THING TODAY.
YOU SAVED ALL THOSE PEOPLE.
WE DIDN'T FIND THANOS.
HE IS...ON EARTH.

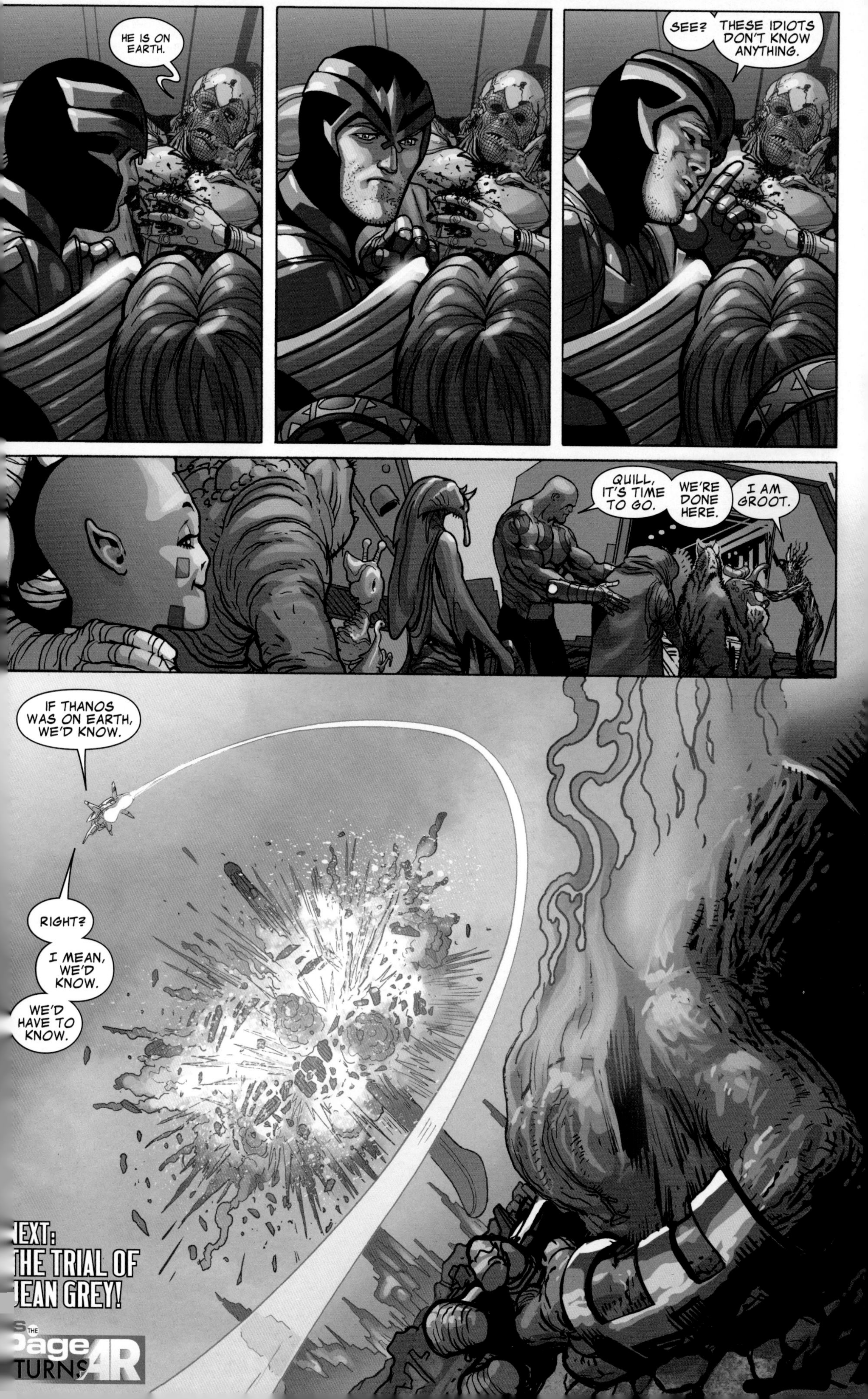
HE IS ON EARTH.
SEE?
THESE IDIOTS DON'T KNOW ANYTHING.
QUILL, IT'S TIME TO GO.
WE'RE DONE HERE.
I AM GROOT.
IF THANOS WAS ON EARTH, WE'D KNOW.
RIGHT?
I MEAN, WE'D KNOW.
WE'D HAVE TO KNOW.
NEXT: THE TRIAL OF JEAN GREY!

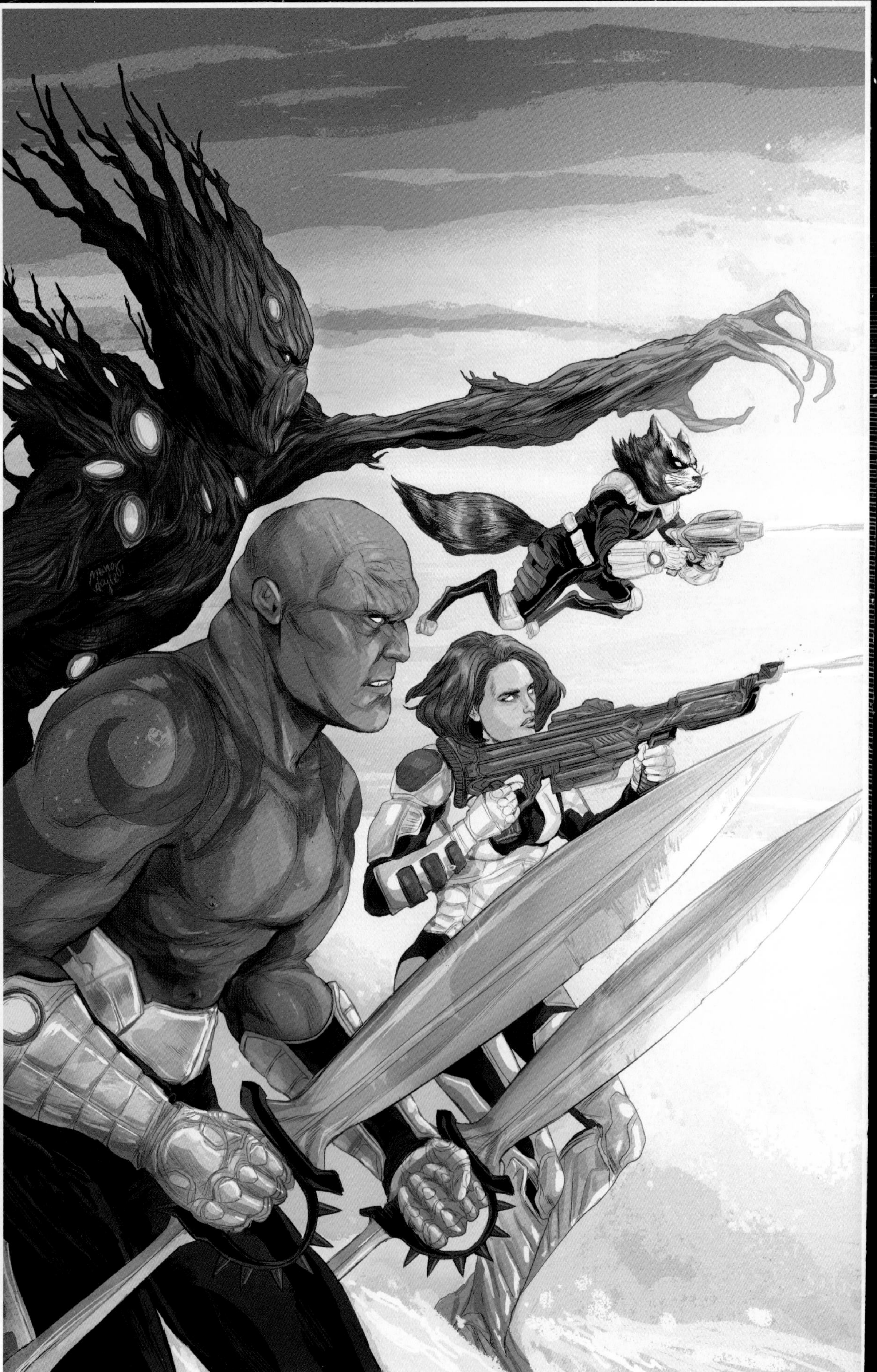

GUARDIANS OF THE GALAXY: TOMORROW'S AVENGERS #1

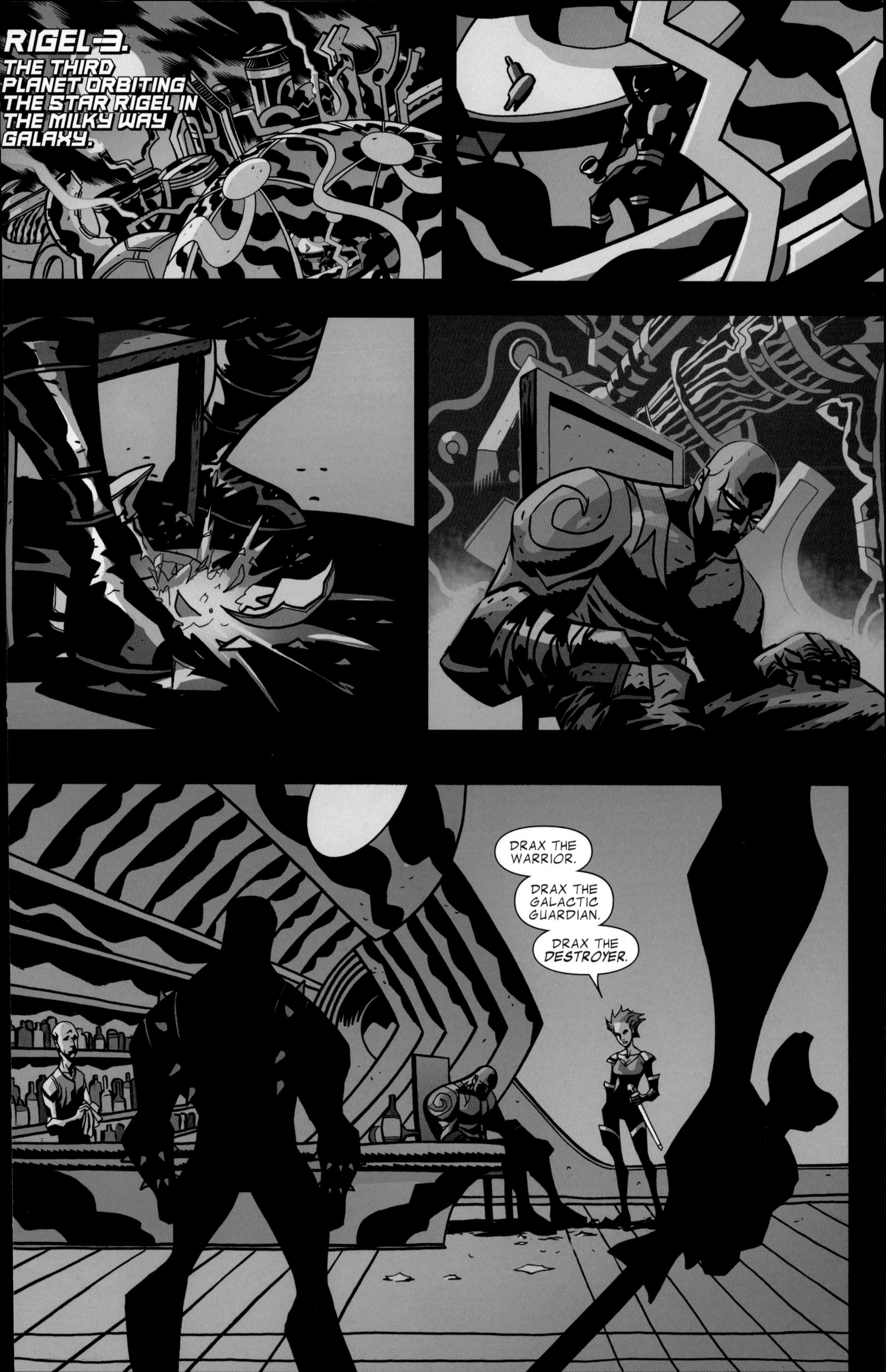
RIGEL-3.
THE THIRD PLANET ORBITING THE STAR RIGEL IN THE MILKY WAY GALAXY.
DRAX THE WARRIOR.
DRAX THE GALACTIC GUARDIAN.
DRAX THE DESTROYER.

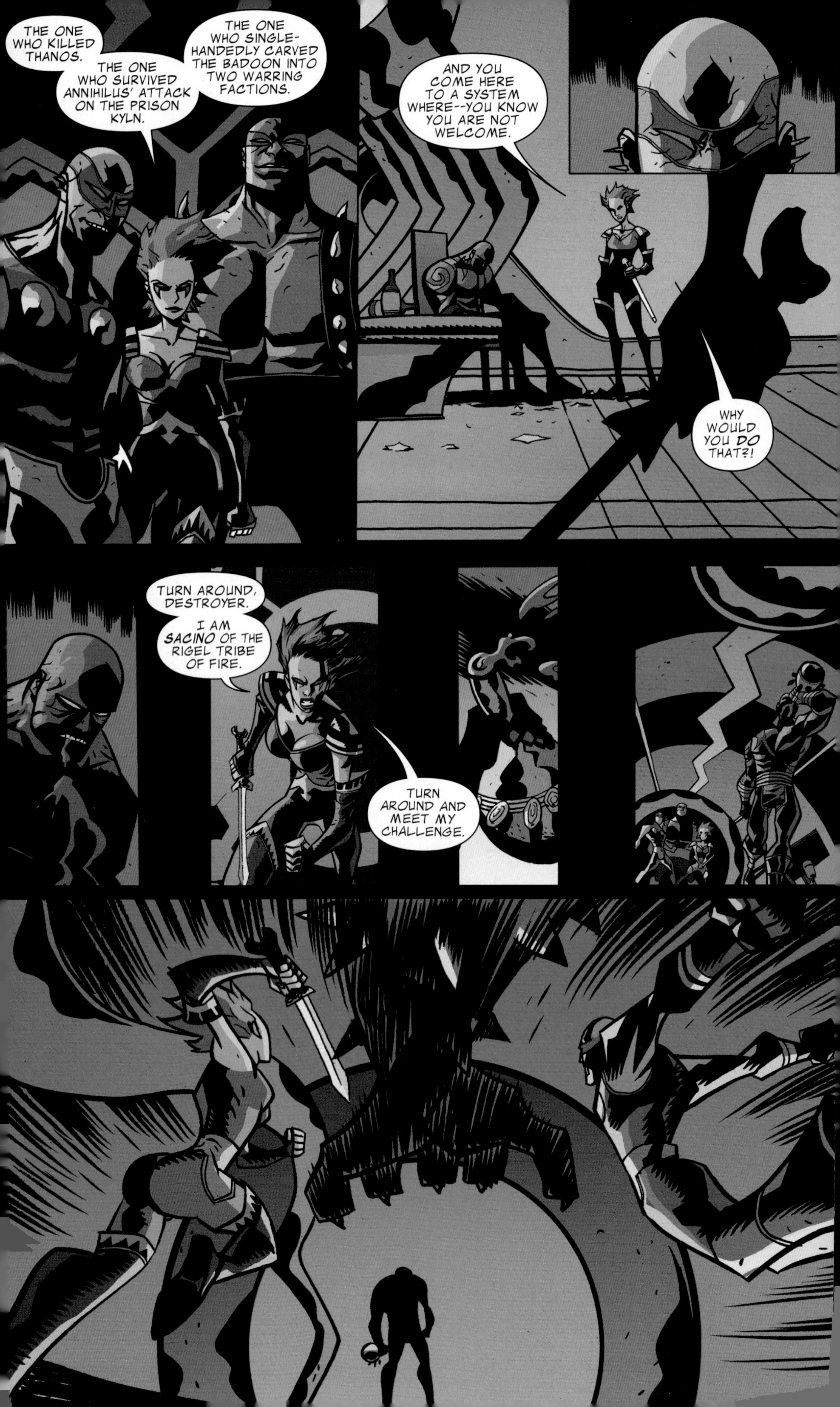
THE ONE WHO KILLED THANOS.
THE ONE WHO SURVIVED ANNIHILUS' ATTACK ON THE PRISON KYLN.
THE ONE WHO SINGLE-HANDEDLY CARVED THE BADOON INTO TWO WARRING FACTIONS.
AND YOU COME HERE TO A SYSTEM WHERE--YOU KNOW YOU ARE NOT WELCOME.
WHY WOULD YOU DO THAT?!
TURN AROUND, DESTROYER.
I AM SACINO OF THE RIGEL TRIBE OF FIRE.
TURN AROUND AND MEET MY CHALLENGE.

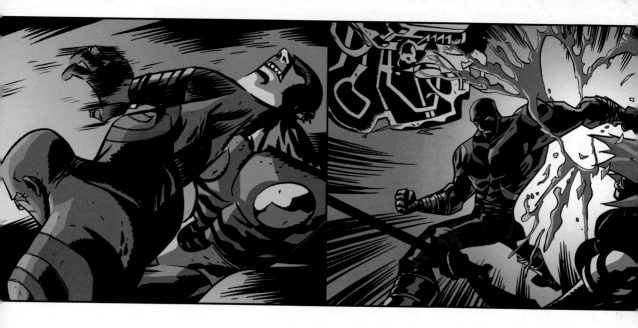

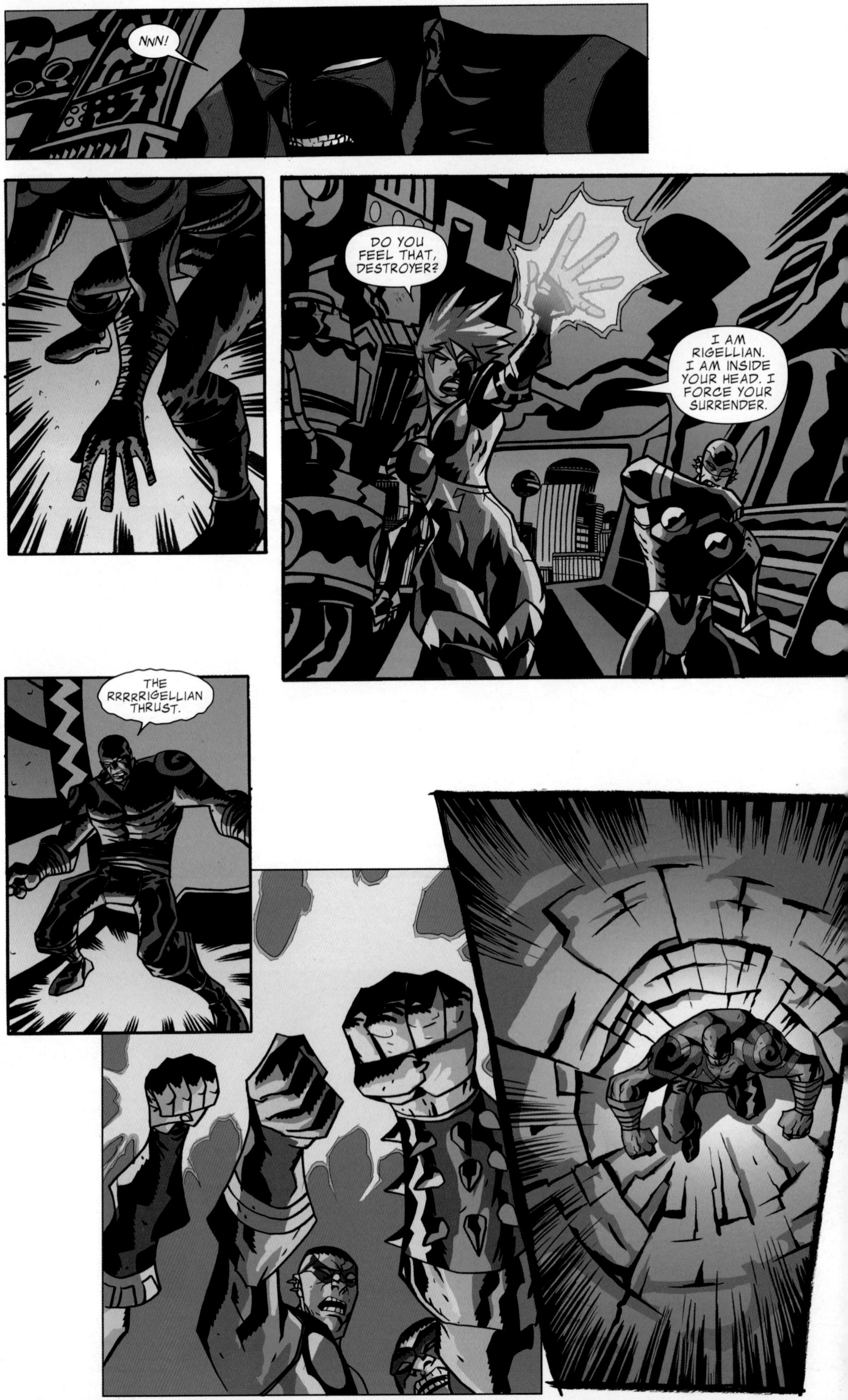
NNN!
DO YOU FEEL THAT, DESTROYER?
I AM RIGELLIAN. I AM INSIDE YOUR HEAD. I FORCE YOUR SURRENDER.
THE RRRRRIGELLIAN THRUST.

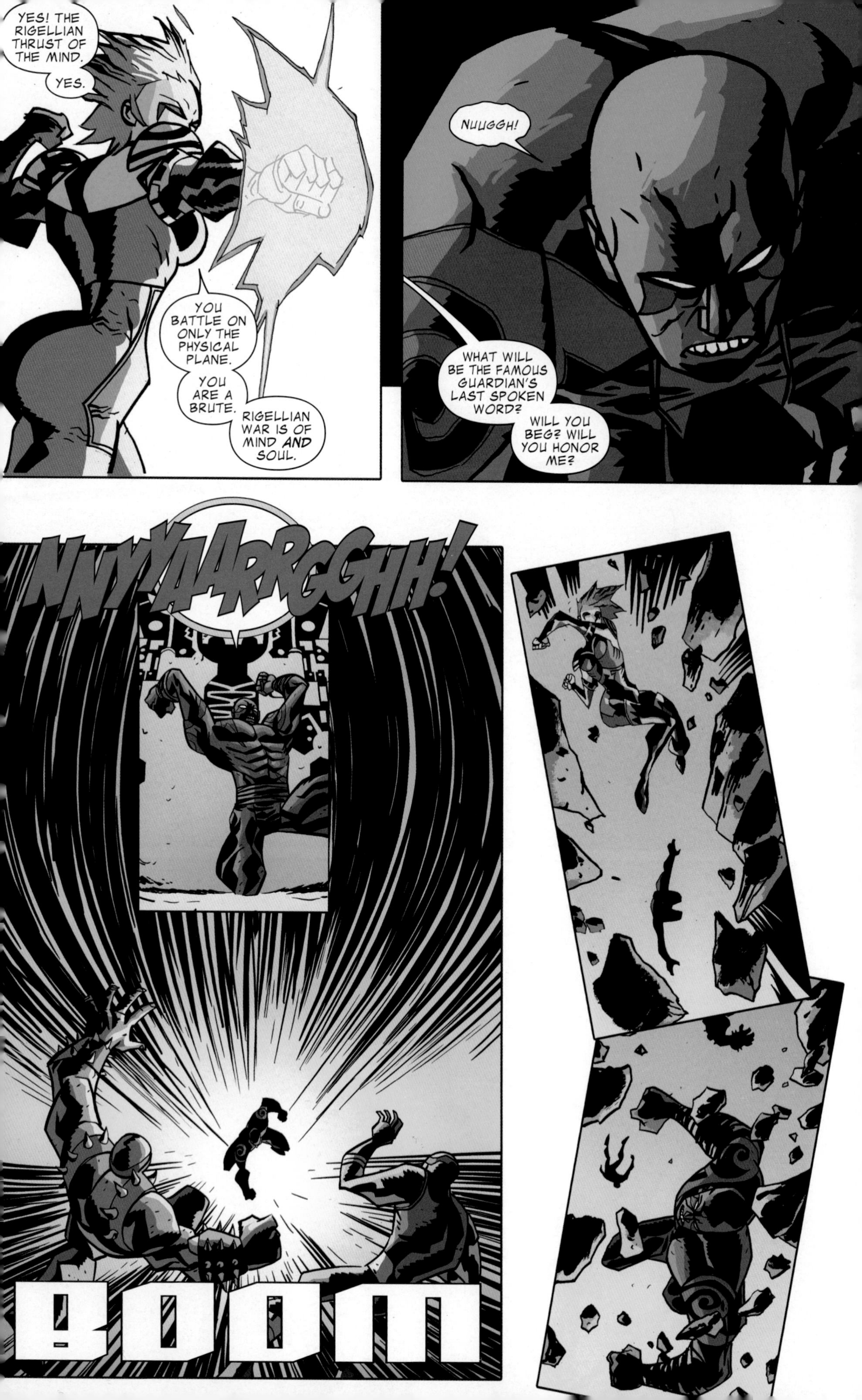
YES! THE RIGELLIAN THRUST OF THE MIND.
YES.
YOU BATTLE ON ONLY THE PHYSICAL PLANE.
YOU ARE A BRUTE.
RIGELLIAN WAR IS OF MIND AND SOUL.
NUUGGH!
WHAT WILL BE THE FAMOUS GUARDIAN'S LAST SPOKEN WORD?
WILL YOU BEG? WILL YOU HONOR ME?
NNYYAARRGGHH!
BOOM

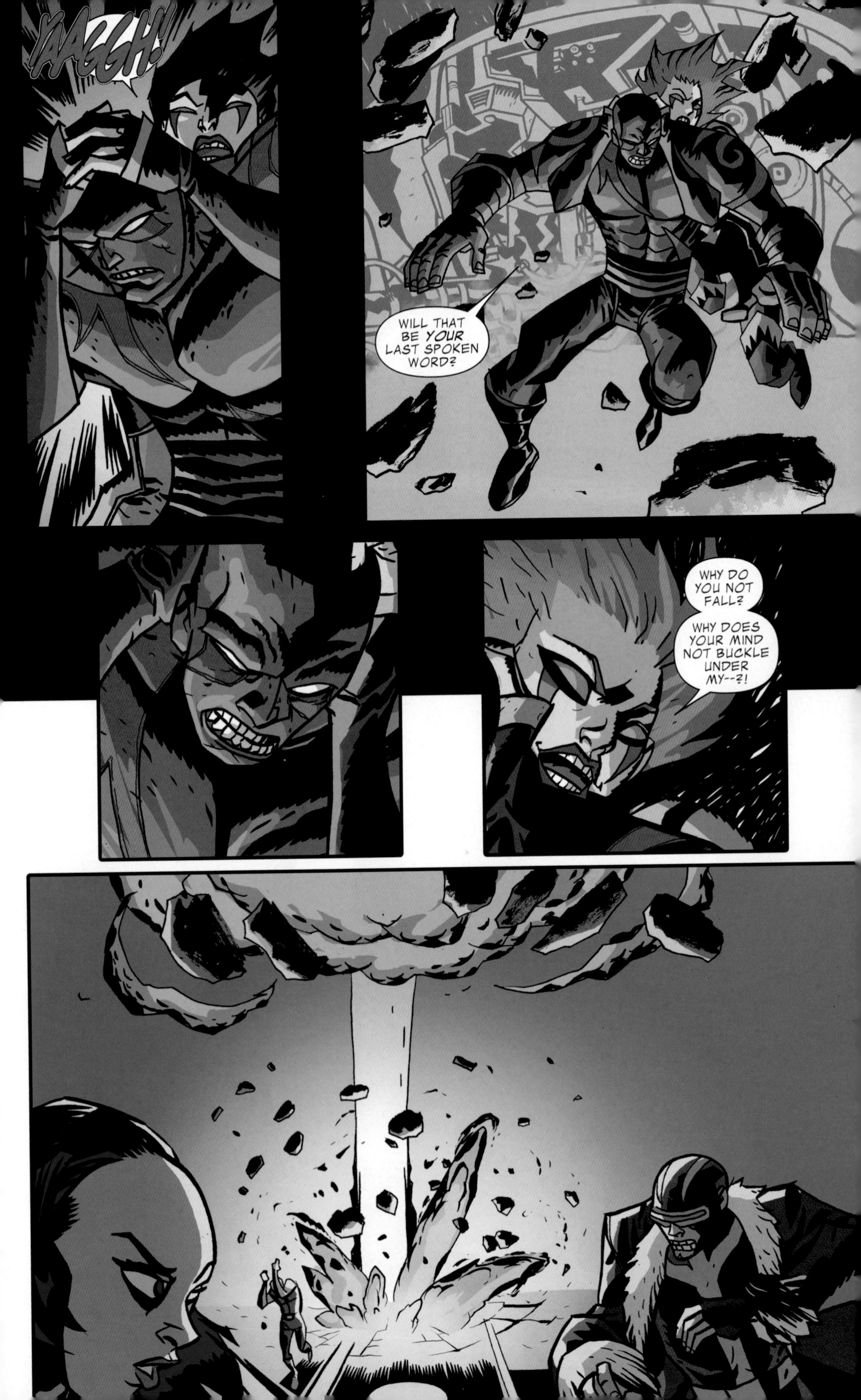
YAAGGH!
WILL THAT BE YOUR LAST SPOKEN WORD?
WHY DO YOU NOT FALL?
WHY DOES YOUR MIND NOT BUCKLE UNDER MY--?!

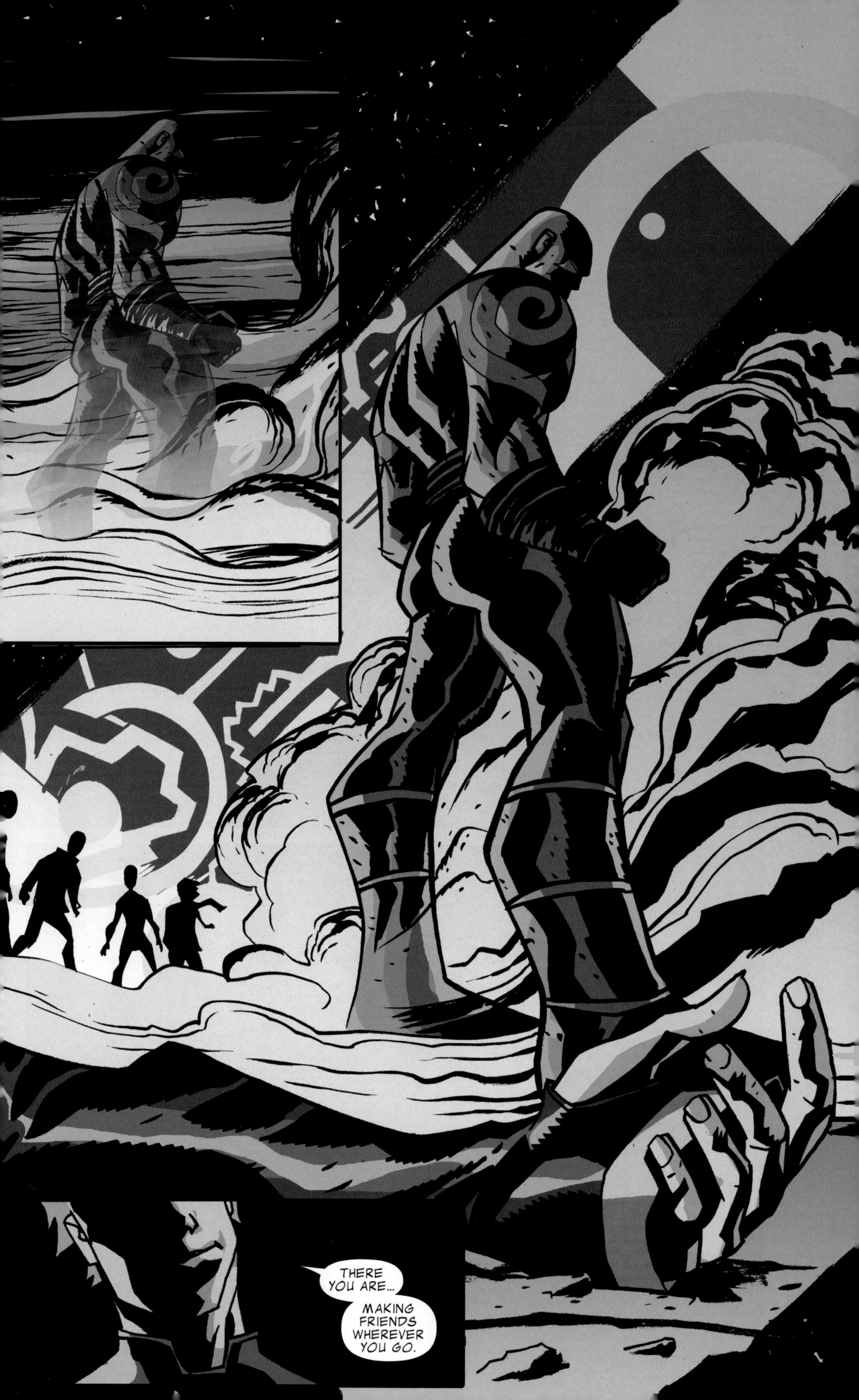
THERE YOU ARE...
MAKING FRIENDS WHEREVER YOU GO.

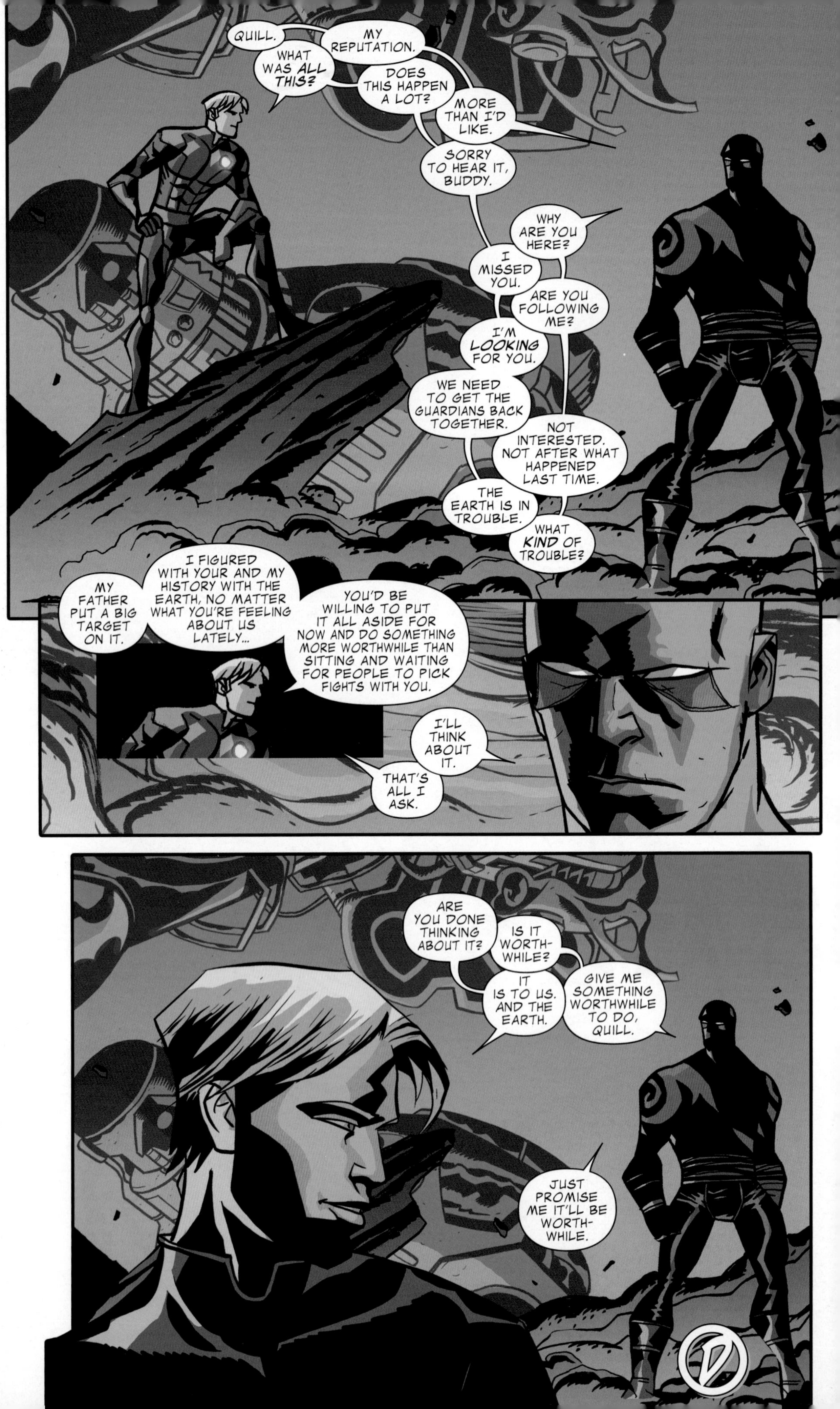
QUILL.
MY REPUTATION.
WHAT WAS ALL THIS?
DOES THIS HAPPEN A LOT?
MORE THAN I'D LIKE.
SORRY TO HEAR IT, BUDDY.
WHY ARE YOU HERE?
I MISSED YOU.
ARE YOU FOLLOWING ME?
I'M LOOKING FOR YOU.
WE NEED TO GET THE GUARDIANS BACK TOGETHER.
NOT INTERESTED. NOT AFTER WHAT HAPPENED LAST TIME.
THE EARTH IS IN TROUBLE.
WHAT KIND OF TROUBLE?
MY FATHER PUT A BIG TARGET ON IT.
I FIGURED WITH YOUR AND MY HISTORY WITH THE EARTH, NO MATTER WHAT YOU'RE FEELING ABOUT US LATELY...
YOU'D BE WILLING TO PUT IT ALL ASIDE FOR NOW AND DO SOMETHING MORE WORTHWHILE THAN SITTING AND WAITING FOR PEOPLE TO PICK FIGHTS WITH YOU.
I'LL THINK ABOUT IT.
THAT'S ALL I ASK.
ARE YOU DONE THINKING ABOUT IT?
IS IT WORTH-WHILE?
IT IS TO US. AND THE EARTH.
GIVE ME SOMETHING WORTHWHILE TO DO, QUILL.
JUST PROMISE ME IT'LL BE WORTH-WHILE.

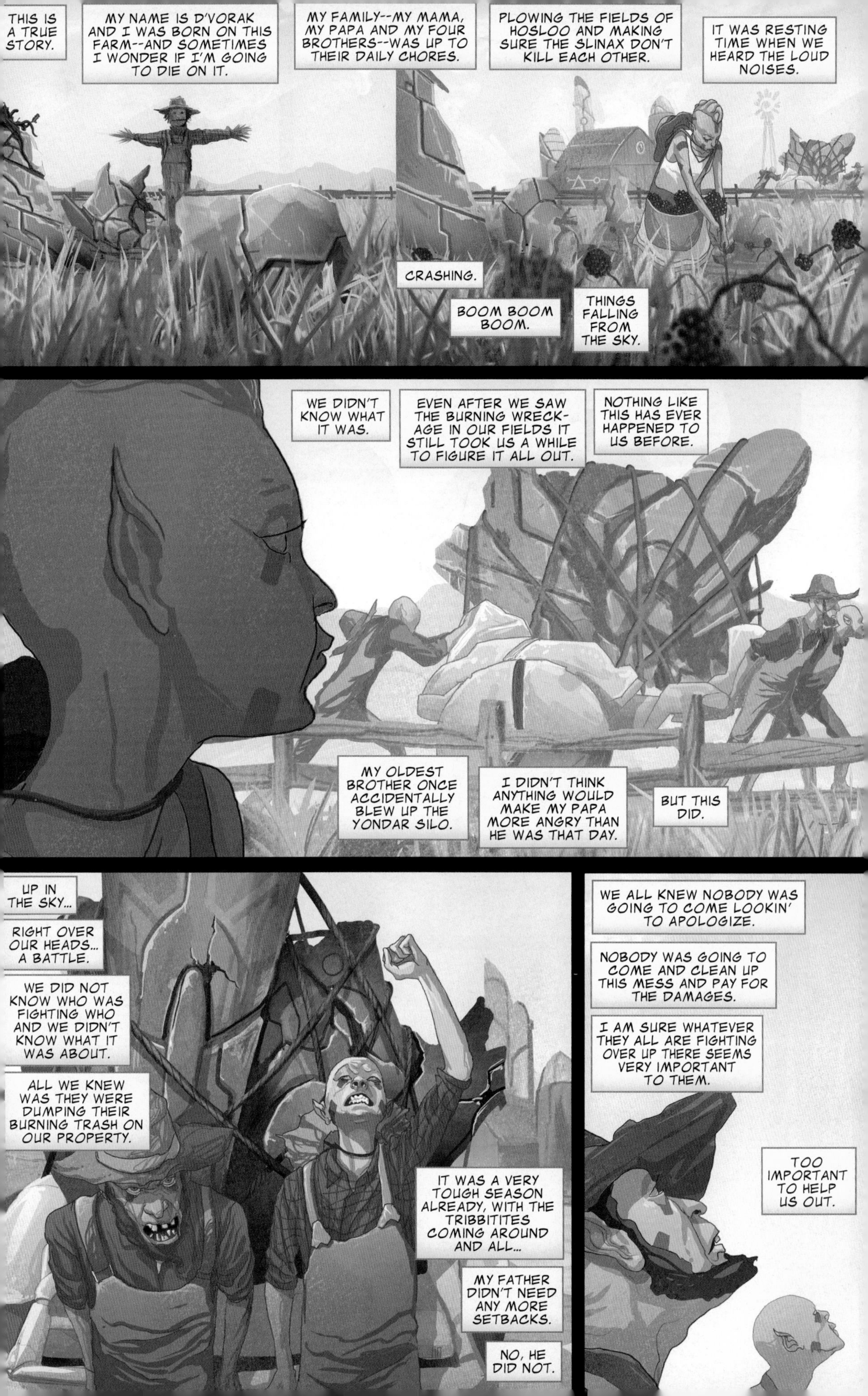
THIS IS A TRUE STORY.
MY NAME IS D'VORAK AND I WAS BORN ON THIS FARM--AND SOMETIMES I WONDER IF I'M GOING TO DIE ON IT.
MY FAMILY--MY MAMA, MY PAPA AND MY FOUR BROTHERS--WAS UP TO THEIR DAILY CHORES.
PLOWING THE FIELDS OF HOSLOO AND MAKING SURE THE SLINAX DON'T KILL EACH OTHER.
IT WAS RESTING TIME WHEN WE HEARD THE LOUD NOISES.
CRASHING.
BOOM BOOM BOOM.
THINGS FALLING FROM THE SKY.
WE DIDN'T KNOW WHAT IT WAS.
EVEN AFTER WE SAW THE BURNING WRECK-AGE IN OUR FIELDS IT STILL TOOK US A WHILE TO FIGURE IT ALL OUT.
NOTHING LIKE THIS HAS EVER HAPPENED TO US BEFORE.
MY OLDEST BROTHER ONCE ACCIDENTALLY BLEW UP THE YONDAR SILO.
I DIDN'T THINK ANYTHING WOULD MAKE MY PAPA MORE ANGRY THAN HE WAS THAT DAY.
BUT THIS DID.
UP IN THE SKY...
RIGHT OVER OUR HEADS... A BATTLE.
WE DID NOT KNOW WHO WAS FIGHTING WHO AND WE DIDN'T KNOW WHAT IT WAS ABOUT.
ALL WE KNEW WAS THEY WERE DUMPING THEIR BURNING TRASH ON OUR PROPERTY.
IT WAS A VERY TOUGH SEASON ALREADY, WITH THE TRIBBITITES COMING AROUND AND ALL...
MY FATHER DIDN'T NEED ANY MORE SETBACKS.
NO, HE DID NOT.
WE ALL KNEW NOBODY WAS GOING TO COME LOOKIN' TO APOLOGIZE.
NOBODY WAS GOING TO COME AND CLEAN UP THIS MESS AND PAY FOR THE DAMAGES.
I AM SURE WHATEVER THEY ALL ARE FIGHTING OVER UP THERE SEEMS VERY IMPORTANT TO THEM.
TOO IMPORTANT TO HELP US OUT.

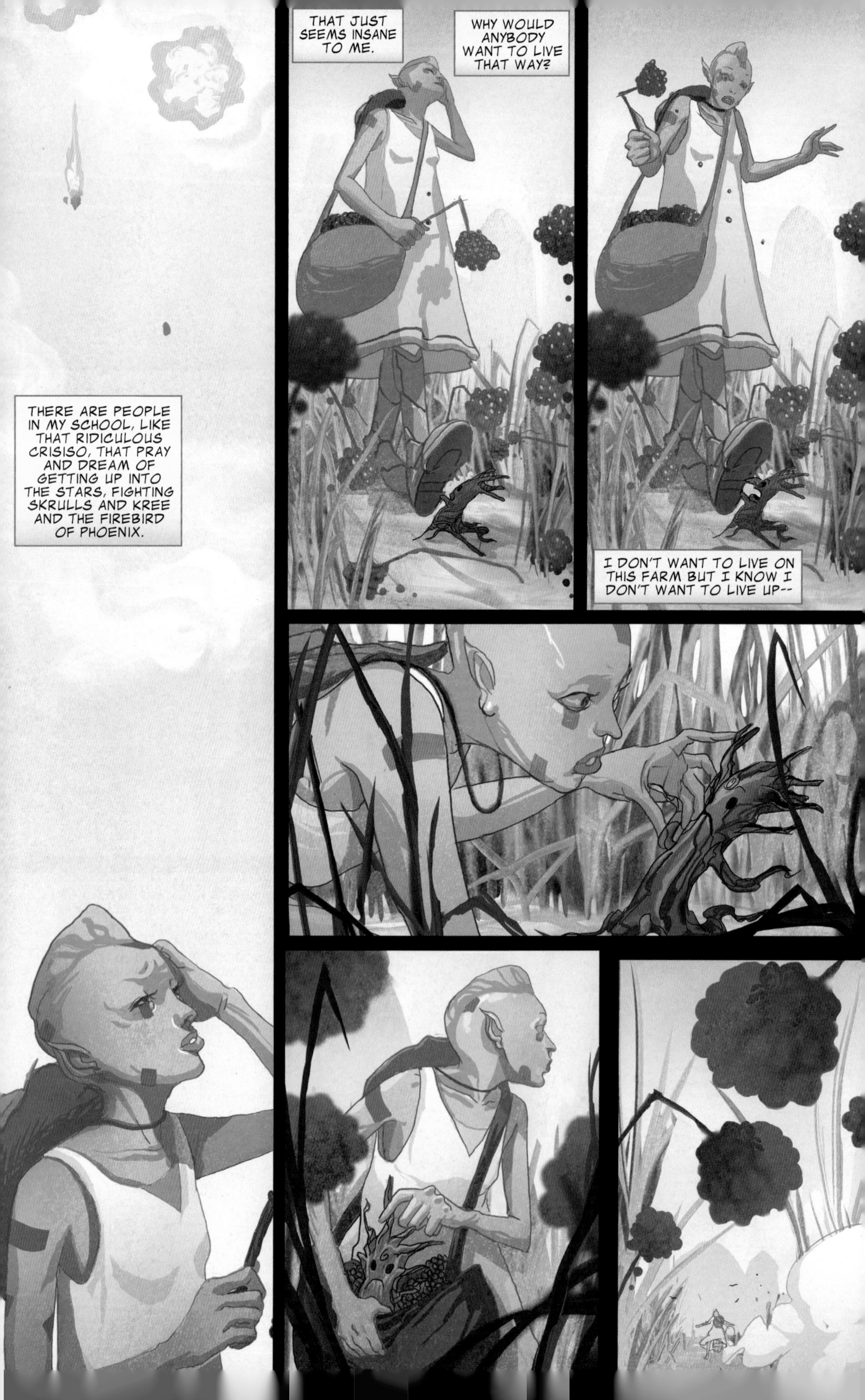
THERE ARE PEOPLE IN MY SCHOOL, LIKE THAT RIDICULOUS CRISISO, THAT PRAY AND DREAM OF GETTING UP INTO THE STARS, FIGHTING SKRULLS AND KREE AND THE FIREBIRD OF PHOENIX.
THAT JUST SEEMS INSANE TO ME.
WHY WOULD ANYBODY WANT TO LIVE THAT WAY?
I DON'T WANT TO LIVE ON THIS FARM BUT I KNOW I DON'T WANT TO LIVE UP--

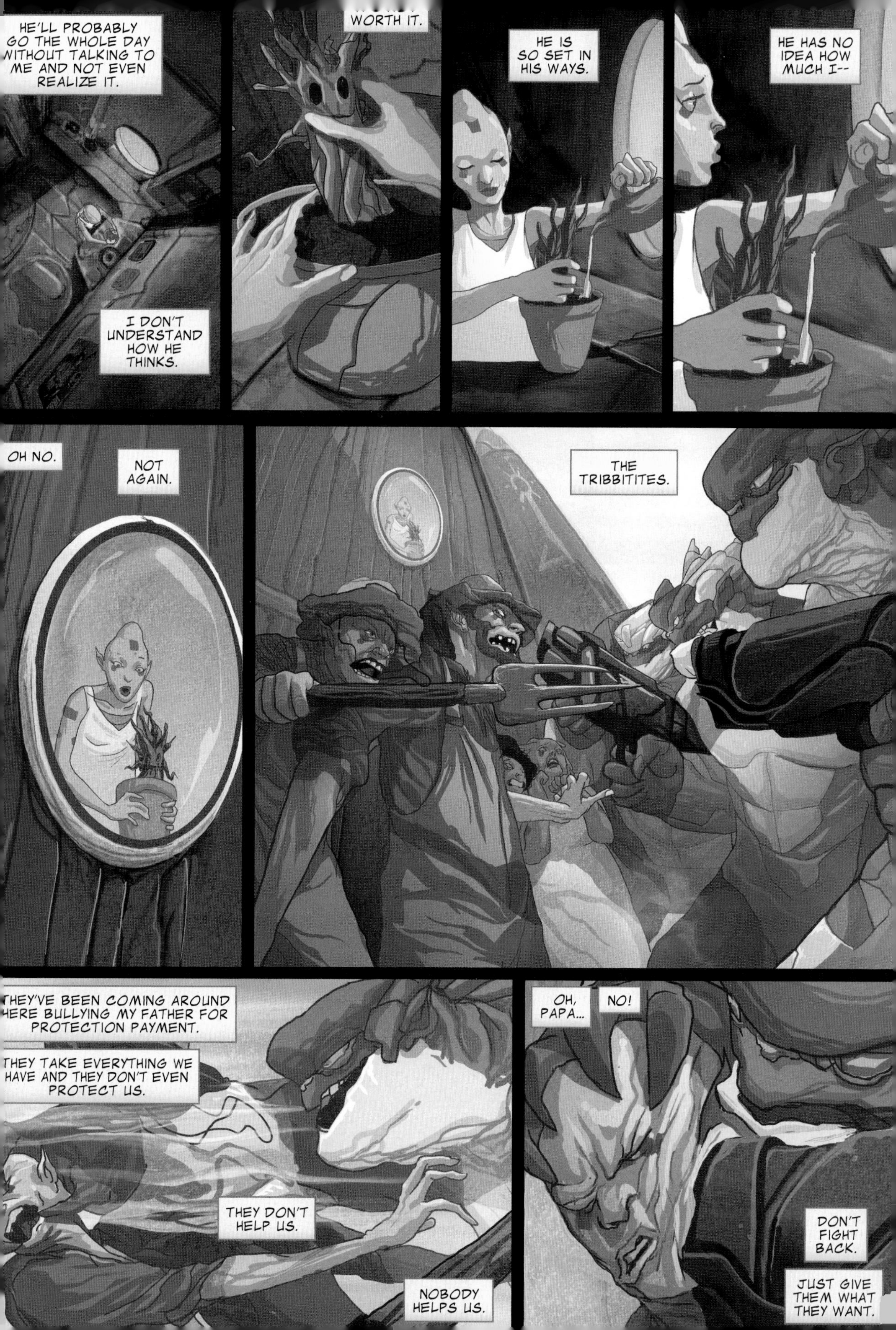
HE'LL PROBABLY GO THE WHOLE DAY WITHOUT TALKING TO ME AND NOT EVEN REALIZE IT.
I DON'T UNDERSTAND HOW HE THINKS.
WORTH IT.
HE IS SO SET IN HIS WAYS.
HE HAS NO IDEA HOW MUCH I--
OH NO.
NOT AGAIN.
THE TRIBBITITES.
THEY'VE BEEN COMING AROUND HERE BULLYING MY FATHER FOR PROTECTION PAYMENT.
THEY TAKE EVERYTHING WE HAVE AND THEY DON'T EVEN PROTECT US.
THEY DON'T HELP US.
NOBODY HELPS US.
OH, PAPA...
NO!
DON'T FIGHT BACK.
JUST GIVE THEM WHAT THEY WANT.

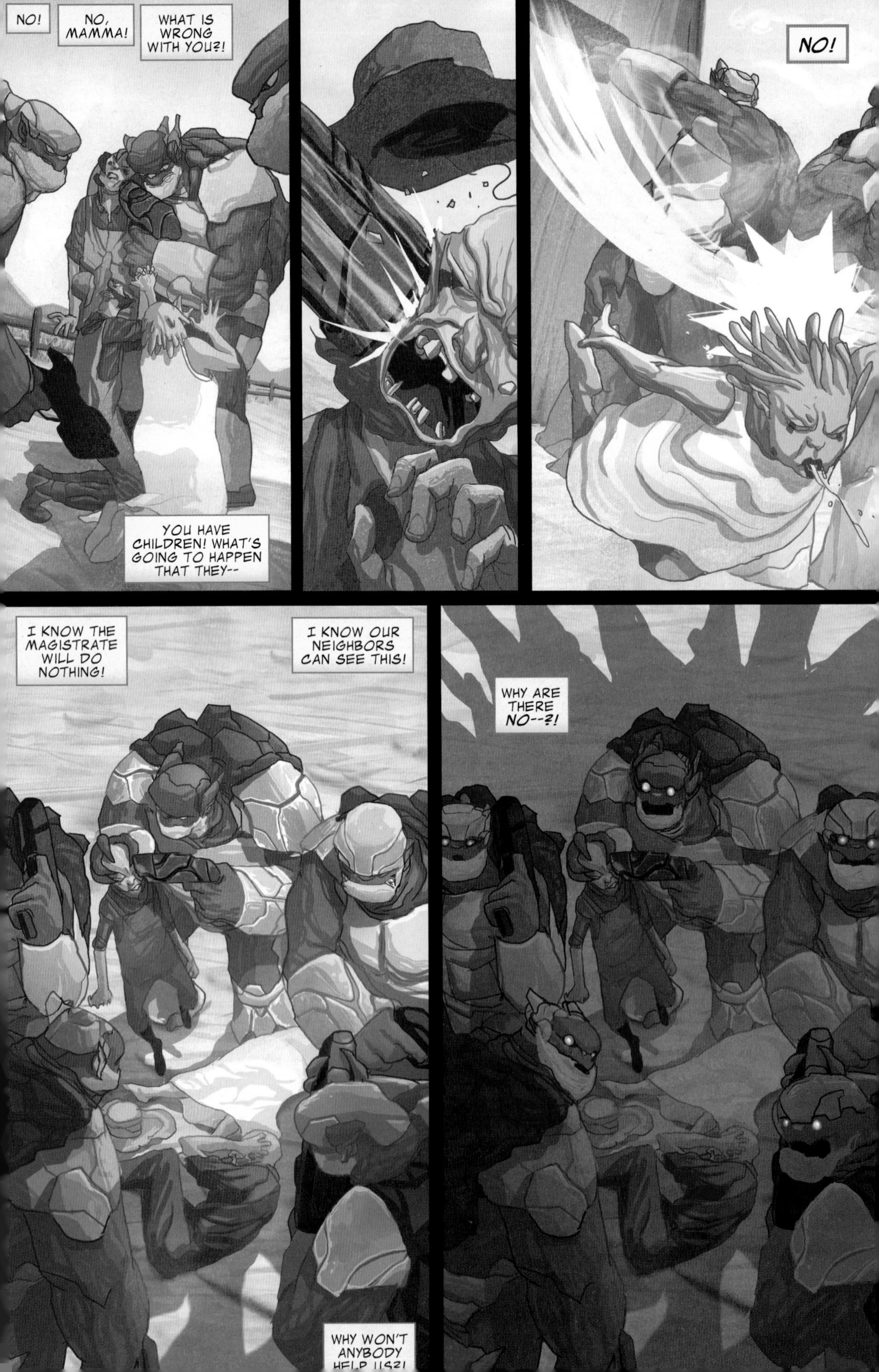

NO!
NO, MAMMA!
WHAT IS WRONG WITH YOU?!
YOU HAVE CHILDREN! WHAT'S GOING TO HAPPEN THAT THEY--
NO!
I KNOW THE MAGISTRATE WILL DO NOTHING!
I KNOW OUR NEIGHBORS CAN SEE THIS!
WHY WON'T ANYBODY
WHY ARE THERE NO--?!

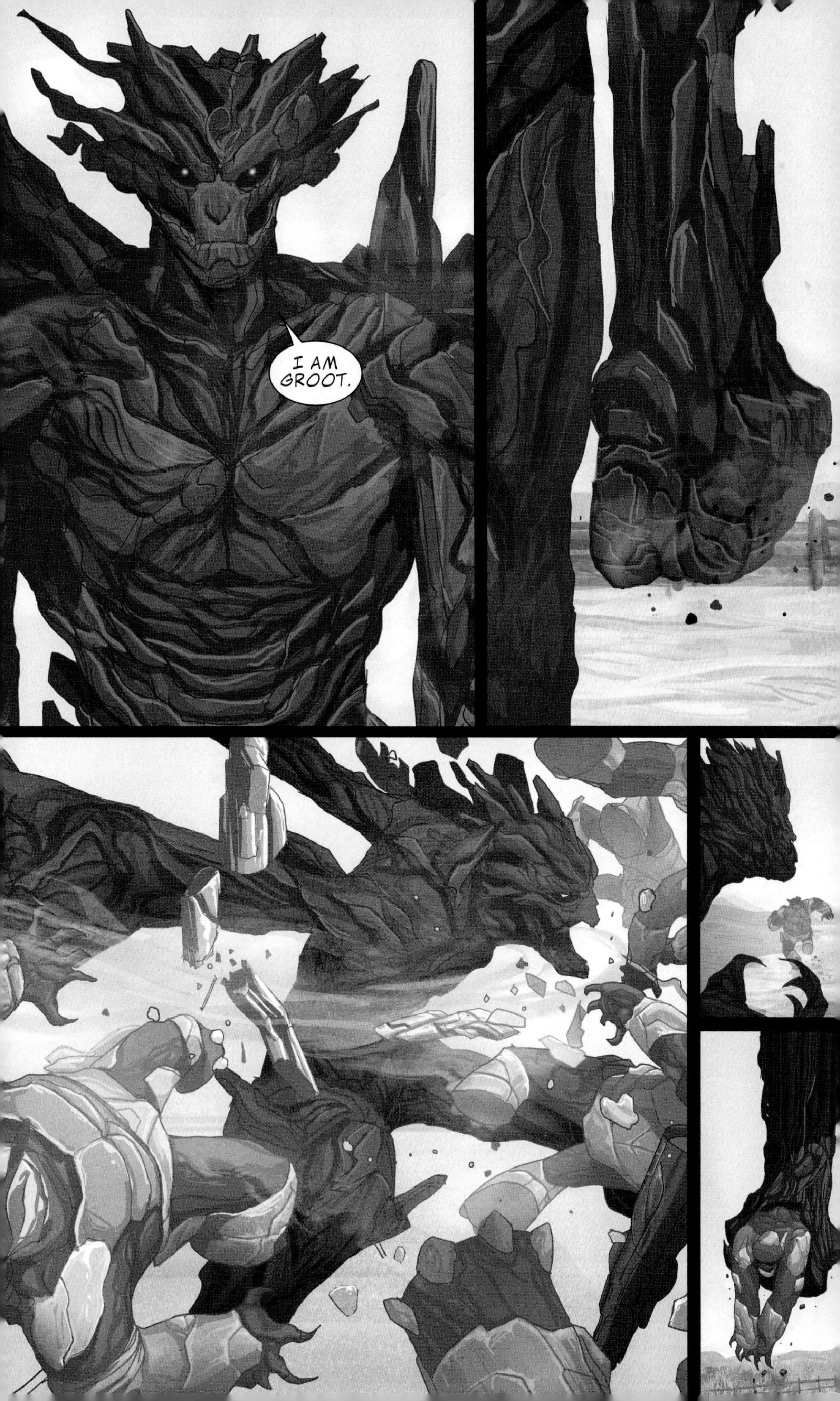
I AM GROOT.

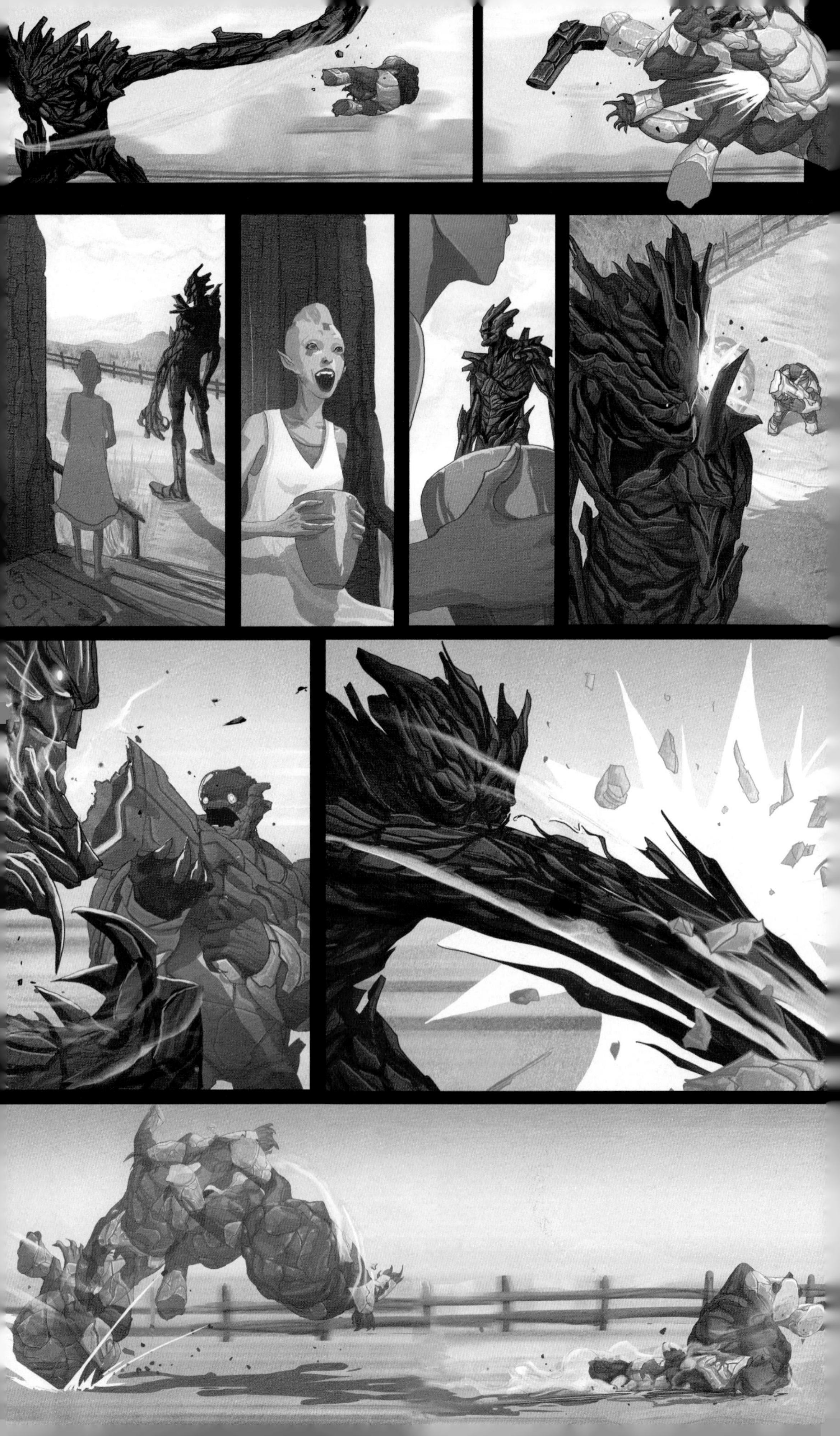

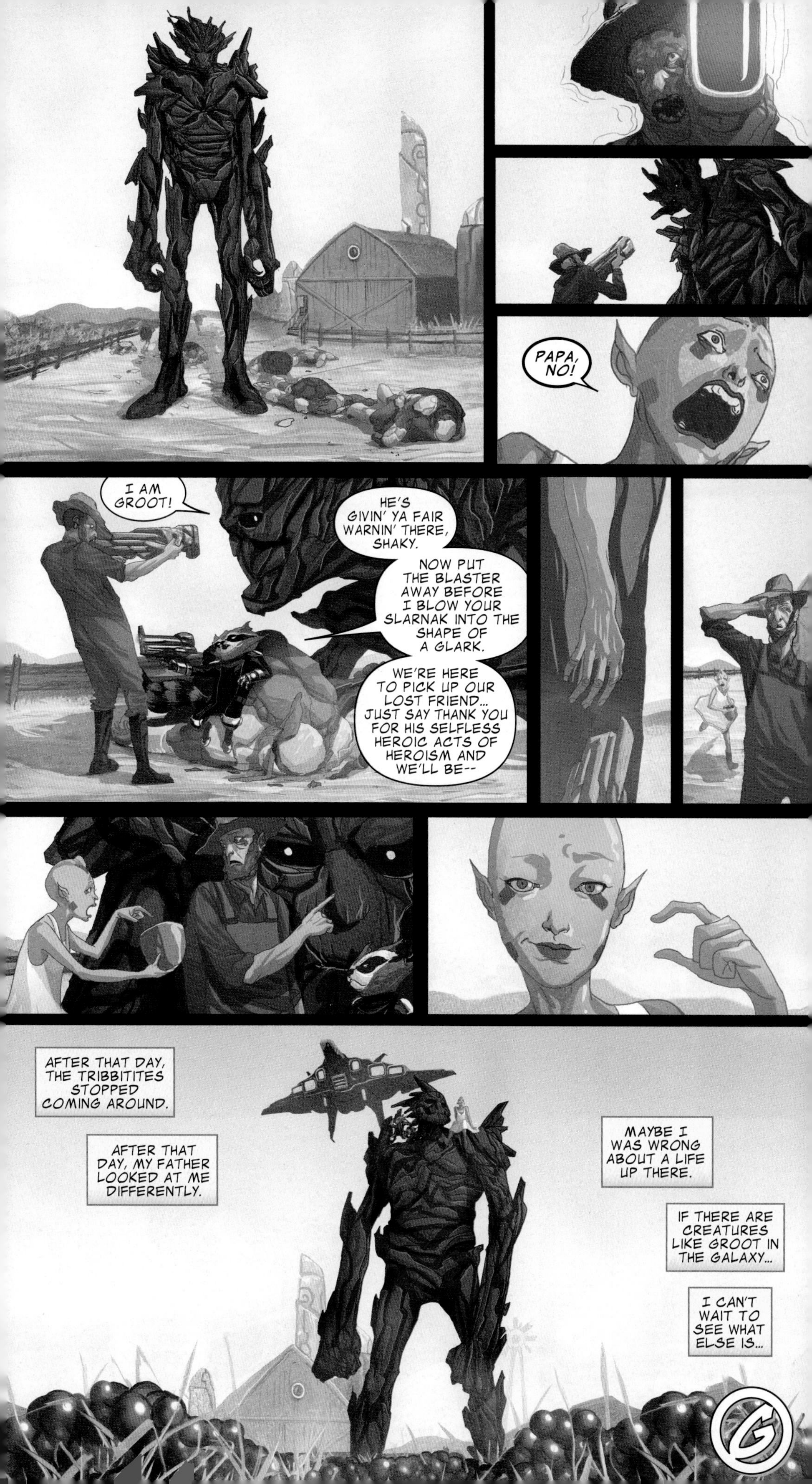
PAPA, NO!
I AM GROOT!
HE'S GIVIN' YA FAIR WARNIN' THERE, SHAKY.
NOW PUT THE BLASTER AWAY BEFORE I BLOW YOUR SLARNAK INTO THE SHAPE OF A GLARK.
WE'RE HERE TO PICK UP OUR LOST FRIEND... JUST SAY THANK YOU FOR HIS SELFLESS HEROIC ACTS OF HEROISM AND WE'LL BE--
AFTER THAT DAY, THE TRIBBITITES STOPPED COMING AROUND.
AFTER THAT DAY, MY FATHER LOOKED AT ME DIFFERENTLY.
MAYBE I WAS WRONG ABOUT A LIFE UP THERE.
IF THERE ARE CREATURES LIKE GROOT IN THE GALAXY...
I CAN'T WAIT TO SEE WHAT ELSE IS...

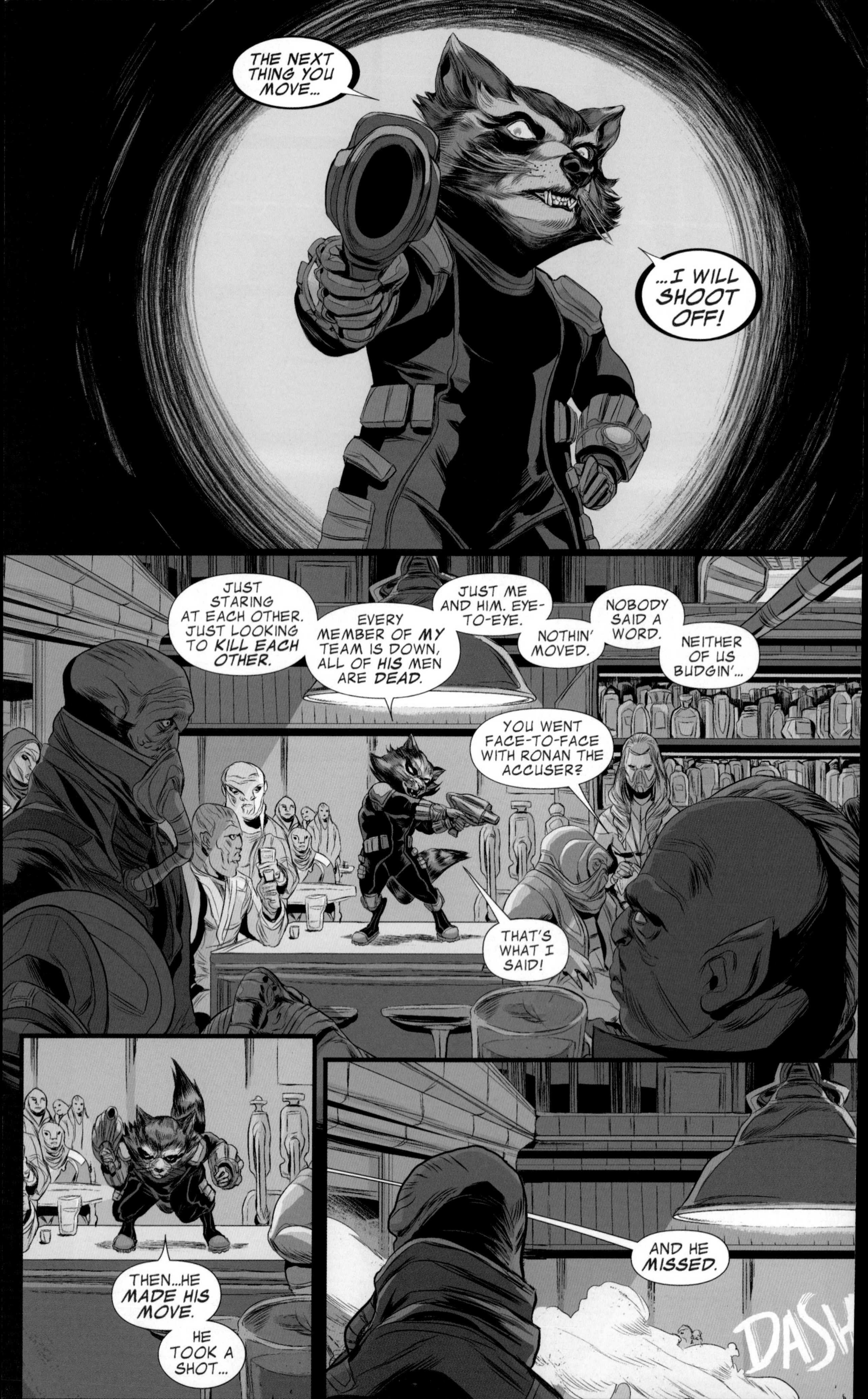
THE NEXT THING YOU MOVE...
...I WILL SHOOT OFF!
JUST STARING AT EACH OTHER. JUST LOOKING TO KILL EACH OTHER.
EVERY MEMBER OF MY TEAM IS DOWN, ALL OF HIS MEN ARE DEAD.
JUST ME AND HIM. EYE-TO-EYE.
NOTHIN' MOVED.
NOBODY SAID A WORD.
NEITHER OF US BUDGIN'...
YOU WENT FACE-TO-FACE WITH RONAN THE ACCUSER?
THAT'S WHAT I SAID!
THEN...HE MADE HIS MOVE.
HE TOOK A SHOT...
AND HE MISSED.
DASH

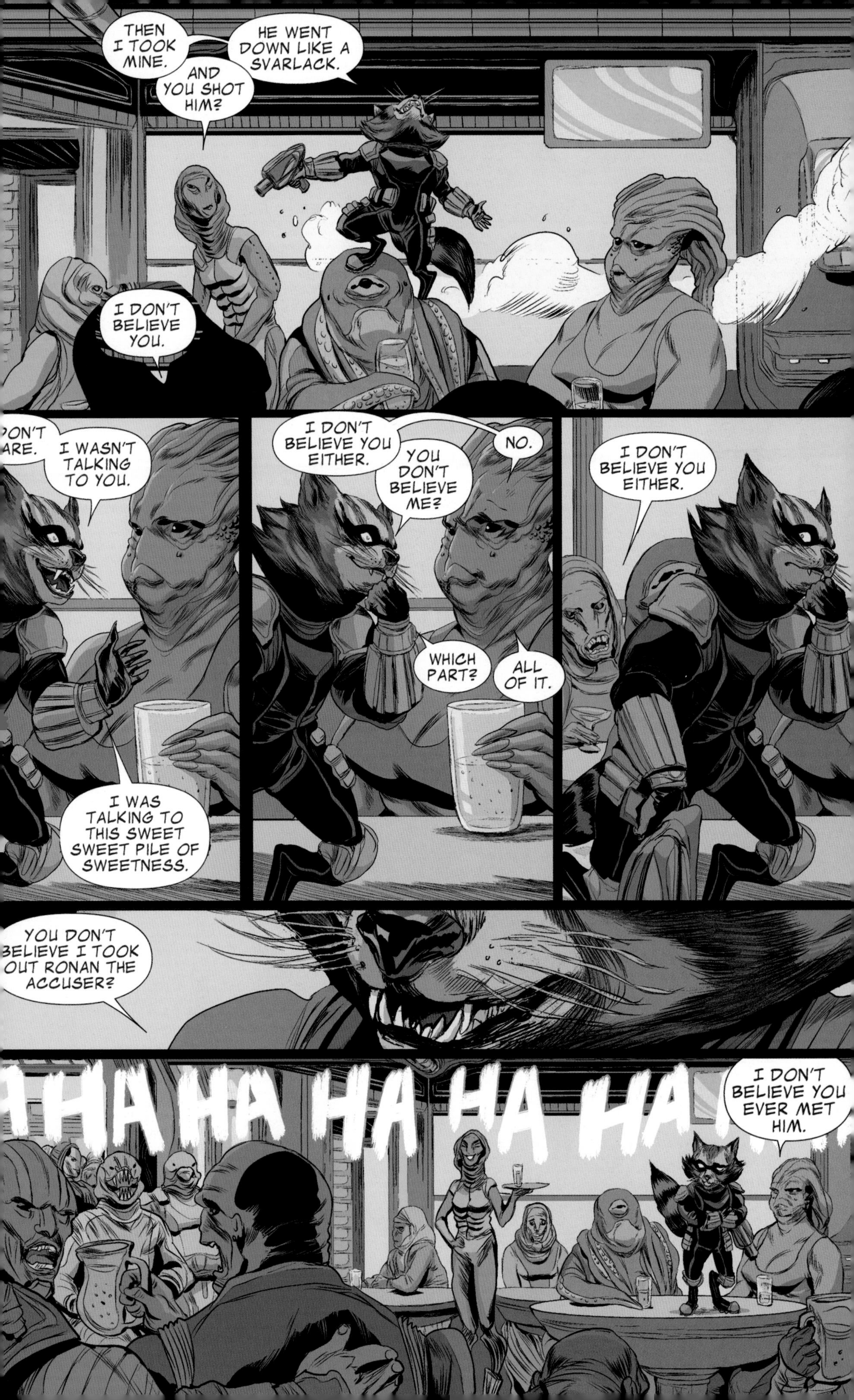
THEN I TOOK MINE.
AND YOU SHOT HIM?
HE WENT DOWN LIKE A SVARLACK.
I DON'T BELIEVE YOU.
I WASN'T TALKING TO YOU.
I WAS TALKING TO THIS SWEET SWEET PILE OF SWEETNESS.
I DON'T BELIEVE YOU EITHER.
YOU DON'T BELIEVE ME?
NO.
WHICH PART?
ALL OF IT.
I DON'T BELIEVE YOU EITHER.
YOU DON'T BELIEVE I TOOK OUT RONAN THE ACCUSER?
HA HA HA HA HA
I DON'T BELIEVE YOU EVER MET HIM.

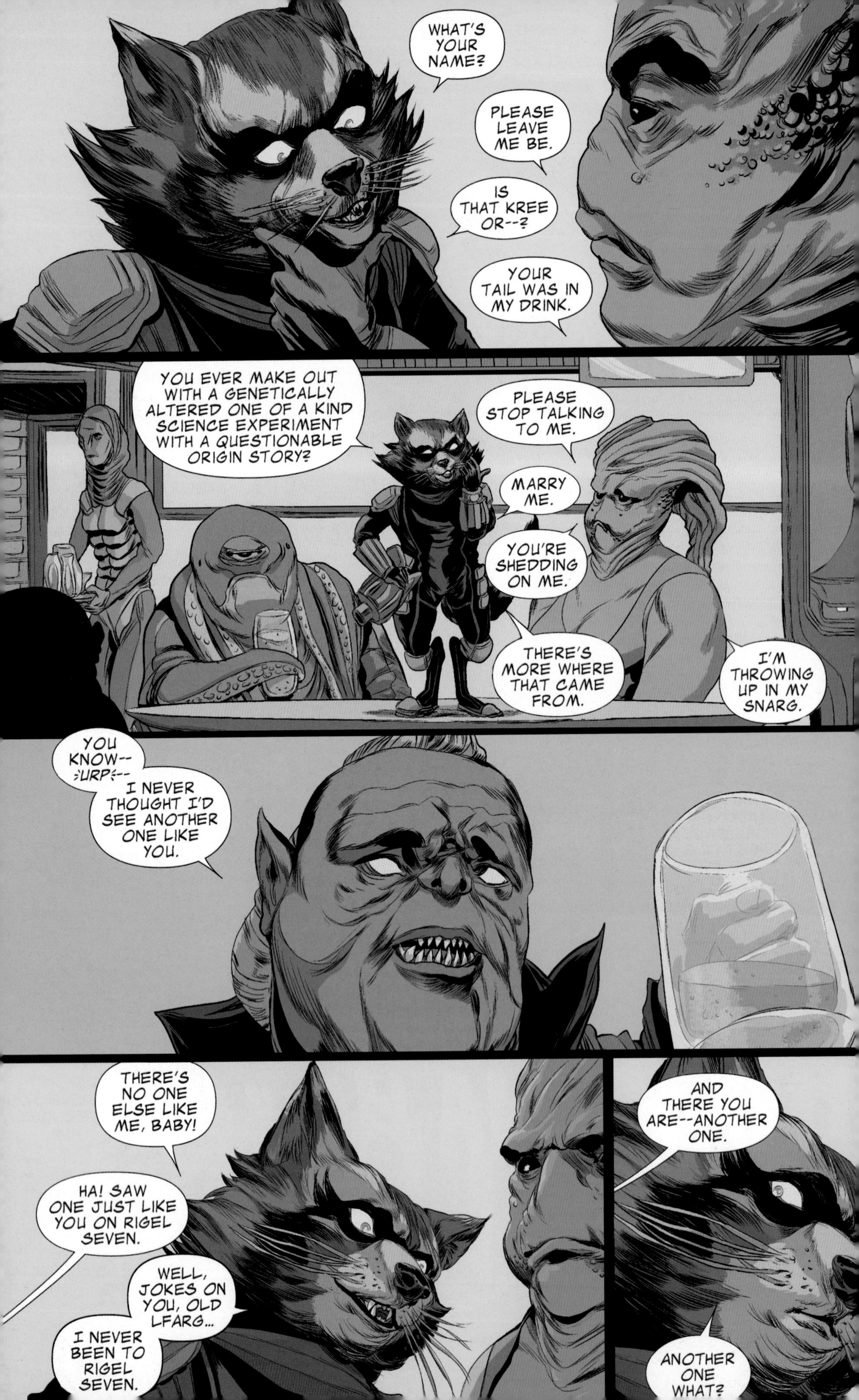
WHAT'S YOUR NAME?
PLEASE LEAVE ME BE.
IS THAT KREE OR--?
YOUR TAIL WAS IN MY DRINK.
YOU EVER MAKE OUT WITH A GENETICALLY ALTERED ONE OF A KIND SCIENCE EXPERIMENT WITH A QUESTIONABLE ORIGIN STORY?
PLEASE STOP TALKING TO ME.
MARRY ME.
YOU'RE SHEDDING ON ME.
THERE'S MORE WHERE THAT CAME FROM.
I'M THROWING UP IN MY SNARG.
YOU KNOW-- URP-- I NEVER THOUGHT I'D SEE ANOTHER ONE LIKE YOU.
THERE'S NO ONE ELSE LIKE ME, BABY!
HA! SAW ONE JUST LIKE YOU ON RIGEL SEVEN.
WELL, JOKES ON YOU, OLD LFARG...
I NEVER BEEN TO RIGEL SEVEN.
AND THERE YOU ARE--ANOTHER ONE.
ANOTHER ONE WHAT?

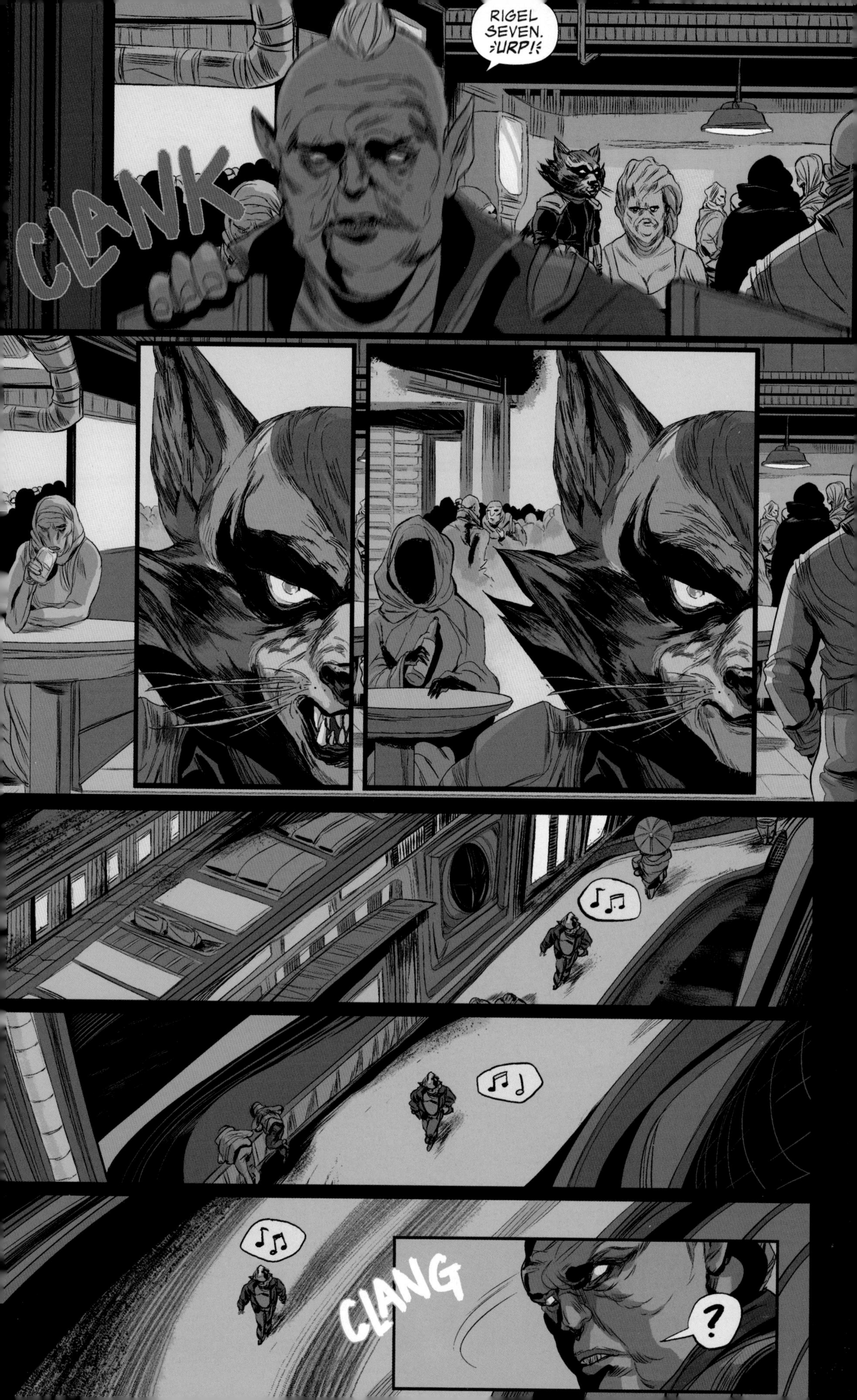
RIGEL SEVEN. URP!
CLANK
♪♫
♫♩
♪♫
CLANG
?

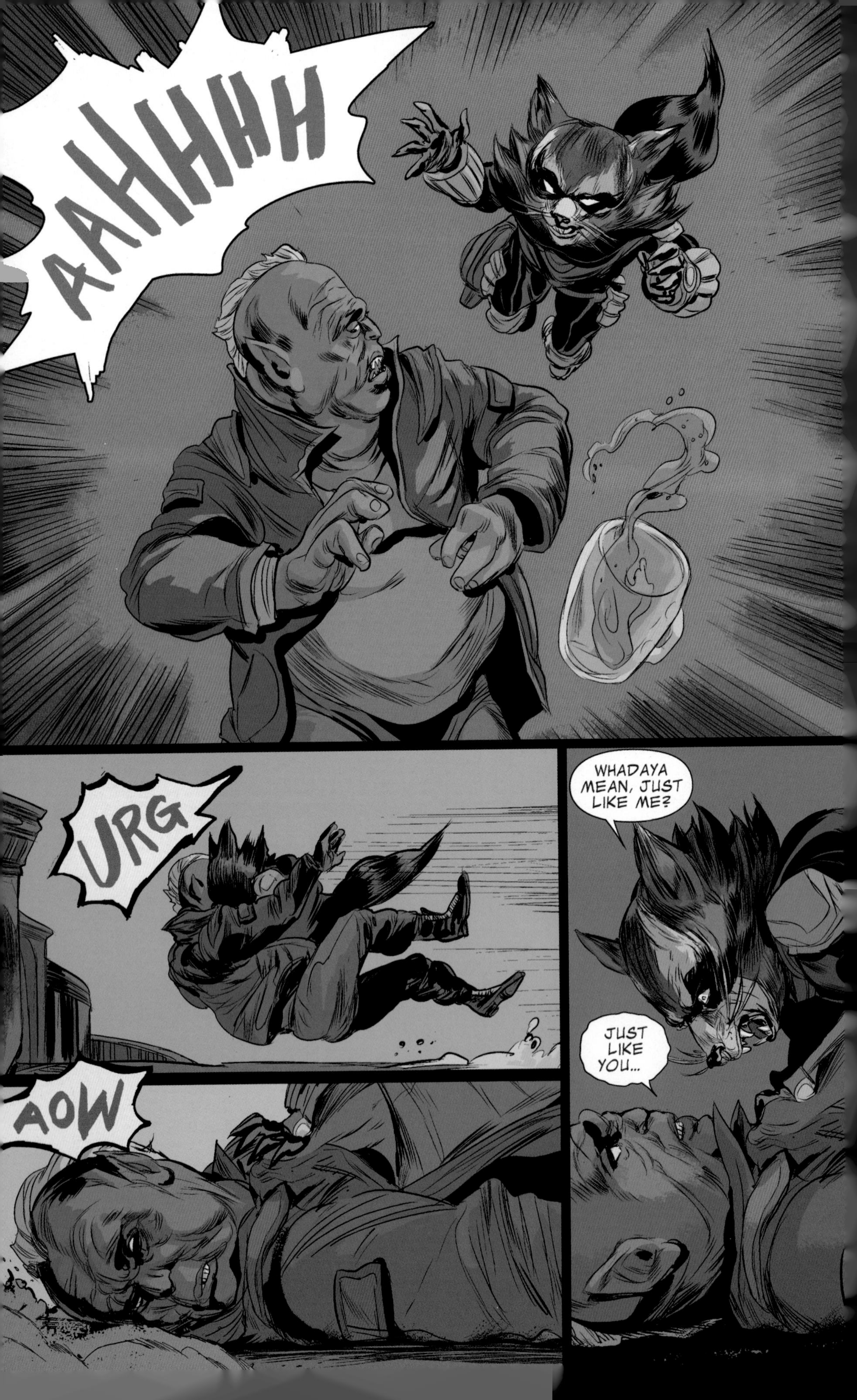
AAHHHH
URG
AOW
WHADAYA MEAN, JUST LIKE ME?
JUST LIKE YOU...

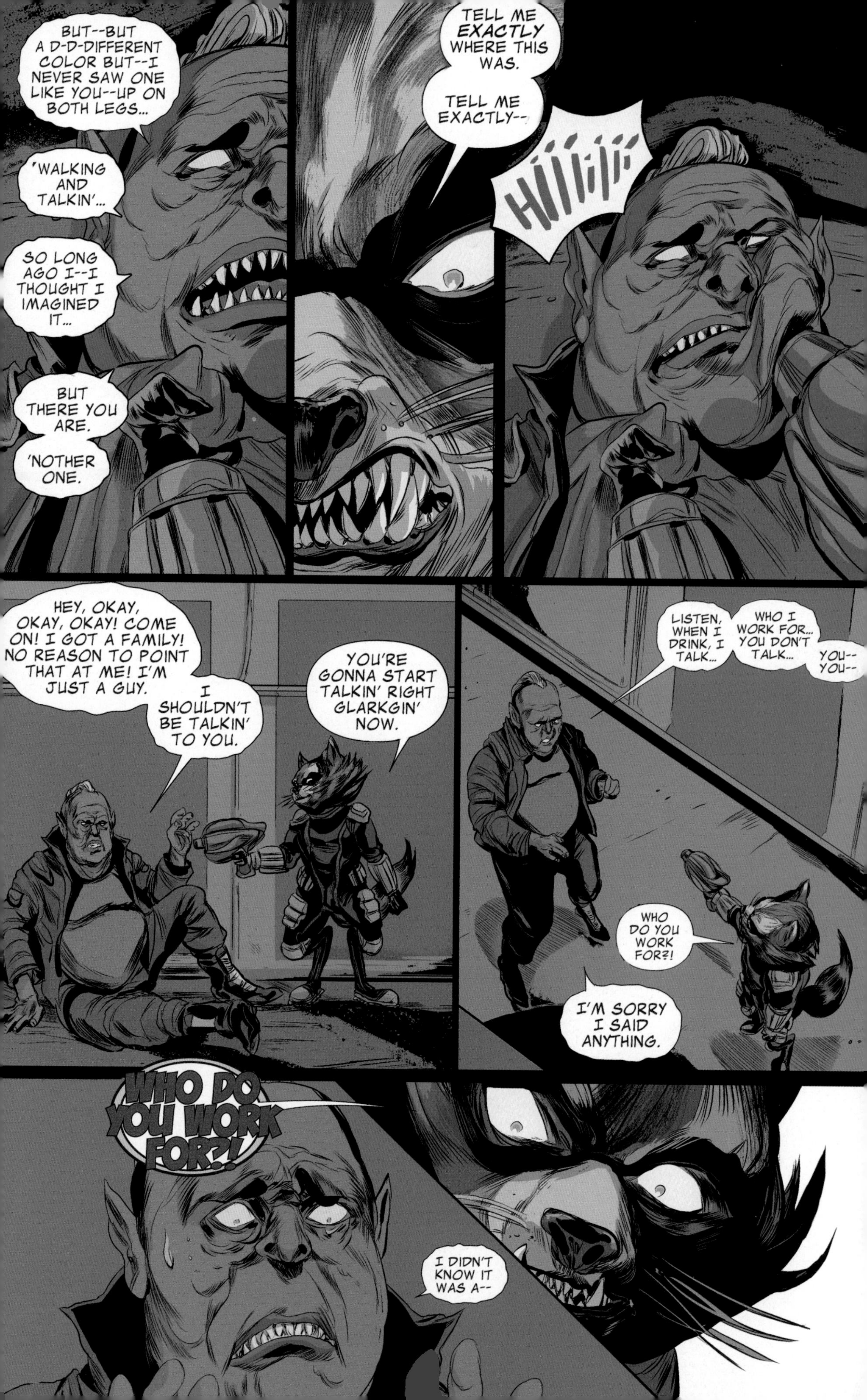
BUT--BUT A D-D-DIFFERENT COLOR BUT--I NEVER SAW ONE LIKE YOU--UP ON BOTH LEGS...
'WALKING AND TALKIN'...
SO LONG AGO I--I THOUGHT I IMAGINED IT...
BUT THERE YOU ARE.
'NOTHER ONE.
TELL ME EXACTLY WHERE THIS WAS.
TELL ME EXACTLY--
HIIIIII
HEY, OKAY, OKAY, OKAY! COME ON! I GOT A FAMILY! NO REASON TO POINT THAT AT ME! I'M JUST A GUY.
I SHOULDN'T BE TALKIN' TO YOU.
YOU'RE GONNA START TALKIN' RIGHT GLARKGIN' NOW.
LISTEN, WHEN I DRINK, I TALK...
WHO I WORK FOR... YOU DON'T TALK...
YOU-- YOU--
WHO DO YOU WORK FOR?!
I'M SORRY I SAID ANYTHING.
WHO DO YOU WORK FOR?!
I DIDN'T KNOW IT WAS A--

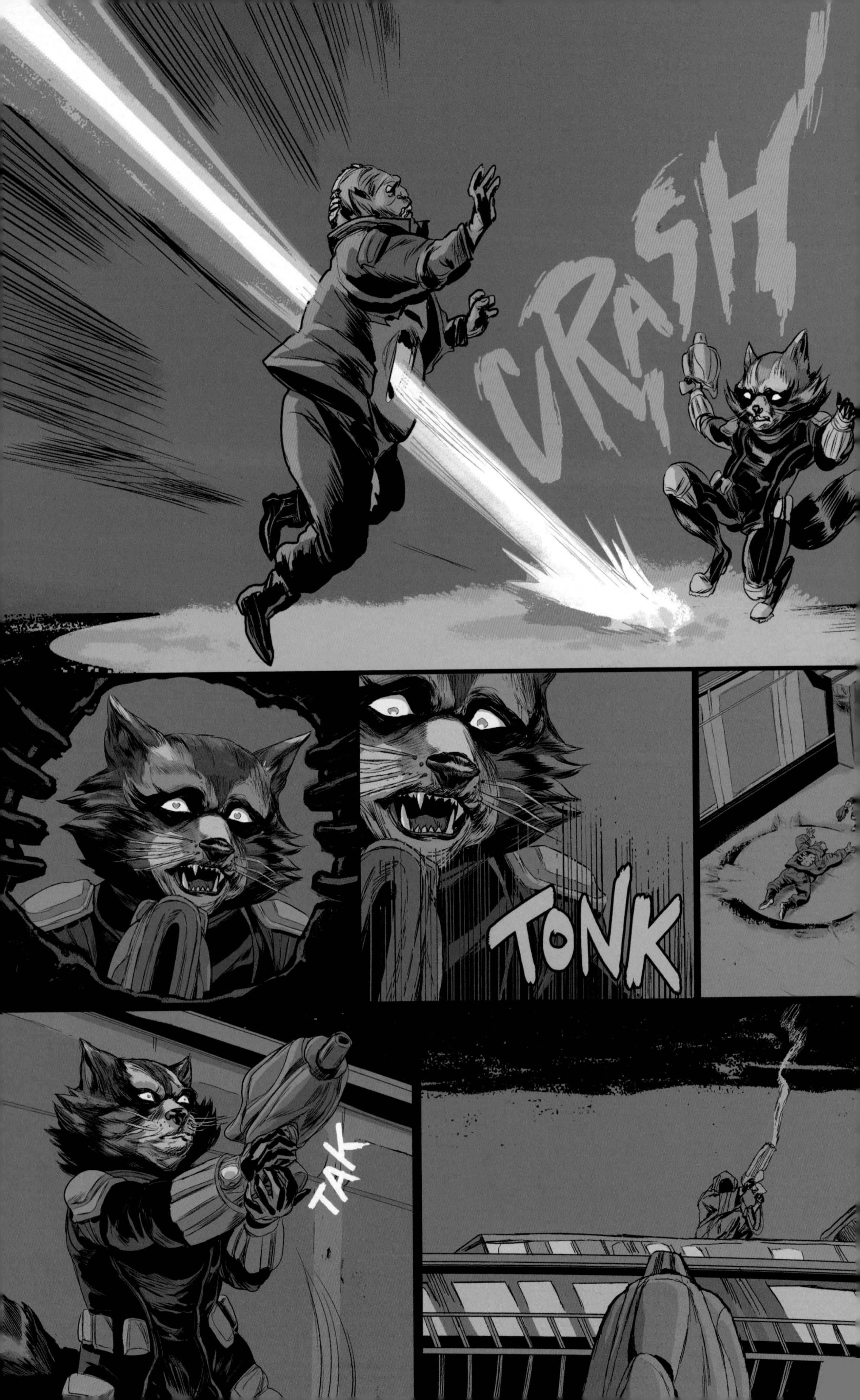

CRASH
TONK
TAK

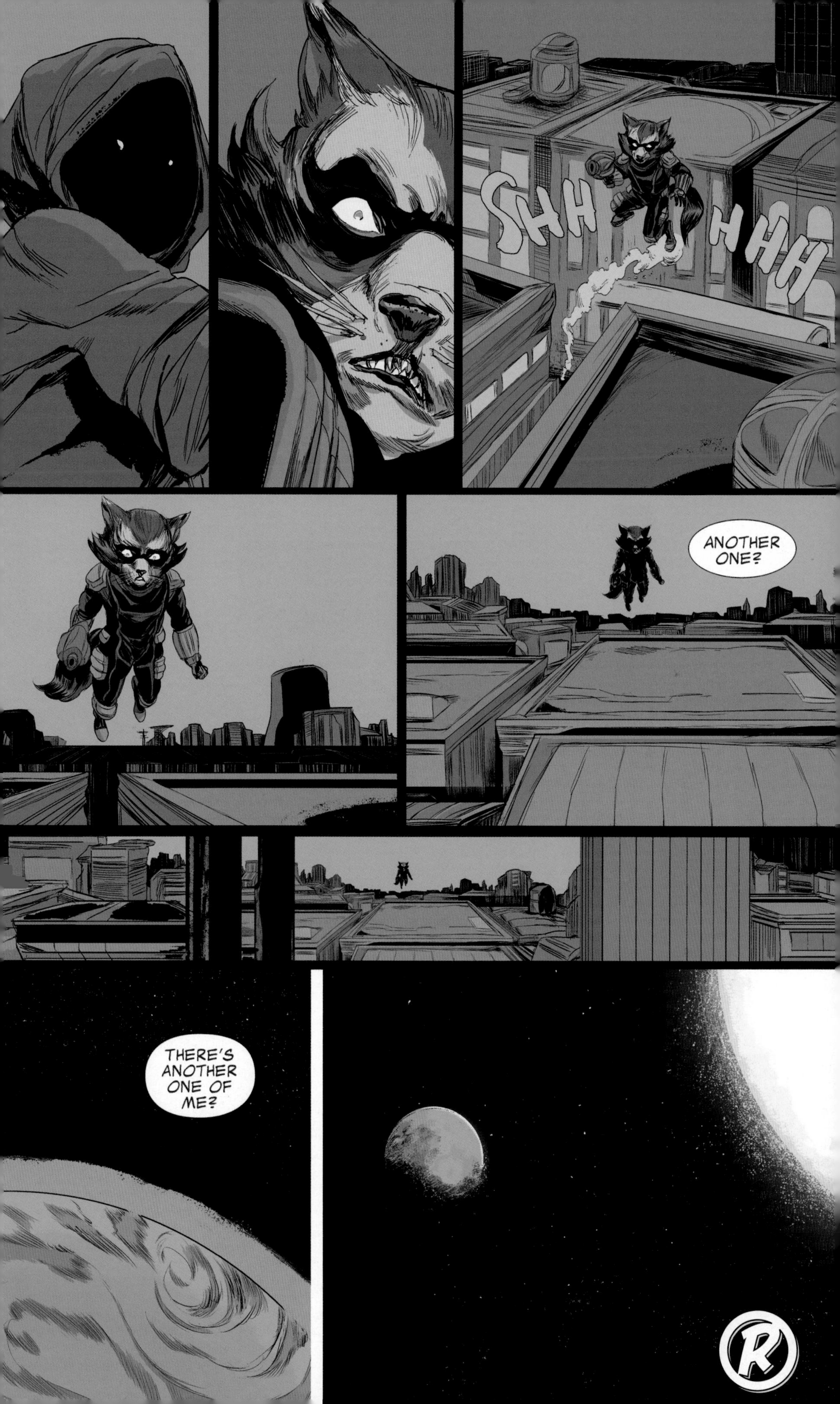
SHHHHHH
ANOTHER ONE?
THERE'S ANOTHER ONE OF ME?

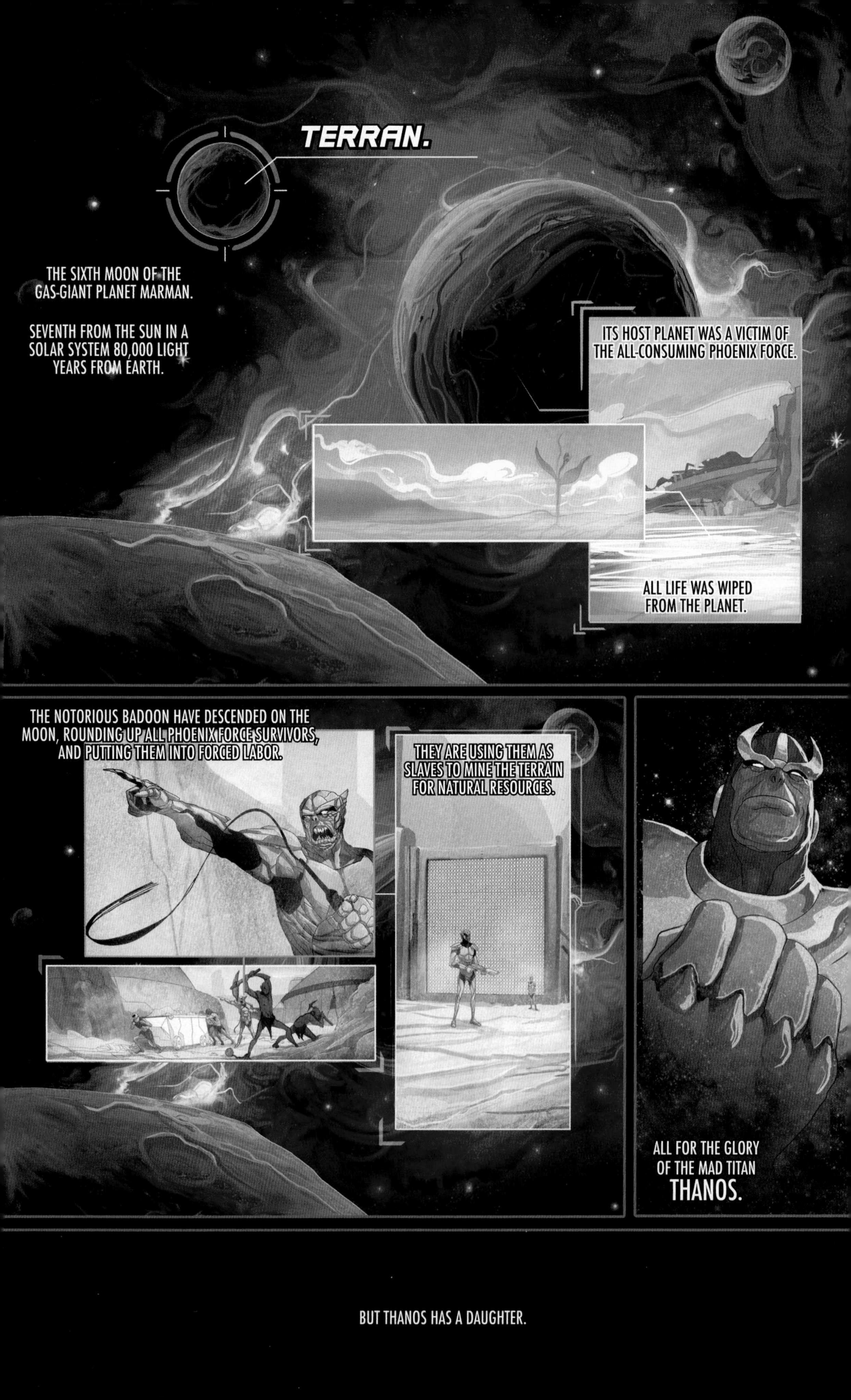
TERRAN.
THE SIXTH MOON OF THE GAS-GIANT PLANET MARMAN.
SEVENTH FROM THE SUN IN A SOLAR SYSTEM 80,000 LIGHT YEARS FROM EARTH.
ITS HOST PLANET WAS A VICTIM OF THE ALL-CONSUMING PHOENIX FORCE.
ALL LIFE WAS WIPED FROM THE PLANET.
THE NOTORIOUS BADOON HAVE DESCENDED ON THE MOON, ROUNDING UP ALL PHOENIX FORCE SURVIVORS, AND PUTTING THEM INTO FORCED LABOR.
THEY ARE USING THEM AS SLAVES TO MINE THE TERRAIN FOR NATURAL RESOURCES.
ALL FOR THE GLORY OF THE MAD TITAN THANOS.
BUT THANOS HAS A DAUGHTER.

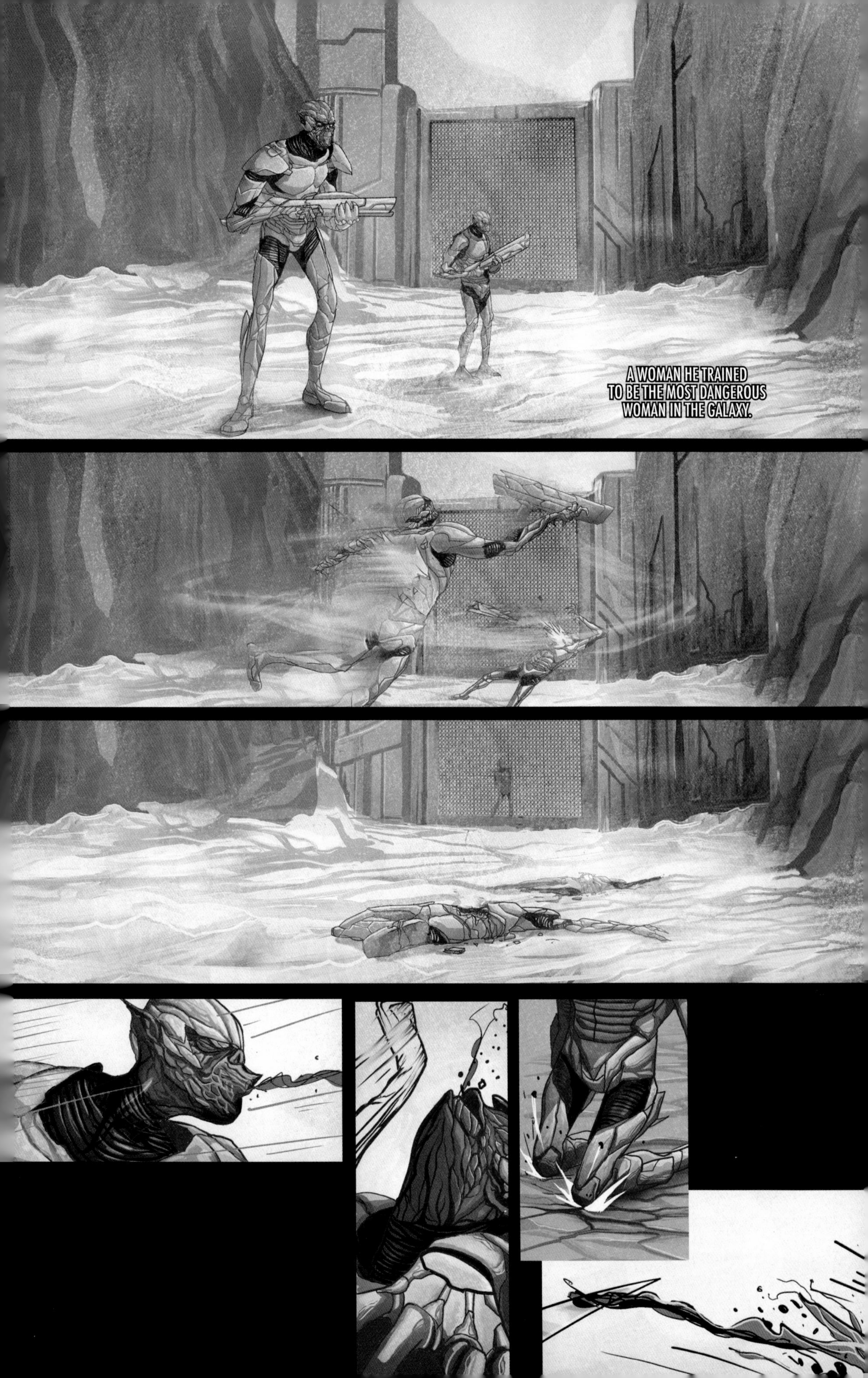
A WOMAN HE TRAINED TO BE THE MOST DANGEROUS WOMAN IN THE GALAXY.

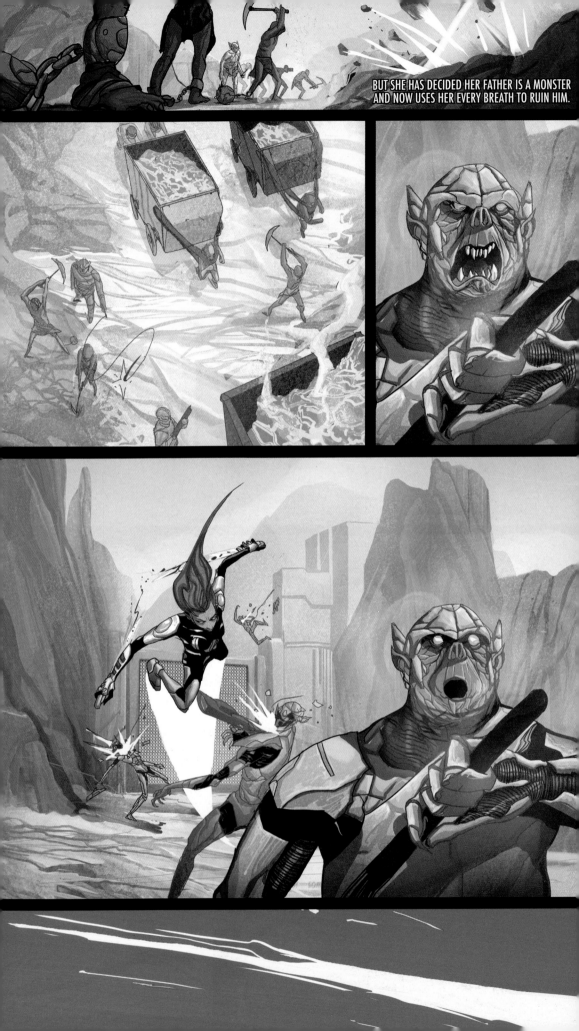

BUT SHE HAS DECIDED HER FATHER IS A MONSTER AND NOW USES HER EVERY BREATH TO RUIN HIM.

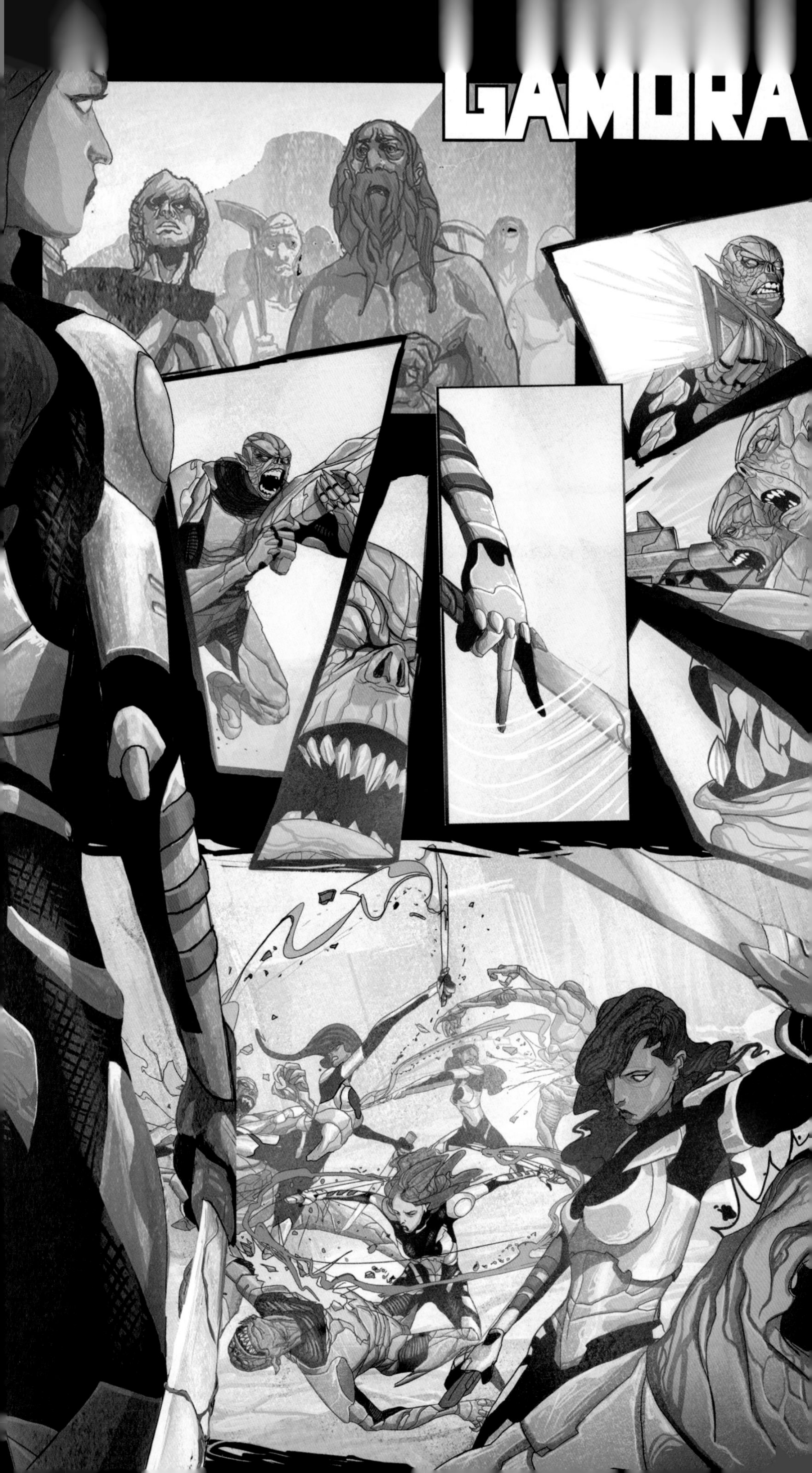
GAMORA

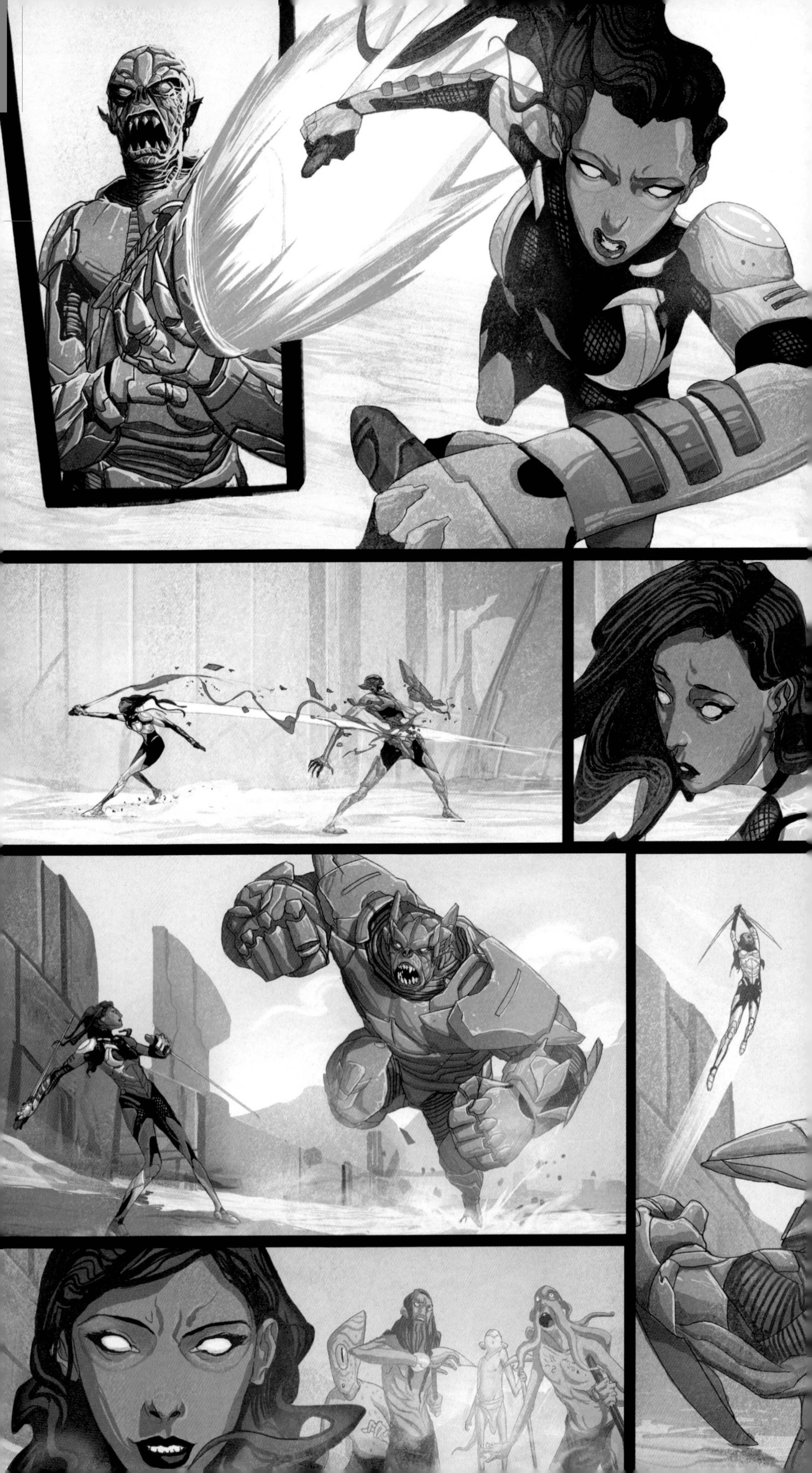

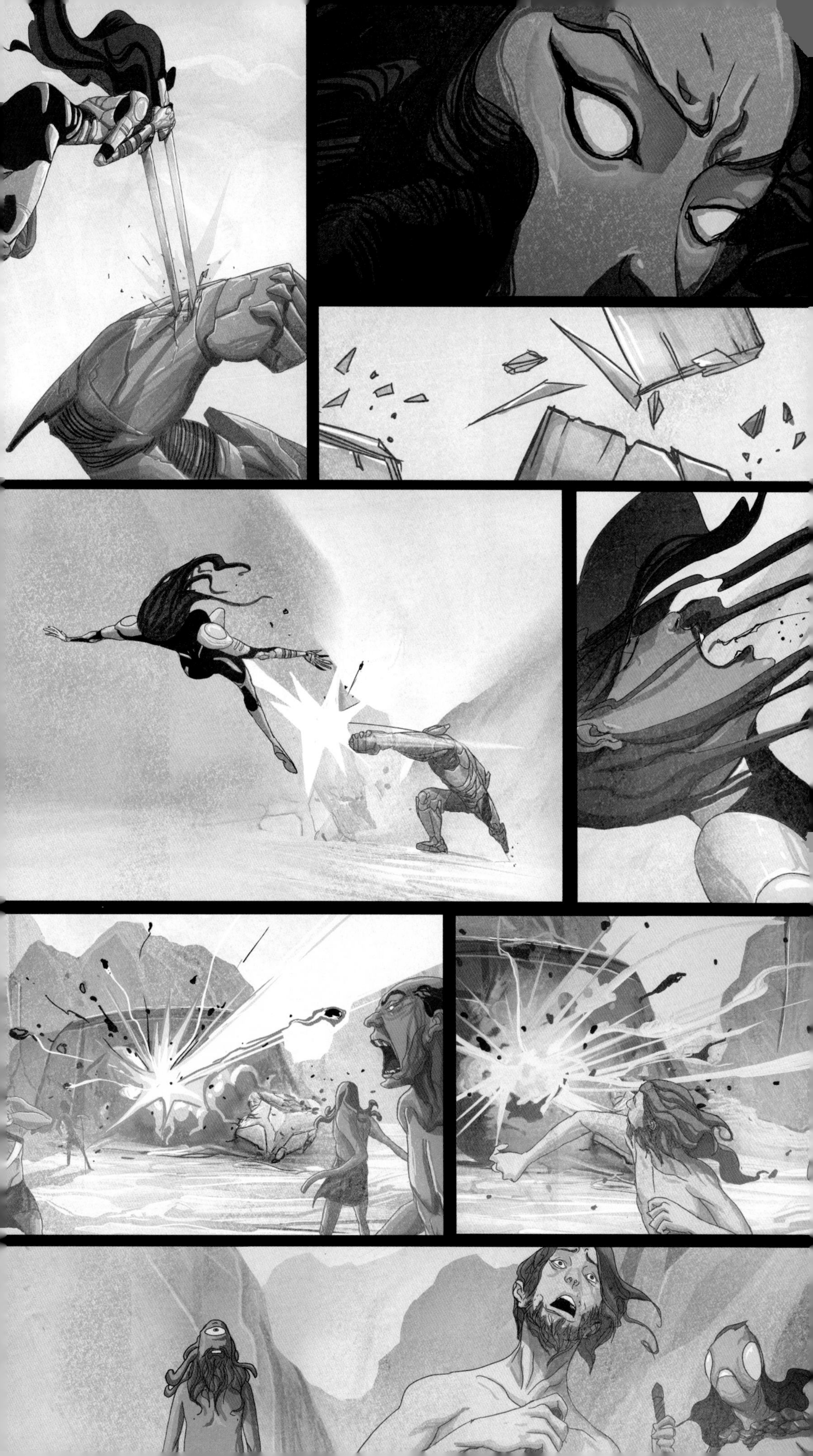

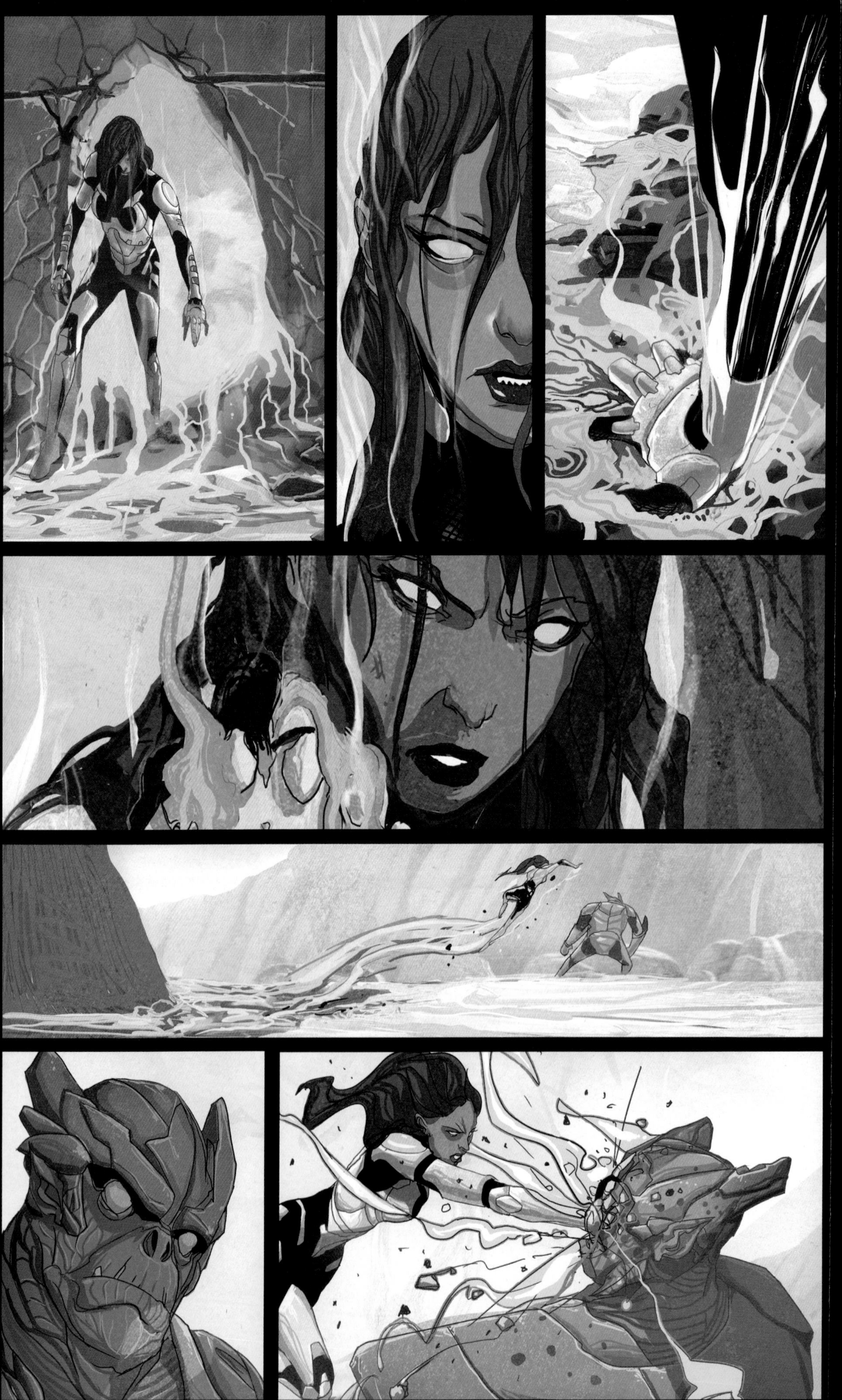

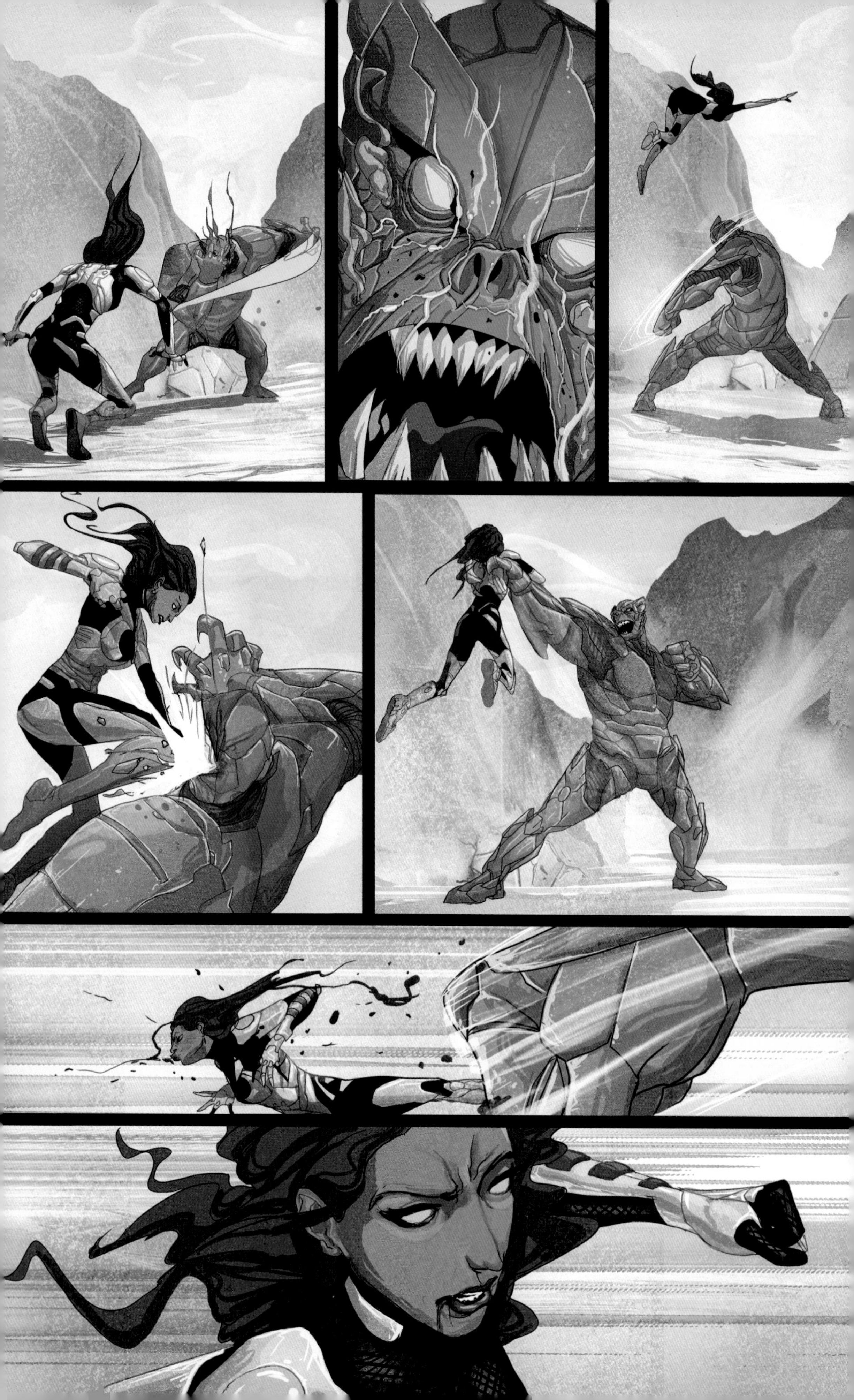

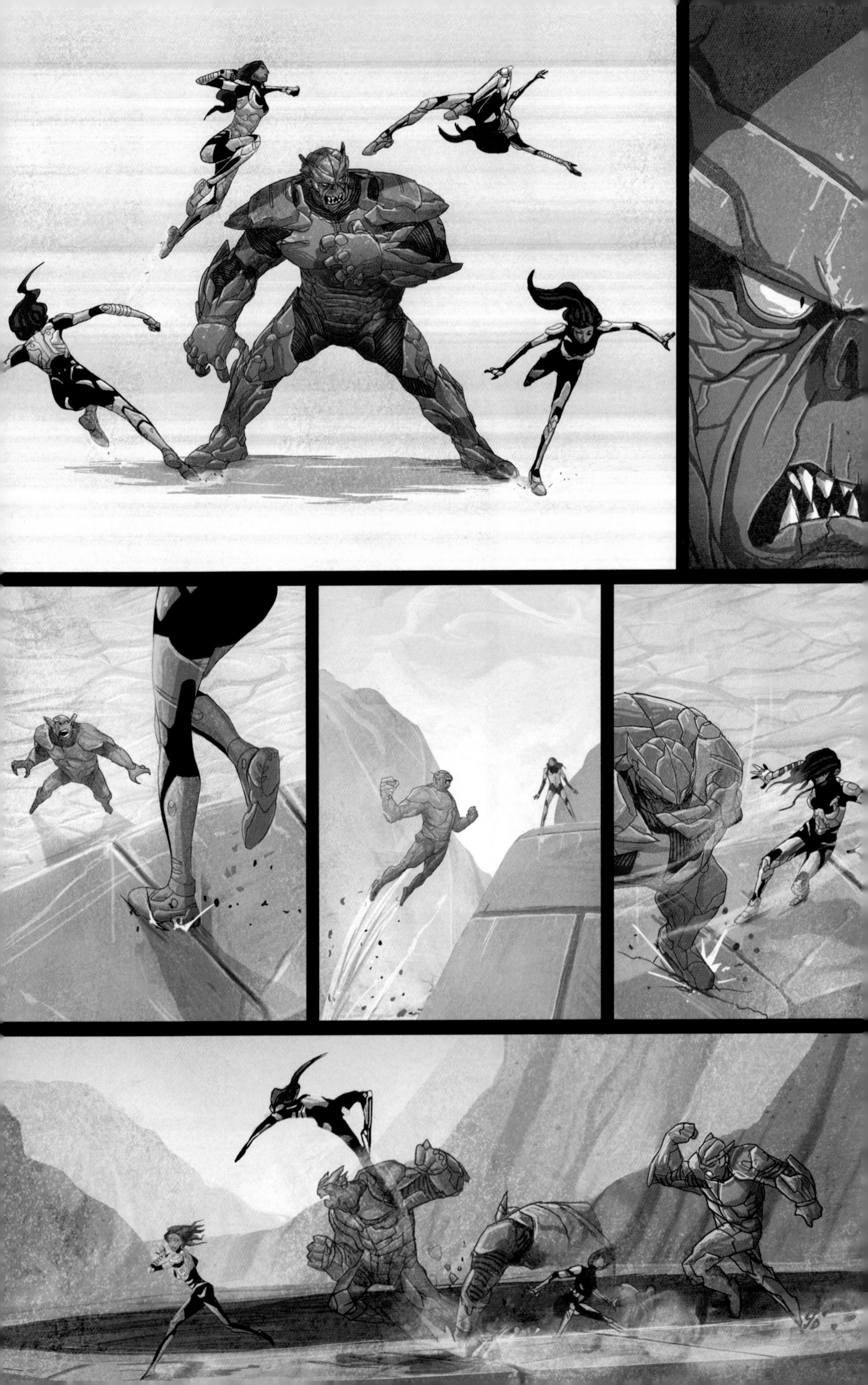

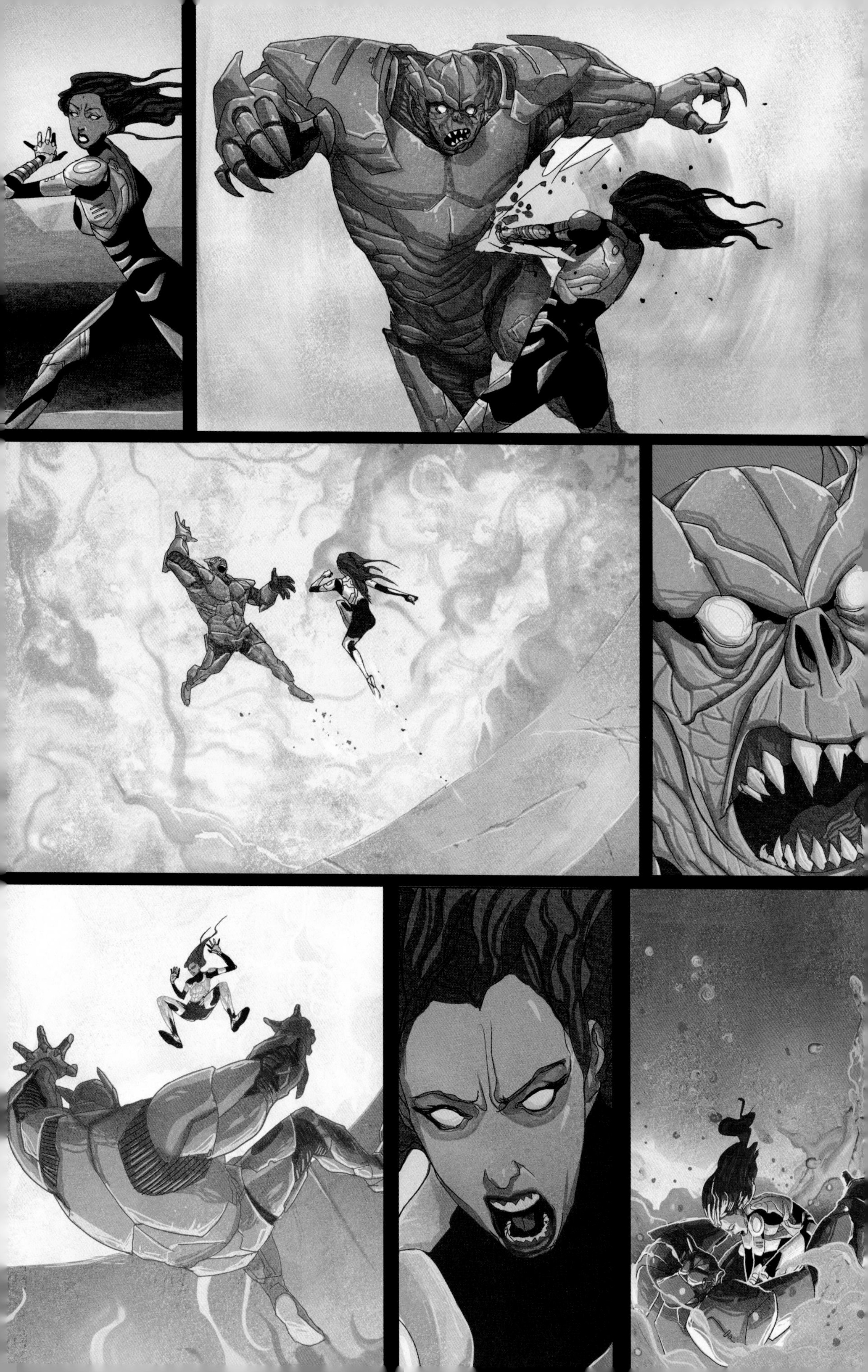

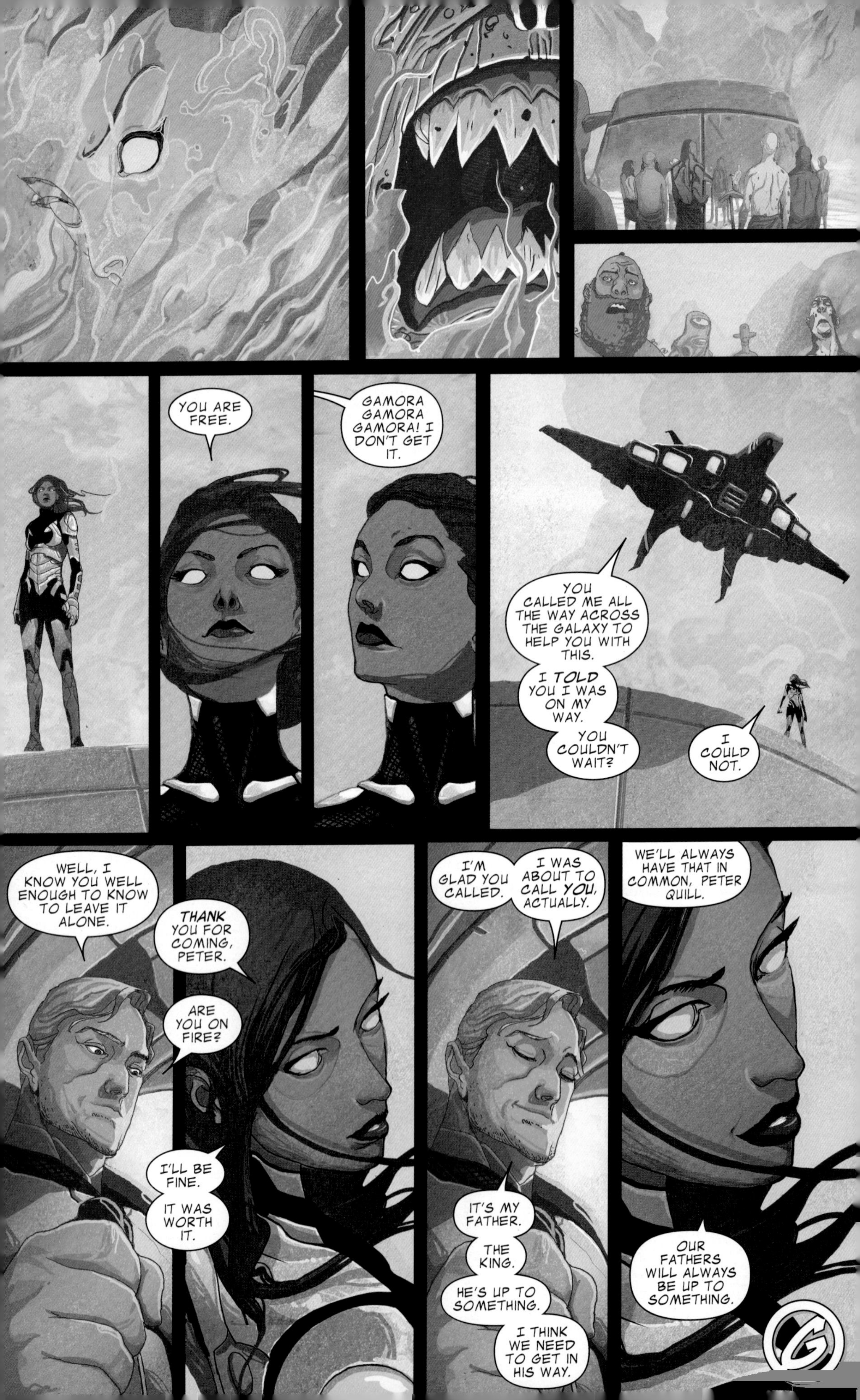
YOU ARE FREE.
GAMORA GAMORA GAMORA! I DON'T GET IT.
YOU CALLED ME ALL THE WAY ACROSS THE GALAXY TO HELP YOU WITH THIS.
I TOLD YOU I WAS ON MY WAY.
YOU COULDN'T WAIT?
I COULD NOT.
WELL, I KNOW YOU WELL ENOUGH TO KNOW TO LEAVE IT ALONE.
THANK YOU FOR COMING, PETER.
ARE YOU ON FIRE?
I'LL BE FINE.
IT WAS WORTH IT.
I'M GLAD YOU CALLED.
I WAS ABOUT TO CALL YOU, ACTUALLY.
IT'S MY FATHER.
THE KING.
HE'S UP TO SOMETHING.
I THINK WE NEED TO GET IN HIS WAY.
WE'LL ALWAYS HAVE THAT IN COMMON, PETER QUILL.
OUR FATHERS WILL ALWAYS BE UP TO SOMETHING.

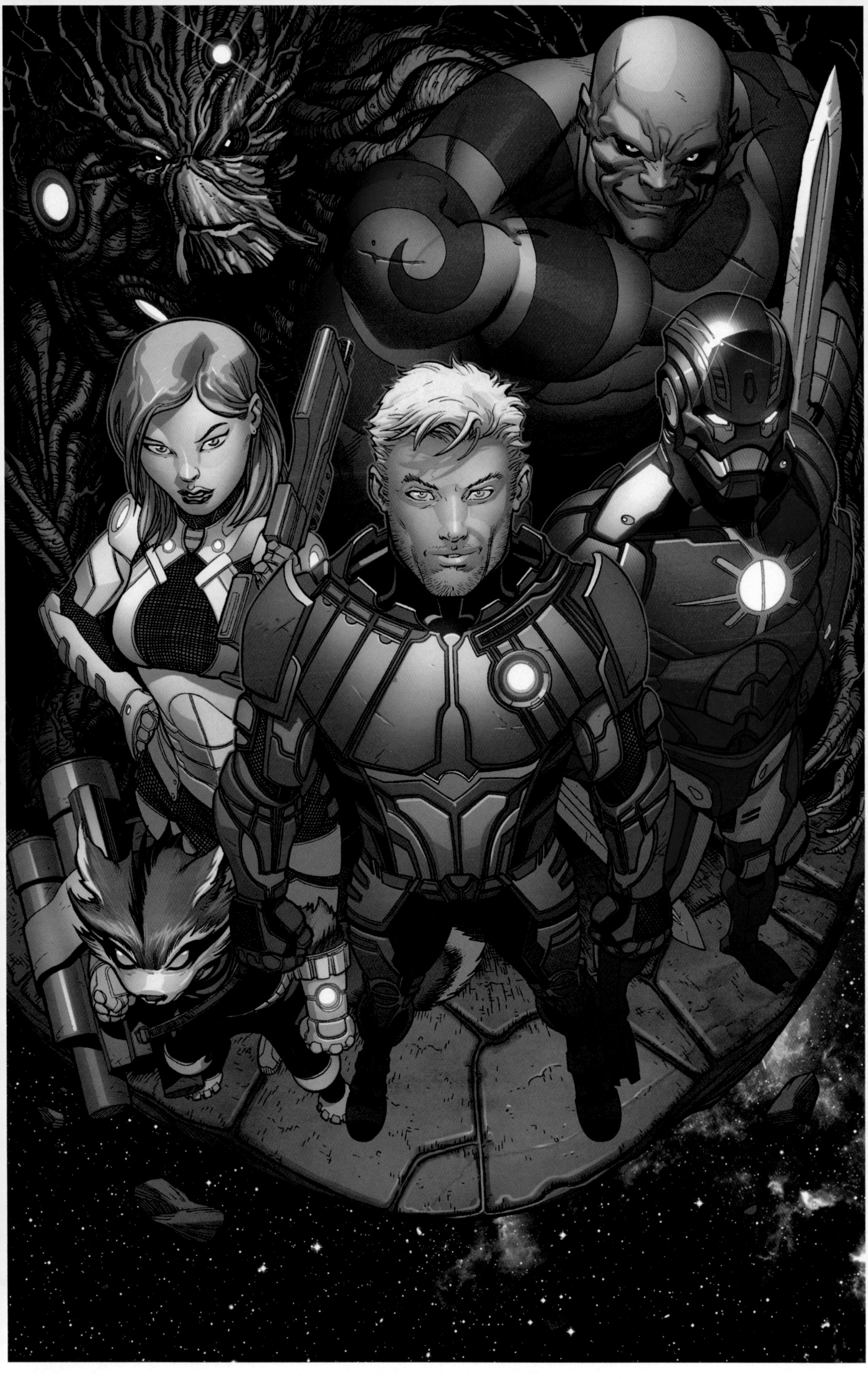

#*0.1* VARIANT BY ED MCGUINNESS & MARTE GRACIA

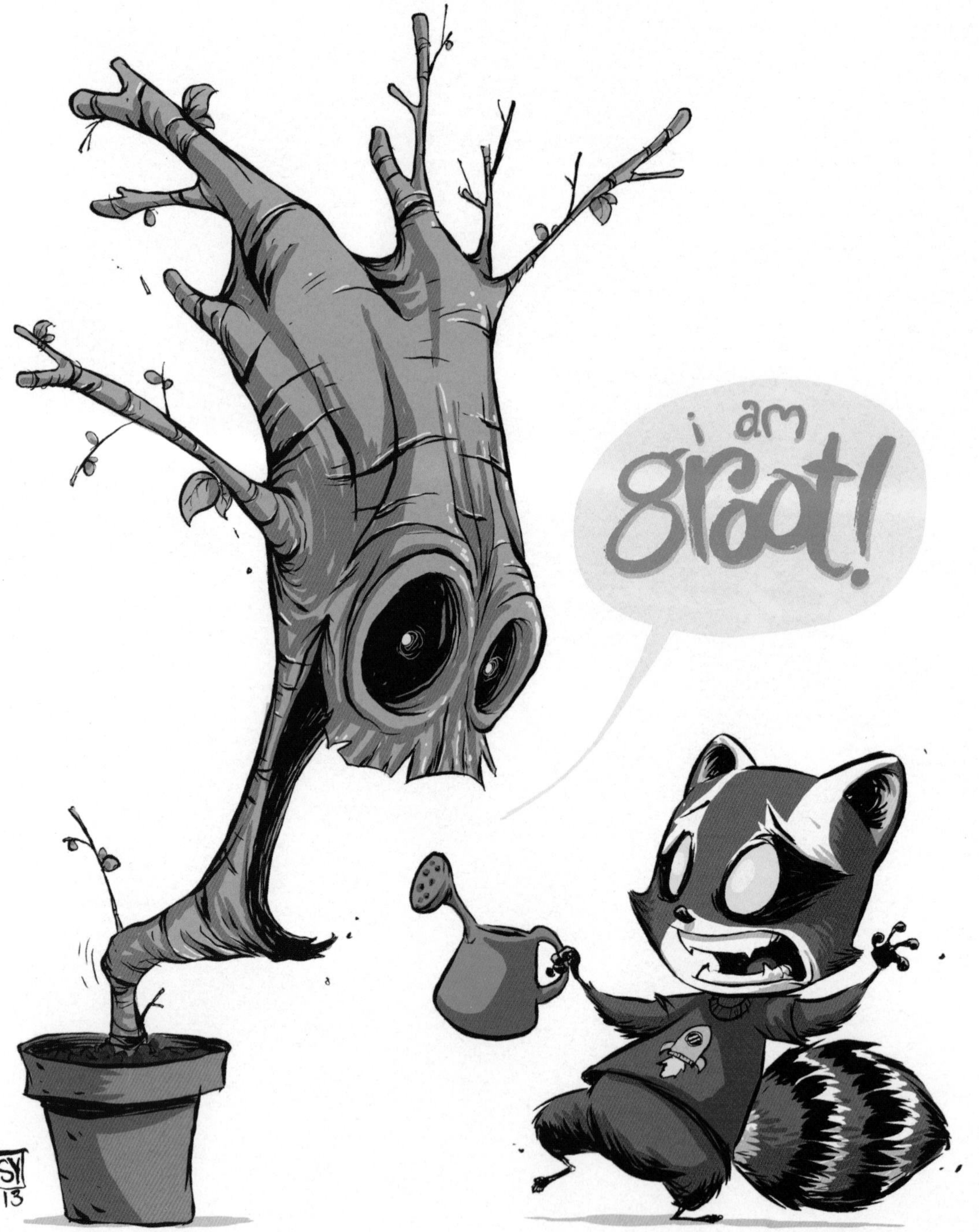
i am groot!
SY
13

#1 **VARIANT** BY SKOTTIE YOUNG

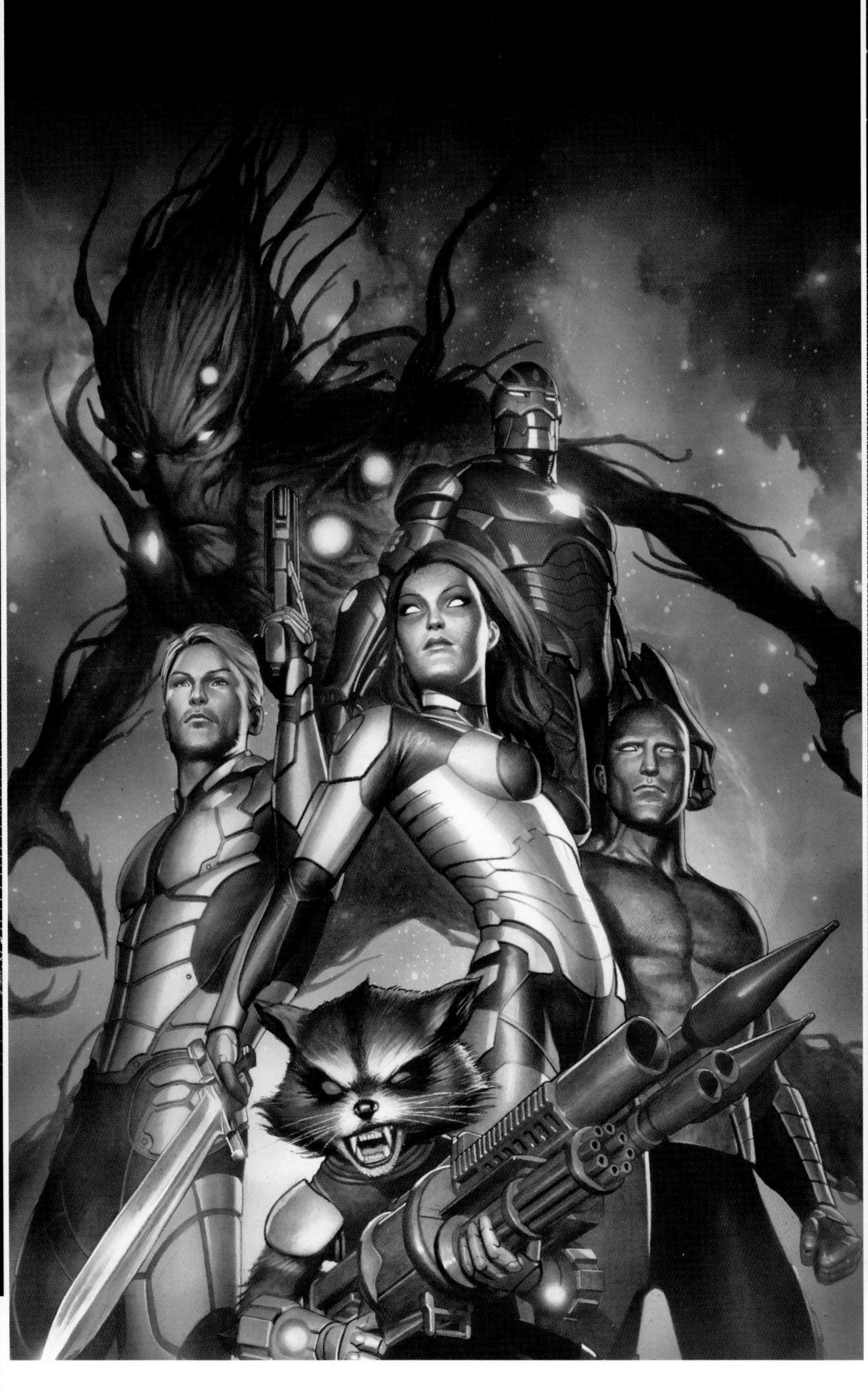

#*1* LIMITED EDITION COMIX VARIANT BY ADI GRANOV

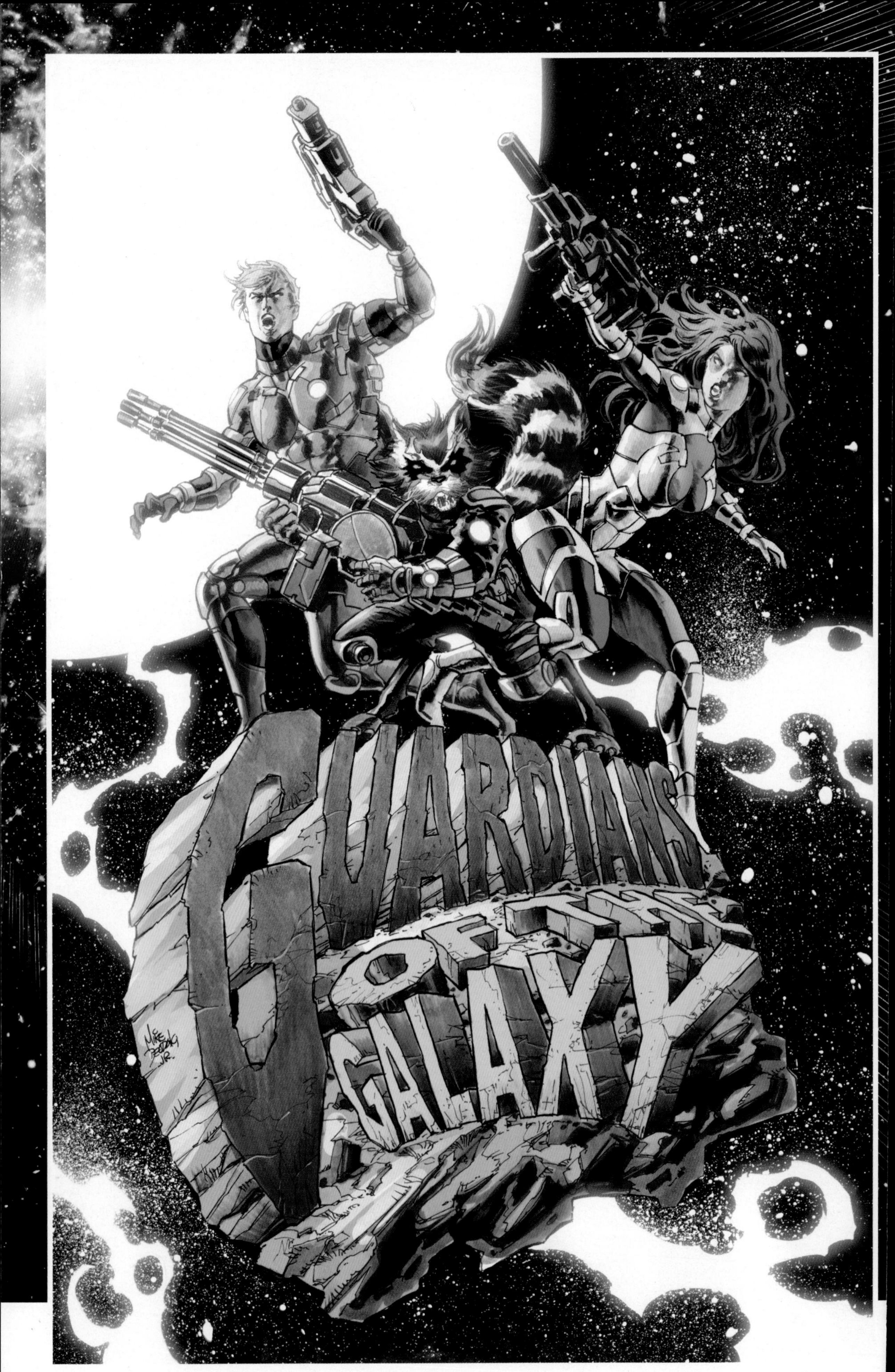
GUARDIANS OF THE GALAXY
MIKE DEODATO JR.

***#1* MILE HIGH COMICS VARIANT** BY MIKE DEODATO & RAIN BEREDO

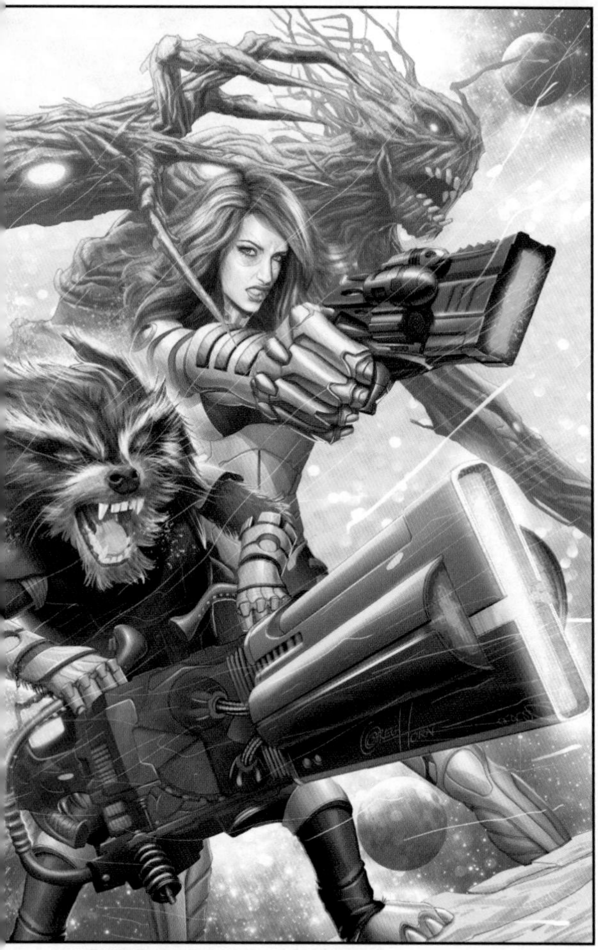

#1 THIRD EYE COMICS VARIANT BY GREG HORN

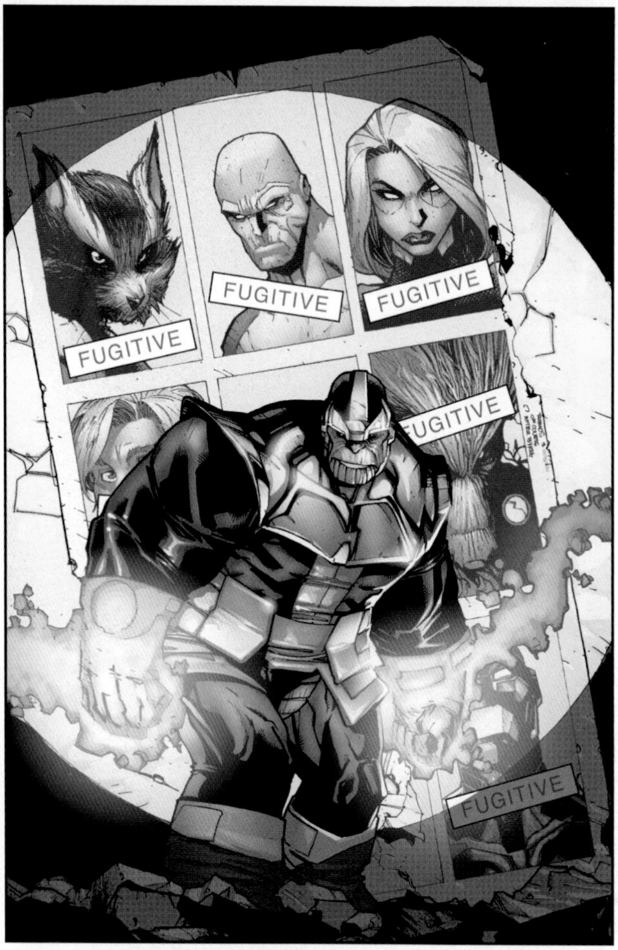
FUGITIVE
FUGITIVE
FUGITIVE
FUGITIVE
FUGITIVE

#1 PHANTOM VARIANT BY HUMBERTO RAMOS & EDGAR DELGADO

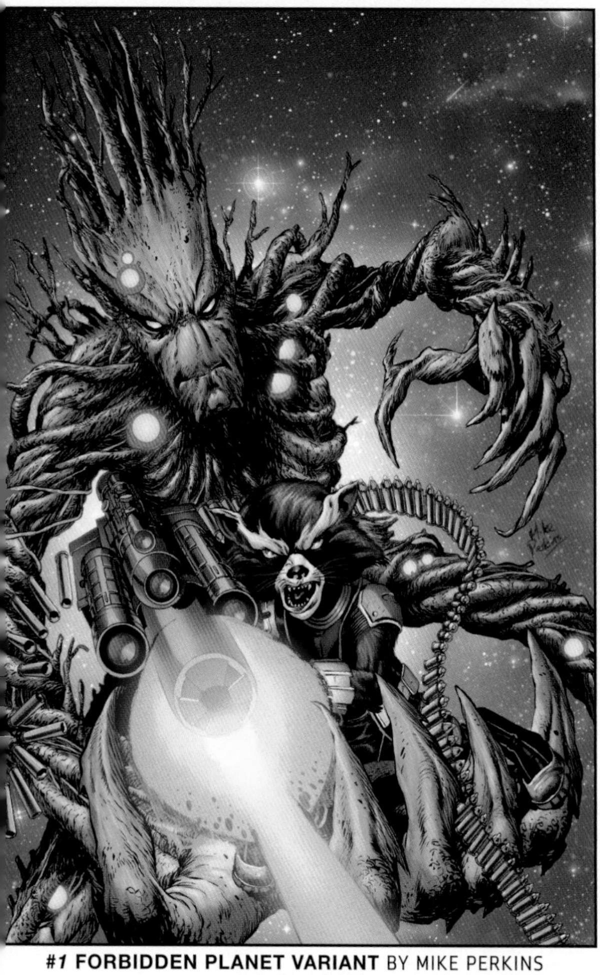

#1 FORBIDDEN PLANET VARIANT BY MIKE PERKINS & ANDY TROY

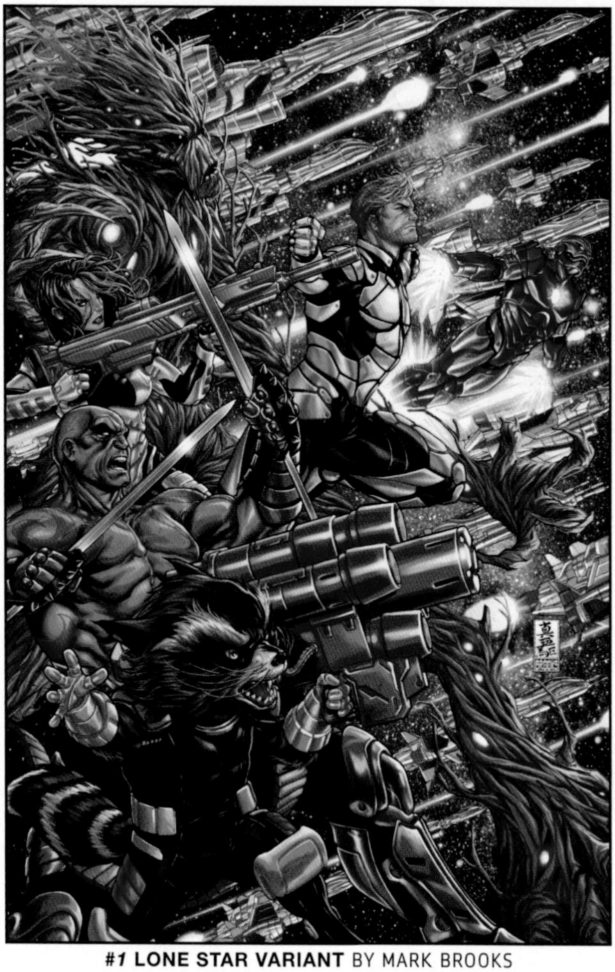

#1 LONE STAR VARIANT BY MARK BROOKS

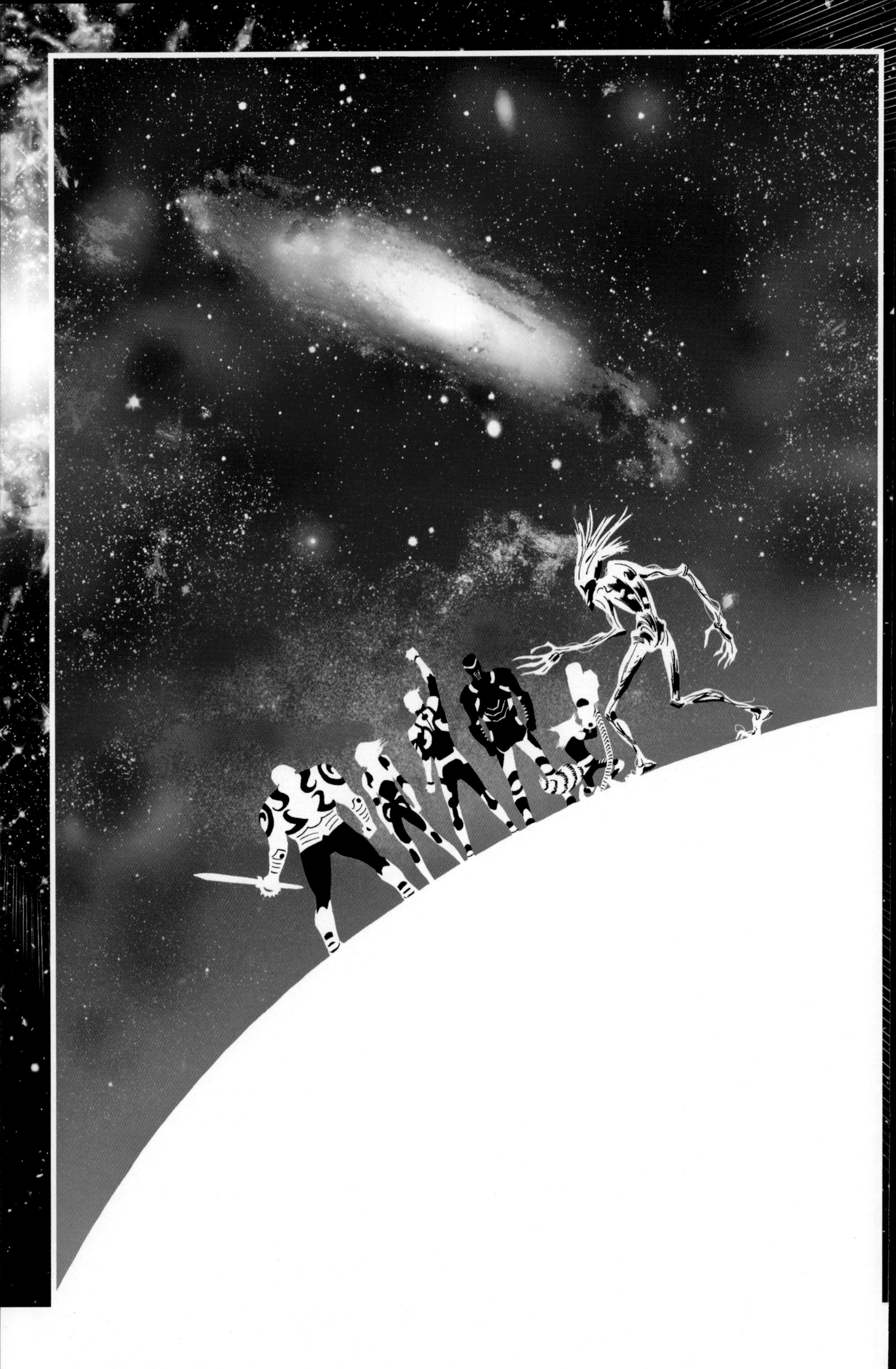

***#1* DETROIT COMIC BOOK STORES VARIANT** BY MARCOS MARTIN

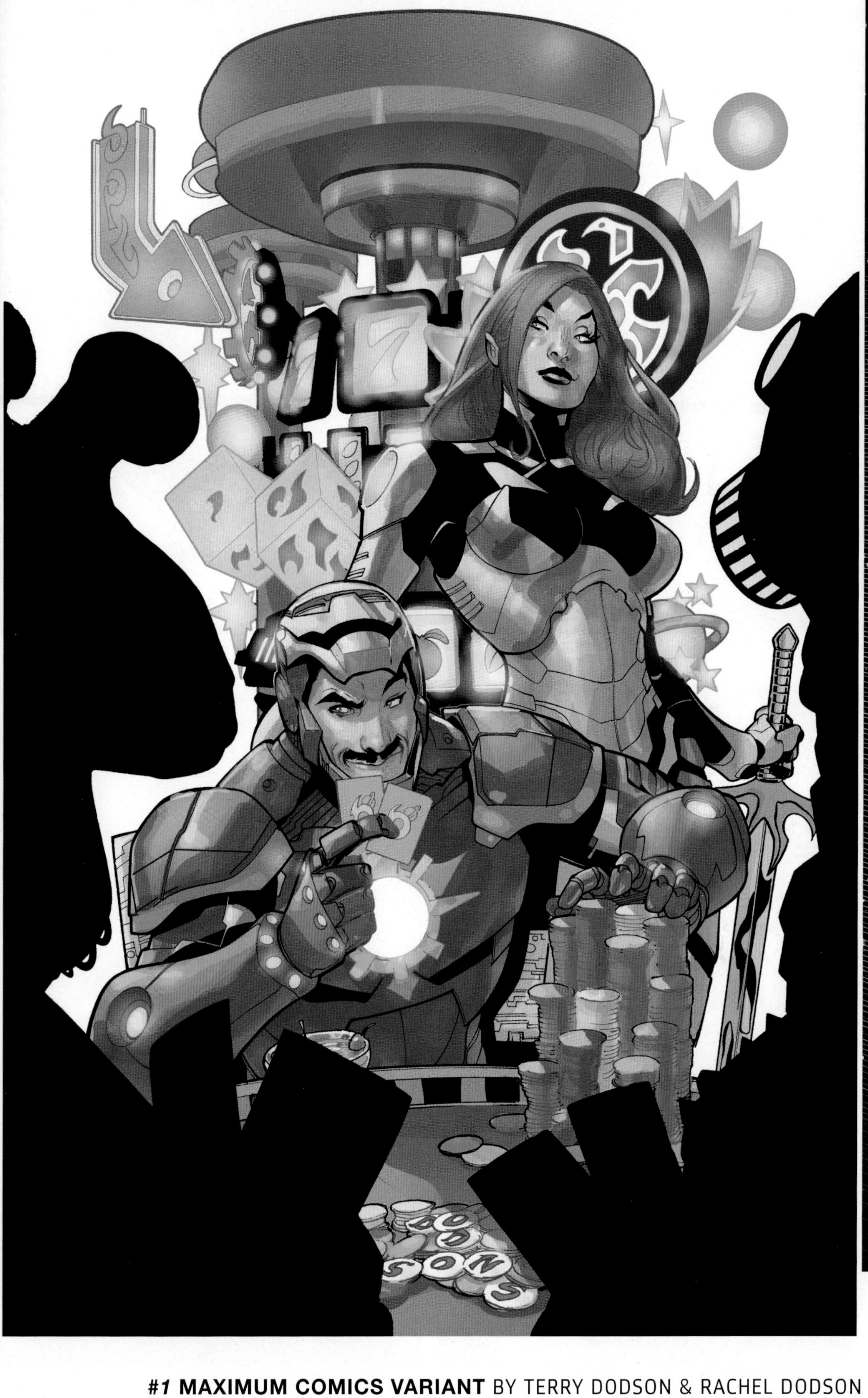

#1 MAXIMUM COMICS VARIANT BY TERRY DODSON & RACHEL DODSON

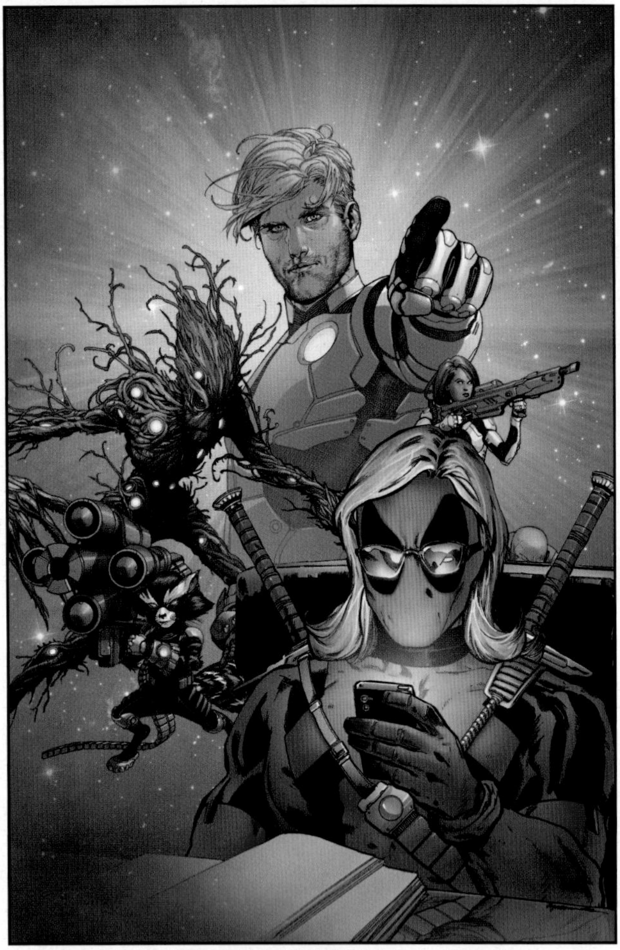

#1 DEADPOOL VARIANT BY PHIL JIMENEZ
& FRANK D'ARMATA

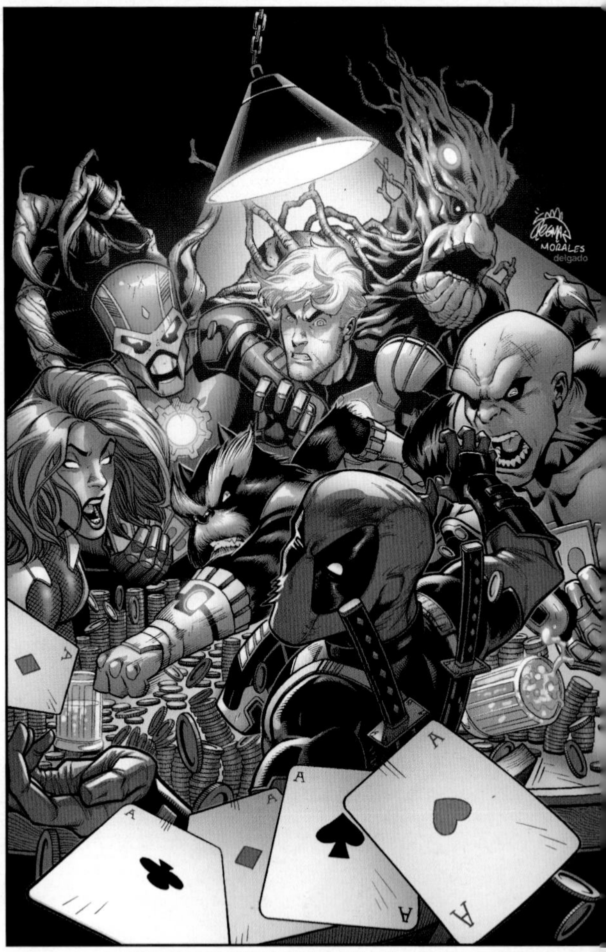

#1 HASTINGS VARIANT BY RYAN STEGMAN,
MARK MORALES & EDGAR DELGADO

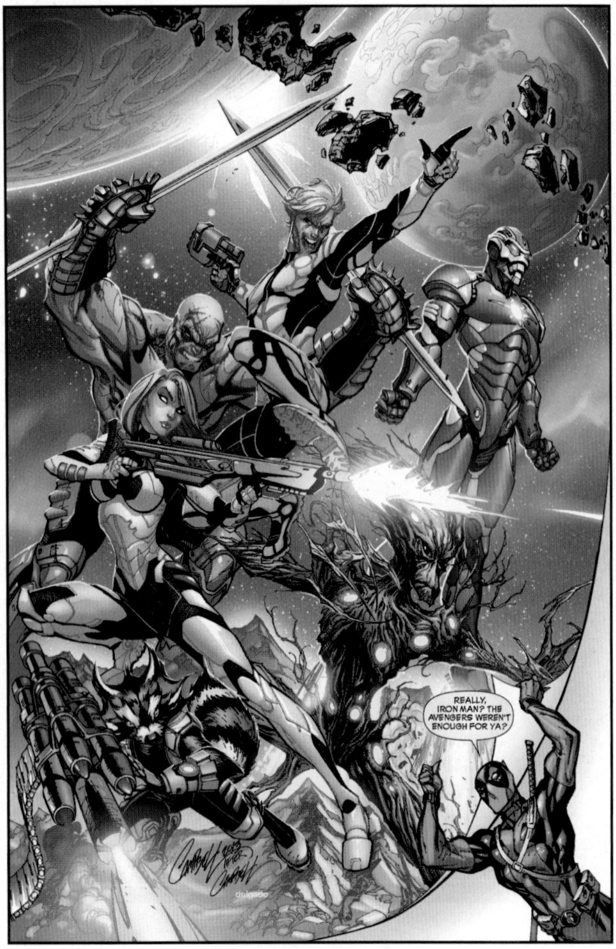
REALLY, IRON MAN? THE AVENGERS WEREN'T ENOUGH FOR YA?

#1 MIDTOWN VARIANT BY J. SCOTT CAMPBELL
& EDGAR DELGADO

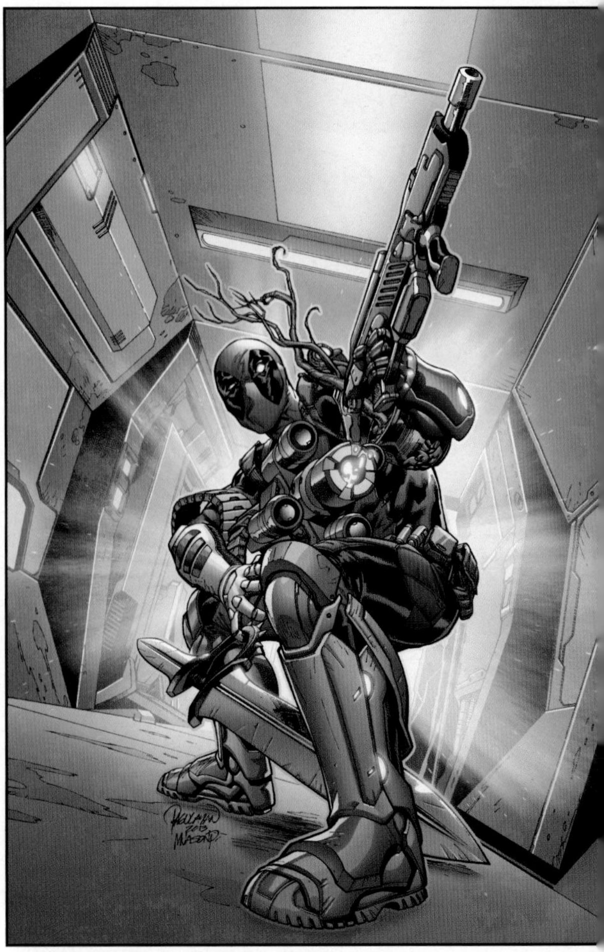

#1 DYNAMIC FORCES VARIANT BY CARLO PAGULAYAN,
JASON PAZ & GURIHIRU

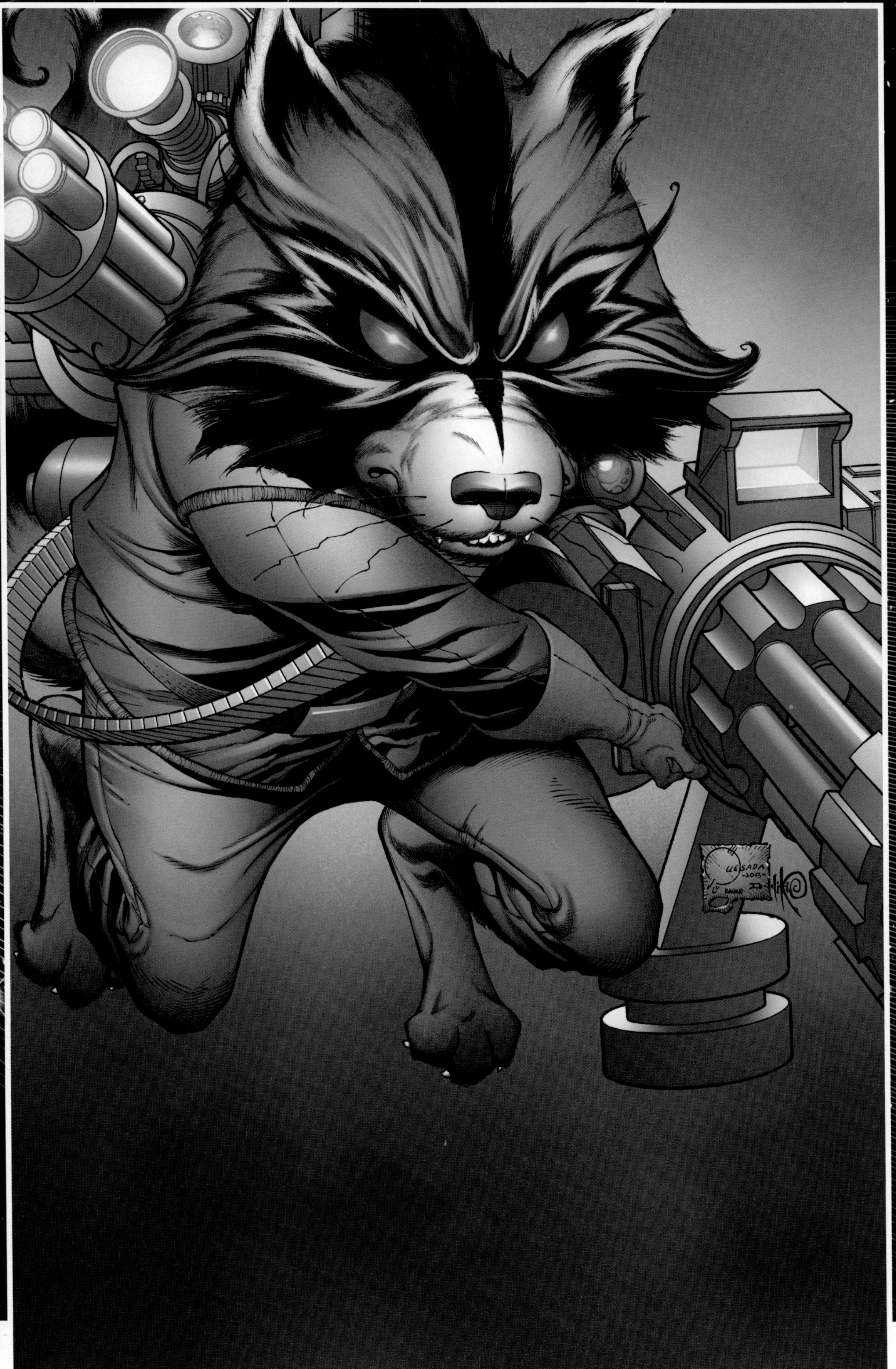

#1 VARIANT BY JOE QUESADA, DANNY MIKI & RICHARD ISANOVE

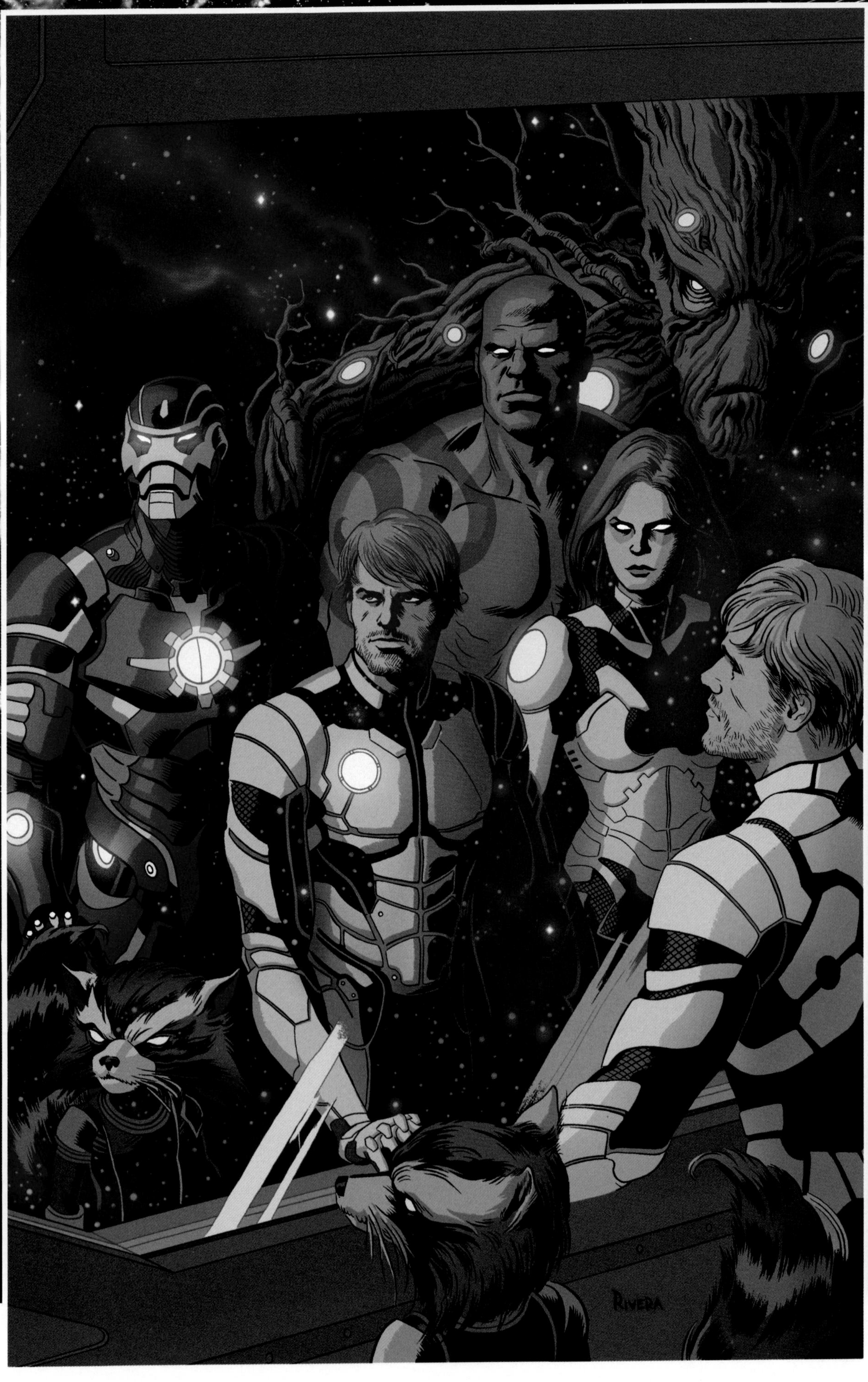
RIVERA

#2 VARIANT BY PAOLO RIVERA

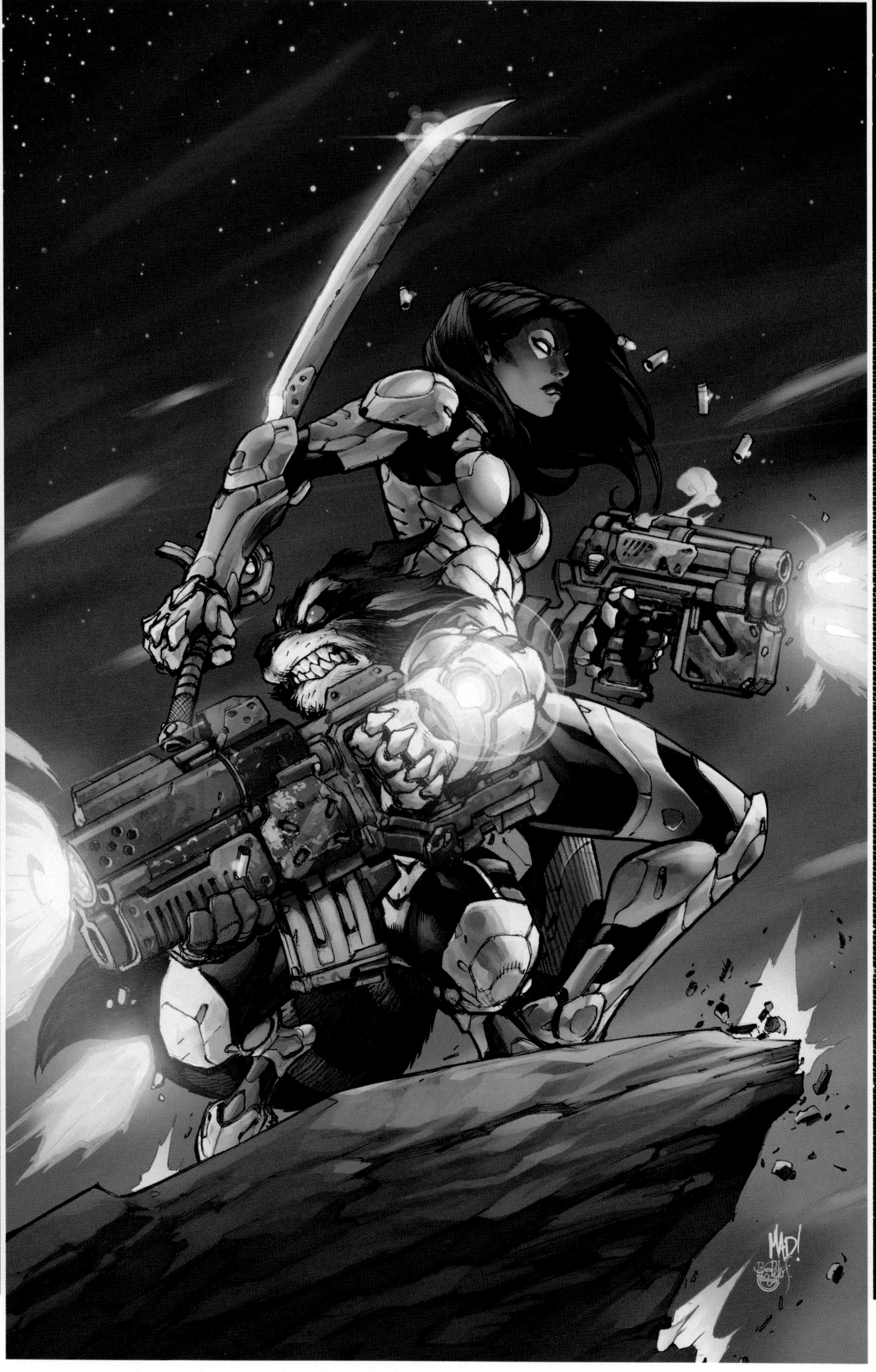

#2 VARIANT BY JOE MADUREIRA & PETER STEIGERWALD

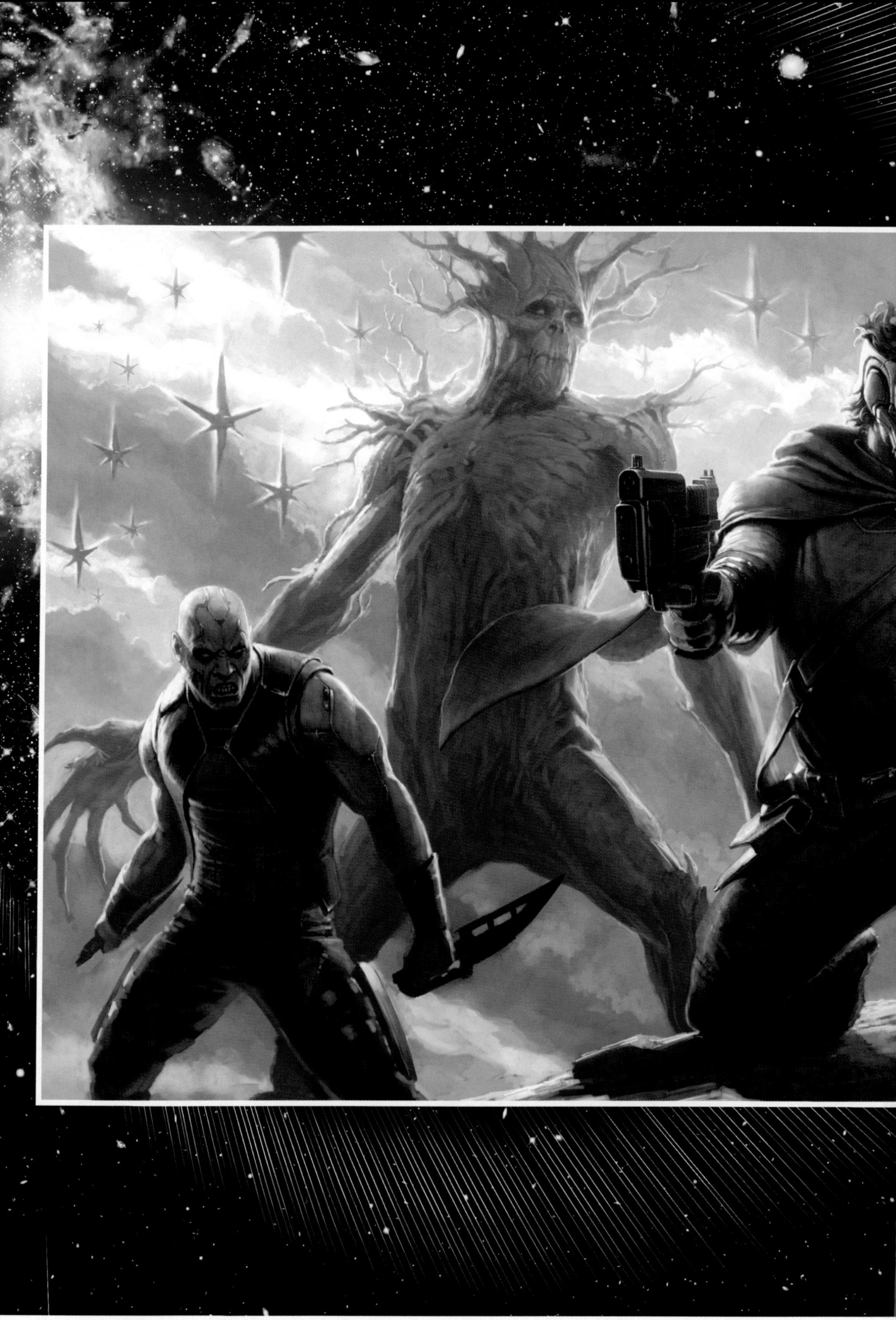

#2-4 COMBINED VARIANTS BY CHARLIE WEN

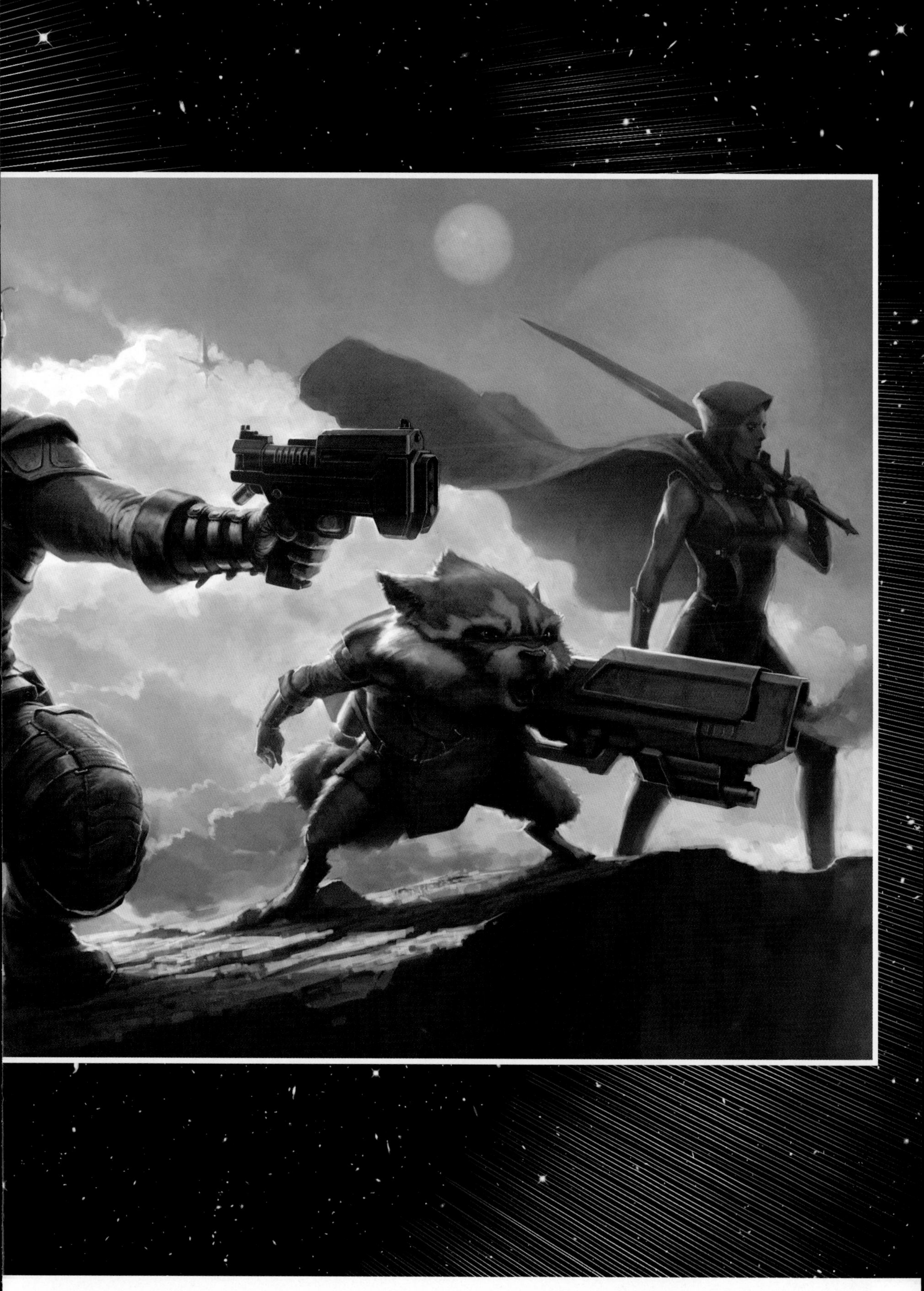

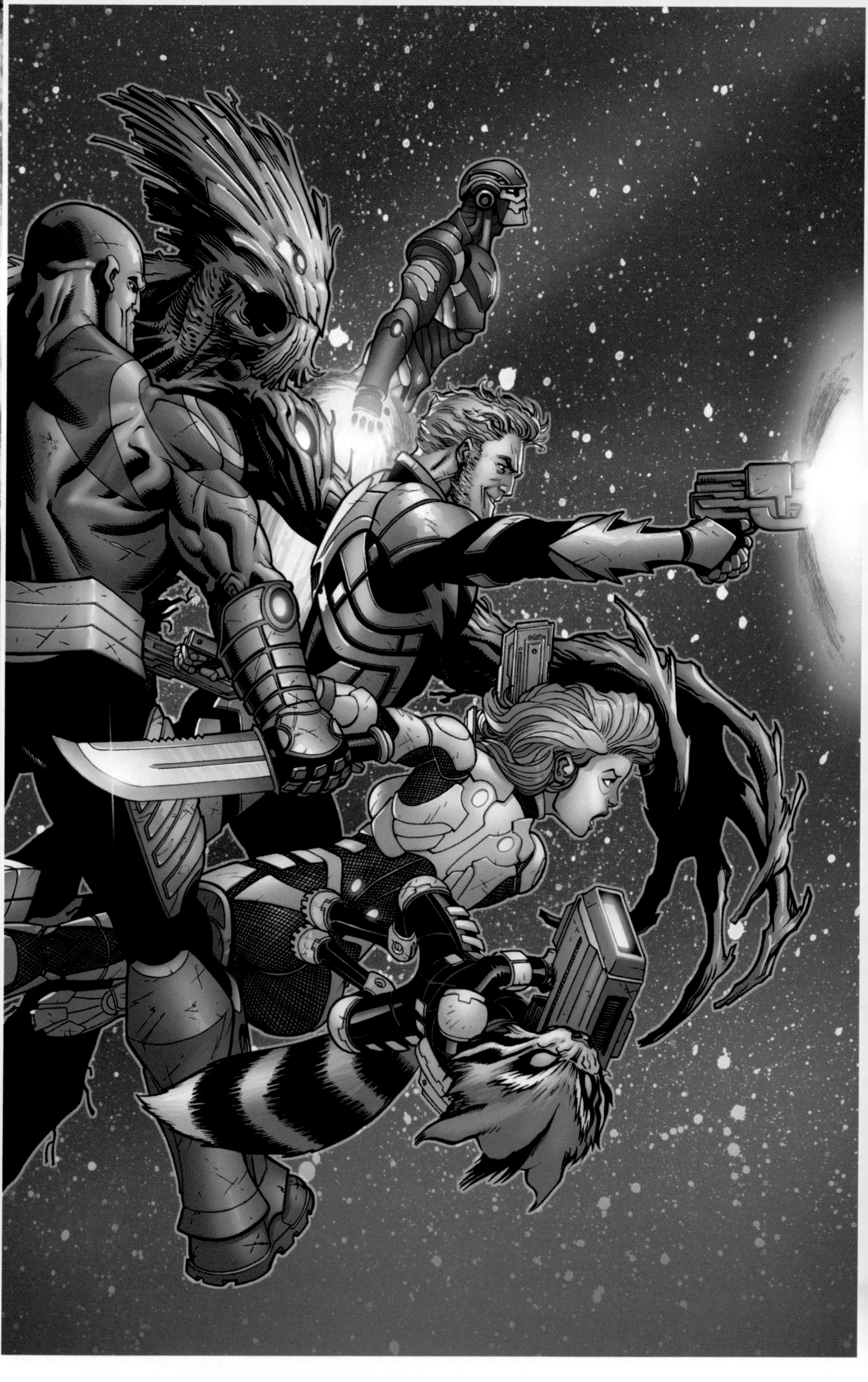

#3 VARIANT BY ED MCGUINNESS, DEXTER VINES & EDGAR DELGADO

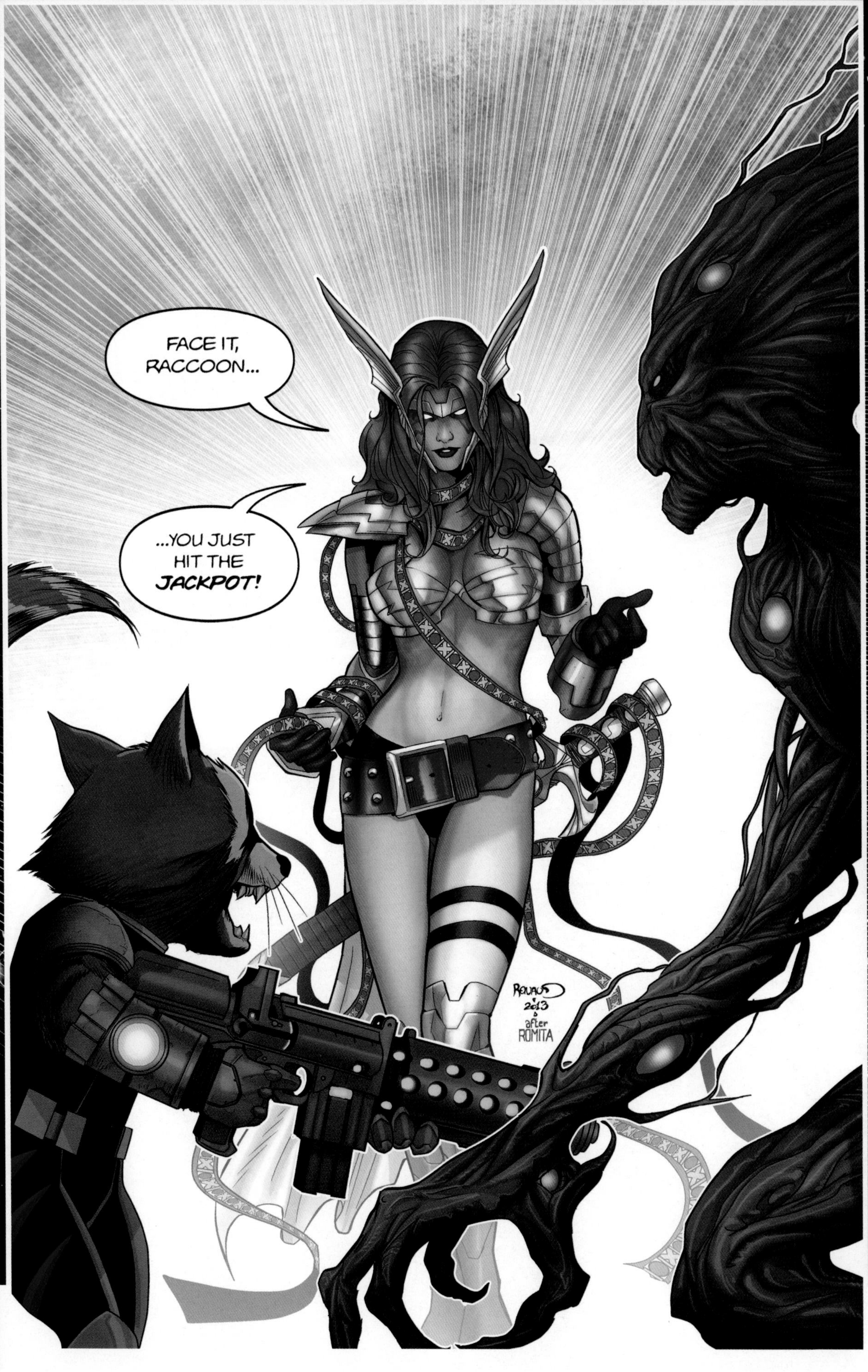
FACE IT, RACCOON...
...YOU JUST HIT THE JACKPOT!
RENAUD 2013 after ROMITA

#5 HEROES AREN'T HARD TO FIND VARIANT BY PAUL RENAUD

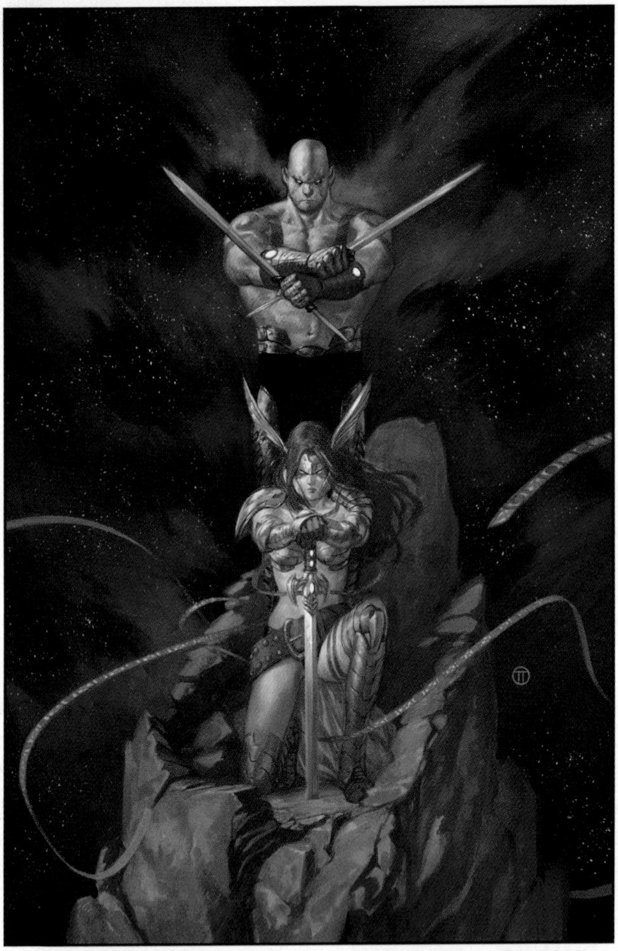

#5 DRAGON'S LAIR VARIANT BY JULIAN TOTINO TEDESCO

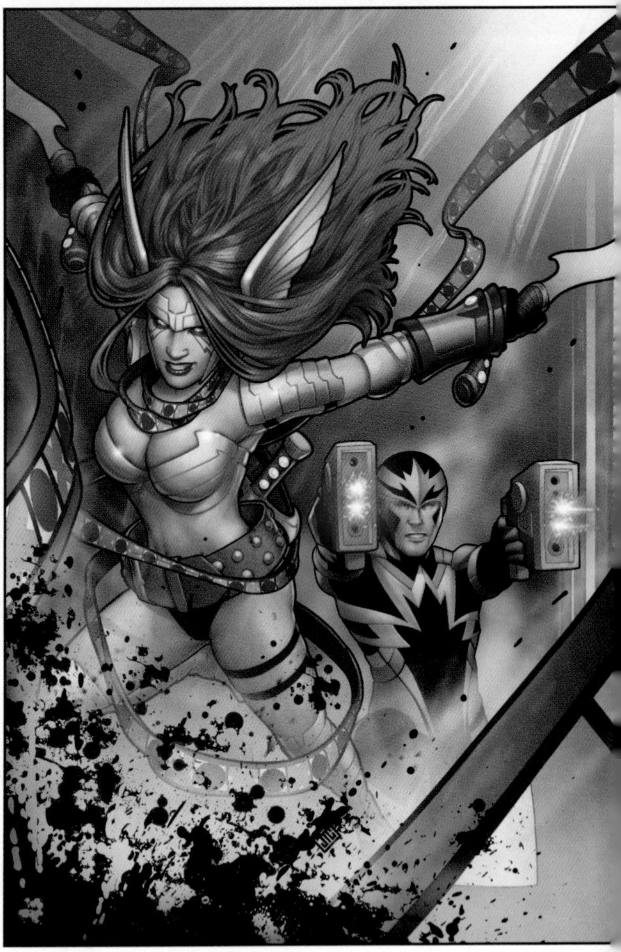

#5 HASTINGS VARIANT BY JOHN TYLER CHRISTOPHER

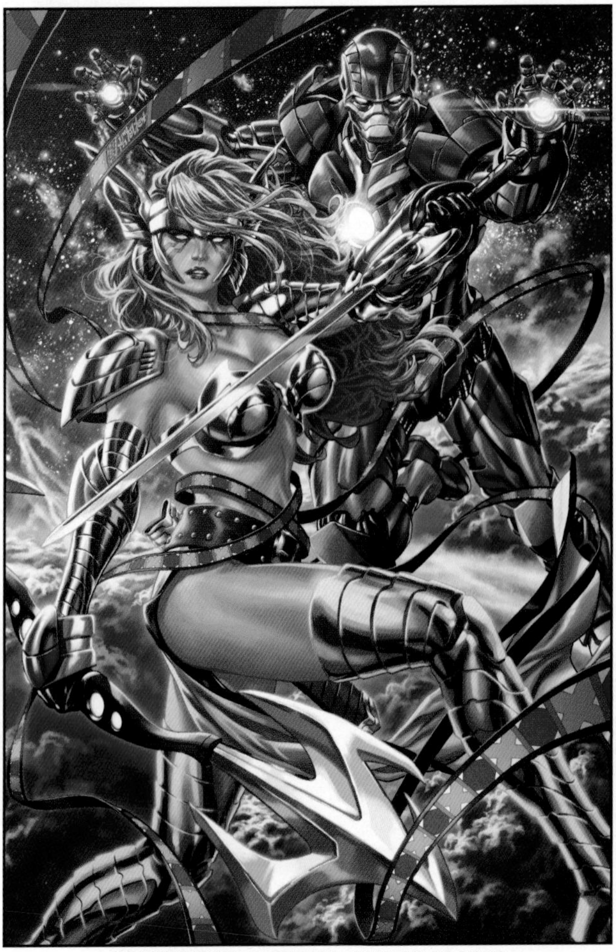

#5 MIDTOWN VARIANT BY MARK BROOKS

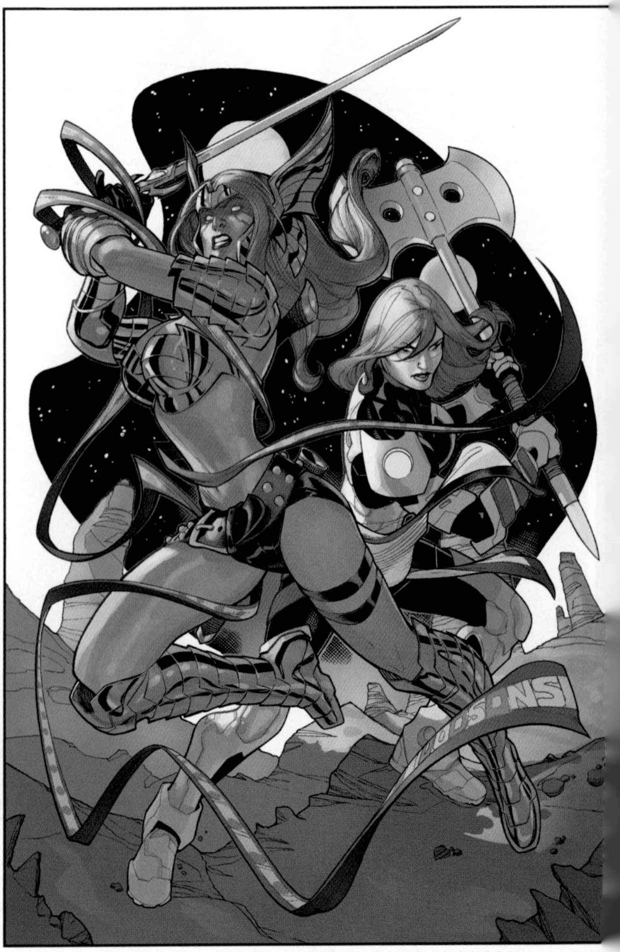

#5 MILE HIGH VARIANT BY TERRY DODSON
& RACHEL DODSON

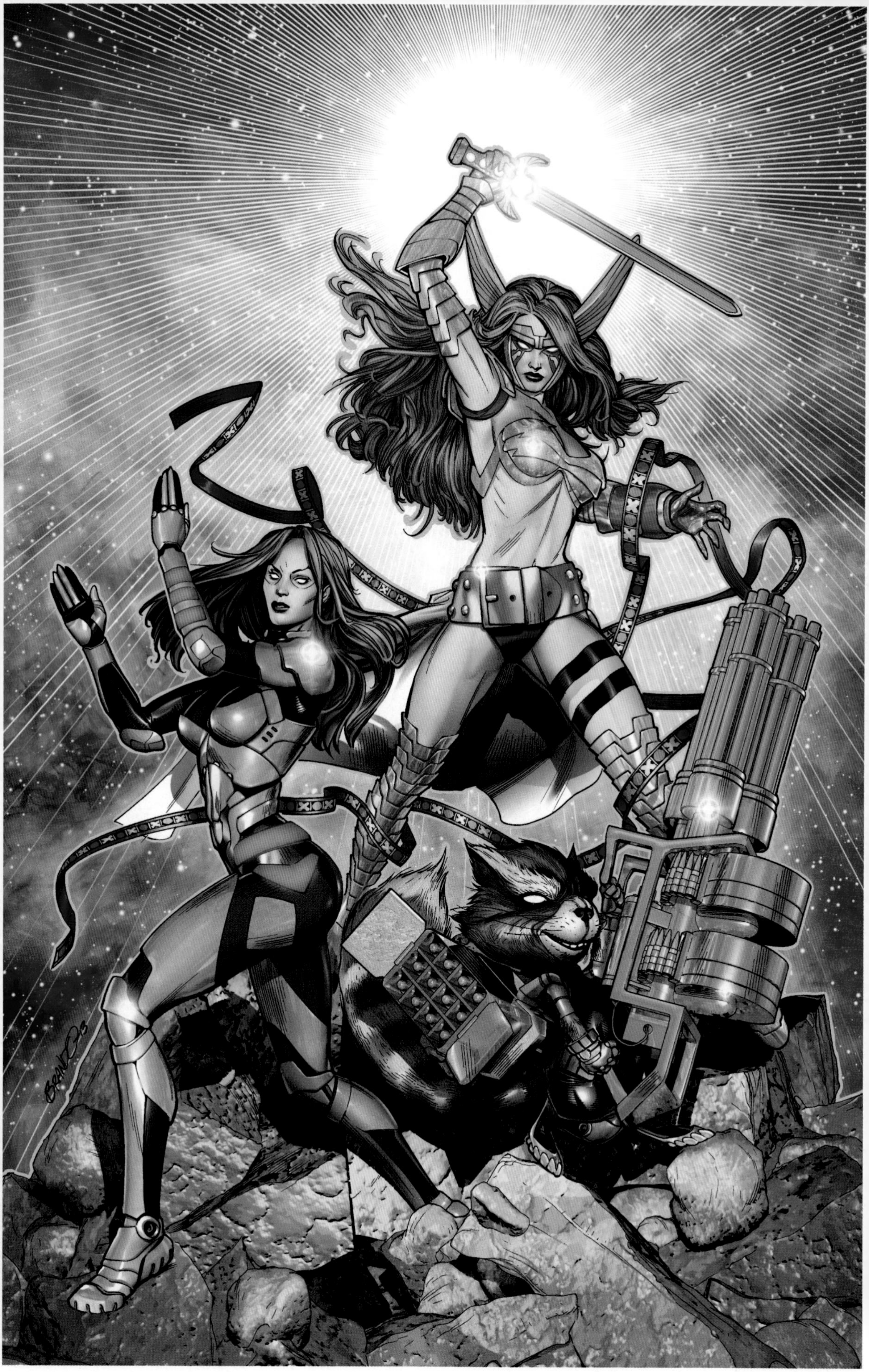

#5 FORBIDDEN PLANET VARIANT BY BRANDON PETERSON

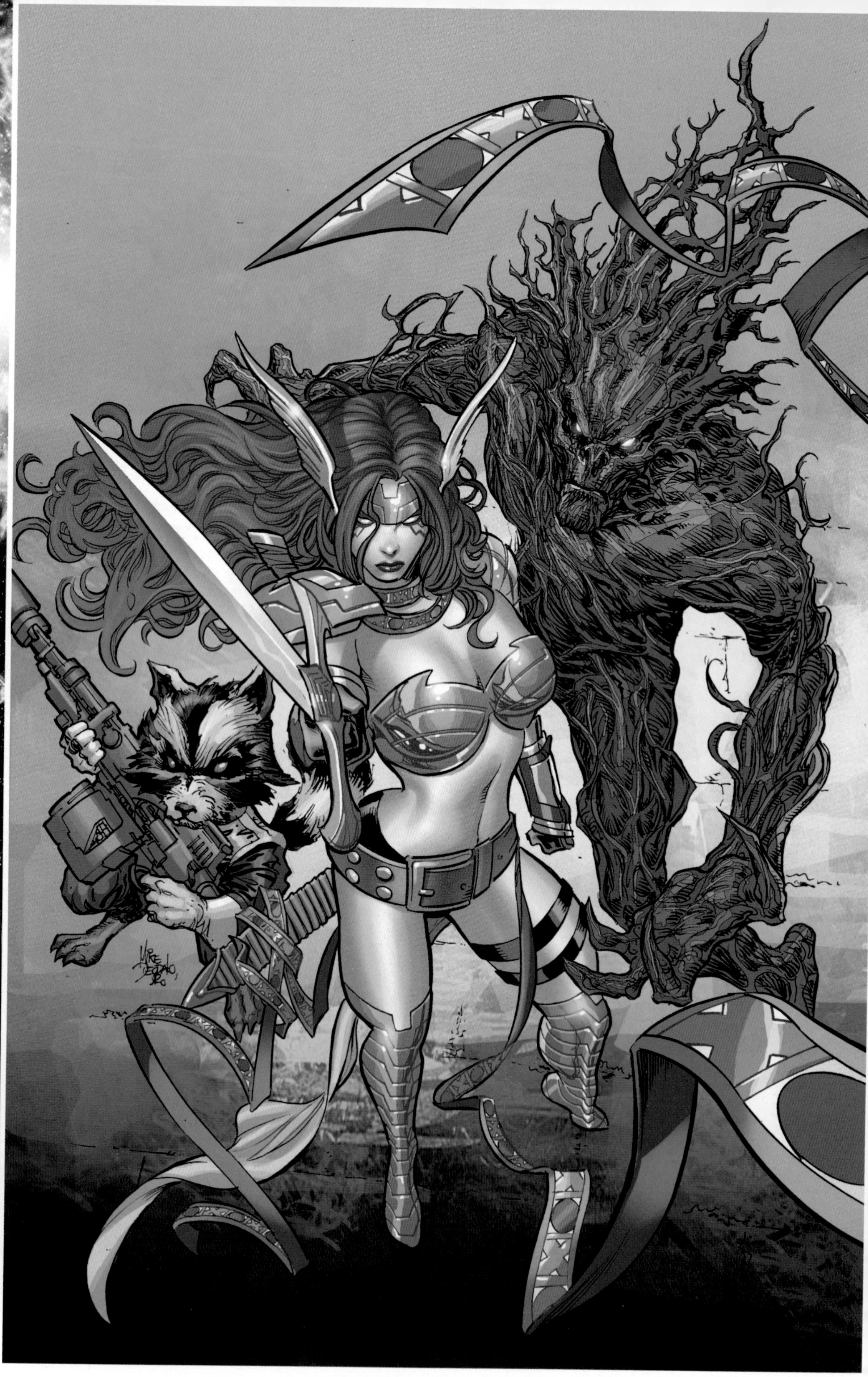

#5 DYNAMIC FORCES VARIANT BY MIKE DEODATO & JUSTIN PONSOR

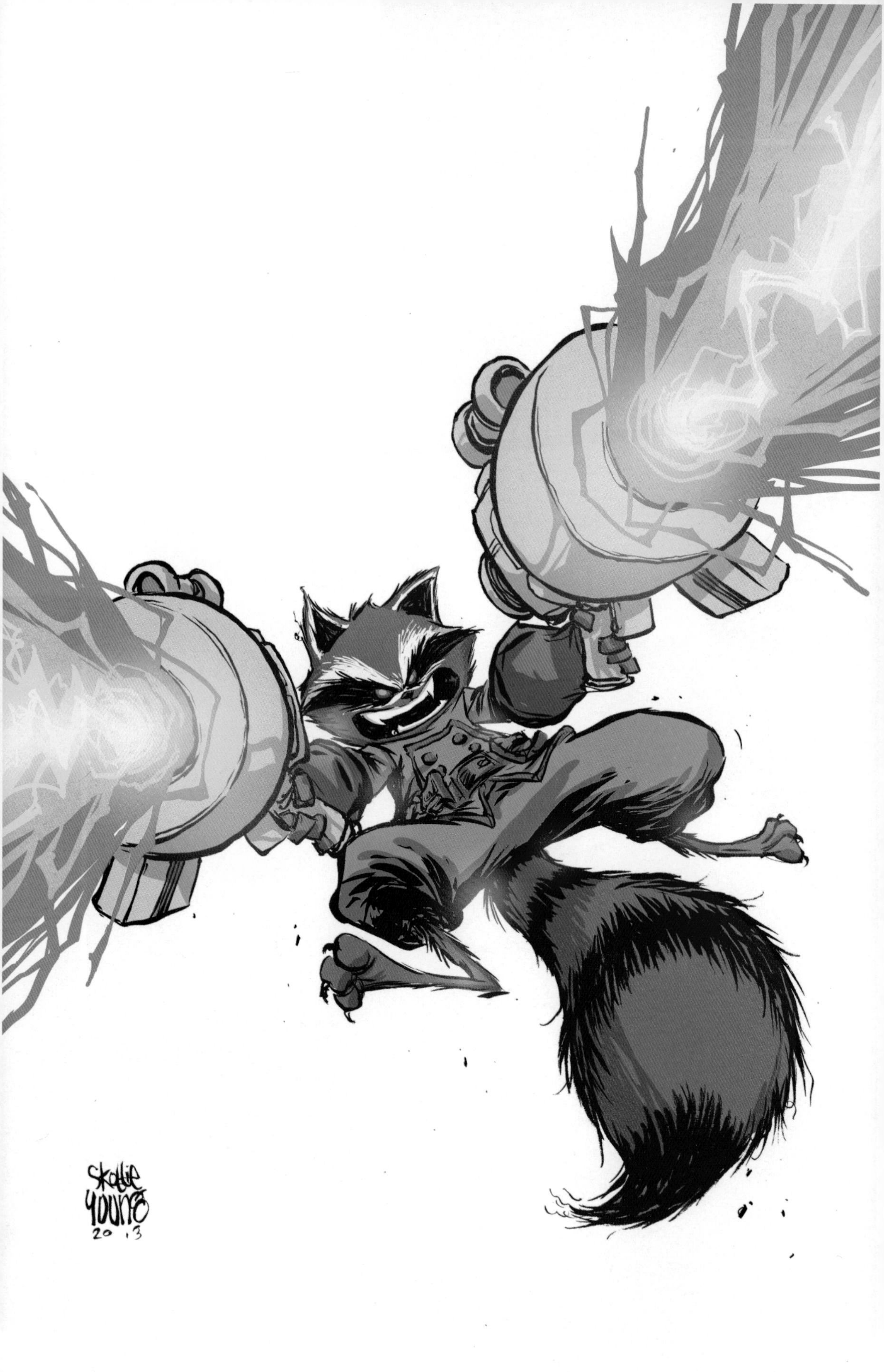
Skottie
Young
20 13

#7 VARIANT BY SKOTTIE YOUNG

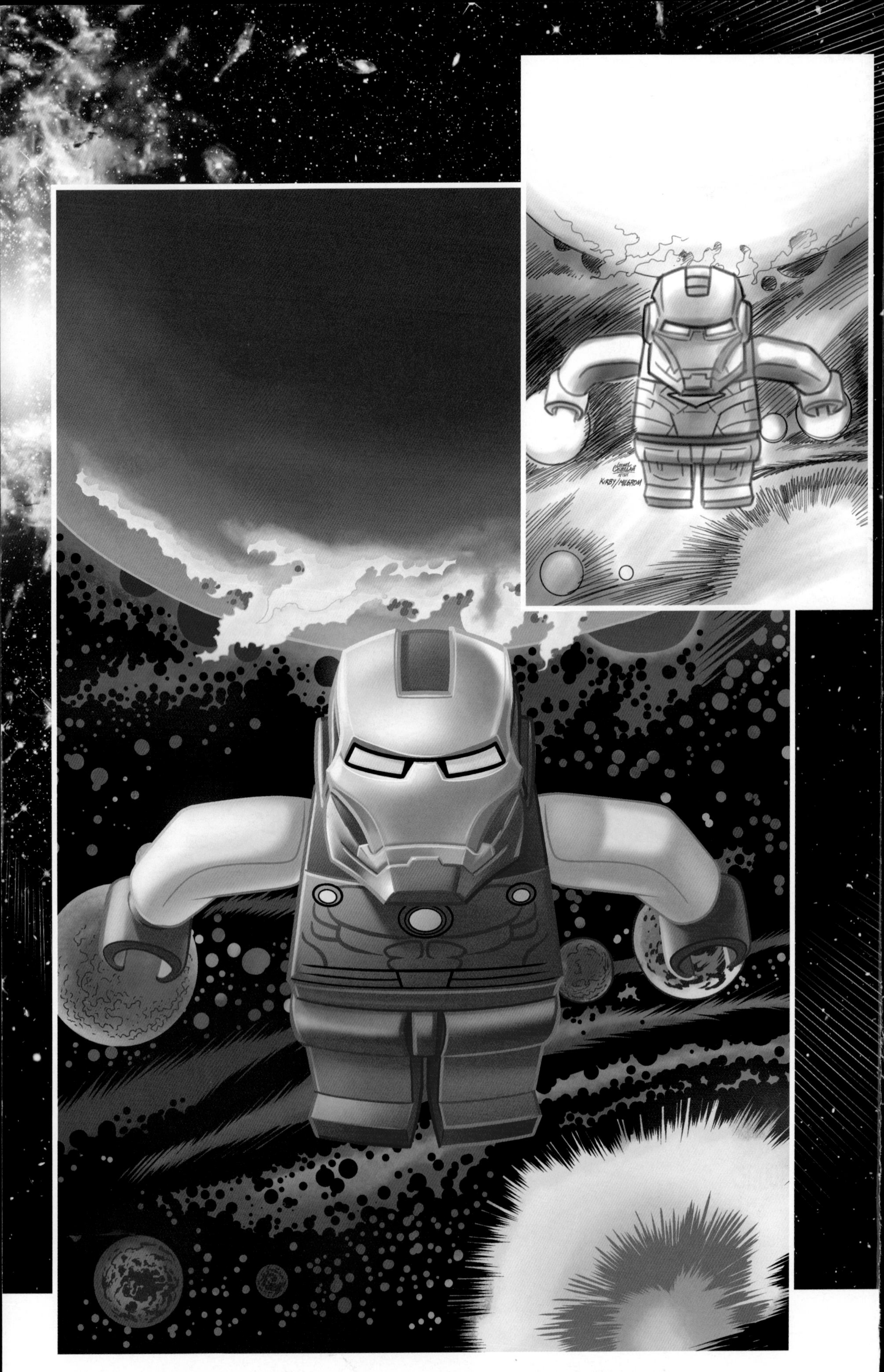
KIRBY/MILGROM

#5 LEGO VARIANT & LEGO SKETCH VARIANT BY LEONEL CASTELLANI

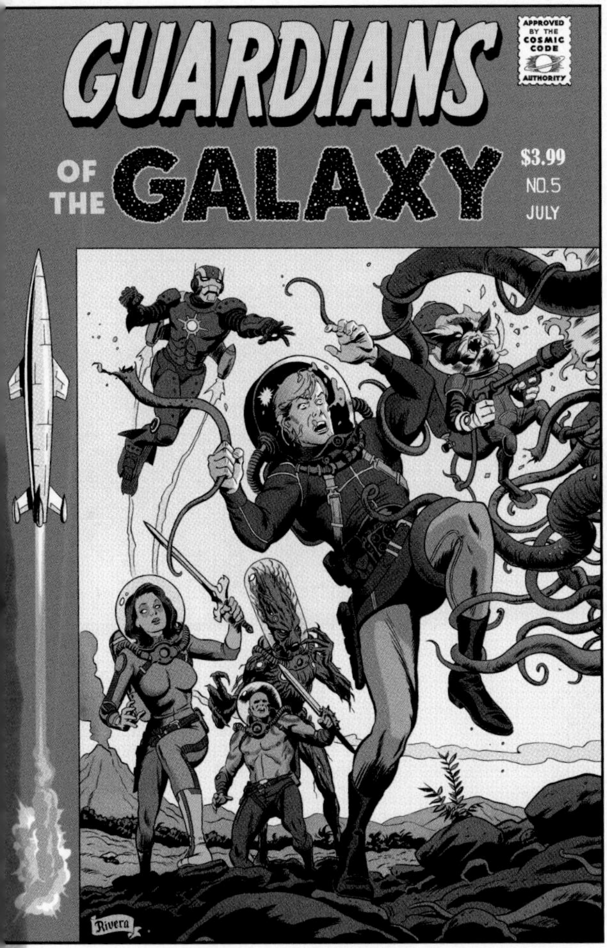

GUARDIANS
APPROVED BY THE COSMIC CODE AUTHORITY
OF THE GALAXY
$3.99
NO.5
JULY
Rivera

#5 VARIANT BY PAOLO RIVERA

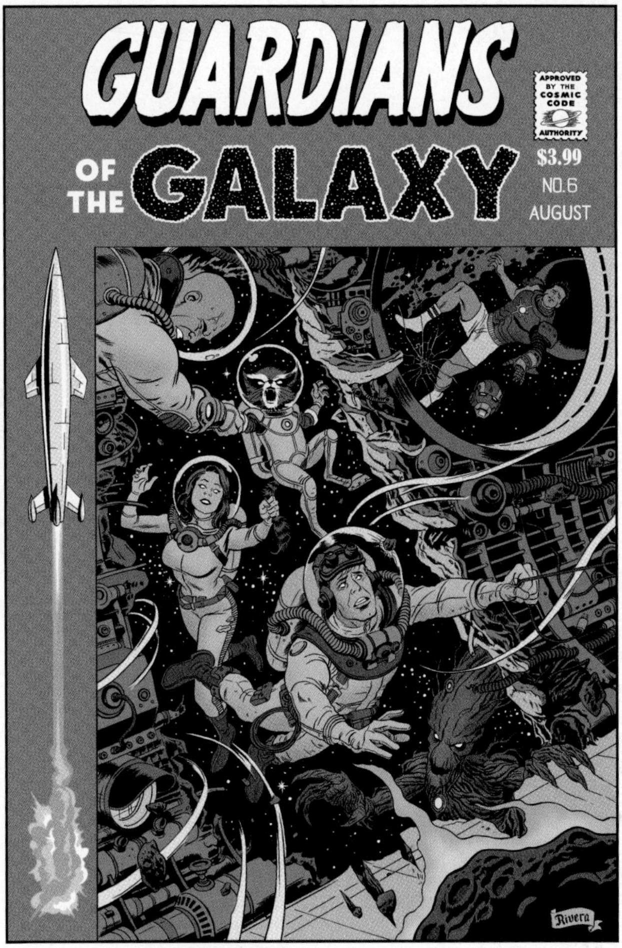

GUARDIANS
APPROVED BY THE COSMIC CODE AUTHORITY
OF THE GALAXY
$3.99
NO.6
AUGUST
Rivera

#6 VARIANT BY PAOLO RIVERA

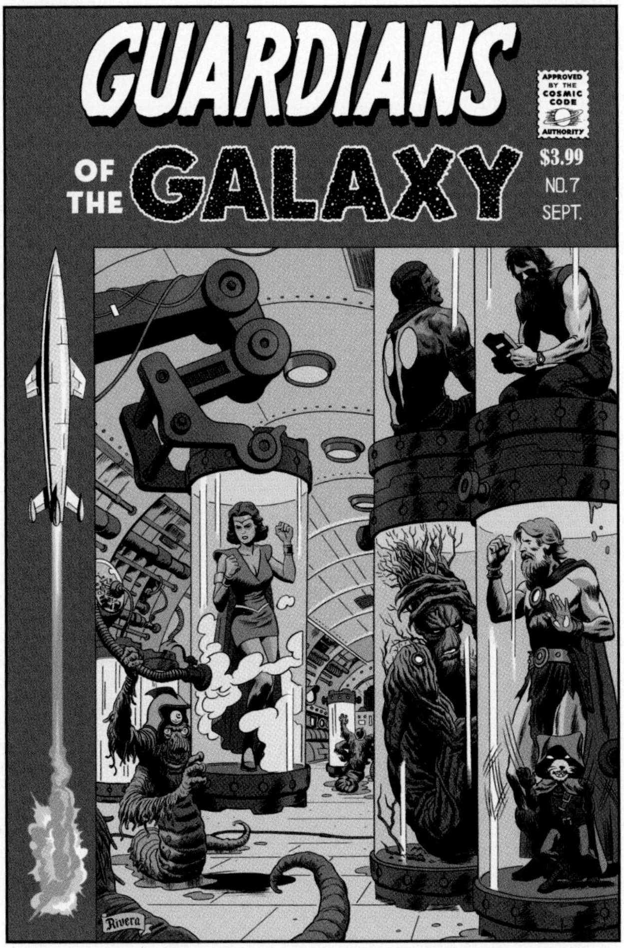

GUARDIANS
APPROVED BY THE COSMIC CODE AUTHORITY
OF THE GALAXY
$3.99
NO.7
SEPT.
Rivera

#7 VARIANT BY PAOLO RIVERA

TO ACCESS THE FREE *MARVEL AUGMENTED REALITY APP* THAT ENHANCES AND CHANGES THE WAY YOU EXPERIENCE COMICS:

1. **Download the app for free via** marvel.com/ARapp

2. **Launch the app on your camera-enabled Apple iOS® or Android™ device***

3. **Hold your mobile device's camera over any cover or panel with the AR graphic.**

4. **Sit back and see the future of comics in action!**

*Available on most camera-enabled Apple iOS® and Android™ devices. Content subject to change and availability.

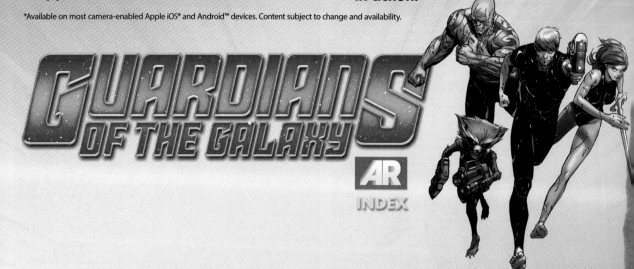

GUARDIANS OF THE GALAXY
AR INDEX